A CHRONOLGY
of
THE PEOPLE'S REPUBLIC
OF CHINA
from OCTOBER 1, 1949

An objective day-by-day chronicle of kaleidoscopic events leading to the emergence of Communist China as a major power, and to its subsequent impact upon world affairs. The book records the daily significant developments from the October 1, 1949 proclamation by Mao Tse-tung formally establishing the People's Republic of China.

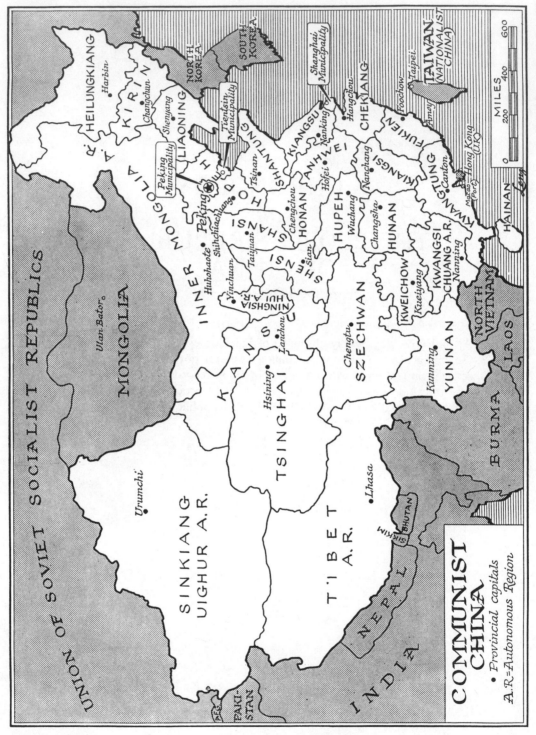

COMMUNIST CHINA

• Provincial capitals
A.R.=Autonomous Region

Copyright • Current History, Inc. 1970

MILES
0   200   400   600

A CHRONOLOGY

of

THE PEOPLE'S REPUBLIC OF CHINA

from OCTOBER 1, 1949

by

PETER CHENG

ASSISTANT PROFESSOR OF POLITICAL SCIENCE

AT THE UNIVERSITY OF NEBRASKA

1972

LITTLEFIELD, ADAMS & CO.

TOTOWA, NEW JERSEY

Printed in the United States of America

PREFACE

✲

Professor Peter Cheng in his Chronology covers the daily recorded events concerning the People's Republic of China from the day of its inauguration in 1949 through 1970. This objective account has been compiled from reports appearing in publications in China, England, France, India, and the United States.

In the Introduction the author has covered major events through August ,1971 when the U. S. formally announced support for the U.N. seating of the People's Republic of China.

Just before going to press other significant events occurred. They have been included in this preface.

The author has included a special index for the Chronology which enables the reader to locate entries pertaining to certain subjects. The index has two major divisions: DOMESTIC AFFAIRS and FOREIGN AFFAIRS.

DOMESTIC AFFAIRS has entries classified under Agriculture; Communist Party of China (CPC); Construction; Cultural Revolution; Economy; Political Reforms; Social, Cultural, and Military Reforms; and Tibet.

FOREIGN AFFAIRS has two sub-divisions. The first, INTERNATIONAL CONFERENCES and MULTILATERAL AGREEMENTS, has entries under Indochina Conference; Korean War; Multilateral Relations and Agreements; United Nations; and Vietnam War. The second, BILATERAL RELATIONS, has entries under the names of 110 countries arranged alphabetically from Afghanistan through Zambia.

On October 25, 1971, Mainland China was voted into the United Nations. The result of the vote was no surprise because the U. S. had reversed its 20 year stand on the admission of Red China to the U.N. The vote was 76 to 35 with 17 abstentions. Peking was admitted and Taiwan was dismissed. The U. S. expressed deep regret over the expulsion of Taiwan and the loss of U.N. support for its "two China" policy.

On October 27, 1971, *The Peking People's Daily* headline read, "A VICTORY FOR THE PEOPLES OF THE WORLD, A SAD DEFEAT FOR U. S. IMPERIALISM."

On November 15, 1971, Mainland China's nine member delegation to the U.N. was seated for the first time. The leaders of the delegation were Deputy Foreign Minister Chiao Kuan-hua and Permanent United Nations Representative Huang Hua, formerly Chinese Ambassador to Canada.

In his first address to the U.N. General Assembly Chiao Kuan-hua demanded the end of the U.N. domination by the superpowers. He blamed U. S. obstruction for the delay in U.N. acceptance of the People's Republic of China. He declared, "The Chinese people are determined to liberate Taiwan and no force on earth can stop us from doing so." He insisted upon the withdrawal of the U. S. from Southeast Asia. He vowed that China would not be the first to use nuclear weapons and he exhorted the U. S. and the Soviet Union to make similar pledges if they truly desired disarmament.

On November 18, 1971, China conducted its first nuclear weapons test in over a year. The test, at Lop Nor in Western China, was an explosion in the atmosphere with a force equal to that of the bombing of Hiroshima. When criticized at a U.N. Assembly committee session the Chinese defended their right to the test. They said the People's Republic of China was involved only in limited nuclear development for defense.

Recently there have been rumors of a major power struggle reported to have resulted in the disappearance of Marshall Lin Piao who was Defense Minister and Deputy Chairman of the Communist Party. Also reported missing are Mr. Lin's wife and several senior military leaders including Chief of Staff of the Armed Forces, Huang Yung-sheng.

Mr. Lin, who was Chairman Mao Tse-tung's closest collaborator, was reported to have been his chosen successor. Chairman Mao is 77, and Premier Chou En-lai is 73 years old. If Mr. Lin has been purged, authorities believe there may be a grave crisis in the leadership of China.

On November 29, 1971, White House officials announced that President Nixon's visit to China will begin on February 21, 1972. This will be the first visit to China by a United States chief of state.

December, 1971   The Editor

ACKNOWLEDGMENTS

I am very grateful to the University Research Council of the University of Nebraska for travel grants to the Library of Congress to gather materials for this study. Special thanks go to the Department of Political Science, University of Nebraska, for its secretarial assistance. Finally, I want to thank my wife, Nelly, and my daughters, Margaret, Elizabeth and Patricia for their patience and encouragement which made the preparation of this book possible.

Bibliographical Sources

The chronology is compiled from the following sources:

1. *Asian Record*, (New Delhi)
2. *China and United States Far East Policy: 1945-1967*, (A publication of the Congressional Quarterly Service)
3. *China Quarterly*, (London)
4. *Current Background*, (United States Consulate, Hong Kong)
5. *Communist China Digest*, (Joint Publications Research Service)
6. *Department of State Bulletin*, (Washington D. C.)
7. *Extracts China Mainland Magazines*, (United States Consulate, Hong Kong)
8. *Chung-hua jen-min Kung-ho Kuo fa Kuei hui-pien*, (Collection of Laws and Regulations of the PRC: Peking, 1954-1963)
9. *Far Eastern Economic Review*, (Hong Kong)
10. *Chung-yang jen-min Cheng-fu fa-ling hui-pien*, (Collections of Laws and Decrees of the Central Peoples Government: Peking, 1949-1954)
11. *Facts on File.*
12. *International Legal Materials*, (American Society of International Law, Washington, D. C.)
13. *Le Monde*, (Paris)
14. *Jen Min Jih-pao*, (People's Daily, Peking)
15. *Jen Min Shou-tse*, (People's Handbook, Hong Kong)
16. *Joint Publications Research Service*, (Washington D. C.)
17. *Keesing, Archives.*
18. *New China News Agency*, (Peking)
19. *New York Times*, (New York)
20. *Times*, (London)
21. *People's China*, (Peking)
22. *Peking Review*, (Peking)
23. *Survey China Mainland Magazines*, (United States Consulate, Hong Kong)
24. *Survey China Mainland Press*, (United States Consulate, Hong Kong)
25. *Chung-hua jen-min Kung-ho-Kuo tiao-yueh-chi*, (Compilation of Treaties of PRC, Peking 1949-1964)
26. *U. N. Treaty Series.*
27. *Chung-hua jen-min Kung-ho-kuo tui-wai Kuan-hsi Wen-Chien-Chi*, (Compilation of Foreign Relations Documents of the PRC, Peking, 1949-1963)
28. *Chung-hua jen-min Kung-ho-Kuo Yu-hao tiao-yueh hui pien*, (Collection of Friendship Treaties concluded by PRC: Peking 1965)

ABBREVIATIONS

ACFDW	The All-China Federation of Democratic Women
ACFTU	The All-China Federation of Trade Unions
ACSF	The All-China Students' Federation
CAS	Chinese Academy of Sciences
CC	Central Committee
CDL	China Democratic League
CPC	Communist Party of China
CPG	Central People's Government
CPGC	Central People's Government Council
CPPCC	Chinese People's Political Consultative Conference
CPSU	Communist Party of the Soviet Union
CPV	Chinese People's Volunteers
CY	League of Communist Youth
CYC	Communist Youth Corps
GAC	Government Administration Council
KMT	Kuomintang
NCNA	New China News Agency
NDC	National Defense Council
NPC	National People's Congress
PA	Peasant Association
PLA	People's Liberation Army
PRC	People's Republic of China
SC	State Council
SPC	Supreme People's Court
SPP	Supreme People's Procuratorate

Unless otherwise indicated all references to Korea mean North Korea, those to Vietnam mean North Vietnam, and those to Germany mean East Germany.

INTRODUCTION

The final cap was put on the cultural revolution in 1970. It transformed China from a fragmented nation into a monolithic state, based on the moral authority of Chairman Mao Tse-tung. Now, China set about repairing the damage caused by that upheaval. She began to restructure party and state organizations with the army as an instrument to provide for political stability. In order to reduce the disparities between city and countryside, and between coastal and interior provinces, an effort was made to re-distribute investment and social services. Above all, an attempt was designed to re-educate China's "bourgeois" intellectuals, revise university admission standards, and revolutionize Chinese culture. Internationally, China launched one of her most success-ful diplomatic campaigns ever.

For state reorganizations, on August 23, 1970, the Party's Ninth Central Committee held its second plenary session and issued a communique (September 6) to announce that preparations were under way for the long-delayed Fourth National People's Congress. The new Congress was expected to name a new state chairman to replace Liu Shao-ch'i, purged during the cultural revolution. In the provincial-level adminis-trations, the party succeeded in restoring control over 25 provinces (out of a total of 29) by August, 1971 with army pragmatists. One exception is Shanshai, which is still in the hands of the educated urban activists who dominated the party before the cultural revolution. Of the provincial bosses, 18 are oldline generals, five vintage bureaucrats, two veterans of service in the state security apparatus. Rural, poorly educated, un-traveled and just plain old—their average age is 62—they are hardly the sort of men to heed Mao's call to accept the new. In fact, a dominant theme of the 25,000-word CPC anniversary editorial on July 1, 1971 was a warning against the evil of "impetuosity."

The same theme appeared in an article published in the first 1970 issue of *Hung Chi* to call for the rebuilding of the CPC. It rejected the contention to admit automatically the extremists to the party on the credentials of their participation in the cultural revolution. It moved the party to a more moderate phase of development by reducing the role of representatives of the revolutionary masses in the party committees. It showed strong resistance against mass organizations' demands for open party meetings and told mass representatives on revolutionary committees to return to their produc-tion posts. It took a hard line toward new applicants for party membership, calling for "strict accordance" to the membership provisions of the new party constitution. It demanded that the new applicants must be "free from the influence of the Right or Left tendencies and that of bourgeois factionalism."

On the military front, significant efforts were made in 1970 to reduce the political role of the Army. Although military cadres retained prominent positions in the political system, they were asked to accept party control. Less emphasis was given to the Army in accounts of the National Day celebration in 1970 and the 1970 Army Day editorial focussed on the Army's strategic tasks rather than on its domestic functions. Gradually, party propaganda teams were replacing Army propaganda teams as instruments for implementing central directives. The most significant indication of China's military capability was the launching of her first satellite on April 24, 1970. The 380-pound probe circled the globe every 114 minutes, broadcasting a popular song praising Mao Tse-tung, *The East is Red*. The announcement caused little surprise in the West. Two months prior to the launching, U.S. Defense Secretary Melvin Laird told Congress that the Chinese would "attempt to test-launch their first ICBM or space booster in the near future." The significant technological progress appeared to demonstrate that China was advancing toward an important goal of building missiles capable of delivering nuclear warheads to U.S. and European targets as early as 1973. On November 23, 1970, the *New York Times* reported that China had deployed a few medium-range (600-1,000 miles) nuclear-tipped missiles while concentrating her efforts on developing an intermediate-range (1,500-2,500 miles) missile. Furthermore, China conducted an atmospheric explosion on October 14, 1970 over its testing grounds in Sinkiang Province in northwest China. The test was detected and announced by the U.S. Atomic Energy Commission. The AEC estimated that the explosion had a force of about three megatons. The test, the eleventh since China entered the nuclear age in October, 1964, was not disclosed officially by Peking. It was the second time that China had failed to announce one of her atomic tests publicly.

Chinese economy showed improvement and a shift of the policy in 1970. A shift in her economic policy aimed at strengthening agriculture and small rural manufacturers. An article in *Hung Chi* stated on June 8 that the policy, called "walking on two legs," was to be defined as "the simultaneous development of industry and agriculture and that of heavy and light industry, with priority given to the development of heavy industry; simultaneous development of industries run by central authorities and of local industries; simultaneous development of large, medium, and small industries and the simultaneous application of foreign and indigenous methods of production under centralized leadership." The article added that the development of small enterprises "can take full advantage of various scattered, limited local resources so that they can produce with what is locally available, and sell their products in local markets in order to cut down transport costs. This will make possible the rational geographical distribution of industry in the interest of preparedness against war." As a matter of the principle, the article concluded that industry must support the technical transformation of agriculture. In a series of statements in 1970 and 1971, references were made to the preparation of the Fourth Five-Year Plan with the revival of the State Planning Commission. China again renewed interest in central co-ordination and planning of the Chinese economy in an effort to create a small but complete industrial system in every province in the process of economic development. As for the statistical data, the Japanese Foreign Office on March 4, 1971, released its estimates on the Chinese economy. It disclosed that in 1969, China's economy recovered to the level before the cultural revolution (1966-1969) and made a further rise in 1970. Among the reported gains listed: industrial production increased 15%-20%; agricultural output was up between 5%-10%; the gross national product grew about 10% and reached $74 billion; 220-230 million metric tons of grain and vegetables were harvested; foreign trade increased slightly to about $4.3 billion. On April 28, 1971, the U.S. Agricultural Department confirmed that China had achieved a record grain output in 1970 and that its soybean production was the highest in three years. The increased food yield was assisted by a record use of fertilizers, more irrigation, mechanization, and newer seeds, the report indicated.

In 1970, schools at all levels began functioning for the first time in four years. NCNA announced on July 21, 1970 the resumption of regular classes at Tsinghua University in Peking, widely regarded as the birthplace of the cultural revolution of 1966. Although ideology still played an important role in school curricula, more attention was being given to traditional subjects such as science, mathematics, and languages.

As for the daily life of the people, *Time* (May 3, 1971) carries the following description: Salaries begin at around 24.5 yuan or $10 a month for a peasant on a commune—an amount that varies by a system of work points awarded according to the work he does, his political zeal, and the harvest. The upper range is around $100 a month for a young army general or experienced technician. But rents are low, from $1 to $3 for a typical one-or-two room apartment. Vegetables in season cost only 1.5 cent to 2 cents per pound, rice 7 cents per pound, and meat from 20 to 40 cents per pound. Milk is higher, at 10 cents a quart, and eggs are 30 cents a dozen. Cereals and cooking oils are rationed, as is China's chief export item, cotton cloth (each person is allowed six yards a year.) Peasants are allowed to own small plots and to sell the produce on a limited free market. City workers spend about one-third of their income on food and are still concerned with the things money can buy; bicycles, radios, cameras, and wristwatches, their status symbols. Most Chinese would have to save for two years to buy a bicycle, which costs $35 to $45. They work eight hours a day, six days a week. Leisure time is spent picnicking, swimming, hiking—in emulation of Mao Tse-tung's long march to the Yenan caves in the 30's—or reading the Chairman's thoughts. The drabness of the austere blue, gray or green uniforms that all Chinese wear on the streets is not entirely a true picture. Many Chinese like to dress up in bright-colored clothes at home.

By far the most spectacular and significant developments for China in 1970 and 1971 were those on the international front. Beginning with the 1970 New Year's Day editorial, official statements consistently emphasized China's willingness to establish or improve diplomatic relations with all countries, regardless of their social systems on the basis of the Five Principles of Peaceful Coexistence. One of the earliest moves toward improved foreign relations came on January 20 when the Sino-U.S. ambassadorial talks in Warsaw resumed after a recess of two years. Exactly one month later the two sides were getting down to substantive issues. Further progress in improving Sino-American contacts might have been possible had not developments in Cambodia interfered. On March 18, 1970, the Left-leading Prince Norodom Sihanouk was ousted as Cambodia's head of state. On March 19, he arrived in Peking and was embraced by the Chinese. Premier Chou En-lai turned out to greet him, and Sihanouk remained in Peking. Late in April the Chinese sponsored a summit conference of Communist representatives from the Indochina states—Cambodia, Laos, and Vietnam. Sihanouk formally joined forces with the Communists, and China became the champion of his cause along with that of the Vietnamese and Laotian Communists. When the United States sent troops into Cambodia on April 30, 1970, any hope of further improvement in Sino-American relations was halted temporarily. Peking announced on May 18 that it was calling off the 137th Warsaw meeting.

China's response to the Cambodian situation itself was extremely cautious. On May Day, Mao Tse-tung and Sihanouk presided at an anti-U.S. rally in Tien An Men Square to condemn American intervention in Cambodia. Mass demonstrations were held throughout China on May 8 denouncing the United States. Military aid to arm the guerrilla forces under Sihanouk's control was stepped up. However, Chinese aid would not include active combat support.

After the Cambodian situation cooled off, improvement in Sino-American relations was speeded up. Washington announced in November, 1970 that it would no longer oppose seating Peking in the United Nations so long as Taiwan retained its seat as well. President Nixon, in his "State of the World" message in February, 1971, referred to the mainland Chinese regime by its official name: the People's Republic of China. In March, the State Department ended the restrictions that have effectively prevented travel to China by U.S. citizens for twenty years. Then in April, "Ping Pong" suddenly became an apt metaphor for the relations between Washington and Peking. The 15-member U.S. table tennis team and three accompanying American reporters were invited to visit China with the teams from Canada, Columbia, England, and Nigeria. The U.S. team was the first to visit China in nearly a quarter of a century. Premier Chou En-lai told the U.S. visitors: "We have opened a new page in the relations of the Chinese and American people."

In the wake of Chou's statement to the Americans, President Nixon released a new statement on trade with China that, in effect, allows Americans to deal with China on nearly the same basis as in the Soviet Union. The President said that the U.S. would welcome visitors from China, abolish currency restrictions for American businessmen dealing with China, allow companies to provide fuel for ships and planes travelling to China, and authorize American ships and planes to carry Chinese cargoes and American-owned foreign flag ships to call at Chinese ports. In June, President Nixon personally approved the catalogue of items that American businessmen may sell to Peking without Washington's approval—some 1,000 in all—representing an end to the 21-year old U.S. prohibition against direct trade with mainland China. In the meantime, the two American biologists, Dr. Arthur W. Galston of Yale University and Dr. Ethan Signer of MIT, were guests of the Scientific Community in Peking in May. James Reston of the *New York Times* and Robert I. Keatley of the *Wall Street Journal* were granted visas to visit China.

On July 15, 1971, in just 15 minutes of television time, President Nixon made a historical announcement which altered many major assumptions and patterns of postwar diplomacy. The President said he would go to Peking to meet Chairman Mao Tse-tung and Premier Chou En-lai before May, 1972. The arrangements had been made by his National Security Adviser, Henry Kissinger, during a secret meeting with Chou in Peking the week before. The aim of the meeting, said the President, "is to seek the normalization of relations between the two countries and also to exchange views on questions of concern to the two sides." The announcement, on the whole, brought an instant and exuberantly favorable response at home as well as abroad. The Nationalist Chinese on Taiwan, though reassured by the President that he would do nothing "at the expense of our old friends," protested angrily, since their claim to the mainland was now finally shattered and their hold on a seat in the United Nations became tenuous at best. But that did not deter the U.S. intention to pursue a more realistic policy toward Peking.

More than twenty years of American opposition to a United Nations seat for Peking ended with Secretary of State William P. Rogers' statement on August 11, 1971. The Secretary said at a news conference: "The United States will support action at the General Assembly this fall calling for seating the People's Republic of China, the mainland government. At the same time the United States will oppose any action to expel the Republic of China or otherwise deprive it of representation in the United Nations." In his 750-word statement and in answering questions later, the Secretary emphasized the Nixon administration belief that the interest of world peace would best be served by the United Nations membership for Peking as well as Taiwan. Underlying Roger's statement was what he termed "the realities of the world today." The new U.S. policy was attacked by both Chinas, since each claims to be the rightful representative of all of China's people. Taipei issued a terse statement that promised a fight for Taipei's "lawful rights and positions" in the United Nations, and warned that the organization could "drift into impotence and total failure" if Peking is admitted. In Peking, the official New China News Agency thundered that the U.S. decision "peddles the preposterous proposition of two Chinas." It described the two-Chinas plan as a "trick" designed to keep Taiwan in the United Nations and thus make it impossible for Peking to accept a seat.

China's coexistence policy began to repair her relations with Yugoslavia, Burma, and India since 1970. Peking also reassigned new ambassadors to return to all China's embassies overseas by the middle of 1971, and received a large number of foreign high level officials from Pakistan, France, Rumania, Tanzania, Zambia, Sudan, Syria, the Congo Republic, Poland, and South Yemen. Furthermore, China signed aid agreements with North Korea, North Vietnam, and Albania, and extended loans to Tanzania, Zambia, Ceylon, and Rumania. The largest Chinese aid commitment was $408,000,000 to build 1,080 miles of railroad to connect the rich copper mines of landlocked Zambia with the Tanzanian port of Dar es Salaam on the Indian Ocean. Work on the railroad started officially in October, 1970. On the Middle-East cease-fire, China denounced it as a "political fraud," and extended moral and material support to the Palestinian commandos. Yasir Arafat, the leader of the Palestine Liberation Front, paid a visit to Peking in early September, 1970, and hailed the Chinese as being the first to provide military assistance to the Palestinian guerrillas. However, Chinese efforts were ineffective in the Middle-East.

A number of foreigners connected with China made news in 1970. In June the American-born writer Anna Louise Strong died in Peking at the age of 84. Miss Strong had lived in China for a number of years and was often received by Mao Tse-tung, Chou En-lai, and other ranking Chinese officials. Catholic Bishop James Walsh, who had been imprisoned in China, serving a twenty-year sentence since the late 1950's, was released in July. And British engineer George Watt, apprehended during the Cultural Revolution for alleged spying activities while supervising construction of a chemical plant in Lanchow China, also was released in August. He had served nearly three years in prison.

China's diplomatic offensive paid off when it won a simple majority for the first time in the United Nations (1970) on the question of whether it should replace Nationalist China in that body. The vote was 51 for Peking, 49 against, 25 abstentions. However, Peking still remained out of the United Nations for another year, because the General Assembly had voted earlier 65-52 (with 17 abstentions) in favor of a U.S. backed resolution declaring the China issue an "important question" requiring a two-thirds majority. Since the latter part of 1970, Peking succeeded in obtaining diplomatic recognition from Canada (October, 1970), Equatorial Guinea (October, 1970), Italy (November, 1970), Ethiopia (December, 1970), Chile (January, 1971), Nigeria (February, 1971), Kuwait (March 1971), Cameroon (April, 1971), Austria (May, 1971), and Turkey (August, 1971). Initially, Peking demanded that each state acknowledge its claim over Taiwan. However, in the end, Peking accepted the so-called Canada formula which allowed each state to announce that the latter "takes note" of the claim without further commenting on the former's claim.

Peking appeared to revise its relations with Moscow after the American invasion of Cambodia at the end of April, 1970. While Mao's statement of May 20 condemned "American imperialism," it made no mention of revisionism or the Soviet Union. In July, 1970, it was announced that the two nations would exchange ambassadors. Soon after his arrival in Peking, Russian envoy Vasily Tolstikov was received by Chou En-lai—Chou's first public meeting with a Soviet official since his conference with Alexsei Kosygin at the Peking airport in September, 1969. Liu Hsin-chuan, the new Chinese ambassador to Moscow, presented his credentials to Soviet President Nikolai V. Podgorny in November, 1970. On November 12, a Soviet trade delegation, headed by a Deputy Minister of Foreign Trade, arrived in Peking, and a trade agreement was signed ten days later. In addition, the Soviet delegation at the United Nations made a last minute appeal on November 19 for the admission of Peking, reversing a position to abstain from the debate as it had done in 1969. Talks on Sino-Soviet problems entered into the second year. While there were no indications of any progress in the talks, there were no reports of further border skirmishes, either. In the meantime, polemic exchange between Peking and Moscow was relatively mild with the apparent indication that both sides agreed to disagree on ideological and doctrinal questions. Although state-to-state relations between the two nations were somewhat improved, Moscow was skeptical about the "Ping-Pong Diplomacy" and President Nixon's projected visit to Peking.

One exception to China's coexistence policy is Japan. Peking expects the rise of Japanese militarism to wage counter-insurgency warfare against Communist forces in Asia. Peking has increased its fear of resurgent Japan because of the following events: (1) Japan stated that both South Korea and Taiwan were essential to Japanese national security in the Tokyo-Washington agreement on the reversion of Okinawa; (2) Japan launched her first earth satellite in February, 1970; (3) the Japanese-American mutual security treaty was automatically extended in June, 1970; (4) Japan issued a defense white paper in October, 1970, and increased trade with the Soviet Union; (5) Japanese investments were substantially increased in Taiwan and Southeast Asia. Since the President's announcement to visit Peking, it seemed particularly worried about Japan's role in Taiwan. The New China News Agency saw dark portents in the recent visit of Chiang Kai-shek's personal secretary, Chang Chua, to Tokyo. Peking seems to fear that Japan is easing into the role of protector of Taiwan, which was under Japanese rule for a half-century before V-J day. Although Sino-Japanese trade increased 25% during 1970, Peking began to undertake a restrictive measure against Japanese firms which have close ties with Taipei. Furthermore, the growing Japanese interest in the Korean peninsula led to an improvement of relations between China and North Korea. In April, 1970, Premier Chou En-lai made an official state visit which was followed by other meetings of Chinese and Korean military leaders. China made specific assurances that it would provide military aid to North Korea against an American or Japanese attack on the latter.

In balance, at the beginning of the 1970's decade, China has entered into an era of revolutionary pragmatism at home as well as abroad. She appears to follow a rational policy on both fronts with some significant developments on her way to becoming a major power. *A Chronology of the People's Republic of China*, with a day-to-day chronicle from the inception of the government from 1949, is designed to provide a better understanding of the kaleidoscopic events leading to the emergence of China as a major power.

1949

October 1: The formal inauguration of the People's Republic of China (PRC) was announced in a proclamation issued by Mao Tse-tung in Peking. In the proclamation Mao declared that the war of the people's liberation had been fundamentally won, and that the Organic Law of the People's Government and of the Republic had been enacted by the Chinese People's Political Consultative Conference (CPPCC). At the same time he announced that a State Administrative Council would be created under the premiership of Chou En-lai.

October 2: Official Soviet recognition of the PRC was announced in Moscow.

October 3: Recognition of the PRC was extended by Bulgaria and Rumania.

October 4: Recognition of the PRC was extended by Poland, Hungary and Czechoslovakia.

The U.S. State Department issued a statement reaffirming the U.S. recognition of the Nationalist government as the legal government of China.

October 5: The Sino-Soviet Friendship Association, headed by Mr. Liu Shao-chi, was established in Peking.

October 9: The First National Committee of the CPPCC held the First Session, which selected its chairman (Mao Tse-tung), vice-chairman (Chu Te), and the members of its Standing Committee.

October 12: U.S. Secretary of State Acheson listed three conditions a new government must meet before receiving U.S. recognition: (1) it must exercise effective control in the country it purports to govern; (2) it must recognize its international obligations, and (3) it must govern with the consent of the people. The secretary doubted whether Communist China adhered to the standards of international behavior required under the second condition.

October 15: Communist forces occupied Canton without resistance.

October 16: Outer Mongolia established diplomatic relations with the PRC.

October 19: The Central People's Government Council (CPGC) appointed the vice-premiers and members of the Government Administrative Council (GAC) and of its various committees, designating the persons in charge of the ministries, commissions and administrations, the president of the Academia Sinica, the managing-director of the People's Bank of China and the vice-chairman and members, the chief of general staff and the deputy chief of general staff of the People's Revolutionary Military Council, etc.

October 24: U.S. Consul General Angus Ward and four other members of the Mukden consular staff, confined to the consular compound since late 1949, were arrested by Communist authorities and held until November 22 on charge of beating a Chinese employee.

October 25: The GAC decided: (1) to set up a Take-Over Committee to take over the Kuomintang (KMT) Central Government and the personnel, archives and materials of its various subordinate organs; (2) to leave the problem of taking over the former North China People's Government and the various units of the provinces under it to the chairman of the CPGC, with an order issued to wind them up, the five provinces and two municipalities to be put directly under the CPGC; and (3) to have all ministers, committees, courts and administrations formally begin office as of November 1.

October 27: East Germany established diplomatic relations with the PRC.

October 28: The GAC passed the "General Rule of Organization of the GAC Offices" and the "Working Rules of the GAC Committee for the Take-Over."

October 31: Mr. Wang Chia-hsiang, Chinese Communist ambassador to the Soviet Union, arrived in Moscow.

November 18: Secretary Acheson appealed to the foreign ministers of thirty countries

1

represented in China for intercession in the Angus Ward case.

A formal demand was sent to Trygve Lie, United Nations Secretary-General, from Premier Chou En-lai, in which Mr. Chou repudiated the legal status of the Nationalist delegation under T. F. Tsiang, and held that it had no right to speak for the Chinese people in the United Nations.

November 22: Consul General Angus Ward and four aides, whose prison sentences by a Mukden people's court were remitted to deportation, were released and authorized to leave China.

November 23: Albania established diplomatic relations with Communist China.

November 26: U.S. Vice-Consul William Stokes was arrested in Mukden and released after being escorted to a Communist espionage trial. The Communist deportation order was extended to include all non-Chinese members of the consulate staff. They left Mukden on December 7 and sailed from Tientsin on December 14.

December 2: The CPGC passed the state budget for 1950 and adopted the organization rules of the people's representative conferences in provinces, municipalities, and counties. It named October 1 as the National Day of the PRC.

December 4: The GAC passed the "General Rules of Organization for All Organizations under GAC." The GAC decided to set up a Regional Military and Political Committee.

December 8: U.N. General Assembly adopted two resolutions on China, calling on all states to be guided by U.N. principles in their relations with China, and authorizing the Interim Committee to study and report upon the Nationalist charges against the U.S.S.R.

December 9: The GAC passed provisional measures on the controlled release of important news of the CPGC and its subordinate organs. The GAC also decided to distribute the 300,000 suits of old cotton clothes stored by the Rear Service of the North China Military District to the poor in Jehol, Chahal, Suiyuan, Northwestern Shensi, Peking and Tientsin.

December 16: The GAC passed the "Rule Governing the Relief Through Production," and the "General Rule of Organization for the Regional Government Committees."

Mao Tse-tung arrived in Moscow and soon afterward entered into secret negotiations with Stalin.

December 17: Burma became the first non-Communist country officially recognizing the PRC.

December 25: Agreement on postal services, protocol on postal services, agreement on tele-communications, agreement on telephone services, protocol on tele-communications and telephone services were signed in Peking beween the PRC and North Korea.

December 29: In the United Nations Security Council, Mr. Malik of the U.S.S.R. stated his government's support of the Chinese Communist application for non-recognition of the Nationalist Chinese delegation.

December 30: Recognition of the PRC was extended by India.

1950

January 4: Recognition of the PRC was extended by Pakistan.

January 5: President Truman announced in Washington that the U.S. would not provide military aid or advice to Chinese forces on Taiwan. Secretary of State Acheson added that the President's decision was proof to the world that the U.S. would keep the promise not to meddle in the internal affairs of China. However, he advised against premature recognition of Communist China.

January 6: Recognition of the PRC was extended by Great Britain, Ceylon, and Norway.

The GAC passed the organizational rules for provincial, municipal, and *hsien* people's governments.

January 8: Premier Chou En-lai sent a telegram to the United Nations Security Council demanding removal of the Nationalist delegation.

January 9: Recognition of the PRC was extended by Denmark and Israel.

January 10: The People's Bank of China had fixed official exchange rate at 23,000 "People's currency dollars" to one U.S. dollar and 4,400 to the pound sterling.

Soviet delegate Jacob A. Malik walked out of a meeting of the United Nations Security Council when it refused to take immediate action to oust the Nationalist Chinese representative.

Secretary Acheson testified at an executive session of the Senate Foreign Relations Committee. In explaining Formosan policy, Acheson said the first line of U.S. defense in the Western Pacific would include Japan, Okinawa and the Philippines, but not Taiwan. He gave no indication that the American government was considering recognition of Communist China.

January 12: President Truman reaffirmed his "hands-off-Formosa policy" at a news conference.

January 13: The Soviet resolution for the removal of the Nationalist Chinese delegation was rejected in the Security Council, whereupon Mr. Malik again walked out after stating that Russia would not consider itself bound by any actions taken by the Security Council in the absence of the Soviet delegation and that it would not recognize any such action as being legal if a Chinese Nationalist delegate were present. The voting was: Against, U.S.A., France, China, Cuba, Ecuador, Egypt; for, U.S.S.R., India, Yugoslavia; abstaining, Great Britain, Norway.

Recognition of the PRC was extended by Finland and Afghanistan.

The GAC approved a directive on the disposal of the farm land in the suburban districts of the old liberated areas.

January 14: Chinese Communist authorities seized U.S., French, and Netherlands compounds in Peking on the grounds that they were military barracks.

The State Department recalled all official personnel from Communist China, following seizure of the U.S. consulate in Peking.

Recognition of the PRC was extended by Sweden.

January 17: Recognition of the PRC was extended by Switzerland.

January 18: Secretary Acheson said that seizure of the Peking consulate made it obvious that Communist China did not want U.S. recognition.

January 19: Communist China officially recognized the government of Ho Chi-Minh as "the legal representative of the will of the Vietnamese people."

January 20: Premier Chou En-lai joined Chairman Mao Tse-tung in Moscow for negotiations with Soviet authorities.

January 27: A regional government for Eastern China was created.

The GAC approved, in principle, the two draft provisional measures governing the industrial and business taxes and commodity taxes.

February 3: The Nationalist Chinese delegate in the United Nations told a Security

Council committee that he would veto a resolution to recognize the right of the Communist regime to represent China in the organization. On February 8, the committee decided that the General Assembly would have to solve the problem of Chinese representation.

February 7: Sino-Soviet agreements on telephone and telegraph communications, and Sino-Soviet agreement on exchange of mails and parcels were signed in Moscow.

February 14: Negotiations between Mao Tsetung, Chou En-lai, Stalin, and M. Vyshinsky ended after eight weeks of discussions. M. Vyshinsky for the Soviet Union and Chou En-lai for China signed (1) a treaty of friendship, alliance, and mutual assistance; (2) an agreement on the Ch'angch'un Railway, Port Arthur, and Dairen; (3) an agreement by which the U.S.S.R. was to extend long-term credits to China.

February 15: Supplements to Sino-Soviet Agreement of February 7, 1950, on exchange of mails and parcels were signed in Peking .

February 24: The GAC passed directive governing the land reform and the collection of public grain in new liberated areas. The GAC also passed a general order strictly prohibiting opium smoking.

March 1: A Sino-Polish agreement on exchange of goods in 1950 was signed in Peking.

March 3: The GAC passed a measure to unify the state financial and economic work. The GAC also passed provisional measures governing the public enterprises' payment of industrial and business taxes and regulation of government treasury.

March 8: U.N. Secretary General Trygve Lie implied in a memorandum to all the delegations that the PRC should be permitted to take China's seat at the U.N. Lie said U.N. policy should be to deal with whatever government exercises "effective authority" in a country and was "habitually obeyed by the bulk of its population." Secretary Acheson replied that the U.S. would not vote to seat the Communists while it recognizes the Nationalists, but would refrain from using the veto and accept the majority decision of the U.N. Acheson's statement was severely criticized in Congress.

March 10: The GAC passed a directive on spring plowing and production, and decisions governing the provisional unified organization of government personnel at all levels, the provisional standard of government provision for 1950, the unified measures of enforcement for all state-operated trades, and the clearance and distribution of supplies in government warehouses.

March 24: The GAC passed decisions on the unified control of the 1950 financial receipts and disbursements, on the unified regulation of public grain receipts and disbursements, on the security work for the financial and economic departments of the state, on the provisional measure to wipe out the gang-labor system in transportation enterprises, on the change of standard for the processing of food and the increase of staple food.

March 27: The Netherlands extended recognition to the PRC.

It was announced in Moscow, and confirmed in Peking two days later, that China and the Soviet Union had signed agreements establishing two mixed Sino-Soviet joint stock companies for the exploitation of the oil and non-ferrous metal resources of the Chinese provinces of Sinkiang. The arrangement would remain in force for 30 years.

April 2: Announcement was made of a 10-year Sino-Soviet agreement, signed on March 27, which created a joint civil aviation company to operate three air routes between Peking and the Soviet cities of Chita, Irkutsk, and Alma-Ata.

April 4: Chinese Communist authorities seized the British compound in Peking on the ground that it was a military barracks. Mr. Hutchinson, British charge d'affaires in Peking, pointed out that British title to the compound was based on the Anglo-Chinese treaty of 1943, whereupon the Chinese Foreign Ministry replied that it was unable to reverse the order but that the proposed action would be limited to "requisitioning" instead of "expropriation."

April 5: Mr. George Yeh, the Nationalist foreign minister, asked the United Nations Security Council to take measures against Russia because of "definite Soviet participation in the military action of the Chinese Communists in violation of the United Nations Charter."

April 10: The New China News Agency (NCNA) announced that the food situation, while serious in the north Chinese provinces, was progressively improving in the deficiency areas in the south as the result of the dispatch of large grain surpluses from Inner Mongolia and of rice consignments from Manchuria, and intensive spring sowing.

April 13: It was announced that the 30-year Sino-Soviet Treaty of Friendship, Alliance, and Mutual Assistance had been ratified by both Communist China and the Soviet Union, as were the agreements on the Ch'angch'un railway, Port Arthur, and Dairen, and the agreement on long-term Soviet credits to China.

April 19: An official statement was issued in Moscow that these agreements had been signed between the PRC and the Soviet Union: (1) a general trade agreement; (2) an agreement on commercial exchange for 1950; (3) a protocol fixing the quantities of equipment and materials that would be given China under the February 14 agreement on Soviet credits.

April 21: The GAC passed the draft Labor Union Law of the People's Republic of China and decided to publish it for preliminary study by the public.

April 23: General Lin Piao's forces occupied Hainan without resistance.

April 25: A Sino-Soviet protocol on the organization of the Chinese Ch'angch'un Railway Company was signed in Peking.

April 30: The Marriage Law was promulgated. The new legislation banned arranged and child marriage, sale of childen, concubinage, polygamy, discrimination against illegitimacy, and interference with the right of a widow to remarry. It gave women equal rights with men in working, in status in and outside the home, in property rights, and in divorce, and allowed them to retain their maiden names.

May 8: *The New York Times* reported that French intelligence had information that Communist China had a secret military aid agreement with Ho Chi-Minh, leader of the Indochinese (Viet Minh) rebels.

May 19: The GAC passed a directive on the relief of unemployed workers and approved the provisional measures of the Ministry of Labor for relief of the unemployed. The Provisional Organic Regulation for Provincial and Municipal Labor Bureaus was promulgated.

June 2: Dr. Malan, Prime Minister of South Africa, announced that his government had decided not to recognize the PRC.

June 6-9: The Third Plenum of the Seventh Central Committee of the Communist Party of China (CPC) met in Peking. Chairman Mao Tse-tung delivered a speech entitled "Fight for a Fundamental Turn for the Better on the Financial and Economic Situation in China." He presented an eight-point program for the solution of China's problems in a report to the meeting. Included in the program were the following considerations: Completion of agrarian reform; reducing the tax burden; partial demobilization of the army; reform in the area of education; relief work; recruitment of new members for the Communist Party; maintaining unity between "all democratic parties"; and suppressing "bandits, spies, despots, and other counter-revolutionary elements."

June 6: U.N. Secretary General Trygve Lie disclosed that he had asked the Big Four Powers to end their deadlock over Chinese representation in the U.N. It was generally understood that Lie wanted the Western Powers to admit Communist China and let Peking occupy China's permanent seat in the Security Council.

June 7: Secretary Acheson told a news conference that the U.S. would not be "coerced" by the Soviet walkout into admitting Communist China to the U.N. He said the U.S. did not favor transfer of Chinese representation to the Communists but would not use the veto to block the transfer if a majority of the Security Council so voted.

June 14: A trade agreement was signed between the PRC and Czechoslovakia.

June 14-23: The National Committee of the CPPCC in Peking, meeting June 14-23, unanimously adopted an Agrarian Reform Law providing for the redistribution of the land in areas recently brought under Communist control. From the outset it was stressed that the basic economic motive of the law was not to raise the living standard of the poor peasant, but rather to strengthen the national economy and to facilitate the transition of collectivization and industrialization. Other legislation approved by the National Committee of the CPPCC provided for the partial demobilization of the army; for the establishment of provincial and city consultative councils, which would be responsible for local government until a provincial and city people's Congress could be elected by universal suffrage; and for the adoption of a new national emblem.

June 16: Construction work on Chengtu-Chungking Railway began.

June 25: North Korean forces invaded South Korea. The United Nations Security Council met on the same day and passed a resolution calling for an immediate cessation of hostilities and withdrawal of North Korean forces to the 38th parallel; asking all member states "to render every assistance to the U.N. in the execution of this resolution, and to refrain from giving assistance to the North Korean authorities"; and asking that the Security Council be kept informed on the implementation of this resolution through the United Nations Korean Commission.

June 27: The Security Council called on U.N. members to "furnish such assistance to the Republic of Korea as might be necessary to repel the armed attack and to restore international peace and security in the area."

President Truman ordered U.S. air and sea forces to support South Korean troops; he also ordered the U.S. 7th Fleet to prevent any attack on Taiwan or action from Taiwan against the mainland, and announced intensified military aid to the Philippines and Indochina.

June 28: Chairman Mao Tse-tung, speaking at the meeting of the CPGC, strongly denounced U.S. aggression in Taiwan and Korea. On the same day, Premier Chou En-lai asserted that Taiwan would always be a part of China and that China would fight "to liberate Taiwan from the grasp of the American aggressor."

June 29: The Trade Union Law was promulgated. It required all unions to report to and be approved by the All-China Federation of Trade Unions; otherwise they shall not be called trade unions.

July 1: It was announced by the Central Committee of CPC that in line with the proposals made by Chairman Mao Tse-tung, certain measures would be taken to "sift out" party members who "have great defects and are unwilling to correct them." This process was to begin with the leadership. At the same time, the Central Committee announced their goal of recruiting one-third of all industrial workers in China into the Communist Party within three to five years.

July 6: Premier Chou En-lai sent a note to U.N. Secretary General Lie to denounce the Security Council resolution of June 27 and American armed aggression against Taiwan.

The U.S. State Department announced that the United States government was requesting that private companies and foreign governments cooperate in an effort to tighten the United States embargo on oil shipments to Communist China. The State Department had also announced that all oil shipments and all materials with possible war potentials had been cut off by the United States government from shipment to the Far East in order to prevent such shipments from reaching countries that might be sympathetic to North Korea. It was also announced that Britain had declined to comply with the request to reduce her shipments.

July 14: The GAC passed the General Organic Rule for Peasant Associations and that for People's Tribunals.

July 20: Sino-Soviet protocol on the completion of transfer to the PRC of all buildings of the Soviet military compound in Peking was signed.

July 21: The GAC reached decisions on the suppression of counter-revolutionary activities, on the relief of unemployed teachers, and on the disposal of students who lost schooling.

July 31: General MacArthur and Chiang Kai-shek held military discussions on Taiwan.

August 1: The Soviet delegate, Jacob A. Malik, returned to the Security Council, ending the six and one-half month Russian boycott without explanation or condition. The same day, the Council voted to override an order by Malik, as President of the Council for August, that the PRC take the Chinese seat in that body.

August 7: A Sino-Soviet protocol on the measures for free transfer to the PRC of Japanese properties in Manchuria taken over by U.S.S.R. in 1945 was signed in Mukden. The agreement on completion was signed on August 28, 1950.

August 12: The Vietnam government in Saigon announced that the Chinese Communists had initiated a large-scale program of military aid to Ho Chi-Minh's Indochinese rebels.

August 17: The British destroyer *Concord* returned fire in self-defense after Communist shore batteries opened fire on it as the ship approached Hong Kong. The *Concord* was not damaged.

August 18: A trade agreement was signed between the PRC and North Korean People's Republic.

August 20: Premier Chou En-lai cabled the United Nations, declaring the PRC's support for the proposal brought forward by the Soviet Union in the Security Council for a peaceful settlement of the Korean question, which included the withdrawal of all foreign troops and participation of the PRC in discussions on Korea.

August 24: Premier Chou En-lai demanded that the U.N. Security Council order U.S. "armed invading forces" to withdraw from Taiwan.

General Yeh Chien-ying Communist chairman of the Kwangtung provincial government, accused the British military and air forces in Hong Kong of "planning to encroach against Chinese sovereignty." He also claimed the "intrusion of a British warship into Chinese waters," and claimed that the warship had fired on Communist positions before going into Hong Kong. At the same time, he claimed that there had also been previous "violations of Chinese territory by British air and military forces in Hong Kong."

August 27: Premier Chou En-lai complained to the U.N. Security Council that U.S. planes had bombed Chinese territory. He repeated his complaint on August 30.

August 31: Answering Communist China's complaint to the Security Council, Secretary Acheson denied that the U.S. had encroached in China, asserted that the status of Taiwan had still to be internationally fixed, and suggested a U.N. investigation into the Communist charges. Acheson said that the Chinese would have no justification for entering the Korean war.

September 11: A Soviet proposal to the Security Council to invite an envoy from Peking to attend discussion of alleged U.S. violation of the Manchurian air space failed by one vote.

September 16: Premier Chou En-lai cabled the U.N. Security Council, declaring that the PRC must be invited to attend discussions of alleged U.S. armed aggression against Taiwan.

September 19: The Chinese Communists were barred from taking China's seat in the U.N. General Assembly. An Indian motion to seat the Communists lost 33-16 with 10 abstentions. A Russian motion to oust the Nationalists lost 38-10 with 8 abstentions.

September 24: The PRC sent a protest to the United Nations alleging that on September 23 a United States plane had dropped bombs on Antung in Manchuria. Three persons were wounded and there had been damage to property.

September 27: The PRC protested to the United Nations that an American destroyer had shelled a Chinese merchant vessel in the Yellow Sea. China demanded that the attacks of September 24 and September 27 be included on the agenda of the General Assembly and that Chinese Communist delegates be present at the meeting "to present their case and take part in the discussions."

The United States government admitted that U.S. aircraft might have dropped bombs in the vicinity of Antung by mistake.

September 29: The Security Council agreed (7-4) to invite a Peking delegation to present its case on alleged American aggression against China.

September 30: Premier Chou En-lai repeated his government's assertions of American "aggression in Taiwan." He also announced that his government was determined to "liberate the people of Tibet and stand on guard at the Chinese frontiers." He reiterated his government's support for the North Koreans in the war in Korea.

October 1: Premier Chou En-lai warned that his government would not stand aside if "the imperialists were to invade the territory of North Korea."

October 10: Conclusion of a trade agreement between the PRC and East Germany was announced in Peking.

A spokesman of the Chinese Foreign Ministry denounced passage of the eight-nation proposal in the General Assembly for a full-scale U.N. force to cross the 38th parallel, and warned that his government would not remain idle.

October 13: The announcement was made by Peking radio to close down the Roman Catholic Fujen University in Peking,

which was established in 1924, and had since that year been operated by the American Fathers of the Divine Ward. The reasons mentioned were that certain of the professors had tried to manipulate the administration of the university, and that American Fathers had tried to force the dismissal of "progressive professors."

October 17: Premier Chou En-lai cabled the United Nations demanding the participation of the PRC in the discussion of the alleged U.S. armed aggression against China in the General Assembly, and protesting against the inclusion of the "Taiwan Question" in the General Assembly agenda.

October 24: The Chinese Communists accepted an invitation to attend a U.N. Security Council discussion of alleged U.S. aggression in Taiwan and appointed Mr. Wu Hsiu-ch'üan to head the Chinese delegation.

Announcement was made by the NCNA of a "political liberation directive" ordering Chinese Communist forces to advance into Tibet "to liberate 3,000,000 Tibetans from imperialist aggression, to complete the unification of the whole of China, and to safeguard the frontier regions of the country."

October 25: Chinese Communist volunteers entered the Korean war in support of the North Koreans. This was confirmed by a spokesman at General MacArthur's general headquarters on October 28. However, it was termed "only a face-saving operation" and he stated that there was no cause for alarm.

Sino-Soviet agreement on working conditions for Soviet experts in the PRC was signed.

October 30: A Communist Chinese note to India asserted that Tibet was a domestic problem and that India's policy was being influenced by foreign governments. India, on October 31, denied any foreign influence on its policy and said that China should not impose a decision in Tibet by force.

November 4: All minor parties in Communist China jointly declared their full support

8

of the "voluntary" aid rendered by the Chinese people to North Korea.

The PRC and East Germany exchanged notes on general conditions for delivery of goods.

November 6: The United Nations Security Council received a report from General MacArthur on the "confirmed fact" of Chinese intervention in Korea.

November 8: The Security Council considered General MacArthur's report and adopted a British resolution to invite the Chinese Communist government to send representatives to participate in the Council's discussion. The invitation was rejected by Peking three days later.

November 10: A six-power resolution presented to the Security Council called on the Chinese Communist government to withdraw its troops from North Korea and reassured the government that its legitimate interests in the border zone of the Yalu River would be respected. The resolution was sponsored by the United States, Great Britain, France, Norway, Cuba, and Ecuador.

November 15: Premier Chou En-lai sent a communication to the United Nations stating that the Peking government would send a delegation to the U.N. to discuss the Taiwan question (an invitation to do so had been sent by the U.N. on September 29), but that they would refuse to take part in the discussion on General MacArthur's report.

Secretary Acheson told reporters that he would welcome direct talks with the Chinese Communists but warned that deliberate precipitation of a war by China would be "a tragedy of the most colossal nature" and would be met by firm U.N. action.

November 23: Peking radio broadcast a statement by the Foreign Ministry accusing the French land and air forces in Indochina of having repeatedly violated the Chinese frontier since December, 1949, of having killed and wounded many soldiers and civilians, and of having assisted KMT guerrillas. No official protest against the alleged incidents was re-

ceived by the French government, and the French military authority in Saigon completely denied all the Chinese charges.

November 24: The United Nations General Assembly suspended consideration of the Tibetan appeal due to the Indian contention that an honorable and peaceful settlement could be reached in the area itself. Meanwhile, the PRC established a "Tibetan Autonomous Region" under its control.

November 25: Peking delegates to the United Nations, headed by Mr. Wu Hsiu-ch'üan, arrived in New York.

November 28: In a Security Council debate on alleged U.S. aggression, Mr. Wu Hsiu-ch'üan told the council that it should penalize the U.S. for "armed aggression against China, Taiwan, and Korea."

November 30: The six-nation resolution was voted on in the Security Council and received nine votes in favor, with India abstaining, but was defeated by the Soviet veto.

December 1: In a special message to Congress, President Truman denounced Chinese intervention in Korea as deliberate and unprovoked aggression.

The General Assembly approved (35-17) a proposal referring Nationalist China's allegation of Soviet intervention and treaty violation to the Interim Committee.

The GAC adopted decisions on the general accounting system, on examination of budget plans for promotion of investments, and on control of currency.

December 3: The Provisional Regulations for private enterprise was promulgated, stipulating in detail the conditions under which such enterprises would be permitted to operate.

December 4-8: A five-day Washington conference of President Truman and British Prime Minister Clement R. Attlee ended with a joint statement that there would be "no appeasement" of Communist China over Korea. Both leaders agreed to abide by their decisions, although they disagreed on whether China should be admitted to the U.N.

December 4: Premier Chou En-lai declared that the proposed Japanese Peace Treaty, contained in the memorandum sent by the U.S. to the Soviet Union in October, completely violated all international agreements with regard to the Allies' policy toward Japan. He charged that the U.S. was turning Japan into a colony.

December 5: The PRC issued a statement accepting Universal Postal Convention (1947) and various postal arrangements.

December 8: The GAC passed the Provisional Regulations Governing the Control of Foreign Trade and General Organic Principles for the Conference of Representatives of the People of a *Hsiang*, and for the People's Government of a *Hsiang*.

December 13: The Asian-Arab cease-fire proposal (creating a three-man cease-fire committee) was approved by the General Assembly's Political Committee by 51 to 5 with 5 abstentions. It was approved by the plenary session of the General Assembly next day by 52 to 5. Lester B. Pearson (Canada), Sir Benegal N. Rau (India), and Nasrollah Entegan (Iran) were appointed to membership.

December 15: The GAC passed Provisional Regulations Governing Industrial and Business Taxes, Provisional Regulations Governing Income Tax on Interest, organic rules governing the democratic assessment committee for industrial and business taxes, and organic rules for the reappraisal committee.

December 16: At a press conference General Wu called the cease-fire resolution a "trap" to let the United States continue its aggression against Korea and Taiwan. He said his government was willing to advise the Chinese volunteers to withdraw from Korea, but only if (1) United Nations forces were withdrawn from Korea; (2) American occupation of Taiwan was ended; and (3) the Peking government was admitted to the United Nations. He left New York after the press conference, and returned to Peking on December 30.

President Truman announced that he intended to proclaim that a national emergency existed in the United States as a result of the international situation. Several steps were taken following this broadcast: American ships and aircraft were banned from trading with Communist China; a ban was placed on the loading or unloading of cargo to any part of the world if there was reason to believe that it might be destined "directly and indirectly" for Communist China; all Chinese Communist assets under American jurisdiction were "frozen."

December 22: Peking radio announced that the three-man cease-fire committee proposal had been rejected by the PRC.

December 23: Premier Chou En-lai asked the U.S. to withdraw the 7th Fleet as a condition for peace in Korea.

December 29: It was announced in Peking that all U.S. assets in China would be "frozen" and placed under government control. Regulations were also issued regarding the cultural, educational, and charitable organizations and religious bodies subsidized by the United States.

1951

January 1: The conclusion of a barter agreement with the Chinese Communist government was announced in New Delhi. The agreement called for an exchange of 50,000 tons of rice for 37,000 bales of jute during the first quarter of 1951.

January 2: Sino-Soviet agreement on navigational procedures and construction on border rivers Amur, Ussuri, Argun, and Sungacha and on Lake Hanka was signed in Harbin.

A decree was issued banning all secret societies in China. The banned organizations were described as "contrary to the best interests of the people."

January 8: Resumption of U.S. military shipments to Chiang Kai-shek was confirmed by the State Department.

January 13: The Political Committee of the United Nations General Assembly approved a five-point truce and conference plan. Premier Chou En-lai rejected the plan (on January 17) to have a cease-fire first, then to have a conference. He suggested holding a seven-nation conference in China, including the five big powers plus India and Egypt, and proposed that the legal status of the Chinese representation in the United Nations should become effective on the date of the convention.

January 16: A Sino-Soviet agreement on direct rail communication was signed.

January 20: Mr. Warren Austin, the United States delegate to the United Nations, introduced a resolution in the Political Committee of the General Assembly calling on the United Nations to declare Communist China an aggressor.

January 22: An agreement on trade and payment was signed between Communist China and Hungary.

January 23: A U.S. Senate resolution demanded passage by the U.N. General Assembly of a resolution declaring Communist China an aggressor in Korea.

January 24: The Political Committee of the General Assembly rejected a proposal, by twelve Asian-Arab nations, to convene a seven-nation conference on Korea.

January 29: Textual modification of the United States resolution was introduced as an amendment by the Lebanese delegate, Dr. Charles Malik. The amendment proposed that the phrase stating that the Peking government "has rejected" all calls for a cease-fire be changed to "has not accepted," and that the report of the Collective Measures Committee for the possible use of sanctions should be deferred until satisfactory progress be reported by the Good Office Committee in its efforts to achieve a peaceful solution to the Korean crisis. The modified U.S. resolution was adopted in plenary session by the General Assembly on January 30.

Conclusion of the Sino-Polish barter agreement for 1951 and agreements on payments, shipping, and the interchange of mails, parcels, and tele-communications were announced.

February 1: Sino-Polish protocol on general conditions for delivery of goods was signed in Peking.

February 2: Premier Chou En-lai denounced the U.N. resolution as illegal and slanderous.

February 13: The GAC announced the target of agricultural production for 1951: an increase of 7.1% in grain production and 36.9% in cotton production over 1950.

February 19: Sino-Hungarian protocol on general conditions for delivery of goods was signed in Peking.

February 23: Peking announced the imposition of the death penalty or life imprisonment for a wide range of "offenses against the state." It was stated that persons liable to these punishments would include those engaged in "rebellion against the Fatherland" or working for imperialism; those bribing the armed forces or the civil service to participate in rebellion; instigators or leaders of rebellions; persons engaged in espionage and sabotage or in directing enemy aircraft and warships to their targets; those supplying military equipment and materials to the enemy within or without the country; members of secret societies; former nationalists who failed to atone for their crimes or who participated in "counter-revolutionary activities"; and persons resisting, or inciting to resist, the requisitioning of grain, the collection of taxes, and other administrative orders.

February 26: The GAC promulgated the Labor Insurance Regulations.

March 14: Another Sino-Soviet agreement on "through rail traffic" was signed in Peking.

March 23: The GAC passed Customs Law of the People's Republic of China, to be enforced on an experimental basis. It was promulgated on April 18.

April 3: Conclusion of the Sino-Soviet cultural cooperation was announced.

April 10: General MacArthur was relieved by President Truman of all his commands and was succeeded by Lieutenant General Matthew B. Ridgway.

April 20: Washington revealed that the Nationalist government would receive increased U.S. arms and the assistance of a military advisory group.

The GAC passed directives on adjustment of cultural organs in Provincial and Municipal People's governments and on reforms of dramas.

April 25: Sino-Indian contract on delivery by the PRC of rice to India was signed in Peking.

April 29: It was announced by the NCNA that Premier Chou En-lai had ordered that all property in China belonging to the Asiatic Petroleum Company (a subsidiary of the Shell Oil Company) be requisitioned in the interests of "national security and the general public."

May 1: Over 186,430,000 people throughout China were said to participate in demonstrations in support of the Resist-America Aid-Korea Campaign and in opposition to the remilitarization of Japan.

May 3: Mr. Ernest Gross, U.S. delegate, presented a resolution to the Additional Measures Committee of the U.N. General Assembly in which he recommended that an embargo be placed on the export of strategic materials to Communist China by all member states. The Additional Measures Committee approved the resolution on May 14. The resolution was approved by the full General Assembly (48-8) on May 18.

May 18: U.S. Assistant Secretary of State for Far Eastern Affairs, Dean Rusk, publicly promised increasing aid to Nationalist China and non-recognition of the Communist regime on mainland China.

May 22: Premier Chou En-lai handed a note to the Soviet ambassador in Peking expressing his government's full support for "the concrete proposals of the Soviet government concerning the preparation of the peace treaty with Japan," and attacking the draft treaty prepared by the U.S. government.

May 23: Conclusion of the Agreement on the Measures for the Peaceful Liberation of Tibet, between representatives of the Central People's Government and the Tibetan local government, was announced. Sino-Indian contract on delivery by the PRC of grain to India was signed in Peking.

May 25: The GAC passed measures governing the employment of civilian labor for building and repair of highways in 1951.

June 1: A Sino-Polish agreement on the establishment of Sino-Polish joint stock shipping company was signed. The Peking National Committee of the Resist-America Aid-Korea Association formally called for the initiation of the three major supporting campaigns: "A patriotic pact movement," a donation campaign for the purchase of airplanes and heavy artillery, and a relief and aid campaign for military personnel and their dependents.

The GAC passed Provisional Regulations for Preservation of State Secrecy and General Rules for Organization of Security Committees of people's government at all levels.

June 3: The NCNA announced that two Roman Catholic nuns had been sentenced to ten years' imprisonment for neglect and ill-treatment of Chinese children. Four other nuns had been expelled from the country.

June 15: Sino-Soviet protocols on exchange of goods and supply of industrial equipment and materials by U.S.S.R. to PRC in 1951 were signed in Peking.

June 21: Conclusion of the Sino-Czechoslovak barter agreement for 1951 and an agreement on payment were announced in Peking. A Sino-Czechoslovak protocol on general conditions for delivery of goods was also signed in Peking.

June 23: A cease-fire and withdrawal from the 38th parallel were suggested in a broadcast by Soviet U.N. delegate Jacob A. Malik. Soviet views were further developed by Deputy Foreign Minister A. A. Gromyko in conversation with U.S. Ambassador Alan G. Kirk on June 27.

June 29: General Ridgway, the U.S. Commander, proposed armistice talks in a broadcast directed to the enemy commander.

July 1: Nation-wide celebration of the 30th anniversary of the Communist Party in China was held.

The Chinese and North Korean Communist commanders accepted the U.N. proposal for a meeting to discuss a cease-fire and suggested the meeting be convened near Kaesong between July 10 and July 15.

July 10: Korean armistice negotiations opened at Kaesong.

July 12: Premier Chou En-lai signed a decree in which all Chinese Christian churches were ordered to sever relations with American missions and with any non-American missions which were "largely supported by American funds." In addition, all American church missions in China which financed "educational, cultural, or charitable work" were ordered to "suspend their activities immediately."

Conclusion of Sino-Hungarian and Sino-East German cultural agreements were announced.

July 13: The GAC adopted decisions on improvement of students' health throughout the country and on augmenting the staff of health workers in national defense enterprises.

July 28: A Sino-Soviet agreement on establishment of the Sino-Soviet Joint Stock Company for Ship Building and Repair was signed in Peking.

August 1: The "Three-Anti" campaign was begun in the Northeastern region and was later taken up on a national scale, covering all government departments, schools, universities, nationalized enterprises, and the Communist Party. The "Three-Anti" campaign was a movement against corruption, waste, and bureaucracy among government employees.

August 3: The GAC passed a decision on the relations of local Consultative Committees at all levels; also passed were supplementary measures on the duty and authority of the Standing Committee of the *hsien* People's Representative Conferences.

August 15: Peking attacked the U.S. and British governments for "audaciously excluding" the People's Republic of China from the San Francisco conference; described the draft treaty as a "violation of international agreements" which was basically unacceptable to the Chinese people. A note setting out the Communist government's objections to the treaty was handed by Premier Chou En-lai on August 17 to the British charge d'affaires and the heads of other diplomatic missions in Peking.

August 23: The Communists broke off negotiations at Kaesong after accusing the United Nations forces of bombing the conference area.

September 4-8: Japan and 48 nations at war with her held a peace conference in San Francisco to sign a peace treaty. The Soviet powers had refused to sign the treaty. Neither Communist nor Nationalist China was invited to attend the conference. On September 8, a U.S.-Japanese mutual security pact was signed.

September 5: Expulsion of the Papal Internuncio in China, Mgr. Riberi, was announced. He had been kept under house arrest in Nanking since the end of June. This was followed by the expulsion or imprisonment without trial (or by trial in the "people's courts") of several other bishops and ecclesiastics.

September 6: General Ridgway offered to renew negotiations at a new site; the offer was repeated on September 27.

September 14: The GAC ratified three documents: (1) Provisional Regulations Governing the Accord of Privileges by the People's Republic of China to Foreign Diplomatic and Consular Personnel; (2) Provisional Regulations Governing the Exemption from Inspection of the Baggage and Possessions of Foreign Diplomatic and Consular Personnel on Entry into, and Departure from, the Country; (3) Provisional Regulations Governing the Exemption from Taxation of Foreign Diplomatic and Consular Personnel.

September 18: Premier Chou En-lai denounced the Japanese Peace Treaty as a violation of international agreements and therefore unacceptable.

October 9: A Sino-East German cultural cooperation agreement was signed in Peking.

October 12: Conclusion of the Sino-East German agreement on the interchange of mails, parcels, and tele-communication was announced.

Publication in Peking of the first of the four volumes of *Selected Works of Mao Tse-tung* was announced.

October 16: The Special Committee of seven members to consider the question of the representation of China rejected a Polish draft resolution calling on the General Assembly to exclude the representation of the Nationalist government of China, and to invite the representatives of the People's Republic of China. The committee authorized the chairman to inform the Assembly that in existing circumstances it had been unable to make any recommendation on the question.

October 23: The third session of the National Committee of the First CPPCC was convened. Chairman Mao Tse-tung and Premier Chou En-lai both reaffirmed Communist Chinese foreign policy aims in their report to the conference. The conference passed a resolution to support the proposal for the big five powers' peace pact on November 1.

October 25: The Korean cease-fire negotiations were resumed at Panmunjom.

November 13: The question of Chinese representation in the United Nations General Assembly was postponed by vote of 37 to 11, with 4 abstentions.

December 6: A Sino-Soviet agreement on technical training for PRC specialists in U.S.S.R. was signed.

December 12: Conclusion of the Sino-Rumanian cultural cooperation agreement was announced.

December 21: The GAC approved Provisional Regulations Covering Control of Publication and Distribution of Books and Provisional Measures for Registration of Periodicals.

1952

January 1: At the New Year celebration, Chairman Mao Tse-tung opened the Three-Anti campaign by calling on the nation to fight corruption, waste, and bureaucracy.

January 9: President Truman and British Prime Minister Winston Churchill, after conferring in Washington for four days, recorded in a joint statement their full agreement that aggression in Korea and Southeast Asia must be blocked.

January 19: Pope Pius XII issued an encyclical letter to Roman Catholics in Red China telling them "to render to everyone, and especially to God, that which in his due." The letter denied that foreign Catholic missionaries in China were anti-Red spies.

February 1: The PRC launched its "Five-Anti" campaign against bribery, theft of state property, tax evasion, theft of state economic secrets, and embezzlement in carrying out government contracts. A "patriotic denunciation campaign" was launched calling for a confession of malpractices and in which shop assistants were encouraged to accuse their employers. Businessmen were classified as "basically law-abiding," "partly law-abiding," and "inveterate law-breakers."

The United Nations General Assembly found that the U.S.S.R. had failed to carry out its 1945 treaty with Nationalist China.

February 4: An official survey of the position of the Roman Catholic church in Communist-dominated countries was issued by the Vatican. Of the 1764 Roman Catholic ecclesiastics still in China, 133 (including 21 bishops) were in prison and a great majority of the others were under house arrest or otherwise prevented from exercising their functions.

February 7: At the closing session of the CPPCC, Mao Tse-tung called for an end to the Korean War and suggested that the remaining questions should be left for later settlement.

February 8: A Sino-Polish plan for cultural cooperation in 1952 was signed.

February 15: The GAC set the agricultural target for 1952: An increase of 8% over 1951 in grain production and 20% in cotton production.

February 22: The GAC passed the Program for Enforcement of National Regional Autonomy, the Provisional Organic Rules for Committees of Nationalities Affairs at All Levels, the GAC Decision on Measures for Setting up Local Democratic Coalition Governments of National Minorities, and the GAC Decision on Protection of Equality Rights of National Minorities Living in Scattered Places. The first two were to be enforced when ratified by the CPG Council.

February 24: Premier Chou En-lai announced Peking's support of the protest of North Korean Foreign Minister Bak Hun Yung against germ warfare in Korea.

March 7: Sir Arthur Morse, chairman of the Hong Kong and Shanghai Banking Corporation, announced in Hong Kong that the bank's offices at Peking, Tientsin, Tsingtao and Swatow had been closed or were in the process of liquidation, since trading arrangements with China were now very largely in the hands of Chinese government departments or their agents.

March 8: Premier Chou En-lai protested against the alleged U.S. intrusion over Chinese territory and its germ warfare in Northeast China.

March 15: The Commission for Investigating the U.S. Crime of Bacteriological Warfare, headed by Li Teh-ch'üan, president of the Chinese Red Cross Society, was formed.

March 27: The GAC passed the Regulation of the People's Republic of China for the Punishment of Corruption. It also passed by-Laws governing establishment of People's Tribunals for the Three-Anti Campaign and approved by-Laws of the CPGC Economy Check-Up Committee for Recovery of Funds and Stolen Articles from the Corrupt.

March 29: A Sino-Soviet protocol on amendment of 1950 protocol on general conditions for delivery of goods was signed in Moscow.

April 1: The Northeast China group of the Commission for Investigating the U.S. Crime of Bacteriological Warfare made public its report on the alleged spreading of germ-laden insects and infected objects in Northeast China by the United States.

April 7: A Sino-North Vietnamese agreement on general conditions for delivery of goods was signed in Peking.

April 8-12: At the International Economic Conference in Moscow, a barter trade agreement between French firms on the one hand and the China National Import-Export Corporation and Chinese National Bank on the other was signed.

April 10: Publication of the second volume of the *Selected Works of Mao Tse-tung* was announced.

April 12: Conclusion of the Sino-Soviet trade protocol for 1952 was announced in Moscow .

April 26: A contract for exporting 100,000 tons of rice from Communist China to India was signed in Peking.

May 5: Premier Chou En-lai protested against U.S. announcement on the effectiveness of the Japanese Peace Treaty.

May 6: Conclusion of the Sino-Czechoslovak cultural cooperation pact, science and technical cooperation, and agreements on the interchange of mails and tele-communications were announced.

May 19: British trading companies in China decided to close because of increasing governmental encroachment in Chinese business and because of increasing restrictions on entry and exit of foreigners and the arbitrary taxation policies of the Chinese government. They said they had been operating at a loss and that the loss might total 250,000 pounds. It was confirmed by British Foreign Secretary Eden.

May 24: A Sino-Czechoslovak agreement on air traffic was signed.

May 28: A Sino-East German protocol on general conditions for delivery of goods in 1952 was signed in East Berlin.

June 1: Conclusion of the Sino-Japanese barter agreement, involving the exchange of commodities to the value of 30 million pounds sterling, was announced in Peking.

June 14: The "Patriotic Denunciation Campaign" was officially called off. The decree stated that in the future law-breaking traders and firms would be tried and fined by "people's courts." Furthermore, they would be required to return any illegally acquired profits and all outstanding taxes by 1953.

June 20: Chingkiang flood diversion project on the Yangtze River in Hupeh province was reported completed after 75 days of arduous labor by 300,000 workers, involving 7,800,000 cubic meters of earthwork, 117,000 cubic meters of concrete work, and the building of a 1,054-meter regulator, the largest in the country.

June 25: A trade agreement was signed between the PRC and West German private businessmen.

June 27: Provisional measures for the control of counter-revolutionaries were issued by the GAC—defining additional punishment measures for lesser counter-revolutionaries. A decree of the Ministry of Home Security set out measures to be followed for ideological education and for reform by labor of counter-revolutionaries. These counter-revolutionaries would be put under a three-year period of "control" and would be required to take part in "productive work," as well as losing certain civil rights.

July 1: The Ch'engtu-Chungking Railway was opened to traffic.

July 2: Construction work began on the Ch'engtu-T'ienshui Railway.

July 11: A Sino-Polish protocol for extension for another year of agreement on general conditions for delivery of goods in 1951 was signed in Warsaw.

July 13: Premier Chou En-lai announced that Communist China had accepted the 1929 and 1949 Geneva Convention on germ warfare, on treatment of the sick, wounded, and war prisoners, and on protection of civilians.

July 14: Conclusion of the Sino-Bulgarian cultural cooperation pact was announced.

July 15: Conclusion of the Sino-Czechoslovak trade protocol for 1952 was announced.

July 21: Sino-Hungarian protocols on extension and revision of the 1951 agreement on exchange of goods and payments, and on general conditions for delivery of goods in 1952, were signed in Budapest.

July 25, 26, 29 and 30: Border clashes took place between Chinese and Portuguese troops at Macao.

July 27: The Minister of Home Security announced a decree directed against former Kuomintang officers and officials captured in the civil war who had not responded to indoctrination.

July 30: Conclusion of the Sino-Rumanian agreement on the exchange of goods and payments for 1952 was announced in Bucharest.

August 2: The second year's work on the project for harnessing the Huai River, started on December 8, 1951, involving 187,000,000 cubic meters of earthwork and 55,000 cubic meters of concrete work, was completed before the flood season.

August 6-8: The creation of five new ministries was approved by the Central People's Government Council. Also approved were the division of the Ministry of Trade and the elimination of the Government Information and News Department.

August 9: A statement on government policy was issued by Chairman Mao Tse-tung after approval by the CPGC. It provided for autonomous regional governments for minority groups, authorized them to administer their own finances and to organize their own security and militia units, and encouraged them to use local languages and to develop indigenous arts and cultures. They could enact legislation after receiving the approval of higher government organs.

August 9: A Sino-French barter contract (not a formal governmental agreement) was signed in Berlin.

A Sino-Soviet agreement on the training of PRC citizens in Soviet institutions of higher education was signed in Moscow.

August 12: New provisional regulations were announced by the Ministry of Public Security for the establishment of security committees in government departments, schools, and factories in order to prevent counter-revolutionary and criminal activities. These committees were to report spies, traitors, bandits, etc., and were empowered to arrest, supervise and reeducate suspects and their families.

August 17: A Chinese government mission, headed by Premier Chou En-lai, arrived in Moscow. Its purpose was to discuss with the Soviet government important political and economic questions. Discussions were held through September 15. Stalin received Chou En-lai on August 20. An agreement was signed calling for (1) The transfer of all Soviet rights of joint administration of the Manchurian Railroad to Communist China, to be completed by December 31, 1952; (2) the maintenance of Russian troops at Port Arthur. It was suggested that the Chinese had "requested" that the U.S.S.R. maintain troops there because there had been no peace treaty with Japan.

August 20: The PRC and Hungary exchanged notes on a 1952-53 plan for cultural cooperation.

August 23: An agreement was signed ending the Sino-Portuguese border dispute at Macao.

August 25: It was announced that the railway line from T'ienshui to Lanchow had been completed. The railway was opened to traffic on September 29.

August 29: A statement on agrarian policy was issued by the Ministry of Agriculture. It was stated that approximately 35,000,-000 peasant families (about 40% of the total) were taking part in 6,000,000 "mutual aid teams" and 3,000 "production cooperatives."

September 2: At a conference of workers in private industry, held in Peking, repre-

17

sentatives of the General Labor Union and the Ministry of Labor emphasized that the main task of the trade union was to increase production, and advised consultation for this purpose between workers and peasants.

September 15: The PRC, Outer Mongolia and the U.S.S.R. signed an agreement to construct the Chining-Ulan Bator Railway.

September 21: A tri-partite agreement was signed between Finland, the U.S.S.R. and the PRC which called for the delivery of paper products to Communist China, while Russia was to send wheat, oil, cars, and iron to Finland, in return for which China was to send Russia unspecified goods valued at thirty-four million rubles.

September 29: The government delegation of the Mongolian People's Republic, headed by Premier Tsedenbal, arrived in Peking. A ten-year agreement for "economic and cultural cooperation" between Communist China and Mongolia was signed on October 4.

October 2: Liu Shao-ch'i arrived in Moscow as head of the Chinese Communist Party (CPC) delegation to the 19th Congress of the Communist Party of the Soviet Union (CPSU). He stayed over three months in the Soviet Union before returning to Peking by air on January 11, 1953.

October 2-12: The Peace Conference of the Asian and Pacific Region was held in Peking, attended by 367 delegates and 37 observers from 37 countries. The conference adjourned after blaming the U.S. for termination of the Korean truce talks and demanding the repatriation of all prisoners of war according to the Geneva Convention of 1949.

October 4: A trade agreement between Communist China and Ceylon was signed. China was to supply 80,000 metric tons of rice in exchange for 50,000 tons of sheet rubber.

October 10: The formation of a State Planning Board, under the chairmanship of Kao Kang, and the setting up of a Ministry of Higher Education, a Committee for

the Elimination of Illiteracy, and a Physical Culture Committee were approved by the Central People's Government Council.

October 13: Conclusion in Peking of a trade contract for selling 50,000 tons of Chinese rice to India was announced.

October 23: Conclusion of a Sino-Chilean trade agreement was announced in Peking.

October 25: The question of Chinese representation in the United Nations was postponed by vote of 42 to 7, with 11 abstentions.

October 27: Premier Chou En-lai cabled the president of the 7th session of the United Nations General Assembly demanding the participation of Communist China in the discussion of the alleged U.S. crime of bacteriological warfare.

November 1: The government readjusted its policies toward business in order to restore the confidence of the private businessman. This was an attempt to revive private trade after the "Five-Anti" campaign resulted in almost a total standstill.

November 6: Sino-Vietnam agreement on exchange of mail was signed in Peking.

November 15: The GAC passed a resolution concerning the establishment of administrative committees for the greater administrative areas and the readjustment of the existing boundaries of some provinces.

November 20: The K'angting-Ch'engtu section of the Sik'ang-Tibet Highway was opened to traffic.

December 3: A plenary session of the United Nations General Assembly approved the Indian 17-point plan for breaking the deadlock over the repatriation of war prisoners and for ending the Korean war. It adopted recommendations of the nonforcible repatriation of prisoners of war by 54 to 5. The resolution was submitted to Premier Chou En-lai on the same day.

Conclusion of the Sino-Bulgarian trade protocol for 1953 was announced.

December 5: Completing a three-day visit to Korea, General Eisenhower disclaimed "panaceas" and "trick solutions."

December 14: In reply to the General Assembly resolution of December 3, Premier

Chou En-lai declared that his government would not accept the resolution because it was "illegal and invalid," had been adopted without the presence of North Korean and Chinese representatives, and was "unfair and unreasonable" in its insistence on non-forcible repatriation.

December 16: A five-year trade agreement was signed in Peking between Ceylon and the PRC. Under the agreement, China was to supply 27,000 metric tons of rice each year, and would purchase from Ceylon 50,000 tons of rubber. Prices were to be negotiated prior to the start of each year.

December 24: Premier Chou En-lai announced that the government planned to hold elections during 1953 to an All-China People's Congress.

A five-year plan for industrial and agricultural development was also to begin in 1953.

December 31: Under the terms of the September 1 Sino-Soviet agreement, control over the Ch'angch'un railway was transferred from Russia to China. Sino-Soviet protocol on transfer of assets and operations of the Soviet Foreign Insurance Administration in Manchuria to the Chinese People's Insurance Company was also signed.

1953

January 9: Conclusion of the Sino-Rumanian technical-scientific cooperation agreement was announced in Peking.

January 11: Liu Shao-ch'i arrived in Peking by air from Moscow after a stay of over three months in the Soviet Union. He arrived in Moscow on October 2, 1952 as head of the CPC delegation to the 19th Congress of CPSU.

January 13: The CPGC adopted the resolution on the convening of the All-China People's Congress and the local People's Congress on all levels.

The GAC Committee of Financial and Economic Affairs called a financial-economic ministers' conference to discuss curtailment of the 1953 building and construction plans. Decision was reached that the total figure of the plans should be cut by about 30%.

January 14: Changes in taxation were announced as follows: A combined income and business tax was to be implemented, and commodity taxes were to be reduced by 20%.

The CPGC re-appointed former chairmen of military and administrative councils as chairmen of the respective administrative councils of their regions: Kao Kang, the Northeast; Jao Shushih, East; P'eng Teh-huai, Northwest; Lin Piao, South-Central; Liu Pe-ch'eng, Southwest.

January 16: A Postal and Tele-communications Agreement between the PRC and the Mongolian People's Republic was signed in Peking.

January 19: Conclusion of the 1953 Sino-Rumanian agreement on barter trade and payments was announced in Peking.

January 21: Premier Chou En-lai issued an official protest against the alleged "intrusion into territorial air of Northeast China" on January 12 of a plane "carrying special agents sent by the U.S. government for strategic reconnaissance."

January 23: Establishment of the Thai Nationalist Autonomous Area in Southern Yunan province (Cheli) adjacent to the Lao-Buran border was announced.

January 28: Conclusion of the 1953 Sino-Polish administrative agreement for cultural cooperation was announced in Warsaw.

February 2: President Eisenhower delivered his first State of the Union message and announced that the U.S. 7th Fleet would no longer prevent Nationalist Chinese attacks on the Communist-held mainland. NCNA comment on the message charged that the U.S. was out to extend war to the entire Far East and denounced the de-neutralization of Taiwan.

February 4: In his political report to the 4th session of the Central Committee of the First CPPCC, Premier Chou En-lai stated that the major tasks ahead were (1) To strengthen aid to Korea and resist American imperialism; (2) to increase the development of agricultural and industrial enterprises during the next five-year plan; (3) the election of the All-China People's Congress and of the local people's congresses; (4) the establishment of 2,000 state farms and 34,000 cooperatives with 141,000,000 members; (5) it was announced that trade had increased with the Soviet Union to the point that in 1952 72% of all trade was with the U.S.S.R.

February 7: Chairman Mao Tse-tung spoke at the closing session of the 4th session of the Central Committee of the First CPPCC and stressed the following points as "imperative": (1) Strengthen the "Resist-America Aid-Korea" struggle; (2) learn from the Soviet Union; (3) oppose bureaucratism among the leading cadres and organs of the government.

February 9: Sino-East German protocol on 1953 plan for cultural cooperation was signed in East Berlin.

February 11: The CPGC adopted the Electoral Law for the All-China People's Congress. A Central Election Committee was also set up, headed by Liu Shao-ch'i.

February 13: The CPC Central Committee called for an end to the agrarian reform program and the implementation of a large-scale program of collectivization. The basis for this shift had been provided by the Decision on Mutual Aid and Co-operation in Agriculture taken by the CPC.

February 14: Liu Shao-ch'i made a statement at the meeting in Peking to celebrate the third anniversary of the Sino-Soviet Treaty of 1950. He stressed the fact that the "main purpose of the Sino-Soviet Treaty of 1950 is to prevent the rebirth of Japanese imperialism and the resumption of aggression on the part of Japan or any other states that would unite with Japan in acts of aggression," and that relations between China and the Soviet Union were "enduring, unbreakable, inalienable, and invincible."

February 15: Peking announced the initiatation of talks on the Japanese repatriation question in Peking between a Japanese delegation and a group representing the Chinese Red Cross Society.

February 20: Peking announced promulgation of the GAC Measures for the Refund of Pre-Liberation Bank Deposits.

February 22: Speaking at Dairen, Premier Chou En-lai charged the U.S. of using germ warfare and extending the war in Korea, sponsoring Nationalist raids on the mainland, and converting Japan into an American military base.

The United Nations Commander repeated an earlier proposal to the Chinese and North Korean commanders for immediate exchange of sick and wounded prisoners.

February 23: Premier Chou En-lai, accompanied by Soviet Ambassador Panyushkin and senior Communist military officers, arrived in Port Arthur-Dairen areas as head of the CPG delegation to visit Soviet garrison troops there. In a speech Chou En-lai thanked Soviet troops for assisting the People's Liberation Army (PLA) in "defending the peace and security of China and the Far East in the past three years." Commenting on the significance of the area, he said, "In the present situation, the garrison of Soviet troops in Port Arthur is of first significance in checking and countering any aggressive schemes of imperialism."

February 24: Conclusion of the Sino-Mongolian Non-Trading Credit Agreement was announced in Peking.

An official order of the Military Control Commission in Canton requisitioned the British property belonging to Butterfield and Swire in that city.

The Peking office of the Dalai-Lama was established.

March 1: The Electoral Law, which had been passed by the CPGC on February 11, was promulgated by Chairman Mao Tse-tung. This law covers the election for the All-China People's Congress as well as for local People's Congresses at the provincial, municipal, county and rural district levels.

March 4: News of serious illness of Stalin was first announced by NCNA. Mao Tse-tung, accompanied by several members of the politburo of the CPC, called on Soviet Ambassador Panyushkin to convey "profound anxiety." Mao sent a telegram to Stalin expressing "deep concern" over his illness, and the CPC Central Committee sent a similar message to Moscow.

March 6: NCNA announced the death of Stalin and issued an order of the CPG proclaiming the period March 7-9 as a period of national mourning throughout Communist China.

March 7: An official Chinese delegation headed by Premier Chou En-lai left Peking for Moscow by air to attend Stalin's funeral.

March 8: It was announced on Peking radio that an agreement had been reached with Japan about the repatriation of some 30,000 Japanese nationals.

March 9: Over 600,000 people attended memorial meeting in Peking in memory of Stalin. Chairman Mao Tse-tung laid a wreath before Stalin's portrait. An article by Mao Tse-tung dedicated to Stalin,

"The Greatest Friendship," appeared in the *People's Daily*.

March 14: Conclusion of the Sino-Pakistan agreement on cotton and a coal contract were announced in Karachi.

March 17: Premier Chou En-lai, head of the Chinese delegation, and Marshal Bulganin, head of the Soviet delegation, flew from Moscow to Prague to attend the Klement Gottwald funeral, who died on March 14 in Czechoslovakia.

March 21: Conclusion of the Sino-Soviet trade proposal for 1953 was announced in Moscow.

March 24: V. V. Kuznetsov, deputy minister of Foreign Affairs of the U.S.S.R., left Moscow by air for Peking to become Soviet ambassador there, succeeding Panyushkin.

March 26: Following extended negotiations in Moscow, announcement was made of the signature in that city of a protocol on trade between the PRC and the Soviet Union, a protocol to the agreement on credits to the PRC on February 14, 1950, and an agreement on the Soviet Union rendering assistance to China in the expansion and construction of new power stations. The announcement stated that the protocol envisaged a further expansion of trade between China and the Soviet Union and specified deliveries from the Soviet Union to China in 1953 of certain industrial and mining equipment as well as "supplies for industry and transport, modern agricultural machinery, pedigreed cattle, seed, and other goods." China was to deliver to the Soviet Union "non-ferrous metals, rice, vegetable oils, oil-bearing seeds, meat, tobacco, tea, fruit, wool, jute, raw silk, silk fabrics, hides and other goods."

The *People's Daily* printed the text of two important documents issued by the CPC Central Committee on agricultural policy: (1) Decision on Mutual Aid and Cooperation in Agriculture (the directive called for moderation in the organization of peasants into agricultural cooperatives); and (2) Directive on Spring Cultivation and Production of the CPC Central Committee to Party Committees at all levels. This document stated that during the period of spring cultivation, production must constitute the central task in rural areas with priority over all other government programs.

March 28: The U.N. Command in Tokyo announced that the Chinese and North Korean authorities had agreed to a proposal by General Mark Clark for an exchange of sick and wounded prisoners of war in Korea, and that they also suggested the resumption of the armistice negotiations at Panmunjom.

March 30: Conclusion of the Sino-Hungarian agreement on barter trade and payments was announced in Peking.

Premier Chou En-lai called for the repatriation of nationals held by the United Nations or Communists for those who desired repatriation, while those who did not request repatriation were to be turned over to a neutral state.

April 1: The GAC Committee on Financial and Economic Affairs issued a directive readjusting the price ratio between grain and cotton in order to favor grain production.

April 3: Central Election Committee adopted two documents: (1) Directive on Election Work at Basic Levels, and (2) Answers to Questions to Electors. Elections of local People's Congresses were to be held between May and October, 1953.

April 6: Resumption of liaison meetings at Panmunjom was announced.

NCNA announced the measures for national census and registration of the population.

April 10: Publication of the third volume of the *Selected Works of Mao Tse-tung* was announced.

April 11: An agreement for the repatriation of sick and wounded captured personnel was signed at Panmunjom.

It was announced that Sino-Soviet Civil Aviation Company would open a new air line from Urumchi to Kashgar in Sinkiang Province. It was hoped the line would be open for traffic by July 1, 1953.

April 17: The GAC passed a directive ordering local governments to stop the "blind influx" of peasants into the cities and to mobilize those already there for return to the countryside.

April 20: The exchange of sick and wounded prisoners of war began at Panmunjom.

April 23: The CPC Central Committee issued a Directive on Theoretical Education for cadres in 1953-54. It set forth extensive courses for the reading of works by Lenin and Stalin during the period from July, 1953 to December, 1954. Its purpose was to enable the cadres to apply Soviet experience to China's economic construction in the light of China's specific conditions.

April 26: The resumption of the armistice negotiations on Korean conflict at Panmunjom was announced.

April 30: Conclusion of the Sino-East German barter and payment agreement for 1953 was announced in Peking.

May 5: The Central Anti-Flood Headquarters, which was established in Peking on April 7 with Tung Pi-wu as Director, issued a general directive on anti-flood work in 1953. The directive admitted that the absence of floods in 1950 and 1951 was mainly attributed to weather and not to public works.

May 7: Goods Exchange and Payment Agreement for 1953 signed in Peking with Czechoslovakia provided for volume of trade 33% larger than 1952. Conclusion of the Sino-Czechoslovak radio agreement was announced in Prague.

May 19: An exchange of notes in Peking provided the 1953 implementation plan for the Sino-Hungarian cultural cooperation agreement.

May 21: A special conference was called in Mukden to discuss the "blind flow of peasants to the cities." During the winter and spring, some 85,000 migrated to the cities of the Northeast from the countryside in Manchuria and North China. Special cadres were organized to persuade them to return to their villages,

and escort them if necessary.

May 22: An exchange of notes in Peking established the 1953 implementation plan for the Sino-Bulgarian cultural cooperation.

May 23: A French trade delegation arrived in Peking from Paris to negotiate on "matters concerning the development of trade relations between the two countries."

May 25: Conclusion of the Sino-Polish trade agreement for goods exchange and payment was announced in Peking.

May 29: The GAC passed the "Decision on Strengthening the Practice of Production in Institutes of Higher Education and Intermediary Technical Schools" and the "Decision on Readjusting the Leadership Relations of the Institutes of Higher Education."

June 3: The Chinese Buddhist Association was founded in Peking to unite the Buddhists of China under the leadership of Central People's government and to link them up with Buddhists of other countries.

June 5: An agreement on goods exchange and payments in 1953 was signed in Peking between the PRC and Finland.

The French Trade Delegation of 16 members signed an agreement with the China National Import and Export Corporation for two-way trade totaling 10,-000,000 francs. The French would sell machinery, drugs and chemicals, and the Chinese would sell agricultural products.

June 8: An agreement on the repatriation of prisoners of war taken in the Korean conflict was signed at Panmunjom.

June 9: A Sino-Rumanian protocol in the 1953 plan for cultural cooperation was signed in Bucharest.

June 13: A new Sino-Japanese trade pact was signed, providing for $74,500,000 (U.S.) of trade each way.

June 15: Basic level elections were started in mid-June and early July in a few areas in the Southwest, East, Central South and Northeast regions. Experimental elections continued to be held in pilot districts throughout the country.

June 24: A Sino-Czechoslovak protocol on

scientific and technical cooperation was signed in Peking. Exchanges of notes also confirmed a plan for cultural cooperation in 1953.

June 25: The GAC passed the "General Rules of People's Supervisory Organs of People's Governments at All Levels to Employ People's Supervisory Correspondents."

June 27: The CPC called a halt to the recruiting of rural members which had been part of the party membership campaign started in June, 1952. The party workers were instructed to devote their efforts to the increase of agricultural production and the consolidation of the present membership.

June 30: The trade agreement with the Japanese trade delegation signed in June, 1952, was extended for an additional six months until December 31, 1953 at the request of Japan.

July 1: On the CPC anniversary, An Tse-wen reported that there were 5,000,000 members of the Party.

July 3: A Sino-German agreement on exchange of weekly press clippings was signed.

July 6: The Chinese National Import and Export Corporation and a mission of 19 British businessmen signed a one-year trade agreement allowing the exchange of £30,000,000 worth of goods.

July 7: The GAC Directive on the Issuance of Farming Credits pointed out that the policy of providing funds to farmers for production purposes has not been properly carried out in many areas and instructed that loans should be granted to both organized peasants and individuals.

July 10: The Ministry of Heavy Industry issued a "Directive on Enforcement of the Responsibility System and the Raising of the Quality of Engineering Work in Capital Construction." The directive pointed out that little progress has been made in the campaign to prevent waste and to adopt the responsibility system, so that in the third quarter it will be necessary to carry on both this campaign and the campaign to enforce quality checks.

July 15: The cornerstone for China's first automobile factory was laid in the Northeast. It will use Soviet designs and equipment.

July 16: The first congress of the All-China Industrial and Commercial Federation met in Peking to discuss ways of increasing the participation of private businessmen in national construction.

Conclusion of the Sino-Hungarian agreement on the interchange of mails and tele-communication was announced in Peking.

July 19: The "deviation of rash advance" in the mutual aid and cooperation movement in North China is reported to be "basically corrected," and the number of agricultural producers' cooperatives has been reduced from 9,000 to 6,000.

July 20: Talks were resumed at Panmunjom for a Korean armistice.

July 24: The Thai and Chingpo Nationalities Autonomous People's Government was set up in Tehhung, Yunan.

July 27: The armistice agreement was signed at Panmunjom by representatives of the U.N. Command and of the Korean People's Army and Chinese People's Volunteers. The armistice agreement created the Neutral Nations Supervisory Commission and the Neutral Nations Repatriation Commission.

July 30: The CPC sent greetings to the CPSU on its anniversary. Virtually all mention of Stalin was omitted in the message which concluded with the statement, "the great friendship between the Soviet and the Chinese people will be consolidated with each passing day."

July 31: Multilateral agreements on "through railway freight traffic" and "through railway passenger traffic" were signed in Moscow by the PRC, the U.S.S.R., Albania, Bulgaria, Czechoslovakia, East Germany, Hungary, North Korea, Mongolia, Poland and Rumania.

August 3: A multilateral agreement on the operation of Red Cross teams in Korea was signed in Panmunjom by delegates of Korea, the PRC Red Cross Societies, and delegates of the national Red Cross Societies of countries participating in U.N. Command in Korea.

August 5: A check on the operations of the consumers' cooperatives reveals, according to the NCNA, that there have been many serious mistakes resulting from too hasty expansion, blind purchases, and lack of systematic investigation and study. This has led to graft and corruption, over-complicated accounting systems devised during the Five-Anti campaign, and inability to handle a job of the dimensions required.

August 8: A Sino-German protocol on supplement to agreement on exchange of goods and payments in 1953 was signed in Peking.

August 11: The U.S.-Republic of Korea Defense Treaty is described by the Chinese Communists as a treaty to prepare for war, an aggressive treaty, and a direct threat to the success of the political conferences on the Korean question.

August 14: The *People's Daily*, in commenting on the speech by Malenkov on August 8, states that he outlined the correct way to ease international tension. It said the Chinese will always work to strengthen their solidarity and cooperation with the Soviet Union.

August 18: A Sino-Czechoslovak agreement on cooperation for prevention of insect pests and plant diseases was signed in Peking.

August 20: A goods exchange and payments agreement for 1953 was signed in Peking between China and Mongolia. It was made on the basis of the Sino-Mongolian Agreement on Economic and Cultural Cooperation signed October 4, 1952.

August 23: Mr. Humphrey Trevelyan, the new "representative of the British government for negotiating the establishment of diplomatic relations with the PRC," arrived in Peking.

August 24: Premier Chou En-lai made a statement on the Political Conference on Korea in which he said it should be a round-table conference; it should first negotiate the withdrawal of foreign troops and the peaceful settlement of the Korean question and then it should discuss other questions; all nations with armed forces in Korea may participate and the U.N. has the responsibility of keeping the Chinese and Korean Communists informed regarding the U.N. decisions on the conference.

August 31: Local elections are reported to have been held during August in some parts of most of the provinces and will continue through September and October, chiefly in cities. In the countryside the elections will be held mostly in the winter and early spring. Following the elections at the lowest level, the People's Congresses at county and provincial level will be elected, and then finally the All-China People's Congress will be chosen.

September 2: Secretary of State John Foster Dulles warned Communist China that a renewal of the Korean conflict or a transfer of Communist forces into Indochina might mean war against the mainland itself.

September 5: The U.S., in a message to the Chinese Communist and North Korean governments, suggested that a political conference be convened on October 15 in San Francisco, Honolulu, or Geneva.

September 13: Premier Chou En-lai sent a telegram to U.N. Secretary General Hammerskjold demanding basic revisions in the two resolutions passed by the U.N. General Assembly concerning the political conference on Korea. The Assembly rejected this proposal on September 22.

September 15: The question of Chinese representation in the United Nations was postponed by a vote of 44 to 10 with 2 abstentions.

The NCNA released the text of a letter from Mao to Malenkov on the question of Russian economic aid to China. The letter expressed China's gratitude to the Soviet Union for its promise to "extend systematic economic and technical aid in the construction and renovation of 91 new industries in China and to furnish aid to the 50 enterprises now being built or renovated."

September 21: The Ceylon government trade

delegation signed two contracts with the Peking regime for the exchange of rubber and rice during 1954 and they agreed to extend for two years the 1952 Trade Agreement.

September 28: Premier Chou En-lai granted an interview to Professor Ikuo Oyama, Chairman of the Japanese National Peace Committee, and ten days later the NCNA carried an unprecedented account of the conversation. Chou said the restoration of diplomatic relations with Japan is impossible so long as Japan is an American "satellite," but trade and cultural exchange were to be encouraged in the meantime.

October 1: Parades and mass meetings throughout the country marked the celebration of the 4th anniversary of the founding of the Chinese Communist regime. The *People's Daily* national day editorial called on the people to implement the "general line of the state in the transition period." "The general task" is to "work for the socialist transformation of the states in stages and to carry out the socialist transformation by the state of agriculture, handicrafts, private industry and commerce, step by step, over a considerable period of time."

October 3: Conclusion of the Sino-Hungarian agreement on scientific and technical cooperation was announced.

October 6: The GAC passed a resolution placing control of all universities and higher technical institutions under the Ministry of Higher Education. The training of specialized cadres by the various departments of government will now have to be regulated through the Ministry of Higher Education.

October 8: Premier Chou En-lai endorsed the Soviet proposal of September 28 for the calling of a five-power conference of foreign ministers, including Communist China, to examine measures for easing international tension. He added that the U.N. must admit Communist China if it is to safeguard world peace.

October 10: Premier Chou En-lai agreed to the holding of preliminary discussions at Panmunjom on the time, place and composition of the political conference to settle the Korean problem. The meeting will begin on October 26.

October 12: Directives on winter schooling for peasants were issued by various administrative regions. They stressed the importance of political instruction in connection with literary work. Special emphasis is to be given the general line, the state grain purchases policy, the mutual aid and cooperation movement, the improvement of agricultural techniques, and the increasing of food production.

October 15: Communist China signed Radio Broadcasting Cooperation Agreements with Bulgaria, Hungary, Poland, and Rumania.

A Sino-Rumanian protocol on scientific and technical cooperation was signed in Bucharest.

October 29: A new Sino-Japanese Trade Agreement was signed between the Chinese Committee for the Promotion of International Trade and the Japanese delegation of Diet members. The agreement provided for 300 million pounds sterling of trade.

October 30: Conclusion of the Sino-East German Agreement on Scientific and Technical Cooperation was announced.

November 1-5: The Overseas Chinese Affairs Commission held its first enlarged conference, with 412 delegates representing most of the major overseas Chinese communities. The delegates heard reports on the general line of the state and agreed to a formula for their representation in the National People's Congress.

November 2: The only remaining French companies were requisitioned by the Chinese in Shanghai. This ended the last foreign ownership of public utilities in this city.

November 7: Mao Tse-tung sent "warm and heartfelt" greetings to Malenkov on the 36th anniversary of the October Revolution, and many other Chinese organs sent messages to their counterparts in the U.S.S.R. These acts opened a period of special meetings, film shows, picture exhibits, study groups, newspaper and radio programs stressing Sino-Soviet cooperation.

November 12: The high-level North Korean delegation led by Premier Kim II Sung arrived in Peking and was given the highest honors by Mao Tse-tung and other high officials of the PRC. On November 23, a Sino-Korean Economic and Cultural Cooperation Agreement was signed in Peking after twelve days of negotiations and elaborate ceremonies. The agreement, which will be in force for 10 years, provides for a grant of approximately $338,-000,000 (U.S.) for the supply of equipment and material for North Korean reconstruction over four years.

November 28: The Sino-East German cultural plan was signed in Peking.

November 30: A Sino-Indonesian Trade Agreement was signed in Peking.

December 2: Pavel F. Yudin was appointed the new Soviet Ambassador to China, replacing V. V. Kusnetsev. Ambassador Yudin arrived in Peking on December 12 and presented his credentials on December 15.

December 7: Premier Chou En-lai sent a note to the Secretary General of the U.N. accusing the U.S. of obstructing the agreement on a conference, the repatriation of prisoners of war, and the peaceful settlement of the Korean problem.

December 8-10: Mao Tse-tung and other Communist leaders in Peking cast their votes in the elections for the basic level assemblies amid wide publicity and fanfare.

December 9: The floating of the 1954 National Construction Bonds will commence in January and the total amount is to be 6,000 billion yen. The bonds will pay 4% interest and are redeemable by lot after one year. More than two-thirds of the bonds will be sold in the cities and more than half to private industrialists and merchants.

December 10: A Sino-German protocol on

banking arrangements to implement noncommercial payments was signed.

December 16: A decision on the further development of agricultural producer cooperatives was adopted by the Central Committee of the CPC. It stressed the need for active and correct leadership by the party in steadily developing agricultural production. The 1954 plans call for the establishment of 20,000 new cooperatives throughout the country, making a total of 35,600.

December 17: A GAC directive on the development of winter agricultural production said that all phases of rural work must be subordinated to agricultural production and that the primary way in which to increase production is to develop mutual aid teams and agricultural producer cooperatives.

December 24: In delivering the Politburo report to the 4th plenary session of the 7th Central Committee, Liu Shao-ch'i credited Mao with having initiated at this meeting a proposal for strengthening party unity. Admitting the need for such a proposal, Liu then spoke out vigorously, but without naming names, against the threat of division within the upper ranks of the party.

December 27: The execution of Beria was hailed by the *People's Daily* as a "major victory in frustrating the imperialist plot against the Soviet Union."

December 31: According to a roundup by the NCNA, basic level elections had been concluded in areas with a total population of about 166,000,000 people, or less than one-third of the country. Local People's Congresses had been convened and secondary elections held in areas inhabited by one-fifth of the population.

Premier Chou En-lai received the government delegation of India headed by Ambassador Raghavan, which will negotiate "with the government of China on matters concerning the two countries in the Chinese territory of Tibet."

1954

January 1: The *People's Daily* editorial declared that the Chinese Communists will concentrate on the development of heavy industry and railways in 1954, with an additional 70% newly built or expanded factories and mines to commence operations; industrial production will increase 17%, as compared to a claimed increase of 30% in 1953. The editorial admitted that grain production in 1953 was no greater than in 1952, and called for an increase of slightly over 3% in 1954. Also called for was an increase in the number of agricultural procedure cooperatives from nearly 15,000 to 35,000, and the convening of a National People's Congress.

In Moscow, a multilateral agreement on "through railway traffic" was signed by the PRC, the U.S.S.R., Poland, East Germany, Czechoslovakia, Hungary, Rumania, Bulgaria, Albania, Mongolia and North Korea.

January 8: Completion of over half of the 1700-kilometer Sikang-Tibet highway was reported in a NCNA dispatch from Ch'engtu. According to the report, the central section of the highway had reached the basin of the Brahamputra River. Meanwhile, construction of the western section of the highway was said to be progressing eastward from Lhasa.

January 11: Details of a plan for the gradual collectivization of agriculture were announced in Peking, after having been adopted on December 16, 1953, by the Central government and the Central Committee of the CPC. It was stated that the scheme would be voluntary, and that it was aimed at increasing the number of agricultural cooperatives from the then existing level of 14,000 to 35,000 by the end of 1954 and to 800,000 by 1957, the last year of the Five-Year plan. While it was emphasized that the "agricultural economy of the small peasants must be transformed into a cooperative economy of organized farms," it was stressed that precipitate haste and adventurism must be avoided at all cost, and that the new measures must be made understandable to the peasant mass to cover the transitional period towards socialism. It was admitted that the goal of 800,000 cooperatives set for 1957 would comprise only about one-fifth of the peasant households of China.

January 12: Secretary Dulles, addressing the Council on Foreign Relations in New York City, outlined the doctrine of massive retaliation.

January 22: The CPC Central Committee issued a directive concerning the strengthening of cultural and educational work for cadres, so as to make them "backbone elements" in carrying out the general line. The immediate objective is declared to be raising less-educated cadres to a level equivalent to senior primary and junior middle school graduates, with a certain amount of higher education provided. Forty weeks a year are to be devoted to such education, on a part-time basis.

January 23: The United Nations Command in Korea released those of its prisoners who, after listening to the required explanations by the Communist side, still refused repatriation. These included 14,-000 Chinese (out of a total of about 20,000), who were then sent to Taiwan.

Conclusion of the Sino-Soviet trade protocol for 1954 and of the protocol on delivery to the PRC of Soviet industrial equipment and materials in 1954 was announced.

January 25: The Foreign Ministers of the Big Four met in Berlin to discuss the German and Austrian questions and the prospect of a conference on Korea.

A Sino-North Korean agreement on "through railway traffic" was signed in Peking.

January 31: The first direct passenger train service between Moscow and Peking was opened with the departure of trains from both capitals. They will run twice a week from each city.

February 6-10: On February 6, the 4th plenary session of the CPC Central Committee convened in Peking, the first such meeting since 1950. Chou En-lai made the formal report, which calls for the strengthening of party unity. However, a significant part of Chou's report was a statement that the policy of complete planning in the purchase and supply of foodstuffs by the State went into operation in the winter of 1953 "to ensure the steady supply of foodstuffs and stability of commodity prices, to overcome the spontaneous tendencies toward capitalism among the peasants, and to counter the opposition to restrictions on the part of the capitalist class."

February 18: The communique issued at the end of the Berlin Conference proposes to hold a meeting in Geneva on April 26 for the purposes of reaching a peaceful settlement of the Korean question and of restoring peace in Indochina.

February 20: Conclusion of the Sino-Polish Trade Protocol for 1954 was announced.

February 23: A Sino-Polish protocol on 1954 plan for cultural cooperation was signed in Peking.

February 27: Announcement was made in Peking that as of March 6 jurisdiction over Suiyuan Province will be transferred to the Inner Mongolia Autonomous Region, and Suiyuan's status as a separate province abolished.

February 28: A GAC order for the enforcement of the planned purchase and supply of grain was promulgated in Peking. By this order all "surplus" grain is to be sold to the state, and citizens in general are to be supplied with special grain purchase certificates. All private merchants formally dealing in grain are forbidden to further engage in the grain trade, and purchase and sale prices are to be strictly regulated by official organs in every section of the country.

March 3: A brief NCNA announcement stated that the PRC has accepted the invitation of the Soviet Union to send its "plenipotentiary representative" to attend the Geneva conference.

March 14: A 400-person North Korean People's Delegation headed by Kim Dug Gi arrived in Peking to begin a three-month visit in China. The accent of the visit is on cultural relations.

March 15: The Ministries of Interior and Labor issued a joint directive calling for a halt in the "blind influx" of peasants into the cities. The directive stated that this phenomenon had been checked for a time after the issuance of the GAC directive in April, 1953, forbidding such population shifts, but that the problem has since recurred and in some places has become even more serious than last year.

March 18: To fulfill the State's "stupendous" agricultural task for 1954, the GAC determined that the main agricultural policies in connection with spring plowing and production shall be (1) acceptance of the fact that increased agricultural production is inseparable from the mutual aid and cooperation movement; (2) all possible steps must be taken by leadership organs to guard against mutual calamities; (3) supplies and equipment needed by the peasants for their production work must be supplied in adequate quantities; (4) fertilizer must be "rationally" distributed, and the masses encouraged to rely primarily on natural fertilizers; (5) credits must be provided, especially through the agencies of credit cooperatives; and (6) leadership strengthened.

March 21: In accordance with the GAC directive concerning the granting of farm credit, announcement was made by the People's Bank of China that 10 tribillion yen will be provided by the state in 1954 as farm credit for the development of farm production and the "implementation of Socialist transformation of small peasant economy." Short-term credit will be provided, primarily to peasants organized into farm producer cooperatives and mutual-aid teams, but also to individual peasants to "tread on the path of mutual-aid and cooperation."

March 23: At the 53rd meeting of the Standing Committee of the CPPCC National Committee, the decision was made to invite "responsible personnel of various democratic parties, groups, people's bodies, and people of all circles" to form seventeen groups to study the first draft of a proposed constitution. Chairman Mao Tse-tung reappeared on the political scene to preside at the first meeting of the Committee for Drafting the Constitution, and submitted the first draft to the committee for consideration. This draft had already been drawn up by the Central Committee of the CPC. An agreement was reached at the meeting to complete all discussion on the revisions of the draft Constitution within two months, so that it may be submitted to the Central People's Government Council for adoption and promulgation. Discussions are to be carried out jointly by the Committee for Drafting the Constitution and the National Committee of the CPPCC.

March 23: The GAC Committee of Financial and Economic Affairs issued a directive authorizing the All-China Federation of Cooperatives to make advance purchases from the peasants of such products as food, cotton, peanuts, tea, silk cocoons, wool, etc. Such purchases are to be on a voluntary basis, and coordinated with the propaganda and education on the general line of the state in the period of transition.

Announcement was made of the adoption by the GAC of provisional rules governing the organization of people's mediation committees. These committees are to be established in each *hsiang* in rural areas and each street or area falling under the supervision of a specific public security substation in the cities. The committee will handle civil disputes and minor criminal cases.

March 25: Conclusion of the Sino-Bulgarian trade protocol for 1954 was announced.

March 29: Mr. Dulles, in his speech in New York, called for "united action" against further Communist aggression in any part of Southeast Asia. He said also that the U.S. would stand firm against recognition of Communist China and against its admission to the United Nations.

The GAC Committee of Political and Legal Affairs defined the main political and legal work tasks for 1954 as follows: (1) The completion of the general elections; (2) strengthening of civil affairs departments to serve production; (3) expediting the disposal of judicial cases involving industrial and mining production, capital construction, and rail and water transportation; (4) expansion of public security to cope with concealed threats to economic work; (5) the continued enforcement of the "self-salvation through production" policy in famine areas.

March 30: Conclusion of the Sino-East German trade protocol for 1954 was announced.

Conclusion of the Sino-North Korean agreement on the interchange of mail parcels was announced.

April 7: Conclusion of the Sino-Mongolian trade protocol for 1954 was announced.

April 15: At a joint meeting of the Central Election Committee and the GAC, the decision was made to convene *Hsien* people's congresses in June and provincial and municipal People's Congresses in July or August. The election by these bodies of people's governments of the same level will be postponed pending the promulgation of the constitution, the decision noted.

April 19: Conclusion of the Sino-Rumanian trade protocol for 1954 was announced.

April 22: A three-year Sino-Burmese trade agreement was signed for the exchange of goods at existing world market prices.

April 26: The Geneva Conference on Far Eastern problems opened at the Palais de Nations. Premier Chou En-lai represented the PRC at the conference.

April 27: Conclusion of the Sino-Czechoslovak trade protocol for 1954 was announced.

Announcement was made in Peking that the Ministry of Labor has "recently" called a National Unemployed Workers Relief Conference to summarize relief work for the unemployed over a four-year period and to lay out future policies in this respect. In the future, the announcement stated, the unemployed are to be taught to rely primarily on their own efforts in locating work, and the government will give relief only to those "really experiencing difficulty in living."

April 29: An "Agreement on Intercourse between the Tibet Region of China and India" was signed in Peking. It provided for the withdrawal of all Indian troops from Tibet, the cession by India to China of control over that part of Tibet's postal, telephone, and telegraphic communications formerly administered by India, the establishment of free travel facilities for religious pilgrims from both sides of the border, and the mutual establishment of three trade agencies by each country in the other country's territory.

April 30: Conclusion of the Sino-Hungarian trade protocol for 1954 was announced.

May 3: The so-called people's organizations in China, including the China Peace Committee and the ACFTU, joined together to form the Chinese People's Society for Cultural Relations with Foreign Countries.

May 3-4: Premier Chou En-lai made his first major address at Geneva, speaking in support of North Korean proposals for withdrawing all foreign troops from Korea and holding free all-Korea elections.

May 4: A Sino-Bulgarian protocol on the plan for cultural cooperation in 1954 was signed in Sofia.

May 5-8: Trade union delegates from China, Burma, Ceylon, India, Indonesia, North Korea, Mongolia, the U.S.S.R. and North Vietnam met in Peking "to strengthen mutual understanding and bonds of friendship." Also present as observers were trade unionists from Japan, Israel, France and Italy. The delegates duly attacked colonialism, deplored a decline in living standards of Asian workers, declared their support for the peaceful settlement of the Indochina and Korean questions, and called for the international solidarity and unity of the working class.

May 7: Dienbienphu fell the day before the Geneva Conference began its discussion on the Indochina question.

May 13: A NCNA release stated that by the end of March, 76,400 new agricultural producer cooperatives had been established throughout China, with 36,000 of these newly established cooperatives located in North China alone. The total number of cooperatives in China has now reached 91,000, the report stated, a figure exceeding by almost four times the target set in December, 1953 by the CPC Central Committee.

May 17: Two contracts were signed in Peking by the PRC and Rumania. The first was on exchange of films, while the second was on exchange of newsreel materials.

May 19: The PRC and Mongolia exchanged notes on a plan for cultural cooperation in 1954.

May 20: A Sino-Korean agreement on currency exchange rate was signed in Peking.

May 28: A Sino-Rumanian protocol on a plan for cultural cooperation in 1954 was signed in Peking.

May 29: A Sino-Soviet contract on distribution of Soviet films in the PRC was signed in Peking.

June 1: Premier Chou En-lai offered a new compromise proposal on Indochina at the Geneva Conference, breaking what had seemed an insurmountable deadlock. The Chinese dropped their demand that rebel forces in Laos and Cambodia be recognized as "government," said those forces would be withdrawn under a ceasefire, and asked that the Viet Minh rebel command represent the Communists in truce talks in Vietnam.

June 3: Through passenger train service between Peking and Pyengyang was inaugurated, according to a New China News Agency release.

June 5: Two members of the American and Chinese delegations to the Geneva Conference, U. Alexis Johnson and Wang Ping-nan, began "direct" bilateral talks at Geneva on repatriation of 76 Americans detained in China and 70 Chinese students in the United States. The U.S. stressed that talks did not imply diplomatic recognition.

June 9: Premier Chou En-lai, at the Geneva Conference, made a tough speech in which he reiterated his frequent accusation that the U.S. was trying to use Indochina as a base for military action against the People's Republic of China.

June 10: Conclusion of the Sino-East German agreement on broadcasting cooperation was announced.

June 11: A GAC directive on developing secondary education, released by the NCNA, stated that senior middle schools have not turned out enough candidates for institutes of higher learning, the political and cultural standards of the students were inadequate, their health was not good enough, and teaching staffs were weak both in numbers and quality. It was revealed that in the past four years only 216,000 students have graduated from senior middle schools, compared to 1,055,-000 graduates from junior middle schools. The directive proposed measures to end these deficiencies.

June 14: At the 30th session of the CPGC the Draft Constitution of the People's Republic of China was "unanimously" adopted. The final version was to be submitted to the first session of the First National People's Congress (NPC) for approval.

June 15: At the Geneva Conference the Korean discussion ended inconclusively.

June 16: At the Geneva Conference the Chinese delegation put forward a six-point proposal for ending the war in Cambodia and Laos.

June 17: A Sino-Finnish protocol on general conditions for delivery of goods by PRC was signed in Peking.

The NCNA announced from Peking that agreement had been reached with the British government to send a Chinese charge d'affaires to London, "having the same position and duties as the British charge d'affaires in Peking."

June 19: At its 32nd meeting the CPGC approved the appointment of many new government officials, including that of Li Hsien-nien as Finance Minister and Vice-Chairman of the Financial and Economic Committee of the GAC. Also appointed vice-chairmen of the People's Revolutionary Military Council were Liu Po-ch'eng,

Ho Lung, Ch'en Yi, Lo Jung-huan, Hsieh Jung-chen, and Yeh Chien-ying, thus expanding the number of vice-chairmen from seven to fourteen.

At the same meeting, according to a subsequent announcement, decision was taken to abolish the major administrative regions; amalgamate the provinces of Liaotung and Liaohsi into a new Liaoning province; transfer the jurisdiction of the municipalities of Mukden, Port Arthur, Dairen, Anshan, Fushun, Penki, Harbin, Ch'ang-ch'un, Wuhan, Canton, Sian and Chungking from the Central Government to the relevant provincial governments; amalgamate Sungkiang Province with Heilungkiang, and amalgamate Ninghsia Province with Kansu. A previous decision to amalgamate Suiyuan into the Inner Mongolian Autonomous Region is ratified.

At the Geneva Conference, after a final plenary session, a communique was issued announcing that unanimous agreement had been reached upon the following steps relating to the cessation of hostilities in Cambodia and Laos: (1) Representatives of the two sides should meet immediately in Geneva or on the spot in Indochina; (2) they should study the question relating to the ending of hostilities in the two states; (3) they should report their conclusions and recommendations to the conference as soon as possible.

June 21: Indian guards at Panmunjom released Korean War prisoners of both sides who refused repatriation.

Conclusion of Sino-Finnish trade agreement was announced.

June 23: Premier Chou En-lai met French Premier M. Mendes-France at the French embassy in Berne to discuss Indochina. It was the first time contact at government level between France and the PRC had been made. Chou repeated his views on the Laos and Cambodia settlement, agreed that there was no urgency about holding an election in Vietnam, and suggested bilateral talks between France and Ho Chi-Minh on the terms of the Vietnamese settlement.

Sino-German protocol on scientific and technical cooperation was signed in Peking.

June 24: Premier Chou En-lai left Geneva.

June 25-28: Premier Chou En-lai visited India to insure against the unlikely possibility that Britain might succeed in drawing the Asian members of the Commonwealth nations into the proposed collective security arrangement in Southeast Asia. In a joint communique, the two nations agreed on the Five Principles governing their relations. The Five Principles were (1) Mutual respect for territorial integrity; (2) non-aggression; (3) non-interference in the internal affairs of others; (4) relations to be based upon mutual equality and benefits; (5) peaceful co-existence.

June 28-29: Premier Chou En-lai visited Burma. In a joint statement with Premier U Nu, Chou announced that they had agreed to base their relations on the Five Principles issued at New Delhi. It was also understood that the talks between Chou and U Nu dealt with Indochina and Southeast Asia problems, and with matters of common interest to Burma and China.

June 28: A Chinese Communist trade mission arrived in London at the invitation of the Federation of British Industries and four other industrial and commercial organizations. The mission will spend some time in England journeying to different industrial areas. Purpose of the mission, according to its head Tsae Chung-shu, was "to find opportunities jointly with those who are interested in developing Sino-British trade and to lay firm foundations for a bright future for the Sino-British trade." The mission later (July 9) issued a statement declaring that two-way trade between China and Britain can reach a total of 100,000,000 pounds sterling annually.

June 30: Conclusion of Sino-North Korean protocol on the exchange of goods was announced.

July 3-5: Premier Chou En-lai met President Ho Chi-Minh at an undisclosed spot on the frontier between China and Indochina. Their conversation dealt with the Geneva Conference, the restoration of peace in Indochina, and related matters.

July 5: The enlarged session of the National Committee of the CPPCC met in Peking, and unanimously approved the lists of candidates for the National People's Congress. On July 8 Chou En-lai made a report to the session on his trip to Geneva, India, Burma, and the meeting with Ho Chi-Minh.

July 7: Conclusion of Sino-North Vietnam trade protocol for 1954 was announced. Sino-Vietnamese protocol on small-scale trading and currency exchange in border areas was also signed in Peking.

July 9: The United States Senate passed a resolution opposing the admission of Communist China into the United Nations. A similar resolution was passed by the House of Representatives on July 15.

July 12-14: The prime ministers and other representatives of the countries taking part in the Geneva Conference reassembled in Geneva. Chou En-lai reached Geneva via Moscow on July 12.

July 13: *People's Daily* published a report of the All-China Federation of Cooperatives, stating that Peking plans to organize five million handicraft workers into cooperatives by 1957. The remainder of China's 20 million handicraft workers will be organized into cooperatives during the second five-year plan.

July 14: Regulations on the conduct of labor in state-operated enterprises, adopted at a meeting of the GAC on May 6, were promulgated in Peking. The regulations aim at "ensuring and consolidating labor discipline, fully and rationally utilizing working time, increasing labor efficiency, and producing goods of superior quality." Workers are required to be punctual in attendance, to devote full time to production, to fulfill production quotas, etc. Strict punishment of delinquents was authorized.

July 17: A Sino-Czechoslovak protocol on a plan for cultural cooperation in 1954 was signed in Prague.

July 21: An armistice agreement on Indochina was concluded at the Geneva Conference.

Peking freed 6 Americans, including 4 civilians, while Washington permitted 15 Chinese students to leave the United States.

Conclusion of the Sino-Polish agreement on scientific and technical cooperation was announced.

A Sino-Indian agreement on tobacco trade was signed in Peking.

July 23: A British Skymaster passenger aircraft was shot down in the sea of Hainan by two Communist fighters. Ten of the eighteen aboard died. The British issued a strong protest and on July 26, Chan Chang-fu, a deputy foreign minister, apologized for the incident and offered compensation over Radio Peking.

July 23-26: Premier Chou En-lai visited East Germany. A joint communique was issued dealing with rearmament of West Germany and Japan, the Geneva Conference on Indochina, etc.

July 26-28: Premier Chou En-lai visited Poland.

July 26: Two Chinese aircraft attacked a United States plane over international waters 13 miles off Hainan. The Chinese note said that there had been an invasion of Chinese air space by U.S. aircraft which had shot down two Chinese planes and strafed ships. In the United States, Admiral Stamp, Commander-in-Chief of the Pacific Fleet, said that U.S. troops had orders to shoot back and be quick on the trigger.

July 28-30: Premier Chou En-lai visited Moscow.

July 31-August 1: Premier Chou En-lai visited Mongolia.

August 1-10: People's Congresses at the Provincial level were held in different parts of the country to elect deputies to the National People's Congress, which is to meet in the fall. Servicemen's congresses are also being held among People's Liberation Army units and districts.

August 2-5: Pham Van Dong, vice premier and acting foreign minister of North Vietnam, arrived in Peking on the invitation of the Chinese Communists. In various speeches made while in Peking he extolled China's world position and its aid in achieving the victory at Geneva, and stated that in the "imminent struggle for consolidating lasting peace in Indochina and in the struggle against the warmongers' scheme," the people of Vietnam are confident that they will receive China's aid.

August 7: The NCNA announced that the Ministry of Finance ordered that all canvassing for the sale of National Economic Construction Bonds will cease on August 10. According to the announcement, subscriptions have reached 9,200 billion yen, exceeding the target of 6,000 billion by 53%.

August 9-15: Attended by some 200 delegates from 50 countries, the Council of the World Federation of Democratic Youth met in Peking.

August 10: Provisional regulations on residence, travel, and exit by foreign nationals were promulgated by the Ministry of Public Security. They supersede all previous regulations. Maximum residence was set at five years (renewable upon application); travel beyond city or *hsien* boundaries and departure from the country require permits which state itinerary, means of transport, and time limits; travelers are subject to police or military questioning. Identity cards in lieu of residence permits will be issued to foreigners without occupations, those who are serving punishments, or who are insane.

August 11: Premier Chou En-lai presented a foreign policy report at the 33rd meeting of the CPGC which called for "determined action to liberate Taiwan." Chou En-lai also strongly attacked the non-Communist plan for a Southeast Asia defense community as a threat to China and to the Indochina agreements, and indicated that Communist China wished to introduce "collective security" to Asia without the inclusion of the Western powers. The United States continued direct negotiations with the Communist

Chinese delegate at Geneva seeking release of 60 Americans detained in China, including 30 civilians and 15 military personnel in jail; three civilians under house arrest, and 12 denied exit permits. It was also reported that 22 Chinese students had obtained exit permits from the United States.

August 14: An eight-member British Labor party delegation headed by Clement Attlee arrived in Peking via Moscow in response to an invitation made earlier by the Chinese People's Institute of Foreign Affairs. The Communist press acclaims the visit, holding out the possibilities of increased Sino-British trade and betterment of relations on the basis of the "Five Principles of Peaceful Co-existence."

August 17: President Eisenhower stated that the 7th Fleet would defend Taiwan.

August 21: A Sino-Soviet agreement on cooperation in radio broadcasting was signed in Moscow.

August 22: The following declaration was issued by the CPPCC: (1) That Taiwan was Chinese territory; (2) that it was occupied by the United States and that this was intolerable; (3) that Taiwan was not to be put under United Nations trusteeship; (4) that the liberation of Taiwan was an exercise of Chinese sovereignty; (5) that the Chinese People's Republic was willing to give amnesty to all but Chiang Kai-shek and that these persons could renounce their past and return to the mainland.

Conclusion of a Sino-Soviet agreement on broadcasting cooperation was announced.

August 29: The abolition of the East China Administrative Committee was announced, while both the Northeast and North China Administrative Committees were abolished on October 15.

August 31: The PRC and Hungary exchanged notes on a 1954 plan for cultural cooperation.

The North China Bureau of the CPC Central Committee was dissolved.

A Sino-German supplementary protocol on exchange of goods in 1954 was signed.

September 1: Conclusion of Sino-Indonesian trade and payment protocol was announced.

September 2: At a meeting, GAC adopted "Provisional Regulations Governing Public-Private Jointly Operated Enterprises." The regulations asserted state control over such enterprises through CPG industrial, commercial, and financial organs, although the "lawful interests" of private shareholders are in theory protected.

NCNA noted that the GAC passed a series of regulations and measures for labor reform entitled, "Labor Reform Regulations of the People's Republic of China," and "Provincial Measures Governing the Settlement and Employment of Labor-Reformed and Acquitted Criminals After Serving Prison Terms." According to Public Security Minister Lo Jui-ch'ing, criminals may "offer" to remain in corrective labor units. He indicated that the Chinese Communist labor reform regulations are patterned after those in the Soviet Union.

Sino-Czechoslovak protocol on scientific and technical cooperation was signed in ?rague

September 3-6: Chinese Communist artillery shelled Quemoy and Little Quemoy islands.

September 4: Nationalist Chinese spokesman saw Chinese Communist invasion of Quemoy imminent.

A Sino-Korean protocol on exchange of goods in 1954 was signed in Peking.

September 5: The prospective withdrawal of seven Chinese Communist divisions from Korea was announced.

The White House said that President Eisenhower was alert to Chinese Communist threats, and that the order to the 7th Fleet had not been changed.

September 7: The Nationalists retaliated with large-scale air attacks against the mainland but discontinued them about a month later, reportedly at U.S. suggestion.

September 8: The Southeast Asia Treaty Organization (SEATO) was signed at Manila.

September 9: Secretary Dulles conferred

36

with Chiang Kai-shek in Taipei and assured him that Nationalist China would not stand alone against a Chinese aggression threat.

September 12: The National Security Council met in special session with the President in Denver to discuss Far Eastern policy in the light of the Manila conference decisions and the Chinese Communist attack on Quemoy. President Eisenhower announced after the meeting that no specific decision had yet been made on the defense of Quemoy. Mr. Dulles saw no early Chinese Communist attempt to invade Quemoy or Taiwan. He held the view that Taiwan could not be taken. On the defense of Quemoy, he said that it was for military men to decide, and that Chiang Kai-shek neither sought nor was given any U.S. commitments in this respect. He reiterated U.S. policy to defend Taiwan and the Pescadores.

September 13: Peking radio reported that H. F. Redmond was sentenced to life imprisonment as a U.S. spy ring member in Shanghai.

September 14: The GAC issued an order imposing "planned purchase and planned supply" of cotton cloth throughout the country, beginning September 15. State monopoly purchase of raw cotton from the peasants is also to be enforced. Thus the two principal agricultural products, grain and cotton, have passed under government control.

The Military Service Law was promulgated. The law is intended to draft 450,-000 men into the PLA between November 1, 1954, and February 28, 1955. All male citizens between the ages of 18 and 22 are eligible; service will be 3 years in the Army, 4 in the Air Force, or 5 in the Navy, as of March 1, 1955. The call-up is declared to be "a step toward gradually carrying out a system of universal military training."

September 15-28: The first session of the First National People's Congress met in Peking with 1141 deputies attending. Chairman Mao Tse-tung opened the session with a brief address in which he spoke of "several five-year plans" for building China into a highly industrialized country. He exhorted the nation to work hard and learn from the advanced experience of the Soviet Union. Mr. Liu Shao-chi reported to the NPC on the draft of the constitution on September 15. The NPC adopted a new constitution to replace the common program and the Organic Law of 1949 (September 20). On September 23 Premier Chou En-lai delivered a report on the work of the government between 1949 and 1954, in which he cited the achievements made in industrializing China, but admitted that agricultural production—although allegedly above 1949 levels—had lagged behind consumer and industrial demands. In domestic affairs, he indicated that the future course of state planning called for further steps toward socialization of agriculture, industry, and handicrafts; strengthening of the struggle against "counter-revolutionaries," and building up "powerful modern national defense forces." In foreign affairs, he stressed the need to strengthen the friendly ties between China, the Soviet Union, and the people's democracies on the "Five Principles"; broaden East-West trade and liberate Taiwan. He made a special reference to the overseas Chinese nationality problem, which he claimed China is willing to "settle" with those Southeast Asian nations which have recognized the regime. The NPC reelected Mao Tse-tung to a four-year term as Chairman of the People's Republic of China on September 27.

September 21: The question of Chinese representation in the United Nations was postponed by vote of 45 to 7, with 5 abstentions.

September 29: A top-level Soviet government delegation headed by Khrushchev and including such figures as Bulganin, Mikoyan, and Shvernik, arrived in Peking to participate in the Chinese Communist National Day celebration on October 1.

October 2: With 6,000 people attending the formal ceremonies, a permanent "Exhibition of Economic and Cultural Achievements of the Soviet Union" opened in

Peking. This exhibition is reported to be the biggest exhibition of its kind sponsored by the Soviet Union in a foreign country. Over 11,000 items of machinery and Soviet-manufactured goods are on display to show purported Soviet industrial, agricultural, and cultural progress.

October 6: An agreement between Ceylon and the PRC on the prices to be paid for rice and rubber in the third year (1955) of the Sino-Ceylonese five-year trade agreement was signed in Peking.

October 7: The Credentials Committee of the 9th U.N. General Assembly voted down as out of order a Soviet proposal to declare the Nationalist Chinese representatives' credentials invalid.

October 8: Two Sino-Ceylonese contracts on rice and rubber trade in 1955 were signed in Peking.

October 10: Premier Chou En-lai sent a message to the United Nations alleging American aggression against Taiwan and asking that the General Assembly urge the Security Council to call for a complete American withdrawal from the Taiwan area.

October 12: Economic aid by the PRC to Albania in the form of a gift of ten million rubles and credit of fifty million rubles over the period 1955-1960 was announced.

After two weeks of negotiations, a series of Sino-Soviet agreements were announced in Peking. The U.S.S.R. agreed to return Port Arthur to China by March 31, 1955; to provide long-term credit of 520 million rubles and equipment, with 400 million rubles for 15 new and 141 previously planned industrial plants; to extend Russian aid in the construction of a railway linking the Soviet Union to China; and to relinquish its shares in four Sino-Soviet joint stock companies by January 1, 1955. On foreign relations they agreed (1) That they would consult each other in the formation of foreign policy; (2) that China and the U.S.S.R. base their relations with others on the Five Principles agreed upon with India; (3) that the United States should leave Taiwan and that its presence there was incompatible with world peace; (4) that a conference should be called to discuss the Korean question; (5) that they opposed the existence of American bases on Japanese soil, they wanted to develop better relations with Japan, and they desired to normalize these relations. Furthermore, the Soviet Union agreed to aid in the mining of metals in Sinkiang and the construction of naval ships at Dairen. Sino-Soviet agreement on scientific and technical cooperation was also signed.

October 14: Conclusion of the Sino-Indian trade agreement in the period 1954-1956 was announced. The two states also exchanged notes agreeing to discuss questions concerning inspection of commodities, navigation, insurance, and transit of merchants.

October 14: Conclusion of the Sino-Albanian cultural, scientific and technical cooperation agreement was announced.

October 15: A Sino-Rumanian protocol on scientific and technical cooperation was signed in Peking.

October 19: A Sino-Indian accord on exchange of tobacco and raw silk was signed in New Delhi.

October 19-30: Mr. Nehru, accompanied by Indira Gandhi and N. R. Pillai (Minister of External Affairs), arrived in Peking on October 19. The Nehru party left China on October 30 after visiting Manchuria, Nanking, Shanghai, Hangchow and Canton. In a summarization of his trip on November 2 in Saigon, Mr. Nehru said that China was anxious to avoid war. He held a view that peaceful co-existence was possible if principles of non-aggression and non-interference were acted upon. It was announced that an agreement on China-India air service was concluded on October 14.

October 28: Peking's charge d'affaires arrived in London.

November 1: Cumpulsory enlistment of 450,-000 men for the PLA began.

The State Statistical Bureau made public details of China's first nationwide census, which set the total population at

601,938,035, including some 12 million overseas Chinese and 7 million Taiwanese. Of this figure, 51.62% are males. Szechwan has the largest population with 62 million people, and Shanghai takes a big lead over other cities with a population of 6.2 million. Peking's population is 2,768,-149. Han Chinese constitute nearly 94% of the total compared to some ten other large racial groups.

November 3: A trade protocol between Burma and China was signed in Peking by which Burmese rice will be exchanged for Chinese export commodities. At the same time, a contract covering the purchase by China of 150,000 long tons of Burmese rice was also signed.

November 4: The Tachen Islands off the coast of Chekiang Province were raided by Chinese Communist aircraft.

November 8: The Northwest Administrative Committee was dissolved on November 8, while the Southwest and Central-South Administrative Committees were abolished as of November 1 and 7 respectively.

November 12: With the visit to Peking of an Argentine "Industrial and Commercial Delegation" at the invitation of the China Committee for the Promotion of International Trade, a "good basis had been laid for future development of trade between China and Argentine," according to the NCNA. The visit of the Argentine delegation marked the first contact between Peking and any South American country in a semi-official way.

November 15: The Central-South Bureau of the CPC Central Committee was abolished.

November 23: The NCNA announced the sentencing of eleven U.S. fliers and two civilians, captured during the Korean war, to prison terms of from four years to life. The U.S. protest was rejected on November 26 (delivered by the British charge d'affaires).

November 27: With the construction of a bridge across the Pa River, the 2255-kilometer motor road from Ya-an in Szechwan to Lhasa is "basically completed," the NCNA announced. The first convoy of

trucks from Sikang arrived in the suburbs of Lhasa. The highway will be completely finished when a bridge across the Indus into Lhasa is erected.

December 1-16: U Nu, Premier of Burma, visited Communist China. The communique issued by Chou En-lai and U Nu on December 12 included (1) Re-affirmation of the Five Principles; (2) establishment of consulates in appropriate cities of each in the near future; (3) opening of air and road traffic and the signing of postal and telegraphic agreements; (4) Chinese import quota from 1955 to 1957 to be 150–200,000 tons of rice in exchange for industrial and other goods; (5) delimitation of the border dispute through diplomatic channels.

December 2: The United States concluded a Mutual Defense Treaty with Nationalist China in Washington.

NCNA announced that 1400 miles of road had been completed, linking Lhasa and Chungking and other Chinese cities.

December 3: Conclusion of Sino-Albanian trade and payments protocol for 1955 was announced. An agreement on long-term credit to Albania, and a protocol on Sino-Albanian 1955 plan for scientific and technical cooperation, were also announced.

December 6: The NCNA announced that the PRC has presented a consignment of food and other products to Albania in honor of the 10th anniversary of the Albanian "liberation."

December 7: The sixteen Korean allies offered a resolution in the General Assembly accusing Communist China of violating the Korean armistice by jailing 13 Americans as spies and detaining other captured U.N. personnel who wanted to be repatriated. On December 10, the General Assembly adopted the resolution and instructed Secretary General Dag Hammerskjold to seek immediate release of the prisoners. On December 11 he sent a letter to Chou En-lai requesting discussions. On December 13 Peking Radio said the U.N. had no right to interfere with the conviction and punishment of the Americans. On December 17 Chou En-lai replied to Dag Hammarskjold's request for talks and said he was prepared to receive the latter. In an additional telegram, Chou said that the U.S. airmen were spies and that he would not compromise on this question.

December 8: Premier Chou En-lai denounced the U.S.-Nationalist Chinese defense treaty and said that the U.S. would be responsible for the consequences if forces were not withdrawn from Taiwan and that Communist China was determined to "liberate Taiwan and liquidate the traitors of the Chiang Kai-shek clique." On December 15 the Soviet Union announced "full support" of the Chinese demands.

December 11: The Japanese government expressed its wish to restore normal relations with Russia and China on mutually acceptable terms without prejudice to its basic collaboration with the free nations. Japan would also welcome opportunities for expanding the volume of trade with both countries.

December 11-28: The first session of the Sino-Soviet Commission on Scientific and Technical Cooperation was held in Moscow, leading to the signing of a Sino-Soviet Scientific Aid Protocol.

December 13: Conclusion of a Sino-Finnish supplementary trade protocol for 1954 was announced.

A Sino-Indian contract on export of silk to India was signed in New Delhi.

December 16: Conclusion of a Sino-Mongolian trade protocol for 1955 was announced.

December 18: The first forum for criticism of the viewpoints in Hu Shih's *History of Chinese Philosophy* was held in Peking.

December 20: A new set of regulations was promulgated governing arrest and detainment without the prior approval of the People's procuratorates in cases of emergency.

December 24: A joint Sino-North Vietnam communique issued in Peking stated that Communist China has agreed to give North Vietnam material and personnel aid in restoring communications and water conservancy work in North Vietnam. The agreements provide for (1) restoration and new construction of a railway connecting Hanoi with the Chinese border; (2) opening of postal and telecommunications between the two countries; (3) Chinese supplies for road transport; (4) Chinese supplies for a civil air service and meteorological station; and (5) equipment for five water conservancy works destroyed during the war. Chinese personnel are to be sent to North Vietnam to carry out the agreements.

December 25: The NCNA announced the completion of Tsinghai-Tibet highway.

The first session of the Second CPPCC, held in Peking (December 21-25), passed a resolution to denounce the U.S.-Nationalist China mutual defense treaty.

December 27: Conclusion of the Sino-East German protocol on the exchange of students was announced. Sino-German agreement on a plan for cultural cooperation in 1955 was also announced.

December 28: A Sino-Hungarian agreement on cooperation to prevent insect pests and plant diseases was signed in Peking.

A Sino-Soviet protocol on scientific and technical cooperation was announced in Moscow.

December 29: A Sino-Indonesian joint communique was issued for preliminary negotiations on dual nationality.

December 30: A joint Sino-Soviet air service agreement was signed in Peking calling for the establishment of air service between Peking and Moscow.

December 31: Conclusion of the Sino-North Korean trade protocol for 1955 was announced. A protocol granting aid and credit by PRC to North Korea in 1955 was also announced in Peking.

Four Sino-Soviet joint stock companies were transferred to Communist China with elaborate ceremonies. The four companies were the Sino-Soviet Civilization Joint Stock Company, the Sino-Soviet Joint Stock Company for Non-Ferrous and Rare Metals, the Sino-Soviet Joint Stock Company for Petroleum, and the Sino-Soviet Stock Company for Shipbuilding and Repair.

1955

January 1: A Moscow NCNA dispatch stated that a "Sino-Soviet Commission on Scientific and Technical Cooperation" has been formed and has agreed upon a wide range of scientific and technical exchanges between the two countries.

January 5-10: Secretary General Dag Hammarskjold arrived in Peking to negotiate the release of the U.S. airmen and U.N. personnel detained in China. He had talks with Premier Chou En-lai on sixth, seventh, eighth and tenth of January. A joint communique was issued on January 10. No indication was given of the immediate release of the prisoners.

January 10: The Tachen Islands were again raided by the Chinese Communists. Some 600 bombers and fighter-bombers took part.

Yugoslavia and the PRC agreed to the establishment of diplomatic relations at the embassy level.

Conclusion of a Sino-Hungarian protocol on scientific and technical cooperation was announced.

January 17: The Soviet Union agreed to give scientific and technical aid in the use of atomic energy to China, Poland, Rumania, Czechoslovakia and East Germany. Included was a reactor capable of producing 5000 kw. of energy.

January 18: Yikiangshan, eight miles north of the Tach'en Islands, was captured by the Chinese Communists.

January 19: The Chinese Communists began an attack on the Tach'en Islands, including the use of some 200 aircraft. The Nationalists counter-attacked in the Amoy and Swatow areas.

President Eisenhower discounted the importance of Yikiangshan and the Tach'ens to Taiwan defense. He also favored the United Nations' effort to arrange a cease-fire.

January 20: A NCNA announcement stated that the PRC and Afghanistan have agreed to establish diplomatic relations and to exchange ambassadors.

The 1955 protocol for the implementa-

tion of the Sino-Hungarian Cultural Cooperation Agreement was signed in Budapest.

The 1955 Sino-Rumanian goods exchange and payments agreement was signed in Peking.

January 21: Peking Radio announced that facilities would be made available for relatives of captured airmen to visit them and would be provided by the Red Cross. The offer had been made by Chou En-lai to Dag Hammarskjold. The United States made it clear that relatives would travel to China at their own risk, and on January 27 Secretary Dulles announced that the United States would not issue passports to those requesting them for a trip to China.

January 24: Premier Chou En-lai issued a statement saying that any U.N. effort to arrange a cease-fire in the Taiwan Straits is an interference with Communist China's internal affairs, as "Taiwan is an inalienable part of China's territory." He declared that all tension in the area is due entirely to U.S. occupation of Taiwan and can be ended by the withdrawal of all U.S. forces from Taiwan and the Taiwan Straits.

President Eisenhower, in his special message to Congress, asked authority to use U.S. forces to defend Taiwan and the Pescadores and to take action against the threatening Communist concentrations on nearby islands and mainlands. He held a view that Congressional authorization would ease the war threat by removing doubt of U.S. intention to preserve free Taiwan. He hoped that the U.N. could arrange a ceasefire but viewed the situation as too critical to await U.N. action.

January 27: The Sino-Bulgarian agreement on exchange of goods and payments for 1955 was signed in Peking.

January 29: Congress adopted a joint resolution—Formosan Resolution—authorizing the President to defend the offshore islands only if he judged a Communist attack on them to be part of an attack on Taiwan.

January 31: The Committee for Reforming the Chinese Written Language announced a "draft plan for simplifying Chinese characters."

U.N. Security Council voted (9-1-1) to adopt the New Zealand proposal to discuss cease-fire on off-shore islands and to invite Communist China to attend debate.

February 2: An order of the State Council was promulgated protecting the remittances of overseas Chinese to their dependents on the mainland. Such remittances are declared to be private property, and dependents have the right to enjoy them without interference, provided that funds are used for living expenses. "Donations" to "patriotic" savings drives and purchase of bonds are to be on a voluntary basis only, although overseas Chinese dependents are to be "encouraged" to invest in construction projects of benefit to the state.

February 3: Chinese Communists rejected a U.N. invitation to participate in Formosan Strait cease-fire discussions. In his message to Hammarskjold, Premier Chou En-lai said that Peking would send representatives to discuss only the U.S.S.R. resolution charging U.S. aggression, and only when the Nationalist representative was driven from the Security Council.

According to the release by the NCNA, a "draft plan for simplifying Chinese characters" has been issued by the Committee for Reforming the Chinese Written Language. The draft plan introduced 798 "simplified characters," abolished the variants of 400 characters, and laid down the methods of reducing strokes of characters and radicals. It has been distributed to "cultural and educational workers and persons of all circles" for comment, and will be implemented later in the year.

February 4: Statements were made in the House of Commons by British Prime Minister Churchill and Foreign Secretary Eden to the effect that the status of

Taiwan remains in doubt and that "two entities" exist, each "claiming to represent China." There was a furious Chinese Communist attack against the two statements.

February 5: The State Department announced that the U.S. 7th Fleet would help in the evacuation of the Tachen Islands.

February 8: The U.S. Senate Foreign Relations Committee approved a U.S.-Nationalist China mutual defense treaty (11-2).

The NCNA reported that construction had begun on the Paotow-Lanchow Railway.

February 9: The NCNA announced the promulgation by Chairman Mao Tse-tung of the "Regulations on the Service of Officers of Chinese PLA" which were adopted at a meeting of the NPC Standing Committee on February 8. These regulations contain the statement that they are "made in line with the change in the country's military service from a voluntary to a compulsory basis and in order to further the building up of the Chinese PLA as a modern, regular army." Fourteen grades of officer ranks were introduced, from junior lieutenant to supreme marshal.

The NCNA announced from Hanoi that track-laying work on the 150-kilometer railway linking Hanoi with the Sino-Vietnam border town of Munanhuan has been completed.

February 11: Conclusion of a Sino-Soviet trade protocol for 1955 was announced.

A Sino-Polish agreement on the plan for cultural cooperation in 1955 was signed in Warsaw.

The U.S. Senate ratified the Mutual Defense Treaty with Nationalist China (in force on March 3).

February 13: The NCNA announced that the PRC had liberated the Tachen Islands as well as the Yashan and Peishan Islands.

February 15: The Chinese government approved conscription regulations which made nearly 80,000,000 men liable for for service—3 years for army, 4 years for air force, 5 years for navy. The regulations applied to all men between the ages of 18 and 40 with the exception of only sons, men responsible for a family, and counter-revolutionaries who had been deprived of citizenship rights.

February 16: Up to the first ten days of February, 500,000 agricultural producer cooperatives had been formed, and 16,000 more were in the process of being set up, the NCNA declared. Thus, "the plan of setting up 600,000 cooperatives in China in the winter of 1954 and the spring of 1955 has been fulfilled."

February 17: The 1955 protocol for implementing Sino-Bulgarian cultural cooperation agreement was signed in Peking.

February 20: A new section of the Lanchow-Sinkiang Railway connecting Lanchow and Wumei was opened to traffic.

February 21: The State Council promulgated an order issuing a new currency to replace the notes presently in circulation, effective March 1. The new *yuan* of the old currency, and foreign exchange rates, prices, and accounts will be changed accordingly.

February 23-25: The Nanchi Islands, 130 miles north of Taiwan, were evacuated and the Communist Chinese reopened fire on Quemoy and Matsu Islands.

February 25: The PRC announced the withdrawal of six divisions from North Korea.

February 28: Two American prisoners were released from the Chinese mainland after three and one-half years of imprisonment.

March 1: The new people's currency started to circulate. Chinese currency was revalued so that 1000 old *yuan* would be exchanged for one new one.

The PRC and Czechoslovakia exchanged notes for the 1955 plan for cultural cooperation.

March 2: The 1955 plan for implementing the Sino-Albanian Agreement on Cultural Cooperation was signed in Tirana.

NCNA announced that a 100-mile railway linking Hanoi with the Chinese frontier had been opened.

March 8: NCNA revealed that the CPC Central Committee recently convened a conference on rural party work at which

expansion of party membership in rural areas was discussed. According to the agency report, party branches had been set up in 170,000 out of a total of 220,-000 village groups, and rural party membership stood at 4 million out of a total of about 6 million. More rural members would be admitted in the next three years.

March 10: The 1955 plan for carrying out the Sino-Rumanian Cultural Cooperation Agreement was signed in Bucharest.

March 12: It was announced in Peking that after six months of negotiations with the Dalai and Panchen Lamas of Tibet, the Tibetan autonomous region was formed. It was to be headed by the Dalai Lama as Chairman of the Preparatory Committee.

March 14: The PRC and Outer Mongolia exchanged notes in Ulan Bator on the 1955 plan for cultural cooperation between the two countries.

March 21: A Sino-Polish agreement on the exchange of goods and payments for 1955 was signed in Peking.

March 23: A Sino-Bulgarian Agreement on Scientific and Technical Cooperation was signed in Sofia.

A State Council directive published in the *People's Daily* called for advance purchase of cotton in order to stimulate production. The directive authorized an advance payment of 10% on contracts and offered cotton growers 10 catties of food and 100 feet of cloth over and above the standard rations for every contract of one picul of ginned cotton. An additional 225,000 tons of cotton will be grown in 1955, the directive declared.

March 24: Chinese Communists withdrew six divisions from Korea.

March 26: As part of the state efforts to mobilize rural credit behind agricultural production, the State Council approved the establishment of an Agricultural Bank of China within the People's Bank of China.

March 28: Barter agreements for the exchange of Chinese metals and steel, construction materials, sanitary equipment, paper, cotton yarn, etc. for Burmese rice were signed in Peking, in accordance with a Sino-Burmese trade protocol of November, 1954.

April 1: A joint Sino-Indian communique from Lhasa stated that the Indian government has agreed to turn over to Communist China without compensation its postal, telegraph, and public telephone services in Tibet and to sell its twelve rest houses in Tibet to Peking for 316,828 rupees.

April 2: The U.S. State Department announced that 76 Chinese students with technical training who had been refused exit permits after the start of the Korean war, because they might have helped the Communists in Korea, were now "free to depart" from the United States.

April 4: It was announced in Peking that Kao Kang, former Deputy Premier and Chairman of the Administrative Committee of the Northeast (Manchuria), had been expelled from the party by the Central Committee for acts against the party and people, and had committed suicide. Jao Shu-shih, a political commissar at the head of the party organization bureau, was expelled for anti-party activity. Teng Hsiao-p'ing stated that Kao Kang had attempted to split the party and take over the leadership of the state and create his own kingdom in the Northeast. Jao Shu-shih was accused of having used deceit in an attempt to gain power.

April 6: A Sino-Czechoslovak goods exchange and payments agreement for 1955 was signed in Peking.

April 8: Peking Radio announced that Chairman Mao Tse-tung had issued a proclamation ending the state of war with Germany.

April 11: A plane carrying an Indian crew, seven or eight Chinese Communist journalists, and one North Vietnamese delegate to the Bandung Conference, crashed near the Great Natuna Island, off Borneo, while en route from Hong Kong to Djakarta. The Chinese Communist government presented a note to Britain alleging that the plane had been sabotaged at Hong Kong by U.S. and Chinese Nationalist

agents with the aim of assassinating the Chinese delegates. Led by Premier Chou En-lai, these delegates were en route to the Bandung Conference of April 13. On April 17, the British replied that there had been nothing to suggest sabotage of the plane and that it had been under guard. At the conclusion of an investigation undertaken by Indonesian authorities, it was found that a bomb had been placed in the wheel well of the aircraft.

April 13: The NCNA announced from Canton that 26 "Chiang Kai-shek agents," accused of attempting to set time bombs in Canton during the 1954 National Day celebrations, had been sentenced before a mass trial attended by 5,000 persons. Nine of the alleged agents were sentenced to death, 16 others received suspended death sentences. All were said to have connections with secret agent organizations in Hong Kong.

April 14: Premier Chou En-lai conferred with Burmese Premier U Nu in Rangoon on his way to Bandung.

April 15: The first issue of the Russian language newspaper *Friendship Daily* was published in Peking.

An agreement on fishing in the Yellow Sea and East China Sea was signed in Peking between delegations of the China Fishery Association and of the Japan-China Fishery Association of Japan. There was also an exchange of letters on demarcation of the PRC military and conservation zones closed to Japanese fishing vessels.

April 18-24: The Conference of Asian and African States, organized by the five Colombo powers, opened at Bandung (Indonesia) and was attended by representatives of 25 countries. In addition to the four resolutions on economic, cultural cooperation, human rights and self-determination, problem of dependent people, and promotion of world peace and international cooperation, the conference also adopted a Declaration on the Problems of Dependent Peoples and a Declaration on the Promotion of World Peace and Cooperation.

April 20: The Headquarters of the Chinese People's Volunteers announced the completion of the withdrawal of six divisions from Korea, in progress since March 31.

April 21: A Sino-North Korean contract on sale and distribution of films was signed.

April 22: A treaty was signed between the PRC and Indonesia which governed the position of the Chinese in Indonesia. According to the treaty, (1) all persons over 18, including married women, were required to choose between Chinese and Indonesian citizenship within two years. Any one failing to do so would automatically be registered as Indonesian or Chinese in accordance with his or her father's descent; (2) children would acquire their father's citizenship, but would be allowed to choose for themselves on reaching the age of 18; (3) nationality would not be affected by marriage, unless the party chose his or her spouse's citizenship at the time; (4) persons choosing Chinese citizenship would be liable to deportation if considered undesirable, while those choosing Indonesian citizenship would not be eligible for protection by the Chinese government. On April 28 a joint statement issued by Chou En-lai and Dr. Sastroamidjojo stated that both countries accepted the "Five Principles" of peaceful co-existence.

April 23: Premier Chou En-lai stated that the PRC would be willing to talk with the United States about the question of relaxing tension in the Far East, especially in the Taiwan area. In Washington the State Department issued a statement asking the Chinese to prove their sincerity by placing an immediate cease-fire in effect in the Taiwan area, releasing American airmen and others, and accepting a U.N. Security Council invitation to participate in discussions to end hostilities in the Taiwan region.

In Bandung, a series of meetings took place between the Chinese, North Vietnamese, Laotian, and Cambodian representatives. As a result of the meetings,

M. Pham Van Dong and M. Katay Sasorith signed an agreement on April 23 whereby Mr. Sasorith affirmed Lao's adherence to the Five Principles of Peaceful Co-existence and M. Pham Van Dong gave an assurance that North Vietnam had no designs on the Laotian provinces controlled by the Pathet Lao movement. Similar assurance of non-interference was given to Cambodia by M. Pham Van Dong, and to Laos and Cambodia by Chou En-lai.

April 24: The 1955 trade and payments agreement between the PRC and East Germany was signed in Peking.

The final communique of the Bandung Conference was issued.

April 26: Secretary Dulles told a press conference that the U.S. would be prepared to enter into bilateral discussions with Communist China, provided there was confidence in the possibility of a cease-fire in the Taiwan Strait, but that it would not negotiate on the rights of the Nationalists in the latter's absence.

The 1955 Sino-Hungarian agreement for goods exchange and payments was signed in Peking.

April 27: A Sino-Soviet agreement on Soviet technical assistance to the PRC in peaceful use of atomic energy was signed.

April 28: In an effort to alleviate the "tense situation" in some areas, which resulted from the peasants' outcry of "grain shortage" and which led to an "extremely abnormal and dangerous" over-sale of grain to the peasants by the government, the State Council and the CPC Central Committee issued a directive calling for the intensified reorganization of planned marketing of grain.

A Sino-Indonesian joint communique was issued on Premier Chou En-lai's visit to deal with the Bandung resolution, dual nationality, Sino-Indonesian relations, etc.

April 30: Quoting a Tass report of April 29, the NCNA announced that the Soviet Union had concluded accords with five Soviet-bloc nations, including the PRC, whereby the Soviet Union would undertake to provide training in atomic physics to technicians from these countries and provide all materials and equipment for setting up experimental atomic piles.

May 1: All publications in the PRC started using the first group of 57 simplified Chinese characters. Later it was stated that the experimental use of these characters proved to be satisfactory, and on August 15 some forty newspapers and magazines in Peking and Tientsin started using an additional 84 simplified characters.

May 2: An exhibition on the history and present situation of Taiwan and the "Chinese people's determination to liberate the island" opened in Peking. The NCNA later reported that over half a million people visited the exhibition during its 80-day run.

May 4: The third Sino-Japanese agreement to promote Japan-China trade was signed in Tokyo by the PRC delegation headed by Lei Jen-min, Vice Minister of Foreign Trade, and representatives of the Japan International Trade Promotion Association and the Japanese Diet Members' Union. The one-year agreement stipulates that the total amount of imports and exports for each country will be 30 million pounds sterling, and the types of exports to be made from each country are listed. Both delegations pledged to implement the decisions on the payments question and the exchange of permanent trade missions, and to urge their governments to conduct negotiations "so that trade relations between the two countries can thereby develop normally."

May 11-21: V. K. Krishma Menon, India's delegate to the U.N., visited Peking at the invitation of Premier Chou En-lai to continue the efforts made at the Bandung conference to find a solution to the Taiwan question.

May 13: Reporting to the NPC Standing Committee on the Asian-African conference, Premier Chou En-lai emphasized the "historical significance" of the conference. He interpreted the conference's joint communique as being fully consistent with the CPG's stand. However,

he did not mention that there was no specific support for the CPG's claim to a U.N. seat in the statement on U.N. membership. Chou reiterated the CPG's willingness to enter into negotiations with the U.S. "to ease tension in the Taiwan area," but stressed that such action does not affect the CPG's "sovereign rights to liberate Taiwan" and that the CPG "can at no time agree to participation by the Chiang Kai-shek clique in any international conference."

May 15: North Vietnam and the PRC established consulates.

May 24: A joint Sino-Soviet communique was issued stating that in accordance with the Sino-Soviet agreement of February 14, 1950, and joint communique of October 12, 1954, the U.S.S.R. had withdrawn its armed forces from the Port Arthur naval base and transferred the installations to the PRC without compensation.

May 25: At a joint meeting of the presidium of the All-China Federation of Literary and Art Circles and the Union of Chinese Writers, Hu Feng was expelled from both organizations; the resolutions also recommended that Hu Feng's status as a NPC deputy be voided, that the Procurate-General take action "to deal with the counter-revolutionary crimes of Hu Feng," and that members of the "Hu Feng clique" must come forward to expose Hu Feng, to criticize themselves and to start afresh with a clean slate. Hu Feng had been under fire for some time for advocating more literary freedom.

A Sino-Vietnam agreement on "through railway traffic" was issued.

May 26-June 3: Reciprocating Chou En-lai's visit in Indonesia after the Bandung conference, Indonesian Prime Minister Ali Sastroamidjojo arrived in Peking for a week's visit. During his talks with Chou En-lai, agreement was reached on the basic principles of trade and cultural relations and on the implementation of the dual-nationality treaty.

May 30: Peking announced that four U.S. airmen shot down in late 1952 over Korea had been tried on May 24, 1955, and found guilty of acts of provocation. However, they were ordered to leave China.

A State Council directive was adopted stating that demobilized servicemen should be given priority for jobs in factories, mines, government, and other organizations. The directive says that all demobilized servicemen who originally came from rural areas should return to those areas to take part in agricultural production.

May 31: Minutes of Sino-Egyptian talks on cultural cooperation were issued.

June 1: Through the Chinese Consul-General in Geneva, the U.S. State Department asked for information on and for the release of fifty-two others held by Chinese Communists.

June 3: Indonesian Prime Minister Sastroamidjojo and Premier Chou En-lai exchanged notes clarifying certain points in the treaty between the two countries on dual nationality; persons who have "implicitly renounced" Chinese nationality need not make a declaration of nationality; a choice of nationality remains valid after the expiration of the treaty's 20-year period of validity; a joint committee will be established in Djakarta to work out the method of implementation of the treaty; before the expiration of the two-year period for choosing nationality, a person's status remains unchanged unless a choice has been made.

June 6: A State Council directive was published calling for the "planned elimination of illiteracy in the rural areas." The target within the next three to five years was "to eradicate illiteracy among the majority of village cadres." The directive states, "political education must be conducted simultaneously with cultural education," and points out that with a few exceptions "all operational funds for spare-time cultural education of peasants should be raised by the masses themselves."

June 8: Sino-Polish minutes on talks between academies of sciences to develop scientific cooperation were issued.

June 10: The People's Bank of China announced the completion of the currency change, which began on March 1 and which involved replacement of the old yuan at a rate of 10,000 to 1 of the new. The announcement stated that prices and foreign exchange rates were unaffected by the change.

June 11: A Sino-Polish protocol on scientific and technical cooperation was signed.

June 13: A Sino-Soviet protocol on scientific and technical cooperation was signed.

June 18: The PRC Red Cross Society announced that three former U.S. soldiers and two Belgians, who had refused repatriation at the time of the exchange of prisoners-of-war in Korea, had been granted permission to leave the country.

June 20: The State Council issued a directive that, "in order to unify the wage system of workers in state organs," the salary system would be instituted in July, replacing the "government provisional" system. There would would be no special compensation for workers with large families who, through the change, would suffer a loss of income, but they could apply for subsidies from the welfare funds of the various organs.

June 22: A Sino-Korean protocol on 1955 plan for cultural cooperation signed in Pyongyang.

June 23: The State Council decided to convene a meeting of the NPC on July 5.

The NCNA reported that a 200-mile railway had been completed linking Litang (on the Hunan-Kwangsi line in South China) with the port of Tsamkeng (on the Leichow peninsula off Hainan Island). The new line runs near the Vietnamese border and gives direct rail access to Peking via the South China railway network and the Peking trunk line.

June 24: China and Sweden exchanged notes agreeing to establish consular relations.

June 25-July 8: President Ho Chi-Minh of North Vietnam visited Peking for talks with Chairman Mao Tse-tung and other Chinese officials. In a communique issued on July 7, a grant of £115,000,000 for the construction of railway and bridges technical aid and health experts. Also were exchanges of trade and students. They also demanded strict observance to the Geneva agreements, paid tribute to the activities of the international control commission, and accused the United States of violations of the Geneva conference agreements.

June 29: After a year's stay in China, the Dalai Lama returned to Lhasa; the NCNA reported that over 50,000 met him. In his speech the Dalai Lama praised "Chairman Mao Tse-tung's great policy of equality and unity for the nationalities."

July 2: According to the directive passed by State Council on June 19 regarding the establishment of a permanent system for the registration of persons, all births, deaths, and permanent changes of address are to be registered; moves outside the original *hsiang* or *chen* require prior permission. The system is under the administrative control of the Ministry of Internal Affairs, but in cities and towns the work is handled by the public security stations.

July 5-30: The NPC met in Peking July 5-30 with the review and adoption of the First Five-Year Plan as the main item on the agenda. Following group discussions and about 150 speeches, all proposals were adopted unanimously. Other than the five-year plan, topics which were most emphasized during the session were the counter-revolutionary problem, the necessity of practicing strict economy, and the grain situation.

July 7: Sino-Vietnamese protocols on cultural cooperation, exchange of goods by local state-owned trading companies in border areas, and small-scale trading in border areas were signed in Peking.

July 11: A Sino-Bulgarian agreement on cooperation for prevention of insect pests and plant diseases was signed in Sofia.

July 12: The PRC and North Korea had an exchange of notes on their 1955 plan for cultural cooperation.

July 13: The Ministry of Education issued a directive which, according to the NCNA, stated that the CPG had decided that "the standard tongue based on the Peking dialect must be vigorously promoted" so that a common language can be established throughout the country. Emphasis is to be put first on the training of primary school teachers in order that the dialect may be used in their schools.

July 16: A report of the Military Service Law, which provides a legal basis for compulsory military service, was given to the NPC by Peng Teh-huai, Vice Premier and Minister of Defense. After its approval by the NPC, the law was promulgated by Chairman Mao Tse-tung on July 20.

A Sino-Vietnamese contract on distribution of PRC films in Vietnam was signed.

July 20: The NCNA reported that work had started on the Yangtze River bridge at Wuhan, "the biggest bridge project in the eastern hemisphere." There was considerable Soviet assistance.

July 23: The Ministry of Public Security promulgated regulations which impose strict controls on the manufacture, repair, possession and shipment of radio equipment, the stated purpose being "to strengthen the control of this equipment and to prevent its use by counter-revolutionaries for subversion, and also with a view toward consolidating the security of the state and safeguarding economic construction."

A 200-mile railway between Litang and Tsamkong was completed.

July 25: Washington and Peking announced that their ambassadors would meet in Geneva on August 1 to discuss the reciprocal repatriation of nationals and other practical matters now at issue between them.

July 30: Premier Chou En-lai told the NPC in Peking that the "number of American civilians in China is small and their problem can be easily settled." He voiced concern over "the extremely unjust policy of blockade and embargo which obstructs trade between countries," and said it should be possible "to remove such barriers so that peaceful trade between all countries will not be hindered." Chou observed that after the Korean armistice and restoration of peace in Indochina, the situation in the Taiwan area has become the most tense in the Far East. He continued: "Provided that the U.S. does not interfere with China's internal problems, the possibility of peaceful liberation of Taiwan will continue to increase. If possible, the Chinese government is willing to enter into negotiations with the responsible local authorities of Taiwan to map out concrete steps for that country's peaceful liberation. It should be made clear that there should be negotiations between the Central Government and local authorities. The Chinese people are firmly opposed to any ideas or plots of the so-called 'two Chinas'."

A NPC resolution established the Ministry of Fuel Industry, the Ministry of Coal Industry, the Ministry of Petroleum Industry, and the Ministry for the Purchase of Agricultural Supplies.

The NPC ratified a State Council decision to abolish Jehol and Sikang Provinces. The Jehol area was transferred to Hopei, Liaoning and Inner Mongolia; the Sikang area to Szechwan.

At the close of an NPC session a People's Parliamentary Group was formed for the purpose of joining the Inter-Parliamentary Union; P'eng Chen was chosen as head.

Conclusion of Sino-Rumanian agreement on the exchange of post mail and tele-communication was announced in Peking.

July 31: Chairman Mao Tse-tung delivered a major policy report, *On the Question of Agriculture Cooperation*, at a meeting of local party secretaries in Peking. In his report, Mao mentioned that 16,900,000 peasant households had joined the cooperatives. The significance of the report was its indication of the end of a period of sharp debate within the party over the tempo of the collectivization drive and its relation to the industrialization program. Mao indicated that the collective form of organization was fundamental for further technological advances.

The State Council issued an order stating that all public security corps, previously under the Ministry of Defense, are to be reorganized by August 1 into the People's Armed Police under the Ministry of Public Security.

August 1: U.S.-Chinese ambassadorial negotiations began in Geneva on release of prisoners and internees, and other matters now at issue between the two nations.

The NCNA announced that the Military Tribunal of the Supreme People's Court has decided to release, before the completion of their sentences, the eleven U.S. airmen who, in November, 1954, had been sentenced to terms of from four to ten year's imprisonment on charges of "espionage."

An agreement was signed in Delhi between the PRC and Nepal establishing normal diplomatic relations between the two nations, based on the Five Principles of Peaceful Co-existence.

The NCNA reported that through rail traffic between North Vietnam and Communist China had been opened. There would be two through passenger trains a week in each direction. The 2,970-km. trip from Peking to Hanoi would take four days.

August 8: A one-year trade agreement between the PRC and Finland was signed in Peking.

August 10: A Sino-Egyptian contract on purchase of Egyptian cotton by PRC was signed in Cairo.

August 13: The NCNA stated that geological prospecting in the Paotow area had been basically completed, and that engineers were setting up a "preparatory organization for the construction of the projected Paotow Iron and Steel Complex," the major part of which would be designed by the Soviet Union. Preliminary work had also been started on the Wuhan Iron and Steel Complex.

August 14: Chu Teh, Vice Chairman of the

PRC, led a Chinese Communist delegation to Pyongyang to participate in the celebration of the tenth anniversary of the liberation of North Korea.

August 16: The CPG Ministry of Foreign Affairs issued a statement labeling as "completely groundless" the complaints made in July by the Japanese government regarding Japanese civilians in Communist China. The statement claimed that about 29,000 of the original 35,000 Japanese civilians have been repatriated, and that the remaining 6,000 "have expressed a desire to remain in China permanently or for the time being." What should be negotiated instead is "the question of Chinese civilians residing in Japan."

A Sino-Soviet agreement on cooperation in the examination, prevention, and control of insect pests and plant diseases was signed in Peking.

August 17: Agreement was reached between the PRC and Albania on the 1956 executive plan for the Sino-Albanian Agreement on Cultural Cooperation.

August 20: A Sino-German protocol on scientific and technical cooperation was signed in Berlin.

August 22: After one year's study in the Russian language, a group of 610 Chinese students left for the Soviet Union to take up higher studies, with 1,280 more scheduled to go during August.

A trade agreement between the PRC and Egypt was signed in Peking. Contracts for the purchase of 15,000 tons of cotton from Egypt, and the sale of 60,000 tons of Chinese rolled steel, were also signed. A Sino-Egyptian joint communique on trade talks was issued on August 26.

August 23: The NCNA reported, "China's largest province, Sinkiang, will become the Sinkiang-Uighur Autonomous Region in September this year."

A rally was held in Peking, under the sponsorship of the Chinese-India Friendship Association, which expressed its support for India and its condemnation of "Portuguese atrocities."

August 25: The State Council adopted two new sets of measures to regulate grain supply in urban and rural areas. In urban areas, for the first time, a nation-wide ration system was established; the rice ration for an adult ranges from 24 to 55 catties per month, depending on occupation. In rural areas, households are to be classified into three categories: grain surplus, self-sufficient, and deficient. The state will purchase 80-90% of surplus grain, and will establish the amount to be sold to grain-deficient households. The figures for state purchase of grain are to remain fixed for three years, with the peasant entitled to retain any increased production.

August 28: A thirteen-member Tunisian Goodwill Mission, headed by Ben Alega Othman, president of the Tunisia-China Society, arrived in Peking.

August 31: The State Council ratified a decision to abolish the "supply system" which had been applicable to some state employees and to place all government employees under the "money wage system." The order was retroactive to July, 1955.

September 1: The Inner Mongolian Autonomous Region People's Council issued a resolution to adopt a new Mongolian language.

September 3: The NCNA reported a decision by the Thai government to permit trade between Thailand and the PRC. The decision was made public in a note from the Thai Ministry of Economic Affairs to the Bangkok Chinese Chamber of Commerce, according to the NCNA.

September 6: The PRC ambassador, Wang Ping-nan, announced in Geneva talks with U. Alexis Johnson, U.S. ambassador to Czechoslovakia, that Peking would release twelve of the forty-one American citizens held in China. The State Department called the action "encouraging" but reaffirmed demands that all of the civilians be released.

September 10: In Geneva ambassadorial talks, the U.S. and the PRC agreed on reciprocal release of internees. With respect to Chinese in the United States, Ambassador Johnson informed Ambassador Wang Ping-nan that (1) The United States recognizes that Chinese in the U.S. who desire to return to China are entitled to do so; (2) the government of India will be invited to assist in the return to China of those Chinese who desire to leave; (3) the U.S. government will give wide publicity to the foregoing arrangements and the Indian embassy in the U.S. may also do so. With respect to Americans in China, Ambassador Wang Ping-nan has informed Ambassador Johnson that (1) The People's Republic of China recognizes that Americans in China who desire to return to the U.S. are entitled to do so; (2) the British government will be invited to assist in the return to the U.S. of those Americans who desire to leave; (3) the government of the People's Republic of China will give wide publicity to the foregoing arrangements and the office of the British charge d'affaires in China may also do so.

Ambassador Wang informed Ambassador Johnson that seven Americans imprisoned in China, and a further three under house arrest would be released within the next few days and sent to Hong Kong.

September 14: Conclusion of a Sino-Bulgarian postal and tele-communication agreement was announced.

At the Geneva ambassadorial talks, Mr. Wang urged discussion on the second item on the agenda: the lifting of trade barriers and preparatory work for Sino-American talks at a higher level. Mr. Johnson, after consultation with Washington, subsequently issued a statement saying that it would be premature to discuss other matters before an announcement about the return of civilians.

September 16: A Sino-East German protocol on additional deliveries of goods in 1955 was signed.

September 20: The question of Chinese representation at the United Nations was postponed by vote of 42 to 12, with 15 abstentions.

September 27: At a ceremony held in Peking, Chairman Mao Tse-tung, acting in accordance with a decision of the State Council and an order issued by himself on September 23, conferred the newly created title of Marshal of the Chinese People's Republic of China on ten military leaders. He also awarded three newly created military titles to several hundred members of the PLA. The new marshals are Chu Teh, Peng Teh-huai, Lin Piao, Liu Po-cheng, Ho Lung, Ch'en Yi, Lo Jung-huan, Hsu Hsiang-ch'en, Nieh Jung-chen and Yeh Chien-ying. Chou En-lai then promoted certain officers of field rank.

September 28: Sino-Albanian agreements on cooperation in radio broadcasting and the 1956 plan for cultural cooperation were signed in Peking.

October 1: The Sinkiang-Uighur Autonomous Region was officially inaugurated and Sinkiang province was abolished. Saifudin was elected Chairman of the region.

October 5: The Exhibition on Economic and Cultural Achievements of the Soviet Union opened in Canton. Travel restrictions were eased to permit several thousand Chinese residents in Hong Kong and Macao to visit the exhibition.

October 7: The arrival in Shigatse from Lhasa of a convoy of motor vehicles marked the opening of a 337-kilometer link between these two cities. The following day the State Council announced a decision to build a 150-kilomoter road from Gyantse to Phaii in southern Tibet. On October 20 a ceremony was held in Lhasa to celebrate the opening to traffic of the Lhasa-Shigatse highway and subsequently the Shigatse-Gyantse highway. Construction of the Gyantse-Phaii road was sufficiently advanced to permit the first trucks to arrive in Phaii on November 14.

October 9: Thirty-three students who left the United States recently arrived in Canton. The most prominent member of the group was aeronautical engineer Chien Hsiieh-shen, former director of the Guggenhein Jet Propulsion Center in California. Ch'ien later was outspoken in his denunciation of the United States.

October 12: The NCNA reported 66 Americans in China (47 free to leave China if they applied for exit visas; 19 charged with breaking the law). It was also reported that 19 cases were under study, and that Mr. Oneill, British charge d'affaires in Peking, would be advised of the findings.

The press announced that beginning November 1 the Ministry of Food, in accordance with a State Council directive, will require residents of towns and cities to present grain cards in order to purchase, according to the local scale, such grain products as noodles, rice, flour or niem-kao (rice head) either locally or when travelling. This is a nation-wide measure.

The widening of the gauge of the Tsining-Erhlien sector of the Tsining-Ulan Bator Railway was completed.

October 14: An agreement was signed in Peking between Ceylon and the PRC providing for the revision of the price of rubber for the period from June 1 to December 31, 1955. Also, contracts were signed for the purchase of rubber and rice in 1956. China will buy 50,000 tons of rubber; Ceylon will buy 270,000 tons of rice.

The NCNA announced that Egypt and the PRC had signed a three-year trade agreement under which Egypt would receive light machinery from China. The two countries would open commercial offices in each other's capitals and would hold to the most-favored-nation clause.

October 15: A communique was issued on the 6th plenary session of the Seventh Central Committee of the CPC which was held October 4 to 11. The session discussed the acceleration of agricultural cooperation based on Mao Tse-tung's July 31 policy directive to the CCPCC. It passed a "Resolution on the Question of Agricultural Cooperation" and the fundamentals of "Draft Model Regulations for Agricultural Producer Cooperatives." It listened to "Explanations on the Draft Resolution on the Question of Agricultural Cooperation" by Chen Po-ta. It

set the stage for the subsequent "high tide of socialization in rural areas." In addition, the Central Committee resolved to convene the Eighth National Party Congress in the latter half of 1956. The main items to be placed on the agenda of the party congress will be a report on the work of the party Central Committee, a report on the revision of the party constitution, a directive on the Second Five-Year Plan for the development of the national economy, and the election of the party's Central Committee.

A Sino-Japanese protocol on a supplement to the trade agreement of May 4, 1955, was issued in Peking.

October 16: A Sino-Ceylonese agreement decreasing PRC rice prices was issued in Peking.

October 17: A Sino-Japanese communique, signed by Peng Chen, Secretary General of the Standing Committee of the National People's Congress of the PRC, and Eikichi Kanbayashiyama, leader of the Japanese Diet Mission, urged normalization of diplomatic relations, abolition of trade restrictions, establishment of permanent trade organizations in Tokyo and Peking, further promotion of cultural exchanges, exchange of the dead of each other's nationals, and unrestricted travel to and from their home country by nationals residing in each country. The PRC announced its intention to make a final disposition of Japanese war criminals.

A Sino-Mongolian-U.S.S.R. agreement on opening through rail traffic between the PRC and the Soviet Union through Mongolia was signed in Ulan Bator. Also, Sino-Mongolian bilateral agreements on border railways and "through railway traffic" were signed in Ulan Bator.

October 18: Secretary Dulles, at a press conference, said that the Geneva ambassadorial talks moved to discuss agenda item 2, although Communist China had not yet fully implemented accord on releasing Americans. He also said that the U.S. reserved the right to reopen item 1 if it believed that the accord was not being carried out.

October 28: Conclusion of the Sino-Rumanian agreement on scientific and technical cooperation was announced in Bucharest.

November 1: Registration for military conscription began.

November 1-21: A major campaign to bring about the socialist transformation of private industry and commerce was given additional impetus by the convening in Peking from November 1 to 21 of the Executive Committee of the All-China Federation of Industry and Commerce. Just before the session began, Chairman Mao Tse-tung called a forum of executive members to explain how China is building socialism and to show the place of private industry and trade in the new scheme of things. Following the meeting, the movement in the direction of joint state-private ownership was greatly accelerated.

November 5: The completion of the Nanwan Reservoir, second largest in the Huai River Harnessing Project, was announced. It is the sixth reservoir in the Huai River basin to be completed thus far.

November 7: Mr. Wang Ping-nan, at the Geneva talks, reportedly proposed that the U.S. and China jointly renounce force as a policy instrument. He also reportedly offered a pledge to respect foreign territorial interests on the China mainland if the U.S. withdrew the 7th Fleet from the Taiwan Strait, withdrew support from Chiang Kai-shek, and ended its trade embargo.

November 8: An air transport agreement was signed in Rangoon between Burma and the PRC which provided that "air service will be provided by the Civil Aviation Administration of China on the Kunming-Mandalay-Rangoon route and by the Union of Burma airways on the Rangoon-Mandalay-Kunming-Canton route."

November 9: The NPC Standing Committee adopted the Draft Model Regulations for Agricultural Producer Cooperatives and the full text was released by the State Council the following day. Nation-wide discussions were to be conducted before the end of March, 1956, to permit necessary revisions before the Draft Regulations were submitted to the next session of the NPC.

November 10: Ambassador Johnson, after the 25th meeting with Mr. Wang in Geneva, made it clear that the U.S. would not negotiate a joint declaration on renouncing force in settling disputes if Taiwan were not specifically mentioned. It was reported that no U.S.-China issue could be settled until all detained Americans were freed.

November 11: Chairman Mao Tse-tung promulgated the "Organic Regulations for People's Congresses at All Levels and People's Councils of All Levels in the Inner Mongolia Autonomous Region."

A goods exchange and payments agreement for 1956 was signed in Prague between the PRC and Czechoslovakia.

November 15: A Sino-Bulgarian protocol on mutual assistance in science and technology was signed in Peking.

November 20: A Sino-East German trade and payment agreement for 1956 was signed in East Berlin.

The press announced that the number of agricultural producer cooperatives in China reached 1,240,000 by November 10. Of these, 590,000 had been established since the end of July, 1955. At the current rate of expansion it is very likely that the target of 1,300,000 set for the spring of 1956 will be exceeded.

November 25: The PRC and North Vietnam signed in Peking an agreement on currency exchange rates as well as "protocols on the exchange of currencies in border areas, trade settlements, aid settlement and non-trade remittance."

November 27: A Sino-Japanese agreement on establishment of liaison facilities to promote cultural exchanges was signed in Peking.

November 29: The PRC and U.S.S.R. made an arrangement on acquisition of each other's film copyrights.

November 30: A Chinese trade delegation opened a Chinese Commodity Exhibition in Osaka. It had been on display in Tokyo since mid-October.

The PRC signed a trade agreement and an agreement on payments with Syria in Damascus.

December 3: A Sino-Czechoslovak protocol on scientific and technical cooperation was signed in Peking.

December 8: Prime Minister Otto Grotewohl, heading an eleven-man East German delegation, arrived in Peking. On December 10, the delegation began negotiations with the Chinese Foreign Ministry which will culminate on December 25 in the signing of a treaty of friendship and cooperation, a Sino-East German agreement on cultural cooperation, a Sino-East German agreement on cooperation in the examination, prevention and control of insect pests and plant disease, and a joint statement by the two governments.

December 9: The joint committee for Sino-Czechoslovak Scientific and Technical Cooperation signed a protocol in Peking providing for an exchange of information and aid on scientific and technical matters.

December 10-January 13: Vice Chairman Chu Teh visited East Germany.

December 16: Soong Ch'ing-ling (Madam Sun Yat-sen) visited India.

December 17: The PRC and Uruguay signed a joint statement in Peking on promotion of trade relations.

The State Council issued a directive on the Protection of Young Animals which deals with the problem created by the unwillingness of certain agricultural producer cooperatives to bear the cost of raising young draft animals which eventually results in a shortage of these animals. The Council proposed such inducements as tax reductions, increases in grain allowances, etc. to encourage livestock breeding.

December 21: The PRC and North Korea signed an agreement in Peking regarding the rate of currency exchange. A new protocol on non-commercial remittances between the People's Bank of China and the Central Bank of Korea was signed also.

A Sino-Polish agreement on the exchange of goods and payments for 1956 was signed in Warsaw.

A Sino-Mongolian agreement on broadcasting cooperation was signed in Ulan Bator.

December 27: The Sino-Soviet trade protocol for 1956 was signed.

Chairman Mao Tse-tung completed the preface for a book entitled *The Surging Tide of Socialism in China's Countryside*. The preface was reprinted in the *People's Daily* of January 12, 1956. He gave the statistical basis for the drastic telescoping of the planned period for the socialist transformation of agriculture. Over 50 million additional households joined the cooperatives.

The Kwanting hydroelectric plant neared completion and commenced generating current on a limited scale. Located on the Youngting River near Peking, it is the first large plant to be built by the Chinese Communists solely on their own efforts. It will supply additional power to Peking, Tientsin, Tangshan, and Kalgan.

December 29: A protocol relating to the exchange of 150,000 long tons of Burmese rice for an equivalent volume of Chinese commodity supplies in the year 1955-56 was signed in Rangoon, to implement the Sino-Burmese trade agreement of 1954.

December 30: Two Sino-Vietnamese contracts were signed dealing with the purchase of five airliners and aircraft equipment from the PRC, and aid by PRC technicians in North Vietnam.

December 31: A Sino-Lebanese trade agreement was signed. In the exchange of letters, the two states agreed on the establishment of the PRC Trade Mission in Beirut and also agreed on matters of trade involving third countries.

1956

January 1: All Chinese newspapers appeared with characters printed horizontally, instead of in vertical form, and reading from left to right.

Jehol Province was officially abolished; the *hsien of* Chengteh, Weichang, Lunghua, Fengning, Luanping, Pingchuan, Chinglung, and Hsinglung, and the municipality of Chengteh were transferred to Hopei Province; the *hsien* of Chaoyang, Peipiao, Chienping, Chienhang, and Lingyuan, and the Kalachin Left Banner to Liaoning Province; and the three *hsien* of Chifeng, Ningcheng, and Wutan, and the Oahan Banner, Kalachin Banner, and Wengtehniu Mengel Nationality Autonomous Banner to the Inner Mongolia Autonomous Region.

January 2-23: Soong Ch'ing-ling visited Burma.

January 3: Chu Teh attended the celebration of the 80th birthday of East German President Wilhelm Pieck in East Berlin.

An agreement for Sino-Czechoslovak cultural cooperation was signed in Peking.

The 1956 Sino-Rumanian trade and payments agreement was signed in Bucharest.

January 4: The new Trans-Mongolian railway linking China with the U.S.S.R. was officially opened. It permits through service between Peking and Moscow via Ulan Bator.

The PRC recognized the Republic of Sudan.

The NCNA announced that a comprehensive program for scientific and technical cooperation between the Soviet Union and the PRC has been worked out, and a civil aviation agreement had been signed in Moscow.

January 6: A spokesman for the Chinese Communist Foreign Ministry indicated that the Chinese government was becoming impatient with the ambassadorial discussions in Geneva, which had recessed for "longer and longer" periods since they began in August 1955. Peking's spokes-man said that Chinese-held American civilians "offended against the law in China and must be dealt with in accordance with Chinese legal procedures, and no time limit can be set for their release."

Otto Grotewohl, East German Prime Minister, announced at the cabinet meeting that he had agreed with the Chinese government on the drawing-up of a five-year trade agreement between the two countries, instead of the existing annual agreements, so as to allow East German industry to plan ahead.

January 12: The 1956 Sino-North Korean trade protocol was signed.

Chairman Mao Tse-tung declared that the rapid progress in the collectivization of agriculture during 1955 had made it possible to envisage (1) the complete semi-socialization of agriculture during the year 1956, and (2) the total socialization of agriculture by 1959 or 1960. Mao also called for a concurrent and rapid increase in the "scale and tempo" of China's industrialization so that the socialist revolution could be basically completed on a national scale within three years. The new policy constituted a radical departure from the earlier official declaration that the socialist transformation of China would take about 15 years to accomplish, and that the collectivization of agriculture could be carried out only through gradual stages.

January 14: A Sino-Korean protocol on transport of timber on the Yalu and Tumen Rivers was signed in Peking.

January 14-16: Chu Teh visited Hungary on the invitation of the Hungarian People's Republic.

January 14-20: The Central Committee of the CPC held a conference on the question of intellectuals, proposing the strengthening of party leadership over intellectuals and over work in scientific and cultural fields as a whole.

January 15: Peng Chen announced "Peking

enters socialism" at a rally in Tienanmen Square in the presence of Mao Tsetung.

January 17-19: Chu Teh visited Czechoslovakia.

January 18: Tientsin proclaimed entry into "socialism."

After 18 meetings without any agreement at the ambassadorial talks at Geneva, the Chinese Foreign Ministry issued a long statement accusing the U.S. government of "dragging out" the talks, to which the U.S. State Department replied on January 21. The two statements showed that the talks had become deadlocked principally over the question of Taiwan. While both sides were prepared to make a statement renouncing the use of force, the Chinese would not agree that such a statement should infringe on their sovereign right to liberate Taiwan. The U.S. on the other hand was not prepared to agree to any declaration on the renunciation of force unless Taiwan was specifically mentioned in this respect, and unless a reservation was made regarding the "inherent right of individual and collective self-defense."

January 19: A Sino-Burmese contract on purchase of Burmese rice by the PRC was signed in Rangoon.

January 21: All private industry and commerce in Peking, Tientsin, Shanghai, Canton, Wuhan, Shenyang, Sian and other major cities completed the switch-over to joint state-private operation between January 10-20.

The 1956 Sino-Bulgarian trade and payments protocol was signed in Sofia, together with Sino-Rumanian protocol on 1956 plan for cultural cooperation, signed on January 19.

January 24: Ton Duc Thang, chairman of the standing committee of the National Assembly of North Vietnam, arrived in Peking on the invitation of Liu Shao-chi.

January 24-February 2: Soong Ching-ling visited Pakistan on the invitation of the Pakistan government.

January 25: A 12-year agricultural development plan, based upon the complete collectivization of Chinese agriculture, was published in Peking. It was submitted to the Supreme State Conference of some 300 Communists and non-party officials, presided over by Mao Tse-tung. The plan envisaged the complete abolition of illiteracy within the 12-year period, in which connection schools for adults would be established in all localities. Compulsory education would be introduced throughout China within a period of five to seven years, and the training of 5 to 6 million technicians to help and direct the collective farms would be undertaken.

January 27: The 1956 Sino-Hungarian trade and payments protocol was signed in Budapest. Also Sino-Hungarian protocol on the 1956 plan for cultural cooperation was signed.

January 28: The Sino-Polish protocol on a plan for cultural cooperation in 1956 was signed in Peking.

January 30-February 2: Chu Teh visited Poland.

February 1: President Eisenhower and British Prime Minister Anthony Eden, who was visiting Washington, announced they had agreed that trade control against Communist China should continue and should be reviewed periodically as to its scope, in the light of changing conditions, so that it might best serve the interests of the free world.

February 2: The 1956 plan for the Sino-East German cultural cooperation agreement was signed in Peking.

February 4-March 20: Chu Teh visited the U.S.S.R. On February 15 he delivered a speech to the 20th Congress of the CPSU in which he hailed Soviet accomplishments proving the superiority of the Soviet system, said the CPSU was a shining example to the CPC, that China and the Soviet Union were inseparable, and that China was grateful for Soviet aid.

February 7: The 1956 Sino-Mongolian trade protocol was signed in Ulan Bator.

February 8: The State Council adopted decisions on socialist transformation of private industry, commerce and handicraft, calling for more considered plans before private industry is socialized, because wholesale socialization occurring since January had resulted in dislocations of supply and production. The State Council issued regulations fixing within a range from 1% to 6% the annual interest which can be paid to private shareholders in joint public-private enterprises.

February 10: The NCNA announced that official approval had been given to a thirty-letter Latin alphabet to replace approximately 30,000 ideographic characters used in written Chinese. The two scripts would be used side by side for some time. It also approved a new Mongolian alphabet in Cyrillic (Russian) characters which would be introduced into Inner Mongolia within the next few years. The State Council also approved the organization of the Central Work Committee for the Popularization of the Standard Spoken Chinese (P'u-T'ung-Hua), with Chen Yi as chairman.

A one-year contract under which Belgium would sell 425,000 tons of chemical fertilizer to Communist China was signed between the China National Import and Export Corporation and the Belgian Cobelaz Company.

February 13: The 1956 plan for implementing Sino-Rumanian cultural cooperation was signed in Bucharest.

February 13-21: Prince Norodom Sihanouk visited China, was entertained by Chou En-lai and Mao Tse-tung, and signed a Sino-Cambodian joint communique on February 18 which affirmed Sino-Cambodian friendship based upon the Five Principles of Peaceful Co-existence, and declared that future economic and cultural relations between the countries were to be encouraged.

February 14: A Sino-Yugoslav agreement on tele-communications and postal services was signed in Belgrade.

February 15: The PRC and Denmark agreed to raise the legations of both countries to the level of embassies.

February 17: A Sino-Yugoslav trade and payments agreement was signed in Bel-

grade; also Sino-Yugoslav agreement on scientific and technical cooperation was signed.

February 19: The PRC and France issued a joint statement on trade talks, and a protocol on commercial payments procedures and payments. The documents were signed in Peking by representatives of the French Economic Mission to the PRC and the China Committee for Promotion of International Trade.

February 24: A Sino-Polish postal and tele-communication agreement was signed.

February 25: A Sino-Mongolian parcel post agreement was signed.

February 29: A Sino-Hungarian protocol on scientific and technical cooperation was signed in Budapest.

March 4: Peking threatened to end the Geneva ambassadorial talks if the U.S. continued to drag them out. It demanded the U.S. accept Peking's proposal of October 27 that both parties agree to settle disputes peacefully under U.N. principles and hold a conference of foreign ministers to end the tension in the Taiwan area. It hinted at military action in the Taiwan area if talks failed. The U.S. reply said that the Peking note contained nothing new.

March 9: The State Council passed Draft Model Regulations for Agricultural Producer Cooperatives and sent them to the Standing Committee of the NPC. It also passed the decision of the Central Committee of the CPC and the State Council on elimination of illiteracy and other measures.

March 11: A Sino-Albanian protocol on scientific and technical cooperation was signed in Peking.

March 13: The 1956 Sino-Albanian trade and payments protocol was signed.

March 14: The State Council inaugurated in Peking a Planning Committee for Scientific Development, with Ch'en Yi as Chairman.

March 17: Model regulations for Agricultural Producers' Cooperatives were promulgated by order of Mao Tse-tung.

March 19: A Sino-Pakistan contract on

the supply of coal by the PRC to Pakistan was signed in Karachi.

March 25: State Council issued general directive on relief work to tide over spring famine. In spite of the general increase in production, said the directive, there exists possibilities for famine in some areas of the vast expanse of China; hence all organs should be prepared to cope with some spring famine.

March 26: The NCNA reported that the route had been fixed for the section of the Lanchow-Sinkiang Railway from Hami to the national border.

It was announced in Moscow, at the end of a six-day conference attended by China and ten other Communist countries, that an Eastern Institute for Nuclear Research would be established jointly in the Soviet Union.

March 27: Through an exchange of notes in Sofia, the PRC and Bulgaria agreed on revision of protocol on general conditions for delivery of goods in 1955.

March 29: The 200-kilometer highway between Gyantze and Yatung, in southern Tibet, opened with a 30-truck convoy entering Yatung. This highway links the southernmost frontier post of Tibet with the rest of China.

March 30: The State Council announced its decision to eliminate illiteracy, a campaign which would be basically completed in 5 to 7 years, with the work among organ cadres to be completed in 2 to 3 years.

March 31: Through an exchange of notes, the PRC and Finland agreed on a reciprocal grant of most-favored-nation treatment in customs duties and navigation.

April 1: The Ministry of Defense issued communiques stating the 1955 draft and demobilization programs had been completed according to schedule. More than 100,000 men will join prospecting and construction work and several hundred thousand others will take jobs in rural areas.

April 4: In separate announcements, Chou En-lai greeted the independence of Morocco and Tunisia.

The CPC Central Committee and State Council issued a joint directive on the running of cooperatives. Extravagance and waste were condemned, as well as attempts to fulfill the 12-year plan in 2 to 3 years. This procedure caused dislocations and a lack of understanding of the overall development of the country and led to wasteful use of resources. Members of the CPC and organ cadres must assist the APC's to operate industriously and economically.

April 5: In reacting to Khrushchev's speech, made at a secret session of the Soviet Party Congress on February 25, the Peking newspapers published a statement issued by the CPC condemning the "cult of the individual." Chinese Communist newspapers criticized Stalin, inter alia, for neglecting the welfare of the peasants, ignoring the German invasion threat, and showing conceit in his later years.

The Sino-North Vietnam agreement on civil air transport was signed in Peking.

April 6-8: A Soviet government delegation headed by A. I. Mikoyan, First Vice-Chairman of the Council of Ministers of the U.S.S.R., arrived in Peking on April 6. On the same day Mikoyan was received by Mao Tse-tung. A Sino-Soviet communique on his visit was issued on the following day. He also signed agreements with Chinese leaders on increased Soviet economic aid to China: (1) Fifty-five new factories were to be built in China with Soviet assistance, and (2) the railway from Lanchow (in northern China) to Aktogai (near Alma-Ata) would be completed by 1960.

April 9: The sixteen countries represented on the United Nations Command in Korea rejected the Chinese Communist proposal to hold a conference on the withdrawal of all foreign forces in Korea and the unification of the country.

April 11: The first scheduled air service between Burma and the PRC, using Soviet-type planes, went into operation on the Rangoon-Mandalay-Kunming route.

April 12: A communique was issued in Khartoum on Sino-Sudanese trade talks, both sides expressing willingness to promote trade and economic relations between the two countries.

April 15: A Sino-Egyptian agreement on cultural cooperation was signed in Peking. A communique regarding trade talks between the countries also issued on April 16.

April 22: A preparatory committee to prepare Tibet for regional autonomy within the PRC was inaugurated in Lhasa with Dalai Lama as chairman.

April 23: A Sino-Polish scientific and technical cooperation protocol was signed in Warsaw.

April 24: A Sino-Cambodian trade and payments agreement was signed in Peking.

Service between Canton and Hanoi started with arrival at Hanoi of a plane from Canton.

April 25: Work began in Tsinghai Province on a highway from Sining, Tsinghai, to Changyeh, Kansu.

April 27: Two Sino-Yugoslav contracts were signed in Belgrade on distribution of films, and exchange of newsreel materials.

April 28: The 1956 Sino-Rumanian trade protocol was signed.

April 29: The 1956 Sino-Hungarian trade protocol was signed.

A Sino-Cambodian joint communique on trade talks was issued in Peking.

May 8: A Sino-Japanese protocol on the extension of a 1955 agreement on fishery regulations in the Yellow and East China Seas to June 13, 1957 was signed in Peking by representatives of the China Fishery Association of the PRC and the Japan-China Fishery Association of Japan.

May 10: The through train from Lanchow to Peking made its first run.

A Sino-Pakistani contract on supply of coal by the PRC to Pakistan was signed in Karachi.

May 11: Daily train service opened between Canton and Shanghai.

May 12: The State Council, upon the recommendation of Chou En-lai, made the following changes in the organization of the government: Established: National Economic Commission, National Tech-

nological Commission, Ministry of Metallurgical Industry, Ministry of Chemical Industry, Ministry of Building Materials Industry, Ministry of Main Products, Ministry of Power Equipment Industry, Ministry of Food Industry, Ministry of Land Reclamation, Ministry of Timber Industry, Ministry of City Construction, and Ministry of City Service. Abolished: Ministry of Heavy Industry, Fluid Ministry of Machine Building, and Ministry of Local Industry.

May 16: It was announced in Cairo that Egypt had formally recognized the People's Republic of China and had withdrawn recognition from Nationalist China.

Britain informed the United States that it planned to expand trade with Communist China by "excepting" a number of items currently on the list of strategic goods not to be exported to mainland China. British officials said that they would move "cautiously" to avoid selling any important strategic goods to the Communists.

May 20: A Sino-Egyptian protocol on 1956-57 plan for cultural cooperation was signed.

May 22: A Sino-East German protocol on additional deliveries of goods in 1956 was signed.

May 26: At a meeting of scientists, specialists in the social sciences, doctors, writers and artists, convened in Peking, Lu Ting-yi, chief of the propaganda department of the Central Committee of the CPC, gave an address entitled, "Let All Flowers Bloom Together, Let Diverse Schools of Thought Contend." This speech, can be assumed to be an elaboration of Mao Tse-tung's remarks at the Supreme State Conference on May 2 when the policy was approved, stated that the policy of permitting all types of literature to bloom and permitting different schools of thought in science is "aimed at exhorting all active elements to give their best to enrich China's literature and art, and to enable China's scientific work to catch up with advanced world levels." Although considered an important statement of Communist China's policy toward intellectuals, freedom of thought is severely restricted by the limitations set forth in the speech.

May 26-29: The first aircraft landed in Lhasa. It took off from Peking the evening before, saw dawn in Tsinghai, and arrived in Lhasa later in the morning. The first passenger aircraft landed on May 29 at ten a.m. after a flight of eleven hours.

May 28: In furtherance of the resolution of the Standing Committee of the NPC on March 10 that elections of deputy congresses of municipality at the *hsien* level and below shall be carried out in 1956, the State Council promulgated regulations concerning the demarcation of electoral districts, qualifications of voters, etc.

May 29: The Foreign Ministry issued a statement on China's sovereignty over the Nansha Islands.

May 30: A Sino-North Korean protocol on a plan for cultural cooperation in 1956 was signed in Pyongyang.

A Sino-Syrian agreement on cultural cooperation was signed in Damascus.

The Ministry of Foreign Affairs, in a formal announcement, urged the United States to come to an agreement with China at Geneva on the basis of the Chinese draft announcement of May 11, which stated that the two powers would agree not to use force against each other, no mention being made of using force against Taiwan, and that a conference of the foreign ministers of the two powers be arranged.

June 1: In an official statement the Ministry of Foreign Affairs expressed regret that the U.N. had rejected a proposal by China and North Korea for a conference of all nations concerned with the Korean question, alleged that the United States and other nations represented in the U.N. Command had thereby frustrated an early settlement of the Korean question, and charged that they were thereby preventing the further relaxation of tensions in the Far East.

Premier Chou En-lai said that hope for peaceful liberation of Taiwan became brighter; that Peking could not agree to continuing present status but would join in a pledge to settle the dispute and would not be frightened by Dulles' brink-of-war policy. The Premier insisted that the dispute on Taiwan was purely internal; he charged that the United States had used Geneva talks to legitimize occupation.

The PRC and the United Kingdom agreed on trademark registration through an exchange of notes.

June 6: Premier Chou En-lai said that China sought talks at the foreign minister level. On June 12 the United States rejected the bid for a foreign ministers' conference as long as Peking failed to renounce the use of force in Taiwan area and held thirteen Americans.

The Indonesian government announced that it would no longer observe the ban on shipments of rubber to the PRC. The statement referred to the British government decision of June 4 to allow Malaya and Singapore to resume limited shipments of rubber to Communist China.

June 12: The Sino-Soviet-North Korea-North Vietnam agreement on cooperation in fishery, oceanographic, and limnological research in western Pacific region was signed in Peking.

June 14: Through an exchange of notes, the PRC and the U.S.S.R. agreed on delivery of commodities.

June 15-30: Delegates numbering 1,025 attended the third session of the first NPC presided over by Liu Shao-chi, Chairman of the Standing Committee of the NPC. A total of 146 delegates addressed the Congress. The budget approved by the Congress provided for a slightly smaller proportion to go to the armed forces. The Model Regulation for the Higher Agricultural Producer Cooperatives was approved.

June 16: The track laid for the Lanchow-Sinkiang Railway reached Yümeng, 792 kilometers from Lanchow.

June 18: Chen Yun, head of the planning commission, stated at the NPC that the minimum interest paid to former owners of private enterprises now under joint private and public ownership would be raised from one to five percent.

A Sino-North Vietnam trade protocol was signed.

June 20: The Soviet cruiser *Dmitri Pozharsky* and two Soviet destroyers sailed into the mouth of the Yangtze River. Welcomed by the Chinese navy in Shanghai.

The Thai government decided to lift the ban on the export of non-strategic goods to Communist China and North Korea.

June 21: China and Cambodia signed an Economic Aid Agreement (economic aid by PRC-gift of 800 million rials in 1956-57 for construction of factories, etc.).

It was announced that 335 Japanese criminals of war had been released by the Supreme People's Procuratorate.

Sino-Polish agreement on trade was signed in Poznan.

June 22: In a report to the NPC, both the minister of public security (Lo-Jui-ch'ing) and the procurator-general (Chang Ting-cheng) admitted that mistakes had been made in the struggle against counter-revolutionaries. Mr. Chang admitted that in some individual cases persons had been wrongly arrested and sentenced, while Mr. Lo emphasized that the government had strictly forbidden the practice of forced confessions, that security officials should not "too easily believe oral testimony, and that they should rely only on material evidence." Mr. Lo also said that during the past year 27 pretenders to the throne had been arrested, some of these men, claiming to be emperors, having wanted to set up new imperial dynasties.

June 23: A newly concluded Sino-Soviet protocol for scientific and technical cooperation was signed in Peking.

June 28: Premier Chou En-lai proposed negotiations with the Chinese Nationalists looking toward "peaceful liberation" of Taiwan. The specific terms suggested in Chou's statement were reported to be as follows: (1) The head of the Nationalist government Chiang Kai-shek, would be Vice-Chairman of the People's Republic of China, and his son, Chiang Ching-kuo, governor of Taiwan; (2) the island of Taiwan and the Pescadores would become a province of the People's Republic of China with full autonomy granted to the inhabitants; (3) Taiwan-made goods would be considered part of Communist Chinese products for custom purposes: (4) all the Nationalist officials who had been declared by the People's government as "war criminals" would be forgiven; (5) in return for these concessions, the Nationalist government would either withdraw from the U.N. or agree with the Communists on a U.N. representative agreeable to both, for whose instructions Peking would assume responsibility; (6) Nationalist embassies and legations abroad would be closed, ending the two-China situation. The proposals were rejected by the Nationalists.

A multilateral regulation on establishment of Organization for Cooperation of Railways was signed in Sofia by the PRC, the U.S.S.R., Mongolia, Rumania, Czechoslovakia, Bulgaria, East Germany, Hungary, North Korea, Albania, and North Vietnam.

A Sino-Japanese joint communique on repatriation of Japanese war criminals, return of the dead, visiting rights between nationals residing in each other's country, and their relatives, etc., was signed in Tientsin.

June 29: In his speech to the NPC, Chou En-lai compared the United States to an ostrich for failing to establish ties with Peking. He again called for a meeting with Secretary Dulles.

July 2: Syria extended diplomatic recognition to Communist China.

July 3: The last steel rail was laid on the 668-kilometer Paoki-Chengtu trunk railway which links Southwest China with Northwest China.

A tripartite agreement between Communist China, North Korea, and the Soviet Union concerning the rescue of persons, ships, and airplanes in the Pacific region was signed in Peking.

July 4: A Sino-Czechoslovak protocol on exchange of essential goods for the period of 1958-62 was signed in Peking.

July 5: A Sino-Soviet agreement on cultural cooperation was signed in Moscow. The 1956 plan to implement this agreement was signed on July 13.

July 6: The Central Committee of the CPC announced the decision to hold the 8th Party Congress on September 15, with the following agenda: (1) Report on the work of the Central Committee; (2) report on the revision of the Constitution; (3) proposals on the 2nd Five-Year Plan; (4) election of the Central Committee.

July 11: The Ministry of Supervision issued emergency notification on the strengthening of supervision and examination of flood prevention work to provincial, regional and municipal supervision departments, stating that this work must be made the first and most important task of these departments because of the present flood situation.

July 13: The first trucks made in China were produced at the No. 1 Motor Car Plant in Changchun. Ten trucks, modeled after the Soviet "Zis 150," were produced. Mass production was expected before October 1.

The last section of the 668-kilometer Paoki-Chengtu railway was completed 13 months earlier than called for in the original schedule. Construction had started on July 1, 1952.

A Sino-Soviet protocol on a plan for cultural cooperation in 1956 was signed in Moscow.

July 14: A Sino-Polish agreement on the exchange of students was signed.

July 25: A spokesman for the Ministry of Higher Education stated that post-graduates will be enrolled this year to study for the degree of associate doctor, this being the first time in China's history that an advanced degree will be obtainable in China. 1,015 graduate students will be accepted this year for studies leading to this degree.

A Sino-Soviet supplementary protocol on mutual supply of goods in 1956 was signed in Peking.

July 26: The PRC and North Vietnam signed an agreement and two protocols: (1) An agreement on exchange of goods and payments in 1956; (2) a protocol on economic aid by the PRC to North Vietnam in 1956; (3) a protocol on technical assistance by the PRC to North Vietnam.

July 28: A directive of the State Council laid down the procedures to be taken with regard to small merchants, owners, handicraft operators and transport cooperatives. It fixed at 5% the interest rate to be given to owners who had their enterprises transformed into joint-state enterprises.

July 31: The Burmese foreign minister stated that Chinese troops had entered Burmese territory and established outposts in the Wa State (on the Chinese frontier east of Mandalay).

A Sino-Finnish agreement on trade in 1956-57 was signed in Helsinki.

August 5: Chou En-lai told an Australian newsman that the U.S. refusal to recognize the Peking government was ostrich-like. He rejected U.S. participation in any discussions on Taiwan, asserting that the island was a Chinese province.

August 6: The PRC offered visas to fifteen United States newsmen who had requested them. The following day, the State Department announced it would continue to bar travel to Communist China as long as Americans were held there as "political hostages."

August 7: Burmese Prime Minister U Ba Swe said at a press conference that there were about 500 Chinese troops on Burmese territory, scattered over an area of 700 to 1,000 square miles. He expressed confidence that a peaceful settlement could be achieved through diplomatic means.

August 13: A Sino-North Korean agreement on cooperation in radio broadcasting was signed in Pyongyang.

August 14-23: Soong Ching-ling visited Indonesia at the invitation of President Sukarno.

August 15: A Sino-Soviet agreement on the joint investigation and development of the national resources of the Heilungkiang River valley was signed.

August 19: The PRC and the Soviet Union reached agreement on plans for joint development of the Amur-Argun river basin, which forms the boundary between Manchuria and the Soviet Union, and for the construction of several hydroelectric power stations. According to details published in the Soviet press, the plan provided for the building of a series of hydroelectric power stations, with an annual output of 70,000,000,000 kilowatt-hours, on the Amur, the Argun, and their tributaries. These stations would supply power for the Chinese cities of Harbin, Mukden, Anshan, and Peking, and for the Chita, Amur, and Buohidjan regions and part of the Khabarovsk territory in the Soviet Union, as well as for the electrification of the Trans-Siberian Railway from Irkutak to Vladivostock.

August 21: Yemen recognized the PRC, and the PRC reciprocated on August 23 with an exchange of letters through their respective embassies in Cairo.

August 21-26: Following the conclusion of the agreement for settlement between Royal Government and Pathet Laos, Prince Souvanna Phouma of Laos paid a visit to Peking, where he and Chou En-lai signed an agreement in which Laos reaffirmed her policy of neutrality. They agreed on August 25 to observe the "Five Principles of Peaceful Co-existence," to develop good-neighbor relations, and to develop economic and cultural ties.

August 22: Trade missions from Singapore (54 members) and from Malaya (28 members) visited China at the invitation of the All-China Federation of Industry and Commerce and the China Committee for the Promotion of International Trade.

The United States navy announced that a patrol plane carrying a crew of 16 was missing after having been attacked 160 miles north of Taiwan and about 32 miles off the Chinese coast. Peking radio announced that a Chiang Kai-shek plane which had intruded over some off-shore islands 300 miles north of Taiwan had been driven off by aircraft and had disappeared in the direction of Taiwan after being hit.

August 27: In reply to inquiries made through the British charge d'affaires in Peking, the Chinese government stated that if the plane proved to be a U.S. naval aircraft, and not a KMT plane as had been believed, they could not but express great regret. However, if this were the case, it proved that the maneuvers of the U.S. 7th Fleet in this area, and the intrusion of large numbers of its aircraft for reconnaissance on August 23-24, were planned provocations in violation of China's territorial air and sea against which the Chinese government must express a serious protest.

August 28: A Sino-Indian agreement on the sale of rice by the PRC to India was signed in Peking.

August 29: An agreement was signed in Ulan Bator under which the Chinese People's Republic undertook to provide economic aid to the Mongolian Republic totaling 160,000,000 rubles during the four-year period 1956-59.

August 31: A joint communique issued by the U.S. State and Defense Departments said that the plane attack of August 22 had been made without warning and announced that compensation would be claimed.

September 2: The Chinese government rejected the U.S. protest and requested compensation for the aircraft incident, and also demanded that the United States stop its provocative activities.

A Sino-North Korean protocol on joint conservation on Tumen River was signed in Genchi.

September 5: A Sino-Czechoslovak protocol on scientific and technical cooperation was signed in Prague.

September 6: It was announced in Peking

that the PRC and Ceylon had reached preliminary agreement on the establishment of diplomatic relations at the ambassadorial level and on closer economic, technical, trade and cultural cooperation.

September 7-27: The Eighth National Congress of the CPC met in Peking, the first held since 1945, during which it adopted a revised party constitution, approved the government's proposals for a Second Five-Year Plan, and elected a new Central Committee with Mao Tse-tung as Chairman. The new Central Committee consisted of 97 full and 73 alternate members, against 41 full and 30 alternate members previously. At its first meeting (September 28) Mao Tse-tung was re-elected Chairman; Liu Shao-chi, Chou En-lai, Chu Teh, and Chen Yun, Vice Chairmen; and Teng Hsiao-ping, Secretary-General.

September 8-14: The Ceylonese government delegation headed by Sir Claude Corea, which arrived in Peking September 8, signed with representatives of the PRC on September 14 a joint communique recommending the establishment of diplomatic relations at the ambassadorial level, negotiations for trade and payments agreements, and a technical cooperation agreement. Promotion of cultural relations was recommended on September 16.

September 10: A United States note demanding full compensation for the loss of life and property resulting from the plane incident of August 22 was delivered by the British charge d'affaires in Peking.

September 13: A Sino-Austrian protocol on promotion of trade was signed in Vienna.

September 16: A Sino-Bulgarian protocol on scientific and technical cooperation was signed in Sofia.

September 18: Deputy Premier Mikoyan re-affirmed close ties with Peking in his speech to the CPC Congress in Peking. In Moscow the PRC and the U.S.S.R. agreed on conveyance of Manchurian archives by the U.S.S.R. to the PRC.

September 20: The PRC and Nepal signed an agreement in Katmandu which affirmed their intention of further developing friendly relations on the basis of the Five Principles of Peaceful Co-existence, abrogated previous agreements regarding Tibet, and detailed new provisions regarding relations between Nepal and the Tibet region of China. Exchange of diplomatic envoys was also agreed upon.

September 21: The Foreign Ministry issued its seventh statement on the Geneva ambassadorial talks, accusing the United States of dragging out the talks, particularly by its tactics on the "renunciation of force" issue, and contended that the two sides should, without further delay, discuss and reach agreement on the question of the trade embargo.

September 24: U.S. State Department said the United States would bar easing the trade curb with China so long as Americans were held. It also said that thirteen months of talks at Geneva had failed to bring about release.

A multilateral statute to establish a Joint Institute of Nuclear Research was signed by the PRC, the U.S.S.R., Czechoslovakia, Rumania, Bulgaria, Albania, East Germany, Hungary, North Korea, North Vietnam and Mongolia.

September 25-October 11: The Prime Minister of Nepal, Prassad Charya, visited China from September 25 to October 11. He issued a joint statement with Chou En-lai on October 7 in Peking. The statement expressed satisfaction with the development of economic, trade, and cultural relations between the two countries. At a press conference the same day Prasad announced that the PRC had agreed to give Nepal 60 million Indian rupees in aid over a three-year period, and that Soong Ching-ling had accepted his invitation to visit Nepal. The two states also agreed on cash payments to Nepalese traders in Tibet under economic aid agreements and foreign exchange facilities.

September 30-October 14: President Sukarno of Indonesia arrived in Peking from the Soviet Union and the Mongolian People's Republic for a state visit September 30. He was the first non-Communist head of state to visit Communist China. On October 14, before Sukarno flew from Kunming to Rangoon on his way home, a joint press communique was issued, which stated that Mao and Sukarno had held talks on various international problems (including the PRC representation in the 9th United Nations General Assembly, West Iran, and support for Egypt in the Suez problem) and on the present relationship between the two countries.

October 2: U Ba Swe announced that the Chinese government had agreed to withdraw its troops to the 1941 boundary line; at the same time, he denied press reports that Chinese forces had entered the autonomous Kachin State in northern Burma.

October 3: The PRC, Malaya, and Singapore issued a joint communique on trade talks in Peking.

October 5: A multilateral agreement on co-operation of agricultural institutes in socialist countries was signed in East Berlin by the U.S.S.R., East Germany, the PRC, and other People's Republics.

October 10: Sixteen persons returned from the United States to mainland China, including nuclear physicist Dr. Chang Wen-yu.

October 13: At an interview with Mr. O'Neill, the British charge d'affaires in Peking, Premier Chou En-lai protested and expressed indignation on the October 10 Kowloon riots in which a number of persons died. He attributed the riots to Kuomintang agents and demanded that British authorities take immediate steps to protect the Chinese population.

October 15: A Sino-Japanese joint statement on trade talks was issued in Peking.

October 16: In his reply to Chou En-lai, Mr. O'Neill stated that the Hong Kong authorities had done their utmost to protect both domestic and foreign interests in very difficult circumstances, and that severe action would be taken against those found responsible when investigation into the causes of the riots were completed.

The PRC Foreign Ministry issued a statement saying that on September 22 Ambassador Wang had presented at Geneva a draft-agreed announcement on the promotion of mutual contacts and cultural exchange, which the United States representative had refused to discuss.

October 18-29: Pakistani Prime Minister H. S. Suhrawardy arrived in Peking for a state visit from October 18 to 29 at the invitation of the Chinese government and held talks with Mao Tse-tung and Chou En-lai. On October 23 the two prime ministers issued a joint statement in which they pledged to work to maintain peace and relax international tension, re-affirmed their faith in the Bandung resolution, and recognized the need for the development of commercial and cultural relations. The statement also announced that Chou En-lai accepted an invitation to visit Pakistan.

October 21: Under an agreement between the PRC and the government of India, a Chinese civil plane flew from Tanghsiung airport near Lhasa over a mountain pass near Yatung and landed at Bugdegra airport in North India. On October 24 an Indian plane took off from Jarhat airport in Assam and landed at Tanghsiung.

October 22: Sino-Egyptian trade protocol and payments agreement were signed in Cairo.

A Sino-Albanian protocol on scientific and technical cooperation was signed in Tirana.

October 22-November 7: U Nu, the former Prime Minister of Burma, visited China from October 22 to November 7. A joint press communique released November 9 in Peking stated that Premier Chou En-lai and U Nu had discussed questions of mutual interest, including the boundary question, "on the basis of the Five Principles of Peaceful Co-existence and in an atmosphere of friendship and mutual understanding." On the border question, the Chinese had put forward "a fair and reasonable proposal" and "in the meantime" the Chinese and Burmese governments had agreed that during the month of December, 1956, Chinese troops would be withdrawn from the area west of the

1941 line and Burmese troops would be withdrawn from Hpimaw, Kangfang, and Gawlum. The statement further said that the two parties believed that the talks had provided a favorable basis for settlement of the boundary question.

October 24: A Sino-East German agreement on cooperation between academies of sciences was signed in Peking.

October 29: A Sino-Polish protocol on cooperation between academies of sciences was signed in Warsaw.

October 31: Multilateral minutes of conference on postal service, tele-communications, hydrography, and meteorology were signed by Mongolia, the PRC, North Korea, North Vietnam, and the U.S.S.R.

November 1: The PRC government issued a statement supporting the Russian declaration of October 31 which protested British and French armed aggression against Egypt.

November 3: Peking sent a protest to British and French governments against their armed aggression against Egypt. Sino-Indonesian agreements on trade, economical, and technical cooperation were signed in Peking. Through an exchange of notes, the two states agreed on supply of export commodities to the PRC over the next three years in settlement of Indonesia's debit balance.

November 5: The NCNA reported the Minister of Interior, Hsieh Chüeh-tsai, announced that the Chinese Communists would demobilize about 800,000 men from the armed forces during 1957.

November 6: The question of Chinese representation in the U.N. was postponed by a vote of 47 to 24 with 9 abstentions.

The official Chinese Communist organ supported the Soviet action in Hungary as entirely just, declaring that Soviet troops had entered Hungary to restore order at the request of the Hungarian government and in accordance with the genuine desire of the Hungarian people.

November 7: A Sino-Czechoslovak agreement on cooperation between academics of sciences was signed in Peking.

November 8: The PRC government issued a statement declaring that it could not stand idly by while Egyptian sovereignty and territory were subjected to encroachment, and promising Egypt an effective measure within its ability, including material aid. On November 10 it was disclosed that the Chinese Communist government would give 20 million Swiss francs in aid to Egypt.

November 10-15: The 2nd plenary session of the 8th Central Committee of the CPC was attended by 84 members, 65 alternates and 147 "leading members of central and local organizations." Liu Shao-chi spoke on the current situation in Egypt, Poland, and Hungary; Chou En-lai on the plan of national economic development and control figures for the 1957 budget; Chen Yun on questions concerning grains and major non-staple foods. Mao Tse-tung, in summing up the events of the meeting, urged all public functionaries to adopt a simple and industrious style of living, combat tendencies to subjectivism, sectarianism, and bureaucracy, and to oppose Han chauvinism regarding national minorities or great-nation chauvinism in international relations.

November 13: The Ninghsia (Kansu) Hui Nationality autonomous *Chou* was officially founded at the first session of the first People's Congress of the *Chou*, attended by 312 deputies representing Hui, Han, Tunghsiany, Paoan, Sala, Tu, and Tibetan nationalities (of the latter, 60% are Moslems).

November 16: The Standing Committee of the NPC approved a decision concerning lenient treatment of and proper arrangements for the remnants of counter-revolutionary elements in urban areas, after hearing a report by Minister of Public Security Lo Jui-ching.

The NCNA announced the first use in China of air surveys for prospective rail lines. Surveys of 2,000 kilometers of routes had been completed, including the entire 920 kilometer route from Sian, Shensi, to Wuwei, Kansu, and parts of the lines from Sian to Hankow and from Sining to the Tsaidam Basin in Tsinghai.

Future aerial surveys were planned for 3,000 kilometers of new lines, including one through Tsinghai to Lhasa, Tibet.

November 17: Premier Chou En-lai left Peking by special plane to visit Vietnam, Cambodia, India, Burma, Pakistan, Nepal, and Afghanistan at the invitation of their respective governments.

November 18-22: Chou En-lai and his party arrived in Hanoi for a four-day visit. Premiers Chou En-lai and Phan Van Dong issued a joint communique November 22 in which they announced support for Egypt and the "Kadar" regime in Hungary, denounced the United States for seeking to help divide Vietnam permanently, accused the South Vietnamese government of refusing to execute the Geneva agreements, called on all powers which took part in the Geneva Conference to thoroughly implement agreements, stressed the unbreakable friendship and cooperation of the two countries, supported the Soviet declaration of October 31, and agreed to abide by the Five Principles Peaceful of Co-existence and to avoid mistakes of chauvinism.

November 22-27: Chou En-lai and his party arrived in Phnom Penh, Cambodia, for a six-day visit. In a joint statement issued November 27, Chou and Cambodian Premier M. San Yun agreed on the desirability of development of friendly relations, especially economic relations, and Chou said that the Chinese residents should abide strictly by the laws and decrees of the country. During his stay at Phnom Penh, Chou told U.S. journalists on November 26 that the time had come to establish better relations between China and the United States and that American journalists would be welcome to visit China if they could obtain permission from their government. He also hinted that he would offer Chiang Kai-shek a top post in Communist China as part of the resolution to the Taiwan problem. Taiwan called the offer nonsense.

November 28-December 10: Chou En-lai and his party arrived in New Delhi where he was welcomed by Mr. Nehru and by the Dalai Lama and Panchen Lama of Tibet, who were visiting India at the time in connection with the Buddha Jayanti Celebrations. While in New Delhi, he had a series of private discussions with Mr. Nehru on political questions. It was reported that Chou En-lai briefed Nehru on China's views to be passed on to President Eisenhower. On December 1 Chou En-lai hinted that Americans imprisoned in China might be released on good behavior. He suggested later that the United States would have to make the next move if it wanted release of the prisoners and a general settlement in the Far East. No joint statement resulted from this visit.

November 29: A Sino-Japanese joint communique on fishery talks was issued in Peking.

December 2: Two former American soldiers of the U.N. Command, Artie Pate and Naron Wilson, were turned over to representatives of the American Red Cross by the Chinese Communist Red Cross at Shumchon, on the Hong Kong border.

December 8: A 1957 executive plan under the Sino-Czechoslovak cultural cooperation agreement was signed in Prague.

December 9: Track-laying on the Yingtan-Amoy railroad was completed by the railway corps of the PLA one year ahead of schedule after 20 months of construction. The line is 700 kilometers long and contains 46 tunnels and 1,973 bridges and culverts.

December 10-20: Chou En-lai and his party arrived in Rangoon for a ten-day visit. In a speech on December 11, Chou said that China must increase the strictness of the demands upon herself in order to put resolutely into practice the principles of peaceful co-existence, and gave an assurance that China's policy towards Burma would not be actuated by "big power chauvinism." It was announced that the Chinese forces completed their withdrawal from the border area on December 12. On December 15, Chou, accompanied by U Ba Swe, flew to Mangshih in Yunan (China) for discussions on the border question, which were continued after their return to Rangoon. A joint statement, issued on December 20, said that talks, conducted in a spirit of cordial and mutual understanding, had led to a further clarification of the Burmese and Chinese points of view and had brought the border problem near to a solution. In a December 18 interview with Edward R. Murrow of the Columbia Broadcasting System, Chou said that United States influence in the United Nations was the main reason China had not recovered her legitimate right of representation in that body.

December 12: A Sino-Rumanian protocol on scientific and technical cooperation was signed in Peking.

December 20: A 1957 executive plan for cultural cooperation between the PRC and Poland was signed in Warsaw.

An agreement on maritime transport was signed between the PRC and North Vietnam.

December 20-30: Chou En-lai and his party arrived in Karachi for a ten-day visit. A joint communique signed by the two prime ministers on December 24 declared that "there is no real conflict of interests between the two countries," and cautiously endorsed the expansion of cultural and commercial relations. At a press conference on December 24, Chou charged the United States would not renounce their defense pact with the Nationalists, whereas Peking was ready to renounce the use of force in the Taiwan area. He also said that he had discussed the Kashmir dispute both with Mr. Nehru and Mr. Suhrawardy, but declined to comment on this question. He subsequently visited the former Northwest frontier provinces Lahore and Dacca (East Pakistan). During the visit to the Batata engineering works in Lahore, he stated that a delegation of Chinese technicians would shortly visit Pakistan and that China would be able to supply steel to Pakistan after the completion of her present five-year plan. On leaving East Pakistan on December 30, he returned to Delhi for

further private talks with Mr. Nehru, before returning to Peking on January 1, 1957.

December 22: The United States announced that only one of twenty-four Chinese held in prisons in the United States desired to return to Communist China. All twenty-four had been interviewed by the Red Cross.

A Sino-Mongolian 1957 trade protocol on mutual supply of goods was signed in Peking.

December 24: A new protocol for extending scientific and technical cooperation between the PRC and the U.S.S.R. was signed in Moscow.

The Ministry of Foreign Affairs announced that Premier Chou En-lai would visit Poland in the middle of January on the invitation of the government of the People's Republic of Poland.

December 28: Peking hailed Communist China's alliance to the U.S.S.R. and denounced Titoism. The U.S.S.R. press, next day, hailed Peking support for Moscow's leadership of world communism.

Chinese ambassador to the Swiss Confederation, Feng Hsuan, delivered to the Swiss government the ratification of the fourth Geneva Convention, which had been approved by the Chairman of the PRC in November, 1956. The four conventions, which were dated August 12, 1949, concerned (1) amelioration of the condition of sick and wounded armed forces in the field; (2) amelioration of the condition of wounded, sick and shipwrecked members of armed forces at sea; (3) treatment of prisoners of war; and (4) protection of civilian persons in time of war.

December 29: Three Sino-Ceylonese trade documents were signed in Columbo: One was an exchange of letters which extended the Sino-Ceylon trade agreement of 1952 to the end of 1957, and the other two were contracts for Chinese purchase of 50,000 metric tons of sheet rubber from Ceylon in 1957, and Ceylonese purchase of 270,000 metric tons of rice from China.

1957

January 4: A Sino-Yugoslav trade protocol for 1957 was signed in Peking extending trade and payments agreement of February 17, 1956 for one more year. A Statute of the Sino-Yugoslav Committee for Scientific and Cultural Cooperation was signed at the same time. Through an exchange of notes, the two states agreed on cooperation in air transport and marine insurance.

January 5: The first Peking-Tardin airline was opened to service.

January 7: Chou En-lai arrived in Moscow for discussions with the Soviet leaders. He also had informal talks with the Hungarian prime minister, M. Kdar, who had arrived in Moscow on January 10. A Sino-Soviet-Hungarian joint statement was issued on socialist solidarity.

January 9: The 190-kilometer highway from Lhasa to Chetang was opened.

January 11-16: From Moscow, Chou flew to Warsaw on January 11 for talks with M. Gomulka, M. Cyrankiewicz, and other Polish leaders, and afterwards made a tour of the main Polish cities. In a public speech in Warsaw on January 12 he expressed his full approval of the recent developments in Poland. A joint statement was issued at the conclusion of the Warsaw talks on January 16, emphasizing that relations between Socialist countries should be based on the principle of equality between them. It was, however, regarded as significant that the statement made no reference to the Soviet claim to leadership of the socialist countries, or to Soviet allegations that the uprising in Hungary had been a "counter-revolutionary" movement instigated by the Western powers, although it expressed support for M. Kadar's government.

January 16-17: Chou En-lai paid a 24-hour visit to Budapest at the end of which he issued a joint statement with M. Kadar denouncing the counter-revolutionary armed uprising prepared by the imperialist reactionary forces and calling upon the Hungarian people to stand solidly with the Soviet Union, leader of the socialist camp.

January 17-18: Chou En-lai returned to Moscow to resume his discussions with the Soviet leaders. On January 18, Chou En-lai and Marshal Bulganin issued a 2,000-word joint declaration, covering the whole field of international affairs, which inter alia pledged support to the countries of the Middle East against any aggression or interference in their affairs as a result of the "Eisenhower Doctrine."

January 18: In Peking, the 1957 plan for Sino-Soviet cultural agreement was signed.

January 19-22: Chou En-lai went to Kabul, Afghanistan, where he discussed international questions with Prime Minister Mohammed Dand Khan. A communique issued on January 22 stated that they had agreed to strengthen the ties between their countries.

January 24: A Sino-North Korean trade protocol for 1957 and a PRC economic aid to North Korea protocol were signed in Pyongyang.

January 24-26: Chou En-lai proceeded to Delhi, where he had a three-day meeting with Prime Minister Nehru.

January 26-30: Chou En-lai continued his journey to Nepal for a five-day visit. At the banquet given in his honor on January 26 by the Nepalese premier (Mr. Tanka Prasad Acharya), Chou gave assurance that China would continue to assist Nepal to build up her economy and safeguard her independence. A joint communique was issued on January 29.

January 28: A Sino-Bulgarian trade and payments protocol for 1957 was signed.

January 31-February 1: Chou En-lai paid a five-day visit to Ceylon at the invitation of the Ceylonese government. He had a number of discussions with Prime Minister Bandaranaike in Colombo. On February 5 they signed a joint statement calling for a new Asian-African conference at the earliest date.

February 6: Secretary Dulles told a news

conference that the State Department had banned travel of reporters to Communist China because China was "trying to get reporters, preferably those it picked, to come," and had "tried to use the illegal detention of Americans" in China to force the State Department's approval of the trips. He added that "the issuance of passports to a regime which is not recognized is something which is never done."

February 13: Mr. Johnson and Mr. Wang Ping-nan resumed their ambassadorial talks at Geneva (their 65th meeting since the opening of the talks in August 1955). It was understood that the discussions dealt with two subjects: The release of Americans still imprisoned in Communist China, and the possibility of a visit to China by United States newspapermen.

February 15: A Sino-Soviet postal and telecommunications protocol was signed.

February 17: Peking issued a statement supporting the Russian proposal on the Mid-East.

February 20: A Sino-Bulgarian cultural plan for 1957 was signed in Peking.

February 21: A Sino-Rumanian cultural plan for 1957 was signed in Peking.

February 27: Mao Tse-tung spoke for four hours to more than 1800 persons attending the Supreme State Conference on "the correct handling of contradictions among the people." The speech, in a text revised and enlarged by Mao himself, was released to the public by the NCNA on June 18. The twelve principal questions discussed concerned (1) The "enemy" and the "people," (2) counter-revolutionaries, (3) agricultural cooperation, (4) industrialists and businessmen, (5) intellectuals, (6) national minorities, (7) over-all planning, (8) free discussion in arts and sciences and the relations between the democratic parties and the Communist party, (9) strikes and demonstrations by small numbers of persons, (10) "Can bad things be turned into good things?" (11) practice of economy, and (12) China's path to industrialization. Enlarging on the CPC slogan, "Let 100 flowers blossom and 100 schools of thought contend," Mao emphasized that

ideological and artistic controversies should be resolved through free discussion and not by crude coercive methods. He stated that the Communist party and other parties should continue to exist side by side and to exercise mutual criticism, although the building of socialism and the leadership of the Communist party must remain the two guiding and unassailable principles by which all views were to be judged.

February 28: The government raised the purchase price of pigs by an average of 13.8%. Retail pork prices were raised an average of 8.24%. The shortage of hogs was blamed on insufficient fodder for pigs, low procurement prices, and confusion over whether APC's or individuals should raise pigs.

March 5-20: The 3rd plenary session of the 2nd National Committee of the CPPC was held from March 5 to 20. On March 5, in his report on foreign affairs, Chou En-lai accused the United States of planning to install guided missiles on Taiwan in an attempt to aggravate tension in the area. He said that Taiwan was Chinese territory, and the problem could be settled only by the Chinese themselves.

March 6: A Sino-Czechoslovak trade and payments protocol for 1957 was signed.

March 7: President Eisenhower said he could not "offer at the moment any change in policy" on newsmen's travel. He said the State Department had "studied this very carefully with a view toward securing more news from China without appearing to be accepting Red China on same cultural basis as we do . . . other nations."

March 8: A Sino-Albanian trade protocol for 1957 and a protocol on use of PRC's economic aid to Albania were signed.

Sino-Mongolian protocol on a 1957 plan for cultural cooperation was signed in Ulan Bator.

March 9-April 16: A Czechoslovak delegation led by Premier V. Siroky arrived by air for a visit in Peking on March 9. During his visit a Treaty of Friendship and Cooperation between China and Czechoslovakia was signed on March 27. The treaty provided for mutual consultation on important matters affecting world peace, mutual economic aid and assistance, and unity among all socialist countries. Separate agreements on cultural and public health cooperation were also signed.

March 12: Mao Tse-tung addressed a National Propaganda Work Conference on "Internal Contradictions Within the People."

March 18: Nepalese armed units in Tibet were withdrawn in accordance with agreement between China and Nepal of September 20, 1956. The CPC Central Committee issued a notification on the running of cooperatives on democratic lines to improve relations between cadres and masses, strengthening unity, and promoting agricultural production.

March 19: State Council issued a directive in advance purchase of grain, oil-bearing crops, cotton, tea, cocoons, hemp crops, wool, and live hogs. The CPC Central Committee and State Council issued joint directives on (1) spring sowing and better harvests, (2) consummation of spring cultivation for bumper agricultural crops in 1957, (3) draft animals to deal with problem of decrease in draft-animal population in several provinces.

March 22-April: Mr. U Nu, former Burmese Prime Minister, visited Kunming, and had a talk with Chou En-lai on March 29.

March 25-April 30: A campaign began on an unpublicized level with municipal and regional discussions of internal contradictions among the people and methods of improving the "blooming of all flowers together."

March 27: A Sino-Soviet protocol on the transfer of a Peking Red Cross hospital to the PRC was signed.

March 28: Father Fulgence Gross was released after six years in prison. He left Shanghai by ship for Hong Kong on April 5.

March 30: A Sino-North Vietnamese protocol on a plan for cultural cooperation in 1957 was signed.

April 1: A Sino-Polish agreement on trade and payments for 1957 was signed.

April 5: A Sino-East German trade payments protocol for 1957 was signed.

April 6-13: A Polish delegation headed by Chairman of Council of Ministers Cyrankiewicz arrived in Peking on April 6 for a visit. A joint statement issued on April 11 called for strengthened solidarity of socialist camp on the basis of "proletarian internationalism" and "equality among nations."

April 8: The PRC and Sweden exchanged notes on trademark registration. Construction of a Wuhan iron and steel combine started. First stage is scheduled for completion in 1961, to produce more than 15 million tons of steel.

April 10: A Sino-Soviet trade protocol for 1957 was signed in Moscow.

A Sino-North Korean agreement on examination, prevention, and control of insect pests and plant diseases was signed in Pyongyang.

April 12: A Sino-Soviet radio broadcasting cooperation pact for 1957 was signed.

A Sino-North Vietnam agreement on traffic of goods between parts of China which must transit Vietnam en route was signed.

State Council reduced the value of cloth ration coupons for May-August by 50%. Over-consumption of cloth in 1956 and non-fulfillment of cotton target in the same year made these steps necessary in order to assure adequate cloth supplies in winter, 1957.

April 13: Excavation work on Sammen Gorge dam began. This dam on the Yalu River will be China's largest hydroelectric project, the first of 46 on the Yalu River, and will be basically completed by 1962.

April 15-May 26: In response to an invitation by Mao Tse-tung on January 6 to visit China in order to "consolidate and develop close cooperation and great friendship" between China and the Soviet Union, Voroshitou, Soviet president, arrived by plane in Peking on April 15. He left Peking for a trip to Indonesia and North Vietnam on May 6 and returned to Peking on May 24. He invited Mao Tsetung to visit the U.S.S.R. in 1957; this was accepted on May 25. On May 26, he left Peking for Outer Mongolia.

April 19: Sino-Rumanian trade protocol payments for 1957 were signed.

April 20: The U.S. State Department announced that the U.S. government, "repeatedly pressed by some of its allies" to relax controls on trade with Communist China, had agreed to consider changes in these controls. An official spokesman emphasized, however, that the U.S. would in no event consider any relaxations as far as her own trade was concerned. The spokesman's reference to "pressure" by some U.S. allies referred particularly to Britain, which had been pressing for over a year for the embargo on trade with the PRC to be reduced to the same level as that applying to the U.S.S.R. and the Soviet-bloc countries. It was pointed out in the British press that there were 207 items on the embargo list for China which were not controlled in the case of the Soviet bloc, where only certain "strategic" items came under the export prohibition or restrictions; these strategic items numbered 200, in addition to atomic energy and munitions items. The Soviet-bloc list covered the following three classes of goods: (1) Strategic goods barred from trade with the Soviet bloc (List No. 1); (2) nonstrategic goods that might have military use and for that reason were limited as to the volume of trade (List No. 2); (3) other goods which by agreement were kept under constant supervision to make sure that they did not have some special value for the Soviet war potential (List No. 3).

April 23: Secretary Dulles told a news conference that the State Department was willing to allow a "pool" of American newsmen to visit Communist China provided existing bans on travel by other Americans to the Chinese mainland could be maintained.

April 25: A Sino-North Vietnamese fisheries agreement was signed.

April 27: The CPC Central Committee issued a directive on a rectification campaign which was to be based on Mao Tse-tung's February and March speeches and to be directed against bureaucracy, sectarianism, and subjectivism. The campaign was to be executed slowly, in small groups, and without large struggles or criticism meetings. Contacts between masses and leaders were to be encouraged by physical labor of party and farmer. Campaign to start with higher level cadres and gradually be popularized. It was to be open to participation by non-party people on a voluntary basis.

April 29: State Council announced price increases in pork, edible oils, woolens, cigarettes, salt. The increase would amount to 2% spread over all consumer goods.

May 6: Details of the United States proposal on relaxation of China trade controls were published in Washington. It was proposed that a complete ban to Communist China should be continued for certain goods in which trade with Soviet-bloc countries was permitted. Although the additional "China list" would be abolished and freedom of trade be permitted for 157 of the 207 items on that list, the remaining 50 items should be transferred to List No. 3 of the Soviet-bloc list and embargoed on the ground that they were sufficiently strategic to warrant their continued restriction. Furthermore, exports to Soviet-bloc countries, even of items in Lists No. 2 and 3, should be restricted where there was "likelihood" of diversion to Communist China. The exceptions procedure should not be used except after advance consultation with the China Committee of the Consultative Group (Chincom) in Paris and on condition that the export to China would produce a benefit to the exporting country equal to the benefit accruing to China. The control system should be tightened to minimize any violations. The United States proposals were discussed by the Chincom, which consisted of the 15 member-countries of NATO (except Iceland) and Japan, with Australia and New Zealand represented by observers.

May 7: The United States and Nationalist China announced that missiles capable of carrying conventional or nuclear warheads were being based on Taiwan "wholly for defensive purpose of deterring and if necessary repelling attack."

May 11: The Ministry of Foreign Affairs, in a statement issued in Peking, accused the United States of turning Taiwan into a base for atomic warfare by the installation of guided missiles.

May 13: An agreement on Chinese loans (100 million rubles) to Hungary was signed. The PRC also granted long-term credit to Hungary.

May 14: Secretary Dulles pointed out that American newspapers could send anyone to Communist China so long as he did not travel on a U.S. passport not validated for travel to that country. Dulles added that there were "ample ways" to obtain news from China "without sending American correspondents into areas where it would involve a conflict with U.S. foreign policy." He concluded that if China released U.S. prisoners "we would certainly take a new look at the situation."

May 15: A Sino-North Vietnamese contract on the mutual supply of books, newspapers, periodicals, records, scores, and prints was signed.

May 23: Kuo Mo-jo announced that an atomic reactor of the heavy water type and a 25-million electron volt cyclotron would be completed with Soviet help before the end of the year.

May 24: After several meetings of Chincom, it became clear that the negotiations had reached a deadlock, as all attempts at a compromise between U.S. views and those of the majority of other members failed. Britain, in particular, while willing to compromise on details, stood firm on the main demand that the differential between permitted trade with Communist China and permitted trade with the U.S.S.R. and other Soviet-bloc countries should be abolished on the grounds that it was anomalous and largely ineffective. This view was reported to have been shared by the other European member-countries, as well as Japan, while Canada was understood to have taken a middle view between the U.S. and British position. Fur-

ther meetings on May 27, 28 and 29 proved equally unsuccessful.

May 25: Mao Tse-tung told youth delegates that "words and actions which deviate from the cause of socialism are utterly wrong. The CPC is the nucleus of the Chinese people without which the cause of socialism cannot succeed."

The two-year trade agreement between India and the PRC of October 14, 1954, was renewed until December 31, 1958, under letters exchanged in New Delhi.

May 26: A Sino-Soviet communique was issued in Peking on talks during President Voroshitou's visit.

May 30: The China Fishery Association and the Japan-China Fishery Association of Japan exchanged notes to extend the 1955 Fishery Agreement.

May 31: In Washington, the State Department declared that the United States was most disappointed by the British action. For its part, the United States contemplated no change in its policy of total embargo on trade with Communist China.

A Sino-Albanian agreement on postal services and tele-communications was signed in Peking.

June 2: Peking papers gave favorable comment on the British decision to ease the China trade embargo, emphasizing it as a new sign of independence on the part of U.S. allies.

June 5: On trade with China, President Eisenhower observed at his news conference: "I do not see as much advantage in maintaining the differential (between restrictions on Soviet and Chinese trade) as some people do, although I have never advocated its complete elimination."

June 7: The plenary session of the State Council decided in Peking to set up two new autonomous regions with the status of provinces in Ningsia Hui on the northwest and Kwangsti Chuang in the south.

The PRC and India exchanged notes on the return of real estate in Yatung.

A Sino-North Korean postal and tele-communications agreement was signed (the extension of 1949 agreements).

A Sino-Yugoslav agreement on cultural cooperation was signed in Peking.

The PRC and Cambodia exchanged notes to extend 1956 trade and payments agreements to June 16, 1958.

June 8: A Sino-Hungarian agreement on exchange of goods and payments in 1957 was signed.

June 11: A new shaft mine was opened in Fuhsin (Liaoning) estimated to produce 1.5 million tons of coal annually. It is the largest coal mine opened during the first Five-Year Plan.

June 14: Charles J. McCarthy and John Alexander Heule, imprisoned as spies since 1953, were released in Shanghai.

June 15: A Sino-East German protocol on a plan for cultural cooperation in 1957 was signed in Peking.

June 18: The NPC session scheduled to open June 20 was postponed to June 26, according to a decision of the NPC Standing Committee.

June 20: The NCNA reported that the Vice Chairman of the Chinese Communist National Defense Committee, General Lung Yun (a former aide to Chiang Kai-shek), had denounced the Soviet Union for removing "huge quantities of industrial equipment" from China after World War II, and for allowing China to pay all expenses of the Korean War. Lung pointed out that the United States had "given up her claims for loans she granted to her allies during the first and second world wars, yet the Soviet Union insists that China must pay interest on Soviet loans." He added that "China could not possibly repay these loans within 10 years or more." On June 23, it was reported that the Kuomintang Revolutionary Committee had renounced Lung and two other generals for "rightist deviation."

June 21: The Italian government announced relaxation of its restrictions on trade with Communist China.

June 21-July 20: A four-man Australian Labor Party delegation, headed by Leslie C. Haylen, reached Peking. Haylen foresaw Australian recognition of China and admission into the U.N. with Australian support. On June 30 they were received by Chou En-lai, afterwards touring the country. Before his departure on July 20, Haylen called for the return of Taiwan to China.

June 22: A Sino-Cambodian contract on implementation of 1956 trade agreement in 1957-58 was signed in Phnom Penh.

June 25: Mao Tse-tung issued new security rules on the eve of the NPC meeting. He listed tasks of "people's police," including duty to deal with counter-revolutionaries and to smooth implementation of socialist construction, as steps in the rectification campaign.

June 26-July 15: A session of the NPC was made the occasion both for public denunciation of the leading "rightists" in the non-Communist parties and for private rectification meetings of deputies from the same city or province. Three ministers belonging to the Democratic League—Mr. Chang Po-chun (Communication), Dr. Lo Lung Chi (Timber Industry), and Mr. Chang Nai-chi (Food), were objects of particularly violent attacks, as a result of which they were finally induced to confess their political errors.

June 28: Secretary Dulles, addressing a convention in San Francisco, made what the State Department called a major policy pronouncement on Communist China. He reaffirmed that the United States would continue to oppose Communist Chinese membership in the U.N., to withhold diplomatic recognition of the Peking regime, and to ban all trade with Communist China. He said: "We can confidently assume that the Communist rule of strict conformity is, in China as elsewhere, a passing and not a perpetual phase."

July 3: A Sino-Syrian trade protocol and payments agreement was signed (revision of 1955 agreement).

July 5: The Central Committee of the CPC sent a message to the Central Committee of the CPSU expressing belief that the ouster of the anti-party group of Malenkov, Kaganovich, and Molotov would help further the unity of the CPSU, and promised to strengthen the great fraternal alliance between China and the Soviet Union.

July 6: Ho Chih-Minh, President of the Vietnam Democratic Republic, arrived in Peking on his way to Korea. He was entertained, and consulted with Chu Teh, Chou En-lai, Liu Shao-chi, and other top Communist leaders. After a visit to nine socialist countries in Europe, he returned via Peking, where he was feted on August 29.

July 15: A written confession by the Democratic League ministers was submitted to the closing session of the NPC. They said that their political ideas were in a "dreadful state," which they attributed to their "feudal-landlord-bourgeois" background. They had proposed that the People's Political Consultative Conference should be converted into an upper house in which Communists would be in a minority, with the right to vote upon decisions of the NPC. They had also helped to set up committees to work for the "weakening of Communist influence in the universities" and the replacement of proletarian dictatorship by "bourgeois democracy"—a policy which they admitted would inevitably have led to a capitalist comeback.

July 16: In conformity with the decisions taken by Britain and a number of European countries, the Japanese government announced that the existing controls on trade with China would be relaxed to the level applying to trade with the U.S.S.R. and the countries of the Soviet bloc.

July 17: A Sino-Soviet protocol on scientific and technical cooperation was signed in Peking.

July 18: A Sino-Hungarian protocol on 1957 plan for cultural cooperation was signed in Budapest.

July 19: The State Council laid down a series of provisions tightening control over students graduating from higher institutions. Those who are to teach or go on to graduate studies must be screened for political reliability, and should be tempered by physical labor for some time on farms and in factories before taking up their new posts. Other students, if they are unwilling to accept the jobs assigned them by the

state, may be given graduation certificates, but the state then has no obligation to find them work, and state enterprises can give work only to those sent them by the authorities. Rightist students are to be sentenced to farm labor in serious cases. Less serious cases are to be given work under observation for one to three years, with a living subsidy instead of pay.

July 24: The Ministry of Foreign Affairs handed a note to the British charge d'affaires in Peking protesting the "forcible eviction" and destruction of houses of Chinese residents in Chek Yun village and other places north of Kai Tak airport. It demanded a cessation of these activities and more compensation for those already evicted.

July 25: The Chinese consul general in Geneva and the Chinese Red Cross Society sent letters to the Japanese consul general in Geneva and three Japanese organizations refusing to allow a mission to come to China to discuss the question of Japanese whose whereabouts are unknown. This question, it was stated, did not exist. Twenty-nine thousand of 35,000 Japanese remaining in China in 1953 had been repatriated and the other 6,000 were staying on at their own request.

July 26-August 20: During this period the Chinese Press published almost daily accounts of the arrest of counter-revolutionaries in all parts of China for plotting to overthrow the government or party, to assassinate officials, or to sabotage collective farms. Such plots were detected in Kwangtung, Shantung, Hupei, Kwangsi, Szechwan, Kiangsu, Chekiang, Anhwei, etc.

July 28: A two-year trade agreement was signed in Kabul between the PRC and Afghanistan.

July 31: Sino-North Vietnam trade protocol and payments agreement were signed in Hanoi. Furthermore, the two states agreed on material aid by the PRC to North Vietnam, exchange of goods by local state-owned trading companies in border areas, and extension of the 1955 protocol on small-scale trade in border areas.

August 1: The NPC Standing Committee ratified measures to give overseas Chinese investors in China further preferential treatment. Their investments will continue to be owned by them after the completion of socialist construction. They may withdraw their capital after 12 years. Their dividends will be 8% per annum, 50% of which may be remitted abroad. They are to have priority in getting employment in the enterprises in which they invest.

August 2: Peking extended recognition to Tunisia.

August 3: The State Council's decree on labor custody, passed August 1, was promulgated by Chou En-lai on August 3. It provided that special farms and factories be set up at which counter-revolutionaries, vagrants, social misfits, intractables, etc., would be "accommodated." They would be paid normal wages, with deductions for the support of their families. They would be "required to work, by compulsion if necessary." The establishments are to be under the joint control of the civil administration and the public security organs.

A Sino-Hungarian protocol on scientific and technical cooperation was signed in Peking.

August 4: A report on the fulfillment of the state economic plan for 1956 was published. It showed that during that year private enterprises had been virtually eliminated in industry and commerce, as well as in agriculture.

August 7: Sino-Finnish trade protocol and payments agreements were signed in Peking.

August 8: The Central Committee of the CPC issued a directive to its members calling for a large-scale program of socialist education among the peasants to enable them to distinguish right from wrong and refute reactionary incitement. The subjects to be discussed included the advantages of cooperativization, planned purchase, work-peasant relations, and the suppression of counter-revolutionaries.

August 9: The State Council passed regulations barring from sale on the free market all food products on the list for planned purchase. Food grains, oil-bearing materials, and cotton are without exception for purchase only by the state.

August 14: Forty-one young Americans left Moscow on a trip to Peking despite warning from the State Department that the United States and Communist China were in a "quasi state of war" and that the trip would be subversive of American foreign policy. The youths attempted to avoid violating American passport laws by obtaining visas from the Chinese Communist government. The forty-one were members of the United States delegation to Russia's Sixth World Festival of Youth and Students in Moscow.

August 22: Secretary Dulles authorized 24 news organizations (newspapers, news services, periodicals, and radio-TV networks) to send correspondents to mainland China for a seven-month trial period. The State Department said that the United States would not accord reciprocal visas to newsmen from Communist China.

August 25: *People's Daily* called the State Department's plan "completely unacceptable to the Chinese people." It denounced the United States for "insufferable arrogance" in agreeing to "send its correspondents to China just on the basis of its own unilateral decision" and "refusing reciprocal visas to Chinese correspondents." The paper asserted that the U.S. State Department "wants to collect intelligence in China through its correspondents and carry out subversive activities." The principle of equality and reciprocity, it added, requires that newsmen of both sides be allowed to stay in each other's country.

August 27: Secretary Dulles told a news conference that if any Chinese newsman applied for entry into the United States, his application would be studied on "its merits." The secretary explained that when travel of American newsmen was authorized, no reciprocal offer to admit Chinese Communist newsmen was made because "we wanted to obviate any claim by the Chinese Communists that they would be entitled as a right to send a corresponding number" of reporters to the United States. "That we could not do under the law," he said, which "hedges about very strictly the possibility of Communists coming to this country." Dulles said there must "be a finding made by the Attorney General to permit any Communist to come. Whether or not he could make these findings I do not know."

September 6: The State Council adopted a decision calling for improvement of relief work and an increase in production in disaster-affected areas, as well as a struggle against pessimism, the disbanding of cooperatives, and the flight of refugees to other areas. Relief is to be given only in case of absolute necessity.

September 8: The first West German delegation of industrialists and businessmen reached Peking, led by Otto Wolff Von Amerongen, president of the Eastern Committee of the West German Economy. An agreement was signed in Peking between the Eastern Trade Committee of the West German Federation of Industry and the Chinese Committee for the Promotion of International Trade, providing for an exchange of goods worth 230,000,000 Deutschemark (nearly £20,000,000) in each direction within the next 12 months. On September 27, through two exchanges of notes, application of trade agreement to West Berlin area and arbitration procedure under trade agreement were agreed upon.

September 10: A Sino-Rumanian communique on scientific and technical cooperation was issued in Bucharest.

September 12: A Sino-Czechoslovak protocol on scientific and technical cooperation was signed in Peking.

The CPC Central Committee issued a directive to extend the rectification campaign and socialist education to industrial enterprises.

September 12-21: In Geneva Wang Ping-nan proposed to Ambassador Johnson that the PRC and the United States permit reciprocal entry of news correspondents. The U.S. rejection was criticized as arrogant, deceitful, and stubborn.

September 14: Three directives were issued by the Central Committee of the CPC aimed at improving the working style of cooperative functionaries, reducing the size of cooperatives to "one-village, one cooperative," or about 100 households, and keeping the upper middle peasants in cooperatives by increasing their financial incentives.

September 14-October 12: A Bulgarian government delegation, headed by Anton Yugov, Chairman of the Council of Ministers, arrived in Peking on September 14 and toured Manchuria; on October 11, after talks with Chinese leaders, a joint Chinese-Bulgarian statement was issued affirming identical views on a series of topics and agreeing on a visit by Chou En-lai to Bulgaria. On October 12 the delegation left for home.

September 16-November 2: A 24-member Japanese trade mission headed by Masanosuke Ikeda arrived in Canton on September 16 and in Peking on September 17. During the trade talks, obstacles were created when the Japanese side raised the issue that the personnel attached to civil trade organizations in each other's country be limited to a specific number. After protracted but inconclusive negotiations, the talks adjourned and the Japanese mission left for home on November 1.

September 19: A new five-year trade and payments agreement (1958-1962) between Ceylon and the PRC was signed in Peking, together with an agreement providing for Chinese economic aid to Ceylon. Sino-Ceylonese communique on economic talks was issued on September 20.

September 20-October 9: The enlarged plenary session of the 8th CPC Central Committee was attended by 153 members and alternates as well as 416 lower party functionaries. It heard reports and adopted resolutions on the rectification movement, improving the administrative system of the state on wages and labor insurance, and in particular adopted the 1956-1967 National Program for Agricultural Development.

September 23: In a report presented to the

CPC Central Committee, the secretary-general (Mr. Teng Hsiao-P'ing) announced that the campaign against "rightists" had been completed.

September 24: The question of Chinese representation in the United Nations was postponed by vote of 47 to 27 with 7 abstentions.

September 25: Trial traffic began today on the Yangtze River bridge at Wuhan when a train with 1,000 passengers steamed across it. The 1,700-meter bridge made through rail traffic possible from Peking to Canton and allows 10,000-ton vessels to pass at the high-water season. The formal opening of the bridge took place on October 15 with widespread celebrations.

September 26: A Sino-East German protocol on delivery and supply of complete sets of equipment in 1958 was signed in Berlin.

September 27-October 5: A Hungarian government delegation headed by Janos Kodar visited China.

A joint communique on international tensions, U.N. intervention in Hungary's domestic affairs, etc., was issued on October 4.

September 30: Details of the fulfillment of the first Five-Year Plan, which covered the period 1953-57, were published. It was stated that coal production for 1957 had nearly reached the target of 120,000,-000 tons, making China the largest coal-producing country in Asia. Steel production for 1957 so far reached 5,000,000 tons, and total steel production for the period of the plan 16,000,000 tons; in consequence, China was able to supply 88% of her current steel requirements. About 67% of the country's demands in machinery and equipment were now produced in China, as against 20% in 1936. Most of the designing for the second Five-Year Plan would be carried out by Chinese technicians, who, it was claimed, were now capable of designing metallurgical complexes with an annual capacity of 1,500,000 tons of steel, blast furnaces, thermal and hydroelectric power stations, refineries, machine-tool plants, and ships of over 10,000 tons.

October 3: A Sino-Mongolian protocol on "through rail service" was signed in Ulan Bator.

October 5: Fourteen of the 41 American youths who had visited Communist China returned to Moscow and were informed by a United States consular official that their passports were valid only for return to the United States.

Peking Radio announced that a motor road linking West Sinkiang with Tibet had just been completed, reducing a month's journey by truck to five days.

October 8: A Sino-North Korean protocol on the Tumen River project was signed in Pyongyang.

October 11: A Sino-Belgium trade agreement for 1958-60 period and a payments agreement were signed.

October 13: Mao Tse-tung called a meeting of the Supreme State Conference, attended by 61 persons. The meeting agreed on the steps necessary to convene a joint meeting of the NPC and the CPPCC Standing Committee to discuss the revised draft of the national program for agricultural development from 1956 to 1957.

A Sino-Moroccan agreement on the exchange of goods in 1958 was signed in Peking.

October 15-22: The Standing Committees of the NPC and the CPPCC met jointly to discuss the 1956-1957 National Program for the Development of Agriculture. They approved the program on October 22, 1957.

October 20: The Ministry of Education ordered three items of pedagogic reform: (1) Political curriculums were introduced in the middle and secondary normal schools; (2) the contents of teaching matter were simplified for part of the curriculums for middle schools, primary schools and secondary normal schools; (3) ideological and political education was intensified in the middle schools, primary schools, and secondary normal schools.

October 22-December 4: The Chinese Economic and Technical Mission headed by Chi Chao-ting arrived in London on October 22. While in Britain the mission toured London, Birmingham, Glassgow, Manchester, Liverpool, Newcastle, and other cities. After a six weeks' tour the mission was to leave London on December 4.

October 22-30: The Afghan premier, Sardai Mohammed Davoud, arrived in Peking on October 22. Chou En-lai and Davoud signed a joint communique on October 26, reaffirming the Bandung spirit. Davoud left China for home on October 30.

October 23: The NPC Standing Committee approved in principle the "Provisional Regulations on Awards and Penalties for Works in Administrative Organs of the State." Regulations were designed to heighten the socialist awareness, activity and creative power of government workers, and to prevent violation of law and dereliction of duty. Regulations were promulgated by the State Council on October 26.

The PRC issued a statement to accept the 1930 International Load Line Convention for Shipping.

October 25: The State Council passed a regulation on pork supply. Under the regulation, pork supply to cadres of organs, schools, factories, etc., will be the same as that for the citizens; the armed forces shall be supplied up to a maximum of 1.5 *shih* catties per capita each month; foreign guests, foreign emissaries, foreign experts and banquets will be assured a pork supply according to actual needs. The State Council also passed regulations providing for the addition of 1.5 *shih* catties of vegetable oil per month to the usual ration for bureau and department directors and higher intellectuals. Finally, the State Council approved a report of the Central Industry and Commerce Administration Bureau concerning city market control. The report called for strengthened supervision over unlicensed merchants and increased control over clandestine factories and speculators.

October 29-November 1: The revised draft Chinese phonetic alphabet was approved by the CPPCC. The draft was not yet a scheme for general alphabeticization of the written Chinese language. It is designed chiefly to help beginners study Chinese and to unify the standard spoken language. The State Council passed this revised draft and decided to publish it for discussion and trial before submitting it to the NPC for decision.

October 29: A Sino-Polish protocol on cooperation in public health work was signed in Peking.

November 1: A Sino-Yugoslav agreement on general conditions for implementation of scientific and technical cooperation was signed in Peking.

Sino-Burmese agreements on postal services and parcel post were signed.

The China Committee for Promotion of International Trade and the Japanese Trade Mission issued a joint statement agreeing to prepare a memorandum concerning establishment of permanent private trade missions in each other's country.

November 2-7: Mao Tse-tung arrived in Moscow, representing the PRC, to attend the meeting of twelve Communist countries celebrating the 40th anniversary of the October Revolution of 1917. He returned to Peking on November 7. The 12-nation declaration, issued by the U.S.S.R., China, Bulgaria, Czechoslovakia, Poland, Hungary, Rumania, East Germany, Albania, North Korea, North Vietnam and Outer Mongolia, was divided into four sections: (1) A denunciation of imperialism, combined with an affirmation of the Communist countries' wish for peaceful co-existence; (2) cooperation between the Communist countries; (3) a denunciation of revisionism and sectarianism within Communist party; and (4) relations between Communist party and non-communist party, with special reference to the transition to socialism in non-communist countries.

November 4: A Sino-Polish protocol on scientific and technical cooperation was signed in Peking.

November 8: The State Council passed draft regulations for the improvement of industrial, commercial, and financial management. On November 18 the State

Council issued three relevant directives calling for partial decentralization of enterprises. Industrial management is to be improved by transferring some enterprises (now under direct control of the central government) to provinces, autonomous regions, and municipalities, increasing the authority of local officials in the distribution of materials and personnel management (giving them 20% of profits), and enlarging the authority of the managers of the enterprises. Commercial management is to be improved by transferring certain enterprises to local officials and dividing authority between the central and local levels. Financial management is to be improved by reallocating revenue and expenditures and increasing the power of local authorities.

A Sino-Swedish trade agreement was signed in Stockholm.

November 9-December 3: A six-member Danish government trade delegation led by Knuth-Winterfeldt arrived in Peking on November 9. China and Denmark signed a trade and payments agreement on December 1, 1957.

November 13: The regulations on 1958 National Economic Construction Bonds, as adopted by the NPC Standing Committee, provided for a total issue amounting to 630,000,000 yen, to be redeemed in ten years.

November 20: The NPC Standing Committee approved: (1) Draft provisional regulations governing leave of workers and staff members, and wages and treatment, aimed at enabling workers and staff members separate from their families to return home for a visit; (2) "draft provisional regulations on wages for ordinary and miscellaneous workers"; (3) draft provisional regulations on retirement of workers and staff members; and (4) draft provisional regulations on apprenticeship and living allowance. They were promulgated by State Council for enforcement on February 9, 1958.

November 21: A Sino-Soviet agreement on a 1958 plan for cultural cooperation was signed in Moscow.

November 25: In a directive the State Council required all government organs to appoint leading personnel to handle the people's letters and interview the people.

The committee of the consultative group in Paris, dealing with efforts by its member-states in countries of the Soviet bloc and Communist China, decided to abolish the fixing of separate effort quotas in respect to goods on List No. 2 (nonstrategic goods that might nevertheless be of military value) to be supplied to Communist China. Accordingly, exports of such goods to China were coordinated as from January 1, 1958, with the general quotas fixed for trade with the Soviet-bloc countries. The United States, while abstaining from voting, did not oppose the decision taken by the committee.

November 27: A Sino-Polish agreement on a 1958 plan for educational cooperation was signed in Peking.

November 29: The NPC Standing Committee decided that elections for deputies to the 2nd NPC should be completed at the ordinary city, *hsien* and *hsiang* level by May 31, and at the level of directly administered municipalities by June 15.

December 1: A Sino-Danish agreement on trade and payments was signed in Peking; there was also an exchange of notes on reciprocal most-favored-nation treatment in customs duties and navigation.

December 2: A Sino-Polish agreement on a 1958 plan for cultural cooperation was signed in Peking.

December 5-11: On December 5, Wang Han, Vice Minister of Supervision and a party member of 25 years' standing, was exposed as an anti-party influence. He was accused of spreading absurd theories against Marxism-Leninism, attacking socialism, applauding the superiority of American guided missiles and the good management of capitalist factories, and opposing the directives and resolutions of the Central Committee concerning supervisory work. The *People's Daily*, on December 11, reported that 15 meetings had been carried on in the Supreme People's Court against Chia Chien (president of the criminal section and a CPC member), Lu Ming-ching (director of the research office, a CPC member), Chu Yao-tang vice president of the criminal section and a member of the China Democratic League), who were tagged "rightists and anti-party and anti-socialist persons. The principal charges were opposition to party leadership, separation of politics and law, endeavors to seek independent judiciary," violation of the party directive and over-leniency toward criminals and counter-revolutionaries.

December 9: The Five-Year Plan for 1958-62, details of which had been announced in September, 1956, was revised in 1957. The revised targets for 1962 were announced on December 9, 1957, by Mr. Li Fu-ch'un (a Vice-Premier and Chairman of the State Planning Commission) as follows (the original targets announced in 1956 are given in parentheses): Steel, 12,000,000 tons (10,500,000 to 12,000,-000 tons); cement, 12,500,000 tons (12,-500,000 to 14,500,000 tons); electric power 44,000,000,000 kw-hours (40,000,-000,000 to 43,000,000,000 kw-hours); coal, 230,000,000 tons (190,000,000 to 210,000,000 tons); grain, 240,000,000 tons (250,000,000 tons); raw cotton, 21,-150,000 tons (2,400,000 tons); chemical fertilizer, 7,000,000 tons (3,200,000 tons). Mr. Li Fu-ch'un forecast that by 1972 China would be producing 35,000,000 to 40,000,000 tons of steel annually. In order to achieve the results envisaged, the Chinese government abandoned its previous policy of relying for industrial output primarily on large industrial complexes built with Soviet aid and requiring several years to construct. Instead, hundreds of thousands of small and medium plants were constructed all over the country.

December 11: The revised draft alphabet for the phonetic annotation of Chinese (Han) characters was issued by the State Council. The revised draft alphabet, consisting of all 26 Latin letters of the alphabet, will be used to help beginners to standardize pronunciation.

A Sino-Soviet protocol on cooperation between academies of sciences for 1958-62 was signed in Moscow.

A Sino-North Vietnamese protocol on 1958 plan for cultural cooperation was signed in Peking.

December 12: After the 73rd meeting, ambassadorial talks at Geneva were temporarily suspended because of the impending transfer of the United States negotiator, Alex Johnson, from the post of ambassador to Prague to the Bangkok embassy.

December 12-January 7: Communist China sent a delegation of 25 led by Kuo Mo-jo to the Afro-Asian Solidarity Congress in Cairo. The delegation left Cairo for Moscow on its way home on January 7.

December 16: A Sino-East German public health cooperation protocol was signed in Berlin.

It was announced in Paris that the various effort quotas had now been fixed by the committee of the consultative group in 1958 with respect to each member-country, covering all the quantitatively restricted goods, without any further distinction between China and other Communist countries affected. The announcement added that all members of the committee had been "completely satisfied" with its decisions.

In Moscow, a multilateral agreement on establishment of organization for cooperation in postal service and tele-communications among socialist countries was signed.

December 18: A new Sino-Finnish trade pact for one year from November 1, 1957, to October 31, 1958, was signed in Peking.

A joint directive, calling for cessation of the flow of rural people into cities, was issued by the CPC Central Committee and State Council.

December 21: A Sino-Soviet agreement on commercial navigation on border waterways and tributary streams and lakes was signed.

December 22: The PRC and the Soviet Union signed an agreement in Moscow providing for free commercial navigation by vessels of both countries on the Hai-lungkiang River, the Sangari, the Cherny Irtepi and other rivers, and Lake Khanka.

A Sino-Egyptian trade protocol for 1958 was signed in Peking.

December 23: The PRC issued a statement to accept 1948 international regulations for preventing collisions at sea.

December 27: A Sudanese trade delegation arrived in Peking. Trade talks were held between Chinese officials and the Sudanese delegates, and on January 9 a communique was published to the effect that the two governments would provide facilities to promote trade relations, arrange exchange of trade missions, hold mutual commodity exhibitions, and expand economic cooperation.

The State Council passed a treaty between the PRC and the Indonesian Republic on the question of dual nationality. It was decided to submit the treaty to the NPC Standing Committee for ratification. The treaty was ratified by the NPC Standing Committee on December 30.

Sino-Yugoslav protocol on scientific and technical cooperation was signed in Belgrade.

December 30: A Sino-Polish protocol on the 1958 plan for cooperation between academies of sciences was signed in Peking.

Sino-Soviet protocol on settlement of non-commercial payments was signed in Moscow.

Sino-North Korean protocol on 1958-59 plan for cultural cooperation was signed in Peking.

December 31-January 13: Emir Seif el Islam Mohammed Al-Badr arrived in Peking on December 31. Following the China-Yemen talks on January 11, treaties of friendship and commerce, an agreement on scientific, technical and cultural cooperation between China and Yemen, and a joint communique were signed on January 12 by Chou En-lai and Yemen Deputy Premier Crown Prince Al-Badr. The Yemen prince left for home via Moscow on January 13.

December 31: A Sino-North Korean scientific and technical cooperation agreement was signed in Pyongyang; also an agreement on cooperation in hydrological work.

1958

January 1: Peking Radio announced the opening of a new 500-mile railway from Yingtan (Kiangsi) to the port of Amoy, and of a 3,000-foot bridge across the Yalu River at Tungkwan (Shensi). The reopening of the railway from Kuoning (Yunan) to Haiphong (North Vietnam), which had been closed by the Indochina war, was announced at the same time.

January 6: The NPC Standing Committee decided to convene the 5th session of the NPC in Peking on January 25. The principal items on the agenda to be a decision on the 1958 national economic construction plan, an examination and adoption of the 1958 state budget, and an approval of the Han language phoneticization plan.

A revised version of the Regulations Governing Requisition of Land for National Construction, first promulgated by the government Administrative Council on November 5, 1953, was approved by the State Council and ratified by the NPC Standing Committee. The regulations are designed to ensure economical use of land requisitioned, to lower the criterion of compensation to APC's from 3-5 years' value of output to 2-4 years' output, and to resettle the persons whose land is requisitioned, mainly in local farm work.

January 7: The mothers of three Americans held prisoner in China were allowed to visit their sons.

January 9: The Standing Committee of the NPC adopted a new set of regulations pertaining to household registration. Under this set of regulations, all visitors to the cities must either qualify for permanent registration after three months or get special permission to extend their stay. Peasants in particular must obtain documents not only from their places of residence but from organs in urban areas to which they wish to go before they may change their residence.

January 13-26: During this period, the China Kuomintang Revolutionary Committee, the China Democratic League, the China Democratic National Construction Association, the All-China Federation of Industry and Commerce, the China Association for Promoting Democracy, the China Peasants' and Workers' Democratic Party, the China Chih Kung Tang, the Chi'u San Society, and the Taiwan Democratic Self-Government League held meetings, at which a number of rightists were removed from various posts.

January 17: An aviation agreement between Communist China and Outer Mongolia was signed in Ulan Bator.

The State Council formally ratified the decision to transfer the Chiating, Paoshan, and Shanghai *hsien* to the jurisdiction of the Shanghai municipalities.

January 18: A protocol on joint Sino-Soviet research in important subjects of science and technology and also on Soviet assistance to China for this research was signed in Moscow. The protocol provides for joint research from 1958 to 1962 on 122 scientific items (cooperation between academies of agricultural sciences, and cooperation between ministries of higher education).

January 17-18: A meeting of party committees of the Central Government organizations held on January 17-18 planned to wind up the rectification campaign by the end of May. In February and March the campaign is to concentrate on "antiwaste," retrenchment and reorganization. In April the campaign is to enter the fourth stage, when every government functionary would examine his thinking.

January 21: A Sino-Korean protocol on exchange of goods in 1958 was signed in Peking.

January 24: Sino-Mongolian agreement on technical cooperation in civil aviation, and a protocol on air transport and mutual services, were signed in Ulan Bator.

January 28: A Sino-Mongolian protocol on exchange of goods in 1958 was signed in Peking.

January 29-31: The State Council, on January 29, decided to relieve Chang Nai-chi of his present duties as Minister of Food, Chang Po-chun as Minister of Communications, and Lo Lung-chi as Minister of Timber Industry. On January 31, the Standing Committee of NPC decided to remove these three from their ministerial posts. Mao Tse-tung issued a decree implementing this decision.

January 31: A Sino-Burmese agreement on tele-communications was signed in Peking.

February 1: The 5th session of the First NPC opened in Peking; it was presided over by Liu Shao-ch'i and attended by 970 deputies. The session adopted a resolution on removing ten rightists from their posts in the Standing Committee and other NPC committees and the National Reference Council; it also decided that 38 rightists, including the ten, should not be seated in this session.

The Japanese Commodity Exhibition opened in Canton with 22,000 items on view. The exhibition closed on February 24 after a 24 days' run, during which 700,000 people were reported to have visited the show.

February 6-16: A Czechoslovak cultural delegation headed by Dr. Jaroslav Havelka, Vice Minister of Education and Culture, arrived in Peking on February 6 and on February 16 signed a Sino-Czechoslovak cultural plan for 1958.

February 7: The PRC proposed that all foreign troops should leave Korea by specified dates, announced that it was prepared to discuss the withdrawal of the Chinese volunteers with the North Korean government, and asked the United States and other countries participating in the U.N. forces to take similar measures to withdraw their troops from South Korea as a preliminary to the re-unification of the country.

February 11: The NPC approved Chou En-lai's proposal to place Tientsin under the administration of Hopei province in-stead of under the direct administration of the central authorities. The change was made for better coordination in industry and agriculture and also to facilitate state administration.

Premier Chou En-lai resigned from the post of foreign minister, which he had held since September, 1949, and was succeeded by Marshal Ch'en Yi, a deputy premier. On the same day, the NPC approved a government reorganization whereby several ministers and commissions were abolished or merged with others. Announcing the government's reorganizational proposal, Mr. Chou said that the 35 ministries and commissions established in 1954 had since increased to 48, and that reorganization was necessary in the light of the rectification campaign against "bureaucracy."

February 15: In an exchange of notes, the PRC and Finland agreed on a revision of the 1953 payments agreement.

February 18: A Sino-Czechoslovak protocol on 1958 plan for cultural cooperation was signed in Peking.

February 19: Premier Chou En-lai and Foreign Minister Ch'en Yi, after talks in Pyongyang, North Korea, with Kim Il Sung, Prime Minister, issued a joint communique announcing that all Chinese forces would be withdrawn from Korea before April 30, 1958.

The State Department announced that the United States would not remove its troops from South Korea but hoped that Communist China would go further "and agree to genuinely free elections" to unite the country.

February 21: The Sino-Mongolian cultural cooperation agreement and its executive plan for 1958 were signed in Peking.

Sino-Burmese agreement on trade was signed in Rangoon.

February 22: A Sino-Polish agreement on non-commercial payments was signed in Warsaw.

February 23: Chou En-lai sent a message of recognition and greeting to the president of the United Arab Republic, Gamal

Abdul Nasser. Mao Tse-tung also sent a message of greeting to Nasser.

February 26: A five-year barter agreement involving 100 million pounds sterling worth of iron ore and coal from the PRC and the same sum in steel materials from Japan was signed between the visiting Japanese steel mission and two Chinese corporations. A protocol for the current year's transactions of 10 million pounds each way was made at the same time.

February 27-April 16: A six-member Czechoslovak government trade delegation led by Otto Kocour, Czechoslovak First Vice-Minister of Foreign Trade, arrived in Peking on February 27. On April 16, the two states signed an exchange and payments agreement for 1958.

February 28: A Sino-Yugoslav protocol on exchange of goods in 1958 was signed in Belgrade.

March 3: The CPC Central Committee issued a directive on the current campaign against waste and conservatism. The directive called upon all party committees and organizations to use two or three months' time to intensify the campaign against waste and conservatism.

March 4: The first issue of the *Peking Review* an English language weekly containing news and views, came out in Peking.

March 4-8: The Joint Sino-Soviet investigation teams for the Amur Valley held a meeting in Peking on March 4-8, attended by over 100 Chinese and Soviet scientists. They were urged to prepare all necessary data for building in 1958 a 2.2 million-kilowatt hydroelectric power station on the border river.

March 5: The fourth Japan-China trade agreement involving 35 million pounds sterling worth of goods each way, and providing for the setting up of permanent peoples' trade mission in each other's country, was signed in Peking between the China Committee for the Promotion of International Trade and the Japanese trade delegation.

March 7: The State Council decided to place under the administration of the Peking municipality five *hsien*—Tung-

hsien, Shunyi, Tahsing, Lianghsiang and Tangshan—and also the Tungchow municipality. All these areas were originally under the jurisdiction of Hopei Province.

March 9: The PRC issued an official statement supporting North Vietnam's peaceful unification proposal contained in Pham Van Dong's letter to the South Vietnam authorities.

March 12: The PRC announced that the first six divisions (about 100,000 men) of the Chinese volunteers would begin to leave Korea on March 15, and would complete their withdrawal by April 30. The total number of Chinese volunteers in North Korea was estimated at about 350,000 men.

A Sino-Albanian protocol on exchange of goods and payments in 1958 was signed in Tirana.

March 13: A Sino-Bulgarian protocol for trade and payments in 1958 was signed in Sofia.

The Ministry of Education issued a notification instructing primary, middle, and normal schools to teach the phonetic alphabet. The notification said that schools for national minorities might also experiment with the phonetic alphabet in teaching the Han language.

March 15: A Sino-Vietnamese agreement on cooperation in radio broadcasting was signed in Hanoi.

March 19: A Sino-Bulgarian protocol on a plan for cultural cooperation in 1958 was signed in Sofia.

March 21: The Sino-Hungarian agreement on exchange of goods and payments for 1958 was signed in Peking.

March 24: An agreement on joint experiment and research in high-tension electrical equipment operating in the wet tropical parts of China has been signed recently at a conference by the PRC, Hungary, the Soviet Union, Poland, Czechoslovakia and East Germany.

March 26: In an exchange of notes, the PRC and Cambodia agreed on extension of 1956 Economic Aid Agreement.

March 27: A Sino-East German protocol on

non-commercial payments was signed in Berlin.

March 28: Chinese leaders sent greetings to Nikita S. Khrushchev on his election as Premier in Moscow.

March 29: The NCNA reported that under the new policy of the decentralization of industry, the four adjacent provinces of Szechwan, Shensi, Yunnan, and Kweichow had concluded an agreement whereby they would exchange services and cooperate in the construction of railways, roads, and other public works.

A Sino-Yugoslav protocol on a plan for cultural cooperation in 1958 was signed in Berlin.

March 30: A trade and payments arrangement for 1958 between Rumania and the PRC was signed in Bucharest.

March 31: It was disclosed that the PRC and four companies, three Canadian and one American, had signed an agreement for shipment of Canadian wheat to China.

The PRC and North Vietnam signed an agreement on mutual supply of goods and payments in 1958 along with an agreement on PRC aid in industrial construction or reconstruction projects in Peking.

April 1: The Communist Chinese press welcomed the Soviet decision to discontinue nuclear weapons tests unilaterally as a move to help mankind eliminate the threat of atomic war.

April 1-24: The Japanese Commodity Exhibition was opened in Peking on April 1 with 22,000 items on display. It closed on April 24.

April 3: A Sino-Hungarian protocol on a plan for cultural cooperation in 1958 was signed in Budapest.

April 5: A Sino-Polish protocol on the exchange of goods in 1958 was signed.

April 6: A Sino-North Korean accord on a flood control plan for the Tumen River was signed in Changchun.

April 7: The CPC Central Committee and the State Council issued a joint directive on the national program of afforestation, calling for efforts to double the national forest area in ten years, i.e., an increase

from 100 million to 200 million hectares.

In a directive the State Council called for collection and utilization of the abundant resources of wild plants to supplement raw materials for light industries.

Furthermore, the CPC Central Committee and the State Council issued a notice convening a National Conference of Advanced Builders of Socialism in Agriculture, to be held in the winter of 1958.

A Polish delegation led by M. Gomulka, the First-Secretary of the United Workers party, and M. Cyrankiewicz, Prime Minister, visited Peking in its Asian tour. After discussion between Cyrankiewicz and Chou En-lai, a joint statement on international problems was issued on April 7 calling for the replacement of antagonistic military blocs by a collective security system; condemning all attempts of the colonialists to obstruct the national liberation movement; emphasizing the importance of strict implementation of the Geneva Agreement on Indochina; expressing their regret at the obstruction of the implementation of the agreement by South Vietnam, supported by external forces; and reaffirming the support of the Polish and Chinese Communist parties for the Kadar government in Hungary. A Sino-Polish agreement on trade in the period 1959-62 was also signed.

A Sino-Russian joint communique was issued on talks during the visit of Chairman Stoica. Subjects included international tensions, disarmament, the German question, and socialist solidarity.

April 9: The PRC Foreign Ministry lodged a strong protest with the British government against its allowing a Nationalist patrol bomber and crew, which had landed in Hong Kong after carrying out "harassing activities" over the mainland, to be flown back to Taiwan.

April 12: Peking Radio reported that the PRC refused to continue the Geneva talks with Ambassador Johnson's successor, B. E. W. Martin, because he did not have ambassadorial rank.

The PRC and Denmark agreed on trademark registration in an exchange of notes.

A Sino-Rumanian protocol on a plan for cultural cooperation in 1958 was signed in Bucharest.

April 16: A Sino-Czechoslovak agreement on the exchange of goods and payments in 1958 was signed in Peking.

April 17: The PRC and Indonesia agreed on a loan by the PRC to Indonesia in an exchange of notes.

April 19: The instruments of ratification of the agreement between the Chinese and Soviet governments on merchant shipping on boundary rivers and lakes, and along rivers which run through both countries, were exchanged in Peking.

April 21: A trade agreement covering 1959 to 1962 was signed in Peking between the PRC and Hungary.

April 23: A 1958 goods exchange and payments agreement was signed in East Berlin between the PRC and the German Democratic Republic.

The PRC and the U.S.S.R. signed a treaty of commerce and navigation in Peking. Along with the treaty, a trade protocol providing for a greater volume of trade than the previous year was signed by the two countries on most-favored-nation treatment.

April 24: The NCNA reported that elections at basic levels were in progress in nine out of every ten counties or cities throughout the country.

April 26: The PRC minister to Yemen, Chen Chia-kang, and Yemeni Premier Prince Badr agreed in principle that the PRC would help Yemen build highways and factories.

April 28: The Rumanian Economic Exhibition, the biggest ever held by Rumania abroad, opened in Peking.

April 29: A Sino-Albanian protocol on a 1958-59 plan for cultural cooperation was signed in Peking.

The first commune, the Weihsing (Sputnik), was formed in Honan Province.

Details were announced in April of a project for building a shale-oil centre in Mowming county (in the Liuchow Peninsula, southwest Kwangtung), where it was estimated that it would be possible to produce 1,000,000 tons of petroleum annually for 100 years. The entire project, scheduled for completion by 1962, envisages an oil refinery producing high-grade gasolines, diesel oil, and fuel oil, a thermal power station, machine repair workshops, and a town of 80,000 inhabitants. To make use of the by-products and provide employment for the workers' families, an ammonium sulphate factory producing 100,000 tons a month will also be erected, together with other factories producing sulphates, gunny sacks, and silk yarn. The discovery of a rich oil field in Szechwan covering 1500 square miles was also announced in April.

May 4: Prince Axel of Denmark and his secretary arrived in Peking on a four-day visit at the invitation of the Chinese People's Institute of Foreign Affairs.

May 5-23: The 2nd plenary session of the 8th CPC National Congress opened in Peking on May 5 and closed on May 23. At the May 23 meeting, the Congress passed a resolution on the report on the work of the Central Committee and another one on the Moscow meetings of Communist and Workers' parties. In the latter resolution, the Congress flayed Yugoslavia for "revisionism." The Congress also adopted the National Program for Agricultural Development. It also elected 25 additional alternate members to the Central Committee.

May 6: The Chinese Communist and North Korean governments said the U.N. Command would have to withdraw all its forces from South Korea before there could be "a peaceful settlement of the Korean question, including the question of holding free elections."

May 7: Referring to the tearing down of a flag of Communist China by two Japanese "gangsters" in Nagasaki, the Peking *Ta Kung Pao* editorially declared the incident "unmasks most clearly the inveterate hostility of the Kishi government toward the Chinese people."

A Sino-Czechoslovak protocol on the exchange of daily necessities was signed in Prague.

May 12: The first automobile of the "East Wind" brand was built in the first automobile manufacturing plant in Communist China.

May 15: The PRC issued a statement condemning foreign interference in Indonesian affairs, and accusing the United States of assisting the rebels.

The 1958 Spring Export Commodities Fair, which opened in Canton on April 15, closed on May 15.

A trade agreement in 1958-59 between the delegation of the Chinese State Trading Company and the Indian State Trade Corporation was reached in New Delhi.

May 17: Sino-Hungarian agreement on cooperation between academies of sciences was signed in Peking.

May 20-24: The leaders of the Soviet Union, the Soviet-bloc countries, and China met in Moscow for a meeting of the Warsaw Treaty Organization and the East European Council of Mutual Economic Assistance. It was announced that China, North Korea, North Vietnam and Outer Mongolia had decided to coordinate their economic planning and to strengthen their mutual economic cooperation with the Soviet bloc.

May 22: A Sino-East German protocol on general conditions for delivery of goods in 1958 was signed in East Berlin.

May 25: The 8th Central Committee of the CPC held its 5th plenary session in Peking. Lin Piao was elected an additional Vice-Chairman of the Central Committee and a member of the Standing Committee of the Political Bureau; Ko Chin-shih, Li Ching-chuan, and Tan Chen-lin were elected additional members of the Political Bureau. Li Fu-chun and Li Hsien-nien were elected additional members of the secretariat of the Central Committee. The session also decided to set up a fortnightly journal of the Central Com-

mittee, the *Red Flag*, with Chen Po-ta as editor-in-chief.

June 1: The first issue of the *Red Flag*, official organ of the CPC Central Committee, appeared today.

June 3: Five procurators of the Supreme People's Procuratorate and 52 procurators at the provincial and municipal levels were dismissed and 34 were appointed. Further, 14 rightists were dismissed, including Chia Chien, division president of the Supreme People's Court.

A Sino-Pakistani contract on barter of PRC coal for Pakistan cotton was signed in Karachi.

New agricultural tax regulations were approved by the NPC Standing Committee and promulgated for enforcement.

June 4: A Sino-Norwegian agreement on exchange of goods and payments was signed in Peking.

A Sino-Albanian protocol on scientific and technical cooperation was signed in Peking.

June 5: The Chinese Communist delegation withdrew from the 31st Congress of the International Federation of Football Associations in Stockholm on June 5 after protesting against alleged "two Chinas intrigue."

The NPC Standing Committee approved a State Council bill on the cessation of the issue of National Economic Construction Bonds and the issue of Regional Economic Construction Bonds.

The PRC issued a statement on "adherence" to the 1929 Warsaw Convention for the unification of certain rules relating to international carriage by air.

June 9: The State Council issued "Regulations to Improve the System of Taxation" for trial operation, delegating power to local governments to administer taxation.

June 10: The Chinese Foreign Ministry sent a note to the office of the British charge d'affaires, strongly protesting the action of the Hong Kong British authorities in interfering with and prohibiting Chinese residents in Hong Kong from flying the Chinese national flag and singing the Chinese national anthem.

June 11: The Chinese Fishery Association announced that the Sino-Japanese People's Fishing Agreement would not be extended at the expiration of its term on June 12.

June 12: A Sino-Hungarian trade protocol was signed in Budapest.

June 14: Joseph Patrick McCormack and Cyril Wagner were released in Shanghai on the expiration of their prison terms. They left China from Shanghai on June 19.

June 15: The bridge crossing the Yalu River at Santaok'an on the Paotow-Lanchow Railway was formally completed today.

June 16: The CPC Central Committee and State Council issued a circular in connection with preparations for the "National Representative Conference of Advanced Units in Socialist Construction of Agriculture." The circular listed quotas on delegations and announced the setting up of a preparatory committee with Ten Tzehui as Chairman.

June 21: New drafts for language reforms based on Latin alphabet for the Uighur, Kazakh, Mongolia, Khalkhas and Hsipe nationalities have been worked out by the committee for studying the languages of nationalities of Sinkiang.

June 28: The PRC and Cambodia agreed on extension of 1956 trade and payments agreement to June 16, 1959.

June 29: The NPC Standing Committee adopted a resolution convening the 1st session of the 2nd NPC in January 1959, with deputies to be elected before the end of October 1958.

June 30: A member of the Atomic Physics Institute in China, Jen Ta-ming, told a gathering of civil servants in Peking that China's first atomic reactor had gone into operation on June 13.

Peking warned that it would abandon the ambassadorial talks with the United States in Geneva unless the United States agreed within 15 days to resume the discussions.

Peking announced that foreign diplomats in China would not be allowed to travel more than 12 miles from Peking without special permission.

July 1: At a press conference, Secretary Dulles rejected the Chinese ultimatum, and said that the United States intended to continue the talks, and the U.S. ambassador to Poland might be named to confer with Chinese Ambassador Wang Ping-nan if Warsaw proved to be an acceptable conference site.

July 2: The member states of the U.N. Command in Korea told the Chinese Communists that U.N. forces would not be withdrawn from South Korea until plans for unification of the country through free elections were definitely agreed upon.

July 3: 4,500,000 people's deputies have been elected at the *hsiang* and *Chen* levels, according to a NCNA dispatch.

July 4: A Sino-Soviet protocol on scientific and technical cooperation was signed in Moscow.

July 9: The NPC Standing Committee ratified the Sino-Soviet treaty of commerce and navigation signed on April 23, 1958.

July 11-August 14: The second group of the Chinese People's Volunteers, comprising six divisions and specialized units totalling 100,000, completely withdrew from Korea to the mainland in the period from July 11 to August 14, according to a communique issued by the headquarters of the Chinese People's Volunteers in Pyongyang.

July 16: The PRC extended formal recognition to the Republic of Iraq, and Iraq reciprocated its recognition to the PRC on July 18.

The PRC government issued a statement demanding the immediate withdrawal of United States troops from Lebanon.

July 17: Over half a million people demonstrated in Peking before the Tien An Men to proclaim Communist China's support for the Iraqi Republic and to denounce the U.S. intervention in Lebanon. In a speech, Mayor Peng Chen described the United States as a "paper tiger."

July 18: A note was presented to the British charge d'affaires in Peking protesting

Britain's armed intervention in Jordan, demanding the withdrawal of British troops from that country, and warning the British that they faced grave consequences if they failed to do so.

July 19: Vast numbers of demonstrators—stated by Peking radio to number 2,000,-000—marched in procession outside the British embassy in Peking, chanting anti-British slogans and beating gongs and tom-toms, but there was no act of mob violence as in Moscow. Similar large-scale demonstrations took place outside the British consulate in Shanghai.

July 21: A long-term trade agreement for 1958-1962 was signed today between the PRC and Rumania.

July 24: A joint Sino-Cambodian declaration issued in Phnom-Penh, Cambodia, announced that Cambodia agreed to establish diplomatic relations with Communist China and that the two countries would exchange diplomatic missions at ambassadorial level.

July 30: The 1,000-kilometer-long Paotow-Lanchow Railway was completed today when the northern and southern sections were joined at Yingchuan, the prospective capital of the Ninghsia Hui Autonomous Region.

July 31: A protocol on Sino-East German scientific and technical cooperation was signed in Peking.

July 31-August 3: Soviet Premier Khrushchev visited Peking for talks with Chairman Mao Tse-tung. The meeting took place under conditions of great secrecy, no intimation of the Soviet leader's presence in Peking being given until August 3. The communique issued at the end of the talks called for the immediate holding of a summit conference, the ending of nuclear testing, and the abolition of military blocs and military bases on foreign soil. It reaffirmed the ideological unity of the Soviet and Chinese Communist parties. The communique made no reference to the Taiwan question. The wording in the communique indicated for the first time China's rise to co-equal status with the U.S.S.R.

August 3: It was announced in Washington that the U.S. ambassador in Warsaw (Mr. Jacob Beam) had been asked to resume ambassadorial talks with Mr. Wang Ping-nan in the Polish capital.

August 4-13: Mao Tse-tung inspected the rural areas of Hopei, Honan, Shantung, and Tientsin with attention being paid mainly to agricultural production. On his way back from Tientsin he visited two cooperative farms in a Peking suburb.

August 5: Transformation of private houses put out to lease is being intensified in many cities. These houses are generally placed under the control of the state agencies, and for a specified period of time the house owners are given a fixed amount of interest-rent amounting to 20 to 40 percent of the original rent.

August 8: An agreement on Soviet technical assistance to China for the construction or expansion of 47 metallurgical, chemical, coal-mining, machine-building, woodworking, building material enterprises and power stations was signed in Moscow.

A Sino-Hungarian agreement on mutual purchase of film distribution rights was signed in Budapest.

The PRC issued a statement in support of the Soviet Union's proposal for the holding of an emergency special session of the U.N. General Assembly.

August 9: The U.S. State Department issued a memorandum to U.S. embassies entitled "U.S. policy regarding non-recognition of the Chinese Communist regime," to bar change in the non-recognition policy.

August 14: Major relaxations in the embargo on exports to Soviet-bloc countries and Communist China were announced in Paris, London, and other capitals concerned on August 14, to be in effect from August 15. The agreements involved the following changes: (1) The first list on which the embargo was based, consisting of strategic items whose export was absolutely forbidden, was reduced from 181 items to 118—a large number of goods being freed but a small number added, while the remaining items were more closely redefined; (2) the second list, which laid down quantitative restrictions for the export of 25 items, was abolished; (3) the watching list, details of which were not published, was retained. It was announced in Washington, however, that while agreeing to the revision of the embargo in respect to trade with the U.S.S.R. and other Soviet-bloc countries, the United States would maintain the complete embargo on all U.S. trade with China, North Korea and North Vietnam.

August 15: A Sino-Czechoslovak protocol on scientific and technical cooperation was signed in Prague.

Prince Norodom Sihanouk and the Cambodian State delegation arrived in Peking. A joint statement was signed on August 24, reiterating the Five Principles of Peaceful Co-existence, PRC economic aid, neutralist policy of Cambodia, etc.

August 17: The NCNA dispatched a report that the Ministry of Education and other ministers of the Central Government have, since July, transferred from 55% to 74% of higher educational institutions, secondary technical schools, and schools for training skilled workers to the local authorities at the provincial, municipal or autonomous region levels.

August 17-30: The political bureau of the CPC Central Committee held an enlarged meeting at Peitaiho, Hopei, on August 17-30. The meeting discussed the National Economic Plan for 1959, the question of industrial and agricultural production, the question of establishing people's communes, and other questions.

August 20: The Chinese Olympic Committee decided today to cease its recognition of the International Olympic Committee in protest against that body's recognition of the sports organization in Taiwan.

August 22: A Sino-Hungarian protocol on scientific and technical cooperation was signed in Budapest.

August 23-28: Quemoy and Little Quemoy were subjected to almost daily bombardments from Communist shore batteries on the mainland.

August 25: A Sino-Egyptian agreement on postal services was signed in Peking.

August 27: President Eisenhower declared that the United States would not "desert our responsibilities or statements we have already made" concerning Taiwan and the offshore islands. Adding that "the Nationalist Chinese have now deployed about a third of their forces to these islands . . . ," the President noted that "that makes a closer interlocking between the defense system of the islands with Taiwan than before."

The PRC Foreign Ministry sent a note to the office of the British charge d'affaires, strongly protesting against intrusion by British military aircraft into the territorial air of China, and against the Hong Kong British authorities for forcibly closing down the premises of the Chung Hua Middle School and the "brutal beating up" by the Hong Kong police of the teachers, staff, and students of the school as well as the Chinese reporters.

August 29: The Peking Radio said that a "landing on Quemoy is imminent," and that the Communists were "determined to liberate Taiwan as well as the offshore islands." The broadcast told Nationalist forces defending Quemoy "to stop resistance immediately and return to the fatherland or be totally destroyed." The same day, the State Department warned that a Communist attempt to change the situation in the Formosa Strait by force could not be a limited operation. The Defense Department announced that U.S. forces in the area were being reinforced.

The CPC Central Committee adopted a resolution on the establishment of People's Communes in the rural areas. The resolution stated that the establishment of People's Communes is a preparation for transition to Communism. Communes should generally be set up on a *hsiang* basis with the merging of farming cooperatives. In general, one commune may be set up for each *hsiang* to embrace 2,000 households. Until conditions are ripe, there is no immediate need to change the collective ownership into ownership by all the people or to change the original system of distribution.

The Political Bureau of the CPC Central Committee adopted a directive on a Socialist and Communist education campaign to be widely launched in the rural areas in the coming winter and next spring.

August 31: A *Pravda* "Observer" article voiced strong Soviet support for Communist China's campaign to liberate Taiwan and offshore islands.

September 1: The U.S. 7th Fleet in Taiwan Straits, comprising some 60 warships, was reinforced during the first fortnight of September by the aircraft carrier Essex (33,000 tons) and four destroyers from the Mediterranean, the 45,000-ton carrier Midway from Hawaii, and the guided-missile cruiser Los Angeles (17,000 tons) from California. It was also disclosed in Washington that the United States air forces in Taiwan had been reinforced during the same period by an undisclosed number of Sabre and Starfighter jets from Hawaii and the United States.

September 4: Secretary Dulles discussed the off-shore island situation with President Eisenhower, then issued the following statement with the authorization of the President. "The United States is bound by treaty to defend Taiwan from armed attack, and the President is authorized by joint resolution of Congress to employ the armed forces of the United States for the securing and protecting of related positions such as Quemoy and Matsu."

The Chinese Communist government issued a declaration extending the limit of China's territorial waters from three to twelve nautical miles, applicable to the Chinese mainland and its coastal islands as well as Taiwan, the Pescadores, and all other islands belonging to China which are separated from the mainland and its coastal islands by the high seas.

September 5-8: The 15th meeting of the Supreme State Conference, called by Mao Tse-tung, opened on September 5 and closed on September 8. At the first-day meeting, Mao made an analysis of the domestic and international situation.

September 6: Premier Chou En-lai reiterated the Chinese Communist government's claim to liberate Taiwan and the Pescadores, and denounced what he described as the U.S.A.'s aggression in these areas and its support for the Chiang Kai-shek clique. At the same time he called for a resumption of the Sino-American ambassadorial talks to make another effort for peace.

September 7: After the National Security Council meeting in Washington, an official United States statement announced that the U.S. ambassador at Warsaw stood ready to promptly meet with the Chinese ambassador there.

In his letter to President Eisenhower, Premier Khrushchev supported Communist China on the Taiwan Strait crisis, asserted Soviet and Chinese Communist security interests were identical, and warned an attack on Communist China was an attack on the Soviet Union. At the same time, he urged that all parties should try to find a common language with the aim of removing the tension which had arisen in the Far East.

September 9: Secretary Dulles told a news conference that a meaningful renunciation of force by Communist China would ease the Taiwan Strait crisis, and he said there might be "further consequences." Dulles hinted that the United States was ready to offer concessions under such circumstances at the proposed ambassadorial talks in Warsaw. He said the United States would seek agreement along detailed, specific lines but could not itself negotiate the future of Quemoy and Matsu, because those islands belonged to Nationalist China.

September 10-29: Mao Tse-tung made an inspection tour of provinces along the Yangtze during September, covering Wuhan, Huangshihkang, Anching, Hopei, Wuhu, Manshu, Nanking and Shanghai, and returned to Peking on September 29. He inspected factories, met functionaries, surveyed crops, and visited people's communes.

September 11: President Eisenhower made a nationwide broadcast about the Taiwan situation, dangerous to peace, which had developed in the Formosa Strait, and expressed his hope on the forthcoming ambassadorial talks to settle the dispute.

September 13: In reply to Khrushchev's letter, President Eisenhower appealed to the Soviet Union to use its influence with China to persuade that country to renounce the use of force in the Formosa Strait area and begin peace negotiations.

September 14: The ambassadorial talks between the United States and Communist China were reopened in Warsaw. Both parties maintained strict silence on the proceedings. It was the 74th ambassadorial meeting since the opening of the Sino-American talks at Geneva in 1955.

September 15: A Sino-Polish protocol on scientific and technical cooperation was signed in Warsaw.

September 15-22: Nationalist Chinese convoys succeeded in running the Communist blockade of Quemoy daily from September 15 to 22 and again from September 26 to 28.

September 15-January 4: The National Industrial and Communications Exhibition, with more than 50,000 exhibits on display, opened in Peking.

September 17: An agreement between Ceylon and the PRC was signed in Colombo whereby China granted Ceylon a loan of 50,000,000 rupees for flood relief and rehabilitation.

September 18: The Nationalist Chinese Defense Ministry claimed that Sabre jet fighters escorting a convoy, although greatly outnumbered, had shot down five Communist MIG-17's and sunk three torpedo boats. Communist sources claimed that a Nationalist plane had been shot down.

A Defense Department spokesman said the United States had sent $90 million in military supplies to Taiwan in the three weeks since the Quemoy crisis began.

The Pentagon announced also that American pilots were authorized to follow a "hot pursuit" policy against any Chinese Communist plane which might attack them, including following the plane over Communist-held territory.

Secretary Dulles told the U.N. General Assembly that debate on the Taiwan and Quemoy-Matsu dispute should be postponed until the outcome of negotiations in Warsaw between the United States and Communist China. He expressed hope that the negotiations there would bring a cease-fire but reserved the right to bring the problem to the U.N. if the Warsaw talks appeared headed for failure.

September 19: In his reply to President Eisenhower's letter of September 12, Premier Khrushchev contended that U.S. support of the Nationalist government was responsible for the crisis, and that there could be no lasting peace in the Far East until the U.S. armed forces were recalled from Taiwan and the Taiwan Straits.

September 20: Chen Yi, the PRC Foreign Minister, made a statement refuting U.S. Secretary of State Dulles' speech at the U.N. General Assembly. Chen said: "The crucial question is not a so-called cease-fire but the withdrawal of U.S. forces. There is no fighting between China and the United States, so the question of cease-fire does not arise. The liberation by the Chinese people of their territory, whether by peaceful means or by armed struggle, is a matter for the Chinese people themselves." He went on to say that if the United States had any sincere desire to settle the dispute between the two countries peacefully, it should respect China's sovereignty and territorial integrity and stop interfering in China's internal affairs.

September 21: Nationalist Chinese navy patrols sank a Communist gunboat off Matsu. The U.S. government formally rejected Khrushchev's note which was returned to the Soviet Foreign Ministry by the U.S. embassy in Moscow. A White House statement declared that the note was "replete with false accusations," was couched in "abusive and intemperate language, indulged in personalities," contained "inadmissivable threats," and was therefore unacceptable under established diplomatic practice.

The Nationalist government announced that the Chinese Communist bombardment of Quemoy from August 23 to September 21, 1958, had resulted in 3,000 civilian and 1,000 military casualties.

September 22: The PRC extended formal diplomatic recognition to the newly established Algerian rebel government.

The Bulgarian delegation, headed by V. Chervenkov, arrived in China for a six-week visit. Chervenkov expressed his admiration of the "Great Leap Forward" and communes on his departure.

An American woman writer, Anna Louise Strong, arrived in Peking as a guest of the Chinese People's Association for Relations with Foreign Countries and the Union of Chinese Writers.

September 22-23: A conference took place in Taipei between Chiang Kai-shek and U.S. military representatives headed by Admiral Felt, Commander-in-Chief of the U.S. forces in the Pacific. Chiang had strongly argued in favor of military action against the Chinese mainland during these discussions, but no official statement was issued.

September 23: The U.N. General Assembly approved, by 44-28-9, a U.S. proposal to postpone for another year any consideration of Communist China's admission to the U.N.

September 24: Nationalist Chinese reported that 10 Communist aircraft had been shot down in an action between 32 Sabres and over 100 MIG-17's. Communist sources claimed that during fighting over the mainland a Communist plane had also been lost. A spokesman of the Ministry of National Defense said that Nationalist aircraft had launched five Sidewinder guided missiles.

A Nationalist Chinese spokesman stated that his government favored immediate aerial bombardment of the Communist batteries and an eventual landing on the mainland.

September 25: A U.S. Defense Department spokesman pointed out that an agreement existed that the Nationalist forces would not attack the mainland without U.S. approval.

The CPC Central Committee and the State Council announced a decision requiring workers of all government organizations, armed forces, enterprises and industries, except those who are too old or too sick to perform physical labor, to spend at least one month a year in such labor.

A Sino-Tunisian agreement on the exchange of goods in 1959 was signed in Tunis.

September 27: The first nuclear reactor in Communist China was put into operation in Peking. Built with the assistance of Soviet specialists, it comprised a 10,000-kilowatt heavy-water research reactor and a 20,000,000-electron-volt cyclotron, to be used in the production of radio-active isotopes and other industrial and medical applications. It was inaugurated at a ceremony attended by Soviet nuclear figures.

Representatives of the PRC and North Korea signed in Peking three economic agreements. The first was a long-term trade agreement covering the period 1959-1962. During the four-year period, China would supply Korea with coal, cotton, cotton yarns, tires, tin, rolled steel, ferromanganese, sulphur, paraffin, and gypsum. From Korea, China would receive iron ore, copper, lead, zinc, high-speed steel, carbon tool steel, calcium-carbide, ginseng, marine and other products. The two countries decided to build the Unbong hydroelectric power station in the upper reaches of the Yalu River. The cost of construction would be shared on an equal basis. Under the second agreement, China would extend to Korea a long-term loan to cover the cost of work undertaken by the Koreans. This loan would be repaid in goods over a ten-year period beginning in 1963. The third agreement covered a Chinese loan to Korea for the purchase of Chinese machinery and equipment for the construction of a textile mill and two cement paper-bag plants. This loan would be repaid in goods over a ten-year period beginning in 1961.

September 30: 90.4% of all peasant households have joined people's communes, according to a NCNA dispatch. There are a total of 23,384 people's communes in China, averaging 4,797 households each.

In Washington, Mr. Dulles declared that the U.S. government would favor the evacuation of the offshore islands by the Nationalist forces if a reasonable dependable cease-fire were arranged.

October 1: In Taipei, Chiang Kai-shek said that he was incredulous at the reports of Mr. Dulles' press conference, and added, "Granted that Mr. Dulles had made the statement attributed to him, it would be only a unilateral declaration, and my government would be under no obligation to keep it."

At a press conference, President Eisenhower denied suggestions that Mr. Dulles' new attitude would be described as "appeasement." He said that as a soldier he believed that it was not a good thing to have so many troops on Quemoy and Matsu, which "as of themselves, as two pieces of territory, are not greatly vital to Taiwan."

October 2: Mr. Dulles, in reply to inquiries from Mr. Drumwright (U.S. ambassador in Taipei), said that he had sent the latter a telegram "straightening out misconceptions in Nationalist circles which gave an exaggerated idea of the shift of position on our part."

October 4: The talks in Warsaw between the United States and Chinese ambassadors were believed to have reached a deadlock by this time, although no official statements were issued. Between the fifth and sixth sessions (held on September 30 and October 4, respectively), Mr. Huang Hua, head of the Western European department of the Chinese Foreign Ministry, arrived in Warsaw from Peking to take part in the discussions.

In exchange of letters, the PRC and Pakistan agreed upon the granting of reciprocal most-favored-nation treatment.

October 5: In a Tass interview, criticizing United States distortions of Soviet position on military support for Peking, Premier Khrushchev clarified the Soviet commitment, saying that the U.S.S.R. would come to the help of the People's Republic of China if the latter were attacked from without. He implied that attack by Nationalist China would be regarded only as an incident of civil war.

A Sino-Hungarian agreement on tourism was signed in Budapest.

October 6: The Communist defense minister, Peng Teh-huai, announced in a message to the Nationalists that he had ordered the bombardment of the offshore islands to be suspended for seven days, and that supplies might be introduced during this period provided there was no United States escort. He also proposed that talks should take place between the Communists and Kuomintang to bring about a permanent settlement, while the issue between China and the United States should be solved through the Warsaw negotiations.

In Taipei, Nationalist China denounced the Communist statement as part of a diabolical peace offensive, but stated that the Nationalist forces would fire only in self-defense.

October 7: Chen Yi, Foreign Minister of Communist China, sent a message to Sekou Toure, Prime Minister of the Republic of Guinea, informing him that the Chinese government had decided to extend recognition to his country.

October 8: The U.S. State Department announced that U.S. warships had stopped escorting Nationalist convoys, but would resume escort activity if the bombardment began again.

October 9: A Sino-East German agreement on the purchase of film distribution rights was signed.

October 10: A Sino-Rumanian agreement on cooperation in radio and television broadcasting was signed in Bucharest.

October 12: The NPC Standing Committee decided to set up a State Capital Construction Commission with Vice-Premier Chen Yun concurrently chairman of the commission.

October 13: On the expiration of the seven days' suspension of the bombardment, the Communist defense minister issued an order extending it for a further two weeks.

A Sino-Indonesian contract on the sale of rice by the PRC was signed in Djakarta.

October 14: Mr. Dulles said at a press conference that the continued suspension of the bombardment was not the dependable cease-fire to which he had referred on September 30. He also said that the United States had no plans whatsoever for urging Chiang to reduce the strength of his forces on Quemoy.

Mr. McElroy, the United States Secretary of Defense, visited Taiwan for discussions with Chiang Kai-shek. He denied reports that the object of his visit was to persuade the Nationalists to agree to a reduction of their garrisons.

October 17: A Sino-North Korean joint communique on withdrawal of Chinese People's Volunteers from Korea and turnover of barracks to Korea was issued in Pyongyang.

October 18: Professors and students of Nankai University in Tientsin were reported to have built an experimental atomic reactor with a maximum permissible power of 3,000 miliwatts, according to a NCNA dispatch.

A Sino-Korean protocol on scientific and technical cooperation was signed in Peking.

October 20: The State Council endorsed a decision to place the four *hsien* of Huaniyu, Miyun, Pingku, and Yengchin within the jurisdiction of Peking municipalities.

Communist Defense Minister Peng Teh-huai issued an order cancelling the cease-fire, on the grounds that U.S. escort vessels had allegedly entered Chinese territorial waters. However, two main factors were believed to have influenced Peking's decision to resume the bombardment: (1) The attitude adopted by Mr. Dulles at his press conference on October 14, which was regarded as an indication that he was less prepared to make concessions than he had been on September 30, and which was interpreted by the Peking *People's Daily* as proving that the

U.S. demand for a cease-fire was merely designed to secure an opportunity for military development under the cover of political bargaining; (2) a Taiwan announcement (on October 17) that the United States would supply the Nationalists with Nike-Hercules missiles and train Nationalist troops in their use.

October 21-23: Dulles flew to Taiwan for talks with Chiang at Taipei. A joint communique issued at the conclusion of the talks stated that under present conditions the defense of Quemoy and Matsu was closely related to the defense of Taiwan and the Pescadores, and that the mission of Nationalist China would not include the use of force against the mainland.

October 25: Peng Teh-huai announced that he had ordered his artillery not to shell Quemoy airfield, the wharf, beach, and ships on even dates.

October 26: Withdrawal of the Chinese People's Volunteers from North Korea was completed pursuant to a declaration of policy made on February 19, 1958.

October 27: A Sino-Moroccan trade agreement was signed in Rabat.

October 31: A State Department press officer Lincoln White told a news conference that Nationalist China could use fire "for self-defense or in the case of a large-scale uprising on the Communist mainland," despite President Chiang Kai-shek's October 23 renunciation of force. White said his statement was aimed at clarifying "misunderstanding."

November 1: The PRC and Indonesia agreed on the extension of a 1956 trade agreement.

In an interview with a Canadian newsman in Peking, Chinese Communist Foreign Minister Chen Yi said: "Quemoy, Matsu, Taiwan, and the Pescadores must be liberated as a whole. We will not allow the handing over of Quemoy in exchange for placing Taiwan under U.N. trusteeship," which "would be nothing but American occupation." "Nor can we accept demilitarization or referring the matter to the U.N. or the International Court of Justice."

It was announced in Rabat and Peking that Morocco and the PRC had decided to establish diplomatic relations at the ambassadorial level.

November 2: Communist Chinese shelling of the offshore islands entirely ceased.

November 6: In accordance with the decision made at the China committee of the consultative group in Paris on August 14, the United States government issued a revised list of goods which might not be exported to Soviet-bloc countries; over 250 items were removed from the restricted category, leaving more than 700 still still under control. The total embargo on shipments to Communist China, North Korea, and North Vietnam was not affected.

November 10: The United States ambassador to Poland, Jacob D. Beam, returned to the United States to report on seven weeks of negotiations with Communist China's ambassador in Warsaw, Wang Ping-nan. The two envoys were scheduled to resume their talks November 25.

November 13: A Sino-Bulgarian protocol on scientific and technical cooperation was signed in Peking.

November 19: A Sino-Korean protocol on the exchange of goods in 1959 was signed in Peking.

November 22-December 9: A delegation of the North Korean government headed by Kim II Sung arrived in Peking on November 22. On December 8, Chou En-lai and Kim II Sung signed a joint statement demanding withdrawal of U.N. forces from Korea, condemning the United States for "encroaching on China's territory," and supporting the North Vietnamese in their efforts for the peaceful unification of Vietnam. Kim and the delegation left for home on December 9.

November 23: Mao Tse-tung appointed Vice-Premier Nieh Jung-chen concurrently Chairman of the Science and Technology Commission.

November 26: Track-laying was completed along the 168-kilometer Nanping-Foochow Railway, the second railway in Fukien.

November 27: The PRC's first ocean-going freighter, LEAP FORWARD, with a loading capacity of 13,400 tons and a displacement of 22,100 tons, was launched at the Dairen shipyard.

A Sino-Bulgarian protocol for cultural cooperation in 1959 was signed in Peking.

November 28-December 10: The sixth plenary session of the Eighth Central Committee of the CPC was held in Wuhan under the guidance of Mao Tse-tung between November 28 and December 10. The main items on the agenda were: The people's communes, the national economic plan for 1959, and the question of not nominating Mao Tse-tung as candidate for Chairman of People's Republic of China for the next term.

The resolution on the people's communes made it clear that the transition from socialism to communism is quite a long and complicated process of development and that completion of this process will take about 15, 20 or more years.

November 28-December 18: A nine-member Chinese Communist delegation headed by Nan Han-chen left for Cairo to attend the Afro-Asian economic conference.

November 29: Foreign Minister Ahmad Khier announced that Sudan had recognized the People's Republic of China.

November 30-December 12: The 1958 National Conference of Overseas Chinese Affairs, held in Canton from November 30 to December 12, recognized the urgent need to solve some problems in respect to dependents of overseas Chinese and returned overseas Chinese who have joined the people's communes. The following points were clarified: (1) After joining the communes, personal means of subsistence (including houses, clothing and furniture), overseas remittances, bank deposits, and cooperative credits would forever remain their own; (2) their property rights would be protected at the present and in the future. Surplus houses may be used by the communes but the ownership will remain unchanged; (3) those who do not desire to sit in a mass hall and do not desire to send their children to a nursery may be allowed to follow their own desires. But ideological education must be carried out among them.

December 1: The Mongolian-Soviet-Chinese-Korean-Vietnamese railway transport planning conference was held in Ulan Bator on December 1-9, at which a protocol of the 1959 transport plan for import, export, and transit cargoes of the five nations was signed.

December 3-20: An Algerian ministerial delegation arrived in Peking on December 3. A joint communique was issued on December 20 to request the withdrawal of foreign troops from Asian and African countries.

December 8: A Sino-Vietnamese protocol on border railways was signed in Kunming.

December 9: A multilateral protocol on rail transportation in 1959 was signed in Ulan Bator by the PRC, North Korea, Mongolia, North Vietnam, and the U.S.S.R.

December 15: A trade and payments agreement for 1959-61 was signed between the PRC and UAR in Cairo after over a month of talks.

December 16: A Sino-Korean protocol on barter in border areas was signed in Pyongyang.

December 17: The CPC Central Committee announced that Mao Tse-Tung, aged 65, would retire as Chairman of the PRC when his current term expired in January 1959. The announcement said Mao was resigning to devote full-time to his job as Communist Party Chairman. Chinese Foreign Minister Chen Yi said Mao was retiring "to conserve himself for still more important tasks." He denied that difficulties with the commune system—which was intended to enable Communist China to make a "great leap forward" in agricultural and industrial production—or the failure to gain control of the offshore islands had anything to do with Mao's decision.

December 18: The 1959 trade protocol on the exchange of goods and payments between the PRC and Bulgaria was signed in Peking.

The Chinese Communist government called a temporary halt to plans to set up large-scale communes in big cities, and pushed reform in existing ones.

December 19: The CPC Central Committee in a directive called upon local party committees to follow the example of Hupeh and pay attention to the living conditions of the people. The measures announced by the CPC Hupeh committee include the following: (1) Eight hours for sleep and four hours for taking meals and relaxation must be guaranteed. Even in the busiest season, work may not exceed 12 hours a day; (2) public mess hall must see that everyone has enough to eat and that the food is as good or better than that prepared at home; (3) a work shed must be built on the work site to provide shelter from storms and snow. Houses demolished must be rebuilt as soon as possible. In housing, human beings must be separated from livestock; (4) the nurseries, kindergartens, and the homes for the aged must be well managed; (5) cultural and recreational activities must be developed.

December 20: In view of the profound changes taking place in production, distribution, exchanges and consumption following establishment of communes, the CPC Central Committee and the State Council announced a decision to improve the financial and trade administration in rural areas. The basic level organizations such as the departments of food, commerce and finance, and banks are to be transferred, both fixed assets and personnel, to communes for administration. In their financial and trade administration, the commune must obey the unified policies of the state concerning market prices, planned purchases, marketing, and other financial matters. They must deliver, and sell to the state, products, and distribute commodities to commune members according to unified state plans. They must guarantee delivery to the Treasury of taxes, income of enterprises, and other receipts after subtracting administrative expenses hitherto defrayed by the state.

Thus the communes serve as the foundation of the rural financial and trade work.

Sino-Algeria joint communique was issued in Peking on talks during visit of Mohmond Cherif, member of "Provisional Government of Republic of Algeria," on such subjects as Algerian independence, nuclear tests, etc.

December 21: The PRC made a statement extending full support for the Soviet proposal on the withdrawal of foreign troops from Berlin and the termination of the occupation of Berlin.

December 23-29: A Mongolian government delegation headed by D. Molomz-hamts, Vice-Chairman of the Council of Ministers, arrived in Peking on December 23 to discuss economic cooperation between the two countries. A Sino-Mongolian economic and technical agreement was signed in Peking on December 29.

December 26: According to the Ministry of Railway, China's total railway building this year was about 2,300 kilometers of new track, including the doubletracking of some old lines. Work had gone forward on 50 new lines, with 20 other lines being doubletracked or improved. Among the new lines built and put into operation this year are the Paotow-Lanchow line, and the one linking Lienkiang with Mowming. The new trunk line from Lanchow to Sinkiang has reached Tienhu in Sinkiang, 1,169 kilometers from Lanchow and only 160 kilometers away from Hami. Another new line, the Lanchow-Tsinghai Railway, is now being built in Northwest China.

December 27: Albanian Vice-Premier Kellegi arrived in Peking on a 3-week economic mission resulting in a 35-million-ruble loan for 1961-65 by Chinese Communists, and a new trade agreement.

The PRC and North Korea signed an agreement on currency exchange rate and non-commercial payments in Pyongyang with protocols on currency exchange in border areas and non-commercial remittances between People's Bank of China and Central Bank of Korea.

December 29: Sino-Mongolian agreement on economic and technical aid was signed in Peking.

1959

January 1: A Sino-Czechoslovak protocol on a plan for cultural cooperation in 1959 was signed.

January 2: Britain announced a number of changes in the embargo list on exports to the Soviet bloc and China. Under the revisions of the embargo list, a wide range of scientific instruments and apparatus were freed from control.

The 168-kilometer Nan Ping Foochow railway was formally opened to traffic this morning.

January 3: A trade and payments agreement between Iraq and the PRC, under which China undertook to supply machinery and equipment in return for dates, wool, cotton, and hides, was signed in Baghdad with an exchange of letters on trade involving third countries.

January 5: A Sino-Mongolian protocol on a plan for cultural cooperation in 1959 was signed in Ulan Bator.

January 16: The PRC and Albania signed two agreements in Peking: (1) Trade in the period 1961-65, (2) PRC loan in the period 1961-65, with a protocol on the exchange of goods and payments in 1959, and a protocol on the use of a PRC loan and gift to Albania in 1959.

Sino-North Vietnamese agreement on cultural cooperation in the period 1959-64 was signed in Hanoi.

January 17: A Sino-Soviet protocol on scientific and technical cooperation was signed in Peking.

January 20-February 12: The delegation of the Vietnam Lao Dong party led by Ho Chi Minh arrived in Peking on January 20 on its way to Moscow to attend the 21st Congress of the Soviet Communist Party. The delegation came back from Moscow on February 9. Mao Tse-tung received Ho Chi Minh on February 10. The delegation left Peking for home on February 12.

January 21: The PRC issued a statement extending full support for the proposal of the Soviet government on the holding of a peace conference to discuss and conclude a peace treaty with Germany.

A multilateral protocol on further scientific cooperation among members of Joint Institute for Nuclear Research was signed in Dubna.

January 22: The maritime arbitration commission of the China Council for Promotion of Foreign Trade was inaugurated in accordance with a State Council decision.

January 22-29: Prime Minister Otto Grotewohl, his wife, and members of the East German government delegation arrived in Peking on January 22. Mao Tse-tung received Grotewohl on January 27. A joint Sino-German statement was signed in Peking by Chen Yi and Grotewohl on January 27. The two parties expressed firm support for the Soviet proposals on Germany. As to Sino-German relations, the two parties agreed to conclude a consular convention and a long-term trade agreement and to establish an East German consulate in Shanghai. The German delegation expressed its admiration of the commune set up in Communist China. The delegation left Peking for Moscow on January 29.

January 23: In accordance with the recommendation of the State Council, the NPC Standing Committee decided to postpone the convocation of the first session of the Second NPC to April, 1959.

A protocol on the PRC aid in construction of roads and of a textile factory in Yemen was signed in Taizz, Yemen.

January 28: Chou En-lai, at the 21st Congress of the Soviet Communist Party held in Moscow, declared that neither the "U.S. imperialist nor the Yugoslav revisionists" would be able to break the eternal and unbreakable friendship between the Soviet Union and China. He spoke of the commune as the best form for developing socialism under Chinese conditions, claiming that China would become a socialist country with highly developed modern industry, agriculture, science, and culture in 15 or 20 years, or a little longer. He read a message from Mao Tse-tung praising Khrushchev's "correct leadership," but made no reference to the latter's proposal for an atom-free zone in the Far East.

January 30: A Sino-Polish protocol for cultural cooperation in 1959 was signed in Warsaw.

A Sino-Mongolian protocol on the mutual supply of goods in 1959 was signed in Ulan Bator.

February 5: England announced changes on the list of strategic goods subject to embargo on exports to the Soviet bloc and China. Under the changes announced, export control was reimposed on the following items: Lithium compounds, various niobium alloys, nickel wire mesh, climatic conditioning chambers, specified military electronic equipment, high-energy military fuels, missile-refueling apparatus, certain noxious gases, nuclear reactors, ammonium perchlorate, zirconium manufactures, specified communications equipment, certain electronic components, and electromagnetic-wave absorbing materials.

A Sino-East German goods exchange and payments agreement was signed in Peking.

February 7: The 605-kilometer Kwangsi Railway, stretching from Kweiyang to Liuchow, was opened to traffic today.

Soviet Premier Khrushchev and PRC Premier Chou En-lai signed a technical aid agreement (1959-1967) in Moscow to provide China with $1.25 billion worth of equipment and assistance by 1967 for construction of 78 heavy industrial installations.

February 13: The PRC and Rumania signed an agreement in Peking on the current exchange rate and non-commercial payments between the two countries.

February 14: A Sino-Polish protocol on general conditions for the delivery of goods in 1959 was signed in Warsaw.

February 18: The PRC and North Vietnam signed seven documents in Peking: (1) Agreement on trade in period 1960-62, (2) agreement on mutual supply of goods

and payments in 1959, (3) agreement on economic and technical aid (including long-term loan of 300 million *yuan*), (4) exchange of notes on PRC aid of 100 million *yuan* without compensation to North Vietnam, (5) protocol on economic and technical aid, (6) protocol on PRC technical aid, (7) protocol on PRC aid in 1959.

A Sino-North Korean agreement on air transport was signed in Peking, with a protocol on reciprocal air services and a protocol on technical cooperation in civil aviation.

February 18-19: Chen Yi issued a statement on the refusal of the government of Laos to continue to implement the Geneva Agreement. It states that Prime Minister Sananikone's refusal to continue to do so "constitutes an unscrupulous violation of the Geneva agreements and forms a part of the U.S. imperialist plot of aggression against Indochina." On February 19, identical notes from Chen Yi to the Soviet and the British foreign ministers as co-chairmen of the Geneva Conference were delivered to Soviet Charge d'Affaires Antonow and British Charge d'Affaires Wilson in Peking.

February 20: A Sino-Polish protocol on a 1959 plan for cooperation between academies of sciences was signed in Warsaw.

February 21: A Sino-North Korean agreement on cultural cooperation was signed in Pyongyang.

February 23: Assistant Secretary of State for Far Eastern Affairs Walter S. Robertson told the Senate Disarmament Subcommittee that Communist China would have to be included in any "sound and workable" disarmament or nuclear test ban treaty. He also said that, during the Warsaw negotiations, the Chinese Communists had refused to negotiate on the offshore islands because to them the offshore islands are "peanuts." He warned, "What they want is to get rid of a rival Chinese government on Taiwan. Their sine qua non is that we get out of Taiwan Strait and . . . out of the Western Pacific."

A Sino-Syrian agreement on the exchange of newsreel was signed in Damascus.

February 26: A Sino-Soviet trade agreement on exchange of goods in 1959 was signed in Moscow.

March 3: A joint statement of the Chinese and Japanese Communist parties was signed in Peking. Both delegations declared they would strive for realization of the proposals for establishment of a nuclear weapon-free zone in Asia. The CPC expressed support for the JCP goals of annulment of the Japan-U.S. security treaty, elimination of U.S. troops and bases from Japan, and return of Okinawa and Ogasawara Islands to Japan. Both delegations urged restoration of diplomatic relations between Communist China and Japan.

A Sino-Czechoslovak agreement on scientific cooperation in 1959-61 was signed in Prague; also a protocol on 1959 plan for cooperation between academies of sciences.

March 5-21: A seven-member delegation of the Japanese Socialist party, headed by Secretary-General Inejire Asanuma, arrived in Peking on March 7. A joint statement was issued on March 17 by Chang Hsi-jo, president of the Chinese People's Institute of Foreign Affairs, and Asanuma, affirming the following points: (1) PRC welcomes Japanese neutrality, (2) setting up an area free from nuclear weapons in the Far East and the Pacific, (3) after Japan has smashed the Japan-U.S. security treaty, achieves complete independence, and concludes non-aggression pacts with Communist China and the Soviet Union, then it can be expected that the military clauses against Japan in the Sino-Soviet treaty naturally will become null and void, (4) political questions have priority over economic questions in Sino-Japanese relations.

March 6: An agreement on goods exchange and payments for 1959 between the PRC and Poland was signed in Warsaw.

March 9: A Sino-East German contract on supply by Germany of equipment for power stations in 1959-62 was signed in Leipzig; also a protocol on the supply of two cement plants by East Germany.

March 10: The military commander in Lhasa, Tibet, sent a special invitation to the Dalai Lama asking him to attend a theatrical performance at Chinese military headquarters. The invitation was duly declined by the Dalai Lama.

A Sino-Rumanian protocol on a 1959 plan for cultural cooperation was signed in Peking.

March 11: A total of 1,226 people's deputies were elected from all parts of the country to the 2nd NPC, according to a public notice by the NPC Standing Committee.

A Sino-Soviet protocol on joint use of the Amur River was signed in Harbin.

March 12: An agreement on goods exchange and payments for 1959 was signed in Peking by the PRC and Czechoslovakia.

March 17: A 1959 goods exchange and payment was signed by the PRC and Hungary in Budapest.

A Sino-German agreement on cooperation between academies of sciences was signed in Berlin.

March 18: A Sino-Yugoslav trade agreement for 1959 was signed in Peking.

A Sino-Soviet protocol on a 1959 plan for cultural cooperation was signed in Peking.

March 19: Peking endorsed the Soviet March 2 proposal to hold a summit conference on Germany.

March 22: A Sino-Rumania protocol on 1959 goods exchange and payments was signed in Peking.

March 24: A Hong Kong newspaper reported Chairman Mao Tse-tung had swum across the Yalu River seven times in September 1958, presumably to disprove reports that he was in ill health.

March 26: A Sino-Ceylonese air transport agreement to establish civil air communications was signed in Peking along with a protocol to the air transport agreement and an exchange of notes on the nationality of pilots.

March 28: First Chinese statement on happenings in Tibet was made by Chou En-lai in issuing an order dissolving the

Tibetan government and replacing it by a 16-member preparatory committee for the Tibetan Autonomous Region, headed by the Panchen Lama, and containing four Chinese officials. Chou also named 18 "traitors," elements of the former Tibetan government, who had been relieved of their posts and would be punished individually according to law.

March 29: First Algerian rebel military delegations arrived in Peking for a one-week stay.

March 30: Prime Minister Nehru, in a speech to the Lower House of Indian Parliament, stated India's desire, on the one hand, to see the people of Tibet "progress in freedom," and on the other, to maintain friendly relations with the great country of China. He counselled "a certain measure of restraint" in the present difficult situation.

March 31: The Dalai Lama, accompanied by members of his family and cabinet ministers, reached the Indian frontier after a dramatic escape from Lhasa, which they left on March 17, 1959; according to reports from Kalimpong and other border areas, Chinese planes had flown many low-level reconnaissance sorties and dropped paratroopers in a number of areas in an unsuccessful attempt to intercept the Dalai Lama's party. This was the second time in history that the Dalai Lama had sought asylum in India. The first time was in 1910 when a Chinese force entered and took control of Lhasa. The Dalai Lama had returned to Tibet in 1912 after the Chinese were expelled from Lhasa by a rebellion.

April 2: Mr. Nehru made a statement to the Lower House reiterating that no subversive or espionage activities were being carried on at Kalimpong, and described as "completely untrue" the allegation that Kalimpong was a command center of the Tibetan uprising.

April 2-5: The 8th Central Committe of the CPC held its 7th plenary session in Shanghai from April 2 to 5. The session was held under the guidance of Mao Tse-tung. Mao made an important speech on the

question of the methods of war. The session discussed and adopted the draft plan for development of the national economy in 1959, reviewed the work of overhauling the people's communes, and decided on the nomination of candidates for leading posts in state organs.

April 3: A Sino-Hungarian protocol on a 1959 plan for cooperation between academies of sciences was signed in Budapest.

April 4: A Sino-Iraqui agreement on cultural cooperation was signed in Baghdad.

April 5: NCNA announced that the Panchen Lama had arrived in Lhasa to take over the chairmanship of the preparatory committee for the Tibetan Autonomous Region. It was stated that he would hold this post during the time that the Dalai Lama is under duress.

April 6: A Sino-Hungarian agreement on cooperation in radio broadcasting was signed in Budapest.

April 8: A Sino-Iraqui protocol on a 1959 plan for cultural cooperation was signed in Baghdad.

April 11: The CPPCC National Standing Committee promulgated the name-list of members of the 3rd National Committee of the CPPCC. The total number is 1,071, a 46% increase over that of the 2nd National Committee. These members include 60 from the CPC, 196 from minor parties, 147 from organizations, 225 from scientific, medical, educational, and artistic circles, and 308 who were specially invited. Scientific, medical, educational, and artistic circles showed the greatest proportionate increase.

NCNA reported that six railway lines were being built and reconstructed in Anhwei, namely, the Huainan Railway (Pangpu to Yuhsikou), the Ninwu Railway (Nanking to Yuanhu), the Wuhsuan Railway (Wuhan to Hsuan Cheng), the Wupan Railway (Wuhu to Fanchang), the Fuhsiao Railway (Fulichi to Hsiaohsien), and the Hsiangwa Railway (Hsiangshan to Maanshan), totalling some 500 kilometers.

April 12: The Dalai Lama arrived at Bomdiha and was met by Mr. P. N. Menon of the Indian External Affairs Ministry, representing Mr. Nehru. On the following day it was announced in New Delhi that the Dalai Lama and his entourage would be allowed to reside at Mussoorie (Uttar Pradesh), the hill station 150 miles north of New Delhi.

April 13: The PRC and Czechoslovakia signed a long-term (1960-62) trade agreement in Prague.

A Sino-Rumanian agreement on cooperation between academies of sciences was signed in Bucharest.

April 15: A short anti-Indian campaign developed in the Chinese press and radio during the latter part of April, including charges of Indian "expansionist" aims in Tibet, attacks on so-called Indian reactionaries, and allegations of Indian interference in Chinese internal affairs.

Mao Tse-tung convened the Supreme State Conference to discuss the list of candidates for leadership posts in state organs to be presented to the NPC, and the list of candidates for leadership posts in the 2nd CPPCC National Committee, to be presented to the 3rd National Committee.

A Sino-Polish agreement on cooperation in radio and television broadcasting was signed in Warsaw.

April 17-29: The first session of the 3rd CPPCC National Committee opened on April 17. Chou En-lai presided over the meeting, which was attended by 911 members. The plenary session at its closed meeting on April 29 elected Mao Tse-tung honorary Chairman and Chou En-lai Chairman of the CPPCC, and adopted a resolution approving the work of the Standing Committee of the Second National Committee. Also approved was a political resolution supporting the reports on government work, the 1959 National Economic Plan, and the 1958 state final accounts, and the 1959 state budget.

April 18-28: The 2nd NPC held its first session in Peking April 18-28.

April 18: In a speech to the NPC meeting, Chou En-lai repeated the allegation that the Dalai Lama had been abducted; ex-

pressed the hope that he would free himself from the duress imposed by the rebels and return to the motherland; and reiterated that Tibet was a part of China and that the suppression was an internal affair. At the same time he welcomed the statement of non-intervention made by Nehru.

Before leaving Tezpur for Mussoorie, the Dalai Lama issued a statement to the assembled press correspondents of many countries, in which he emphasized that he left Tibet of his own free will, denied the Chinese allegation that he had been under duress, and accused the Chinese of destroying monasteries, killing lamas and monks, and deporting Tibetan officials to China for forced labor.

April 20: A Sino-Albanian agreement on non-commercial payments was signed in Tirana.

April 21: The Dalai Lama reached Mussoorie and took up residence in a villa placed at his disposal by the Indian government.

April 22: In a speech to the NPC, the Panchen Lama said that the reactionaries in India, following in the footsteps of the British imperialists, have always harbored expansionist ambitions in Tibet and have carried out various sabotage activities unfavorable to the friendship between China and India.

April 23: Peking radio claimed that units of the Chinese army had crossed the Tsangpo River, captured over 30 villages and towns held by Tibetan guerrillas, and occupied all vital strongholds in the area between the Tsangpo and the Himalayas and eastward to Gyantse, the second town of Tibet. It was claimed that over 2,000 guerrillas had been killed or wounded in these operations.

A Sino-Bulgarian agreement on cooperation between academies of sciences was signed in Sofia.

April 24: Defense Minister Peng Teh-huai led a military mission to Eastern Europe and Moscow. Peng made only one public appearance after his return.

Mr. Nehru had a four-hour meeting

with the Dalai Lama at Mussoorie, after which he held a press conference. Asked about the Panchen Lama's speech to the NPC in Peking, Mr. Nehru said that it was obviously made in a state of excitement and did not do justice to India, China, Tibet or the Panchen Lama. He refuted the allegation of Indian expansion.

April 25: A Sino-East German agreement on cooperation in radio and television broadcasting was signed in Berlin.

April 27: At a meeting of the NPC, Liu Shao-chi was elected Chairman of the Chinese People's Republic in succession to Mao Tse-tung, receiving 1,156 votes against one vote for Tung Pi-wu. Although the Constitution provides for only one vice-chairman of the Republic, two were elected: Madame Soong Ching-ling (Mrs. Sun Yatsen), and Mr. Tung Pi-wu. A new Standing Committee of the NPC was elected, with Marshall Chu Teh as its chairman; also elected were 16 vice-chairmen, who included both the Dalai Lama and the Panchen Lama. Mr. Hsieh Chueh-tsai (minister of the interior) succeeded Mr. Tung Pi-wu as president of the Supreme Court. Mr. Liu's first action was to propose the re-election of Mr. Chou En-lai as prime minister. Mr. Chou's new State Council, which was approved by the closing session of the NPC on April 28, contained 16 vice-premiers, 4 of whom were new appointments: Tan Chen-lin, Lu Ting-yi, Lo Jui-Chung (Minister of Public Security), and Hsi Chunhsun (Secretary General of the State Council).

April 28: At its closing session, NPC adopted 21-billion-dollar budget with a call to the people to achieve a bigger leap forward in building socialism. NPC in a resolution reiterated that Tibet is an inalienable part of China and no foreign interference in China's internal affairs can be tolerated.

April 30: A Sino-Czechoslovak agreement on cooperation in radio and television broadcasting was signed in Prague.

May 6-19: A national trade fair, jointly organized by the Ministries of Commerce and Light Industry, opened in Shanghai on May 6 and closed on May 19.

May 6: A Sino-Hungarian friendship and cooperation treaty was signed in Peking. Also made public was the communique on talks during a visit of Hungarian party and government delegates, led by Premier Muennick.

May 15: A Sino-Finnish trade agreement for 1959 was signed in Helsinki.

May 18: With reference to the announcement by the Kingdom of Laos that it has ordered two battalions of the former Pathet Lao fighting units to surrender their arms with 24 hours, the Ministry of Foreign Affairs in Peking issued a statement protesting against such action and declaring: "China cannot look indifferently at the serious actions of the government of the Kingdom of Laos in completely repudiating the Geneva agreements and endangering peace in Indo-China."

May 20: A Sino-Czechoslovak protocol on scientific and technical cooperation was signed in Peking.

May 21: A Sino-North Korean protocol on scientific and technical cooperation was signed in Pyongyang.

May 25: Letters were exchanged between the PRC and India in New Delhi, extending until the end of the year the validity of the Sino-Indian trade agreement concluded in 1954.

Chen Yi has sent a letter to the U.S.S.R. and Britain, co-chairmen of the Geneva Conference on Indochina, calling on the two nations to adopt measures at once to check the "serious actions of the Royal Laotian government in violation of the Geneva Agreements," and instructing the International Commission in Laos to convene a meeting immediately and resume its activities at once.

May 30: The PRC and Cambodia exchanged notes to extend 1954 trade and payments agreements.

May 31: The annual Demographic Yearbook published by the U.N. estimated China's population at 640,000,000.

June 1: A Sino-Soviet protocol on a 1959

plan for cooperation between academies of sciences was signed in Peking.

June 12: The U.S. State Department announced it would give visas to any bona fide athletes sent from Communist China to the winter olympics in Squaw Valley, California.

June 13: A Sino-Ceylonese trade protocol on exchange of goods in 1959 was signed in Colombo along with the two contracts on exchange of PRC rice and Ceylon rubber.

June 18-23: A six-day conference was called by the CPC Central Committee to discuss non-staple food and handicraft production. The conference considered it necessary to adopt the policy of self-dependence supplemented by outside help in solving the problem of non-staple food in cities. As to handicraft production, the conference laid down the policy of energetically restoring and developing this art.

June 20: At a news conference in Mussoorie to representatives of the world press, the Dalai Lama accused the Chinese Communists of continued inhuman persecution of the Tibetan people. He challenged the Peking government to allow an international commission to visit Tibet, stating that he and his government were willing to abide by the verdict of such a body. He alleged that the Chinese Communists had killed over 65,000 Tibetan civilians since 1956, deported large numbers to China, destroyed 1,000 monasteries, done their utmost to exterminate Buddhism and settled more than five million Chinese in Tibet.

A Sino-North Vietnamese agreement on the currency exchange rate and on non-commercial payments was signed in Hanoi.

June 23: A Sino-Soviet consular treaty was signed in Peking.

Track-laying along the Sino-Soviet "Friendship Railway," linking the Aktogai station on the Turkestan-Siberia line to the Soviet-Chinese border, was completed on June 23, NCNA reports from Moscow, quoting Soviet papers.

June 25: The State Council approved in principle the "Report by the Science and Technology Commission on the Unification of China's Weighing and Measuring System." The report recommends the international metric system as China's basic system of weights and measures. It suggests three measures: (1) Retain the Shih system, (2) abolish the English system and other old systems, (3) unify the Chinese terms of the metric system of weights and measures.

June 27: A Sino-North Vietnamese protocol on a joint survey of the Gulf of Tonkin was signed in Hanoi.

July 4: A Sino-Soviet protocol on scientific and technical cooperation was signed in Peking.

July 8: A program of reform in Tibet, involving large-scale redistribution of land and the abolition of serfdom and other feudal customs, was announced in Peking.

July 11: A Sino-Albanian agreement on cooperation in radio broadcasting was signed in Tirana.

July 17-August 25: Between mid-July and mid-August, drought spread to seventeen provinces and regions in mainland China with more than 320,000,000 persons affected, in nine provinces—Honan, Shantung, Anhwei, Kiangsu, Hupeh, Hunan, Shensi, Szechwan and Shansi. The Ministry of Agriculture and the CPC and State Council issued emergency directives respectively on July 27 and August 13, urging intensified campaign against drought. On August 25 the Ministry of Agriculture claimed that, relying on water conservancy projects and irrigation facilities, drought fighters had watered more than 200,000,-000 *now*, 60% of the drought-affected area, and that the area of crop failure "is estimated at some 50,000,000 *now* only." Further, the Ministry claimed that the watered crops "are doing well."

August 2-16: Following a plenary session of the Central Committee of the CPC at Lushan, a communique was issued containing an official admission that production in 1958 was much lower than the targets fixed for that year. The fall in production was attributed to a variety of factors, including lack of experience in assessing and calculating the output of an unprecedented bumper harvest, shortage of agricultural labor, and severe floods and droughts in the Yangtse and Yalu River basins, affecting Kwangtung and Kwansi Provinces. The communique was particularly critical of the small steel furnaces scattered through the country, saying that the steel produced in such units was suitable only for rural requirements; it was added that the output of backyard-produced metal would no longer figure in the State's economic plans. Regarding the rural people's communes, it was claimed that they had taken root and were demonstrating their advantages; the principal threat to the communes lay in the growth of rightist opportunists' ideas among certain cadres who underestimated the great achievements of the leap forward movement and over-emphasized the seriousness of certain defects due to lack of experience, which defects have now been overcome.

August 5: A *People's Daily* editorial welcomed the Khrushchev-Eisenhower exchange of visits but warned that the sincerity of the U.S. government was to be proven.

August 6: A Sino-Bulgarian agreement on cooperation in radio broadcasting was signed in Tirana.

August 13: Ho Chi-Minh, President of North Vietnam, arrived in Peking from the Soviet Union, and was welcomed by Chen Yi and others. Liu Shao-chi entertained Ho on August 21. He left for home on August 25.

August 20: In a statement from Mussoorie, issued after a meeting of the Tibetan cabinet in exile, the Dalai Lama announced his intention of bringing the Tibetan situation to the attention of the U.N., since there had been no response to his appeal of June 20, 1959.

August 24: Liu Shao-chi convened the Supreme State Conference to discuss the "leap forward" in 1959 and expansion of the higher output and economy campaign. Chou En-lai made a report, reviewing

fulfillment of the national economic plan during the first half of this year and pointing to the tasks ahead.

August 25: A Sino-Korean agreement on fishery regulations in the Yellow Sea was signed in Peking.

August 26: The State Statistics Bureau stated that the 1958 agricultural figures released in the past were in some cases too high. The bureau revised the statistical figures as follows: Total food grain output, 500 billion catties; total cotton output, 42 million piculs; increase in percentage in the output of other major crops as compared with 1957—soybean 4%, peanuts 9%, cured tobacco 40%, jute and ambary hemp 3%.

The NPC Standing Committee at its enlarged session adopted a resolution readjusting the major targets in 1959 economic plan as follows: 12 million tons of steel (not including steel produced by simple, improvised methods); 335 million tons of coal; 10% increase over the verified output of food grain and cotton for 1958.

August 28: A Sino-Bulgarian protocol on scientific and technical cooperation was signed in Peking.

September 4: Indian Prime Minister Nehru announced that the Chinese had accused India of "aggression" and demanded that India evacuate "one or two areas which they claim to be Chinese territory." Nehru called the dispute "rather absurd" and said it was "not a question of two or three miles of territory, but of national prestige and self-respect."

September 5-14: Prince Sardar Mohammed Naim, deputy prime minister and foreign minister of Afghanistan, arrived in Peking on September 5. He was welcomed by Chou En-lai at the airport. On September 9 a Sino-Afghan joint communique was signed by Chen Yi and Prince Naim, agreeing to continue to strengthen and develop the economic and cultural ties and expand technical cooperation between the two countries. Prince Naim left for home on September 14 after visiting

Chengchou, Shanghai, Hangchow, and Wuhan.

September 7: A White Paper containing notes, memoranda, and letters exchanged between the government of India and China from 1954 to 1959 was presented to the Indian parliament by Mr. Nehru. The paper contained the text of three letters exchanged between Mr. Nehru and Mr. Chou En-lai from December 1958 to March 1959 concerning the border incidents and the question of Chinese claims to Indian territory based on Chinese maps. The correspondence showed that Mr. Chou En-lai accepted the McMahon line as the northeastern border between India and China in 1957, but had subsequently retracted from his commitment.

September 8: The text of Mr. Chou En-lai's reply to Mr. Nehru's letter of March 22 was made public in Delhi. The Chinese prime minister maintained that the boundary between the two countries had never been formally delimited, declared that China absolutely does not recognize the so-called McMahon line, and said that the Chinese government could not accept India's unilateral claim to sovereignty in the disputed area of Ladakh. He also accused Indian forces of trespassing and provocation across the frontiers and of shielding armed Tibetan rebels, adding that India would be held fully responsible for these actions. At the same time, he repeated his proposal for the maintenance of the status quo pending a negotiated settlement of frontier questions, and gave an assurance that China would not commit any aggression against Bhutan or Sikkim; in the latter connection, he said that China's boundaries with these two Himalayan hill states "do not fall within the scope of our present discussions."

September 8-13: Meeting on September 8-13, the NPC Standing Committee heard speeches by Chou En-lai and Chen Yi on the Sino-Indian border issue. Some members condemned India's unilateral claim and the anti-China movement in India. A resolution adopted by the NPC Standing Committee stated: "An over-all settlement of the Sino-Indian boundary question should be sought by both sides. Pending this, the two sides should maintain the long-existing status quo, and not seek to change it by unilateral action, still less by force."

September 9: The Soviet government, in a Tass statement, adopted a position of official neutrality in the Sino-Indian border dispute unprecedented in relations between states of the Communist bloc.

The Dalai Lama sent a cable to the U.N. Secretary-General formally asking for the intervention of the U.N. in view of the inhuman treatment and crimes against humanity and religion to which the people of Tibet were being subjected.

September 9-23: Tanzan Ishibashi, ex-Japanese Prime Minister, made a two-week visit to Peking on September 9-23 at the invitation of Chou En-lai. On September 20, Chou En-lai and Ishibashi issued a communique on their talks agreeing to "develop their political and economic relations in a coordinated manner."

September 10: In a strongly worded note presented in Peking, India declared that it stood firmly on the McMahon line, though it was prepared to discuss the exact alignment at places where it departed from the geographical features marking the international boundary.

September 15: Chou En-lai sent a message of congratulations to N. S. Khrushchev on the successful landing on the moon of the Soviet cosmic rockets.

Peking issued a statement on the situation in Laos, expressing full support for the Soviet proposal to quickly call a meeting of the participants of the 1954 Geneva Conference. It held that the meeting should hear the report and suggestions made by the International Commission in Laos.

September 15-27: Premier Khrushchev visited the United States amid press and other public conjectures over possible unfavorable Peking reaction to the trip.

September 17: Major changes in the cabinet and the high command of the Army were announced in Peking. Marshal Lin Piao was appointed Minister of Defense. General Lo Jui-ching was appointed Minister of Public Security.

Municipalities under direct Central authority and relatively large municipalities may have jurisdiction over *hsien* and autonomous *hsien*, according to a resolution adopted by the NPC Standing Committee and an order issued by Liu Shao-chi. The decision was aimed at coping with the development of socialist construction and promoting mutual support between industry and agriculture.

The NPC Standing Committee approved a proposal by the Central Committee of the CPC to grant an amnesty to a number of war criminals on the occasion of the 10th anniversary of the founding of the Communist government on October 1. No numbers were given of those to be released.

September 22: The question of Chinese representation in the U.N. was postponed by a vote of 44 to 29, with 9 abstentions.

September 23: In a joint directive the CPC Central Committee and the State Council required the commercial departments to organize and guide rural fairs so as to facilitate exchange of commodities among commune members and between town and country.

September 25: At the U.N. General Assembly the Irish Republic and Malaya agreed to co-sponsor a resolution deploring recent events in Tibet and calling for the restoration of the civil and religious liberties of the Tibetan people.

To cope with the increased task of transport (the volume of freight in the fourth quarter was expected to be 70% above the third quarter) and ship out the stock-piled supplies (for instance, 13,-000,000 tons of coal was stockpiled in localities within 30 kilometers of railway lines), the CPC Central Committee and the State Council in a joint directive urged a mass short-distance transport campaign to supplement the existing capacity of the transport departments.

September 26: In a letter to Mr. Chou En-lai, in reply to his letter of September 8,

Mr. Nehru reiterated that India's northern border was beyond dispute, adding that no discussion could be fruitful unless outposts on the Indian side of the traditional frontier, now held by Chinese forces, were first evacuated by them and further threats and intimidation cease. While India was willing to discuss minor frontier rectifications, they could not discuss the Chinese claims to nearly 40,000 square miles of what had been for many decades, and in some places for centuries, an integral part of Indian territory.

September 29: A map depicting China's territorial claim on India, compiled from the official maps circulated in China, was published by the Ministry of External Affairs in New Delhi. It showed that about 40,000 square miles of Indian and Bhutanese territory (an area larger than West Bengal) were claimed as part of China, affecting almost the whole length of the 2500-mile Himalayan frontier from Ladakh in the west to the northeast frontier agency in the east. In addition, the map indicated a Chinese claim to some 5,000 square miles of Pakistan-controlled territory in the Gilgit region of Kashmir.

September 30: Mr. Khrushchev and Mr. Gromyko arrived in Peking to attend the celebration of the tenth anniversary of the Chinese People's Republic. They were welcomed at the airport by Mr. Mao Tse-tung and other Chinese leaders, and later in the day Khrushchev was the guest at a banquet attended by 5,000 people. Mr. Chou En-lai congratulated Khrushchev on the success of his mission to the United States as an envoy of peace, and welcomed the communique on his talks with President Eisenhower. In reply Khrushchev emphasized that war must be precluded as a means of settling international disputes, gave a warning against testing the capitalist system and declared that socialism could not be imposed by force of arms. He omitted all references to Chinese Communist foreign affairs.

A Sino-Moroccan agreement on trade in 1959-60 was signed in Peking.

October 1: The 200-kilometer railway section from Lanchow to Sining was opened to traffic.

In an article in the Peking *People's Daily,* Minister Lin Piao said that political control must be supreme in the Army and warned of rightist tendencies among the military.

October 3: Indian Prime Minister Nehru sent a note to Premier Chou En-lai stating that "no discussion can be fruitful unless the posts on the Indian side of the traditional frontier now held by Chinese forces are first evacuated by them and further threats cease." Chou, replying October 7, said in a note to Nehru that the border dispute between the two countries was "merely an episode in our age-old friendship." On the following day, Nehru told newsmen that he was somewhat optimistic about the Chinese note and that India would not "start military operations at this stage, when we are dealing with this matter on a political level." He added that another Chinese attack would be fully resisted.

October 4: It was announced in Peking that diplomatic relations between Guinea and the PRC had been established.

While in Peking, Khrushchev, Gromyko, and Suslov had a series of meetings with Mao Tse-tung, Liu Shao-chi, and Chou En-lai. The Russian leaders left Peking without a joint communique being issued. Before leaving Peking, Khrushchev made a short speech at the airport in which he reaffirmed his belief that it was possible to rule out war for all time as a means of solving international disputes, and said that the Soviet Union would take advantage of any possibilities in order to end the cold war.

October 6: The NPC Chairman, Chu Teh, accused the United States of failing to show any interest in the disarmament question and of viciously distorting the Soviet disarmament proposal.

Chou En-lai declared that the PRC must have a say on all major international questions which concerned its interests and the interests of world peace.

October 7: A cultural cooperation between the PRC and Guinea was signed in Peking.

U.S. Secretary of State Herter said that the U.S.S.R., if it claimed Communist world leadership, must accept some degree of responsibility for China's actions.

October 7-11: Dr. Subandrio, Indonesian Foreign Minister, arrived in Peking on October 7. He was welcomed and entertained by Chen Yi, was received by Chou En-lai and Mao Tse-tung respectively on October 9 and 11. Chen Yi and Dr. Subandrio held talks on October 8-9 and issued a joint communique on October 11. Among other things, the two foreign ministers supported the right of Communist China to "recover Taiwan" and the right of Indonesia to recover West Irian; welcomed the recent communique on talks between the United States President and Khrushchev; considered that, in the process of economic development and stability in Indonesia, the proper rights and interests of the Chinese nationals there should be restored.

October 12: A protocol on Sino-Soviet scientific and technical cooperation was signed in Peking.

October 15: Chairman Liu Shao-chi defended the case for communes against opposition at home and hostile forces abroad in problems of peace and socialism.

October 18: NCNA reported that the Lanchow-Sinkiang railway would extend northwestward from Weiya in Sinkiang, which is more than 2,300 kilometers from the Sino-Soviet border. The 1,170-kilometer section from Lanchow to Weiya had already been completed.

October 20-21: An incident occurred in the Chang Chemo Valley of Southern Ledakh, when Chinese troops patrolling 40 miles inside the Indian frontier killed nine members of the Indian police patrol and captured ten others.

October 21: The Irish-Malaya proposed resolution on Tibet situation was adopted by General Assembly after a two-day debate, 45 to 9, with 28 abstentions. The Soviet delegation protested the resolution strongly.

October 22: Khrushchev, in a letter to Eisenhower, said that the U.S.S.R. fully backed Communist China's claim to Taiwan.

As stated in the Delhi announcement, the Chinese government had lodged a protest with the government of India alleging that the incident had occurred in Chinese territory and that Chinese forces had fired in self-defense against armed provocations by Indian personnel.

October 23: A Peking broadcast described the U.N. Irish-Malayan resolution as "illegal," "unlawful" and "slanderous," and as another criminal act of the United States government in press-ganging the majority of the U.N. members to interfere in China's internal affairs.

Eisenhower disputed Khrushchev's claim that the Taiwan and Communist Chinese dispute is an internal affair, and cited a number of nations recognizing Taiwan as an independent nation.

October 25: The Chinese government informed the government of India that the members of the Indian patrol were in Chinese hands and that the bodies of nine others killed in the Ladakh incident had been recovered; they offered to return the ten prisoners and to hand over to the Indian authorities the bodies of the nine men who lost their lives.

November 10: A Sino-Hungarian protocol on a 1960 plan for cooperation between academies of sciences was signed in Peking.

November 14: The ten Indian policemen captured during the Ladakh incident, together with the bodies of nine who had been killed, were handed over by the Chinese border authority to an Indian police patrol at a previously arranged rendezvous.

November 15: In a speech to the Supreme Soviet, Khrushchev rejected the United States suggestion that U.S.S.R. could be held responsible for Peking's actions. He held that Herter and Under-Secretary Dillon had destroyed the nature of Mos-

cow-Peking relations and had cast doubt on Peking's sovereignty in policy decisions.

November 15-21: The CPC Central Committee convened in Chungking the second national conference on production of non-staple foods in cities. The conference urged medium and large cities to develop production of domesticated animals, with emphasis placed on hog-raising, while consolidating, raising and developing the output of vegetables. Cities should also adopt measures to develop production of oil and fats, aquatic products, fruits and other non-staple foods while diversifying their management of production.

November 17: After a meeting with the Chinese ambassador in Djakarta (Mr. Huang Chen), Dr. Subandrio announced that the ambassador had agreed to support the implementation of the Indonesian government order, but had asked that possible excesses should be avoided. Mr. Huang Chen, however, issued a press statement immediately afterwards denying that he had promised his support, and alleging that some Chinese nationals had been beaten in West Java.

A Sino-Hungarian protocol on scientific and technical cooperation was signed in Peking.

November 18: The Indonesian government retaliated by forbidding members of the Chinese embassy staff to leave Jakarta without official permission.

November 19: The West Java military administration ordered all Chinese consular officials to leave the area until further notice, due to the implementation of regulations ordering all foreign traders in rural areas to close their businesses by January 1 and to sell them to Indonesian citizens or to cooperatives.

November 20: In reply to Chou En-lai's proposal for reducing border tension, Mr. Nehru rejected Mr. Chou's suggestion for a mutual withdrawal along the entire length of the Himalaya border. He proposed the creation of a "no-man's land" in Ladakh, covering 12,000 square miles, under an arrangement whereby (a) Indian troops would withdraw to the line which China claimed as her boundary, and (b) Chinese troops would withdraw to the line claimed by India as her border.

November 21: The PRC and Cambodia exchanged notes on reciprocal tariff concessions.

November 27: Liu Shao-chi promulgated the "Organic Law of People's Congress and People's Council of Ninghsia Hui Autonomous Region" which had been approved by the NPC Standing Committee.

December 4: It was announced by the West Java Military Administration that large numbers of Chinese who had refused to leave their homes had been arrested and placed in detention camps.

It was announced in Peking that the Supreme People's Court had granted amnesty to 33 former Nationalists and Kuomintang leaders hitherto held as war criminals. Among those pardoned were Henry Pu-Yi, the last emperor of China and subsequently emperor of the puppet state of Manchukuo, and a number of former high-ranking Kuomintang generals and political personalities.

December 5: A Sino-Bulgarian protocol on a plan for cultural cooperation in 1960 was signed in Sofia.

Multilateral protocols on technical aspects of railway construction were signed in Peking by the PRC, U.S.S.R., Bulgaria, Hungary, North Vietnam, East Germany, North Korea, Poland, and Czechoslovakia.

December 8: NCNA reported that since September the higher people's courts of various provinces, municipalities and autonomous regions had pardoned 12,082 "counter-revolutionary criminals and ordinary criminals."

December 9: The Chinese foreign minister, Chen Yi, protested against the "intolerable situation" in West Java in a note, and put forward a proposal for a settlement: (1) Both governments should immediately exchange instruments of ratification of the dual citizenship agreement of 1955; (2) the Indonesian government should protect the legislative rights and interests of overseas Chinese who wished to retain Chi-

nese nationality, or whose choice of Indonesian nationality was not approved, and should check any discrimination against or persecution of them. The Chinese government would appeal to the persons concerned to abide by Indonesian laws and regulations; (3) Chinese who had become homeless, lost their means of livelihood, and did not wish to remain in Indonesia should be allowed to return to China with the money obtained from the sale of their property. The Chinese government would arrange for them to earn a livelihood in China.

December 10: The 820-meter double track railway bridge in Chungking was open to traffic.

A Sino-Czechoslovak agreement on cooperation in agricultural research between academies of sciences was signed in Prague.

December 11: A Sino-Hungarian agreement on civil aviation was signed in Budapest.

A multilateral agreement on arrangements of state banks for currency exchange and cash movements was signed in Moscow by the PRC, U.S.S.R., Albania, Bulgaria, Czechoslovakia, North Korea, East Germany, Hungary, Mongolia, Poland, Rumania, and North Vietnam.

December 12: A Sino-Soviet agreement on currency exchange and cash movements was signed in Moscow.

December 13: Indonesia rejected the Chinese government's recent allegations and protested against the activities of Chinese embassy officials in Indonesia.

December 16: A bilateral trade agreement for 1959-60 was signed in Peking between Finland and the PRC.

December 17: Chou En-lai, in a letter of reply to Indian Prime Minister Nehru, proposed that the Chinese and Indian Prime Ministers begin talks either in China or in Rangoon for the purpose of reaching some agreement of principles as guidance to concrete discussions and settlement of the boundary question.

December 21: In contrast to Moscow, Peking praise for Stalin on the anniversary of his birth emphasized his opposition to imperialism, and lauded his achievements as far outweighing defects.

Indian Prime Minister Nehru told the Indian parliament he had rejected a new proposal from Premier Chou En-lai that the two leaders meet to seek a basis for settlement of their border dispute. Nehru said he turned down the offer because of "complete disagreement about the fact" involved. He noted that the Chinese proposal rejected provisions for total military evacuation of the areas concerned and was "merely a reiteration of Chinese claims to extensive areas . . . which, by history, by custom or by agreement have long been integral part of India." He added that his country would "negotiate to the bitter end" because the only alternative is "war."

December 22: A Sino-Mongolian agreement on non-commercial payments was signed in Ulan Bator.

December 26: The Chinese Ministry of Foreign Affairs sent a note to the Indian embassy in Peking giving a detailed account of the "historical facts" about the Sino-Indian boundary. It asserted that the Sino-Indian boundary had never been formally delimited and maintained that an over-all settlement of the question should be sought through negotiations. It expressed the hope that the Prime Ministers of both countries would hold talks to reach agreement in principle. It proposed that, pending the formal delimitation of the boundary, the status quo of the border be effectively maintained. Finally it said: "At no time in the future will China become a threat to its neighboring countries."

December 31: A Sino-Soviet cultural cooperation plan for 1960 was signed in Moscow.

A Sino-Cuban contract on the PRC purchase of Cuban sugar was signed in Peking.

A Sino-North Vietnamese protocol on PRC technical aid in 1959 was signed in Peking.

1960

January 3: A Sino-Ceylon agreement on the exchange of Ceylon rubber and PRC rice was signed in Colombo.

January 13: The Indonesian Foreign Minister, Dr. Subandrio, stated that the Chinese People's government had accepted the Indonesian government's ban on alien traders in rural areas, which had come into force January 1, 1960, and that relations between the two countries were almost normal. The restrictions which had been imposed in November on the movements of the Chinese embassy staff were lifted on January 11. Instruments of ratification of the dual citizenship agreement of 1955 were exchanged on January 20, and a joint Sino-Indonesian commitee was set up in Jakarta on January 25 to study its implementation.

January 15: An up-to-date woolen textile mill built by the PRC for Mongolia was handed over to the Mongolian government and put into operation. This mill is one of the projects provided by the agreement on economic aid signed in 1956.

January 18: A Sino-East German treaty on commerce and navigation was signed in Peking along with an agreement on exchange of goods in 1960-62.

January 19: A Sino-East German communique on talks during the visit of an East German delegation to the PRC was signed in Peking.

January 20: The Lanchow oil refinery, built with the help of the Soviet Union, was inaugurated. The refinery was completed in September, 1958.

January 21: In a statement to the NPC in Peking, Chen Yi said that while China would "unhesitatingly" carry out all international obligations to which she was a signatory, any international disarmament agreement which was arrived at without the participation of the Chinese People's Republic and the signature of its delegates could not have any binding force on China. A resolution to this effect was adopted by the NPC, together with a resolution supporting the Soviet Union's disarmament proposals.

January 23: Replying to a Chinese note of December 24, 1959, Dr. Subandrio emphasized that the Indonesian government had no intention of driving traders out of Indonesia, but hoped to make use of their activities in new places and in certain sectors of the Indonesian economy. If, however, the overseas Chinese concerned still wished to return to their homeland, the government would use all means at its disposal to facilitate the fulfillment of their wishes.

January 25: A "Committee for Receiving and Resettling Returned Overseas Chinese" with Liao Chen-chih as Chairman was established, according to a State Council directive. The committee will assume over-all responsibility for receiving and resettling returned overseas Chinese.

January 28: In a five-day meeting in Peking the Prime Ministers of China and Burma (Chou En-lai and Ne Win) signed a treaty of friendship and non-aggression, and also an agreement settling the Sino-Burmese border problems. The non-aggression treaty, valid for ten years, stated that each country recognized and respected the independence, sovereign rights, and territorial integrity of the other. The terms of the border settlement (published on January 31), provided: (1) Burma would cede to China two small tracts of territory in the Kachin and Wa states; (2) China would cede to Burma the Namman tract between the Kachin and Wa states; (3) the Sino-Burmese border would be delimited by a joint committee along the traditional line, except for the areas to be exchanged under (1) and (2). The reference to the traditional line involved implicit Chinese acceptance of the McMahon Line border between China and Burma, although the term was not used in the official statement.

January 29: A Sino-Soviet agreement on forest protection and prevention of forest fires was signed in Moscow.

January 31: U.S.S.R., as one of the chairmen of the International Control Commission for Laos, formally acknowledged indefinite adjournment of the I.C.C., even though Peking supported North Vietnamese demands for resumption of the I.C.C. to deal with the crisis there.

February 2: Discussions between Chinese Ambassador Huang Chen and the Indonesian Foreign Ministry on the repatriation of the overseas Chinese subsequently opened in Djakarta.

A Sino-Czechoslovak protocol on the exchange of goods and payments in 1960 was signed in Peking.

February 4: At a meeting of the Warsaw Pact countries, Chinese People's Republic observer Kang Sheng delivered a speech sharply attacking imperialism and revisionism and calling for increased bloc unity.

February 5: A plan for the carrying out in 1960 of the cultural cooperation agreement between the PRC and North Korea was signed in Peking.

February 8: A protocol regulating trade exchange between Ceylon and the PRC during 1960 was signed in Peking.

February 11: The 1960-61 executive plan of cultural cooperation agreement between the PRC and Poland was signed in Peking.

February 15: A letter from Indian Prime Minister Nehru to Chinese Communist Premier Chou En-lai, inviting the latter to India for talks on the Indian-Chinese border dispute, was made public.

February 16: The PRC and Rumania signed a 1960 plan for implementation of the Sino-Rumanian Cultural Cooperation Agreement in Bucharest.

The PRC and Hungary signed a 1960 plan for implementation of the Sino-Hungarian Cultural Cooperation Agreement in Budapest.

The PRC and North Vietnam signed a protocol on 1960 plan for cultural cooperation in Peking.

February 19: The 1960 Executive Plan of the Cultural Cooperation Agreement between the PRC and Czechoslovakia was signed in Peking along with the 1960 plan for cooperation between academies of sciences (signed on the previous day).

February 20: A further expansion of contacts in various branches of science was provided in the plan of cooperation for 1960 between the Soviet and Chinese academies of science signed in Moscow today.

February 22: A Sino-Polish agreement on turnover of goods and payments in 1960 was signed in Peking.

February 23: The 1960 Executive Plan of the Cultural Cooperation Agreement between the PRC and Mongolia was signed in Peking along with a protocol on mutual supply of goods in 1960.

February 24: A Sino-Soviet plan for scientific and technical cooperation in 1960 was signed in Moscow.

The PRC and UAR issued a joint communique on trade talks in Peking and signed a protocol on trade in 1960.

February 26: Premier Chou En-lai accepted Nehru's invitation. He said that the friendship between the Chinese and Indian people is eternal and it was possible to settle the boundary issue in a peaceful manner.

February 28: An agreement on the exchange of goods and payments for 1960 was signed between the PRC and Hungary in Peking.

February 29: A protocol on exchange of commodities in 1960 between the PRC and North Korea was signed in Pyongyang.

A Sino-Rumanian agreement on a 1960 plan for cooperation between academies of sciences was signed in Peking.

A Sino-Finnish agreement on establishment of direct telegraphic services between Shanghai and Helsinki was signed in Peking.

March 4: A plan for cultural cooperation in 1960 between the PRC and Albania was signed in Tirana.

March 5: The completion of the dam and dikes of the Schumchun reservoir was celebrated at the reservoir.

March 6: The *People's Daily* carried an editorial acclaiming Khrushchev's visit to India, Burma, Indonesia, and Afghanistan. The editorial emphasized the far-reaching significance of the tour in the struggle against "colonialism and imperialist aggression" and in strengthening unity and cooperation between the socialist countries and the countries which have won national independence.

March 7: The PRC and North Vietnam signed an agreement and protocol on commodity exchange and payments, a protocol on extending Chinese aid to North Vietnam in 1960, and a document concerning trade along the boundaries of the two countries.

March 13: Peking commentary on the eve of Geneva disarmament talks reiterated Chen Yi's January 21 statement rejecting international agreement made without Chinese participation.

March 15: A 1960 protocol for exchange of goods and payments was signed in Peking between the PRC and Rumania.

A Sino-Albanian protocol on goods exchange and payments for 1960 and a protocol on the use by Albanian loans and aid funds in 1960 were signed in Tirana.

A protocol on goods exchange for 1960 was signed in Sofia between the PRC and Bulgaria along with the 1960 plan for cooperation between academies of sciences.

March 17: The Roman Catholic Bishop of Shanghai, Ignatius Kung Ping-Mei, was sentenced by a Shanghai court to life imprisonment for "serious crimes of high treason," twelve other Chinese Catholics receiving prison sentences of five to twenty years on similar charges. On the following day the same court imposed a 20-year prison sentence on Bishop James E. Walsh, an American national, and head of the Maryknoll Mission in Shanghai, on charges of "counter-revolutionary activities" and espionage.

March 21: Agreements on Sino-Nepalese border questions and on Chinese economic aid to Nepal were signed during a 12-day visit to China by the Nepalese Prime Minister, Mr. B. F. Koirala. The border agreement stated that "the contracting parties consider that except for discrepancies in certain sections their understanding of the traditional customary border line is basically the same." Both countries also agreed to withdraw all armed personnel from an area within 12 miles of the frontier.

March 22: The allegations against Bishop Kung, Bishop Walsh, and the other accused were described as "completely false" by leading Roman Catholics in the United States, including Cardinal Spellman, and also by Secretary Herter in a statement on March 18. On the instructions of the Secretary of State, the U.S. ambassador in Warsaw (Mr. Jacob D. Beam) met the Chinese ambassador (Mr. Wang Ping-nan) on March 22 to express the deep revulsion and indignation of the United States government and people at the sentence imposed on Bishop Walsh. Bishop Walsh had been under varying degrees of surveillance and house detention from 1949, when the Communist forces entered Shanghai, until his arrest in October 1958.

March 23: A Sino-East German protocol on exchange of goods and payments in 1960 was signed in Berlin.

March 24: A joint communique issued at the conclusion of Mr. Koirala's Peking visit said that Mr. Chou En-lai had accepted an invitation to visit Katmandu after his forthcoming visit to India in order to discuss a treaty of peace and friendship, and that China and Nepal would open diplomatic missions in each other's capitals.

March 25: A protocol on goods exchange for 1960 was signed in Belgrade between the PRC and Yugoslavia.

Instruments were exchanged in Berlin between the PRC and East Germany on the 1960 plan for implementation of the cultural cooperation agreement between the two countries.

March 26: In reply to the Chinese note of March 15, Dr. Subandrio gave an assurance that the Indonesian government would implement Chinese proposals to enable those Chinese who so desired to be repatriated within the shortest possible time and agreed to study the issue to permit Chinese desiring to return to China to sell their properties and bring back their money and belongings, and to permit dismissed Chinese workers to bring back all their wages. A first group of 1,365 Chinese left Djakarta on February 12 on a Dutch liner chartered by the Chinese government, and by the end of March about seven thousand had returned to China.

March 27: NCNA reported that the 3-kilometer double-track railway bridge spanning the Yalu River at Chengchou has in the main been completed. Work on this bridge started in May 1958.

March 28: Sino-North Vietnamese protocol on PRC aid to North Vietnam in establishment of farms and agricultural school was signed in Peking.

March 29: A Sino-Soviet protocol on exchange of goods in 1960 was signed in Peking.

March 29-April 11: The Third CPPCC National Committee opened its 2nd session in Peking on March 29, presided over by Chou En-lai. The session came to a close on April 11 after adopting a resolution calling on all people, parties and organizations to implement the NPC resolutions and to fulfill and over-fulfill the 1956 economic plan and the 12-year agricultural program.

March 30-April 10: The 2nd NPC held its second session in Peking between March 30 and April 10. 1,063 deputies and top leaders, including Mao Tse-tung, Liu Shao-chi, Chu Teh and Chou En-lai, attended the session. Members of the CPPCC National Committee attended as observers. The Congress heard a report by Li Fu-chun on the 1960 National Economic Plan, a report by Li Hsien-nien on state budget and the 1959 Final State Accounts, and a work report by the NPC Standing Committee. At its closing session on April 10, the Congress ratified the 1960 National Economic Plan, the Final State Accounts for 1959, the State Budget for 1960, and the 12-year National Agricultural Program.

April 1: Construction of the 256-kilometer Peking-Chengtu Railway was completed, and the railway formally opened to traffic.

April 6: Vice-Premier Tan Chen-lin told the NPC that the commune system had been extended to the vast majority of China's rural population. He stated that 24,000 rural communes existed, each with an average membership of 5,000 households, an average work force of 10,000, and an average area of 10,000 acres. He added that 73% of China's population (about 400,000,000) ate in commune-run public dining rooms.

April 10: Premier Chou En-lai's speech to the NPC, published only in summary, said that the United States was forced to make a gesture toward peace by strength of peace forces, but was continuing aggressive policies. He repeated his rejection of any agreement made without Chinese participation. He raised the idea of an atom-free zone in Asia and the Western Pacific for the first time in a year and supported summit and other Soviet peace proposals. Finally, he asserted that it was China's sacred sovereign right to liberate Taiwan and that no outsider could interfere. He went on to say that the United States had seized Taiwan by force and was trying to create two Chinas to legitimize the island's separation from China.

April 11: Liu Shao-chi issued an order promulgating the National Program for Agricultural Development (1956-1967) endorsed by the NPC.

April 13: Some 10,000 returned overseas Chinese were resettled in state farms in Kwangtung, Fukien, Kwangsi, and Yunnan, and some were resettled in factories, mines, and enterprises of rural communes. This was disclosed at a meeting of overseas Chinese organization in Peking.

A Sino-East German protocol on scientific and technical cooperation was signed in Peking.

April 15-19: In his visit to Burma, Premier Chou En-lai held talks with Burmese Premier U Nu on the demarcation of the frontier in accordance with the agreement concluded in January 1960. The two prime ministers agreed that the survey of the frontier should be concluded as quickly as possible in order that a boundary treaty might be signed, if possible on October 1.

April 19-25: Premier Chou En-lai met with Indian Prime Minister Nehru in New Delhi in an attempt to settle the dispute involving 51,000 square miles of territory claimed by both and partly occupied by China. Differences were not resolved. However, in a joint communique issued on April 25, both agreed that PRC and Indian officials would meet for further discussion of the boundary question.

April 25: At a press conference in Delhi, Mr. Chou En-lai listed six points which, he suggested, could form the basis for Sino-Indian border settlements. (1) There exists a dispute with regard to the boundary between the two sides; (2) there exists between the two countries a line of actual control up to which each side exercises administrative jurisdiction; (3) in determining the boundary between the two countries, certain geographical principles, such as watersheds, river valleys, and mountain passes, should be equally applicable to all sectors of the boundary; (4) a settlement of the boundary question between the two countries should take into account the national feeling of the two peoples towards the Himalayas and the Karakoram mountains; (5) pending a solution of the boundary question through discussion, both sides should keep to the line of actual control and should not put forward territorial claims as preconditions; however, individual adjustment might be made; (6) in order to ensure tranquility on the border and thereby facilitate discussions, both sides should continue to refrain from patrolling along all sectors of the boundary. He stated that the Chinese would avoid any friction so that the talks planned for June to work out a solution could proceed in an atmosphere conducive to settlement.

April 26: Chou En-lai sent messages of greetings to Sylvanue Olympio, prime minister of Togo, on the occasion of the proclamation of independence of the Togo Republic.

April 26-29: Mr. Chou En-lai and Marshal Chen Yi visited Katmandu on their return from India for talks with Mr. Koirala, the Nepalese prime minister. The premiers signed on April 28 a treaty of non-aggression and friendship, stating that the relations between the two countries would be based on the Five-Principles of Peaceful Co-existence. The Sino-Nepalese border agreement, concluded in Peking in March, was ratified at the same time.

April 28: At a press conference at Katmandu, Mr. Chou En-lai said that although Chinese maps showed Mt. Everest as inside China, the Chinese government was now prepared to accept the Nepalese maps which showed it as the Nepalese-Tibetan border.

April 29: Mr. Nehru told the Lok Sabha that he had information that the Chinese had built a new road in Ladakh about the middle of 1959, west of the road along the Aksai Chin caravan route, which they had built in 1957-58. He had raised the matter during his talks with Chou En-lai, and had been surprised to find that the latter did not know much about it.

May 3: While supporting the forthcoming summit conference, Mao Tse-tung told foreign visitors "our common enemy was U.S. imperialism," and that "we were standing on the same front and need to unite and support each other."

May 4: A 50,000-strong rally in Peking voiced support for the just patriotic struggle of the Turkish people. "U.S. imperialists" and the Menderes gang of reactionaries" were strongly condemned for "enslaving and slaughtering the patriotic Turkish people."

May 5-9: Mr. Chou En-lai and Marshal Chen Yi paid a visit to Cambodia during which the former opened a radio station near Phnom Penh and a textile factory at Kompang-Chem, both of which had been built with Chinese aid. In a speech on May 6, Prince Sihanouk thanked the Chinese leaders for the aid given to Cambodia, while recalling that France and the United States had also rendered considerable assistance to his country. A joint communique was issued on May 8.

May 6: A Sino-Mongolian agreement on cooperation in radio broadcasting was signed in Peking.

May 7: A consular treaty between the PRC and Czechoslovakia was signed in Peking.

Peking reported on Khrushchev's U-2 accusations and seconded the Khrushchev speech on the U-2 incident.

May 8: Chou En-lai, at a press conference in Cambodia, stated that the PRC would not participate in disarmament discussions unless it was recognized by other participants.

May 9: A mass rally of over 1,000,000 persons was held in Peking to express support for the Japanese people, who were undertaking their 16th nationwide action against the Japan-United States military alliance.

May 13-20: The Algerian government delegation headed by Krim Belkacem returned to Peking on May 13 after visiting North Korea. The PRC and the Algerian delegation signed a joint communique on May 19 to express warm approval in the matter of Algeria establishing its diplomatic representative organ in Peking at a time it would deem appropriate.

May 14: Mao Tse-tung told visitors the U-2 incident showed "no unrealistic illusion should be cherished with regard to imperialism" and expressed hope that those who cherished illusions would be awakened by these facts. He supported the summit conference whether the conference would make achievements or not, or whether the achievements were big or small.

In a joint communique from Hanoi Chou En-lai and Pham Van Dong welcomed Soviet efforts to relax tension, praised Khruschchev's visit to the United States and other countries and expressed

hope that the summit conference would achieve results favorable to world peace.

The PRC and Burma exchanged the instruments of ratification of the "Treaty of Friendship and Mutual Non-Aggression" and the "Agreement on the Question of the Boundary between the Two Countries" in Rangoon.

May 15: The 1960 executive plan of the cultural agreement between the PRC and Iraq was signed in Peking.

May 16: At the first and only summit meeting, Khrushchev demanded the United States condemn reconnaissance flights, renounce further flights, punish those guilty of flights, and make apology as conditions for holding a conference. President Eisenhower announced suspension of flights.

On the question of exchange of correspondents between the United States and the PRC the spokesman for the PRC Foreign Ministry issued a statement explaining why the PRC insisted upon first reaching a formal agreement based on the principles of equality and reciprocity. It said: "The impediment to the exchange of visits between Chinese and American correspondents is not on the Chinese side but on the American side."

May 20: A Peking rally was held against the U.S. sabotage of summit talks.

May 23: A protocol on the final clearing of accounts concerned with the Agreement on Economic and Technical Assistance of 1956 given by the PRC to Mongolia was signed.

A Sino-Korean agreement on border river navigation was signed in Peking.

May 25: Sino-Iraqui trade and payments agreements in 1960-1961 were signed in Peking.

May 31: A treaty of friendship and mutual assistance was signed in Ulan Bator at the end of a five-day visit to the Mongolian capital by Chou En-lai and Marshal Chen Yi. An economic aid plan was also signed whereby China granted Mongolia a long-term loan. A communique was issued stressing Sino-Mongolian unity and friendship and expressing support for the unremitting efforts of the

Soviet Union to ease international tension. A Sino-Mongolian agreement on scientific and technical cooperation was also signed.

June 3: A Sino-Guinean protocol on a 1960 plan for cultural cooperation was signed in Conakry.

June 5-9: The Eleventh session of the World Federation of Trade Unions opened in Peking on June 5. The session closed on June 9 with adoption of the general resolution asserting that, thanks to Communist strength, a real possibility had been created for eliminating the danger of destructive atomic war—a formulation which fell short of the Soviet concept, expressed earlier in Soviet delegate Grishin's speech, that by 1965 bloc economic growth would create premises excluding world war from the life of society.

June 10: NCNA reported a new 98-kilometer railway had been completed and opened to traffic between Leuti and the Shaoyang city of Hunan.

A Sino-Soviet agreement on cooperation between academies of medical sciences was signed in Peking.

June 15-July 25: As agreed during Mr. Chou En-lai's visit to Delhi, talks between Indian and Chinese officials were held in Peking (again in Delhi from August 19 to October 5) to discuss the location and natural features of the frontier; the basis of boundary alignments in treaties, agreements, tradition, and custom; and question of administration and jurisdiction in border areas.

June 18: President Eisenhower, on a tour of Asian countries, arrived in Taiwan aboard the St. Paul which had been heavily escorted by units of the U.S. Seventh Fleet. The night before his arrival in Taiwan, the Chinese Communist batteries on the mainland shelled the Nationalist-held Quemoy islands exceptionally heavily, and carried out another heavy bombardment on June 19.

June 19: Foreign Minister Chen Yi cabled a message to Prime Minister Medibo Keita congratulating the independence of the Mali Federation and informing him that the PRC had decided to recognize the Mali Federation.

A Chinese delegation to the Rumanian party congress arrived in Bucharest after a 3-day stopover in Moscow, where reports said they conferred with Soviet Communist party presidium members.

June 20-25: The Third Congress of the Rumanian Worker's Party held in Bucharest made the occasion a meeting of party leaders from all Communist countries of Eastern Europe and Asia except Yugoslavia. The representation of the 12 Communist parties concerned approved on June 24 a communique reaffirming their support for Mr. Khrushchev's policy of peaceful co-existence. Addressing the Bucharest Congress on June 21, Mr. Khrushchev reaffirmed his view that Lenin's theory of the inevitability of war under capitalism no longer applied. The speech of Mr. Peng Chen, on June 22, was in striking contrast to that of Mr. Khrushchev. Although he endorsed the 1957 Moscow Declaration, he refrained from endorsing the Soviet peaceful co-existence policy; however he made no criticism.

June 21: The Ministry of Agriculture issued a notification calling all areas to popularize the production of chlorella, a kind of fodder crop, as an important means of solving the present shortage of food.

Mao Tse-tung reiterated his call for formation of broad united front against the United States. He told Japanese visitors that the tactics of uniting the broadest possible forces used by the United States was a good method under present circumstances.

June 21-27: The PRC declared a week of Taiwan liberation and anti-U.S. propaganda.

June 25: Chou En-lai sent a cable to the President of the Malgasy Republic, informing him that PRC had decided to recognize the Malgasy Republic.

Chen Yi sent a cable to Mohamed Haji Ibrahim Egal, Prime Minister of Somaliland, extending congratulations on proclamation of the independence of Somaliland and informing him that the PRC had decided to recognize that state.

June 26: Chen Yi sent a message to the Foreign Minister of the Congo Republic informing him that the PRC had decided to recognize that republic.

A Chinese note informed the Nepalese government that Chinese troops had entered the zone within 20 kilometers of the Nepalese frontier to suppress a Tibetan revolt and prevent the rebels from escaping into Nepal; an assurance was given that the troops would not enter Nepalese territory and would be withdrawn immediately the revolt was crushed.

June 27-July 5: The Joint Chinese-Burmese Boundary Committee held its first session from June 27 to July 5. The joint committee reached an agreement on the working procedure, specific tasks, and organization and dispatch of joint survey teams and investigation teams. The communique in these respects was issued on July 6.

June 28: In a frontier incident, a Nepalese officer was killed in a clash with Chinese troops.

June 30: Chen Yi sent a message of congratulations to Somali Prime Minister Abdulahi Issa, informing him that the PRC had decided to give recognition to the Republic of Somalia.

Mr. Chou En-lai apologized for the incident of June 28 but asserted that it had not occurred on Nepalese territory. Expressing deep regret at the incident, the Chinese government said that it had ordered the prisoner and the body to be handed over to the Nepalese authorities and was willing to pay compensation. The prisoner and the body were handed over on July 4 and 50,000 rupees (about $14,-000) was paid on July 18 as compensation for the killing of the Nepalese officer.

July 3: A rally, attended by Chinese leaders and African guests, was held in Peking to celebrate the independence of the Cameroons, Togo, the Federation of Mali, Malgasy, the Congo, and Somalia, and the founding of the Republic of Ghana.

July 4: A Sino-Korean agreement on cooperation between academies of sciences was signed in Pyongyang.

July 4-11: Huang Chen, the PRC ambassador to Indonesia, lodged a serious protest with the Indonesian government in connection with the killing of two Chinese women on July 3 by Indonesian army men and police in Tjimaki, West Java. On July 11 the PRC Foreign Ministry lodged a strong protest with the Indonesian government. It demanded apology, punishment of the murderers, pensions to the families of the overseas Chinese victims, and speedy release of the arrested overseas Chinese. It also demanded that the Indonesian government stop at once the compulsory evacuation and various persecutions of the overseas Chinese.

July 5: It was announced in Peking that Ghana and the PRC had decided to establish full diplomatic relations and to exchange ambassadors. Ghana was the second African country to recognize the PRC.

July 6: A PRC note to the U.S.S.R. supported the Soviet position in breaking off 10-nation disarmament talks in Geneva.

The PRC and Cambodia exchanged notes to extend 1956 trade payments and economic aid agreements.

July 11: Chen Yi pledged, in a letter to Foreign Minister Pham Van Dong of North Vietnam, all-out support of the request to the co-chairman of the Geneva Conference that American military personnel, arms and ammunition "illegally" introduced into South Vietnam be withdrawn and that measures be taken to compel the authorities in South Vietnam to stop their "reprisals" and discrimination against former members of the resistance.

July 19: The CPC Central Committee and the State Council issued a directive calling on all areas to step up production of autumn vegetables.

The PRC issued a statement supporting the Congolese people's struggle against the "imperialist aggression and intervention."

July 23: A Chinese trade mission headed by Lu Hsu-chang signed an agreement with the Cuban government whereby the PRC undertook to buy 500,000 tons of Cuban sugar for the years 1960-65 (a total of 2,500,000 tons) along with agreements: (1) Scientific and technical cooperation, (2) cultural cooperation.

July 25: A Sino-Soviet protocol on border railway was signed in Mutankiang.

July 25-August 1: The Chinese-Burmese Joint Boundary Committee met in Peking on July 25-August 1 and reached agreement on the following questions: (1) Determining the extent of the area of Hpimaw, Gawleen, and Kangfang to be returned to China; (2) determining the extent of the areas under the jurisdiction of the Panhung and Panlao tribes to be returned to China in exchange for the Meng-Mao Triangular area (Nemwan assigned tract) of China; (3) setting the question of the boundary-line-interested villages on the "1941 line" in a fair and reasonable manner. The communique of the meeting was issued on August 2.

August 1: Chou En-lai and Chen Yi sent messages of greetings to Prime Minister of the Republic of Dahomey Hubert Maga, congratulating the proclamation of independence of the Republic of Dahomey.

Mr. Chou En-lai called for a "peace pact" with the United States and other Pacific powers to create a non-nuclear-weapon zone in Asia and the Western Pacific. State Department spokesman Lincoln White said Chou's proposal was a "propaganda gesture" and added that the offer had never been discussed at the Chinese-American meetings in Warsaw.

August 1-31: The controversy between the Soviet and Chinese parties reached an acute phase during August 30, after they had failed to resolve their differences at the Bucharest Conference. Articles from the Soviet press condemning "dogmatism" were broadcast by Soviet radio in its Chinese service; a Chinese-language magazine published in Moscow for circulation in China, and a Russian language magazine published in Peking, both ceased to appear; an international conference of orientalists in Moscow was boycotted by the Chinese; and it was reported that many Soviet technicians and students were being recalled from China, and Chinese students from the Soviet Union.

August 2: Chen Yi cabled a message of greeting to Premier Hamani Diori of the Republic of Niger and informed him that the government of the PRC had decided to recognize that republic.

August 4: Chen Yi cabled a message of greeting to President Maurice Yameogo of the Republic of Upper Volta and informed him that the PRC had decided to recognize that republic.

August 6: Chen Yi cabled a message of congratulations to President Felix Houphouet-Beigny of Ivory Coast and informed him that the PRC had decided to recognize that republic.

August 10: Chen Yi in a message of greeting informed Prime Minister of the Republic of Chad Francois Tombalbaye of the decision of the Chinese government to recognize the new republic.

August 11: The Sino-Nepalese joint boundary commission set up under the March agreement was formally inaugurated.

August 12: Chen Yi in a message of congratulations informed Prime Minister David Dacke of the Republic of Central Africa that the PRC had decided to recognize the new republic.

August 15: Chen Yi in a message of greetings informed Foreign Minister of the Republic of Cyprus Nicos Kranidiotis that the PRC had decided to recognize that republic.

August 16: Chen Yi in a message of greetings informed Leon M'Ba, Premier of the Gabon Republic, that the PRC had decided to recognize that republic.

August 26: A multilateral protocol on passenger rail service in 1960-61 was signed by the PRC, U.S.S.R., North Korea, and North Vietnam.

A Sino-Afghanistan treaty of friendship and non-aggression was signed by Chen Yi, who arrived in Kabul on August

2, and Sardar Mohammed Naim. In addition, the existing commercial and payments agreement between the two countries was renewed. King Mohammed Zahir accepted an invitation to visit China. Chen Yi returned to Peking on August 29, breaking his journey at Alma Ata, the capital of Outer Mongolia.

September 1: A communique on the first session of the Sino-Nepalese Joint Boundary Committee held in Katmandu was issued. Unanimous agreement was reached on the following questions: (1) Tasks and working procedure of the joint committee; (2) general arrangement for the settlement of the entire boundary question; (3) agreement satisfactory to both sides was reached on the settlement of the question of ownership of those sections of the boundary as listed in Clause 3, Article 3 of the Agreement on the Question of Boundary between the two countries; (4) sending out of joint teams to the above-mentioned section to carry out investigation and survey and settling the questions of the tasks, composition, time of dispatch and working methods of the joint teams; (5) fixing the location of survey points along the entire boundary line.

September 2: Fidel Castro announced the decision to recognize the PRC and to break off diplomatic relations with the Chinese Nationalist government.

September 5: Chou En-lai received the British correspondent, Felex Greene, in a television interview and answered questions.

A Sino-Burmese communique on boundary demarcation was issued in Rangoon after the third session of Sino-Burmese joint boundary committee.

September 10: Soviet delegates to the Vietnamese Party Congress, Communist party presidium member Mukhitdinov and Chinese Communist delegate Li Fu-chun, met for an exchange of opinions on many questions, but their communique omitted the usual mention of a harmony of views.

September 13: Guinea President Toure and Premier Chou En-lai signed treaties of friendship and economic and technical cooperation in Peking. In addition they signed trade and payments accords and China provided a loan for economic development. A joint communique on President Toure's visit was also issued.

September 14: On the situation in the Congo, a message of support to Prime Minister Lumbumba was sent by the China Peace Committee. The PRC voiced protest against the "arbitrary and shameless crimes of aggression and intervention committed by imperialism headed by the United States in the Congo."

September 20: An agreement on the dispatching of workers by the PRC to help Mongolia in its construction was signed.

September 24: In a joint press communique the PRC and Burma agreed on the signing of a forthcoming boundary treaty (October 1, 1960), exchange of visits by Premier Chou En-lai and U Nu, and gifts by each government to inhabitants of border areas in each other's country.

September 28-October 4: A Burmese delegation, headed by U Nu, visited Peking for the celebration of the Chinese National Day. The boundary treaty, which incorporated the boundary agreement and full details of the frontier line as agreed on by the joint committee, was signed by Chou En-lai and U Nu on October 1. A communique issued on October 4 stated that Mr. Chou En-lai had accepted an invitation to attend the celebrations of the Burmese National Day on January 4, when instruments of ratification of the treaty would be exchanged. In a Sino-Burmese exchange of notes on October 1, both governments agreed that any inhabitants of the exchanged areas who did not wish to be transferred to the other country could (1) within one year of the coming into force of the treaty express their wish to retain their existing nationality, (2) within two years of the treaty's entry into force, move into the territory of the country to which they originally belonged.

September 29: A new volume, the fourth volume of the *Selected Works of Mao*

Tse-tung, in Chinese edited by the publications committee of the CCP Central Committee for the Selected Works of Mao Tse-tung, was published.

September 30: Chen Yi and Chou En-lai sent messages of congratulation to Prime Minister Tabawa Balema of the Federation of Nigeria on the proclamation of independence of the Federation. In his message Chen Yi informed the Prime Minister that the PRC had decided to recognize the Federation of Nigeria.

October 1: Chen Yi, addressing Peking ceremonies marking the PRC's eleventh anniversary, said that his government would not accept an Asian settlement based on the existence of two Chinas. He denounced a series of Warsaw meetings as senseless in view of the United States' refusal to negotiate fundamental issues and its plans for two Chinas.

October 5: A Sino-Algerian communique was issued on the visit of Premier Ferhat Abbas of provisional government of Republic of Algeria.

October 6: A Sino-Burmese communique on boundary demarcation was issued in Peking after fourth session of Sino-Burmese joint boundary committee.

October 7: Senator John F. Kennedy and Vice-President Richard M. Nixon held their second radio and television debate of the presidential campaign. The nominees disagreed about defense of Quemoy and Matsu. Senator Kennedy said: "These islands are a few miles, five or six miles, off the coast of Red China within a general harbor area, and more than 100 miles from Taiwan. We have never said flatly that we will defend Quemoy and Matsu if they are attacked . . . I think it is unwise to take the chance of being dragged into a war which may lead to a world war over two islands which are not strategically defensible, which are not essential to the defense of Taiwan." Vice President Nixon answered: "I think as far as Quemoy and Matsu are concerned that the question is not these two little pieces of real estate. They are unimportant . . . It is the principle involved.

These two islands are in the area of freedom . . . We should not force our Nationalist allies to get off and give them to the Communists. If we do that, we start a chain reaction, because the Communists aren't after Quemoy and Matsu. They are after Taiwan." On October 13, one of the chief questions at issue in the Nixon-Kennedy debate was again Quemoy and Matsu.

October 8: The question of Chinese representation in the U.N. was postponed by a vote of 42-34 with 24 abstentions.

October 9: A Sino-Polish agreement on cooperation between academies of sciences was signed in Peking.

October 12: The PRC and Mongolia exchanged in Peking instruments of ratification of the Treaty of Friendship and Mutual Assistance.

October 13: Two agreements between North Korea and the PRC providing for the latter a loan of 420 million rubles were signed in Peking along with the agreement on supply of whole sets of equipment and technical aid by the PRC to North Korea.

October 17: Chou En-lai and Chen Yi sent separate messages to the president of the Republic of Mali, Nodibo Keita, informing him that PRC had decided to recognize Mali as an independent sovereign state.

October 18: A protocol on scientific and technical cooperation between the PRC and North Korea was signed in Peking.

The Sino-Albanian Joint Committee for Scientific and Technical Cooperation signed a protocol in Tirana.

October 20: A Sino-Hungarian protocol on scientific and technical cooperation was signed in Budapest.

October 24: The 1961-1962 executive plan of the Sino-Albanian cultural cooperation agreement was signed in Peking.

A Sino-Burmese communique on trade talks was issued in Rangoon along with an accord for the PRC purchase of rice from Burma.

October 26: A Sino-Nepalese communique was issued in Katmandu after the first session of the Sino-Nepalese Joint Boundary Committee.

November 1-10: Chou En-lai and Chen Yi, in a series of interviews granted to Japanese journalists and United States writer Edgar Snow respectively, discussed differences with the Soviet Union with usual candor. Admitted differences exist and played down the importance of Soviet economic assistance to the PRC.

November 2-4: Liu Shao-chi, Chou En-lai, Chu Teh, Teng Hsiao-ping, and other party and government leaders welcomed Ho Chi-Minh, president of the Democratic Republic of Vietnam, who arrived in Peking on November 2 enroute to Moscow to attend the celebration of the 43rd anniversary of the October Revolution.

November 5: A Sino-Bulgarian protocol on scientific and technical cooperation was signed in Sofia.

November 6: The PRC delegation to revolutionary celebrations, headed by Chairman Liu Shao-chi, arrived in Moscow. He was welcomed by Brezhnev, Suslov, and Khrushchev at the airport. Speaking at the airport, Liu Shao-chi said, "The Chinese people heartily thank the Soviet Union for the tremendous assistance that country has rendered to the Chinese revolution and construction." "Everlasting and unbreakable friendship and unity," he said, "have been forged between the peoples of China and the Soviet Union in their joint struggle against enemy." He added, "In all circumstances, no matter what great storms or difficulties might happen in the world, people will witness that the 860,000,000 people of China and the Soviet Union will always stand together."

November 7: The third and final series of talks between India and Chinese officials, at which the two sides examined documentary material put forth in support of their respective claims on the boundary question, was held in Rangoon.

November 10: The PRC government and the Mongolian government signed in Rabat the trade agreement for 1960-61.

November 10-December 1: A Communist "summit" attended by party leaders from 81 countries met in Moscow. Mao was significantly absent. The meeting continued long beyond its scheduled closing of November 15, lending credence to reports that it had become enmeshed in arduous arguments over the correctness and applicability of varying Chinese and Soviet views on key issues. It dealt fully with such controversial issues as "peaceful coexistence" and the "inevitability of war," and put forth plans for future Communist tactics, notably in the underdeveloped countries. These had threatened to split the international Communist movement. Albania openly supported the Chinese viewpoint, while others were believed to have reservations on the Soviet government policy. The conference took place under conditions of strict secrecy.

November 15: An agreement on the supply of water from Kwangtung Province to Hong Kong for an indefinite period was signed by representatives of Hong Kong administration and the People's Commune of Proan County, Kwangtung Province.

November 17: The Laotian cabinet announced its decision to establish relations with the PRC.

November 21: A conference of the Fisheries Research Commission for the Western Pacific, composed of the PRC, the Soviet Union, North Korea, North Vietnam and Mongolia, closed in Peking after meeting for eight days. The session approved proposals for cooperation among member countries concerning fishery research, oceanography, and limnology in 1961.

November 28: The PRC Supreme People's Court pardoned and released another group of "war criminals" who "really repented and turned over a new leaf."

An agreement on scientific and technical cooperation between the PRC and North Vietnam was signed in Peking.

November 30: Khrushchev and Liu Shao-chi conferred in Moscow. It was the first mention of Liu's presence in the Soviet capital since the November 6-7 revolution anniversary celebrations.

At the end of Major Guevara's visit

to the PRC, it was announced that both countries had concluded an economic agreement providing for (1) the Chinese purchase of 1,000,000 tons of Cuban sugar and other Cuban exports; (2) the purchase by the Cuban government of Chinese exports of an equivalent value; (3) an interest-free loan by China to Cuba of 246,000,000 rubles for the five-year period 1961-65; (4) implementation of scientific and technical cooperation agreement of July 23, 1960.

A Sino-Tunisian agreement on trade in 1960-61 was signed in Rabat.

A Sino-Polish protocol on scientific and technical cooperation was signed in Warsaw.

December 1: Representatives of 81 Communist parties, meeting in Moscow, issued a manifesto proclaiming unity in the fight against capitalism. It was reported that Soviet Premier Khrushchev and Chinese President Liu Shao-chi had debated ideological differences for at least ten days before a compromise was reached. Because the manifesto's wording was more aggressive than that of previous Soviet statements, it was thought the Russians had made some concessions to Chinese demands. China's views were believed to have had the support of representatives of Communist movements in Latin America, Albania, and some sections of Asia. The Soviet position was said to have been supported by the majority of the participants, most of them from the East European nations.

December 3-6: Ho Chi-Minh, President of North Vietnam, and his party arrived in Peking on December 3 en route for home from Moscow. They were welcomed at the airport by Chou En-lai and subsequently received by Mao Tse-tung. The party left Peking on December 6.

December 4: Liu Shao-chi hailed U.S.S.R.-Chinese amity in a speech in Leningrad.

December 8: Liu Shao-chi left Moscow on December 8 and returned to Peking on December 9; he was welcomed at the airport by Mao Tse-tung, Chu Teh, Chou En-lai, and others.

December 9: The evacuation of Longju, which the Chinese had occupied since August 1959, had been announced by Mr. Nehru, who said that the Chinese had abandoned the post because of epidemic and had withdrawn about three miles to the north. He said that the Indian government did not propose to reoccupy Longju, as he had proposed that neither side should occupy the post—a proposal which, however, had not been accepted by the Chinese.

Chinese Foreign Minister Chen Yi protested against the "intolerable situation" of the Chinese people living in West Java. He put forward proposals for a settlement which would include: The immediate exchange of instruments of ratification of the dual citizenship agreement of 1955; the Indonesian government should protect the legitimate rights and interests of overseas Chinese who wished to retain Chinese nationality; Chinese who had become homeless, lost their means of livelihood, and did not wish to remain in Indonesia should be allowed to return to China with the money obtained from the sale of their property.

December 12: Instruments of ratification of the Treaty of Friendship and Mutual Non-Aggression between the PRC and Afghanistan, signed in Kabul on August 26, were exchanged in Peking.

December 13: The Indonesian government issued a rejection to the Chinese protest of December 9. The note said that the Indonesian government considered the regulation of Chinese traders a necessary step towards a guided economy and, although incidents had taken place, they had been "grossly exaggerated."

December 15: The PRC and Indonesian governments signed in Djakarta on December 15 arrangements for implementing the Dual Nationality Treaty. Notes on ratification of such arrangements were exchanged on December 21.

December 18: Chou En-lai proposed that he should meet with Mr. Nehru on December 26 for discussions on the Sino-Indian border dispute, but this was rejected.

December 19: Prince Sihanouk (Cambodia) visited Peking where he signed a treaty of friendship and non-aggression and two protocols dealing with technical and economic cooperation. A joint communique was issued on the Chinese proposal for a non-aggression pact between the Asian and Pacific countries and the establishment of a "non-nuclear zone" in that area. Furthermore, Sino-Cambodian agreement on cooperation in navigation was signed, and, in exchange of letters, the two states agreed on dispatch by the PRC of railway and agricultural experts and technicians.

December 24: A Sino-Burmese communique on boundary demarcation was issued in Peking after the fifth session of Sino-Burmese joint boundary committee.

December 28: Chen Yi sent a letter on the present serious situation in Laos to the co-chairmen of the Geneva Conference on the Indochina question, A. A. Gromyko (Russia) and A. F. D. Home (Britain), requesting them "to take energetic action and effective measures to stop the action of the United States government in violating the Geneva Agreements and in intervening and committing aggression against Laos."

December 29: Peking radio and major Communist newspapers reported that more than one-half of Communist China's cultivated farm land (180,000,00 acres) had been ravished in 1960 by natural calamities, including drought, floods, typhoons, and insect pests, said to be the worst in a hundred years. Of these, between 46,-000,000 and 64,000,000 acres were seriously affected. Only two areas escaped—Tibet and Sinkiang.

1961

January 2-9: Chou En-lai paid an official visit to Rangoon, accompanied by Chen Yi and other leaders. Burmese Prime Minister U Nu and Chou En-lai exchanged on January 4 the instruments of ratification of the Sino-Burmese frontier treaty signed in October 1960. Both countries also signed on January 9 an economic and technical cooperation agreement and a payments agreement along with a joint communique.

January 14: In a message to Prince Sihanouk, head of state of Cambodia, Chou En-lai expressed agreement to the latter's proposal for convention and enlarged meeting of the Geneva Conference to seek ways to safeguard the Geneva Agreements and restore peace in Laos.

January 20: The Central Committee of the CPC, after a four-day meeting in Peking under the chairmanship of Mao Tse-tung, issued a communique calling for a strengthening of the agricultural front in 1961 so as to overcome the serious natural calamities, the most severe in a century, which have affected agricultural production in two successive years. The communique made it clear that emphasis would be shifted from heavy industry and capital construction to output of consumer goods during the coming year.

January 21: The CPC Central Committee published a declaration of policy condemning the United States as the "main enemy of the peoples of the whole world." The declaration noted that "revolution is the affair of peoples in various countries" and should not be exported. At the same time Communists "oppose the imperialist export of counter-revolution" and (imperialist interference) in the internal affairs of people . . . who have risen in revolution."

The PRC will buy 1,000,000 tons of Cuban sugar this year at four Cuban cents per pound, according to a contract signed in Cuba. The two countries also signed another contract covering the export of 5,000 tons of copper ore from Cuba to Communist China.

January 25: President Kennedy told a news conference that the United States might consider sending food to Communist China if a request should be made.

January 31: Khrushchev's January 6 speech was belatedly released by Peking in long summaries which were apparently carefully selected and tailored to reflect Chinese views on Sino-Soviet differences.

Look Magazine published an interview by Edgar Snow with Premier Chou En-lai. Chou told the American journalist that although the Soviet Union and Communist China had differences, they agreed on the desirability of disarmament and peaceful co-existence. He said a settlement with the United States would be possible only after the U.S. had accepted Peking's position that Taiwan was a Chinese internal problem. United States forces would have to be withdrawn from the island.

The PRC and North Vietnam signed six documents: (1) Agreement on PRC loans over the period 1961-67; (2) protocol on mutual supply of goods in 1961; (3) protocol on transit of cargo; (4) exchange of notes to extend the 1955 protocol on small-scale trading in border areas; (5) exchange of notes to extend the 1955 protocol on exchange of goods between local state trading companies in border areas; (6) protocol on the PRC technical aid and supply of complete sets of equipment.

February 1: President Kennedy, queried about the five Americans imprisoned in China, replied: "This is a matter of continuing concern, and as long as those men are held, it will be extremely difficult to have any kind of normal relations with the Chinese Communists. There are other matters which affect those relations, too, but this is certainly a point of the greatest possible concern. Now, we have asked for a delay in the meetings in Warsaw between the United States representative and that of the Chinese Communists, from February to March, because they have become merely a matter of form and nothing of substance happens. But I want to make it very clear we are concerned about the men in China."

February 2: The announcement that 40,-000,000 bushels of Canadian grain were to be sold to Communist China at a value of slightly less than $60,000,000 was made in Ottawa by Mr. Alvin Hamilton, the Canadian minister of agriculture. Comprising the shipments were 28,000,-000 bushels of wheat and 12,000,000 bushels of barley. It was described as the largest Canadian shipment ever contracted for. The transaction followed several months of negotiations in Hong Kong.

At the end of a three weeks' visit to Peking by an Albanian delegation headed by the First Deputy Premier, Mr. Spiro Koleka, seven documents were signed by the representatives of the two states: (1) Press communique on economic and trade talks; (2) Sino-Albanian treaty on commerce and navigation; (3) protocol on exchange of goods and payments in 1961; (4) agreement on loan by the PRC to Albania; (5) protocol on Albania's use of the PRC loan in accordance with loan agreement; (6) protocol on Albania's use of the PRC loan in 1961; (7) protocol on settlement of commodities by the PRC in 1960 in accordance with 1954 credit agreement and with notes exchanged in November and December, 1956.

February 4: A Sino-Soviet protocol on a 1961 plan for cultural cooperation was signed in Peking.

February 5: The PRC and the United Arab Republic signed in Cairo a trade protocol for 1961, the third year under their trade agreement concluded in 1958.

February 6: The sale of Australian wheat (1,050,000 tons) and flour (40,000 tons) to the PRC with a value of slightly less than $60,000,000 was announced by the Australian wheat board. The board noted that this sale was the largest since Britain bought 3,000,000 tons during the First World War. This was to be the first direct wheat shipment from Australia to mainland China since 1939.

Secretary of State Dean Rusk told his first Washington press conference that the United States had "strong commitments" to Nationalist China, and "that commitment is firm" even though Communist China considers Taiwan a "major obstacle" to a settlement with the United States. Rusk added that the United States was studying ways to include Communist China in disarmament discussions.

February 12: The 11th anniversary of the signing of the Sino-Soviet Treaty of Friendship, Alliance and Mutual Assistance was marked with messages of greeting and with meetings and various activities in the major Chinese cities.

February 14: A statement protesting the murder of Patrice Lumumba by the "imperialist bloc and its agents" was issued by the PRC government. "The United States," it stressed, "bears unshirkable responsibility for this crime of the imperialist bloc."

February 15: A Sino-Cuban agreement on exchange of television films was signed in Peking.

A Sino-Nepalese communique on boundary demarcation was signed in Peking after the second session of Sino-Nepalese joint boundary committee.

February 23: The White House announced that President Kennedy had rejected a proposal by Representative Thomas J. Lane (D., Mass.) that the United States send food to Red China in exchange for release of Americans held prisoner there. It was reported two days later that Chinese Foreign Minister Chen Yi had said that China would not "stoop to beg for food from the United States."

February 24: A Sino-Czechoslovak protocol on scientific and technical cooperation was signed in Prague.

February 28: A trade and payments agreement between the PRC and the Republic of Mali was signed in Bamako on February 28.

March 2: A Sino-Soviet press communique

was issued on economic and trade talks in Peking.

March 4: A Sino-Mali joint communique on trade talks was issued in Peking.

March 7: The PRC and Laos exchanged notes agreeing on exchange of cultural and economic delegations.

United States-Chinese Warsaw talks resumed with U.S. Ambassador to Poland Jacob D. Beam proposing that he and Chinese Ambassador Wang Ping-nan discuss an exchange of newsmen between their two countries, the release of imprisoned Americans in China, and a general settlement of United States-Chinese disputes. Wang immediately rejected all three proposals, saying that nothing could be negotiated until the United States withdrew its forces from Taiwan.

March 8: The PRC and Cuba exchanged notes agreeing on remittance of money by Chinese in Cuba to their relatives in the PRC.

The 1961 executive plan for the Sino-Hungarian Agreement on Cultural Cooperation was signed in Peking.

A Sino-Bulgarian protocol on exchange of goods and payments in 1961 was signed in Peking.

March 15-April 29: An exhibition of Communist China's achievements in economic construction opened in Havana on March 15. It closed on April 29.

March 17: The 1961 executive plan for the Sino-Rumanian Agreement on Cultural Cooperation was signed in Peking.

March 18: Sino-North Korean protocol on mutual supply of goods in 1961 was signed in Peking along with a protocol on the PRC supply of complete sets of equipment and technical aid to Korea.

March 19: The PRC voiced full support for the demands of the North Vietnamese government to the co-chairman of the Geneva Conference. The co-chairmen were asked to take measures to force the United States government to immediately withdraw all its military personnel from the southern part of Vietnam, cease introducing into that region all arms for reinforcement, and stop the "Ngo Diem

clique's terrorist policy of slaughtering the people there."

March 20: A Sino-Soviet agreement on currency exchange and cash movement was signed.

March 23: An exhibition on the friendship between the Chinese and Latin American people, sponsored by the Chinese Latin American Friendship Association, was opened in Peking. On display at the two-week exhibition were 200 photos recording the friendly contacts and mutual support between the Chinese and Latin American people.

March 27: A Sino-Hungarian protocol on a 1961-62 plan for cooperation between academies of sciences was signed in Budapest.

March 28: Sino-North Korean protocol on the PRC and several light industrial construction projects was signed in Peking.

A Chinese Communist decision to sever all economic and trade relations with the Union of South Africa, "in support of the South African people's just struggle," was announced in a letter sent by China Council for the Promotion of International Trade to the South Africa United Front.

March 28-April 2: Chen Yi and his party arrived in Djakarta on March 28. A treaty of friendship between the PRC and Indonesia, a cultural cooperation agreement and a joint communique were signed. In the communique, Chen Yi reaffirmed Communist China's support for Indonesia's struggle to "recover West Irian" and Dr. Subandrio reaffirmed Indonesia's support for Communist China's struggle to "recover Taiwan" and for Peking's admission to the U.N. Chen Yi left Djakarta for home on April 2. Stopping in Rangoon on his way home, he called on Burmese Prime Minister U Nu on April 3, leaving Rangoon for home on April 4.

March 31: The PRC and North Korea signed in Pyongyang a 1961 plan for the implementation of their agreement on cultural cooperation.

April 4: A protocol covering the exchange of commodities between Ceylon and the

PRC in 1961 under the Sino-Ceylonese trade and payments agreement of 1957 was signed in Colombo.

The PRC and Czechoslovakia signed a plan in Prague for 1961 on the implementation of the cultural cooperation agreement between the two countries.

In exchange of notes, the PRC and Norway agreed on exemption of visa fees.

April 7: The Soviet Union and the PRC signed: (1) Protocol on exchange of goods in 1961; (2) agreement on postponement of repayment by the PRC of debts owed to U.S.S.R. on trade deals contracted in 1960; (3) protocol on delivery of raw sugar from the U.S.S.R. to the PRC.

A cultural cooperation plan for 1961 between the PRC and Mongolia was signed in Ulan Bator.

April 8: Differences in United States-British policies toward the PRC and its admission to the U.N. were reported to have been discussed at three days of talks between President Kennedy and British Prime Minister Harold MacMillan at the White House.

Joint Sino-Soviet communique announced conclusion of long-drawn-out trade talks, and its text had undertones of Soviet condescension toward Chinese agricultural difficulties.

April 8-10: A PRC government economic, scientific, and technical delegation arrived in Moscow on April 8. A plenary session of the PRC and Soviet government economic, scientific and technical delegation was held in Moscow on April 10 to discuss problems concerning the execution of the Sino-Soviet economic agreements and agreements on scientific and technical cooperation.

April 10: A 1961 plan for cooperation between the PRC and Czechoslovak academies of science was signed in Prague.

April 11: A Chinese-Finnish trade agreement for 1960 to 1961 was signed in Helsinki along with an exchange of notes on amendment of the 1953 payments agreement.

April 12-27: A. Kelleiz, Vice-Chairman of the Albanian council of ministers and

head of the Albanian government economic delegation, arrived in Peking on April 12. Four documents were signed on April 23 between Communist China and Albania. They were: (1) On the complete sets of equipment and technical assistance to be provided to Albania by China; (2) on the living conditions of the specialists, technicians, and trainees; (3) the No. 2 protocol on the use of the Chinese loan by the government of the People's Republic of Albania in pursuance of the Sino-Albanian loan agreement of February 2, 1961; (4) exchange of notes on supply of grains and other principal food-stuffs by the PRC to Albania.

April 15-May 15: The 1961 spring Export Commodities Fair opened in Canton on April 15 and closed on May 15.

April 16: At the end of Premier U Nu's visit to Peking, a joint communique was issued dealing with technical aid, support for convening Geneva Conference on Laos, Kuomintang troops in Burma, etc.

April 18: The PRC and North Vietnam signed a 1961 plan for the implementation of the cultural cooperation between the two countries. The PRC and Indonesia agreed on economic and technical cooperation in exchange of notes.

April 20: An executive plan for scientific cooperation for 1961 to 1962 between the academies of sciences of the PRC and Bulgaria was signed in Sofia.

A Sino-Cuban protocol on a 1961 plan for cultural cooperation was signed in Peking.

Sino-Laotian joint statement on talks during visit of Premier Souvanna Phouma and Prince Souphanouvong, Chairman of Neo Loo Haksat, in Hangchow to support convening Geneva Conference on the Laotian situation.

April 26: Chen Yi sent a message of congratulations to Minister for External Affairs John Karefa of Sierra Leone on the Proclamation of Independence of Sierra Leone, and informed him that the PRC government had decided to recognize that country.

April 26: A Sino-Mongolian communique on

trade talks was issued in Ulan Bator along with a treaty of commerce, and a protocol on exchange of goods in 1961.

April 28: The 1961 executive plan of the scientific cooperation agreement between the PRC and Rumanian academies of science was signed in Bucharest.

May 4: The PRC government issued a statement voicing support for the convocation of the Enlarged Geneva Conference.

Sino-Ceylonese minutes on talks on administration of air services were issued in Canton.

May 7-July 9: A report proposing the termination of the Panchen Kanpo Lija Committee was passed at the recent meeting of the Standing Committee of the Preparatory Committee for the Tibet Autonomous Region held in Lhasa with Panchen Erdeni in the chair. A decision on the determination of the Panchen Kanpo Lija Committee was passed at the plenary session of the State Council on July 9.

May 9: A Sino-Burmese communique on boundary demarcation was issued in Peking after the 6th session of the Sino-Burmese joint boundary committee.

May 10-June 9: The Chinese trade delegation, headed by Nan Han-chen, chairman of the China Council for the Promotion of International Trade, was received by President Quadros of Brazil on May 10 during its stay in Brazil. The delegation arrived in Buenos Aires on June 1 and was received by Argentine Under-Secretary of State of Commerce Doctor Garat on June 2. The delegation left for home on June 9.

May 10: A Sino-East German protocol on a 1961 plan for cultural cooperation was signed in Peking.

May 11: Chen Yi, the head of the PRC government delegation to the Enlarged Geneva Conference for the Peaceful Settlement of the Laotian Question, arrived in Geneva on May 11.

May 15: A Sino-Polish agreement on currency exchange and cash movements was signed in Warsaw.

A Sino-East German protocol on the exchange of goods and payments in 1961 was signed in Pcking.

May 17: At the press conference in Geneva on May 17, the spokesman of the PRC government delegation, Wu Leng-hsi, said the delegation fully supported the "two important proposals set forth by the Soviet delegation at the session on May 17— the draft declaration on neutrality of Laos and the draft agreement on the withdrawal of foreign troops and military personnel from the territory of Laos, and on the terms of reference of the International Commission."

May 24: In a speech at the session of the Geneva Conference on May 24, Chen Yi pointed out that any solution of the Laotian question must not run counter to the following principles: (1) It must be based on the 1954 Geneva Agreements; (2) it must strictly insure the neutrality of Laos; (3) it must respect the independence and sovereignty of Laos; (4) it must draw a sharp distinction between the internal and international aspects of the Laotian question. The internal problems can be solved only by Laotians themselves. Any international agreement must in no way interfere in the internal affairs of Laos; (5) all the participating nations must take part in, and strictly abide by, the common agreement.

A new civil airline linking Canton with the city of Samah, in the South of Hainan Island, was formally inaugurated, according to an NCNA dispatch.

May 25: An agreement on broadcasting and television cooperation between the PRC and the Soviet Union was signed in Peking.

The 1961 executive plan for the Sino-Bulgarian Cultural Cooperation Agreement was signed in Peking.

May 26: A Sino-Soviet agreement on cooperation between academies of sciences was signed in Moscow.

May 30-June 2: The Meeting of the Sino-Soviet joint committee for navigation on rivers bordering the two countries was held from May 30 to June 2 in Heiho in Northeast China's Heilungkiang Province.

June 4: The exchanges of territory under the Sino-Burmese frontier treaty of 1960 were carried out. In effect from date, the villages of Hpimaw, Gawleen and Kangfang (an area of 56 square miles) became Burmese territory; and the Namwan assigned trace (an area of 80 square miles) became Burmese territory; and the adjustment of the 1941 treaty line between the High Conical Peak and the Izurazi Pass was implemented, China taking the villages of Ywang Hok and Longnai, and Burma the villages of Umhua, Pangkeing, Pangnawng, and Pangwai.

June 8: The instruments of ratification of the Consular Treaty (signed on May 7, 1960) between the PRC and Czechoslovakia were exchanged in Peking.

June 12: Speaking at the session of the Geneva Conference on June 12, Chen Yi said that the draft protocol proposed by France "tramples on the sovereignty of Laos and interferes in its internal affairs." The British delegates asserted that protection of Laos by the Southeast Asia Treaty does not contradict the status of or respect for Laotian neutrality, the nonparticipation of Laos in military alliances, and the abstention of the other countries concerned from dragging Laos into any military alliance in South Vietnam. Referring to the above, a statement was issued by the PRC Ministry of Foreign Affairs stressing that the co-chairman and the other participating nations of the Geneva Conference should take effective steps to check U.S. intervention and aggression in South Vietnam, insure the implementation of the Geneva Agreement, and peace in Indochina and Southeast Asia.

June 13-15: President Sukarno and his party arrived in Peking on June 13, and were met at the airport by Liu Shao-chi. Sukarno was received by Mao Tse-tung in the afternoon and given a banquet by Liu Shao-chi in the evening. During the stay a ceremony for the exchange of the instruments of ratification of treaty of friendship between the two countries, and notes on the approval of the agreement on cultural cooperation between the two countries was held. Mao and Sukarno had

breakfast together on June 15 shortly before the guest left for home.

June 15: A friendly joint communique was signed between Chou En-lai and Mr. Pham Van Dong, after a visit by the Prime Minister of North Vietnam to Peking. The communique deals with anti-imperialism, U.S. intervention in South Vietnam, Geneva Conference on Laos, the PRC representation on U.N., etc.

A Sino-East German agreement on currency exchange and cash movements was signed.

June 15-19: A 25-member economic mission from Nigeria headed by F.S. Okotie-Eboh visited Communist China June 15-19.

June 19: The delegation of the Chinese-African People's Friendship Association returned to Peking on June 19 from a four-month African tour covering such areas as Guinea, Mali, Ghana, Niger, Upper Volta, Senegal, Togo, and Dahomey.

Agreements on Sino-Soviet economic, scientific and technical cooperation were signed in Moscow.

June 21: A protocol on scientific cooperation between the academies of sciences of the PRC and Soviet Union and a program for its implementation were signed in Moscow.

June 27: Secretary of State Dean Rusk said that United States "moratorium formula of seeking postponement of issue at beginning of each U.N. General Assembly session would no longer suffice." He also said that the United States would try to have the issue handled as substantive matter, requiring a two-thirds majority vote, instead of mere credential matters.

July 1: The 40th anniversary of the CPC was celebrated at meetings and gatherings in all parts of Communist China. In a speech at a grand rally of over 10,000 people in Peking, Liu Shao-chi gave the present total number of party members as 17,000,000, of which 80% had joined the party since the founding of the PRC and 10% since 1953.

Instruments of ratification of the treaty

of friendship between the PRC and Guinea, signed on September 13, 1960, were exchanged.

July 2: The *London Sunday Times* reported that Soviet Premier Khrushchev had sent a letter to the leaders of all Communist parties denouncing the Chinese for what he felt was an overly aggressive policy. Peking's Taiwan policy was said to have come in for special criticism because it risked all-out war. On the same day it was learned that no Soviet officials had attended the celebration in Peking of the 40th anniversary of the founding of the CPC.

July 4: Contracts on the exchange of documentary film copies and on distribution of Chinese films in Guinea were signed in Conakry by the Chinese Film Corporation and the cinema office of the Guinean ministry.

July 7: A protocol on the exchange of goods and payments for 1961 between the PRC and Rumania was signed in Bucharest.

July 10: A Sino-Polish protocol on general conditions for delivery of goods was signed in Warsaw.

July 11: Kim Il Sung and Chou En-lai signed a treaty of friendship, cooperation, and mutual assistance between the PRC and North Korea. In this, provisions were as follows: (1) Military assistance to the other state if attacked; (2) conclude no alliance directed against the other; (3) consultations on international issues affecting both; (4) strengthening cultural and economic contacts; (5) unification of Korea carried out in a peaceful and democratic manner; (6) aid in maintaining peace in the Far East. A joint communique was issued on July 15.

July 12: A contract on distribution of Chinese films in Mali was signed in Bamako by the China Film Distribution and Exhibition Corporation and the Mali Ministry of Interior, Information and Tourism.

July 13: A Sino-Polish agreement on trade turnover and payments for 1961 was signed in Warsaw.

July 14: Sino-Tunisian accord on organiza-tion of week-long festival of PRC films in Tunisia was signed in Peking.

July 15: The 1961 protocol on exchange of goods in 1961 between the PRC and Yugoslavia was signed in Peking.

A protocol on goods exchange and payments between the PRC and Hungary for 1961 was signed in Budapest on July 15 along with an agreement on currency exchange and cash movements.

July 20: A Sino-Vietnamese protocol on a 1961 plan for scientific and technical cooperation was signed in Hanoi.

July 22: The instruments of ratification of the Treaty of Commerce and Navigation signed on February 2, 1961, between PRC and Albania were exchanged by the two governments.

August 3: The PRC and Cambodia exchanged notes in Phnom Penh to agree on the extension of 1956 trade and payments agreements.

August 6: The successful flight of the second Soviet manned spaceship, "Vostok II," was warmly hailed in Communist China. Messages of congratulation were sent by the Chinese party and government leaders.

August 7: An agreement on the establishment of a cotton textile mill by the Ceylonese government with aid from the PRC was reached in Colombo by exchange of letters.

The Canadian Minister of Agriculture, Mr. Hamilton, stated in Ottawa that on instructions from the Chinese Communist government part of the wheat bought by China from Canada earlier this year was being shipped to Albania, the quantity involved being 2,200,000 bushels, worth $3,000,000.

August 13: Chinese Communist party hierarchy held a conference in Hangchow to discuss economic problems, administration, mass discontent, and the general uncertainty of national diirection.

August 14-20: President Nkrumah of Ghana, during his extensive tour of the Soviet Union, the East European countries, and China, arrived in Peking for a six-day state visit. President Nkrumah's visit ended with the signing of a treaty of friendship between China and Ghana and of agreements on economic and technical cooperation, trade and payments, and cultural cooperation. A joint statement, issued in Peking on August 18, expressed the hope that the forthcoming Belgrade conference of unaligned countries would make a positive contribution to the struggle of the Asian, African, and Latin American peoples against imperialism and colonialism and in defense of peace; expressed Ghana's support for the admission of the PRC to the U.N. and her condemnation of the "plot of two Chinas"; and expressed China's support for Ghana and other African countries in winning the complete liberation of Africa, opposing the imperialist attempt to split Africa, and strengthening the solidarity of the African peoples.

August 21: The PRC and Brazil signed an agreement on trade and payments.

August 24: The PRC and Nepal issued a communique on boundary demarcation in Katmandu after the third session of Sino-Nepalese Joint Boundary Committee.

August 26: A Sino-Soviet communique on trade talks was issued in Peking.

August 31: A Sino-Mongolian protocol on joint railways was signed in Huhehot.

The PRC government issued a statement supporting the Soviet government's decision to conduct experimental explosions of nuclear weapons.

September 5: The PRC and Ethiopia issued a communique in Peking on promotion of political, economic, and cultural cooperation.

A Sino-Nepalese protocol on economic aid was signed in Katmandu along with the exchange of letters on working conditions for the PRC experts and technicians in Nepal.

September 7: At the Enlarged Geneva Conference of Laotian Question, Chang Han-fu made a statement on September 1 rejecting the article in the United States draft which stipulated that the Laotian parties inform the International Commission of national defense secrets of Laos.

September 8: The spokesman for the in-

formation department of the Ministry of Foreign Affairs announced the PRC government's decision to withdraw the Chinese embassy in the Congo (Stanleyville).

September 10: Letters of ratification of the Sino-North Korean treaty of friendship, cooperation and mutual assistance were exchanged in Pyongyang (signed on July 11, 1961).

September 11: A Sino-Cuban agreement on the exchange of feature films was signed along with another agreement on exchange of newsreels and documentary films.

September 17: Changes in administrative demarcation in Communist China as effected from January 1 to July 31, 1961, and from August 1 to August 31, 1961, were published in the September 17 issue of the *People's Daily*. Changes in administrative demarcations as effected in Communist China from September 1 to October 31, 1961, were made public in an NCNA dispatch on November 19.

September 18: A Sino-Guinean protocol on economic and technical aid was signed in Conakry.

September 20: A Sino-Polish protocol on scientific and technical cooperation was signed in Peking.

September 21: A protocol for implementing the current Sino-Afghan agreement on the exchange of goods and payments in 1961 was signed in Kabul.

The U.N. General Assembly's steering committee voted to recommend debate on the question of Chinese representation. In a change of policy, the United States supported the proposed debate instead of seeking to have it postponed a year.

September 22: It was announced in Conakry that Guinea and the PRC had signed an agreement under which Chinese engineers and technicians would work on a number of projects in Guinea, including a new National Assembly building and a tobacco factory (Sino-Mali agreement on economic and technical cooperation was signed in Peking).

A resolution on setting up the election committee of the Tibet Autonomous Region to direct the election of deputies to the People's Congresses at various levels in Tibet was passed on September 19 at an enlarged meeting of the Standing Committee of the Preparatory Committee for the Tibet Autonomous Region. It was also declared at the enlarged meeting that the State Council had passed a resolution appointing seven vice-chairmen for the Preparatory Committee for the Tibetan Autonomous Region to strengthen its work.

September 23: The PRC and Denmark exchanged notes in Copenhagen to agree on reciprocal tax exemptions to students.

September 25-October 19: Queen Elizabeth, grandmother of the Belgian King, and her party of eight arrived in Peking on September 25 and visited Kweilin, Shanghai, and other cities of China before leaving Peking for home on October 19.

October 1: The 12th anniversary of the Communist takeover celebrated in Peking, with the absence of any important Soviet delegates. Economic plight and widespread apathy discussed along with the report that the heavy cost of grain imports had major effect on the economy.

October 2: The PRC and Cuba issued a joint communique in Peking on the talks during visit of President Porticos, covering such subjects as anti-imperialism, PRC representation in U.N., Guantanamo Base, Taiwan, etc.

October 5: King Mahenara of Nepal and President Liu Shao-chi signed a Sino-Nepalese boundary treaty in Peking.

The State Council made a decision on setting up customs houses in the Tibet Region, and the "Provisional regulations governing the levying of import and export duties for the Tibet Region of the PRC."

October 6: A Sino-Soviet protocol on scientific and technical cooperation in first half of 1962 signed in Peking along with a plan for cooperation between academies of sciences during fourth quarter of 1961 and first half of 1962.

October 7: The PRC and royal government of Laos agreed to establish consulates at Phong Saly in Laos and at Kunming in China respectively.

A Sino-Ceylonese protocol on exchange of goods in 1962 was signed in Peking.

October 8: A Sino-Ceylonese joint communique on trade talks was issued in Peking.

October 11-12: Chen Yi and Maamun Kugbari, Premier and Foreign Minister of the Arab Syrian Republic, exchanged cables on October 11 and 12 in connection with the establishment of diplomatic relations.

October 11: A Sino-Indonesian agreement on economic and technical cooperation was signed in Peking.

October 13: Foreign Minister Chen Yi and Dr. Qiri signed an agreement on the building of a highway from Tibet to Katmandu, providing for Chinese aid and technical assistance for the section of the read inside Nepal. A joint communique on talks during King Mahendra's visit was also issued dealing with the Five Principles of Peaceful Co-existence, the ten principles of the Bandung Conference, Sino-Nepalese economic cooperation, etc.

October 18: An agreement for renewal of the trade agreement concluded between the PRC and Iraq in May 1960 was signed in Baghdad along with an extension of the 1960 trade agreement.

October 19: At the Soviet Communist Party Congress, Chou En-lai expressed full support for the Soviet government's foreign policy and the principles of peaceful co-existence and general disarmament, but declared that as long as imperialism was preserved, there would be soil for aggressive war. However, he deplored any public one-sided censure of a fraternal party, although without referring explicitly to Albania. He left for Peking on October 23 without waiting for the end of the Congress, although the other members of the Chinese delegation remained in Moscow.

A new 68-kilometer long high-tension transmission line went into operation to power pumping stations being built on the Pearl River in southern-most Kwangtung Province.

October 20: A Sino-Czechoslovak protocol

137

on exchange of goods and payments in 1961-62 was signed in Prague.

October 21: A Sino-Cuban agreement on tele-communications and postal services was signed in Havana.

October 27: A payments agreement was signed between the PRC and Morocco in Rabat.

October 30: A Sino-North Korean protocol on scientific and technical cooperation was signed in Pyongyang.

November 1: The PRC and Ghana signed the following six documents in Peking: (1) Protocol on implementation in 1961-62 of trade and payments agreement of August 18, 1961; (2) exchange of letters on a 1962 plan for cultural cooperation; (3) exchange of letters on trade; (4) exchange of letters on economic and technical cooperation; (5) undertaking on a technical banking arrangement for implementation of Economic and Technical Cooperation Agreement of August 18, 1961; (6) undertaking on a technical banking arrangement for implementation of the Trade and Payments Agreement of August 18, 1961.

November 2: The PRC and Ghana issued a joint communique on trade talks in Peking.

November 8: The CPC Central Committee asserted in a message to the Albanian Communist Party on its 20th anniversary that the Chinese-Albanian alliance "can be shaken by no force on earth."

Lin Piao issued an order commending the anti-aircraft unit which shot down a U.S.-made P-2U plane of the Nationalist government on November 6 over Liatung Peninsula in Northeast Asia.

November 22: New "Regulations Governing Joint Inspection of Ships Clearing or Entering Ports" were made public by the Ministries of Transport, Foreign Trade, Public Security, and Public Health.

November 24: The PRC and North Korea agreed to an extension of the 1956 protocol on the transportation of timber on the Yalu and Tumen Rivers.

November 25: The 1961-62 executive plan

for the Sino-Iraqui cultural cooperation agreement was signed in Baghdad.

December 3: A Sino-Ceylonese agreement on exchange of Ceylonese sheet rubber for price from the PRC was signed.

December 6: The PRC Foreign Ministry, in a statement dated December 6 on the Sino-Indian boundary question, refuted the charge made recently by the Indian government and Prime Minister Nehru that Communist China had renewed incursions and aggressive activities against India. The texts of eight notes exchanged between the PRC and Indian governments were published in full by all Peking papers.

December 7-21: A 31-member government economic delegation of Burma headed by Thakin Tin, minister of finance, arrived in Peking on December 7. A protocol to the Sino-Burmese agreement on economic and technical cooperation and a Sino-Burmese protocol on the purchase of Burmese rice in 1962 were signed in Peking on December 13. Two letters were exchanged between the Chinese and Burmese governments on December 21. One is a supplement to the protocol to the Sino-Burmese Agreement on Economic and Technical Cooperation and the other concerns Sino-Burmese technical cooperation.

December 8-11: Chou En-lai and Chen Yi sent messages of greeting to the Prime Minister of Tanganyika on December 8, congratulating him on the proclaiming of independence of Tanganyika. They also sent messages on December 11 greeting the establishment of diplomatic relations between the two countries.

December 14: The Chinese Communist Party tightened control over the army through new regulations, giving wide power to the political commissars.

December 15: The U.N. General Assembly, by 48-37-19, rejected a U.S.S.R. resolution to unseat Nationalist China and seat the Chinese Communists. It approved, by 61-34-7, the five-nation proposal providing that any new General Assembly resolution dealing with Chinese representation would require a two-thirds majority vote for adoption. It also rejected, by 45-30-20, the three-power proposal to admit Communist China without expelling Nationalist China.

December 17-25: The NPC Standing Committee adopted a decision to grant pardons to a group of "war criminals of the Chiang Kai-shek clique" and the puppet "Manchukuo." The PRC Supreme People's Court pardoned and released on December 25 sixty-eight "war criminals."

December 19: The PRC issued a statement supporting the Indian government in recovering Goa.

December 21: The Canadian minister of agriculture announced that Canada had signed a new agreement with Communist China for sale of $71 million worth of wheat and barley.

December 26: An agreement on the formation of a Sino-Albanian joint stock shipping company was signed between the PRC and Albania in Peking.

December 27: A ceremony for handing over the Ulan Bator Tizhogoited power station to Mongolia was held in Ulan Bator. The station was built by the PRC in the form of a long-term loan to Mongolia.

December 31: Chou En-lai sent a message of congratulations to the head of Western Samoa on the proclamation of independence of that country.

The Chinese Communist Party and state leaders exchanged New Year greetings with Soviet Communist party and state leaders. A message of greetings was addressed jointly to N. S. Khrushchev and L. I. Brezhnev by Mao Tse-tung, Liu Shao-chi, Chu Teh, and Chou En-lai. They received in return greetings from the two Soviet leaders.

1962

January 5: The first session in 1962 of the 7-month Enlarged Geneva Conference on the Laotian question unanimously adopted a message from the co-chairmen to the three Laotian princes.

January 8: The 1962 Sino-North Korean goods exchange agreement was signed in Pyongyang.

January 13: The PRC and Laos signed in Khang Khay, provincial capital of Laos in Xieng Khouang Province, an agreement on the building of a highway from Yunnan Province and Phong Saly. Also signed was an air transport agreement.

The 1962 executive plan of the cultural cooperation agreement between the PRC and Mongolia was signed in Peking.

The PRC and Albania signed the following five documents: (1) Agreement on the granting of a loan by the PRC; (2) exchange of notes on supply of complete sets of equipment and technical aid by the PRC; (3) protocol on exchange of goods and payments in 1962; (4) protocol on use of the PRC credits by Albania in 1962; (5) protocol on scientific and technical cooperation.

January 15: A Sino-Albanian press communique on economic talks was issued in Peking.

January 20: A Sino-North Vietnamese protocol on the mutual supply of goods and payments in 1962 was signed in Hanoi. The two states also exchanged notes to extend their 1955 protocol on small-scale trading in border areas and their 1955 protocol on exchange of goods between local state training companies in border areas.

The work of receiving declarations of choice by those adults who hold dual nationality in accordance with the Treaty of Dual Nationality between the PRC and Indonesia was concluded on January 20.

January 23: A Sino-Soviet protocol on a plan for cultural cooperation in 1962 was signed in Moscow.

January 27: A radio and television cooperation agreement and a protocol of the agreement for 1962 were signed in Havana between the Chinese Broadcasting Administration Bureau and the Cuban Office of Orientation and Coordination of Radio Broadcasting.

February 2: The 1962 executive plan of the Sino-Hungarian cultural cooperation agreement was signed in Budapest.

February 7: The PRC and Ceylon exchanged notes in Colombo agreeing on reciprocal recognition of ships' papers.

February 14: At a news conference, President Kennedy said the Chinese Communists would have to be included in any disarmament among the world powers before the United States "would be able to have any confidence in" such an agreement.

February 17: The 1962 executive plan of the cultural cooperation between the PRC and Rumania was signed in Bucharest.

February 18: A protest note handed over by the PRC Ministry of Foreign Affairs to the Indian embassy on January 24 was published in Peking on February 18. The note dealt with the encroaching by an Indian plane on China's territorial air, its illegal air-dropping on a Chinese frontier post, and deliberate provocation.

February 24: The PRC Foreign Ministry charged the United States action in South Vietnam was "a direct threat" to North Vietnam and therefore "seriously affects the security of China and the peace of Asia." It charged that a recently established military command in South Vietnam was "by no means merely one for military assistance but an operational command of the United States imperialists for direct participation . . . The United States is already in an undeclared war in South Vietnam." Peking urged Britain and the Soviet Union, co-chairmen of the 1954 Geneva Conference, to take "appropriate measures" regarding U.S. intervention in the area. The Soviet Union echoed Chinese sentiments, but the British replied that "the tension in South Vietnam arises directly from the North Vietnamese effort to overthrow the established government by force."

The PRC denounced the Japan-South Korea talks which, it was pointed out, were being manipulated by "U.S. imperialism" to "throw together a Northeast Asian military alliance."

February 25: A Sino-Mongolian protocol on the mutual supply of goods in 1962 was signed in Peking.

February 28: The 1962 executive plan for the implementation of the agreement of cultural cooperation between the PRC and Poland was signed in Warsaw.

The Peking Museum of National History was formally opened to the public after several years' preparation. The 5,000 specimens as well as large numbers of models, paintings and dioramas on display give a vivid picture of the revolutionary changes and developments of animal and plant life since earliest times.

March 2: An agreement was signed between the PRC and Pakistan, which provided for the setting up of a joint border commission to determine the border between the respective countries. (It must be noted here that the area which is under negotiation is under dispute between India and Pakistan also.) After the announcement of the agreement an Indian note was sent to Communist China and Pakistan saying that they had no legal right to negotiate on this question.

March 6: Chen Yi sent a message to the Burmese Foreign Minister, U Thi Han, informing him that the PRC had decided to recognize the new government of Burma.

March 7: A Sino-Czechoslovak agreement on currency exchange and cash movements was signed in Peking.

March 9: The Chinese Communist press denounced the U.S. resumption of atmosphere nuclear tests. The *People's Daily* carried an editorial entitled: "Nuclear Weapons Will Not Destroy Man, Man Will Destroy Nuclear Weapons."

March 11: A contract for the purchase of 24,000 tons of Iraqui dates by the PRC was signed in Baghdad.

March 16: Indian Prime Minister Nehru told the parliament in New Delhi that the Chinese Communists had expressed hope that the two countries could reach an "early" settlement of their border dispute. Nehru said he had replied that "Peaceful withdrawal of Chinese forces from territories which have traditionally been a part of India is necessary to lay the foundations for fresh negotiations."

March 17: The PRC and the UAR signed a trade agreement, a payments agreement, and the 1962 trade protocol in Peking.

March 18: The PRC and Yemen signed a protocol in Taizz, under which the PRC will send ten experts and an interpreter to Yemen to help in the maintenance of the Sana-Hodeidan highway built with Chinese assistance.

March 23-April 18: The third session of the 3rd National Committee of the CPPCC was held in Peking from March 23 through April 18. The session adopted a resolution approving Chen Shu-tung's report and warmly supporting the report made by Chou En-lai on government work. It also adopted a resolution on the examination of motions.

March 27: The PRC State Council at its plenary meeting decided to put the civil aviation administration of China, originally under the Ministry of Communications, directly under the State Council. It also approved certain changes in administrative divisions of *hsien* (autonomous region) and municipalities in the provinces of Hopei, Shansi, Kiangsu, Honan, Kwangtung, Kwangsi, and Yunnan.

A Sino-Polish protocol on extension of the 1961 protocol on general conditions for delivery of goods was signed in Peking.

March 27-April 16: The second NPC held its 3rd session in Peking from March 27 to April 16. The session adopted a resolution on the government work reported by Chou En-lai. It also approved the report on the work of the NPC Standing Committee, the report of budget committee, the views of the motions examination committee and the report of the credentials committee on the examination of the credentials of deputies elected in by-elections.

Chou En-lai's work report showed that hereafter emphasis would be laid on the development of agriculture. More daily necessities would be available, as he called for "making a rational arrangement for the production of light and heavy industry and increasing the output of daily necessities as much as possible." He also pointed out in his report that "it is necessary to continue to unite the patriotic elements of the national bourgeoisie and help them further in educating and remolding themselves and to prolong the period of paying a fixed rate of interest to them for three years beginning with 1963."

March 28: A Sino-Polish goods turnover and payments agreement for 1962 was signed in Peking.

Instruments of ratification of the treaty of friendship between the PRC and the Republic of Ghana were exchanged in Accra (signed on August 18, 1961).

The PRC negotiated another in a series of grain purchases with Canada. This provided for the sale of 39,800,000 bushels of wheat worth approximately $73,000,-000.

March 29: A Sino-Finnish agreement on trade in 1961-62 was signed in Peking.

March 30: The 1962 protocol on goods exchange and payments between the PRC and Bulgaria was signed in Sofia.

At a press conference, President Kennedy tried to discourage the view that the United States would back Nationalist attacks on Communists. He said that the United States must consider the responsibility. Although Chiang Kai-shek urged early action to overthrow Communists in Taipei, American administrative officials said that the United States would not back an invasion attempt.

A Sino-Hungarian agreement on exchange of goods and payments in 1962 was signed in Peking.

April 3: The 1962 executive plan for Sino-

Czechoslovak cultural cooperation agreement was signed in Peking.

April 7: The Chinese reply to the Soviet letter (February 22) proposed, as preliminary steps toward a new international communist conference, the ending of public attacks; bilateral or multilateral talks between parties; and the restoration of normal relations between the Soviet and Albanian governments and Communist parties, with the U.S.S.R. taking the initiative.

April 11: The NCNA and the Albanian Telegraph Agency (ATA) signed a cooperation agreement in Tirana.

April 12: The NCNA reported that 50,000 relics, including prehistoric human fossils, tombs, utensils and remains of ancient buildings have been unearthed in recent years in Inner Mongolia.

April 13: The Sino-Albanian Joint Stock Shipping Company opened a general office in Durrea.

The PRC Ministry of Foreign Affairs made public seven notes on the Sino-Indian boundary question exchanged between the Chinese and Indian governments.

April 15: The 1962 spring export commodities fair opened in Canton on April 15 and closed after a nine-month run.

April 17: The PRC and the U.S.S.R. adopted a joint resolution for a joint survey of the Heilungkiang River valley.

April 18: A 1962 plan for the implementation of the cultural cooperation agreement between the PRC and Bulgaria was signed in Sofia.

April 20: A Sino-Soviet protocol on exchange of goods in 1962 was signed in Peking.

April 21: A report prepared by a United States government agency for Congress, details of which were published, estimated the total membership of Communist parties throughout the world at about 40,000,000 including over 16,000,000 in countries of the Communist bloc. China was reported to have 17,000,000 members, representing the largest communist party in the world.

April 22-27: A conference on international railway traffic through North Vietnam, China, North Korea, Mongolia, and the Soviet Union was held in Peking from April 22 to April 27. The conference examined the implementation of the plan for international through freight traffic in the past year, and worked out the 1962 plan and measures for insuring its fulfillment. A protocol was signed.

April 23: India notified the PRC that a 1954 trade agreement, due to expire June 3, would not be renewed until Chinese forces had withdrawn from traditionally Indian territory.

April 25: The PRC Ministry of Foreign Affairs published a note to the Indian government dated April 21, 1962, seriously protesting against the further violation of Chinese territory by Indian military men who repeatedly crossed the boundary in the western sector and intruded into the Sinkiang-Uighur Autonomous Region of China.

A Sino-Cuban protocol on trade in 1962 was signed in Havana.

April 29: Liu Shao-chi and Chou En-lai sent formal congratulations to Chairman Brezhenev and Premier Khrushchev on their reelections. The formality was seen as a sign of strain in U.S.S.R.-China ties.

April 30: A Sino-North Korean protocol on a plan for cultural cooperation in 1962 was signed in Peking.

May 2: The PRC government lodged a strong protest with the Indian government against the "intrusions of Indian troops into China's Sinkiang region, the establishment of new Indian military posts, continued provocative activities and menace to the security of a Chinese frontier post."

May 3: Official announcement was made in Peking and Rawalpindi that China and Pakistan agreed to conduct negotiations for the delimitation and demarcation of their common border. A protestation by India stated that Pakistan had no legal right to initiate border talks since there was no common border between Pakistan and China.

May 7: A Sino-Soviet accord on shipping survey and registration was signed in Peking.

A Sino-Albanian protocol on shipping was signed in Tirana.

May 8: The PRC Foreign Ministry sent a note to the Indian embassy in Peking expressing great surprise and regret at the rude impolite rejection by the Indian government of the invitation sent by the All-China Federation of Trade Unions to the All-India Trade Union Congress to send delegates to visit China and take part in May Day celebrations.

May 12: All Peking papers devoted wide coverage to six poems written by Mao Tse-tung between 1929 and 1931. They described the growth of the peasant movement and the widespread unfolding of the land reform movement in the revolutionary base of Kiangsi Province, and the continuing victories of the workers' and peasants' Red Army, with the support of the peasant masses, in wiping out "reactionary troops of the Kuomintang."

May 13: A protocol to the Sino-Soviet agreement of June 19, 1961, on economic cooperation was signed in Peking by the trade and economic delegation of the PRC and the Soviet Union.

May 14: The PRC government lodged a serious protest with the Indian government against the "intrusion and provocation" by Indian troops in the area south of Spanggur Lake in western Tibet.

May 19: The PRC government lodged a serious protest with the Indian government against "the act of provocation by Indian troops which constituted a grave violation of Chinese territory at Longju in the Tibet region of China."

May 22: A Sino-Polish protocol on a 1962 plan for cooperation between academies of sciences was signed in Peking.

May 23: President Kennedy at his press conference said that the United States would ease its Chinese immigration quota to admit several thousands of most eligible refugees. On the prospects of a Food for Peace Program for mainland China, he commented, "There has been no indication of any expression of interest or desire by the Chinese Communists to receive any food from us as I have said from the beginning, and we would certainly have to have some ideas as to whether the food was needed and under what conditions it might be distributed. Up to the present, we have no such indications."

A Sino-Sudan agreement on trade was signed in Peking.

The PRC and Cambodia exchanged notes agreeing on reciprocal recognition of ships' papers.

May 28: The PRC government lodged a strong protest with the Indian government against its "further intrusions and provocations" and demanded that India immediately evacuate its military strongpoints set up recently in Chinese territory and put an end to all its "unlawful intrusions."

The PRC and Ceylon exchanged notes to extend their 1957 economic aid agreement.

May 29: The 1962 protocol on Sino-Rumanian goods exchange and payments was signed in Peking.

May 30: The PRC government lodged a serious protest with the Indian government and demanded that it immediately stop recent "intrusions" of Indian aircraft into China's air space.

May 31: India protested to China that proposed negotiations between China and Pakistan over the Kashmir border formed a part of China's "aggressive designs" against Indian territory. India asserted that Pakistan had no right to negotiate a Kashmir border agreement because Kashmir belonged to India. The Chinese replied that India was pursuing a policy of "out-and-out power chauvinism." On June 2 India announced it would not renew its trade agreement with Tibet because of China's refusal to discuss Indian-Tibetan border problems.

The PRC and Mongolia made a joint arrangement to implement their 1960 agreement on scientific and technical cooperation.

June 1: The PRC Ministry of Foreign Affairs made public a note dated May 29, 1962, sent by the Ministry to the Indian embassy in Peking, which lodged a protest with the Indian government against its confiscation of the news bulletins of the PRC embassy in India.

June 3: The first Chinese family got a United States entry visa under the Kennedy emergency program.

June 4: The PRC Foreign Ministry published the note dated May 31, sent by the PRC government to the Indian government, categorically rejecting the "unjustifiable" protest of that government, which is contained in an Indian note dated May 10, against Sino-Pakistan negotiations for a provisional boundary agreement.

A Sino-Mongolian protocol on a plan for scientific and technical cooperation in 1962 was signed in Peking.

June 7: The PRC Foreign Ministry sources told NCNA that the charges raised by Indian government officials recently about the PRC having imposed special restrictions on the movements of Indian diplomatic personnel in Communist China was utterly unfounded.

June 11: Chou En-lai sent a message of greeting to Prince Souvanna Phouma on the complete agreement reached by the three Laotian princes for the formation of a Laotian National Union Government.

June 15: The annual executive plan of the scientific cooperation agreement between the academies of sciences of the PRC and North Korea was signed in Peking.

June 17: The PRC Ministry of Education announced regulations governing enrollment of new students at institutes of higher learning in 1962.

The PRC shelled Quemoy. It was reported that Communist troops and jet planes opposite Quemoy and Matsu constituted the largest build-up since 1950, sufficient for attack on offshore islands, but not Taiwan. United States sources linked build-up to Nationalist invasion threats.

June 18: The PRC government lodged a strong protest with the Indian government against the "atrocity" committed by Indian troops in a recent serious border incident. In the incident, it was pointed out, Indian troops intruded north of the MacMahon Line and shot peaceful inhabitants of Tibet, on the eastern sector of the Sino-Indian boundary.

June 19: The PRC government banned construction of all non-productive buildings.

June 21: White House press secretary, Mr. Salinger, issued a statement expressing "serious concern" of the United States government at a large build-up of Chinese ground and air forces on the mainland opposite the Nationalist-held islands of Quemoy and Matsu.

June 22: Bulgaria, Hungary, North Vietnam, East Germany, North Korea, Poland, Rumania, the U.S.S.R., Czechoslovakia, and the PRC signed a multilateral protocol for adoption and revision of various regulations on railway cooperation and administration.

June 23: Chen Yi sent a message to Quinim Pholsena, Minister of Foreign Affairs of the Laotian government, stating China had decided to recognize the Laotian Provisional National Union government.

A Communist Chinese broadcast alleged that the Nationalists were preparing "a large-scale military adventure" against China, with firm support from the United States. It gave warning to U.S. Ambassador John M. Cabot in Poland against military action by the United States.

A Sino-Soviet protocol on a 1962-63 plan for scientific and technical cooperation was signed in Moscow.

June 25: A protocol on scientific and technical cooperation between the PRC and Poland was signed in Warsaw.

June 26: The United States told Peking that it would not support Nationalist attempt to attack mainland. The stand was conveyed by Ambassador Cabot to Chinese Ambassador Wang Ping-nan at Warsaw with warning that the United States was committed to defend Nationalists against an attack on Taiwan and the Pescadores.

June 27: President Kennedy told newsmen that the United States would "take necessary action to assure the defense of Tai-

wan and the Pescadores" provided for in the 1955 Congressional Taiwan Resolution if Communist China were to take "aggressive action against" Quemoy and Matsu. Kennedy said that any threat to the off-shore islands must be judged in relation to its wider meaning for the safety of Taiwan and the peace of the area.

June 28: A commodity exchange protocol for 1962 was signed in Belgrade between the PRC and Yugoslavia.

The PRC government lodged a serious protest with the Indian government and demanded that it immediately stop "its intrusions into China's air space."

June 30-July 21: The PRC government delegation to the Enlarged Geneva Conference, led by Chang Han-fu, arrived in Geneva on June 30. Following the installation of the coalition government in Vientiane, the 14-nation Geneva Conference on Laos resumed its work. Members of the Conference, besides Britain and the U.S.S.R. (co-chairmen) were the United States, France, India, Communist China, Cambodia, Laos, Canada, Poland, North Vietnam, South Vietnam, Thailand, and Burma.

The Laotian government announced on July 2 that it had decided to exchange diplomatic representatives at the ambassadorial level with Communist China, North Vietnam, East Germany, Poland, and Czechoslovakia.

Chen Yi, head of the delegation of the PRC to the Enlarged Geneva Conference on Laos, arrived in Geneva via Moscow on July 17. Chen Yi spoke at the Geneva Conference on July 21. He said: "What is most important is that peace should be restored in South Vietnam. The tension in South Vietnam was created by the United States government's refusal to undertake the international obligations under the 1954 Geneva Agreement and its perpetration of armed intervention there . . . So long as the flames of war are kept alive in South Vietnam, peace cannot be regarded as consolidated."

On July 21, the Geneva Conference

held its final plenary session and passed a declaration on the neutrality of Laos and a protocol to the declaration (signed by Burma, Cambodia, Canada, France, India, Poland, Thailand, the United Kingdom, the United States, the U.S.S.R., North Vietnam, South Vietnam, and the PRC).

July 1: Chen Yi sent a message to Andre Muhirova, Prime Minister of the Kingdom of Burundi, congratulating him on the proclamation of independence of Burundi and informing him of the decision of the PRC government to recognize that country.

Chen Yi sent a message to Gregorie Kayibanda, Prime Minister of the Republic of Rwanda, congratulating him on the proclamation of independence of Rwanda and informing him of the decision of the PRC government to recognize that country.

A Sino-Czechoslovak protocol on scientific and technical cooperation was signed in Peking.

July 2: Soviet Premier Khrushchev warned during a television broadcast from Moscow that "anyone who dares attack Communist China" will meet a crushing rebuff from the great Chinese people, the people of the Soviet Union, and the whole socialist camp." On the same day Secretary of State Dean Rusk called Khrushchev's statement "nonsense." He said the United States instead of being "aggressive" had urged the "abandonment of force in settling matters in the Taiwan Strait."

July 3: Chen Yi sent a cable to Saad Dahlab, Foreign Minister of the provincial government of the Republic of Algeria, congratulating him on the proclamation of independence of Algeria and informing him that the PRC government had decided to recognize that state.

July 5: The PRC and Cambodia exchanged notes in Phnom Penh to extend 1956 trade and payments agreements.

July 8: The PRC government lodged a strong protest against "a recent fresh serious instrusion by Indian troops into the Sinkiang region of China."

July 9: Guinea and the PRC concluded a trade protocol for 1962 in Conakry.

July 10: A New Delhi announcement stated that an Indian post in Ladakh had been surrounded by some 400 Chinese troops who had taken up positions within 50 yards of the outpost. China replied by a note denying the Indian charges and accusing India herself of setting up four military strongpoints in Sinkaing province as a smokescreen for an armed invasion— an allegation described by the Indian External Affairs Ministry as a "tissue of lies."

July 13: The PRC Foreign Ministry in a note to the Indian embassy in Peking made a further statement on the "Indian troops" intrusion into the Galway Valley in China's Sinkiang Province in a deliberate attempt to provoke an armed clash and refuted the note sent by the Indian government on July 10.

July 16: The PRC Foreign Ministry in a note to the Indian embassy in Peking protested strongly against the "establishment of three additional strongpoints by Indian troops in Asi, Tibet, China, and against serious new Indian military intrusions and provocations."

July 17: The 1962 goods exchange and payments protocol between the PRC and Czechoslovakia was signed in Peking.

A Sino-Rumanian protocol on scientific and technical cooperation was signed in Bucharest.

July 18: The 1962 protocol for exchange of goods between the PRC and the Kingdom of Afghanistan was signed in Kabul.

July 20: The PRC Ministry of Finance made an announcement concerning the redemption of state economic construction funds with interest.

The 1962 executive plan for the Sino-Cuban cultural cooperation agreement was signed in Havana.

The PRC and Czechoslovakia exchanged notes in Peking to extend their 1952 agreement on scientific and technical cooperation.

A Sino-German protocol on scientific and technical cooperation was signed in Berlin.

July 21: A Sino-Soviet protocol on a plan for cooperation between academies of sciences in 1962 was signed in Moscow.

July 22-26: The PRC Foreign Ministry delivered a note to the Indian embassy in Peking protesting most strongly against "an armed attack on Chinese frontier guards by Indian troops which have intruded into the Chip Chop Valley, Sinkiang, China." An NCNA report on July 26 said that the Indian government's statements in Sino-Indian border situation were full of contradictions.

July 30: A Sino-Mali contract on the distribution of PRC films in Mali and exchange of newsreel materials was signed in Bamako.

July 31-August 3: The Cambodian civil aviation delegation arrived in Peking on July 31 and had talks with a Chinese delegation on the technical arrangements for the establishment of air communication between the PRC and Cambodia. The delegation left for home on August 3.

July 31: A Sino-North Vietnamese protocol on scientific and technical cooperation was signed in Peking.

August 1: The PRC and Ceylon agreed to extend for another three years the 1958 agreement on loans to Ceylon for flood relief and rehabilitation.

August 4: A protocol on goods exchange and payments for 1962 between the PRC and East Germany was signed in Berlin.

The NPC Standing Committee and the CPPCC National Committee held an enlarged joint meeting. Chen Yi, who had led the PRC delegation to the Enlarged Geneva Conference for the peaceful settlement of the Laotian question, made a report on the conference.

August 5: Peking papers front-paged the PRC's decision to recognize Jamaica, and the messages on Jamaica's independence sent by Chou En-lai and Chen Yi.

August 7: The PRC Foreign Ministry made public its approval of the Indian government's suggestion for further discussions on the Sino-Indian boundary question on the basis of the report of the meeting of Chinese and Indian officials in 1960. The PRC, in addition, proposed that such discussions be held as soon as possible, and that the level, date, place, and other procedural matters for these discussions be immediately decided upon by consultations through diplomatic channels.

August 13: Indian Prime Minister Nehru said in parliament that India was "prepared to discuss what measures should be undertaken to remove the tensions that exist" between India and Communist China. He reported that there had been a number of incidents in which Chinese troops had fired on Indian forces. "The situation remains serious . . . and is likely to remain serious in the future."

August 14: The PRC and Nepal exchanged notes in Katmandu on the choice of nationality, trans-frontier cultivation of lands, and trans-frontier pasturing by the inhabitants of certain border areas.

A Sino-East German protocol on a plan for cultural cooperation in 1962 was signed in Berlin.

August 21: NCNA reported that the most extensive classified catalogue of collections of ancient books in China had been compiled by the Shanghai Library.

Chen Yi received in Peking Aberrahmane Kioriane, head of the diplomatic mission of the Algerian Republic to the PRC. The vice-premier informed him that the PRC government had decided to present the political bureau of the Algerian government with 9,000 tons of wheat, 3,000 tons of rolled steel for use in construction, and 21 tons of medicine.

August 22: A Sino-North Vietnamese protocol in protection of fish resources in the Red River was signed in Peking.

August 23: A protocol on the execution of the Sino-Cuban agreement on scientific and technical cooperation for 1962 was signed in Havana.

August 27: Chou En-lai sent a letter in reply to Prince Nirodon Sihanouk, head of state of Cambodia, expressing full support for Prince Sihanouk's proposal for an international conference to be attended by the countries which met last month in Geneva, to formally recognize and guarantee the neutrality and territorial integrity of Cambodia.

August 28: A document in the fulfillment of the plan for mutual goods deliveries between the PRC and the Soviet Union in the first half of 1962 was signed in Moscow.

August 30: Chen Yi sent a message to Dr. Eric Williams, foreign minister of Trinidad and Tobago, announcing the PRC's recognition of those nations.

September 2: A Sino-Guinean contract on the distribution and exhibition of the PRC films in Guinea and exchange of newsreel materials was signed in Conakry.

September 7: The PRC and Laos issued a joint communique on the establishment of formal diplomatic relations and the exchange of diplomatic representatives at the ambassadorial level.

September 8: Minutes of talks on performance of the Sino-Polish trade agreement of March 28, 1962, were signed in Peking.

September 9: A U-2 reconnaissance aircraft of the Chinese Nationalist air force was shot down over the Chinese mainland by a Chinese Communist air force unit.

A U.S. State Department spokesman subsequently confirmed that two U-2 aircraft had been sold to the Chinese Nationalist government in 1960 by the manufacturers (the Lockheed Aircraft Corporation) with U.S. government permission, but stressed that operation of the aircraft was solely the concern of the Nationalist authorities.

A new railway, about 200 kilometers in length, was completed recently in the Greater Khingan Mountains in Northeast China, NCNA reports.

September 13: President Kennedy stated that Nationalist China was the only country to which U-2 aircraft had been sold, and that there were no plans to sell any more U-2's to allied countries or to issue export licenses for them.

The PRC Foreign Ministry reaffirmed in a note that the PRC and Indian governments should quickly hold further discussions on the Sino-Indian boundary question, on the basis of the report of the officials of the two countries, without setting any pre-conditions.

A Sino-Bulgarian protocol on scientific and technical cooperation was signed in Peking.

September 15: Representatives of the PRC and Ceylon, after negotiations conducted in Colombo, reached an agreement on the terms of a third five-year trade and payments agreement between the two countries.

September 19: India accepted an invitation from Communist China to discuss their border dispute, the talks to start October 15 in Peking.

September 20: The Sino-American ambassadorial talks were held in Warsaw.

An NCNA report said that "following the intrusion by a U-2 espionage plane sent by U.S. imperialists over East China, a U.S. warship recently made new prolonged and provocative reconnaissance along the East China coast."

September 22: A Sino-North Korean protocol on scientific and technical cooperation was signed in Peking.

September 28: A Peking communique ending the 10th plenum of the 8th Central Committee of the CPC reasserted the correctness of Peking's foreign policy and called for vigilant and resolute opposition to various opportunists' ideological tendencies in the party. The communique noted "modern revisionists" among those gloating over Chinese difficulties were still the main danger to international Communist movement.

The Communist Party Central Committee reported only a "slight gain" in China's agricultural and industrial production in 1962. It said: "Some of our work is not well done." For instance, because of incompetence of leading cadres, some production teams, some factories, and some business establishments have produced less or have become unwelcome to the masses. The committee conceded that the "transition from capitalism to communism would last scores of years or even longer."

September 30: A scientific cooperation agreement for 1962-66 between the Chinese and Czechoslovakian academies of sciences was signed.

On the eve of the 13th anniversary of Communist rule in China, Premier Chou En-lai said at a reception in Peking that "the imperialist reactionaries of many countries and modern revisionists" had "launched anti-Chinese campaigns in an attempt to isolate China and also to compel China to change the just stand it takes in international affairs." But, Chou said, "their attempt is completely futile; it is they themselves who have become more isolated." Turning to the economy, Chou admitted the "Socialist construction work of Chinese people has no plain sailing." He pointed out that "serious natural disasters for three consecutive years, from 1959 to 1961, and shortcomings and mistakes in work, have indeed caused difficulties," but he insisted that "a preliminary foundation has been laid for an independent, comprehensive, and modern national economy."

October 3: The PRC Foreign Ministry, in a note to the Indian embassy in Peking, proposed once again that discussions on the Sino-Indian boundary question be started at once between the two governments on the basis of the report of the officials of the two states; and that during the discussions neither side should refuse to discuss any question concerning the boundary that may be raised by the other side.

The PRC and Ceylon signed the following five documents: (1) A joint communique concerning trade and economic and technical cooperation; (2) an agreement on trade and payments in 1962-67; (3) an agreement on economic and technical cooperation; (4) a protocol on exchange of goods in 1963; (5) two contracts on exchange of rice and rubber in 1963.

October 6: Chen Yi, in a message to the Foreign Minister of Arab Republic of Yemen, Mensen Mohamed Ahmed El Aini, notified him of the PRC's decision to recognize that republic.

The PRC Foreign Ministry in a note to India refuted the misrepresentation in the three Indian government notes dated September 17, 21 and 25, of the incidents of bloodshed which broke out in Chedong on the eastern sector of the Sino-Indian boundary, and in Chedong.

October 8: Chen Yi sent a message to Prime Minister Apollo Milton Abote of Uganda congratulating him on the proclamation of independence of Uganda and informing him of the decision of the PRC government to recognize that state.

October 10: Australia announced it had agreed to sell 67,000 tons of wheat to Communist China.

Serious fighting broke out between Chinese Communist and Indian troops near the Indian outpost of Dhola on the northeastern frontier. At least six Indians and 22 Chinese were killed in a battle that lasted twelve hours.

October 13: France announced it was selling surplus cereals to the PRC.

Premier Khrushchev received departing Chinese People's Republic Ambassador Liu Hsiao and emphasized the "warmth" of Sino-Soviet friendship.

The PRC Foreign Ministry in a note to the Indian Embassy lodged a strong protest with the Indian government against further intrusion on October 11 by Indian troops, who had crossed the illegal McMahon Line and "intruded into Chedong, Tibet, China, and into areas to the east and north of the lower reaches of the Kechilang River." It also protested strongly against the "continual air-dropping of aggressive Indian troops in the Changto area in preparation of war."

October 15: Nehru said at a press conference that India would be willing to negotiate when Chinese troops were cleared from its territory. He charged China with attempting to seize territory and then negotiate.

October 17: The PRC Foreign Ministry sent a note to the Indian embassy in Peking refuting the Indian government's denial of the fact that Indian aircraft had encroached upon China's air space. In another note to the Indian embassy in Peking, the PRC Foreign Ministry lodged a serious protest with the Indian government against the numerous intrusions into China's territorial air by Indian aircraft and deliberate aggravation of tension on the Sino-Indian border.

October 18: An official joint communique on the establishment of diplomatic relations between the PRC and Uganda was signed in Kampala.

The protocol of the Sino-Ghana agreement on economic and technical cooperation was signed in Accra.

October 20: The State Council passed the organizational regulations governing the people's council of Lichiang Nahsi National Autonomous *Hsien* of Yunnan Province. It also approved certain changes in administrative demarcation at *hsien* and municipal level in Hopei, Szechwan, Keichow, Yunna, and Tibet.

October 21: The U.S. State Department said the United States was "shocked at the violent and aggressive action of the Chinese Communists against India." A State Department official said that any Indian request for aid would be "considered sympathetically."

In a note delivered to Charge d'Affaires ad interim P. K. Banerjee of the Indian embassy in Peking, the PRC government lodged the most urgent, most serious and strongest protests with the Indian government against the "massive general attacks launched by the Indians simultaneously on the eastern and western sectors of the Sino-Indian border."

The spokesman for the PRC Foreign Ministry made a statement protesting the Indian government's decision to ask the Kingdom of Bhutan to allow Indian forces to enter Bhutan. "The lie about alleged Chinese threat or ambition towards Bhutan," the statement said, "will only serve to expose the ulterior motives of the lie-teller."

October 22: Nehru declared in a broadcast to the Indian nation that China's aggres-
sion was a menace that threatens the freedom of our people and the independence of our country. He said India would have to fight "a powerful and unscrupulous opponent" and must direct its energies and resources to the one end of strengthening itself militarily.

October 22-28: During this week a pro-Cuban, anti-American campaign was sponsored in the PRC in response to the Cuban missile crisis.

October 24-November 4: Chou En-lai sent a letter to Nehru on October 24 putting forward the three proposals of the PRC government for stopping the border conflicts: (1) Both countries should withdraw their armed forces 20 kilometers (12 miles) from the line of actual control at both ends of the Himalayan border; (2) they should agree not to cross that line; and (3) talks should be held between Chou En-lai and Nehru for a friendly settlement of the border dispute either in Peking or New Delhi. On October 27 Nehru rejected the Chinese proposals, insisting that Chinese troops should withdraw to the position they held on September 28, 1962. On November 4 Chou En-lai again wrote to Nehru appealing to him to consider and respond positively to the said proposals put forward by the PRC government.

October 26: The Soviet Union termed China's proposal "a display of sincere concern over relations with India and a desire to end the conflict." The *People's Daily* carried in full *Pravda*'s editorial of October 25 supporting the PRC government's statement on the Sino-Indian boundary dispute.

India declared a state of emergency and appealed to the United States, Britain, France, and Canada for military aid. All four countries immediately responded affirmatively.

Chou En-lai sent a reply to UAR President Nasser's telegram dated October 21 which expressed concern over the Sino-Indian border clashes. In his reply, Chou En-lai reiterated the PRC's stand of "striving consistently for a peaceful settlement of the Sino-Indian boundary question." He expressed the same desire in a separate message to Indonesian President Sukarno, Cambodian head of state Prince Norodom Sihanouk, and other heads of state of governments of Asian and African countries listed in Nasser's telegram.

October 28: A *People's Daily* editorial carried a thinly veiled attack on Khrushchev's decision to dismantle Soviet rocket bases in Cuba, declaring it is the Cuban people who are heroic, for they have stood firm against all threats of intimidation from the United States. It was argued that Cubans "know better than anyone else how to deal with the threat of aggression posed by U.S. imperialism," citing Cuban revolution as evidence that the resolution of the "masses" is more important than modern weapons.

October 28-November 10: Tatsunosuke Takasaki, former Minister of International Trade and Industry and Diet member of the Liberal Democratic party of Japan, and his party of 42 arrived in Peking on October 28. On November 9, a memorandum on the further development of non-governmental trade between the PRC and Japan on the basis of equality and mutual benefit was signed. The two sides agreed to develop long-term, comprehensive trade by exchange of goods, with 1963-67 as the first five-year period for trade arrangements.

October 30: U.N. General Assembly, by 56-42-12, rejected a U.S.S.R. move to unseat Nationalist China and seat Communist China. The margin against Communist China was slightly higher than in 1962.

November 1: A Sino-Indonesian agreement on radio and television broadcasting co-operation was signed in Peking.

November 3: The first planeload of U.S. small arms arrived in India. Within three days, one United States plane was landing every three hours. On November 10, the State Department announced that the arms airlift to India had been completed.

November 4: Again massive pro-Cuban and anti-American demonstrations took place

in Peking with over a million people participating.

November 5: A *Pravda* editorial marked retreat from its slight show of siding with Peking in the Sino-Indian border conflict. It did not endorse Peking proposals and called for a cease-fire as the next move in the drama.

A *People's Daily* editorial labelled the Soviet backdown in Cuba another "Munich" and a "crisis of carrying out an appeasement policy toward U.S. imperialist aggression." The editorial insisted that all Communists have a duty to support the Cuban revolution and Fidel Castro's five demands.

The PRC and Korea signed the following four documents: (1) A communique on trade talks; (2) a treaty on commerce and navigation; (3) an agreement on mutual supply of major goods in 1963-67; (4) a protocol on mutual supply of goods in 1963.

November 6: The 45th anniversary of the October Socialist Revolution was marked with a message of greeting sent jointly by Mao Tse-tung, Liu Shao-chi, and others to N. S. Khrushchev and other Soviet leaders. A reception was given by the Soviet ambassador in Peking. Chen Yi reminded Soviet hosts that, on the Cuban question, "all revolutionists must adopt a clear stand without any ambiguity."

A Sino-Mali protocol on economic and technical cooperation was signed in Bamako.

November 13: The PRC government handed a note to P. K. Banerjee, charge d'affaires ad interim of the Indian embassy in Peking, protesting against the Indian government's "violation of acknowledged international practice and its discriminatory and restrictive measures against the personnel of the Chinese embassy and consulates in India."

November 17: The PRC State Council passed provisional regulations governing the functions and powers of accounts.

November 18: All Peking papers gave front-page prominence to the letter dated November 15 by Chou En-lai to the heads of Asian and African states and governments, giving them a comprehensive account of the background of the Sino-Indian boundary question and the position of the PRC government. He appealed to them to "uphold justice and use their influence to facilitate a peaceful settlement on a fair and reasonable basis."

November 19: Chou En-lai and Chen Yi received P. K. Banerjee, charge d'affaires ad interim of the Indian embassy in Peking. They talked on the present conflict on the Sino-Indian border (again, on November 20).

Nehru, in a letter to President Kennedy, detailed the state of India's defense and appealed for a massive U.S. military aid program. On the same day, Chou En-lai charged that the United States "was overtly sending military aid to India," planned to "station a big supply mission" there. Chou asserted that such action would only enlarge the area of conflict.

November 20: The NPC Standing Committee ratified the organic law of the People's Congress and the People's Council of Lichiang Nashi Autonomous *Hsien* in Yunnan.

November 21: The PRC government issued a statement on its decision to take initiative measures to order the Chinese frontier guards to cease fire along the entire Sino-Indian border and withdraw. The said measures are as follows: "Beginning November 22, the Chinese frontier guards will cease fire along the entire front; beginning December 1, they will withdraw to positions 20 kilometers behind the line of actual control which existed in 1959; China will set up checkposts at a number of places on its side of the line of actual control."

November 26: A statement issued by the Indian government said: "While making an apparent show of substantial withdrawals, the Chinese want to retain effective control not only of large areas of Indian territory they had acquired by force prior to September 8, 1962, but also to retain control of further areas both in Ladakh and the North East Frontier

Agency that they have occupied since their invasion September 8 and their massive attacks on October 20." The statement concluded that if the Chinese were "really keen on a settlement," they should "accept the easier and straightforward Indian position—restoration of the status quo prior to September 8."

November 28: In a letter, Mr. Chou En-lai warned Mr. Nehru that the disengagement of troops along the border could not be achieved merely by a Chinese withdrawal without a reciprocal withdrawal by the Indian side. Should India refuse to cooperate, he added, "the cease-fire which has been effective is likely to be upset."

November 29: Mao Tse-tung, Liu Shao-chi, Chu Teh, and Chou En-lai have received a message of thanks from Khrushchev and Brezhnev for their greetings on the 45th anniversary of the October Socialist Revolution.

December 1: A new Sino-Soviet protocol on air transport and reciprocal services was signed in Peking.

The State Council passed the tentative regulations governing registration and administration of industrial and commercial enterprises.

The PRC announced it was beginning to withdraw its troops in accordance with its own cease-fire proposal.

December 2-9: The NCNA reported on the following withdrawal of Chinese frontier guards on the Sino-Indian border: (1) Withdrawal from Chile and Samuneceich to Penchiung and the area to its north on December 1; (2) withdrawal from the Uingke Pass on December 1; (3) withdrawal from Penchiung, Hsilung, Chiya, Dongmuti, Kamu, Sati, Wati, Keli, and other places on December 9.

December 3: Kozlov, speaking at the Italian Party Congress, and Brezhnev, addressing the Czechoslovak Party Congress a day later, attacked Albania and defended Moscow's Cuban policy. Both demanded Communist conformity with Soviet interpretation of international affairs. Kozlov chided Albania for not agreeing to meet with the CPSU to discuss differences. Brezhnev stressed that current national party congresses should serve as forums in which basic policies for international movement could be laid down. He implicitly rejected Peking demands for a broad conference. The head of the CCP at the Czechoslovak Party Congress in Hsiu-chuan called for an end to Albanian criticism from the other parties.

December 4: In a Sino-Laotian joint press communique, issued in Peking, the PRC agreed to furnish a long-term loan, technical aid, and equipment for the construction of industrial projects.

December 5: The PRC and North Vietnam signed the following five documents in Peking: (1) a communique on trade talks; (2) a treaty on commerce and navigation; (3) a protocol on mutual supply of goods and payments in 1963; (4) an exchange of notes to extend their 1955 protocol on small-scale trading in border areas; (5) an exchange of notes to extend their 1955 protocol on exchange of goods between local state trading companies in border areas.

December 5-31: The NCNA reported on December 5 that the Chinese frontier guards released at Bombila 64 sick and wounded personnel of the Indian army. The Indian Red Cross Society was notified on December 8 that another 140 sick and wounded Indian army personnel would be released. On December 12 the Chinese frontier guards released 17 wounded officers and men of the Indian army. On December 13, 80 sick and wounded Indian army personnel were released in Dirang Dzong. On December 15, 78 sick and wounded Indian army personnel were released in Waling. On December 19, 368 more sick and wounded Indian army personnel were released in Dirang Dzong, Tibet. On December 31, 108 sick and wounded captured Indian soldiers were released at Jang.

December 6: The Indian External Affairs Ministry decided to close the Indian consulates in Shanghai and Lhasa on December 15, because restrictions imposed by the Chinese authority on consular person-

nel had made it impossible for them to carry out their normal duties.

The PRC in its note once again asked the Indian government to give serious consideration to the three proposals put forward in the PRC government's statement of October 24 and to make a positive response.

December 9: The Chinese government informed New Delhi that its Calcutta and Bombay consulate offices would be closed, at the same time accusing the Indian government of having unscrupulously obstructed their functioning.

The PRC Foreign Ministry in a memorandum delivered to the Indian embassy located in Peking demanded from the Indian government clear and definite reply to the following three questions: "Does the Indian government agree, or does it not agree, to a cease-fire; that the armed forces of the two sides should disengage and each withdraw 20 kilometers from the November 7, 1959, line of actual control; and that officials of the two sides should meet and discuss matters relating to the withdrawal by both sides to form a demilitarized zone, the establishment of checkpoints, and the return of captured personnel."

December 10: Several Chinese officials were asked to leave Czechoslovakia; the reason given was that they were distributing anti-Czech propaganda.

Mrs. Sirimavo Bandaranaike, Prime Minister of Ceylon, at the Colombo Conference, proposed discussions for bringing India and China together in order to prevent further deterioration of the situation caused by the border dispute. Agreement was offered by the Indian government only if the Chinese agreed in toto to the proposals. The Chinese government accepted the proposal in principle, but not the Indian demand.

December 11: A Sino-Albanian protocol on a 1963-64 plan for cultural cooperation was signed in Tirana.

December 12: Khrushchev's speech to the U.S.S.R. Supreme Soviet session was marked by a most derogatory attack on the Sino-Albanian position, including charges that Albanians and "those who push them" are Trotskyites. The speech, which capped a succession of attacks on Khrushchev's bloc critics at Sofia, Budapest, Rome, and Prague, combined a defense of his policies in Cuba, on global co-existence strategy, and on interpretation of doctrine, with a spirited attack on his detractors. For the first time, Soviet leaders engaged at length and in great detail in public polemics with Chinese Communists.

A Sino-Albanian protocol on scientific and technical cooperation was signed in Tirana.

December 13: The PRC and Tanganyika signed an agreement on cultural cooperation in Dar-es-Salaam.

December 14: A Sino-Hungarian protocol on scientific and technical cooperation was signed in Peking.

December 15: An article in the *People's Daily*, reportedly written by Mao Tse-tung, proposed a meeting of the world's Communist parties "to clarify what is wrong, to strengthen unity, and to stand together against the enemy." The article said the Soviet Union had been "scared out of its wits" during the Cuban missile crisis. Soviet leaders were denounced for neutralism in the Chinese-Indian border dispute and for recent friendly relations with the "Tito Clique" in Yugoslavia.

December 18: Communist China agreed to buy 34,000,000 bushels of wheat from Canada at a price of $60,000,000.

The NPC Standing Committee at its meeting decided to convene the 4th session of the 2nd NPC in the second quarter of 1963. It also decided that the election

of deputies to the third NPC would take place in the second half of 1963.

December 24: A Sino-North Vietnamese protocol on a 1963-64 plan for cultural cooperation was signed in Hanoi.

December 26: A Sino-Mongolian boundary treaty was signed in Peking.

December 27: A Sino-Japanese protocol on trade was signed in Peking by representatives of the China Council for Promotion of International Trade and of Japanese trade delegations.

December 28: The PRC and Pakistan reached complete agreement in principle regarding the alignment of the common border of China's Sinkiang and of the contiguous areas the defense of which is the responsibility of Pakistan.

It was announced that Communist China had purchased from Australia 46,000,000 bushels of wheat at an approximate cost of $88,000,000.

December 31: Mrs. Sirimavo Bandaranaike, Ceylonese Prime Minister, arrived in Peking to exchange views with Chinese leaders on the promotion of direct negotiations between the PRC and India for a peaceful settlement of the Sino-Indian boundary question, as suggested by the conference of six Afro-Asian countries.

People's Daily carried a 14,000-word editorial entitled: "Differences Between Comrade Togliatti and the U.S.," elaborating the Chinese Communist position on principal contested issues in the Sino-Soviet polemic. This editorial went to great length to rebut Khrushchev's observation that the "paper tiger" has "nuclear teeth." It said that no matter what kind of teeth imperialism might have, its decadent and paper-tiger nature could not change.

A Sino-Burmese protocol on trade in 1963 was signed in Rangoon along with a joint communique on trade talks.

1963

January 1: *Red Flag* published four articles denouncing "modern revisionism" and pledging that Communist China will "incessantly expose the shameful behavior of modern revisionists who have betrayed Marxism-Leninism."

January 2: Chou En-lai reaffirmed in Peking: "The Chinese government fully supports the Indonesian government in its efforts to convene a 2nd Afro-Asian Conference."

January 2-8: Dr. Subandrio, Deputy Chief Minister and Foreign Minister of Indonesia, and his party arrived in Peking on January 2 for a visit. A joint communique of the PRC and Indonesian governments was issued in Peking on January 8.

January 5: A tele-communications agreement between the PRC and the UAR was signed in Peking.

The PRC and Pakistan signed a trade agreement in Karachi. A joint communique on trade talks was also issued.

January 7: A joint communique issued by Mrs. Bandaranaike, Prime Minister of Ceylon, who arrived in Peking on December 31, 1962, and Chou En-lai said that the Chinese government had given positive response to the Colombo proposals.

A *Pravda* editorial, for the first time in direct comment, named Chinese together with their sins. *Pravda* made a systematic, point-by-point rebuttal of China's most recent broadside. The editorial charged Albania and the PRC with violating the "general line" of peaceful co-existence, with opposing "unanimous opinion" of the world movement as embodied in 1957 and 1960 party statements, and with breaking "international proletarian discipline." On bloc differences, *Pravda* asserted they were subjective in nature and could be easily overcome. Moscow accepted the principle of a Communist conference, but set preconditions, making it quite clear that a reconciliation must be made on Soviet terms. It foreshadowed Khrushchev's move with a demand that opposition abandon its dogmatic attacks on the Soviet and other Communist parties.

January 10: An accord for the renewal of the trade agreement concluded between the PRC and Iraq in 1960 was signed in Baghdad.

A Sino-Somalian cultural cooperation agreement was signed in Magadishu.

January 13: A spokesman of the PRC Ministry of National Defense issued a statement on the continued withdrawal of the Chinese frontier forces, on their own initiative, along the entire Sino-Indian border.

A protocol for the construction of the Katmandu-Lhasa highway between the PRC and Nepal was signed in Katmandu.

January 16: The NCNA reported that the PRC would import from Japan 200,000 tons of ammonium chloride and export to Japan 450,000 tons of raw salt in 1963, according to two trade contracts signed recently in Peking.

At the Sixth Congress of the East German Socialist Unity Party, held in East Berlin, Khrushchev appealed for a truce in polemics between Communist parties and referred to Albania in more conciliatory terms than in previous statements, at the same time rejecting the Chinese Party's proposal for an international communist conference.

January 17: Up to the end of 1962, basic-level elections had been completed in succession in 473 *hsiang* in 48 *hsien* and municipalities, accounting for 24 percent of all the *hsiang* in the Tibet Autonomous Region, an NCNA report said.

The visiting Albanian government trade delegation signed in Peking the "protocol on exchange of goods and payments for 1963 between the two countries" and the protocol on the use in 1963 by Albania of loans from the PRC. A joint communique was also issued on the following day.

January 18: The NCNA carried the full text of Wu Hsiu-chuan's speech at the East German Communist Congress to call for a

Communist unity conference and proposed suspension of interbloc press and radio attacks in the meantime.

January 19: Chou En-lai sent a message to Mrs. Bandaranaike, Prime Minister of Ceylon, on January 19 in reply to her message of January 14. Chou En-lai's reply said that the "Chinese government accepts in principle the proposal of the Colombo Conference as a preliminary basis for meetings of Chinese and Indian officials but maintains two points of interpretation of the Colombo proposals." The proposals, made public January 19, said: (1) India would maintain its present military position in Ladakh, but would not reoccupy territory captured by Chinese Communist forces, which must withdraw 215 miles; (2) until there was a final solution, the vacated area would be demilitarized; (3) in the eastern sector, the boundary recognized by both governments would serve as a cease-fire line; and (4) in the middle area, the dispute would have to be solved by peaceful means.

January 20: A Sino-Nepalese protocol on boundary demarcation was signed in Peking.

January 21: A photograph exhibition on the "Cuban Revolution" opened in Peking.

January 22: A Sino-Japanese memorandum on fishery regulations in the Yellow and East China Seas was signed by representatives of the China Fishery Association and the Japan-China Fishery Association of Japan.

January 23: Nehru told the Indian parliament that India had accepted the Colombo proposals. He said: "There can be no talks to settle the points left for decision by direct discussions between the governments of India and China, unless the government of China accepts in toto the Colombo Conference proposals and their clarifications."

The PRC and Ghana issued a joint press communique in Peking on talks during the visit of a Ghanaian government good-will delegation.

January 27: A *People's Daily* editorial sharply criticized treatment given a Chi-

nese delegate at the Sixth Congress of the East German Socialist Unity party, including an ominous note that a serious split was imminent unless immediate steps were taken to work out accord. Editorials reminded Khrushchev that he was first to use the party congress to openly attack another fraternal party and that CPC representatives at 1957 and 1960 Moscow meetings acted against their better principles to safeguard bloc cohesion. Khrushchev was warned that the international Communist movement was at a "critical juncture" and that the Moscow declarations were on the verge of being discarded.

January 29: A new railway was opened to traffic in the biggest Foochow Bay salt field in Liaoning Province, Northeast China, according to an NCNA report.

February 2-27: The general political department of the "Chinese PLA" called an All-PLA political work conference from February 2 through February 27. The conference reviewed the results of the efforts at strengthening political and ideological work in the whole army in 1962, summed up the basic experiences in the creation of "four-good" campaign in the recent two years, studied the future political tasks, and discussed the draft of the amended regulations for political work.

February 8: NCNA reported ten big and numerous small water-control projects had been built to make the Haiho River one of the biggest and most diversified rivers in China, serving greater areas of farm land.

A multilateral agreement on non-commercial payments was signed in Prague by the U.S.S.R., the PRC, Albania, Bulgaria, Czechoslovakia, North Vietnam, East Germany, North Korea, Mongolia, Poland and Rumania.

February 8-27: Prince Norodom Sihanouk, head of state of Cambodia, and his wife arrived in Kunming on February 8 and in Peking on February 12. They were welcomed at the airport by Liu Shao-chi and by hundreds of thousands of people lining the main thoroughfare of the city. Mao Tse-tung met with the prince on February 15. The text of the joint communique of

Liu Shao-chi and Sihanouk was released in Peking on February 27.

February 10: A *Pravda* editorial reacted to Peking's January 27 attack. Maintaining the non-polemic pose adopted by Khrushchev at Berlin, *Pravda* seemed to speak more in sorrow than in anger. The editorial suggested that the Chinese were trying to continue the polemic, denied that the movement was on the brink of an abyss, and said that agreement was possible. *Pravda,* however, rejected China's demand that Moscow denounce Yugoslavia as a price for bloc unity, and also indicated that it did not tolerate persisting "left opportunist" errors. Moscow's recent effort to shift the focus from a dogmatism versus revisionism issue to a contrast between Moscow reasonableness and Chinese intransigence was maintained. *Pravda* again displayed Soviet willingness to talk bilaterally at any level at any mutually agreeable time.

February 12: Chen Yi in a message to the Foreign Minister of the Republic of Iraq, Talib Hussain Al-Shabeeb, notified him of the PRC government's decision to recognize the new Iraqui government.

February 15: The PRC and Yemen issued a communique on the decision of the two governments to raise their diplomatic representatives from ministerial to ambassadorial level.

February 19: An agreement on inspection and prevention of plant diseases and insect pests was signed in Tirana between the PRC and Albania.

February 20: The 114th session of the Sino-American ambassadorial talks was held in Warsaw.

February 21: The Central Committee of the Soviet Union, in a letter to the Chinese Communist Party, expressed "serious concern" that "open, ever-sharpening polemics were shaking the unity of the fraternal parties" and suggested a high-level meeting in preparation for an international conference.

The PRC and Syria signed three trade documents in Peking: (1) Agreement on trade; (2) agreement on payments; (3)

agreement on economic and technical cooperation.

February 22: The PRC and Cuba signed three trade documents in Peking: (1) Protocol on general conditions for delivery of goods; (2) agreement on loan by the PRC to Cuba; (3) protocol on trade and payments in 1963.

February 23: Mao Tse-tung received Soviet Ambassador Chervonenke for the first time since his arrival in 1959.

In a reply to the Indian embassy in Peking with reference to the note of the Indian Ministry of External Affairs dated December 28, 1962, the PRC Foreign Ministry said, "The Chinese government reiterates that the Indian government is held fully responsible for all the losses suffered by China as a result of the closing down and taking over of the establishments of the Bank of China in India, and the Chinese government reserves its full right to ask for compensation."

A Sino-Soviet protocol on a 1963 plan for cultural cooperation was signed in Peking.

February 24: The PRC and Syria exchanged notes in Peking to adjust a PRC loan in the event of change of the gold standard value of the Swiss franc.

February 26: A Sino-Cuban joint communique on economic talks was issued in Peking.

February 27: *People's Daily* published a 14,000-word editorial in reply to anti-CPC attacks by French Communist boss, Maurice Thorez, and other comrades. The editorial held that there was no reason to reply to specific Thorez charges since they merely repeated other people's stale arguments. Advent of bloc dissension was dated "around the time of the Camp David talks in 1959" when certain comrades put forward views which violated the Moscow declaration. According to the editorial, dispute was first published on September 9, 1959; a *Tass* statement on the Sino-Indian border dispute, said *People's Daily,* provided for the first time in history the spectacle of a Socialist country condemning another fraternal Socialist country when the latter was confronted with armed "capitalist" provocation.

February 28: A Sino-Cuban agreement on purchase of films from each other was signed in Havana.

March 1: A spokesman of the PRC Ministry of National Defense issued a statement announcing that "the Chinese frontier guards have completed their plan of withdrawal along the entire Sino-Indian border on China's own initiative." The statement pointed out that now the Sino-Indian border situation has eased. But the Indian side "has kept sending Indian military personnel and military aircraft to intrude into our territory and air space for provocation and harassment."

Peking announced that the local authorities in Tibet and Sinkiang had established 26 civilian check-posts within the 20-kilometer zone on the Chinese side of the line of actual control as of November 7, 1959, along the Sino-Indian border, from which the Chinese frontier guards had withdrawn.

March 2: In a press communique issued in Peking, the PRC Foreign Ministry said that the PRC and Afghanistan had agreed to conduct negotiations for the purpose of formally delimiting the boundary existing between the two countries and signing a boundary treaty.

The PRC and Pakistan signed an agreement in Peking on the boundary between "China's Sinkiang and the contiguous areas, the defense of which is under the actual control of Pakistan."

March 3: The first contract for the exchange of newsreel material between the PRC and Sudan was signed in Khartoum.

Chou En-lai sent a letter to Nehru urging negotiations concerning the border dispute. He said Chinese forces had withdrawn from contested areas and pledged that the border would not become tense again, "provided that the Indian side refrain from provocations and from re-entering the demilitarized zone."

March 4: A Sino-Pakistani joint communique was issued in Peking (on talks during Foreign Minister Bhutto's visit).

March 5: Chou En-lai clarified his stand on the previous statement (January 19, 1963). He said that Communist China did not accept the Colombo decision as an international tribunal, but merely as suggestions, and that if negotiations were to be successful, reciprocal moves would have to be made on the part of the Indian government.

A Sino-Bulgarian agreement on exchange of goods and payments in 1963 was signed in Peking.

March 6-10: Sri Savang Vatthana, king of Laos, and his party, including Laotian Premier Prince Souvanna Phouma, arrived in Peking on March 6 and were welcomed at the airport by Liu Shao-chi and others. A joint communique was issued in Peking on March 10.

March 9: Vice-Premier Teng Hsiao-ping presents Soviet Ambassador Chervonenke with letter affirming the "necessity of holding talks between the two parties on important questions concerning the international movement at present." The Chinese letter responded to a February 21 Soviet letter.

March 10: Nehru replied to Chou En-lai's request for immediate talks on the border dispute. Nehru said India accepted "without reservation" the proposals of the Colombo Conference and charged that Communist China did not.

March 11: The NCNA and the Laotian Ministry of Information, Publicity and Tourism signed an agreement on the exchange of information in Vientiane.

March 13: Peking released contents of the March 9 letter. In addition to endorsing a Chinese-Soviet meeting to iron out differences, the letter revealed that the CPC Central Committee extended an invitation to Khrushchev or another responsible comrade to stop over in Peking en route to Cambodia for inter-party talks and an exchange of views preparatory to an international meeting of Communist parties.

March 14: The West German Chamber of Commerce announced that a Chinese trade delegation was negotiating with two West German steel and engineering concerns.

The statement said Communist China had been seeking contracts with the West since the Soviet Union had withdrawn its technicians from China.

The Chinese embassy in India in a note to the Indian Ministry of External Affairs said that the government will send the first ship to India during March to bring back the victimized Chinese nationals in India and asked the Indian government to give due cooperation.

March 15: Chen Yi in a message to the Foreign Minister of the Syrian Arab Republic, Salah Eddine Bittar, notified him of the PRC government's decision to recognize the new Syrian government.

March 18: India lodged a formal protest to the U.N. Security Council over the Sino-Pakistani border agreement.

A Sino-Mongolian protocol on the mutual supply of goods in 1963 was signed in Ulan Bator.

March 20: The 1963 executive plan for the Sino-Bulgarian cultural cooperation agreement was signed in Peking.

Her Majesty Queen Therese Kanyonga of Burundi arrived in Peking for a week's state visit.

March 21-April 12: Lu Hsu-chang, the PRC Vice-Minister of Foreign Trade, and his party arrived in London on March 21 for a three-week visit. In a written statement to the press at the airport, Lu Hsu-chang said that he would explore and study with the British government and the British industrial and commercial circles the possibility of expanding Sino-British trade.

March 25: The Chinese Foreign Ministry sent a note to the Indian embassy in Peking, strongly protesting the Indian government's using the Tibetan rebel clique to interfere in China's internal affairs.

Ratification instruments on the Sino-Mongolian boundary which was signed on December 26, 1962, were exchanged in Ulan Bator.

March 26: A Sino-Ghanan agreement on maritime transport was signed in Accra.

March 29: A Sino-Korean protocol on a plan for cultural cooperation in 1963 was signed in Pyongyang.

March 30: A Sino-Moroccan trade agreement was signed in Peking.

The 1963 executive plan of the Sino-Mongolian cultural cooperation agreement was signed in Ulan Bator.

The NPC Standing Committee at its meeting discussed and passed, on the recommendation of the State Council, a decision to pardon a number of war criminals of the Chiang Kai-shek clique, the puppet Manchukuo, and the puppet Inner Mongolian Autonomous government who had truly changed and turned over a new leaf. Liu Shao-chi issued an order granting pardons to these people. In accordance with Liu Shao-chi order, the Supreme People's Court on April 5 pardoned and released a group of 35 war criminals. The meeting also adopted a decision approving the regulations covering the election of People's Congresses of all levels in Tibet Autonomous Region.

The State Council adopted the State Council tentative provisions for readjusting the burden of industrial and commercial tax and improving the methods of collection, and tentative provisions for price control. It also passed a decision to set up a national price committee. It approved changes in the *hsien* administrative divisions in Inner Mongolian Autonomous Region.

April 1: China's longest inland shipping route, along the Yangtze River between Shanghai on the coast and Chungking in Southwest China, was opened to service.

April 2: The PRC Foreign Ministry announced that all 3,213 Indian soldiers captured during the Chinese-Indian border conflict would be released beginning April 11. The Indian government reciprocated on April 14, returning 800 Chinese troops.

April 3: A Soviet reply to the Chinese, in response to the March 9 letter from Peking, presented a counter-invitation to Mao Tse-tung to visit the U.S.S.R.

April 10: The 1963 goods exchange and payments agreement between the PRC and Hungary was signed in Budapest.

April 12-20: PRC Chairman Liu Shao-chi and Foreign Minister Chen Yi visited Indonesia. A joint communique issued by Liu Shao-chi and President Sukarno on April 20 expressed the hope that the favorable climate created by the Colombo Conference could be exploited, solving the Sino-Indian border dispute by direct negotiations; denounced the Malaysian Federation plan as a form of neo-colonialism; advocated the reunification of Vietnam and Korea; condemned outside interference in Vietnam; and announced China's full support for the Indonesian proposal for a second Afro-Asian conference.

April 14-19: 1.7 million voters in Peking and some of the outlying districts went to the polls to cast their votes for their district people's deputies. Elections of deputies to the 5th local people's congresses at district, *hsien*, and *hsiang* levels were completed in Peking on April 19.

April 16: The NCNA reported that construction of the 80-kilometer highway from the Sino-Laotian border to Phong Saly, Northern Laos, had been completed after more than a year's work. The project was undertaken by the PRC as aid gratis to Laos.

The Chinese Foreign Ministry issued a statement accusing the United States of directing "a series of political murders and armed conflicts" in Laos. The statement suggested that if the situation deteriorated further, Britain and the Soviet Union should consider reconvening the Geneva Conference.

April 17: The British Foreign Office replied to the Chinese statement that there was "absolutely no evidence" for the Chinese accusations, and pointed out that the correct procedure under the Geneva Agreement was to seek an investigation by the I.C.C.

April 19: A Sino-Czechoslovak goods exchange and payments agreement for 1963 was signed in Prague.

April 20: The 1963 executive plan of the cultural cooperation agreement between the PRC and Poland was signed in Peking.

A Sino-Soviet protocol on exchange of goods in 1963 was signed in Moscow along with another protocol on pre-term payment by the PRC of a debt to the U.S.S.R. for trade transactions in 1960. The trade talk communique was issued on April 21.

April 20-26: Liu Shao-chi and Chen Yi visited Burma. A communique issued by Liu and Ne Win on April 21 urged that all the countries concerned should respect the independence and neutrality of Laos and strictly abide by the provision of the Geneva Agreement; called for direct negotiations between China and India on the basis of the Colombo proposal; and stated that Ne Win accepted an invitation to visit China.

April 21-25: Alt Sabry, Chairman of the Executive Council of Ministers of the UAR, and his party arrived in Peking on April 21 for a visit. After talking to Chinese leaders, he left Canton for Hong Kong on April 25. The full text of a joint communique between the two governments was published in Peking on April 25.

April 22: The PRC and the Sudanese government issued a joint communique on the forthcoming state visit to China by Ibrhim A. Bond, President of the Supreme Council of the Armed Forces of the Republic of Sudan.

April 27: The government of the PRC and the Somali Republic issued a joint press communique on the forthcoming visit to China by Somali Prime Minister Abdirashed Ali Shermarde at the invitation of Chou En-lai.

April 30: A trade and payments agreement for 1963 was signed in Warsaw between the PRC and Poland.

May 2: A Sino-Albanian protocol on management of a Sino-Albanian shipping joint stock company was signed in Peking.

A Sino-Guinean protocol on trade in 1963 and a supplementary protocol on economic and technical cooperation were signed in Peking.

May 1-5: Liu Shao-chi and Chen Yi arrived in Phnom Penh for a visit to Cambodia. Strict security precautions were taken during their stay; the Cambodian government subsequently revealed that a plot against Liu's life had been discovered on April 28, several "foreign agents" being arrested and a store of explosives seized. A communique issued by Liu and Prince Norodom Sihanouk on May 5 stated that China would oppose any attack on Cambodia's sovereignty and neutrality, and recommended increased cooperation between their two countries.

May 4: A Sino-Polish protocol on scientific and technical cooperation was signed in Peking.

May 6: Regulations governing the establishment and operation of radio stations were promulgated by the PRC State Council.

May 9: In response to a March 30 Soviet letter proposing that Mao visit the U.S.S.R. for high level talks, Chou En-lai informed Soviet Ambassador Chervonenko of a CPC decision that Party Secretary-General Teng Hsiao-ping and Politburo member Peng Chen would lead the Chinese delegation to Moscow for talks; it was also proposed that the date of the talks be changed to mid-June.

May 10: Anti-Chinese demonstrations broke out in Indonesia and continued through the week. Rioters looted, burned, and destroyed Chinese shops and homes. On May 17 President Sukarno ordered restrictions on political meetings and imposed a curfew in Bogn, where there had been serious rioting.

May 12: PRC Chairman Liu Shao-chi, in a Hanoi speech, charged the CPSU with violating the primary responsibility common to every bloc country. The speech further advanced independent Chinese concepts of Communist strategy toward West and tactics for winning revolutions in underdeveloped nations.

May 15: The 1963 executive plan of the Sino-Czechoslovak cultural cooperation agreement was signed in Prague.

A Sino-Somalian agreement on trade and payments was signed in Peking.

The PRC and Mali signed the following three documents in Peking: (1) Agreement on cultural cooperation; (2) contract on exchange of documentary film material; (3) contract on distribution of PRC films in Mali.

May 16: Moscow announced that Peking agreed on May 14 to the CPSU proposal to meet in July in Moscow.

A joint communique issued by PRC Chairman Liu Shao-chi and President Ho Chi-Minh of North Vietnam, after a six-day visit to Hanoi by the former, attacked "revisionism" as the main danger to the international Communist movement, and condemned "bourgeois ideologies" which kill the revolutionary spirit of Marxism-Leninism. The statement was regarded as a concession to Chinese pressure by Ho Chi-Minh, who in the past had attempted to play a medial role between China and the Soviet Union.

May 17: A Sino-Mali protocol on PRC aid to the national film board of Mali in the production of weekly newsreels was signed in Peking.

May 20: The State Council adopted the regulations of forest protection.

May 23: Meetings were held by the Taiwan Democratic Self-Government League and its branches in Peking and other cities to organize the "6th anniversary of the patriotic, anti-U.S. demonstration in Taiwan." At a Peking meeting, Hsu Meng-Shan, Secretary-General of the Taiwan Democratic Self-Government League, said that "the U.S. imperialist attempt to perpetuate its occupation of Taiwan by creating 'two Chinas' would never succeed."

May 25: The 1963 executive plan of the Sino-Hungarian cultural cooperation agreement was signed in Peking.

A spokesman of the PRC Ministry of National Defense issued a statement on the completion of the release and repatriation of all the captured Indian military personnel.

Sino-Mongolian minutes on boundary demarcation talks were issued. The states also exchanged notes on the change of an executive organ under the 1960 agreement on scientific and technical cooperation.

May 29: A trade agreement for 1963 between the PRC and the Republic of Finland was signed in Helsinki.

May 31: The sale of Australian wheat to Communist China was announced by the Chairman of the Australian wheat board, M. J. V. Moroney; shipment under this transaction was to take place between June and October, and payment was to be made within 12 months.

June 6-23: Choi Yong Kun, President of the Presidium of the Supreme People's Assembly of the Korean Democratic People's Republic, and his party arrived in Peking on June 6. After a warm reception in Peking and a visit to Northeast China, a joint communique of Liu Shao-chi and Choi Yong Kun was issued in Peking on June 23. Both sides stressed that "the struggle against modern revisionism has an important bearing on the future of the revolutionary cause of the proletariat and working people of the world as well as the destiny of mankind."

June 7: The 1963 executive plan of the cultural cooperation agreement between the PRC and East Germany was signed in Peking.

June 8: A new scientific and technical cooperation agreement between the PRC and Rumania was signed in Peking.

June 10: Sino-North Korean protocol on a 1963 plan for cooperation between their academies of sciences was signed in Pyongyang.

June 13: A Sino-Pakistani press communique on boundary demarcation was issued in Peking.

June 14: Instruments of ratification of the agreement on cultural cooperation between the PRC and Tanganyika were exchanged in Dar Salaam (signed on December 13, 1962).

June 15: The PRC and Cambodia exchanged notes in Phnom Penh to extend 1950 trade and payments agreement.

June 16: *People's Daily* printed the text of a 22,000-word reply to a March 30 Soviet letter. The Chinese reply, dated June 14, repeated the usual charges against Soviet leadership and cited 25 issues which the

Chinese held would have to be taken up at CPC-CPSU talks.

June 18: Moscow announced the decision of the CPSU Central Committee plenum not to publish the CPC letter "at the present time," since it contained unwarranted attacks on the Soviet and other Communist parties.

A cultural agreement plan between the PRC and Norway was signed in the Norwegian capital.

June 19: The 1963 executive plan for scientific cooperation between the PRC and Bulgarian academies of sciences was signed in Peking.

A Sino-Soviet protocol on a 1963-64 plan for scientific and technical cooperation was signed in Peking.

June 20: "A U.S.-made P-2U plane of the Chiang Kai-shek gang was shot down by a unit of the PLA air force last night when it flew over East China on a harassing mission," an NCNA report said.

June 21: Moscow announced that the CPSU plenum had unanimously adopted a resolution to hold talks with Chinese Communist delegates on July 5.

A Sino-Korean protocol on scientific and technical cooperation was signed in Pyongyang.

June 22: A Sino-East German agreement on exchange of goods and payments in 1963 was signed in Peking.

June 25: "149 servicemen of the Chiang Kai-shek gang crossed over the border of Yunnan and gave themselves up to the frontier guards of the PLA in the more than ten months ending May 31," an NCNA report said.

A Sino-Cuban protocol on a 1963-64 plan for cooperation between academies of sciences was signed in Peking.

June 27: The display windows for news photos in front of the Chinese embassy in the Soviet Union were smashed by four Soviet citizens, an NCNA report said. The Soviet Foreign Ministry expressed the greatest regret to the Chinese embassy over this incident.

June 29: The Women's Congress in Moscow closed in what the NCNA described as an "organized uproar," with the delegates of China, Albania, North Korea, and Indonesia voting against the congress program, and Japan, Laos, South Vietnam, and North Vietnam abstaining.

The spokesman of the PRC Foreign Ministry issued a statement on the Soviet government's unreasonable demand that the Chinese government recall three staff members of the Chinese embassy and two other Chinese from the Soviet Union. The spokesman said, "The Chinese government hopes that the Soviet government will not take further rash steps detrimental to Sino-Soviet unity and the relations between the two states . . ."

June 30: The five Chinese expelled from the U.S.S.R. were welcomed home.

July 1: A CPC Central Committee statement announced that the Chinese party would still send a delegation to the Moscow talks, despite CPSU moves to worsen relations.

July 4: The PRC Ministry of Foreign Affairs handed a note to the Soviet embassy in Peking lodging a strong protest against the unreasonable demand of the Soviet Union for the recall of five Chinese.

The Central Committee of the CPSU explained that the five Chinese who had been ousted from the Soviet Union had interfered in the "internal affairs of our party." A second statement asserted that the Chinese embassy in Moscow had been warned about the unauthorized distribution of leaflets before expulsion was demanded.

July 5: The Chinese delegation to the talks arrived in Moscow, having been seen off at Peking by 200 Chinese party and government functionaries.

A statement issued by the CPC Central Committee said that the committee cannot agree to the distortions, accusations, and attacks which were made in a statement of July 5 by the Central Committee of the CPSU. However, the CPC Central Committee "has instructed its delegation to exercise the greatest patience and make the greatest efforts to strengthen the unity of the Chinese and Soviet parties."

July 5: A Sino-Rumanian protocol on a 1963 plan for cultural cooperation was signed in Peking.

July 6: A Sino-Rumanian agreement on cooperation between academies of sciences was signed in Peking along with the 1963-64 plan for cooperation between academies of sciences.

July 7: Peking publicized a rally for the five expellees at which Foreign Minister Chen Yi spoke. The CPSU, in a Central Committee statement on July 8, protested the rally as part of a "deliberate campaign of aggravation."

July 8: At a meeting of the NPC Standing Committee, Chou En-lai made a report on the domestic and international situation. The meeting passed a resolution approving the report of the adjusted plan for the last two years of the Second Five-Year Plan and its implementation, and the report on the final accounts of the state for 1961 and 1962.

July 10: The CPC Central Committee issued a statement repudiating the Soviet attack on the rally and countered with the charge that the CPSU was carrying out an anti-Chinese campaign in the U.S.S.R.

July 13: The *People's Daily* carried an editorial entitled, "We Want Unity, Not a Split."

July 14: Peking publicized a rally welcoming Afro-Asian and Latin American delegates from the recent Moscow Women's Congress.

The Russian letter reviewed the history of the Sino-Soviet split, blaming Communist China for every phase, and then refuted one by one the 25 points the Chinese had sought to have debated at the Moscow meeting. It accused the Chinese government of reducing by "almost 67 percent in the past three years" the volume of China's trade with the Soviet Union and asserted that "the Chinese leaders did not tell their people truthfully through whose fault trade relations were curtailed."

The 1963 protocol for a Sino-UAR trade agreement was signed in Cairo.

July 15: Talks between the United States,

Great Britain, and the U.S.S.R. on a treaty to limit nuclear tests opened in Moscow.

A Sino-Czechoslovak protocol on scientific and technical cooperation was signed in Prague.

July 18: Peking staged a massive rally to welcome its delegations home from the Moscow Women's Congress.

A Sino-North Vietnamese protocol on scientific and technical cooperation was signed in Hanoi.

July 19: An editorial in *People's Daily* called the nuclear test-ban talks in Moscow a "capitulation in the face of imperialist nuclear blackmail." The same article disclosed that on July 16, 1960, the Soviet Union had suddenly told Peking it had decided to "withdraw all the 1,300 and more Soviet experts in China within a month, to scrap the hundreds of agreements and contracts it had signed, and to discontinue supplies of many important items of equipment and materials." This action "inflicted incalculable difficulties and losses on China's economy, national defense, and scientific research."

Khrushchev, at the Soviet-Hungarian friendship rally in Moscow, reasserted basic Soviet policy and obliquely attacked the CPC.

Peking reported that on July 8 the Czech government had demanded the recall of NCNA correspondents accused of distributing CPC polemical documents, that on July 13 the PRC had rejected the demand, and that on July 17 Czechoslovakia had given the PRC a 48-hour deadline to comply; the PRC Foreign Ministry protested Czechoslovakia's behavior.

July 20: The full text of the July 14 Soviet open letter was published in the *People's Daily* together with an editorial describing the letter as a "distortion of facts."

July 22: The CPC and CPSU released a communique on the conclusion of the Moscow talks, indicating Soviet assent to a CPC proposed "recess" and more meetings in the future.

July 24: A Sino-Cuban 1963 plan for cultural cooperation was signed in Peking.

July 25: A Sino-Ceylonese agreement on

maritime transport was signed in Colombo.

July 26: It was reported from Perth, Canada, that a 12,000-ton shipment of the wheat bought by China was being dispatched to Albania on Chinese instructions.

July 31: The PRC Foreign Ministry statement denounced the nuclear test-ban treaty initiated in Moscow on July 25 by the United States, U.S.S.R. and Great Britain as a "dirty fraud," and proposed the complete prohibition and destruction of nuclear weapons.

August 1: President Kennedy was asked at a news conference to appraise the power and threat of Communist China. He said that China, with its 700 million people, with a "Stalinist internal regime," with its determination for war "as a means of bringing about its ultimate success," and with its future potential as a nuclear power, might present in the next decade a "potentially more dangerous situation than any we faced since the end of the second war."

A cooperation agreement was signed in Rangoon between the NCNA of the PRC and the News Agency Burma of the Union of Burma.

August 2: It was announced by the Federal Minister of Trade and Commerce, Mr. Mitchell Sharp, that the PRC government had entered into an agreement with Canada involving 186,700,000 bushels of grain to be sold to China in the period August 1, 1963, through July 31, 1966.

August 3: Chou En-lai addressed a letter to the leaders of all nations proposing a world conference to discuss the "complete, thorough, total, and resolute prohibition and destruction of nuclear weapons."

August 3-4: The Soviet press carried an official reply to the July 31 Chinese attack on the test-ban treaty. Attention was focused on the "broad program" of the CPSU to strengthen peace. The Soviet "nuclear rocket" shield, it was asserted, protects the security of all Communist countries, including the PRC.

August 3: The PRC and Afghanistan issued a joint press communique on boundary negotiations in Kabul along with minutes of talks.

August 5: The treaty to ban nuclear tests in the atmosphere, in outer space, and under water was signed in Moscow by the United States, Great Britain and the U.S.S.R. France and the PRC had refused to sign the treaty.

The PRC Foreign Ministry issued a statement describing repeated Soviet efforts since 1959 to block Chinese acquisition of a nuclear weapon capability. It was charged that Moscow, on June 20, 1959, "tore up" an October 1957 agreement and refused to provide a sample of the atomic bomb and technical data for its manufacture, shortly after Khrushchev's visit to the United States.

August 7: A Sino-American ambassadorial talk was held in Warsaw.

August 9: A Sino-Somalian agreement on economic and technical cooperation was signed in Peking.

August 10: A Sino-Somalian joint communique was issued in Peking on talks during Premier Shermarke's visit.

The PRC and North Vietnam exchanged notes on the change of executive organs under their 1960 agreement on scientific and technical cooperation.

August 12: *People's Daily* published a statement by Mao Tse-tung appealing to people everywhere to "unite against the racial discrimination practiced by U.S. imperialism and to support the American Negroes in their struggle against racial discrimination." Mao's statement had been requested by Robert F. Williams, a militant U.S. Negro living in Cuba.

August 15: A spokesman of the PRC Ministry of Post and Tele-communications repudiated India's attempt to deny its responsibility for breaking the Sino-Indian agreement on the exchange of mail, an NCNA dispatch said.

August 17: The PRC and Czechoslovakia exchanged notes to extend their 1953 agreement on cooperation for prevention of insect pests and plant diseases.

August 20: The Japanese government approved a contract for construction in the PRC of a $20-million synthetic textile plant by a private Japanese company.

August 21: The Soviet news agency Tass published the Soviet government's reply to Red China's criticism of the Soviet Union on August 5. Moscow said that China's opposition to the nuclear test-ban treaty demonstrated its lack of regard for "how nuclear arms spread among the capitalist states as long as the Chinese leaders get a chance to lay their hands on a nuclear bomb and see what it is like." The Soviet statement criticized China for publicizing "classified information relating to the defense of the Socialist community." It noted that even if China were capable of producing "two or three bombs", it would still depend on the Soviet Union's "nuclear shield for protection." But there were "some people in Peking ready to sacrifice half the population of their country, half of entire mankind, in a war involving nuclear weapons."

A *People's Daily* editorial, "No One Can Save the Indian Reactionaries from Political Bankruptcy," bitterly criticized Soviet military support for the Nehru government, charging that quantities and forms of Soviet assistance to India have mounted in direct relationship to the intensity of Indian provocation against the CPR and collaboration with the United States.

August 28: The PRC and Burma exchanged notes on reciprocal recognition of ship's papers.

August 29: A Sino-Vietnamese agreement on fishery cooperation in the Gulf of Bakho was signed in Peking.

Mao Tse-tung said in a broadcast over the Peking radio: "Setting itself against all the people of South Vietnam, the U.S.-Ngo Dinh Diem clique now finds itself besieged by them. . . The Ngo Dinh Diem regime will inescapably end in total isolation and disintegration, and U.S. imperialism will finally have to get out of South Vietnam."

An air transport agreement between Pakistan and the PRC was signed in Karachi.

August 30: A Sino-Pakistani agreement on air services was signed in Karachi.

Khrushchev, in Yugoslavia, praised Yugoslavia's economic achievements and criticized the Chinese leaders for "behaving irresponsibly" when the serious threat of nuclear war faced all countries.

People's Daily criticized the U.S.S.R. for accepting the 2-Chinas policy engineered by U.S. imperialism.

A Peking rally of 10,000 people expressed support for the "just, patriotic struggle" of the Buddhists and other sections of the people of South Vietnam against "the U.S.-Ngo Dinh Diem clique."

August 31: A Sino-Mali agreement on cooperation in radio broadcasting was signed in Peking.

September 1: Five Japanese war criminals in custody in the PRC were released in advance of the expiration of their prison terms.

A PRC Foreign Ministry statement rebuted an August 21 Moscow statement charging the Peking regime with being willing to risk the destruction of half of mankind in a nuclear holocaust. The statement summarized China's views on war: (1) China wants peace and not war; (2) it is the imperialists and not we who want to fight a war; (3) world war can be prevented; (4) "even in the eventuality that imperialism should impose a war on the people of the world and inflict tragic losses on them, it is the imperialist system and not mankind that would perish and the future of mankind would still be bright."

The PRC and Sudan signed an accord on the establishment of direct telegraphic services between Shanghai and Khartoum.

September 5: The PRC and Pakistan issued a press communique on boundary demarcation.

September 6: Peking released the first of a series of joint *People's Daily-Red Flag* articles entitled, "The Origin and Development of the Differences Between the Leadership of the CPSU and Ourselves— Comment on the Open Letter of the Central Committee of the CPSU (of July

14)." The article asserted flatly that Sino-Soviet relations had been brought to a "new stage of unprecedented gravity," and that the Sino-Soviet treaty of friendship, alliance, and mutual assistance had already been violated. The article also charged that the Soviet Union had been involved in subversion within China's borders.

A Moscow dispatch said that China's charges of subversion in Sinkiang confirmed reports that about 50,000 Kazakh nomads had fled from that province of China into the Soviet Union because of hunger and religious persecution.

September 11: A Sino-Algerian agreement on cultural cooperation was signed in Algiers.

September 13: The editorial departments of the *People's Daily* and *Red Flag* published jointly an article entitled, "On the Question of Stalin—Comment on the Open Letter of the CPSU Central Committee (II)." The anti-Stalin campaign was condemned as a weapon used by Khrushchev in the CPSU leadership struggle without regard for the harm it brought to the Soviet Union and world Communism.

The NCNA reported that the Soviets illegally detained a train, train crew, and 92 Chinese at Naushki returning from Soviet Union. It charged that an international railway agreement had been violated by Russian authorities, also reporting an incident in which Soviet border guards had "high-handedly" searched the baggage and had seized the property of five Chinese military returning to the U.S.S.R. to continue their studies.

September 15-27: Liu Shao-chi with other members of his party was in Pyongyang September 15-27. On September 27 Liu Shao-chi and North Korean President Choi Yong Kung issued a joint statement to reaffirm a "complete identity of views" on all policy matters and noted "the common opposition of the two countries to the policies of the Soviet Union."

September 16: A PRC Foreign Ministry note rejected the charges made by the Soviet Foreign Ministry against the crew members and Chinese passengers on board the Chinese train running on the Peking-Ulan Bator-Moscow line, which entered Soviet territory on September 7; the note lodged a strong protest with the Soviet government against alleged "brutality" at the Maushki station.

The PRC and Pakistan signed an accord to open direct tele-communications between Peking and Karachi.

September 21-22: The Soviet press printed a lengthy government statement purportedly answering the PRC Foreign Ministry statement of September 1. The Chinese were charged with having "systematically violated" Soviet borders since 1960 with soldiers and civilians, including more than 4,000 violations in 1962 alone. Peking was warned against setting off on the "very dangerous path" of calling for a review of "historically established boundaries."

September 23: A Sino-Japanese agreement on trade in 1963-64 on the basis of a 1962 Liao-Takasaki memorandum was signed in Peking.

September 25: The installation of a fourth new generating unit, 72,000 kilowatts in capacity, was begun at the hydroelectric power station on the Sinan River in East China, which had begun to supply electricity three years before.

September 26: The editorial departments of the *People's Daily* and *Red Flag* published jointly an article entitled, "Is Yugoslavia a Socialist Country?—Comment on the Open Letter of the Central Committee of the CPSU (III)." The editorial charged Khrushchev with "wallowing in mire with the renegade Tito clique."

September 27: The 1963 executive plan for the cultural cooperation agreement between the PRC and Mali was signed in Bamako.

September 28: The NPC Standing Committee amended and approved the "Regulations governing the service of officers of the Chinese PLA," and decided to set up 5th and 6th Ministries of Machine Building of the PRC.

A French economic mission arrived in Peking. Visits by various French officials followed, and the French press reported that China's leaders were openly encouraging France to recognize the Peking regime.

September 29: "The inauguration of the so-called Malaysia Federation had made the confused situation in Southeast Asia worse and brought a new threat to peace in that region and Asia as a whole," said the *People's Daily* observer in a commentary.

September 30: A barter-trade agreement was signed between the PRC and Pakistan (exchange of cement from PRC for jute from Pakistan).

October 9: More than 700 Chinese workers, who went to Mongolia in 1960 to help in its work of construction under a Sino-Mongolian government agreement, returned to Communist China on the expiration of their terms.

A new exchange of goods and payments agreement and a protocol on the exchange of goods for the year 1963 to 1964 between PRC and Afghan government were signed in Kabul.

October 10: The meeting of the NPC Standing Committee and of the CPPCC were held jointly. The meeting decided that the 4th session of the 2nd NPC and the 4th session of the 3rd National Committee of the CPPCC would be held simultaneously in mid-November this year.

A Sino-Ceylonese protocol on the exchange of goods in 1964 was signed in Peking.

October 11: The PRC and Britain signed an accord to exchange television films in Peking.

The PRC agreed to provide the Algerian government with a long-term interest-free loan. The loan amounted to 250,000,000 French francs or 25,000,000,000 old francs. A communique on the loan was issued by the Algerian Foreign Ministry.

Premier Chou En-lai told a reporter for *Reuters* that the Sino-Soviet treaty of friendship and alliance was still in effect despite the ideological differences

169

between the two countries. Chou had declared earlier that a diplomatic break between the Soviet Union and Communist China was impossible.

October 13: A Sino-Soviet protocol on border railways was signed in Harbin.

October 14: A Sino-North Korean protocol on the mutual supply of goods in 1964 was signed in Pyongyang.

October 15: A Sino-East German protocol on scientific and technical cooperation was signed in Peking.

A Sino-Albanian protocol on scientific and technical cooperation was signed in Peking.

October 16: The PRC and Indonesia exchanged notes on economic and technical cooperation in Peking.

October 21: Chinese Communist representation issue at the United Nations General Assembly was rejected by 41-57 with 12 abstentions.

The editorial department of the *People's Daily* and the *Red Flag* published jointly an article entitled, "Apologists of New-colonialism—Comment on the Open Letter of the Central Committee of the CPSU (IV)." Soviet leadership was criticized on its attitude toward national liberation movements. It was protested that the CPSU, not the CPC, was insisting on racial hatred by the colored against the white race.

October 23: A Sino-Burmese protocol on the 1964 purchase of Burmese rice by the PRC was signed.

October 24: The PRC Foreign Ministry issued a statement to the effect that the United States had again manipulated the U.N. General Assembly into obstructing the restoration of China's legitimate rights in the U.N.

The PRC and North Vietnam signed the following three documents: (1) Protocol on mutual supply of goods and payments in 1964; (2) exchange of notes to extend 1955 protocol on small-scale trading in border areas; (3) exchange of notes to extend 1955 protocol on exchange of goods between local state trading companies in border areas.

October 25: A contract was signed for the purchase of complete equipment for a synthetic ammonia plant by the China National Import Corporation from Humphreys and Glasgow, Ltd., of Britain.

October 28: An agreement on economic and technical cooperation between the PRC and Algeria was signed in Algiers.

A Sino-Finnish agreement on trade in 1964 was signed in Peking.

November 2: The Peking radio announced that a high-altitude reconnaissance U-2 plane "of the Chiang Kai-shek bandit gang" was "shot down by the air force" near Shanghai while flying "on a harassing mission." On November 2 the Nationalist Chinese admitted the loss of a U-2.

November 5: A Sino-Yugoslav protocol on the exchange of goods in 1963-64 was signed in Peking.

November 6: The 46th anniversary of the October Socialist Revolution was marked with an exchange of greetings by Mao Tse-tung, Liu Shao-chi, Chu Teh, and Chou En-lai, and with reception given by the Soviet ambassador and attended by Chou En-lai, Chen Yi and others. At a Kremlin reception, according to Tass, Khrushchev said he was sure "we shall come to agreement with the Chinese comrades sooner or later."

November 9: The PRC and Japan signed the following three documents: (1) Agreement on fishery regulations in Yellow and East China Seas; (2) exchange of letters on exclusion of Japanese fishing boats from PRC military security areas and conservation zone; (3) exchange of memoranda on prevention of fishing disputes in Yellow Sea.

November 14: President Kennedy, asked at a press conference what would be the conditions for resumption of trade with Communist China, said: "We are not planning on trade with Red China, in view of the policy that Red China pursues. If the Red Chinese indicate a desire to live at peace with the United States, with other countries surrounding it, then quite obviously the United States would reappraise its policies."

A Sino-Cuban memorandum on a commodity list of import and export trade in 1964 was signed.

November 15: The PRC and Cuba signed a protocol in Havana on the execution of the scientific and technical cooperation agreement between the two countries.

November 17-December 3: The 4th session of the 2nd NPC was held between November 17 and December 3. Mao Tse-tung, Liu Shao-chi, Tung Pi-wu, Chu Teh, Chou En-lai, and Teng Hsiao-ping were among the leaders of the party and state who attended the session. In the afternoon of December 3, the session adopted a state budget, the 1964 plan for the national economy, and the preliminary planning of the 1964 state budget.

November 18: The editorial departments of the *People's Daily* and the *Red Flag* published jointly an article entitled, "Two Different Lines on the Question of War and Peace—Comment on the Open Letter of the Central Committee of the CPSU (V)." The article said: "Guided by this theory of nuclear fetishism and nuclear blackmail, the leaders of the Soviet Communist Party maintain that the way to defend world peace is not for all existing peace forces to unite and form the broadest united front against United States imperialism and its lackeys, but for the two nuclear powers, the United States and the Soviet Union, to cooperate in settling the world's problems."

November 18-December 4: The 4th session of the 3rd National Committee of the CPPCC opened November 18, presided over by Chou En-lai. It was decided that during the current session, the whole body of CPPCC National Committee members would attend the 4th session of the 2nd NPC to hear a report on government work.

November 20: PRC Foreign Minister Chen Yi pledged that his country would give Cambodia "resolute support" in its "just and patriotic struggle against imperialism." On November 19, Cambodia Chief of State Prince Norodom Sihanouk ordered termination of all U.S. military and economic aid to his country.

A Sino-Czechoslovak agreement on currency exchange and cash movements was signed in Peking.

November 22: President Kennedy was assassinated in Dallas, Texas, and Vice-President Lyndon Baines Johnson was sworn in as his successor. Communist China's press announced the assassination without comment.

A treaty formally delimiting the 40-mile frontier between the PRC and Afghanistan was signed in Peking. A press communique on boundary demarcation was issued in Peking on November 24.

The NCNA attacked U.S. President Johnson as a supporter of late President Kennedy's policies.

November 25: The PRC and Cambodia signed an agreement on air transport in Phnom Penh.

A Sino-North Korean protocol on cooperation in exploiting and utilizing the Yalu and Tumen Rivers in 1964 was signed in Changchun.

November 26: A Sino-Bulgarian protocol on scientific and technical cooperation was signed in Sofia.

A Sino-Cambodian protocol on agency business and reciprocal services in civil aviation was signed in Phnom Penh.

November 27: The Chilean government announced it had signed an agreement to sell Communist China 10,000 tons of copper.

November 28: The NPC Standing Committee approved an "Explanation on the number of deputies to be elected to the next 3rd NPC and on questions concerning the election."

The PRC and Indonesia signed an accord on the joint filming and production of a color documentary film of first games of newly emerging forces to be held in Djakarta.

November 29: A Sino-Soviet 1963-64 plan for cooperation between academies of sciences was signed in Peking.

November 30: Ex-Premier Faure reported to President De Gaulle on his recent visit to Peking. It was Faure's view that France must sever ties with Nationalists if France wanted diplomatic relations with Communist China. French officials, however, made no early move for recognition.

December 1: The Indonesian government announced it had signed an agreement to buy from Communist China 40,000 tons of rice to help alleviate a food shortage in Indonesia caused by flood and rodent damage.

December 4: Representatives of 80 countries attending a Communist-dominated World Peace Council, held in Warsaw, repeatedly rejected pro-Chinese and anti-Soviet resolutions.

The Canadian government announced that the PRC had ordered 18,700,000 bushels of wheat from Canada at a cost of $35 million.

In an editorial entitled, "Continue Striving to Build an Independent, Complete, Modern National Economic System," the *People's Daily* charged that the withdrawal from China of Soviet experts and economic aid had been responsible for disarrangement of their original economic plan because it had come at a time when China was having "enormous difficulties." The article said: "They suddenly and unilaterally decided to withdraw in July 1960 all their experts, totalling 1,390, who were assisting China in its work; tore up 343 contracts, and annulled 257 items of scientific and technical cooperation. After that, they heavily slashed the supply of whole sets of equipment and crucial parts of installations. This caused heavy losses to China's construction work and dislocated its original plan for the development of the national economy, greatly aggravating our difficulties."

December 5: Chou En-lai received the British writer, Felix Greene, at the latter's request for a television interview, and answered the questions raised by him.

December 6: The PRC and Albania signed the following three documents in Tirana: (1) Protocol on exchange of goods and payments in 1964; (2) protocol on Al-

bania's use of PRC loan in 1964; (3) joint communique on trade talks.

A *Pravda* editorial said that "open polemics have gone too far," and recalls the CPSU "proposal for termination of polemics and for solution of controversial issues by means of bipartite talks and by holding conferences of Communist parties."

December 8-10: Chen Yi sent a cable on December 8 to Jomo Kenyatta, Prime Minister of Kenya, congratulating him on the independence of Kenya and informing him of the PRC's decision to give recognition to that state. On December 10, the PRC and Kenya decided to establish formal diplomatic relations and exchange diplomatic representatives of ambassadorial rank.

December 11: The PRC and Afghanistan issued a press communique on talks concerning establishment of air services.

A Sino-Hungarian protocol on scientific and technical cooperation was signed in Budapest.

December 12: The editorial departments of the *People's Daily* and *Red Flag* published an editorial entitled: "Peaceful Co-existence—Two Diametrically Opposed Policies—Comment on the Open Letter of the Central Committee of the CPSU (VI)." Khrushchev was denounced for not understanding that "the imperialists' cold war against the socialist countries is one of the manifestations of the international class struggle which inevitably goes on, now in an acute and now in a relaxed form." The article added that "the heart and soul of the general line of peaceful co-existence pursued by the leaders of the Soviet Communist Party is the Soviet-U.S. collaboration for domination of the world."

The spokesman of the PRC Foreign Ministry issued a statement stressing once again the Chinese government's unswerving support for the efforts of the Asian and African countries for an increase in their seats in the principal U.N. organs.

December 13: U.S. Assistant Secretary Hilsman, at the meeting of Commonwealth

Club of San Francisco, said that the United States kept the "door open" for talks with Communist China when Chinese leaders ended venomous hatreds. He declared that the Chinese were "dangerously over-confident" and "wedded to out-dated theories, but pragmatic when their existence is threatened." He conceded that, "We have no reason to believe that there is a present likelihood that the Communist regime will be overthrown," but he said there was "some evidence of evolutionary forces at work in mainland China" among the intellectuals and the "more sophisticated second echelon of leadership" which would one day come into power. Hilsman added that U.S. defense of Formosa was a matter of "basic principle" and there could be no "basic improvement" in U.S.-Chinese relations until Communist China accepted that fact.

December 13: Chou En-lai and Chen Yi started a tour of Africa.

December 14: A contract was signed for the purchase of two sets of chemical fertilizer equipment from the Italian "Montecatini" General Corporation of the Mineral and Chemical Industry by the China National Technical Import Corporation.

December 14-21: Chou En-lai was in Cairo for a conference with Egyptian leaders. A communique, issued on December 21, affirmed the UAR's support for China's claim to Taiwan and for the admission of Communist China to the U.N. and China's support of Arab unity, and in particular for the claim of the people of Palestine, Yemen, and Oman. Both countries would strive for a peaceful settlement of the Sino-Indian conflict, and supported the peaceful efforts initiated by the Colombo Conference. During his visit, Chou En-lai admitted that the PRC had "serious differences with the leaders of the CPSU." But, he added, those countries that "want to profit by these differences are doomed to disappointment, because China and the U.S.S.R have between them a treaty of friendship, alliance and mutual assistance," and in case of

attack, "the Chinese and Soviet peoples will without fail stand by each other."

December 17: U.S. Supreme Court Justice Douglas raised the two-Chinas policy issue in dissenting from a U.S. Supreme Court refusal to revive deportation to Taiwan of two mainland-born deportable Chinese. The Supreme Court majority "upheld the U.S. view that, for deportation purposes, Taiwan was China." Douglas urged that the United States first ask Communist China, the country of their birth, to accept them as required under U.S. immigration laws.

The Soviet Union voted against a proposal before the U.N. General Assembly to revise the U.N. Charter to enlarge the Security Council and the Economic and Social Council to give greater representation to Asian and African nations. The Soviet delegates said they voted against the resolution because they felt there should be no expansion until the PRC became China's representative in the U.N. On December 18 *People's Daily* said that the Soviet Union had misrepresented Communist China by voting against the resolution. On December 21, the Soviet Foreign Ministry criticized Communist China for failing to disclose its position on the resolution until after the vote had been taken.

December 19: An agreement on the purchase of a petroleum-refining combined plant was signed between the China National Technical Import Corporation and the SNAN Company of Italy.

December 20: 540 kilometers of narrow-gauge railway and 140 kilometers of motor roads have been built in the Northeast China timber areas by the railway corps of the PLA this year, an NCNA report said.

December 21-27: Chou En-lai flew to Algeria for a week's stay, during which he visited a number of cooperative farms and nationalized factories and had talks with President Ben Bella. In a speech to the leading members of the Algerian NLF, Chou warned against "neo-colonialists" who "disguise themselves as friends of the oppressed peoples." Chou was reported to have offered Algeria a Chinese loan for the construction of a motor road across the Sahara from El Golla to Timbuktu (Mali). President Ben Bella was reported to have offered Chinese oil-prospecting rights in the Sahara. A joint communique was issued on December 27.

December 27-31: Chou En-lai visited Morocco for talks with King Hassan. It was believed that the subjects discussed included a possible increase in trade between the two countries and the border dispute between Algeria and Morocco, in which China had previously supported Algeria. A communique, issued on December 31, said that China favored negotiations between African countries to revise the frontier fixed by the colonial power—a procedure which Algeria had rejected. On December 29, Chou was interviewed in Rabat by a French television network. He said: "We believe it possible that countries with different social systems could co-exist peacefully." He added that war was "not inevitable between the socialist and imperialist camp," but he accused the United States of impeding peaceful coexistence by "its policy of hostility toward China," and by holding the "Chinese territory of Taiwan, maintaining military bases around China, and violating Chinese air-space and territorial waters." Chou said he hoped a "normalization of relations between the PRC and France might result in establishment of cultural and economic ties between the two nations."

December 27: The Tunisian government decided to recognize the PRC and invited Chou En-lai to visit Tunisia.

December 27: A Sino-Rumanian agreement on exchange of goods and payments in 1964 was signed in Peking.

December 30: The State Council approved: "Basic flight rules of the PRC"; flight rules governing foreign civil aircraft; a cultural cooperation agreement between the PRC and Algeria; and a goods exchange and payments agreement between the PRC and Afghanistan.

A Sino-Mali supplementary protocol on economic and technical cooperation signed in Bamako.

1964

January 1: Mao Tse-tung stressed Chinese-Soviet friendship in a New Year's message to Khrushchev.

The PRC and Mexico signed a contract on the exchange of films in Mexico City.

January 2: A Sino-Albanian agreement on cooperation in public health work was signed in Peking.

January 6: Sino-Syrian accord on establishment of tele-communications between Peking and Damascus was signed.

Prince Sihanouk of Cambodia announced that China had agreed to supply Cambodia with military assistance of 100 lorries, some 75 mm. guns, and other equipment.

January 7: A Sino-Guinean protocol on trade in 1964 was signed in Conakry.

January 8: Chou En-lai, speaking in Albania, accused the Tito clique of plotting to overthrow the Albanian leaders. He arrived in Albania on December 31, 1963, for a week's visit during a brief interruption of his African tour. A joint Sino-Albania communique condemned the nuclear test-ban treaty and accused Tito of betraying the Socialist camp and joining the American imperialists in attempting to destroy the world revolution.

January 9: The PRC and Hungary exchanged notes in Budapest to extend their 1953 agreement on scientific and technical cooperation.

January 9-10: Chou En-lai, continued his African tour, arriving in Tunis. A joint communique announced they "agreed to strengthen the friendship between their people and develop economic and human exchanges" and to establish diplomatic relations. The communique also affirmed their determination to support the peaceful settlement of international conflicts without recourse to armed force and their desire for general disarmament and a complete ban on nuclear weapons. The communique was issued on January 10.

January 11: A contract for the purchase of complete equipment for an N-butyl alcohol and ethylhexyl alcohol plant was signed between the China National Technical Import Corporation and the delegation of French companies—Speichim Corporation and S. A. Mele.

January 11-16: Chou En-lai visited Ghana. A joint communique called for an "anti-imperialist conference" of African, Asian, and Latin American peoples and endorsed preparation for an Afro-Asian conference. It also proposed a conference of the world's heads of government to sign an international convention to prohibit the development and use of nuclear weapons and to provide for the destruction of all existing stockpiles. The communique was issued on January 16.

January 13-17: The second session of the executive organ for scientific and technical cooperation was held in Ulan Bator January 13-17. A protocol was signed on January 17.

January 14: The Sino-Cuban cultural cooperation agreement for 1964-65 was signed in Havana.

January 15: The 1964 protocol for China-Cuba trade and payments agreement was signed in Havana.

January 16: A Sino-East German protocol on extension and amendment of a 1953 agreement on cooperation in technology and technical science was signed in Peking.

January 16-21: Chou En-lai visited Mali where 40,000 people awaited him, the the most enthusiastic reception of his tour. A joint communique was issued in Banako on January 21.

January 17: Chen Yi cabled Abdul Rahman Mohammed Bahn, Minister of External Affairs of the Republic of Zanzibar, informing him of the PRC's recognition of the government of that republic.

January 19: A Sino-Mongolian protocol on scientific and technical cooperation was signed in Ulan Bator.

January 20: The 1964 Sino-Mongolian goods exchange protocol was signed in Peking.

U.S. officials confirmed that the United

States had pressed Nationalist China not to break ties with France when the latter recognized the PRC.

Tass denied an NCNA January 12 allegagation that the Soviet embassy in Tokyo had detained a member of a PRC delegation, Chou Hung-ching, who was reported by western press to have tried to defect to the U.S.S.R.

January 21-27: Chou En-lai visited Guinea. A joint communique stated that Chou's talks with President Toure had revealed a "broad identity of views" between them. A joint communique was issued in Conakry on January 26.

January 22: A French parliamentary delegation arrived in Peking.

January 23: Cuban Premier Fidel Castro, winding up a nine-day visit to the Soviet Union, declared his support for the U.S.S.R. in its ideological dispute with the PRC.

The 1964-65 executive plan of the Sino-Rumanian cultural cooperation agreement was signed in Bucharest.

January 24: The PRC, the U.S.S.R., North Vietnam, and North Korea signed a protocol on a 1964 plan for cooperation in railway transport in Hanoi.

January 26: Peking refrained from giving France any public assurance that it would set up relations on a two-China basis.

In Tokyo, U.S. Secretary of State Dean Rusk had a conference with Japanese Foreign Minister Ohira to explore means to avert the spread of general movement for recognition of Communist China.

January 27: The establishment of diplomatic relations between France and the PRC was announced. It was the first recognition by any major power since 1950. The communique issued simultaneously in Paris and Peking stated that both countries agreed to designate ambassadors within three months.

It was announced that Chou En-lai would not visit Kenya, Tanganyika, or Uganda following the request of all three countries for British troops to help suppress army mutinies.

January 27-30: Chou En-lai visited Sudan.

A joint communique called for a second Afro-Asian conference on January 30.

January 28: The PRC and Indonesia signed a contract on implementation of the 1961 agreement on economic and technical co-operation in Djakarta.

January 29: Secretary of State Dean Rusk, in a Tokyo speech, held the view that free nations must not reward Communist China militancy; that world peace could hinge on whether they believed aggressive policies were profitable. He charged that Communist China scorned basic conditions necessary for peace. He said that the United States would be loyal to commitments to Taiwan.

January 30-February 1: Chou En-lai visited Ethiopia. A joint communique stated that Emperor Haile Selassie had accepted an invitation to visit China following "normalizing" of relations between the two countries. It also supported China's "legitimate rights" in the United Nations. The communique was issued February 1.

January 31: A Sino-Hungary broadcasting and television cooperation agreement was signed in Peking.

February 1: Commenting on French recognition, President Johnson said at his press conference, that other nations must not reward China for aggressive policies.

February 1-4: Chou En-lai concluded his African trip by visiting the Somali Republic. During a speech there he stated that revolutionary prospects are excellent throughout Africa. A joint communique called for a second Afro-Asian conference and for the liquidation of foreign military bases in Africa. The communique was issued on February 1.

February 2: Chou En-lai restated his opposition to a two-China policy in an interview with Edgar Snow.

February 3: The editorial departments of the *People's Daily* and the *Red Flag* journal published an article entitled: "The Leaders of the CPSU Are the Greatest Splitters of Our Times—Comment on the Open Letter of the Central Committee of the CPSU (VII)." The article said that divided movement is better than revisionist movement and rejected a recent proposal to halt polemics.

February 5: Chou En-lai returned to Peking after his eight-week tour, having visited eleven countries.

A Sino-Polish agreement on transfer of goods and payments in 1964 was signed in Peking.

The PRC and Ghana signed a protocol in Accra on exchange of goods in 1964.

February 6: The PRC and North Vietnam signed an agreement on cooperation between the PRC Academy of Sciences and the State Commission of Sciences and Technology of North Vietnam.

The government of the Kingdom of Burundi invited Chou En-lai to visit that kingdom. The PRC Premier accepted this invitation, the visit to be made at a suitable time.

A new manual alphabet for the deaf and dumb in China has been issued by the Ministries of the Interior and Education and the Committee for Reforming the Chinese Written Language, NCNA reported.

February 13: China celebrated the 14th anniversary of the signing of the Sino-Soviet treaty of friendship in spite of their quarrel. Soviet Ambassador S. V. Chervanenko attended.

France announced the appointment of Claude Chavet as charge d'affaires in Peking; China appointed Sung Chih-kung as its charge d'affaires in Paris.

February 14: Soviet Premier Khrushchev told a plenary meeting of the Soviet Communist party's Central Committee that the U.S.S.R. was attempting to restore "the monolithic unity of the world socialist system." He said: "We have fought and will continue to fight against revisionists, dogmatists, the newly backed Troskyites who, while making high-sounding revolutionary phrases about the struggle against imperialism, undermine in fact the unity of the world Communist movement by splitting their activities."

February 14-18: Chou En-lai and Chen Yi visited Burma for talks with General Ne Win, Chairman of the Burmese Revo-

lutionary Council. A joint communique expressed hope that China and India would open direct negotiations regarding their border dispute on the basis of the Colombo proposal. The communique was issued on February 18.

February 19: The PRC and Pakistan signed a joint communique on boundary demarcation.

February 18-26: Chou En-lai and Chen Yi visited Pakistan. A joint communique indicated Chinese support of Pakistan in the Kashmir dispute and called for another Afro-Asian conference. The communique was issued on February 23.

February 19: Argentina signed an agreement to sell to the PRC 400,000 tons of wheat.

A *People's Daily* article rejected the "Open Door" offered by the United States for eventual talks leading to understanding between the United States and Communist China. The article was regarded as a reply to Assistant Secretary Hilsman's December 1963 speech.

February 20: The Central Committee of the CPC sent a letter to the Soviet party demanding a copy of a Soviet letter of February 12, 1964, which had been sent to other Communist parties but not to the Chinese party. A similar letter was sent on February 27.

February 22: Chou En-lai sent a cable to Bascal Lissouba, Prime Minister of the Republic of Congo (Brazzaville), greeting the decision of the two governments to give each other recognition and establish diplomatic relations of ambassadorial rank.

President Ayub Khan offered Pakistan's good office to bring about some Peking-Washington agreement.

February 25: Negotiations between the Soviet Union and China opened in Peking to solve their border dispute.

In his speech at the West Pakistan Assembly, Chou En-lai hailed Pakistan for opposing the "imperialist plot to create two Chinas." He said that China would welcome Pakistan's efforts for United States-Chinese amity.

Secretary of State Dean Rusk, addressing a world affairs conference in Washington sponsored by the AFL-CIO International Union of Electrical, Radio and Machine Workers, said: "We have special and very grave concerns about Communist China. And here let me clear away a myth. We do not ignore the Chinese Communist Regime . . . We talk with it regularly through our respective ambassadors to Warsaw. There have been 119 of these talks. And what the Peiping regime itself says to us is among the reasons why we continue to have very grave concerns about it. Peiping continues to insist upon the surrender of Taiwan as the sine qua non of any improvement whatever in the relations with the United States. We are loyal to our commitments to the government of the Republic of China; and we will not abandon the 12 million people of Free China on Taiwan to Communist tyranny. Peiping incites and aggressively supports the aggression in Southeast Asia in violation of the Geneva Agreements of 1954 and the Geneva Accords of 1962. Peiping attacked India and occupies a position from which it continues to threaten the subcontinent of South Asia. Peiping is attempting to extend its tactics of terror and subversion into Africa and Latin America. In other words, Peiping flouts the first condition for peace, leave your neighbors alone. And we in the United States have not forgotten Peiping's aggressive intervention in Korea—an act for which it stands condemned by the U.N. The American people cherished their close and cordial ties with the people of the Chinese mainland. They look forward to the time when it will be possible to renew this historic friendship."

While touring in East Pakistan, Chinese Premier Chou En-lai demanded at a press conference that the United States withdraw its military personnel from Vietnam and end its "armed intervention" in Laos. He reiterated the conditions for an improvement in relations between the United States and China—a change in America's "hostile policy toward China"

and a withdrawal from Taiwan and the Taiwan Strait.

February 26-29: Chou En-lai visited Ceylon for talks with Mrs. Bandaraneke, Prime Minister of Ceylon. A joint communique issued on February 29 expressed interest in the second Afro-Asian conference. Mrs. Bandaraneke strongly urged Mr. Chou during their talks to agree to the Colombo proposals, as a preliminary to a meeting with Mr. Nehru. Chou was reported to have said that if India agreed to discussion, China would be willing to consider the withdrawal of her remaining posts in the demilitarized zone in Ladakh, but he did not agree to the establishment of Indian posts in this zone, as envisaged in the Colombo proposals. A Sino-Ceylonese trade contract was signed on February 28 along with a contract on the sale of cotton to Ceylon.

February 29: A Sino-Soviet cultural cooperation agreement was signed in Moscow.

The Central Committee of the CPC sent a lengthy reply to the CPSU in response to the latter's letter of November 29, 1963. It expressed a willingness to negotiate their boundary dispute; it rejected Soviet offers for economic aid, and called for a world Communist conference on Chinese terms.

March 2-11: A Rumanian delegation visited Peking to continue its efforts of mediation between the Chinese and Soviet parties. The talks produced little result.

March 3: The Canadian government announced the sale of 16.3 million bushels of barley to Communist China.

The World Health Organization rejected a French proposal to seat Peking in place of Formosa.

March 5: A Sino-Albanian agricultural cooperation agreement was signed in Peking.

March 8: Protocol and related documents on technical and operational arrangements for the air service between the PRC and Pakistan were signed in Peking.

March 9: A Sino-North Vietnamese protocol on border railways was signed in Hanoi.

March 15: A planeload of arms arrived in Cambodia from the PRC. At the airport,

Prince Sihanouk told the Chinese Communist ambassador: "Since our liberation from conditional American aid, our two armies have been able fraternally to extend hands . . . Our only worry is to have sufficient military force to dissuade instigators of imperialistic war who menace the Cambodian peace."

The PRC and Pakistan issued a press communique on boundary demarcation in Karachi.

March 21: The 1964 plan for the implementation of the Sino-Bulgarian cultural cooperation agreement was signed in Sofia.

March 24: The 1964 plan for the implementation of the Sino-Hungarian cultural cooperation was signed in Budapest.

March 25: The PRC and Albania signed an accord on cooperation between the PRC Academy of Sciences and the State University of Tirana in Peking along with the 1964-65 plan.

March 28: The Sino-Hungarian goods exchange payments agreement for 1964 was signed in Peking.

March 30: The PRC and Poland signed the 1963-64 plan for cooperation between the Academies of Sciences in Peking.

March 31: The editorial departments of the *People's Daily* and *Red Flag* published an article entitled, "The Proletarian Revolution and Khrushchev's Revisionism—Comment on the Open Letter of Central Committee of the CPSU (VIII)." The article refuted Khrushchev's contention that a peaceful transition from capitalism to socialism is possible and accused him of leading the Soviet Union back to capitalism. It called upon the international Communist movement to repudiate his leadership. It was the harshest and most devastating in the series of blasts at Khrushchev personally.

The PRC Foreign Ministry rejected, in a note, the Indian government's protesting against the setting up of stone cairns by the Chinese troops on the western sector of the Sino-Indian border to mark the line of actual control between the PRC and India.

April 1: Soviet Premier Khrushchev said in a speech delivered on a visit to Budapest: "There are people who call themselves Marxist-Leninists and at the same time say there is no need to strive for a better life. According to them, only one thing is important—revolution. What kind of Marxism is that?" He asserted that the key to Communism's victory was increased "productivity of labor in the socialist countries."

April 3: Moscow released a 30,000-word indictment of the Chinese delivered February 1 at a Central Committee plenum by Presidium member Suslov. It insisted that Moscow had done all it could to conciliate the Chinese, but implied Soviet concern that continued silence would encourage Peking in moves to split the world Communist movement. It read the CPC off as petty bourgeois, chauvinists, and Trotskyites, with Mao characterized as the personification of Stalinism and the personality cult. *Pravda* made a brief reference to a report that the CPSU had recently offered Peking a three-stage plan for a conference of Communist parties: A bilateral meeting, a drafting committee, and an all-party meeting, all to take place before the end of 1964.

April 4-8: Prince Souvanna Phouma, Premier of Laos, arrived in Peking on April 4, to appeal for assistance in bringing peace to his country. He was welcomed at the airport by Chou En-lai. They had an exchange of views on the current situation in Laos, the development of the friendly relations between the PRC and Laos, and other questions. The China-Laos joint communique was signed on April 8 to deal with the 1962 Geneva Agreement on Laos support for conference to guarantee neutrality of Cambodia, etc.

April 5: Australia announced the sale to the PRC of 21 million bushels of wheat for about $35.8 million. This transaction brought the three-year total of Australian wheat sold to China to 300 million bushels valued at $448 million.

April 10-16: A Chinese delegation attended a conference in Indonesia of 21 Afro-

Asian states in preparation for a second Afro-Asian conference in 1965. A final communique on the meeting was signed by the PRC, Afghanistan, Algeria, Cambodia, Cameroon, Ceylon, Ethiopia, Ghana, Guinea, India, Indonesia, Iran, Iraq, Liberia, Morocco, Nepal, Pakistan, the Philippines, Syria, and Tanzania.

April 11: The executive program on a Sino-UAR cultural cooperation agreement was signed in Cairo.

April 14: A Sino-Bulgaria 1964 goods ex-exchange and payments agreement was signed in Sofia.

The 1964 executive plan for the Sino-Algerian cultural cooperation agreement and Sino-Algerian radio and television cooperation agreement were signed.

April 15: Mao Tse-tung sent greetings to Khrushchev on his 70th birthday, proclaiming the unity of Russia and China.

April 17: A supplementary protocol to the agreement on economic aid between the PRC and Nepalese governments was signed in Katmandu.

April 18: The 1964-1965 executive plan for a Sino-Korean cultural agreement was signed in Peking.

A Japanese trade mission reached agreement in Peking to increase trade between the two countries, including the export of Japanese fertilizer to China and the exporting of Chinese iron-ore and coal to Japan. Three series of minutes on talks between the staffs of Liao Cheng-chi and the Japanese trade mission were signed: (1) Trade based on Liao-Takasaki memorandum; (2) exchange of correspondents; (3) exchange of representatives and setting up of liaison offices.

April 19: The Laotian coalition government under Prince Souvanna Phouma was ousted by a rightist military junta. On April 22, the PRC charged that the United States had engineered the coup. The military junta announced on April 23 that Prince Souvanna Phouma had been reinstated as Premier.

April 20: In a speech at the Press Association luncheon in New York, President Johnson said: "So long as the Communist Chinese pursue conflict and preach violence, there can be and will be no easing of relationships . . ." The President added that no one should "doubt our unalterable commitment to the defense and liberty of free China."

April 24: A Sino-Czechoslovak agreement on exchange of goods and payments in 1964 was signed in Peking.

April 26: The 1964 plan for executing the Sino-Malian cultural cooperation agreement was signed in Bamako.

April 27: A publication trade contract for 1964-65 was signed by the PRC and North Vietnam.

People's Daily carried full texts of three CPSU documents released April 3 in Moscow: Suslov's February 14 report, CPSU party plenum resolutions, and a *Pravda* editorial. Peking also made reference to Khrushchev's 12 "anti-China speeches or statements made April 3-18." Khrushchev's remarks were said to read like "abuse hurled by a harridan in the street."

Chou En-lai reported to the National People's Congress Standing Committee on a recent visit abroad; he summed up the Peking foreign policy position as readiness to practice peaceful co-existence with capitalist countries, including the United States; he blamed the United States for the lack of results in Chinese-U.S. ambassadorial talks.

April 29: The 1964 executive plan for a Sino-Korean scientific cooperation agreement was signed in Peking.

A supplement to the Sino-North Vietnamese cultural cooperation was signed in Peking.

April 30: Congratulations were sent by Liu Shao-chi on the founding of the Tanganyika and Zanzibar United Republic.

May 4: Moscow issued a "government statement" addressed to Asian and African countries to rebut the Chinese argument that the Soviet Union should not participate in the Afro-Asian conference scheduled for 1965 because the U.S.S.R. is neither an African nor an Asian country.

May 6: Letters on the promotion of economic and trade relations between the PRC and the Netherlands were exchanged in Canton.

The PRC Foreign Ministry sent a note to the Brazilian government to demand the release of the nine Chinese personnel arrested by the Brazilian authorities.

May 7: A CPC letter rejected the Soviet proposal for a world Communist meeting in 1964. It laid down a Chinese timetable which included bilateral talks with Moscow in May 1965 or later, a 17-party preparatory meeting sometime thereafter, and a world meeting not until perhaps four or five years later or even longer.

May 8: Peking released the contents of seven letters exchanged with Moscow since November 1963. Among other things, the letters revealed that Moscow had sent a conciliatory message offering to resume economic assistance, and that Peking had not even bothered to reply.

The CPC Central Committee, in a letter to a U.S.S.R. counterpart, called old China-Russia border treaties unequal but offered to respect them as a basis for reasonable settlement of disputes.

May 9: In a joint communique, representatives of the PRC and Indonesia denounced the action of the International Olympic Committee against Indonesia, and upheld Games of Newly Emerging Forces.

A Sino-North Korean technical cooperation agreement was signed in Peking.

The PRC and Sudan exchanged notes in Khartoum on an amendment to their 1962 trade agreement.

May 12: A Sino-Malian trade protocol was signed.

The protocol for a cultural cooperation agreement between the PRC and Guinea was signed in Conakry.

A passenger airliner made a successful trial flight from Phnom Penh, Cambodia, to Canton via Hanoi for the new Sino-Cambodian airline.

May 13: A Sino-Soviet trade protocol for 1964 was signed in Peking.

A Sino-Chilian trade agreement was signed for the purchase by the PRC of 20,000 tons of niter from Chile valued at 310,000 pounds.

The PRC Foreign Ministry in a note to the UAR embassy expressed firm support for the people of Aden and South Yemen in their struggle against British colonial rule.

A Sino-Indonesian joint communique on scientific and technical cooperation was issued in Peking.

PRC Foreign Minister Chen Yi sent letters to Foreign Minister R. A. Butler of Britain and Andrei Gromyko of the Soviet Union charging that the United States had promoted the rightist military coup of April 19 in Laos to "endeavor to completely undermine the Laotian government of National Union, rekindle the flames of civil war in Laos, and to create the division of Laos." Chen Yi said that "Laos is now faced with the dangers of all-out civil war as a result of provocations of U.S. imperialists and the Laotian right wing." He proposed a new Geneva conference on the entire Indo-China question.

May 15: The PRC and Nepal exchanged letters on boundary demarcation procedures in Katmandu.

May 16-19: The President of Sudan, Ibrahim Abboud, arrived in Peking for a state visit and was met by Mao Tse-tung in one of his rare public appearances. During his visit the Sudanese President signed an agreement with China for export of Sudanese cotton in return for machinery and electrical equipment. A joint communique was issued on May 19.

May 18: The 1964 executive plan of a cultural cooperation agreement between the PRC and Poland was signed in Warsaw.

May 19: A Sino-Nepalese trade agreement was signed in Katmandu.

Pathet Lao attacks on loyalist forces in Laos were continuing successfully. On May 19 Britain asked Communist China to use its influence to end the hostilities. Peking refused the request a week later and again charged that the United States was guilty of aggression in Indo-China. The Chinese proposed that the foreign ministers of the countries represented at

Geneva in 1962 meet at Phnom Penh, Cambodia, to confer on Southeast Asia, and that they take up the question of Laos first.

May 20: It was announced that China had agreed to make a grant of $3 million to Kenya to help balance its budget, and an interest-free loan of 65 million Swiss francs for development projects over the next five years.

May 21: A day after French President De Gaulle had called for a reconvening of the Geneva Conference, Ambassador Adlai E. Stevenson said in the U.N. Security Council: "There is no need for another such conference. Another Geneva Conference, if it reached any agreement at all, would prove no more effective than the agreements we already have." The United States later said it was agreeable to "consultations" in the Laotian capital of Vietiane of representatives of the 14 nations that signed the Geneva accords.

May 23: The protocol of the 3rd meeting of the administrative council of the Sino-Albanian Joint Stock Shipping Company was signed in Tirana.

May 25: A Sino-Iraqui cultural cooperation plan for 1964-65 was signed.

May 26: Chen Yi's reply to the British Foreign Secretary's message of May 19 said that the uprising of the neutralist troops in the Plain of Jars was the inevitable outcome of the military coup in Vietnam and that the Chinese government hoped that the British government would give serious consideration to its suggestion and effectively perform the duty of upholding the Geneva agreements. Furthermore, in a letter to the co-chairmen and participating nations of the Geneva Conference, Chen Yi put forward a suggestion that the 14-nation Geneva Conference of Foreign Ministers should be held in Phnom Penh, the capital of the Kingdom of Cambodia, in June to discuss first the Laotian question.

May 27: A Sino-Czechoslovak cultural cooperation plan was signed.

Condolence was expressed by Chou En-lai in a message to Madame Indira Gandhi on Prime Minister Nehru's death.

May 29: The U.S. State Department announced that a diplomat at the PRC's embassy in Burundi had defected and was being given asylum in the U.S. embassy there. The Chinese embassy in Burundi charged that the diplomat, Tung Chin-ping, had been "kidnapped." The Burundi government attempted to block Tung's departure from the country, but on July 31 the United States embassy announced that Tung had "disappeared." On August 4 he reappeared in New York and told a news conference that China was using Burundi as a "stepping stone to the Congo," because, according to the strategy of Mao Tse-tung, "when we grab the Congo, then we can grab the whole of Africa."

May 30-31: The PRC government statement (May 30) and *People's Daily* "Observer" article (May 31) disputed Moscow's claim to be an Asian power and thus entitled to a voice at the Bandung Conference. Chinese pronouncements dismissed the size of the Soviet territories in Asia as not germane to the issue and defined the U.S.S.R. as a traditional European power on the basis of the location of its political center, distribution of population, etc.

June 1-11: President Sallal of Yemen visited Peking and signed the following documents on June 9: (1) Joint communique, (2) treaty of friendship, (3) agreement on economic and technical cooperation, (4) agreement on cultural cooperation.

June 3: 3,500 Chinese personnel who had been helping Mongolia with its construction left Ulan Bator for home.

June 5: A State Council meeting decided to set up a commission for economic relations with foreign countries and to divide the Ministry of Education into two ministries—Ministry of Higher Education and Ministry of Education.

June 5-July 31: The 1964 festival of Peking opera on contemporary themes was held from June 5 through July 31. 35 long and short operas were performed to packed houses and audiences. Two thousand five hundred actors, directors, and playwrights of Peking opera and writers and artists from 19 provinces, cities, and autonomous regions attended the performances and made studies of them. Mao Tsetung and other Chinese leaders received on July 17 performers in the festival and those attending the festival for study.

June 6: The NCNA reprinted Indonesian Communist Party Chairman Aidit's May 2 speech in which he defended his earlier rejection of a Soviet request to join in the attack on Albania and argued that Peking was justified in continuing the polemic with Moscow after the July 1963 CPSU open letters.

June 10: A Sino-Korean protocol on maritime transport was signed.

June 11: A Sino-Yugoslav protocol on exchange of goods in 1964 was signed in Belgrade.

June 12: The first Chinese freighter to sail on the direct Sino-Korean lines, "PEACE NO. 60," left Shanghai for Nampo, Korea.

A "Chiang Kai-shek gang's" plane was shot down when it flew over North China on a harassing mission on the night of June 11, said an NCNA report.

Khrushchev asserted at a Soviet-German friendship rally in the Kremlin that Sino-Soviet relations could be normalized despite outstanding differences; he attacked Peking for attempting to weaken economic, military, and cultural ties of socialist countries, and claimed that Chinese nationalism is the primary cause of current bloc difficulties.

June 13: The PRC government issued a statement protesting against "U.S. aircraft bombing the quarters of the Chinese economic and cultural mission in Laos." A protest was also made in a letter by Chen Yi to the two co-chairmen of the 1962 Geneva Conference.

June 14: Sino-Mongolian minutes on talks of boundary demarcation were issued.

June 15: Letters were exchanged between representatives of the Chinese and Ceylon governments turning the loan of 50 million rupees granted by the PRC to Ceylon in 1958 into an interest-free loan.

The Foreign Ministry of Cambodia delivered a statement to the Chinese embassy in Cambodia expressing warm support for the PRC government's proposal on the reconvening of the 14-nation Geneva conference of 1962 to bring about a peaceful settlement to the Laotian question.

June 16: The PRC and Tanzania signed an agreement on economic and technical cooperation in Peking.

June 17: A Sino-Mongolian cultural cooperation executive plan was signed.

June 19: A Sino-Polish scientific cooperation protocol was signed in Warsaw along with a protocol on extension of the 1954 scientific and technical cooperation agreement.

June 27: Japan and the PRC agreed to exchange trade representatives. The United States and Nationalist China both strongly objected.

June 29: Peking protested the visit of a ten-member delegation of Indians to Taiwan.

June 30: A Sino-Mongolian protocol on boundary demarcation was signed in Ulan Bator.

July 4: Chen Yi sent a message to Hastings Banda, Prime Minister of Malaivi, informing him that the PRC government had decided to give recognition to Maliavi.

July 5: Sino-Rumanian protocol on scientific and technical cooperation was signed in Bucharest.

July 6: Chen Yi, in a reply letter to Xuan Thuy, Minister of Foreign Affairs of North Vietnam, declared: "China and the Democratic Republic of Vietnam are fraternal neighbors closely related like the lips and the teeth. The Chinese people cannot be expected to look on with folded arms in the face of any aggression against the Democratic Republic of Vietnam."

July 7: The PRC and Ceylon signed an agreement on the PRC gift of the passenger train and trucks to Ceylon.

Irrigation and drainage facilities for more than 3 million hectares of farmland have been built in China since last winter, according to the Ministry of Water Conservation and Electric Power.

The Ministry of Finance issued a notice concerning the redemption of principal and payment of interest on national economic construction bonds.

July 9: A Sino-East German protocol on scientific and technical cooperation was signed in East Berlin.

July 11: The Chinese government agreed to extend a loan without interest to the government of the Republic of the Congo (Brazzaville) for its economic development. An agreement was signed in Brazzaville on July 10.

July 10-12: Chou En-lai and Chen Yi were welcomed at the airport on July 10 by Ne Win and Foreign Minister U Thi Han in Rangoon. During the visit, lasting from July 10 to 11, Chou En-lai and Ne Win exchanged views on matters of common interest to the two countries as well as on current international problems, particularly those pertaining to Southwest Asia. In a joint communique issued on July 11, the PRC agreed to take the necessary measures to speed up the implementation of the Sino-Burmese agreement on economic and technical cooperation and expand trade.

Mao Tse-tung held an interview with a group of Japanese socialists in which he criticized the Soviet Union for its territorial acquisitions following World War II. He also called for a revision of the Sino-Soviet frontier.

July 14: Peking issued the 9th *People's Daily-Red Flag* article in reply to the July 14, 1963 CPSU open letter. Entitled, "On Khrushchev's Phony Communism and Its Historical Lessons for the World," the article ridicules Khrushchev for having paved the way for the restoration of capitalism in the U.S.S.R. and savagely denies the legitimacy of Soviet leadership. It calls for an anti-Khrushchev movement within the Soviet Union, declaring that the issue confronting the Russian people is not how to build Communism but rather how to resist and oppose Khrushchev's efforts to restore capitalism.

July 15: An agreement of friendship and cooperation was signed between the NCNA and the Algerian press service.

A supplementary agreement to the 1963

agreement on economic and technical cooperation between the PRC and the Ghanaian governments was signed in Accra.

July 17: A 1964-65 working plan for the agreement on cultural cooperation between the PRC and Ghana was signed in Accra.

A Sino-Pakistani communique on economic and trade talks was issued in Peking.

July 20: Liu Shao-chi sent a cable to A. I. Mikoyan congratulating him on being elected president of the Presidium of the U.S.S.R. Supreme Soviet.

July 21: Khrushchev in Warsaw admitted that differences with the CPC had probably acquired a particularly serious character, but insisted that these difficulties would be overcome.

July 22: The State Council approved the draft regulations for propagation and protecting of aquatic resources.

July 23: An agreement of friendship and cooperation was signed in Karachi between the NCNA and the Associated Press of Pakistan.

A Sino-Congo (Brazzaville) agreement on trade and payments was signed in Brazzaville.

July 27: A contract for the purchase of crude oil cracking and olepin separation equipment by Communist China was signed between the China National Technical Import Corporation and a delegation of Lungil Gesellschaft Fuer Nimeraloeltechnik of West Germany.

July 29: A Sino-Vietnamese agreement on postal services and tele-communications was signed in Hanoi.

July 30: An NCNA and Ghana News Agency exchange agreement was signed in Accra.

The CPC announced that it had rejected the Soviet Party's proposal for a world meeting of Communist parties. The July 28 letter of rejection said: "We will never take part in an international meeting, or any preparatory meeting, which you call for the purpose of splitting the international Communist movement."

July 31: A Sino-North Vietnamese health cooperation agreement was signed in Peking.

Pakistan announced it was to receive an interest-free $60 million loan from the PRC for the purchase of heavy machinery, sugar mills, and cement plants, and would repay the loan over a 30- to 40-year-period with agricultural and manufactured goods.

August 1: A Sino-East German 1964 trade and payments agreement was signed in Berlin.

August 2: Peking replied to Moscow's July 25 communication on Laos. It obliquely criticized Soviet performance as Geneva co-chairman in Laos by expressing hope that Moscow would truly shoulder its responsibilty in this capacity. It encouraged Moscow to drop its threat to withdraw a co-chairman.

August 5: An accord on cooperation between the Broadcasting Administrative Bureau of China and the National Radio Division of Guinea was signed in Conakry.

August 11: A Sino-Cuban protocol on economic cooperation was signed in Havana.

August 12: A Sino-Vietnamese 1964 scientific cooperation protocol was signed in Peking.

August 20: M. Tshombe, Prime Minister of the Congo, sent a note to U Thant charging the Chinese with subversive activities in the Congo, and with supplying aircraft to the rebels in Stanleyville.

August 24: A Sino-UAR joint communique was signed on the development of scientific and technical cooperation between the two countries.

August 25: An exhibition on Chinese people's support for the Vietnamese people's resistance to U.S. "aggression" was opened.

August 30: The CPC Central Committee reiterated its stand for an international meeting of the Communist parties to be held after ample preparation, declaring: "We are firmly opposed to your schismatic meeting." This was in reply to the July 20, 1964 letter of the CPSU Central Committee.

August 31: Yang Hsien-chen, a leading member of the Central Committee of the CPC and a veteran Communist philosopher, was sharply criticized as siding with the Russians in opposition to Mao Tsetung.

An eleven-day symposium of over 300 scientists from across the world was concluded in Peking. China announced it was establishing a permanent liaison officer for non-European scientists to rival the Moscow-dominated World Federation of Scientific Workers.

The PRC and Guinea signed a contract in Conakry on distribution of PRC films in Guinea and a contract on exchange of newsreel materials.

September 2: The PRC and East Germany signed in Peking a cultural cooperation plan for 1964.

Peking released new materials supporting earlier accusations of subversion and sabotage by Moscow in Sinkiang, introduced in September, 1963, and reaffirmed during the March 14-26, 1964, Sinkiang-Uighur Autonomous Region Congress. An NCNA report, released this day, notes that at a second session of the Regional Congress (August 26-29) Chairman Irhali declared that economic achievements in Sinkiang had been made in the course of a struggle against the Khrushchev revisionist clique. Irhali also asserted that since April, 1964, Moscow propagandists had been engaged in a "strenuous effort" to spread lies slandering the leadership of the CPC, and charged the Khrushchev clique with creating constant incidents and disruptive activities in the border area.

September 7: Khrushchev in a radio-television report on his trip to Czechoslovakia stated that those parties which have agreed to take part should go ahead with plans for the mid-December preparatory meeting in the face of the CPC and pro-Chinese parties' refusal to attend, adding that the only correct solution is for those parties which are defending the unity of the movement to discuss questions "ripe for solution."

September 8: An article by a *People's Daily* commentator on a possible Khrushchev visit to West Germany inveighed Khrushchev's maneuvers for a "dirty political deal" and a "sellout" to the East German regime. It proclaimed that the "days of Munich are gone for good."

September 10: A multilateral protocol on passenger-train time-schedule was signed by North Korea, Mongolia, the U.S.S.R., and the PRC.

September 12: The Peking Municipal Congress elected 101 deputies to represent Peking in the National People's Congress. Among those elected were Mao Tse-tung and Chou En-lai.

The PRC and North Vietnam signed a civil aviation protocol in Hanoi.

The protocol of the 1964 meeting of the Sino-Korean border railway joint commission was signed at a ceremony in Kirin.

September 13: The PRC and Dahomey issued a joint communique in Cotonou on talks during a visit of the PRC government good-will delegation which dealt with development of economic, technical, and cultural cooperation.

September 14: Describing the Malawi cabinet crisis as a family squabble, Dr. Barda, the Prime Minister, repeated his allegation against the Chinese embassy in Dar-es-Salaam.

September 14-22: An Algerian government economic delegation visited China from September 14 to 22. A trade agreement, a payments agreement, and a protocol on the economic and technical cooperation between the PRC and the Algerian government were signed on September 19.

September 15: Khrushchev held an interview with Japanese Socialists in which he compared Mao to Hitler (published on the 20th).

September 16-24: The World Youth Forum in Moscow witnessed a clash of Soviet and Chinese viewpoints on how to win supporters both inside and outside the Communist movement. Moscow accused the Chinese delegation of "disruptive" tactics; the latter refused to sign a communique at the close of the conference.

September 18: The permanent delegation of the South Vietnam National Front for Liberation to the PRC, led by Tran Van Flank, its head, and Nguyen Min Phuong, its deputy head, arrived in Peking.

September 20: Chen Yi in a cable to Maltese Prime Minister Giorgio Borg Olivier informed him that the PRC has decided to give recognition to his country.

September 22: Contracts on the exchange of newsreels and on the exchange and distribution of sports between the PRC and Ghana were signed in Accra.

September 23: The PRC and Iraq signed a trade agreement in Peking.

September 23-November 16: Noted American Negro leader Robert Williams and his wife and two children arrived in Peking on September 23 to attend the Chinese national celebrations. They visited Shanghai, Nanchang, and other parts of the country.

September 24: The 1964-65 plan for scientific cooperation between the Chinese and Bulgarian Academies of Sciences was signed in Sofia.

September 27-October 6: Prince Sihanouk of Cambodia paid a state visit to Peking for the ceremonies of the 15th anniversary of the Communist regime. A joint statement reaffirmed China's willingness to give Cambodia full support in the event of aggression against Cambodia, and to denounce the alleged U.S. violation of the 1954 and 1962 German agreement on Indo-China. It was issued on October 5.

September 28: China ordered ocean-going cargo ships from France under an agreement signed between the China National Machinery Import and Export Corporation and French companies.

A Sino-Czechoslovak protocol on scientific and technical cooperation was signed in Peking.

China sent a note to the Indian embassy in Peking protesting alleged Indian intrusion into Chinese territory by crossing the China-Sikkim boundary.

September 28-October 3: Alphonse Massemba-Debatm, President of the former French Congo republic, visited Peking. A joint statement of October 3 with Chinese head of state Liu Shao-chi said that China supported the republic against imperialist threats, interference, and subversion emanating from the former Belgian Congo. A day earlier, Massemba-Debatm had signed a treaty of friendship and an economic and technical cooperation agreement along with one on maritime transport.

September 28-October 5: A Nepalese government delegation arrived in Peking on September 28. They signed, October 4, a protocol between the governments of the PRC and Nepal on the construction of the canal headworks and the western main canal for irrigation purposes.

September 29: Malian President Modico Keita arrived in Peking for a state visit. Before his departure on November 3, a joint communique was issued to deal with the Congo crisis, support for a second Afro-Asian conference, PRC representation in United Nations, Taiwan, disarmament, etc.

The Central African Republic exchange of diplomatic relations with China was announced. Economic, technical, and cultural agreements were also signed in Banghui.

Secretary of State Dean Rusk stated that the United States expected China to conduct an atmospheric nuclear test in the near future.

September 30: A protocol on the supply of goods and payments between the PRC and North Vietnam was signed in Peking. Through exchange of notes, the two states agreed to extend their 1955 protocol on small-scale trading in border areas and their 1955 protocol on exchange of goods between local state trading companies in border areas.

October 1: The 15th anniversary of the PRC was celebrated throughout the country. Over 700,000 people participated in celebration in Peking.

October 2: A contract between the China International Travel Service and the Japan-China Travel Agency was signed.

The PRC and Kenya issued a press communique on trade talks in Peking.

October 3: A radio-television cooperation agreement was signed between the Broadcasting Administrative Bureau of China and the Radio and Television Committee of Rumania.

October 4: A contract for the distribution of films between the PRC and Sudan was signed in Peking.

A Sino-Nepalese protocol on canal construction for irrigation purposes was signed in Peking.

October 5: Leaders of 47 non-aligned nations met in Cairo for their second conference (the first was in Belgrade in 1961). On October 7, Indian Prime Minister Lal Bahadui Shastri proposed that the conferees "consider sending a special mission to persuade China to desist from developing nuclear weapons."

October 8: Cambodia announced Chinese aid would include equipment and arms for 22,000 men, plus two textile factories, a paper mill, and an international airport.

October 9: The PRC declared it was ready to start negotiations with India on their border dispute on the basis of the Colombo proposals.

October 10: A Sino-Albanian protocol on exchange of goods and payments for 1965 was signed in Peking along with the two documents: (1) Protocol on Albania's use of the PRC's loans under 1961 loan agreement; (2) agreement on cooperation in customs services.

October 11: China's first factory producing rolled-steel railway wheels and wheel-rims has gone into formal operation, according to an NCNA report.

A Sino-Nepalese cultural cooperation agreement was signed in Katmandu.

The Congo (Brazzaville) announced China had granted it an interest-free loan of 7,300,000 pounds.

October 13: The China National Technical Import Corporation and the French Societe d'Etudesgn Rechersches, Constructions, Alectroneques signed a contract in Peking for the purchase of petroleum exploration equipment by the Chinese corporation from French company.

October 13-15: The Ministry of Foreign

Trade revised and promulgated customs control measures governing personal postal matter coming from and going to Hong Kong and Macao and also customs control measures governing postal matter sent in and out of the country, according to Hong Kong *Ta-Kung, Pao.*

October 14: The ouster of Khrushchev—at his own request in view of his age and deteriorating health, according to *Pravda* —on October 16 initiates a period of calm and watchful waiting in world party circles.

October 15: In Peking the recently held national conference on semi-mechanized farm equipment and implements decided that at present and for a long time to come, continued efforts must be made in the agro-technical reform to implement the policy of simultaneously developing mechanization and semi-mechanization (with emphasis on the latter). Also to conduct a movement for innovating farm tools, to supply the countryside with various kinds of good quality and cheap semi-mechanized farm equipment and implements. This is to further the building of stable and high-yield fields, development of agricultural production, and consolidation of the collection economy of the people's communes.

October 16: The PRC government, after consulting with the government of the Polish People's Republic, has decided to re-establish its consulate in Gaansk, Poland.

Peking sent warm greetings to Brezhnev, Mikoyan, and Kosygin on their appointments in messages signed by Mao Tse-tung, Liu Shao-chi, Chu Teh, and Chou En-lai.

China detonated her first atomic bomb, becoming the fifth nuclear power. The United States announced it was near Lop Nor in the central Asian province of Sinkiang and that it had an explosive power of 20,000 tons of TNT. The NCNA announcement accused the United States, Britain, and the Soviet Union of nuclear blackmail in the test-ban treaty. It again called the atom bomb a paper tiger. China

will never be the first to use nuclear weapons; they are only for defense, it stated. It also called for a summit conference to prohibit the use of nuclear weapons. Britain expressed deep disappointment and stated that it would not alter the balance of military power. Japan and India made strong protests to the Chinese government. Albania sent a telegram expressing "great joy."

October 18: President Johnson addressed the American people, deploring the Chinese nuclear test. He called the nuclear test a tragedy for the Chinese because of their poverty.

October 19: Brezhnev's initial speech as the CPSU first secretary stressed that Moscow wants a world conference of all parties, but failed to give any indication whether the new leadership would modify Khrushchev's tactics in the Sino-Soviet polemics or follow in the path already marked out.

October 20: Chou En-lai sent messages to all heads of governments calling for a summit conference on nuclear disarmament.

October 22: A Sino-Burundi trade and payments agreement was signed in Brejumbura, capital of Burundi.

October 24: Chen Yi sent a message of greetings to Simon Kapinepine on the occasion of the proclamation of independence of the Republic of Zambia and informed him of the Chinese government's decision to give recognition to his republic.

A protocol on exchange of goods for 1964-65 between the governments of the PRC and Afghanistan was signed in Kabul.

The PRC and Ceylon signed three trade documents in Colombo: (1) Protocol on exchange of commodities in 1965; (2) contracts on exchange of rice and rubber in 1965; (3) agreement on grant of interest-free loan by the PRC for the period 1965-67.

October 27: A multilateral protocol on cooperation in postal services and telecommunications was signed at a conference ministers of post and tele-communications of Socialist countries.

A multilateral protocol on "through-passenger railway service" was signed at a meeting of the Railway Cooperation Organization of Socialist Countries.

Sino-North Korean protocol on scientific and technical cooperation was signed in Peking.

October 28: Chou En-lai reiterated the Chinese government stand that it would never under any circumstances be the first to use nuclear weapons. However, he said that China would resist if the United States used nuclear weapons against it.

October 30-November 13: King Mohammed Zahir Shah and his queen of Afghanistan visited China on a state visit.

October 31: Feng Ting has been assailed by the press for his bourgeois thought and subjective idealism. His three books— *Communist Philosophy of Life* (860,000 copies), *Commonplace Truth* (390,000 copies), and the *Historic Task of the Working Class* (400,000 copies)—all contain new points that ought to be criticized in principle, according to the *Red Flag* editor.

November 1: The NCNA reported that new U.S.S.R. leaders had cabled an appreciation for Chinese leaders, sending a congratulatory message and urging "unbreakable" friendship between the U.S.S.R. and China.

November 2-14: A British industrial exhibition was held in Peking at the invitation of the PRC.

November 3: The PRC and Mali signed three documents in Peking before President Keita's departure: (1) Treaty of friendship; (2) agreement on supply of equipment for industrial projects by PRC to Mali; (3) protocol on film cooperation in 1965.

November 4: Chou En-lai accepted the U.S.S.R. invitation to attend a Moscow fete marking the Bolshevik revolution anniversary. He would head a 7-man delegation.

Peking published the October 19 speeches by Brezhnev and Kosygin at a Red Square rally for Russian cosmonauts reaffirming the policy lines of the 20th, 21st, and 22nd CPSU party congresses in domestic and foreign affairs.

November 4-5: Indonesian President Sukarno and his party arrived in Shanghai November 5. Welcomed at the airport by Chou En-lai. The two held talks the same day. They exchanged views on matters of common interest and complete accord was reached. Sukarno and his party left Shanghai for home November 5.

The Peking press carried statements and communiques on Khrushchev's removal by the leaders of 18 Communist parties, including some which praise Khrushchev for his contribution to peaceful co-existence, de-Stalinization, and economic reforms.

November 5-13: Chou En-lai visited Moscow for talks with the new Soviet leaders and to attend the 4th anniversary of the October Revolution. He was welcomed by Kosygin when he arrived in Moscow on November 5. A joint communique was issued in Moscow at the conclusion of Chou En-lai's visit stating that the talks had proceeded in a frank and comradely atmosphere. Chou En-lai's return from Moscow was reported by the NCNA without comment on November 14.

November 6: A multilateral protocol on "through-freight railway service" was signed at a meeting of the Railway Cooperation Organization of Socialist Countries in Peking.

An agreement on air communications between the governments of the PRC and the Republic of Indonesia was signed in Peking. A protocol on agency business and offering of services between the General Administration of Civil Aviation of China and Ganda Indonesian Airways was also signed.

Brezhnev's October Revolution anniversary speech reiterates standard Soviet positions and policies that are anathema to Peking; calls for gradual steps to restore Communist party unity; leaves the impression that Moscow is unwilling to make concessions of principle to placate Peking.

November 9-27: The conference of experts in the economics of posts and tele-communications of socialist countries was held in Peking November 9-27. A protocol was signed. Delegations from 12 socialist countries were present.

November 12: The PRC and Cuba signed in Havana a protocol on broadcasting and television cooperation.

The African state of Dahomey announced it would establish diplomatic relations with the PRC.

November 15: Peking announced it shot down an American pilotless plane over Central-Southern China.

November 22: *People's Daily* announced that Communist China had rejected U.N. Secretary General U Thant's proposal that the five nuclear powers hold disarmament talks and that Communist China participate in the 17-nation Geneva disarmament conference. *People's Daily* said the Geneva conference was "in fact still under the manipulation and control of the United States" and "serves as a smoke-screen for U.S. imperialist armament expansion and war preparations."

November 25: The PRC and Ceylon signed three contracts in Colombo on gift by the PRC of machinery, equipment, and materials for construction of textile mill in Ceylon.

November 26: The annual executive plan for scientific cooperation between the Academy of Science of China and the German Academy of Sciences in East Berlin was signed in Peking.

November 28: Chinese Communist Party Chairman Mao Tse-tung personally announced China's full support for the Congolese rebels and called on all the peoples of the world to "unite and defeat the United States aggressors'.' On the next day, 700,000 people demonstrated in Peking against the U.S. policy in the Congo.

A Sino-Albanian protocol on scientific and technical cooperation was signed in Tirana.

November 30: An agreement on the establishment of non-official commercial representatives bureaus of China and Italy in each other's country had been reached in Rome between the China Council for the Promotion of International Trade and the Italian Foreign Trade Institute.

November 30: A Sino-Bulgarian protocol on scientific and technical cooperation was signed in Peking.

December 3: The protocol on exchange of goods for 1965 between the PRC and the Republic of Ghana was signed in Accra.

The China National Technical Import Corporation and the Swedish International Sipomex Ab reached agreement on the purchase by China of complete sets of equipment for producing porous silica material. A contract was signed in Peking.

December 1: A Sino-Cambodian protocol on the supply of military equipment by the PRC was signed.

December 2: The PRC and Nepal agreed to extend their 1960 economic aid program.

December 3: In Djakarta, a Sino-Indonesian press communique was issued on talks during Foreign Minister Chen Yi's visit which dealt with PRC support for Indonesian policy of confrontation with Malaysia, joint support for second Afro-Asian conference, etc.

December 6: Malawi announced it had decided to recognize the Peking government and called for its admission into the United Nations.

December 7: The PRC and Austria signed an agreement on promotion of economic relations in Vienna.

December 9: The Chinese Red Cross Society sent a cable to the Brazilian Foreign Ministry asking for entry visas for members of the families of the Chinese personnel "unjustifiably" arrested by the Brazilian authorities.

A Sino-Rumanian agreement on exchange of goods and payments in 1965 was signed in Bucharest.

December 10: A protocol of the agreement on economic and technical cooperation between the PRC and Kenya was signed in Nairobi along with exchange of letters on dispatch of the PRC technical experts to Kenya.

A Sino-Mongolian protocol on scientific and technical cooperation was signed in Peking.

December 12: *Pravda* announced postponement of preparatory meeting to March 1, 1965, as the result of mutual consultation among the parties, with the aim of better preparation both for the preliminary meeting and for an eventual world conference of parties.

The 1965 Sino-Bulgarian goods exchange and payments agreement was signed in Peking.

The NPC Standing Committee met and adopted a notification concerning the publication of the names of the deputies to the 3rd NPC. It also decided to pardon a group of war criminals, which was recommended by the State Council.

December 17: The State Council decided to dismiss the Dalai Lama from his posts as Chairman and member of the Preparatory Committee for the Tibet Autonomous Region.

December 18: Liu Shao-chi convened the Supreme State Conference. At the conference, Chou En-lai gave an account of the main contents of the report on government work to be made at the first session of the 3rd NCP. Peng Chen gave an account of the agenda of both the first session of the 3rd NPC and the first session of the 4th National Committee of the CPPCC and other important matters in relation to the two sessions.

"A U.S.-made RF-101 reconnaissance plane of the Chiang Kai-shek gang was shot down somewhere over East China this afternoon by an air unit of the navy of the Chinese PLA," an NCNA report said.

The PRC and Kenya signed a trade agreement in Nairobi.

December 19: The PRC and Mongolia exchanged notes on change of the PRC executive organ under a 1960 agreement on scientific and technical cooperation.

December 20: The first session of the 4th

National Committee of the CPPCC opened on December 20. Presided over by Chou En-lai, the meeting adopted an agenda and elected a presidium of 84.

December 21: China and the United Arab Republic signed an agreement on economic and technical cooperation along with exchange of notes extending for three years the China-UAR trade and payments agreement and a protocol for trade in 1965.

December 21-January 4: The first session of the 3rd NPC was declared open by Liu Shao-chi on December 21, after having been elected in September, 1964, with the number of deputies increased from 1226 to 3040. Chou En-lai, in a state of the nation speech, confirmed reports that it was a Chinese initiative to send a high-level party and government delegation to Moscow for the October Revolution anniversary. He also announced the third five-year plan would begin in 1966, the second one having ended in 1962. In a speech at the December 29 meeting, Chou En-lai said that China would spur broadest united front of nations against the United States; that U.S. power had declined, while China's prestige and influence had gained; that the United States was informed in Warsaw talks that settlement of any problems with China was out of the question until the United States withdrew forces from Taiwan and Taiwan Strait.

December 22: A statement was issued by the PRC government protesting against the sentence passed on Chinese personnel by the Brazilian authorities.

December 25: A Sino-Algerian agreement on scientific and technical cooperation was signed in Algiers.

December 27: An agreement for cooperation in radio and television broadcasting between China and North Korea was signed in Peking.

December 28: In accordance with an order of the Chairman of the PRC issued on December 12, the Supreme People's Court pardoned and released 13 war criminals who had truly changed and turned over a new leaf.

In a note to the Indian embassy to China, the PRC Ministry of Foreign Affairs lodged a strong protest with the Indian government against the "recent intrusions by Indian aircraft into China's air space over extensive areas well inside Tibet and Sinkiang for long-duration reconnaissance and harassment.

December 29: Peking protested against the dispatch of American nuclear submarines into Pacific waters, calling it a "shameless act of nuclear blackmail."

Cambodia announced that Peking had agreed to supply that country with anti-aircraft guns and bazookas.

December 30: The United States disclosed that it rejected China's proposal for mutual pledge not to use nuclear arms against each other.

Liu Shao-chi called Supreme State Conference. Soong Ching-ling, Tung Pi-wu, Chu Teh, and Chou En-lai were among the 177 people attending the meeting. Liu Shao-chi spoke on the current international and domestic situation and on important questions of work.

December 31: The PRC and Cuba signed five trade documents in Peking: (1) Agreement on trade in period 1965-70; (2) protocol on trade in 1965; (3) agreement on payments in period 1965-70; (4) protocol on general conditions for sale of crude sugar to the PRC by Cuba; (5) protocol on general conditions for delivery of goods between foreign trade organizations of the two countries.

1965

January 2: The NCNA claimed the shooting down of another pilotless high-altitude reconnaissance military plane of the United States over Central-South China.

January 3: The Soviet news agency Tass reported that the Soviet Union had informed the PRC of its support for the latter's proposal for a world conference on the outlawing and destruction of all nuclear weapons.

The NPC re-elected the highest leaders of the PRC: Liu Shao-chi, Chairman; Mm. Soong Ching-ling and Tung Pi-wu, Vice-Chairmen; Chou En-lai, Prime Minister; Chu Teh, Chairman of the Standing Committee of the NPC.

January 4: The NPC approved the membership of the State Council, headed by Chou En-lai as Prime Minister. Among the other appointments, Mr. Lu Ting-yi, as Minister of Culture, was considered the most significant as indicating the importance attached by the party to ideological questions.

The CPPCC met in Peking concurrently with the NPC. Mao Tse-tung was elected Honorary Chairman and Mr. Chou En-lai, Chairman.

The PRC and Cuba issued a joint communique on trade talks in Peking.

January 5: A Sino-Tanzania economic and technical agreement was signed in Dar-es-Salaam along with exchange of letters of dispatch of PRC experts and technicians to Tanzania.

January 9: The ratification instruments of treaty of friendship between the PRC and the Republic of the Congo were exchanged in Brazzaville (signed on October 2, 1964).

January 10: The NCNA reported that a Taiwan U-2 reconnaissance plane had been shot down over North China.

January 12: An agreement of cooperation in tourism was signed in Peking by the Chinese and Indonesian travel service organizations.

January 13: The PRC and the United Arab Republic signed a scientific and technical cooperation agreement in Cairo.

Chen Yi wrote to the two co-chairmen and foreign ministers of other participating nations of the 1954 Geneva Conference on Indo-China regarding the "U.S. scheme to drag South Korean puppet troops into the U.S. war of aggression in South Vietnam."

January 14: A Sino-Algerian contract on the purchase of short-length Chinese films was signed in Algiers.

The PRC and Central African Republic signed a protocol on economic and technical cooperation in Bangui.

January 18: The PRC in a note to India charged that Indian troops and reconnaissance planes had violated Chinese territory. It was the second such charge made by the Chinese. The Indian government had rejected the first as a "fantastic fabrication." During the first week of 1965, the Indian government had arrested more than 800 Communists on charges that they were Chinese agents preparing "subversive and revolutionary action."

January 19: The 3rd Standing Committee meeting discussed and adopted a decision on the length of active service of non-commissioned officers and privates in the PLA.

January 20: Chen Yi sent a letter to the Geneva Conference co-chairmen of the invasion of Laos by U.S. F-100 fighter-bombers and their wanton bombing of Ban Ban in the Xieng Khourang liberated areas.

January 21: A provisional agreement on direct postage exchange between the PRC and Nepal was signed in Katmandu.

Indonesia's departure from the U.N. took formal effect when Ambassador L. N. Palar handed U.N. Secretary General U Thant a letter of resignation.

January 22: Peking Radio announced that a "Patriotic Front," similar to National Liberation Front in South Vietnam, had been established in Thailand. Premier Thanom Kittikachorn had warned the previous week that Chinese Communist agents were infiltrating Thailand from Laos.

January 23: Details of new written languages for China's Uighur and Kazakh nationalities, using a slightly modified Latin alphabet, have been officially published in Sinkiang.

January 23-28: Indonesian Foreign Minister Dr. Subandrio visited Peking. A joint statement said that during Dr. Subandrio's talks with Chinese government leaders "the two parties held that the present development of the world is increasingly favorable to all revolutionary people and progressive forces" and that no peaceful co-existence is possible between the imperialist and anti-imperialist forces. The Chinese government had warmly praised and expressed firm support for President Sukarno's wise decision to withdraw from the United Nations. Both parties held that the United Nations has become increasingly discredited and must correct its mistakes and be thoroughly reorganized. The statement condemned the U.S. imperialists' expansion of the war of oppression in Indo-China and the British imperialists' sending of military reinforcements to Malaysia. It also denounced Malaysia as a tool for suppressing the revolutionary movements of the people of Malaya, Singapore, Sarawak, and Sabah, and for establishing a military base for aggression in Southeast Asia which poses a direct menace to Indonesia. The Chinese government, the statement added, has solemnly declared that should the British and U.S. imperialists dare to impose a war on the Indonesian people, the Chinese people will not sit idly by. During Dr. Subandrio's visit, an agreement on economic and technical cooperation was signed, and also an agreement under which China undertook to grant Indonesia economic credits of £35,000,000. It was also decided to expand trade and develop maritime transportation between the two countries to strengthen their friendly contacts in the military fields,

and to exchange military, economic, and other delegations. Mr. Chou En-lai and Chen Yi accepted an invitation to visit Indonesia. Chou En-lai said: "A revolutionary United Nations may well be set up so that rival dramas may be staged in competition with that body which calls itself the United Nations but which, being under the manipulation of U.S. imperialism, is capable only of making mischief and can do nothing good." (These documents were signed on January 28.)

January 25: Canada announced the sale of 27 million bushels of wheat to Communist China.

January 26: A Sino-Burmese protocol on the sale of Burmese rice to the PRC in 1965 was signed in Rangoon.

January 30: The Chinese embassy in Burundi delivered a note to Foreign Minister Marc Maninakiza protesting against the Royal Burundi government's "unjustifiable" breaking off of diplomatic relations with China.

February 2: The President of Niger, Hamani Diori, charged that the PRC had plotted and financed an unsuccessful revolt against his government in the fall of 1964. He denounced Chinese Communist influence in Africa.

February 5: Soviet Premier Aleksei Kosygin received a cool reception in Peking, where he stopped on his way to Hanoi. NCNA released two highly perfunctory reports on Kosygin's arrival in Peking and welcome by Chou En-lai, Chen Yi, and ten government and military officials.

February 6: Two protocols for implementing the Sino-Congolese (Brazzaville) loan agreement and economic cooperation agreement were signed in Brazzaville.

February 7: Responding to major attacks by Viet Cong guerrillas against U.S. installations in South Vietnam, American and South Vietnamese aircraft engaged in "joint retaliatory attacks" on North Vietnamese training and staging areas. The attacks continued on February 8 and 11. Announcement of the first U.S. attack was made February 7 by President Johnson, who said it had been launched in response to provocation ordered and directed by the Hanoi regime.

February 8: The PRC called the first air strike an "extremely serious provocation by U.S. imperialism to extend the war to North Vietnam once again in defiance of world condemnation and in an effort to avert total defeat in South Vietnam.

February 10: Kosygin met with Mao Tsetung in Peking before departure for North Korea.

The PRC and Tanzania signed a trade agreement in Peking along with a protocol on exchange of commodities for the period 1965-69.

February 11: A protocol was signed in Algeria for the implementation of the agreement under which China is to supply gratis equipment for the Algerian militia.

February 12: Kosygin said in a speech at Pyongyang, North Korea, that the imperialist provocations in Vietnam had made the Soviet Union, the PRC, and North Korea unanimous in their desire to support the heroic people of Vietnam.

February 13: A direct radio-telephone service was started between the PRC and Pakistan.

In a second statement, Peking recalled that it had declared long since that aggression against the Democratic Republic of Vietnam means aggression against China, and the Chinese people have long been prepared and know how to aid the people of Vietnam and Indochina in driving out U.S. aggressors.

February 14: The PRC and the Soviet Union exchanged messages on the 15th anniversary of the signing of their treaty of mutual assistance and friendship. The Chinese note was far more militant, especially against the United States, than the Soviet message, which did not mention the United States as an enemy or Vietnam as a problem.

February 15: *People's Daily* published an editorial warning that if the United States sent troops beyond the 17th parallel Communist China would enter the Vietnamese conflict and also reopen the Korean war.

If the United States expands the war in Vietnam, the editorial warned, the front will extend from Vietnam to Korea.

February 16-23: President Nyerere of Tanzania visited Peking. On February 20 the two countries signed a treaty of friendship and in a joint statement issued on February 23 condemned the imperialists.

February 17: The PRC and Kawait issued a press communique in Peking on talks of economic cooperation and development of trade.

February 18: Secretary of Defense McNamara told the House Armed Services Committee that Communist China, while threatening India, Nepal, and other Asian nations, had decided to make South Vietnam the decisive test. "We intend to stand fast against the present implacable animosity of Communist China until that nation realizes that its security and progress can be better served by a more peaceful policy," he concluded.

The PRC and Pakistan signed an egreement on a loan and the dispatch of experts and technicians by the PRC.

February 19: A goods exchange and payments agreement for 1965 signed in Peking between the PRC and East Germany.

February 21: A one-week meeting for formulating the 1965 through traffic plan of China, North Vietnam, North Korea, Mongolia, and the Soviet Union closed in Ulan Bator. The meeting stipulated the volume of through railway traffic for this year among the five socialist countries and the measures they proposed to undertake. A protocol was signed.

February 26: Kosygin in his TV report on his trip to the Far East notes that his talks in Peking "touched on" questions of Sino-Soviet economic and cultural relations, adding that a practical solution of these questions was of great importance.

Peking released the third column of Khrushchev's statement assertedly as part of a project to publish the remainder of his works in some 30 volumes. An editorial note prefacing volume explained that the reason for resuming publication of the Khrushchev flood of "putrid verb-

195

osity" is because the sinister spirit of Khrushchev has not departed even here in China.

February 27: The PRC Foreign Ministry in a statement supported the "just stand of the government of the Democratic People's Republic of Korea and the just struggle of the Korean people to oppose the South Korean-Japan basic treaty and talks."

The U.S. State Department issued a 14,000-word White Paper documenting North Vietnamese aggression against South Vietnam.

February 27-28: Peking press ran a spate of NCNA articles describing anti-Chinese materials recommended for study in the Soviet Union. One article asserted that CPSU Secretary Ponomarev's book, "The International Revolutionary Movement of the Working Class," reveals the hypocrisy of those who, while talking about reinforcing solidarity, actually deepened the split. The book was taken as additional proof that Khrushchev's downfall merely meant a change of signboard.

March 1: The PRC and Tunisia agreed to renew their 1960 trade agreement of one year.

March 1-5: Delegations from 19 Communist parties met in a suburb of Moscow to lay plans for a unity conference of the world's 81 Communist parties. The parties of Albania, Communist China, Indonesia, Japan, North Korea, North Vietnam, and Rumania had turned down invitations to attend. The meeting, held in secret, ended March 5. A public statement, issued March 10, supported the plan for a global conference to re-establish unity in the world Communist movement but only after several years of preparation, which would include bilateral party talks and a preliminary meeting of the 81 parties. The statement called meanwhile for an end to the public polemics, which have a character which is unfriendly and offensive for fraternal parties.

March 2-9: President Ayub Khan of Pakistan arrived in Peking on a state visit. On March 5 he told a Peking audience

that the war in Vietnam should not be allowed to expand and urged negotiations for peace in honor to all interested parties. In a joint communique issued on March 7, Pakistan reaffirmed its support for the immediate restoration of the legitimate rights of the PRC in the United Nations and reiterated Pakistan's opposition to schemes for creating two Chinas. They reaffirmed that the Kashmir dispute should be resolved in accordance with the wishes of the people of Kashmir as pledged to them by India and Pakistan. Chairman Liu Shao-chi accepted the invitation to visit Pakistan at a mutually convenient time.

March 4: The March 2 bombing of North Vietnam by aircraft of the United States and its "lackeys" was denounced as an "undisguised" act of war by the *People's Daily* editorial. Two thousand Russians, Asians (many Chinese), African, and Latin American students broke through police barricades in Moscow to storm the U.S. embassy in protest against American air strikes on North Vietnam.

People's Daily devoted its entire third page to extracts of twelve articles in the Soviet press which the Chinese newspaper said "preach Khrushchev revisionism." Peking also announced the publication of a book "of great and theoretical significance" entitled "Polemics in the General Line of the International Communist Movement." Contents said to include a CPC 25-point proposal of July, 1963, on the "general line," the nine *People's Daily-Red Flag* articles on the July, 1963, CPSU open letters, and the November 21, 1964 *Red Flag* article, "Why Khrushchev Fell."

March 6: Chinese Ambassador to the Soviet Union Pan Tzu-li called on Soviet Foreign Minister Andrei Gromyko at his office. He handed to the minister a Chinese embassy's note of protest against the violence used by the Soviet troops and police against the Chinese students in Moscow during the March 4 demonstration of foreign students against the U.S. imperialist aggression in Vietnam. On the same day a crowd of about 400 demonstrated in front of the Soviet embassy in Peking.

March 8: Changes in administrative divisions in China made during the period from September 1 to December 31, 1964, were published.

Thirty-five hundred United States marines landed in South Vietnam to defend the United States base at Danang.

March 12: Soviet Foreign Ministry note rejected Peking's March 6 protest concerning Soviet militia brutality against Asian students who demonstrated against the United States embassy in Moscow. It said that Chinese students in the demonstration were using "iron rods, stones, and sharp objects" against "unarmed Soviet policemen."

A Sino-Albanian 1965-66 plan for cultural cooperation was signed in Peking.

March 13: Peking Radio said that the landing of U.S. Marines in South Vietnam further blocked the way to a political settlement of the Vietnam question.

March 14: Peking press featured the return of four injured Chinese students from Moscow, two of whom are depicted being lowered from an airplane on stretchers by sober-faced orderlies.

March 15-April 9: The delegation of the NPC of China, led by Liu Ning-yi, made a visit to African countries: March 15-March 20 in Guinea; March 20-March 27 in Mali; March 28-March 30 in Central African Republic; April 1-April 4 in the Congo (Brazzaville); and April 5-April 9 in Ghana.

March 15: Through an exchange of notes, the PRC agreed on Chinese aid in construction of an international conference building and other buildings in Ceylon.

March 16: A Sino-Indonesian agreement on scientific and technical cooperation was signed in Djakarta.

A formal Chinese note demanded that Moscow admit error in putting down student demonstration and apologize to beaten students.

A Sino-Polish agreement on turnover of goods and payments in 1965 was signed in Warsaw.

March 17: In denouncing President Johnson's statement of March 13, *People's Daily* said that discussion of a peaceful settlement in Vietnam was nothing but the most flagrant, most shameless war blackmail by the United States.

A protocol on building the Segou Textile Combine was signed between the PRC and Mali in Bamako.

March 18: "A U.S.-made RF-101 plane of the Chiang Kai-shek gang was shot down by a unit of the Chinese PLA air force this morning when it turned over the coastal areas of Southeast China on a reconnaissance mission," an NCNA report said.

The landing of South Korean "puppet troops" in Saigon on March 16 was "(another step taken by U.S. imperialism to escalate the war in Indochina," said the *People's Daily* commentator.

The PRC and Syria signed a cultural cooperation agreement in Peking along with 1965 plan.

March 19: The PRC and Pakistan issued a press communique on boundary demarcation in Karachi.

March 20: Chou En-lai said in an interview in the Manila *Times* that his country was against world war and would never provoke it, "and that China had shown restraint in Vietnam, although our restraint has limits." He added that China was not afraid of the United States since the latter's forces were scattered all around the globe.

March 21: Chinese Communist Foreign Minister Chen Yi said, in an interview with an Italian journalist, that Communist China would actively fight in Vietnam if U.S. troops invaded North Vietnam or the North Vietnamese government requested them to enter the war.

Chinese leaders congratulated Soviet leaders on successful flight of space ship "Voskhod-2."

March 22: A Sino-Albanian protocol on shipping was signed in Peking.

A joint *People's Daily Red Flag* editorial denounced the Moscow-sponsored Communist party meeting in a most explicit attack on Soviet policy toward Vietnam. The editorial declared that "Moscow hopes to gain political capital for their dealing with U.S. imperialists and to carry out plots for peace talks in a futile attempt to extinguish revolution struggle of the South Vietnamese people against U.S. imperialism and its lackeys." The editorial promised to expose the intrigues of the new Soviet leaders in their "love feast" with the United States.

The PRC and Cambodia signed an agreement on scientific and cultural cooperation along with 1965 plan in Phnom Penh.

March 23: A protocol on building the Sanaa textile factory was signed in Sanaa between the PRC and Yemen.

March 23-27: The Chinese party and government delegation led by its head Chou En-lai arrived in Bucharest on March 23 to attend the funeral of Ghenghe Gheorghiu-Dej, first secretary of the Central Committee of the Rumanian Workers' Party and president of the Rumanian State Council. Chou En-lai and his party left Bucharest for Albania on March 27.

March 24: The PRC and Afghanistan signed three documents in Kahil: (1) Protocol on boundary demarcation; (2) agreement on economic and technical cooperation; (3) agreement on cultural cooperation. (Chen Yi visited Afghanistan from March 22 to March 25.)

A protocol on goods exchange for 1965 between the PRC and Mongolia was signed in Ulan Bator.

The 1964-65 executive plan for scientific cooperation between academies of sciences of China and Czechoslovakia was signed in Prague.

A 1956 trade agreement between the PRC and Finland was signed in Helsinki.

March 25: In a message to Nasser, Chou En-lai said, ". . . The Chinese government and people resolutely support you in your struggle against U.S. imperialism and Zionism and support the resolutions to the conference of Arab Foreign Ministers."

People's Daily said that the PRC, in response to the March 24 declaration of the National Liberation Front, would join the people of the whole world in sending all necessary material aid, including arms and other materials, to the heroic South Vietnamese people who are battling fearlessly. It concluded: "All negotations with the U.S. imperialists at this moment are utterly useless if they still refuse to withdraw from South Vietnam."

March 25-30: Chen Yi and his party arrived in Rawalpindi from Afghanistan on March 25. A boundary protocol and a cultural cooperation agreement between the PRC and Pakistan were signed on March 26. Chen Yi and his party left Dacca for Nepal on March 30.

March 26: A goods exchange and payments agreement for the current year between the PRC and Hungary was signed in Budapest.

March 27-30: Chou En-lai and his party arrived in Tirana from Rumania on March 27, conducting talks with Enver Hoxha and other Albanian party and government leaders on March 27 and 28. The Chinese delegation left Tirana for Algeria on March 30. A joint press communique on Chou En-lai's visit was issued on March 30.

March 28: In a message to Foreign Minister Xuan Thuy of North Vietnam, Chen Yi said, "We firmly support the March 24 statement of the South Vietnam National Front for Liberation."

March 29: A *Pravda* editorial stressed the measures Soviet leaders had taken since Khrushchev ouster to reach an accommodation with Peking, citing recent C. C. plenum as proof of Moscow's will to "spare no effort" to attain world party unity on its own terms.

Multilateral minutes on railway administration were signed in Hanoi at the tenth Ministerial Conference of Railway Cooperation Organization of Socialist Countries.

March 30: The PRC and Indonesia signed in Djakarta a document and a supplementary note concerning talks on the implementation of 1961 economic and technical co-operation agreement between the two countries.

The NCNA charged that two U.S. fighters had machine-gunned a Chinese fishing boat off Hainan.

March 30-April 1: Chou En-lai conferred with President Ben Bella of Algeria regarding the proposed Afro-Asian Conference to meet in Algiers. A joint communique was issued on April 1.

March 30-April 3: Chen Yi and his party arrived in Katmandu from Pakistan on March 30. He had a friendly talk with Kirti Hidhi, foreign minister of Nepal, and issued a China-Nepal press communique on April 3.

March 31: "A pilotless high-altitude reconnaissance military plane of U.S. imperialism, intruding into China's territorial air space over the area of South China on a spy mission, was shot down by an air unit of the navy of the Chinese PLA," an NCNA report said.

April 1: Chou En-lai and his party arrived in Cairo, UAR, to discuss the proposed Afro-Asian Conference with President Nasser.

April 2: Chou En-lai and his party visited Karachi for talks with President Ayub Khan. They held a two-hour meeting and left the following day for Burma.

April 3: "Another pilotless high-altitude reconnaissance military plane of U.S. imperialism, which intruded into China's territorial air space over the area of Central South China shortly after noon today on a reconnaissance mission, has been shot down by an air force unit of the Chinese PLA," an NCNA report said.

Sino-Indonesian minutes on talks of construction of paper factory by the PRC in Indonesia were issued in Djakarta.

April 3-4: Chou En-lai and his party arrived in Burma on April 3. He had talks with General Ne Win on April 3 and 4. The Chinese delegation left Rangoon for home on April 4.

April 6: Chou En-lai replied through an intermediary on Secretary General U Thant's appeal for negotiations to end the Vietnam conflict. Chou said that any negotiations would have to be undertaken directly with the Viet Cong rather than with the PRC or North Vietnam.

Mao Tse-tung told an Arab delegation visiting Peking: "Asia is the largest continent in the world. The West wants to continue to exploit it because the West likes neither us nor you. We must all understand this fact. The Arab battle against the West is actually a battle against Israel, so you Arabs must boycott Europe and America." Mao added that the PRC was winning in all the battles being fought, especially in Vietnam.

April 7: It was reported that the PRC and the U.S.S.R. had reached agreement on shipment of military equipment from the U.S.S.R. through China to North Vietnam.

April 8: A Sino-Czechoslovak agreement on the exchange of goods and payments in 1965 was signed in Prague.

April 9: Contract for Chinese import of Italian chemical fertilizers was signed in Mutan.

The Peking Radio charged that President Johnson's speech at Johns Hopkins University in Baltimore on April 7 was "full of lies and deceptions." It viewed the proposals as an old device presented in new form for the sole purpose of luring the South Vietnamese people to lay down their arms."

The PRC asserted that MIG jet fighters of its air force had been involved in a dogfight with 16 U.S. jets over the Chinese islands of Hainan in the South China Sea. Peking said that one U.S. jet had been shot down by a missile fired from another U.S. plane. According to the U.S. version, the encounter had taken place 35 miles from Hainan Island, and they had lost one of their own. The United States insisted that the American aircraft had not violated Chinese air space and had not been able to determine whether the other aircraft were Chinese or North Vietnamese.

April 12: The China National Machinery Import and Export Corporation and the French Chantiers de l'Atlantique signed a contract in Peking for the purchase of passenger and cargo ships from the French shipyard.

It is not suitable for a special representative of the British government to contact the Chinese government on the problems of Vietnam and Indochina, and he is not welcome, the PRC Foreign Ministry informed the British government in a note.

The *People's Daily*, in an editorial commenting on U.N. Secretary-General U Thant's expressed intention to visit China and North Vietnam, said that Mr. Thant "should condemn the war crimes committed by the United States and demand that it immediately cease its aggression against South Vietnam and its bombing of North Vietnam."

April 17: A 1965 executive plan for Sino-Mali cultural agreement was signed in Bamako.

The nine Chinese trade personnel and newsmen, who had been "illegally detained and victimized by the Brazilian authorities for twelve and a half months," left Rio de Janeiro for home via Switzerland.

April 17-19: Chou En-lai attended the tenth anniversary of the Bandung Conference in Indonesia. He said on his arrival that the Asian and African countries should unite still closer together, hold and support each other, smash all imperialist schemes for aggression and war, and carry to the end the struggle to win and safeguard national independence and defend world peace. He later added that China no longer sought a seat in the U.N. and said that she was considering a new world body which would be progressive and revolutionary.

April 18: An NCNA report says that another U.S. pilotless high-altitude reconnaissance military plane was shot down in Central South China.

Following a meeting of Soviet and North Vietnamese officials in Moscow, the Soviet Union said that if the war in Vietnam intensified, it would allow Russian volunteers to join the fighting forces of North Vietnam whenever Hanoi asked for them. Two days later a similar offer was made by the PRC.

April 19: Chou En-lai had talks with a special envoy of the Japanese prime minister in Indonesia, the first diplomatic meeting between the two countries in twenty years. Dr. Kawashima said after the meeting that he had told Chou En-lai that Japan harboured no ill will towards China and did not endorse the U.S. policy of attempted containment, and added that the meeting had removed Chinese misunderstanding over Japanese arrangements for financial exports.

April 21: The PRC and Uganda signed an agreement on economic and technical cooperation in Peking.

April 22: Commenting on the 17-nation appeal, a *People's Daily* editorial said, "The 17-nation appeal makes no mention at all of the U.S. imperialist intervention and aggression in Vietnam, but instead makes general and vague charges against foreign intervention in various forms. What else can it be if not a deliberate attempt to absolve U.S. imperialism, the arch criminal, from its crime?"

April 26: A Sino-Polish protocol on scientific and technical cooperation was signed in Peking.

April 29: A Sino-Soviet trade agreement for 1965 was signed in Moscow.

April 30: The State Council adopted the frontier inspection regulations. It also approved administrative division changes affecting certain *hsien* and municipalities.

The NCNA, commenting on American intervention April 28 in the Dominican Republic said: "The new intervention on the part of the United States, which came at a moment when U.S. imperialism was wildly extending its aggression in Vietnam, threw further light on its hideous role as the international gendarme."

May 1: An exhibition was opened in Canton on reproductions of 230 rare objects discovered in the underground in the Ming tombs northwest of Peking, an NCNA report said.

The decision of the Australian authorities, under United States instigation, to dispatch an infantry battalion to take part in the U.S. war of aggression in Vietnam is a fresh step taken by "U.S. imperialism to internationalize its war of aggression there," the *Ta-Kung-Pao* commentator said in an editorial.

May 2: An agreement between the PRC and UAR relating to air services was signed in Peking.

The PRC government in a statement fully endorsed and firmly supported the three conditions laid down by the Royal Cambodian government in its May 1 statement for convening an international conference on Cambodia.

May 3: The 1965 executive plan for Sino-Yemeni cultural cooperation agreement was signed in Peking.

The 1965 executive plan for the cultural cooperation agreement between the PRC and the German Democratic Republic was signed in Peking.

The PRC and Ghana issued a joint press communique in Peking on talks during Foreign Minister Botsio's visit.

May 5: The first contingent of 8,000 marines landed in South Vietnam, bringing the total number of U.S. personnel to 42,000 men.

The 1965 executive plan for cultural cooperation agreement between the PRC and Poland was signed in Peking.

The Chinese Foreign Ministry in memorandum to the Soviet embassy in Peking protested against the Soviet government for expelling four Chinese students from Soviet institutions of higher education where they had been studying.

May 6-June 9: The Albanian government economic delegation arrived in Peking on May 6. Accompanied by Chou En-lai, the Albanian delegation visited the nationally famous Tachai village in Shansi Province on May 21, arrived in Hangchow on May 25, and returned to Peking from Shanghai on May 28. On June 8 the two countries signed four documents:

"Agreement on the loan granted by China to Albania"; "Agreement on goods exchange and payments for 1966-79"; and two other protocols on economic cooperation. A press communique on economic talks was issued on June 9.

May 7: At a Moscow rally celebrating the anniversary of VE Day, Premier Kosygin, referring to the Chinese Communists, said that some people contend that "only a new world war can bring about the unity and solidarity of the international Communist movement." He added: "We decisively reject such a position. We have no more important task than to prevent a new world conflagration."

May 9: The "new proposal" of the Indian government on the Vietnam question is a new plot to use the South-Asian countries to serve the "U.S. aggression against Vietnam," said the *People's Daily* observer.

May 11: The PRC and Yugoslavia signed a 1965 goods exchange protocol in Peking.

May 12: An agreement for the exchange of news between the NCNA and the Congolese Information Agency was signed in Brazzaville.

May 13: The 1965 executive plan for Sino-Bulgarian cultural cooperation agreement was signed in Peking.

President Johnson, speaking to the Association of American Editorial Cartoonists, said that Communist China wanted the Vietnam war to continue, not for the fulfillment of Vietnamese nationalism but to erode and to discredit America's ability to help prevent Chinese domination over all of Asia. The president repeated his offer of economic assistance to Southeast Asia and again called for "unconditional discussions."

May 13-18: U.S. bombing raids on North Vietnam were suspended from May 13 until May 18.

May 14: China detonated her second nuclear explosive at Lop Nor in Sinkiang Province. The U.S. Atomic Energy Commission issued a compilation of announced nuclear explosions by the five nuclear countries: United States, 337; Soviet

Union, 127; Britain, 24; France, 5; Communist China, 2.

May 15: A Sino-Rumanian scientific and technical cooperation protocol was signed in Peking.

May 19: An agreement on scientific cooperation between the academy of sciences of the PRC and Ghana was signed in Accra.

May 20: The PRC Ministry of Foreign Affairs delivered a note to the Indian embassy in Peking on May 17 categorically rejecting the notes of the Indian Ministry of External Affairs dated March 10 and April 17, 1965, which lodged so-called protests in connection with the signing of the protocol by China and Pakistan on the demarcation of the boundary.

May 21: The Sino-Cuban 1964-65 scientific and technical cooperation protocol was signed in Peking.

May 21-June 5: A delegation of the CPC and a delegation of the NPC, both led by Peng Chen, arrived in Djakarta on May 21 to attend the celebration of the 45th anniversary of the founding of the Indonesian Communist Party. Peng Chen and his party left Indonesia for home on June 5 via Burma.

May 23: People's communes along the lower Yellow River in Shantung province are turning the high bed of this historically unruly river from a disadvantage into an advantage, an NCNA report said. Since last autumn they have built twenty-seven "syphon" irrigation systems for rice culture. Now all Shantung has these pipes, which channel fertile silt-laden water from the river to a total of 18 thousand hectares of rice fields.

May 24: The meeting of the NPC Standing Committee held on May 22 decided to abolish the system of military ranks in the Chinese PLA. The State Council in a decision announced the hat insignia, collar badge, and some changes in the military uniform for the Chinese PLA which would go into effect June 1, 1965.

May 24-28: A contract for the purchase of 6,000 tons of Chilean electrolyzed copper was signed in Santiago. Another contract for the purchase of 1,500 tons of refined copper by China was signed on March 28.

May 25: A Sino-Soviet 1965 cultural cooperation plan was signed in Peking.

May 28: A Sino-Hungarian protocol on scientific and technical coperation was signed in Peking.

May 29: *Lin's Shon*, a film adapted by Nsia Yen in 1958 from a novel under the same title (written and published by Shen Yen-ping under the pen name of Mao Tung), was the subject of attack by leading national newspapers during its recent run. This came at a time when Shen Yen-ping and Hsia Yen had been ousted as Minister and Vice-Minister of Culture, respectively.

May 30-July 27: The great majority of provinces (autonomous regions) in whole country have recently held in succession rural conferences on part-farming and part-study education or administrative conferences on education at the provincial (autonomous region) level.

June 2: Chou En-lai arrived in Rawalpindi for talks with President Ayub Khan of Pakistan. It was reported that the two leaders had expressed identical views on the desirability of confirming invitations to the proposed Afro-Asian conferences in Algiers to countries pursuing the Bandung principles, on tension in the Indo-Pakistan subcontinent, and on increased U.S. activity in Vietnam.

June 3: An executive plan of the Sino-Algerian culture agreement on cultural cooperation for 1965 was signed in Algiers.

June 4-8: Chou En-lai arrived in Tanzania on June 4 at President Nyerere's invitation. On June 8 Chou and Nyerere urged in a joint statement that an international conference be convoked to discuss elimination of all nuclear weapons. Prior to Chou's visit, the PRC had increased its economic and military aid to Tanzania.

June 5: The 1965 executive plan for a Sino-Guinean agreement on cultural cooperation was signed in Conakry.

The 1965 executive plan for the Sino-Hungarian cultural cooperation agreement was signed in Peking.

June 7: The Berliet Company of France

confirmed it had agreed to supply 1,035 heavy trucks to China at a cost of $30 million.

June 9: The PRC and Mongolia signed in Ulan Bator their plan for the execution of the Sino-Mongolian cultural cooperation agreement.

June 10: The PRC and Kuwait issued a joint press communique in Kuwait on talks during visit of the PRC good-will delegation.

Chou En-lai returned to Peking, having interrupted his journey first at Addis Ababa for a brief talk with Ketema Yipu, the Ethiopian foreign minister; then at Cairo, where he was greeted by Kamaluddin Rifact, a deputy prime minister, and finally at Damascus, where he had talks lasting 75 minutes with President Hafez, after which the two countries confirmed their resolute struggle against colonialism and imperialism in Vietnam and Zionism in Palestine and expressed their readiness to develop friendship and effective cooperation in economic and commercial fields. Chou's African trip was only partly successful because Chou did not receive hoped-for invitations to visit Kenya, Uganda, and Zambia.

June 11: *People's Daily* said in an editorial that the Johnson administration's order of June 8 for direct combat action by U.S. ground forces in South Vietnam shows that "U.S. imperialism" is accelerating the fighting in Vietnam toward a Korean-type war. It warned that the PRC and all other countries reserved their rights to send volunteers of their armies if necessary to participate in the war against U.S. imperialism.

June 12: A Sino-Soviet protocol on scientific and technical cooperation was signed in Moscow.

June 13: Moscow announced that China had withdrawn from the joint nuclear research program for Socialist countries being conducted near Moscow.

The *People's Daily* and *Red Flag* article, "Carry the Struggle Against Khrushchev Revisionism Through to the End," accused the new Soviet leaders of not departing from the essence of Khrushchev's policies—revisionism, great-power chauvinism, and Soviet-American cooperation for the domination of the world.

A Sino-Congo protocol on the agreement of economic and technical cooperation was signed in Brazzaville.

June 14: An arms shipment from China arrived in Tanzania as part of Chinese aid program.

June 16: U.S. Secretary of Defense McNamara announced that United States military strength in Vietnam would be increased to between 70,000 and 75,000 men, including 21,000 ground-combat troops. The total current strength in Vietnam was 54,000 men.

June 18: Sino-North Korean contract on film distribution was signed in Pyongyang.

The Standing Committee of the NPC at an enlarged meeting adopted a message to the presidium of the Supreme People's Assembly of the Korean Democratic People's Republic, pledging full support for the "just and solemn stand" taken by the government of the Korean people to thoroughly smash the South Korean-Japan talks.

A Sino-Czechoslovak 1965 plan for cultural cooperation was signed in Prague.

June 19: The Soviet party, which had refrained from open polemics against China since Khrushchev's removal from office, replied in an editorial in *Pravda* deploring the Chinese attack, and appealing for international Communist unity against U.S. aggression in Vietnam.

A 1965 executive plan of Sino-Vietnamese cultural cooperation agreement was signed in Peking.

June 23: The 47 Chinese scientists who had been working at the Joint Nuclear Research Institute at Dubna in the U.S.S.R. returned to Peking, an NCNA report said.

June 25: Peking officially rejected the Commonwealth mission's approach for talks on Vietnam.

June 26: A ceremony for the signing of two protocols to modify the trade and payments agreements signed on April 24,

1956, between the PRC and Cambodia was held in Phnom Penh.

Chen Yi attended a foreign ministers' meeting in Algiers in preparation for the Afro-Asian Conference which was postponed until November 5, 1965.

June 28-30: Chou En-lai attended a meeting in Cairo with President Ayub Khan, Nasser, and Sukarno which endorsed the decision to postpone the Afro-Asian Conference until November 5, 1965. A press communique in this respect was issued on June 30.

June 30: A Sino-American ambassadorial talk was held in Warsaw.

July 10: The Ministry of Finance issued a public notice regarding the redemption of principal and payment of interest on state economic construction bonds.

July 11-16: Dr. Obote, Prime Minister of Uganda, visited Peking at the invitation of Chou En-lai. A joint communique expressed the agreement of both parties on such questions as the condemnation of colonialism, imperialism, and neo-colonialism and of armed aggression in Vietnam and in the Congo (Leopoldville), and pledged firm support for the national independence struggle of the peoples of African countries still under colonial rule (issued on July 16).

July 11-13: Le Thanh Nghi, member of the political bureau of the Central Committee of the Vietnam Workers' Party, arrived in Peking on July 11. Chou En-lai had a friendly talk with him on July 13. An agreement on economic and technical assistance to Vietnam by the PRC was signed on July 13. A press communique was issued on July 17.

July 13: China agreed to supply the Ceylon government with 162 items of carriages and wagons under an agreement signed in Colombo.

July 14: A Sino-Burmese memorandum on amendments to 1955 air transport agreement was issued in Rangoon.

Radio Lhasa announced that 5,000 Chinese troop reinforcements had been sent to southern Tibet to quell widespread revolt.

The PRC and Mali signed a contract on the construction of a textile plant in Mali by the PRC.

A multilateral protocol on postal services and tele-communications was signed in Peking at the sixth conference of ministers of post and tele-communications of Socialist countries.

July 18: The governments of the PRC and Cuba approved the extension for five years of the Sino-Cuban cultural cooperation agreement signed in July 1960.

July 19-August 5: M. Andre Malraux, French Minister of State for Cultural Affairs, visited Peking. During his visit he had talks with Mao Tse-tung, Liu Shaochi, Chou En-lai, and other Chinese leaders. According to French official sources, on the Vietnam question the Chinese leaders had not moved from their existing known position, reiterating that there could be no peace in Southeast Asia until the Americans left.

July 20: General Li Tsung-jen, 74, formerly Vice-President of Nationalist China, returned to Peking with his wife after 16 years of self-imposed exile, mostly in the United States.

A protocol on the mutual supply of supplementary goods between the PRC and the Soviet Union in 1965 was signed in Peking.

July 21-28: President of Somali Aden Abdulla Osman and his party arrived in Peking on July 21 for a week's visit. A joint press communique was issued on July 28.

July 24: Liu Shao-chi said in Peking, "The Chinese government and people firmly and unreservedly support the fraternal Vietnamese people in their just struggle to liberate the south, defend the north, and reunify their country, and will join all other peoples of the world in the continued fight to check the U.S. imperialist aggression against Vietnam and to defend Asian and world peace." He was speaking at the state banquet he gave for Burmese Prime Minister Ne Win, who arrived in Peking on July 24 for a week's visit.

A Sino-Indonesian accord on maritime transport was signed in Peking.

July 26: Mauritania established diplomatic relations with the PRC in an agreement signed in Nouakchett.

July 30: A Sino-North Korean scientific cooperation plan for 1965 was signed in Pyongyang.

August 1: A Sino-Burmese joint communique on talks during General Ne Win's visit was issued in Peking.

August 2: The Chinese Foreign Ministry in a note to the Indian embassy on July 29 lodged a strong protest against the frequent Indian intrusions into Chinese territory and air space on the Sino-Indian and China-Sikkim border during the first half of this year.

August 3: Commenting on President Johnson's July 28 statement, the *People's Daily* editorial said, "Smash the U.S. adventurous plan for war in the course of its creeping escalation."

August 5: An agreement on agricultural technical exchange between the PRC and Japan was signed in Peking.

The PRC and Ghana signed a protocol on dispatch of PRC military experts to Ghana.

August 6: "A naval fishing boat escort fleet of the Chinese PLA sank two U.S.-made warships of the Chiang Kai-shek gang on the Southeast China coastal front," an NCNA report said.

August 7-19: A delegation of the Chinese NPC, led by Li Hsueh-feng, arrived in Djakarta on August 7 for a two weeks' visit.

August 9: An article in *People's Daily* denounced the recent Tito-Shastri Vietnam proposals. They were denounced because these proposals failed to mention any conditions of U.S. withdrawal of troops, a demand which the Chinese felt was necessary before any meaningful solution could be effected.

August 13: A 1965 plan for the execution of the PRC-Congo agreement on cultural cooperation was signed in Brazzaville.

August 15-22: The Chinese government delegation led by Chen Yi arrived in Djakarta on August 15 to attend the 20th anniversary celebrations of the proclamation of Indonesia's independence. He left Djakarta on August 22, arrived in Rangoon for a one-day stay.

August 16: "The decision of the Park Chung Hee regime in South Korea to send a combat division of 15,000 men to South Vietnam at the call of U.S. imperialism is a new and serious step in the internationalization of its aggressive war in South Vietnam," said the *Ta-Kung Pao* commentator.

August 17: The 1965 executive plan of the Sino-Somali cultural cooperation agreement was signed in Magadishu.

William C. White, a former U.S. prisoner of war, with his wife and two children, left Canton for home.

August 21: "Another U.S. pilotless high-altitude reconnaissance military plane was shot down over the area of Hainan Island," an NCNA report said.

August 25: The NPC Standing Committee ratified the establishment of the Tibet Autonomous Region.

August 25-30: Kirtidihi Bista, Vice-Chairman of the Nepalese Council of Ministers, arrived in Peking on August 25. He signed a protocol between the two nations on the construction of east-west highways in Nepal on August 29.

August 27: The PRC Foreign Ministry in a note to the Indian embassy in Peking strongly protested against "Indian acts of aggression in flagrant disregard of China's sovereignty, disturbing the tranquility on the China-Sikkim border and menacing the security of the Chinese inhabitants there."

August 28: "Hua Tse-hsin, a member of the entourage of Chiang Kai-shek, ambassador of the Chiang Kai-shek clique to the Cameroons, has severed relations with the clique and returned to the embrace of the motherland," an NCNA report said.

A Sino-Algerian joint communique on talks during visit of Minister of State Bitat was issued in Peking.

September 1: The NCNA reported that China was firmly opposed to U.N. intervention in the Vietnam question. It asserted that the United States was seeking to make use of the U.N. to further its peace-talk scheme which had met with rebuffs everywhere.

September 1-9: The nine-day session of the First People's Congress of Tibet Autonomous Region reviewed the history of the revolutionary struggles of the Tibetan people in the past 15 years, discussed and decided the tasks in the revolution and construction for the years to come, elected the leaders of the autonomous region and adopted regulations governing the organization of People's Congresses and People's Council at all levels in Tibet.

September 2: Marshal Lin Piao published a 50,000-word article as a new doctrinal statement of Chinese Communist military strategy on a global basis, based upon the theories of Mao Tse-tung. He foresees the "encirclement" of both the United States and Europe by a world-wide revolutionary movement characterized by "people's wars" in the underdeveloped world.

An Indian note rejected the August 27 Chinese allegations.

September 1: In Bamako, the PRC and Mali signed minutes for talks on PRC aid for three construction projects in Mali.

September 2-9: The conference of representatives of the railways of China, the Soviet and Mongolia, and the meeting of the Sino-Mongolian Border Railway Joint Commission took place in Peking.

September 3: A program of cultural cooperation between Nepal and the PRC for 1965 was signed in Katmandu.

September 4-20: Chen Yi and his party visited the following countries: Pakistan on September 4-5: Syria on September 5-7; Algeria on September 7-8; Mali on September 9-15; Guinea on September 15-17; Algeria on September 17-18; Syria on September 18, and Afghanistan on September 20.

September 8: The PRC and Nepal issued a press communique for talks during visit of Vice-Chairman Bista in Peking.

Peking replied to an Indian note of September 2 demanding that India dismantle the military structures built on or beyond the Sikkim border. Peking Radio announced that the Chinese forces on the Indian border had been put on the alert.

September 9: The Tibet Autonomous Region formally came into being, bringing the number of autonomous regions for national minorities in China to five.

Speaking in Peking, Chou En-lai said that the "Indian reactionaries could not have embarked on such a serious military adventure without the consent and support of the United States." He reiterated the firm support of the Chinese government for Pakistan's "just struggle for freedom and right of national self-determination."

September 12: The Indian government replied, denying the Chinese allegation, and proposing that an independent and neutral observer should visit the Sikkim border to see for himself the actual state of affairs.

September 14: Two agreements, one on postal exchange and the other on the establishment of tele-communications, were signed in Peking by the governments of the PRC and Guinea. Minutes for talks on economic and technical aid were also issued.

A protocol on Sino-Indonesian cooperation in the building of a hall for the conference of New Emerging Forces was signed in Djakarta by the two countries.

September 15: "The landing of the first U.S. cavalry division in South Vietnam on September 12 has given the lie to the Johnson administration's professions of a desire for peace talks and for a settlement in accordance with the Geneva Agreement," said a *People's Daily* commentator.

A Sino-American ambassadorial talk was held in Warsaw.

September 16: 1966 executive plan for Sino-Vietnamese public health cooperation agreement was signed in Hanoi.

The Chinese government sent India an ultimatum rejecting the Indian proposal. The Chinese note threatened that unless the Indian government dismantled all military works within three days, stopped all intrusions into China, returned the kidnapped inhabitants and livestock, and pledged to refrain from further raids across the border, it must bear full responsibility for all the consequences.

The NCNA and Agence Khmere de Presse of Cambodia signed an agreement on the exchange of press information in Phnom Penh.

September 17: The Indian government replied rejecting the Chinese allegation in toto as "completely groundless." In Moscow Mr. Kosygin assured the Indian ambassador that the Soviet Union would continue its regular arms supplies to India. In Washington Mr. William F. Guad (deputy administrator of AID), after talks with Indian ambassador and Mr. Rusk, said that if India were attacked by China he expected that the United States would resume military aid to India.

September 18: The PRC and Japan signed an accord on implementation of Liao-Takasaki memorandum for trade in 1966 in Peking.

September 19: Peking replied to an Indian note of September 17 extending China's three-day ultimatum to India for another three days.

September 20: Peking said one of its planes had shot down an American jet fighter over Hainan Island and that the pilot had been captured.

Peking charged Indian troops had intruded 2½ miles into Chinese territory in the Ladakh sector and fired on Chinese civilians. India had previously charged China with firing upon Indian forces. The protest was rejected by the Indian government, which maintained that it was Chinese troops who had crossed into Indian territory and fired on a police party.

The headquarters of the general staff and the general political department of the Chinese PLA recently held a conference on the work of the people's militia in the course of the socialist education movement. It paid special attention to questions of carrying through more fully the instructions of Mao Tse-tung to put the work of the people's militia on a solid basis organizationally, politically and militarily.

September 21: U.N. Secretary General U Thant urged that the PRC be admitted to the U.N. "Both the Vietnam situation and disarmament impasse," Thant said, "point once again to the imperative need for the U.N. to achieve universality of membership as soon as possible."

September 21: Peking withdrew its ultimatum to India, claiming that the Indian forces had retreated from the four passes between September 16-20 and had dismantled installations on the Sikkim border.

September 22-October 16: Norodom Sihanouk of Cambodia and his wife and party arrived in Chengtu on September 22 to attend China's National Day celebration. Upon arrival in Peking on September 28, Prince Sihanouk and his party were given a rousing welcome by Liu Shao-chi, Tung Pi-wu, Chu Teh, and Chou En-lai at the airport. Mao Tse-tung had a cordial talk with Sihanouk on September 29. Sihanouk attended a mass demonstration on October 1. A joint statement was issued by Liu Shao-chi and Sihanouk on October 3 which stated that the U.N. would disintegrate unless it could shake off the domination of certain big powers, notably the United States. Sihanouk and his party left Peking for Korea on October 4. Continued their visit to China after concluding a tour in Korea from October 10 to 16.

September 23: United States ambassador to the U.N. Arthur J. Goldberg, appealed to the U.N. to keep Communist China out of the organization. He described the "incredible manifesto" of Lin Piao as "the antithesis of everything this organization stands for."

A multilateral communique on Games of Newly Emerging Forces was signed in Peking after second meeting of Council of GANEFO Federation.

September 26: Peking announced it was severing all relations with the International Red Cross because of its invitation to Formosa to attend the 20th I.R.C. conference.

September 27: The Chinese Foreign Ministry, in a note to the Indian embassy dated September 26, lodged a strong protest with the Indian government against a mob of Indian hooligans making provocations before the Chinese embassy in New Delhi on September 24.

September 29: At his press conference in Peking, Chen Yi laid down conditions for entry of the PRC into the U.N. The U.N. must oust the Chiang Kai-shek clique, must cancel its 1951 resolution condemning China and North Korea as aggressors, and adopt a resolution condemning the United States as aggressor in Korea. Furthermore, the U.N. charter must be reviewed and revised by all countries, big and small; all independent states should be included in the U.N.; and all imperialist puppets should be expelled.

September 30: Seven documents including an agreement on economic and technical cooperation, a trade agreement, payment agreements and four unspecified economic matters between the PRC and Indonesia were signed in Peking.

The Indonesian armed forces crushed what appeared to be a coup d'etat against the regime of President Sukarno.

October 1: Mao Tse-tung, other Chinese leaders, and Prince Sihanouk, Cambodian head of state, watched an estimated 700,-000 people march in a Peking parade celebrating the 16th anniversary of the establishment of the PRC.

An agreement was signed between France and the PRC establishing cultural, technical, and scientific exchanges.

October 2: A contract on distribution of Chinese films and the exchange of newsreel materials between the PRC and Guinea was signed in Peking.

October 4: A Sino-Indonesian joint statement on talks during the visit of a delegation from People's Assembly of Indonesia was issued in Peking.

October 6: A protocol for cooperation in broadcasting and television between the PRC and Syria was signed in Camaseus.

A Sino-Albanian protocol on scientific and technical cooperation was signed in Peking.

October 10: Chinese civilian personnel returned the bodies of three Indian soldiers, together with their personal belongings and four rifles, to the Indian side of the Shanggier area.

October 12: A Sino-Ceylonese protocol on exchange of commodities in 1966 was signed in Peking.

October 15: A contract was signed in Peking between the China National Technical Import Corporation and the Italian Innocenti Society to cover the purchase by China of a tube-expanding plant for seamless tubes of large diameters made by the Italian concern.

October 18: Peking sent a strong protest note to Indonesia complaining about the "lies and slanders and anti-Chinese outcries" in Indonesia. They charged that 40 soldiers had broken into the Chinese embassy in Djakarta on October 16, protested specially against the forcible searching of the Chinese commercial counselor's office in that city, and demanded an apology and the punishment of those responsible.

October 19: The first direct postal exchange between the PRC and Nepal was opened at the Friendship Bridge on the Chinese-Nepalese border.

October 22: Changes in administrative demarcation in various parts of the country were announced.

October 23: NCNA reported that Indonesian soldiers and police had forced their way into the Chinese Communist embassy in Djakarta and pried about the whole place. Indonesian army officers and newspapers had complained that Communist China was sneaking weapons into the country through the embassy.

October 26: The Chinese ambassador to Indonesia, Yang Chung-ming, met with Indonesian President Sukarno for the first time since the abortive September 30 coup. After the meeting, the Chinese embassy said that the relations between China and Indonesia remained firm although there were elements trying to alienate the two countries.

A Sino-Czechoslovak protocol on scientific and technical cooperation was signed in Prague.

October 27: Peking announced it would not participate in the Asian African "summit" conference scheduled for November 5 because of the possibility of the Soviet Union attending and because of the lack of enthusiasm for China's demand that a major theme of the conference be the condemnation of American imperialism.

October 28: It was announced that the PRC had signed another three-year wheat purchase agreement with Canada to purchase 112,000,000 bushels over the period August 1, 1965, through July 31, 1969.

November 1: The PRC and Pakistan signed an agreement on the PRC economic aid in construction of plants, factories, and workshops in Pakistan.

A Sino-Korean protocol on scientific and technical cooperation was signed in Pyongyang.

November 3: About 100,000 Moslems and other anti-Communist demonstrators attacked the Chinese consulate in Medan, Indonesia, tearing down the Chinese flag.

November 4: A strong protest note was sent to Indonesia demanding an apology for attacks on the Chinese consulate at Medan. It also demanded the punishment of those responsible and assurances against a recurrence.

November 6: A Sino-Afghanistan protocol on exchange of goods during 1965-66 was signed in Peking.

November 8: An agreement was signed between the PRC and Australia for the purchase of 500,000 tons of wheat.

November 9: A Sino-Bulgarian protocol on scientific and technical cooperation was signed in Sofia.

November 9: An agreement on cooperation in public health services between the PRC and North Korea and the executive plan for 1965-66 were signed in Pyongyang.

Instruments of ratification of the treaty of friendship between the PRC and the United Republic of Tanzania were exchanged at a ceremony held in Dar-es-Salaam (signed on February 20, 1965).

November 10: A Shanghai newspaper de-

nounced a play, "Hai Jui Dismissed From Office," and its author, Wu Han, deputy mayor of Peking, thus marking the opening of a new campaign against intellectuals.

A violent attack on the Soviet party, entitled "Reputation of the New Leaders of the CPSU on United Action," appeared in *People's Daily* and *Red Flag*. The article asserted that the Soviet Union regarded U.S. imperialism as its closest friend and the Marxist-Leninists of the world as its principal enemy. The article said that efforts by the United States and the Soviet Union to curb proliferation of nuclear weapons were only in the interest of maintaining the monopoly of the two nuclear overlords against China and all other independent countries. It accused the new Soviet party leaders of "still pursuing Khrushchev's line, but with double-faced tactics more cunning and hypocritical than his," and of allying themselves with U.S. imperialism by trying to preserve the monopoly of the two nuclear overlords. It also accused the new Soviet leaders of having openly sided with India against China on the Sino-Indian border question. It denied Soviet charges of Chinese obstruction to the transit of Soviet military equipment to North Vietnam. Finally, it stated that if China's leadership is usurped by revisionists in the future, the Marxist-Leninists of all countries should resolutely expose and fight them.

November 11: Three Red Chinese pilots defected to Nationalist China in a Russian-made bomber. The plane crashed while landing and one of the three defectors died.

November 12: A Sino-Albanian protocol on exchange of goods and payments in 1966 was signed in Tirana along with a protocol for Albania's use in 1966 of credits granted by the PRC.

November 13: A naval battle took place in the Taiwan Strait between a Nationalist naval patrol unit and Chinese Communist ships. Both sides claimed victory.

The 1965 plan for cooperation between the PRC academy of sciences, the North

Vietnam state commission of sciences and technology, and academy of social sciences was signed in Hanoi.

November 14: The PRC government issued a statement on the situation in Southern Rhodesia, strongly condemning the declaration of independence by the colonial authorities of that country.

The Nationalist Defense Ministry in Taipei announced that a naval patrol unit had destroyed four Chinese Communist gunboats and severely damaged another in a battle in the Taiwan Strait. In Peking, however, a naval victory over the Chiang Kai-shek clique was claimed off the coast of Fukien Province in which one Chiang ship had been sunk—the frigate Yung Chang (945 tons)—and another damaged—the submarine-chaser Yungtai, which was claimed to have fled in panic. The Peking statement made no mention of any losses of Chinese Communist warships.

November 16: *Pravda* and *Izvestia* replied that the Chinese article from beginning to end is full of impermissible, utterly groundless, slanderous, provocative fabrications, permeated with a spirit of hostility toward the Soviet people and toward the Communist party of the Soviet Union. The Soviet accused the Chinese Communist party of rejecting unity of action with the Soviet Communist party and other Marxist-Leninist parties against U.S. aggression. It had been Soviet policy since the ouster of Khrushchev to ignore the Chinese attacks, but both the November 10 Chinese article and the Soviet reply were given publicity by Soviet news media.

November 17: The U.N. General Assembly defeated a resolution to award China's seat in the U.N. to Communist China and expel the representatives of Nationalist China. The vote was a 47-47 tie, with 20 abstentions.

November 18: A protocol of a Sino-North Korean border railway joint committee was signed in Sinjiju.

The Chinese ambassador to Tunisia strongly protested repeated statements made by Tunisian President Habib Bour-

guiba slandering China and viciously attacking the Chinese state leaders.

A Sino-Soviet 1965-66 plan of cooperation between Academies of Sciences was signed in Moscow.

November 19: *People's Daily* commented: "China may as well stay out of a U.N. like this." It added that the vote had been a "humiliating setback" for the United States, which had strained every nerve and worked overtime to get the resolution voted down by a simple majority. The article asserted that "the U.N. must free itself from the control of the United States, rectify its mistakes, and undergo a thorough reform."

November 22: Sino-East German protocol on scientific and technical cooperation was signed in Peking.

The Chinese Foreign Ministry in a statement strongly protested "the bombing by the United States and its followers of Khang Khay, former seat of the Royal Government of Laos, and the compounds of the Chinese Economic and Cultural Mission and the NCNA branch there on November 20."

Chinese experts and Nepalese technicians began survey work for the 200-kilometer long Katmandu-Pokmara highway to be built with Chinese aid in accordance with the protocol signed by the Chinese and Nepalese governments last August.

November 23: A 1966 trade agreement between the PRC and Finland was signed in Peking.

November 25: The Chinese Foreign Ministry in a note to the Indian embassy informed India that the Chinese government is ready to "consent to the collection by India of the bodies of the three Indian soldiers killed during their intrusion on November 24, and to its receiving of the three Indian soldiers captured during their intrusion on September 26 . . ."

November 26: Lin Piao gave instructions in Chinese PLA work in 1966. The overall requisite for the work of the whole army during the coming year was continued emphasis on politics, as had been the case this year. Specially, there would be five items of work.

November 26-27: The PRC embassy in Indonesia, in its two notes dated November 26 and 27 to the Ministry of Foreign Affairs of Indonesia, lodged two very strong protests in connection with "recent cases of serious persecution of Chinese nationals which were stage-managed and organized by Indonesian right-wing forces in Ambon in Maluku, Bonthain in South Sulamesi, and in many places in Central Java."

November 28: The Chinese Foreign Ministry issued a statement expressing full support of the "just stand and demands of the Democratic Republic of Vietnam" as made clear in the DRV Foreign Ministry statement of November 26. The DRV demanded that the United States end its "war of aggression" in South Vietnam.

November 29: The U.N. General Assembly approved a resolution urging convocation of a world disarmament conference, not later than 1967, that would include the PRC. The vote was 112-0 with France abstaining and Nationalist China absent.

December 1: The PRC and Morocco signed an agreement on renewal of 1963 trade agreement for one year.

The 1965-66 executive plan for cooperation between Chinese and Rumanian Academies of Science was signed in Bucharest.

Peking declared that China would never enter into relations with the U.N. or any conference connected with it before the restoration of her legitimate rights in the U.N. and expulsion of the Chiang Kai-shek government from the organization.

December 2: A United States naval expert drew attention to the rising strength of Communist China's navy. It was reported that China had, in addition to warships, 28 submarines, 24 submarine-chasers, 38 mine sweepers, and a land-based naval air force equipped with bombers and fighters. Most vessels were of Soviet design, some Chinese constructed. Since the cessation of Soviet assistance, China's

naval growth had been delayed, but only temporarily.

The PRC and North Korea signed agreement on river navigation cooperation in Mukden.

December 3: The Polish Communist party criticized Communist China for its November 10 attack on the Soviet Union, which it termed incredibly aggressive and lacking any foundation.

The protocol on Sino-Vietnamese scientific and technical cooperation was signed in Hanoi.

December 4: "Within the past three months 141 officers and men belonging to the remnant Chiang Kai-shek force that fled beyond the Chinese border of Yunnan province, gave themselves up to the frontier garrison of the Chinese PLA," an NCNA report said.

December 5: The PRC and North Vietnam signed an agreement on loan by the PRC in Peking along with a protocol on mutual supply of commodities and payments in 1966.

December 8: A joint statement on cultural exchange for 1966 between the people of China and Japan was signed in Peking.

The Chinese and Algerian governments signed in Algiers a protocol under which another Chinese medical team would be sent to Algeria.

December 10: Two thousand Indonesian demonstrators attacked Communist China's consulate in Medan, North Sumatra. Three persons were killed when police fought to keep the demonstrators from entering the building. Homes and business establishments of Chinese residents also were attacked.

December 14: A contract for the purchase of an LD-steel plant from the Austrian steel combine, "Voest," was signed in Peking between the China National Technical Import Corporation and "Voest."

December 15: The Chinese embassy in Indonesia in a note to the Indonesian Foreign Ministry dated December 15 expressed its great indignation at the "extremely serious second raid on the Chinese consulate in Medan by hooligans organized by the Indonesian right-wing forces on December 10." It lodged a strong protest with the Indonesian government against the raid.

The 1965-66 executive plan for co-operation between the Chinese and Polish academies of science was signed in Warsaw.

December 17: A joint statement and an agreement on fishing on the Yellow and East Seas for the period of 1965-67 were signed in Peking by delegations of the Fishery Association of China and the Japan-China Fishery Association, along with a memorandum to limit the number of trawlers in designated areas.

The PRC and Somali signed an agreement in Mogadishu under which China would build a Somali national theater, a gift from the Chinese government to the Somali government.

December 18: President Sukarno of Indonesia appealed to Indonesians to stop attacking Chinese in that country, and the Peking regime, because, he said, "We are against imperialism and we cannot do it alone."

December 19: The Ministry of Commerce has decided, beginning in 1966, to introduce a revolutionary reform in commercial units in the whole country—to abolish the debit-credit bookkeeping methods and adopt the addition-subtraction method.

December 20: Peking sent a note to Indonesia protesting the sacking of Chinese homes and shops in Singaraja and other towns of Bali by several hundred hooligans.

Speaking at the reception in celebration of the fifth anniversary of the founding of the National Liberation Front in South Vietnam in Peking, Chou En-lai accused the Soviet Union of "sowing discord in an attempt to undermine the Vietnamese people's unity against U.S. aggression and the unity of the Vietnamese and Chinese people against U.S. imperialism."

December 21: A barter and payments agreement for 1966 was signed in Peking between the PRC and Rumania.

December 23: A Sino-Czechoslovak 1966-67 plan for cooperation between academies of science was signed in Prague.

December 28: The Chinese Foreign Ministry in a statement strongly condemned "U.S. imperialism" for its "war threats against the Kingdom of Cambodia" and expressed firm support for the "solemn stand of the Royal Cambodian government to reply to any violation of the frontier with the military means at its disposal."

December 29: A protocol on 1966-67 plan for cultural cooperation between the PRC and Cuba was signed in Peking.

212

1966

January 1: The U.S. State Department's announcement on easing passport restrictions to China and other countries is branded as "nauseating hypocrisy" by the *People's Daily* in a short commentary.

China claimed it had built a modern oil field, as advanced as any in the world, 250 miles northeast of Peking. Work on the oil field began six years ago.

January 2: Cuban Premier Fidel Castro announced that the PRC was reducing its trade with Cuba from an exchange of $250 million in 1965 to $170 million in 1966. He revealed that Peking was cutting its rice shipment to Cuba by 50% and that it was not taking the quantity of sugar from Cuba agreed upon in 1964.

The PRC launched a new five-year plan aimed specially at boosting farm production. The plan called for the building of more factories, the bolstering of national defense, basic industry, communications, and transport.

A new railway, the Hankow-Tanchiang-k'ou Railway, linking with Hsiangfang in the northwestern part of Hupeh, was completed and opened for traffic.

January 2-April 29: Vice-Mayor of Peking, Wu Han, has been the target of a literary and art rectification campaign. Among his writings under attack are *Javelin-Throwing*, a collection of satirical essays written by Wu Han in the forties (published in June-July, 1959), the play "Dismissal of Hai Jui" (published June 1959), and the article "Hai Jui Reproaches the Emperor" (published January 1961). An article by Wu Han criticizing his own writings appeared in the *People's Daily*.

January 3: General Soglo, the new military ruler of Dahomey, broke off diplomatic relations with Peking and gave the staff of the Chinese embassy in Cotonou 72 hours in which to leave the country. The Chinese ambassador, Mr. Li Yun-chuan, accordingly left Cotonou on January 5, after delivering a strongly worded protest from the Chinese government.

The Chinese Foreign Ministry in a statement strongly condemned "U.S. imperialism" for "instigating recently the armed forces of Thailand to commit aggression against Cambodia in its border areas." It reaffirmed China's all-out support for the Cambodian people's "just struggle against U.S. imperialism and its lackeys."

January 4: A Chinese note accused the Soviet Union of spreading "lying rumors" that China had hindered the supply of Soviet military aid to North Vietnam and demanded that these reports should be officially denied. Both the Soviet embassy in Peking and the Soviet Foreign Ministry refused to accept the note.

January 5: A statement lodged a serious protest with the Dahomey government against its "extremely grave action of unilaterally and unreasonably tearing up the agreement between the PRC and Dahomey on the establishment of diplomatic relations and disrupting the relations between the two countries."

January 6: President Bokassa of the Central African Republic broke off diplomatic relations with Peking and demanded all Chinese nationals leave the country as soon as possible. Chinese Ambassador Mr. Meng Yeng, who was said to have been in close contact with certain officials of the former regime, and his staff of 30 members, left for Brazzaville on January 8, while M. Mamadon, the newly appointed Central African ambassador in Peking, who had arrived there on December 12, left for Bangui via Moscow on January 10.

January 7: The *Mansfield Report on Vietnam* was made public by the U.S. Senate Foreign Relations Committee.

January 8: A *People's Daily* commentator wrote that the point of departure of the Johnson administration's "14-point" formula on Vietnam is that "the Vietnamese people are engaged in 'aggression' and

U.S. imperialism is trying to halt this 'aggression'."

January 9: "A U.S.-made plane of the Chiang Kai-shek gang was shot down over the coastal area of East China," an NCNA report said.

An NCNA dispatch called Fidel Castro a liar and an obstacle to Sino-Cuban relations.

January 11: Chou En-lai sent a message of condolence to the Indian President on the death of Indian Prime Minister Shastri.

January 12: An agreement was signed for the supply by China of electrical equipment to the value of Rs 1,000,000 to the East Pakistan Water and Power Development Authority.

Peking radio announced the formation of Malayan Organization to liberate the Malays and "crush Malaysia."

Peking strongly protested to Indonesia the "savage slaughter" of more than 20 Chinese on the island of Lombok.

January 15: A trade contract for chemical fertilizer was signed in Peking by Wang Han-min, acting general manager of the China National Chemicals Import and Export Corporation, and Yoshio Suzuki, head of the delegation representing Japanese ammonium sulphate and urea factories.

In a memorandum to the Soviet ambassador in Peking, the Chinese government pointed out that it had always met the reasonable requests of the Soviet government and had provided all possible facilities and assistance in the transport of arms which were required by the Vietnamese side and which the Soviet side agreed to supply. Nevertheless, the Soviet side "fabricated all sorts of slanderous rumors against China, alleging that it hindered the transport of Soviet military aid supplies destined for Vietnam and even asserting that China demanded from the Soviet Union payment in U.S. dollars for the transport of these supplies in transit."

January 17: In a note to Indonesia, Peking protested the provocative demonstrations on January 10 and 15 in front of the Chinese embassy in Djakarta by thousands of people organized by right-wing forces.

A national conference on schools for financial and trade cadres was held recently in Shanghai under the sponsorship of the political department for finance and trade of the CPC Central Committee. The conference stressed the importance of bringing politics to the fore and indoctrinating financial and trade cadres in the thought of Mao Tse-tung.

January 18: The general political department of the Chinese PLA concluded in Peking its conference on political work in the army. During the twenty days of the conference a serious study was made of the important instructions given by the Central Committee of the CPC and Mao Tse-tung on building up the army and on its political work. It discussed implementation of the five-point principle put forward by Lin Piao of keeping politics in the fore, summed up the experience of political work in the past two years, and made arrangements for political work in 1966.

January 22: Representatives of the China Committee for Promotion of International Trade Promotion Association signed a joint statement on promotion of trade, technical exchanges, exhibitions, and maritime and other transport in Peking.

January 25: All Chinese Communist newspapers carried a report written by Hsiao Hua, chief of the general political department of the Chinese PLA. He indicated that it was essential to keep politics in the fore, strengthen our political and ideological work, arm all our commanders and fighters with Mao Tse-tung's thinking, ensure absolute leadership over the army by the party, make our army the party's most responsive instrument, which most faithfully carries out its line, its principles and its policies, thus ensuring that the guns are always in the hands of the most reliable people.

January 26: A spokesman of the All-China Journalists' Association made a statement on the association's acceptance of the request by the permanent secretaries of various of the Afro-Asian Journalists' Associations to get together in Peking following their temporary withdrawal from Djakarta.

January 28: In his letter to Liu Shao-chi, Ho Chi Minh pointed out that the 4-point stand put forward by the DRV "is an expression of the essential provisions of the 1954 Geneva Agreements on Vietnam." In conclusion he wrote, "In face of the extremely serious situation brought about by the United States in Vietnam, I firmly believe that the people and government of the fraternal People's Republic of China will extend increased support and assistance to our people's just struggle . . ."

January 30: Liu Shao-chi sent a letter in reply to the January 28 letter of Ho Chi Minh expressing firm support to the "just stand of the DRV" set forth in Ho's letter.

January 31: The Chinese Foreign Ministry in a note to the Indian embassy in Peking lodged a strong protest with the Indian government against India's "incessant provocations and serious intrusions into China's territory and air space along the Sino-Indian border and the China-Sikkim border in the latter half of 1965."

A strong protest was made by China to Britain alleging that Hong Kong was being used for warlike purposes by American ships. Asserting that U.S. warships had entered Hong Kong more than 300 times during 1965, the note called upon Britain to take immediate effective measures to prevent Hong Kong from being used as a base for U.S. aggression; it added that Britain would eat bitter fruit of her own making if she continued to act as a willing accomplice of U.S. aggressors.

February 1: *People's Daily* charged that the purpose of the high-level Soviet mission to North Vietnam in January was to "say clearly that the Vietnamese people must sit down around a conference table with the American aggressors." Soviet leaders were attacked also for sponsoring the negotiations that led to a settlement between Pakistan and the Indian aggressors.

February 1-8: *Hsieh Yao-huan*, a play by Tien Han (a Communist and one of the leaders in the theatrical circles of Com-

munist China) was attacked by three articles in *People's Daily*.

February 9: A Sino-Guinean protocol on trade for 1966 was signed in Peking.

February 2: *People's Daily* charged that the Soviet Union was supporting U.S. efforts to achieve the military encirclement of China. The article claimed that Soviet policy on Vietnam, India-Pakistan and Japan questions completely conforms with the requirements of U.S. imperialism, especially with the latter's policy of encircling China.

The Chinese Foreign Ministry in a statement denounced "U.S. imperialism's resumption of bombing of the DRV" and its "attempt to carry on its plot of peace talks through the instrumentality of the U.N."

February 4: A Sino-Czechoslovak agreement on exchange of goods and payments in 1966 was signed in Peking.

February 6: The NCNA indicated that the PRC would not be represented at the 23rd Congress of the Soviet Communist party, due to open March 29.

February 7: "A pilotless high-altitude reconnaissance military plane of U.S. imperialism was shot down over the area of Southwest China," an NCNA report said.

February 7-20: There has been a widespread campaign in China to emulate Mai Hsien-te and Chiao Yu-lu. Notifications and circulars have been issued by various organizations urging people to follow them as an example.

February 11: The executive plan for 1966-67 of Sino-Rumanian cultural cooperation agreement was signed in Peking.

February 12: The Chinese Foreign Ministry in a statement on the Honolulu Conference severely condemned "U.S. imperialism" for "insisting on expanding its war of aggression against Vietnam."

February 14: A letter to the Communist parties of Eastern Europe sent by the Central Committee of Soviet Communist party gave details of Soviet proposals for cooperation with China and of Soviet aid to North Vietnam, and accused the Chinese party of wishing to bring about war between the United States and the Soviet Union.

February 19: *People's Daily* described the "illegal 'agreement' between the U.S. imperialists and the Chiang Kai-shek gang on the status of the U.S. aggressor forces in Taiwan" as "an important move by the U.S. imperialists in pursuit of their futile efforts to perpetuate their forcible occupation of China's territory of Taiwan and to turn the island into a base for the expansion of their aggressive war against Vietnam."

The Chinese Foreign Ministry, in a statement today, strongly protested against "the criminal attack by U.S. aircraft yesterday on the Chinese consulate in Phong Saly of Laos, during which serious damage was done to the buildings and other property of the Chinese consulate," said an NCNA report.

February 20: NCNA said that Secretary of State Rusk's testimony before the Senate Foreign Relations Committee (February 18) was to threaten the Vietnam and Chinese people with a big U.S. brinkmanship. It warned that China was fully prepared to take up the challenge and fight to the end if U.S. imperialism insists on carrying the war into their country.

A Sino-Hungarian agreement on exchange of goods and payments in 1966 was signed in Peking.

February 22: *People's Daily* accused Castro of following mistaken policies based on Soviet advice. It accused him of continuing the imperialist legacy of sugar-cane monoculture.

February 24-28: Dr. Kwame Nkrumah, president of the Republic of Ghana, arrived in Peking on February 24. He was greeted at the airport by Liu Shao-chi, Chou En-lai and other leaders; a military coup d'etat ousted President Nkruman while he was en route to Peking. He left Peking on February 28.

February 25: A Sino-North Korean 1966-67 plan for cultural cooperation was signed in Peking.

February 27: Chen Yi and Tao-Chu talked about some important questions concern-

ing socialist literary creation when receiving the author of *Song of Ouyang Hai*. They praised the novel as a work of epochal significance, and stressed the need for writers to arm themselves with the thoughts of Mao Tse-tung, continuously improve their ideology, and go deep into the world of practical struggle.

"The Chinese Foreign Ministry lodged its strongest protest with the Indonesian government against the barbarous outrage of attacking the Chinese consulate in Makasan and assaulting and injuring the Chinese consul and consulate personnel by hooligans organized by the Indonesian right-wing forces," an NCNA report said.

March 1: The new regime in Ghana ordered all Soviet, the PRC, and East German personnel and their families to leave the country. About 130 Russians and 150 Chinese departed during the first week of March.

March 3: *People's Daily* called the debate in the United States on the administration's Vietnam policy only "camouflage" to hoodwink the people. The article said both the hawks and doves were a "bunch of fools" who would not abandon the U.S. policy of aggression in Vietnam and Asia or advocate withdrawal of U.S. forces from Asia.

A national conference on state farms and land reclamation held recently in Peking urged farm workers in various localities to excel in the operation of farms by energetically bringing politics to the fore.

March 4: "The announcement by U.S. Secretary of Defense Robert S. McNamara that the United States will send an additional 20,000 troops to South Vietnam is a clear signal that the Johnson administration is continuing to widen the war of aggression there," said the *People's Daily* in a commentary.

"In the past two months, three officers and 25 soldiers of the remnant Chiang Kai-shek troops, who had fled beyond the Chinese border from Yunnan province, have given themselves up to the frontier defense units of the Chinese PLA in Yunnan province," an NCNA report said.

March 5: China's 1966 National Sports Conference has called for a mass sports movement to be carried through under the guidance of Mao Tse-tung's thinking.

"A pilotless high-altitude reconnaissance military plane of U.S. imperialism was shot down over Central South China," an NCNA report said.

March 6: Peking rejected an official note from Ghana which accused China of giving assistance to the deposed regime of Nkrumah.

March 7: Secretary of Defense McNamara expressed concern over China's growing nuclear ability, saying that within two to three years they could launch a nuclear attack on countries within 700 miles of China, but that it would take a decade or more before they would be able to support the aggressive statements of its leaders "with instruments of war of the most terrible kind."

March 8: The U.S. Senate Foreign Relations Committee began a series of hearings on United States policy towards mainland China.

March 8-13: A strong earthquake occurred in the Singtai area of Hopei Province, North China. Relief and rescue work was promptly carried out.

March 9: It was disclosed that President Johnson had decided to ease travel restrictions for scholars wanting to visit Albania, China, North Vietnam, North Korea or Cuba.

A mob of Indonesian students broke into the offices of the Chinese Communist New China News Agency in Djakarta, destroying the building and the News Agency's cars. In another part of the city, student mobs attacked the Chinese consulate, injuring 25 persons. The Chinese embassy again protested and demanded an apology from the Indonesian government, severe punishment for the culprits and those who instigated them, compensation for losses, and a guarantee against recurrence of incidents.

Referring to Chinese setbacks in Cuba,

Ghana, and Indonesia, a *People's Daily* article said: "The anti-U.S. struggle does not advance in a straight line. There will be many ebbs and flows until final victory."

March 11-April 1: Once criticized with Shen Yen-ping for the film *Lin's Shop* in May 1965, Hsia Yen found himself the target of another literary and art rectification campaign. Under attack were his Collected Works on Motion Pictures, *Sai Chin Hua* (a play), and other works.

March 14: Sino-Albanian relations appeared to have entered a critical stage. The two countries failed to reach an agreement on economic aid.

March 15 and 19: In two notes, Peking protested against the Ghana government's action in declaring the first secretary, Mr. Hu Ting-yi, and two other officials of the Chinese embassy in Accra, to be undesirable, and rejected a Ghanian complaint accusing China of deliberately intervening in the internal affairs of that country.

March 16: A Sino-U.S. ambassadorial talk was held in Warsaw.

Sino-Bulgarian goods exchange and payments agreement for 1966 was signed in Sofia.

March 18: The West German government announced a DM 150,000,000 contract between the PRC and some German firms for machinery and hardware.

March 21: 198 United States experts on China affairs called upon the United States to drop its opposition to admitting China to the U.N. and to seek the establishment of diplomatic relations with China.

A Sino-Vietnamese protocol on border railway was signed in Hanoi.

March 22: Changes made in administrative demarcation in various parts of China were announced.

A Sino-Polish agreement on exchange of goods and payments in 1966 was signed in Peking.

March 23: The CPC announced that it had refused an invitation to send a delegation to the 23rd Congress of the CPSU which met in Moscow March 29-April 8.

Two strong earthquakes struck the Singtai, Hengshui, and Shihchaing-chuang areas of Southern Hopei Province, North China.

"A pilotless high-altitude military reconnaissance plane of U.S. imperialism was shot down over Southwest China," an NCNA report said.

March 25: A Sino-East German agreement on goods exchange and payments for 1966 was signed in East Berlin.

March 26-31: Chairman of State Liu Shao-chi arrived in Rawalpindi on March 26 for a state visit to West Pakistan. The formal talks between Liu Shao-chi and President Ayub Khan began on the same day, continuing until March 28. A joint communique issued on March 31 reaffirmed China's support for Pakistan on the Kashmir question and Pakistan's support for the admission of the PRC to the U.N. It contained no reference to the Vietnam question, although according to the Pakistan official spokesman this had been one of the subjects discussed between the two presidents.

March 27: A Chinese note lodged the strongest protest with the Indonesian government against the "barbarous outrage of violently raiding on March 24 the residence of the Chinese consul general in Djakarta and kidnapping of its personnel by armed hooligans organized by the Indonesian reactionary right-wing forces."

March 28: United States ambassador to the U.N., Arthur J. Goldberg, said that U.N. members were currently less favorably disposed to seating Communist China in 1965. He said the reason was due mainly to China itself and its self-imposed isolation.

A Sino-Mongolian protocol on mutual supply of goods in 1966 was signed in Peking.

March 29: The 23rd Soviet Communist Party Congress convened in Moscow. In the opening speech, Communist Party First Secretary Leonid I. Brezhnev stressed unity and called relations with the PRC and Albania unsatisfactory. He said the Soviet Communist party condemned "with deep indignation the anti-Communist terror in Indonesia."

The Chinese embassy in Indonesia protested against occupation of embassy villa by organized Indonesian "hooligans."

March 30: An exhibition of archives, documents, and other articles relating to the Paris Commune opened in Peking under the auspices of the Chinese People's Association for Cultural Relations with Foreign Countries.

The PRC embassy in Kenya protested against Kenyan Senate's anti-China motion.

March 31: "The Chinese embassy in Accra, in a note to the Ghana Foreign Ministry, lodged the strongest protest against the fabrications in its note of March 24 and aide memoire of March 25 villifying and slandering China and worsening the relations between the two countries," an NCNA report said.

A Sino-Cambodian 1966 plan for cultural and scientific cooperation was signed in Peking.

April 2: National conference of industry and communications and national conferences of political work on fronts of industry and communication were held in Peking.

The national conference of electric power industry and national political work conference of water conservation and electric power were recently held jointly to discuss the problem of how politics should be brought further to the fore and Mao Tse-tung's thinking be applied in running an enterprise.

April 3: The PRC embassy protested a "hooligans' " attack on the Chinese consulate in Medan and "Indonesian hooligans' " raids on Chinese schools and organizations in Lampung, Djambi.

April 4: A Sino-Soviet agreement on civil air transport was signed in Moscow.

April 4-8: Chairman of State Liu Shao-chi paid an official visit to Afghanistan during which he had talks with Prime Minister Mr. Maiwandwal. A joint communique issued on April 8 expressed their satisfaction at the development of friendly relations and cooperation between the two countries and reaffirmed Afghanistan's support for the admission of the PRC to the U.N. Mr. Maiwandwal accepted an invitation to visit China.

April 5: All Chinese schools (about 50) in the Djakarta district of Indonesia were closed by the Indonesian army. Similar schools in other districts were closed on March 30 and April 7.

April 9: The Chinese Foreign Ministry in a statement declared firm support for "the just stand by the government and people of the Kingdom of Cambodia in opposition to the act of aggression committed by Thailand against their country."

April 11: A strong protest note was sent to Indonesia regarding the closing of Chinese schools there and alleging the beating up and torturing of Chinese nationals.

April 12: The PRC Foreign Ministry's note to Indonesian embassy requests arrangements to ship back Chinese nationals.

April 13: Peking radio announced a U.S. A-38 plane had been shot down over Southwest China.

April 14: The U.S. State Department disclosed that several American universities had been notified that scientists and scholars from Communist China would be permitted to visit the United States. The offer was rejected by Communist China two days later.

April 14: A Sino-Congolese executive plan of cultural cooperation for 1966 was signed in Brazzaville.

The 30th meeting of the NPC Standing Committee heard a report by Shih Hsi-min, Vice-Minister of Culture, on the socialist cultural revolution. In a speech Kuo Mo-jo criticized himself for his not having been reformed ideologically according to Mao Tse-tung's doctrine.

April 15: A mob of 2,000 Chinese citizens of Indonesia raided the Chinese embassy in Djakarta following an anti-Peking rally attended by over 40,000 Chinese Indonesians. The mob ransacked the building, but its employees were protected by Indonesian soldiers.

April 15-17: Chairman Liu Shao-chi paid a visit to Dacca, the capital of East Pakistan, during which he had further talks with President Ayub Khan.

April 16: The PRC protested the embassy riot and charged that "right-wing reactionary soldiers" and "American imperialists" were responsible. On the same day, the Indonesian ambassador to Peking defected to the PRC.

Supreme People's Court granted special pardon to 57 war criminals and ordered their release.

In a special section devoted to criticism of *Sanchia Village* and *Night Causerie at Yanshan, Pei-ching Jih Pao* splashed three whole pages with comments denouncing a number of articles from *Notes on Sanchia Village* written for *Chien Hsien* magazine by Wu Han, Teng To, and Liao Mo-sha under one common pen name of "Wu Nan-hsing," as well as *Night at Yenshan*, under the nom de plume of "Ma Nan-tsun." These articles and works were condemned as representative of a countercurrent against the party and socialism.

April 17: The U.S. House Foreign Affairs Subcommittee on the Far East and the Pacific made public a part of testimony given before the subcommittee March 16 by Secretary of State Dean Rusk. He summed up the elements of future United States policy toward China as a policy of containment as well as of non-isolation.

April 17-19: Chairman Liu Shao-chi visited Burma. A communique issued on April 19 by Liu and Ne Win, prime minister of Burma, stated that both parties pointed out that the Afro-Asian countries should further strengthen their unity in order to eradicate colonialism and neo-colonialism and defend world peace. The Burmese side reaffirmed its support for the restoration of legitimate rights of the PRC in the United Nations.

April 18: The PRC Foreign Ministry notified Indonesian government on stoppage of assistance to contract textile mill in Bandjaran.

The NCNA called Secretary Rusk's testimony "a mixture of hostilities to China and deception." The Nationalist Chinese government characterized the secretary's policy statement as appeasement.

A *People's Daily* article condemned the

History of Development of Chinese Motion Pictures as a "big anti-party, anti-socialist poisonous weed" for its praising highly the works of Hsin Yen, Tien Han, and others.

April 19: The Ministry of Communications published "Regulations Covering Foreign Ships on Bordering Rivers."

Arthur J. Goldberg, speaking at the National Press Club in Washington, outlined the minimum conditions under which the United States would agree to Communist China's admission to the U.N. Peking would have to abandon its demand for expulsion of Taiwan; withdraw its demand that the U.N. rescind its condemnation of Peking for aggression in Korea and brand the United States as the aggressor; withdraw its demand that the U.N. be reorganized and that unnamed "lackeys" of the United States be expelled; and promise to observe the provisions of the U.N. Charter.

A Sino-Soviet protocol on exchange of goods in 1966 was signed in Peking.

April 20: A Sino-Syrian 1966-67 plan for cultural cooperation was signed in Damascus.

April 21: Soviet Defense Minister Marshal Malinovsky repeated in a speech earlier allegations that China was hindering the transit of Soviet military material for North Vietnam.

April 21: The NCNA dismissed Mansfield's proposal of April 18 that negotiations for peace in Vietnam should be sought with greater vigor in the Asian area.

April 22: The protocol for Sino-Vietnamese scientific and technical cooperation was signed in Peking.

The Chinese Foreign Ministry strongly protests against seizure of Chinese diplomatic agency and living quarters by Indonesian troops.

The PRC and Tanzania signed a memorandum on the establishment of Sino-Tanzanian Maritime Transport Joint Stock Company in Dar-es-Salaam.

April 25: "All 33 Chiang Kai-shek naval officers and men, captured when the U.S.-made CHIENMEN and CHANG-CHAING war-

ships of the Chiang gang were sunk by the naval forces of the Chinese PLA on August 6 last year, have been released by the PLA," an NCNA report says.

The PRC protested seizure of more Chinese embassy premises in Djakarta.

April 26-May 11: The Albanian delegation, led by the Prime Minister Mahmet Shehu, visited Peking. A joint communique asserted that "Marxist-Leninists of the whole world must carry through to the end the struggle against modern revisionism, whose center is the leading group of the CPSU, and never allow it any respite." (The communique was issued on May 11.)

April 27: The PRC embassy protested to Indonesian Foreign Ministry at "Fascist atrocities" against Chinese nationals in Bima.

April 30: The 1966-67 plan for cultural exchange between the PRC and Norway was signed in Peking.

A Sino-Guinean 1966 plan for cultural cooperation was signed in Conakry.

May 1: Liu Shao-chi, Soong Ching-ling, Tung Pi-wu, Chou En-lai, Chu Teh, Teng Hsiao-ping, and other party and state leaders attended the May Day celebrations in Peking with the participation of guests from some 60 countries. More than three million people turned out in the capital. At Peking rally, Chou En-lai officially announced the beginning of the "Great Proletarian Cultural Revolution" which was to become the most sweeping purge in China since 1958. He called for the wiping out of "bourgeois ideology in the academic, educational, and journalistic fields, in art, literature, and all other fields of culture." The *New York Times* reported that Chinese Communist Party Chairman Mao Tse-tung had not appeared in public for five months and that there had been no indication as to his whereabouts. Although Mao was absent from the May Day celebrations, people shouted: "Long Live Chairman Mao!" and "Mao Tse-tung's thinking is supreme guide in all fields of work!"

A Sino-Yemini protocol on extension of

1964 agreement on economic and technical cooperation was signed in Sanaa.

May 2: In Peking, the PRC and Nepal signed an agreement on trade and related questions between Nepal and the Tibet Autonomous Region of the PRC.

May 3: A statement by the Chinese Foreign Ministry declared that "Malinovsky is a liar," and stated that in 1965 China had transported 43,000 tons of Soviet military aid to North Vietnam, at high speed and free of charge. The statement also alleged that the Soviet Union had sent a deplorably meager amount of military aid; that most of this consisted of old weapons of its own armed forces, which had been replaced, and which even included some that were worn out and of no use at all; and that even the weapons of comparatively new types were already outmoded.

May 4: A protocol on the meeting of the administrative council of the Sino-Albanian joint stock shipping company was signed in Tirana.

The PRC and the UAR signed a protocol on trade in 1966 in Cairo.

The PRC Foreign Ministry in a note to the Indian embassy in Peking refuted the "groundless counter-charges about Chinese 'intrusions' into Indian territory, made by the Indian government in its three notes of February 2, 3, and 8, 1966."

May 4-August 21: The whole army is being urged to push forward the current nationwide mass movement for the study of Mao Tse-tung's work.

May 7: The PRC embassy in Indonesia strongly protested against "forcible occupation" of Chinese consulate in Makasar.

A Sino-Tanzanian cultural cooperation plan for 1966 was signed in Peking.

The PRC and the UAR signed an executive program for cultural cooperation agreement in Cairo.

May 9: "At 1600 hours (Peking time) China successfully conducted over its western area a nuclear explosion which contained thermonuclear material," an NCNA report said. As in the case of the first two Chinese nuclear tests, an assurance was given that "in no circumstances will China be the first to use nuclear weapons."

The Peking radio disclosed that Teng To, director and former editor of the Peking *People's Daily,* had been denounced by the Chinese Communist leadership for bourgeois tendencies and Soviet revisionism. Three Peking newspapers, *People's Daily,* the *Peking Evening News* and *Front Line,* were attacked for letting themselves be used by Teng to send poison arrows against the socialist system. The three papers published joint statements accepting these criticisms and said they would correct their mistakes and participate in the great socialist cultural revolution. Also denounced was Professor Wu Wan, Peking's Vice-Mayor and a leading playwright, who was accused of being a "right-wing opportunist." It was indicated, in addition, that the Mayor of Peking, Peng Chen, may have been purged.

May 10: The NCNA reported that Chairman Mao had met with Albanian leaders in Peking a few days earlier. A picture of Mao and the Albanians was published.

May 11: A 1966 plan for cultural cooperation between the PRC and Czechoslovakia was signed in Peking.

May 12: The Chinese Communist Youth League Central Committee replied to Soviet Komsomol Central Committee turning down an invitation to attend the 15th Congress of the Soviet Youth Committee League.

May 13: The PRC embassy protested against Indonesian "right-wing reactionaries' anti-Chinese activities."

May 13: The PRC and Mali signed a 1966 plan for cultural cooperation in Bamako.

May 16: "Circular of the Central Committee of the Communist Party of China" and "CPC Central Committee's Comment on the Transmission of the Report of the Work Group of the Central Committee Concerning Lo Jui-ching's Mistakes and Problems" were issued.

May 18: The PRC Foreign Ministry sent a note to Indonesia on sending ships to receive "persecuted Chinese nationals."

May 19: The U.S. House Foreign Affairs

Subcommittee on the Far East and the Pacific issued a report on open hearings, held between January 25 and March 10, 1966, on United States policy toward Asia. The Subcommittee concluded that Communist China was not interested at present in attaining peaceful accommodation with the remainder of the world except on terms which clashed with principles of the western world.

The PRC and Japan signed minutes on trade talks on basis of Liao-Takesaki Memorandum.

May 20: Additional protocol of Sino-Moroccan trade agreement was signed in Rabat.

Chen Yi accused the Soviet Union of provoking over 5,000 incidents between July 1960 and the end of 1965, concentrating troops on the Chinese frontier, and of conducting military maneuvers which presupposed that China was the enemy. He also alleged that the Soviet Union had rejected a Chinese proposal to settle frontier disputes on the basis of the treaties concluded between China and the Russian Tsars, and had insisted on going beyond these unjust treaties.

U.S. Atomic Energy Commission stated that the Chinese nuclear device exploded on May 9 had an explosive force equal to at least 200 kilotons (200,000 tons of TNT), considerably greater than the first estimate.

May 23: Sino-Yemeni 1966-67 plan for cultural cooperation was signed in Sana.

May 24: A 1966 plan for Sino-Afghan cultural cooperation agreement was signed in Kabul.

The Sino-Albanian 1966-67 plan for cooperation between the PRC Academy of Sciences and State University of Tirana was signed in Tirana.

May 25: The *New York Times* correspondent in Hong Kong reported that Li Chi, director of the propaganda department of the Communist party's Peking branch, had been purged. Li was attacked as a Soviet revisionist and for protecting other antiparty elements.

A Sino-American ambassadorial talk was held in Warsaw.

May 25-June 3: First decision on May 25: The editorial board of *Peking Jih Pao* and *Peking Wan-Pao* to be abolished, Fan Chin dismissed as its director. Second decision on June 3: Sung Shih, deputy director of University Scientific Work Department of CPC Peking Municipal Committee, to be relieved of all his duties.

May 26: A Sino-Cuban protocol on trade in 1966 was signed in Havana.

The first section of a 20-kilometer canal has been completed in the Tibet Autonomous Region, according to NCNA report.

May 27: Sino-Cuban 1965-66 plan for cooperation between Academies of Sciences was signed in Havana.

May 28: The PRC protests against alleged seizure of overseas Chinese institutions in Indonesia.

A Sino-Vietnamese 1966 plan for cultural cooperation was signed in Hanoi.

May 30: A Protocol for Chinese-Mongolian scientific and technical cooperation was signed in Ulan Bator.

June 1: A Sino-Pakistan 1966-67 plan for cultural cooperation was signed in Rawalpindi.

Sino-North Korean agreement on preventing animal diseases was signed in Pyongyang.

An air communications agreement between France and China was signed in Paris providing for a weekly Paris-Shanghai service by airlines of the two countries. The service was expected to be inaugurated in September.

People's Daily denounced the President of Peking University, Lu Ping, and two other university officials for attempting to suppress the "strong revolutionary demands" of faculty members and students for participation in the "cultural revolution."

A Yugoslav news agency reported that Peng Chen, Mayor of Peking, and Lo Jui-ching, chief of the army's general staff, had been removed from their offices.

June 2: The PRC and Guinea signed in Conakry an agreement on exchanging news between the NCNA and the Guinean Press Agency along with a memorandum of talks on PRC aid in construction of cinema in Guinea.

June 3: The PRC embassy lodged strongest protest against alleged wrecking and occupying of Chinese consulate in Bandjara-asin.

The minutes of the talks between the PRC and Cambodia on China's aid in building 12 laboratories and a factory for the Cambodian Royal University of Kompong Chan were signed in Phnom Penh.

"The Central Committee of the CPC has decided that Comrade Li Hsueh-feng, First Secretary of the North China Bureau of the Party's Central Committee, be appointed concurrently First Secretary of the Peking Municipal Committee of the party, and Comrade Wu Te, First Secretary of the Kirin Provincial Committee of the Party, be transferred to the post of Second Secretary of the Peking Municipal Committee of the party, for a reorganization of the Peking Municipal Party Committee," an NCNA report said. The ousting of Peng Chen was thus confirmed. The dismissal of Lu Ping, President of Peking University, and of Peng Pei-yung, a member of the higher education department of the municipal committee, also was confirmed.

June 4: The 1966-67 executive plan of the Sino-Iraqui cultural cooperation agreement and a Sino-Iraqui radio and television broadcasting cooperation protocol were signed in Baghdad.

June 6: The entire editorial boards of *Peking Daily* and the *Peking Evening News* were dismissed and publication of *Front Line* was suspended.

June 8: A Sino-Tanzanian agreement on economic cooperation was signed in Peking.

June 9: The Ministry of Finance issued a public statement on 1966 payments of principal and interest for national economic construction bonds.

The PRC Foreign Ministry's note to Indonesian government refuted the "slanders" spread by the Indonesian government in its note of May 2.

The PRC and Mali signed an agreement for granting of loans by the PRC to Mali.

June 9-10: A meeting of Afro-Asian Writers' Bureau was held in Peking. A communique was issued.

June 10: A 1966 Sino-Yugoslav goods exchange protocol was signed in Belgrade.

June 11: The 1966 executive plan of a Sino-Somali cultural cooperation agreement was signed in Magadishu.

June 13-18: The PRC decided to change completely the old system of entrance examinations on the enrollment of students in institutes of higher learning, and to postpone the enrollment for 1966 by half a year. The decision was announced in a notice issued on June 3 by the CPC Central Committee and the State Council.

June 14: "Sailing 100 *Li* Against the Wind," the film produced by Chuchiang Film Studios in Kwangtung, was the target of criticism by commanders and fighters of the PLA.

June 15: It has been decided that Li Li-king, Secretary of the Shansi Provincial Committee of the Chinese Communist Youth League, be transferred to the post of First Secretary of the Peking Municipal Committee of the league, that Wang Ching-han, Secretary of the Kaingsu Provincial Committee of the league, be transferred to the post of Second Secretary of the Peking Municipal Committee of the league, and that Yu Chung-hao, Secretary of the Tsinan City Committee of the league, be transferred to the post of Vice-Secretary of the Peking Municipal Committee of the league. It has also been decided that Wang Chia-liu, most responsible member of the Peking Municipal Committee of the league, be dismissed from his post of Vice-Secretary of the Committee.

June 16: Work teams organized by State Council and new CPC Peking Municipal Committee help in reaping summer harvest in various *hsien* and suburbs around Peking.

The Peking radio announced that Huang Ya-ming, Director of Nanking University, had been ousted from his post because of his "ignoble and villainous conspiracy to suppress the revolutionary movement" in the university.

June 16-24: Chou En-lai paid an official visit to Rumania during which he had talks on international problems with the Rumanian leaders. In subsequent public statements, during his visit, Chou avoided attacks on "revisionism" and concentrated on praising Rumania's independent policy. On June 17 Chou told a luncheon audience in Bucharest that China was undergoing a "cultural revolution." He said: "We want to liquidate entirely by this great 'cultural revolution' all the old ideas, the entire old culture, all the old habits and customs created by the exploiting classes in the course of thousands of years of poisoning people," and "We want to create and form in the ranks of the broad masses of the people, the new ideas, the new culture, the new habits and customs of the proletariat." He asserted that "the main cutting edge of this cultural revolution is turned against a handful of bad elements that are waging dirty anti-Communist activity under the cover of a false communism." A joint communique of talks was issued on June 24.

June 17: Chin Mu, a well-known writer in South China, was attacked by a number of workers in Canton for his "anti-party, anti-socialist crimes."

In a *People's Daily* article, Chen Chi-tung, deputy director of both the culture and propaganda sub-departments of the general political department of the PLA, was condemned for his work, *A Searching Anatomy*.

June 19: The North Vietnamese News Agency denied that Soviet military aid was encountering difficulties in transit through China.

Peking press highlighted Lin Piao's letter on living study and application of Mao Tse-tung's works.

June 20: A Sino-Polish protocol on scientific and technical cooperation was signed in Warsaw.

A Peking daily announced that the PRC had rejected a United States proposal that the two countries pledge not to use nu-

clear weapons against each other and that China adhere to the nuclear test-ban treaty.

The emergency meeting of the Afro-Asian Writers' Bureau, held in Peking, strongly condemned the "splittists meeting in Cairo, usurping the name of the Afro-Asian Writers' Bureau from Colombo to Cairo, a crime committed by the Soviet splittists to create an open split in the Afro-Asian people's movements."

The PRC is to help Algeria build an exhibition house in Algiers for holding national exhibitions and Algiers international fair. A memorandum of the talks on this project was signed in Algiers.

June 23: A protocol for the building of a heavy machinery complex with Chinese assistance was signed between the PRC and Pakistan in Karachi.

June 24: The 1966 executive plan for Sino-Polish cultural cooperation was signed in Warsaw.

Liao Mo-sha was attacked for his reactionary political countenance in a signed article in *People's Daily*.

It was reported that Ho Wei, Minister of Education, and Chiang Nan-hsiang, Minister of Higher Education, had been dismissed from their posts.

June 24-28: Chou En-lai flew to Triana for a visit to Albania. A joint communique reaffirmed the opposition of the Chinese and Albanian parties to modern revisionism, with the leading group of the Soviet Communist party as its center (issued on June 28).

June 25: Li Chi, formerly Head of the Department of Propaganda of the CPC Peking Municipal Committee, was accused of rabid opposition to the Communist party and voiced support for Khrushchevian revisionism in his book, "Simple Explanation of On Contradictions."

June 25-July 13: H. R. H. Birencha Bir, Bikran Shah Deva, the Crown Prince of the Kingdom of Nepal, arrived in Shanghai June 25 on his way to Peking. Arrived in Peking on June 26. Received by Mao Tse-tung, Liu Shao-chi, Chou En-lai, and other leaders before leaving Shanghai for home on July 13.

June 27: Chu Shao-tien, First Secretary of the former Party Committee of Suhan University, and Ho Ting-hua, Vice-President of the university were the targets of an attack through "big-character posters." Ho Ting-hua was suspended from his office by an order of the CPC Hupeh provincial committee on June 2.

A Sino-Soviet cultural cooperation plan for 1966 was signed in Moscow.

June 27-July 9: The Afro-Asian Writers' emergency meeting was held from June 27 through July 9. One hundred and sixty-one delegates from 53 countries and regions and observers from five international organizations took part in the 13-day discussions. An urgent appeal condemning "the heinous crimes of U.S. imperialism" and calling on the people of Asia and Africa and the whole world to "give firm support to the Vietnamese people . . ." was adopted at the June 30 meeting.

June 28-30: Chou En-lai visited Pakistan on his return from Albania and had talks with President Ayub Khan, at which international questions, including Kashmir and Vietnam and the extension of economic cooperation between the two countries, were discussed.

June 30: The PRC embassy in Indonesia protested the alleged murder of overseas Chinese and alleged anti-China, anti-Chinese atrocities in Atjeh.

Chou Yang, the Deputy Director of the party's propaganda department, was denounced in *Red Flag* as a "big red umbrella which covers up all the monsters and demons."

A supplementary Sino-Nepal agreement on maintenance of Katmandu-Kodari highway was signed in Katmandu.

July 1: The 1966 executive plan for a Sino-Bulgarian cultural cooperation agreement was signed in Sofia.

July 2: An agreement on aid by the PRC in setting up farms for North Vietnam was signed in Peking.

July 3: Peking strongly condemned the bombing of Hanoi and Hai-phong by the United States and reaffirmed their support for North Vietnam.

Ke Lin, First Secretary of the Party Committee of Chungshan Medical College and concurrently President of the college, and Lin Chih-ming, Deputy Secretary of the Party Committee and concurrently Vice-President of the college, were accused of being an "anti-party, anti-socialist black gang" and dismissed from all their posts.

July 4: A Sino-Pakistan barter agreement was signed in Rawalpindi.

A Sino-East German protocol on scientific and technical cooperation was signed in Berlin.

July 5: Mr. Lin Mo-han, a Deputy Minister of Culture, was denounced for installing the extreme rightist Chou Yang on the throne of supreme master of the literary and artistic world.

A joint statement on cultural exchange between the people of China and Japan was signed in Peking.

The PRC embassy strongly protested against "illegal occupation" of NCNA Djakarta office.

A Sino-North Korean protocol on scientific and technical cooperation was signed in Peking.

July 6: A Sino-Cuban scientific and technical cooperation agreement was signed in Havana.

July 7: It was announced in Dar-es-Salaam that Tanzania and the PRC had signed an agreement for a joint shipping line to operate between the two countries.

July 10: The NCNA referred to Mr. Tao Chu as head of the propaganda department, while stating that Chen Po-ta was leader of the group in charge of the cultural revolution under the party's Central Committee.

July 11: The PRC suspended most visas and closed China's doors to foreign travelers, with the exception of visitors whose business was considered essential to the Chinese state.

July 12: President Johnson asserted in a nationally televised speech to the American Alumni Council at White Sulphur

Springs, West Virginia, that eventual re-conciliation with Communist China was necessary and possible, and that the United States would persist in efforts to reduce tensions between the two countries.

July 13: Lin Ying-chun, a soldier in an artillery company in one of the PLA units under the Shenyang command, died a "hero" as he tried to prevent a shaft horse from running into a group of people. He was praised by the general political department of the Chinese PLA as a "model revolutionary fighter who took Chairman Mao's works as the supreme instruction in all his actions."

July 16: The U.S. State Department relaxed restrictions on tourist travel to the PRC. The only condition imposed by the new regulations was that the traveler's business or professional stature be such that his trip would benefit the United States. Communist China, meanwhile, refused to grant visas to Americans.

July 18: A canal leading to the Kashgar River has just been completed and put into use. It will benefit 70,000 hectares of farmland in the Ili area of Sinkiang, Northwest China.

July 19: The Chinese Charge d'Affaires in The Hague, Mr. Li En-chu, was ordered by the Netherlands government on persona non grata to leave the country within 24 hours, following the mysterious death of a Chinese engineer, Mr. Hsu Tzu-tsai, who was attending a conference of the International Institute of Welding in the Dutch capital.

July 20: The 1966 executive plan for Sino-Hungarian cultural cooperation was signed in Budapest.

Senator Edward M. Kennedy (D., Mass.) said in the Senate that both Communist China and Nationalist China should be seated in the U.N. Later in the day, President Johnson told a news conference that although the administration would do everything it could to increase our exchanges with Communist China, it was not ready to adopt a "two-China" policy.

July 22: As a reprisal, Peking declared Mr. Geruit Jongejans, the Netherlands Charge

d'Affairs in Peking, to be persona non grata, but refused to allow him to leave the legation until the Chinese delegates to the conference had been allowed to return.

A Sino-German 1966 plan for cultural cooperation was signed in Berlin.

July 22-25: A Peking rally was held on July 22 to voice support for North Vietnam with the participation of Liu Shao-chi, Soong Ching-lin, Tung Pi-wu, Chu Teh, Chou En-lai and Teng Hsiao-ping. A statement of support by Liu Shao-chi was read at the meeting presided over by Li Hsueh-feng. Tao chu and Liu Ning-yi spoke at the rally. Meetings and demonstrations were held in many other cities supporting Liu Shao-chi's statement of support for North Vietnam and Ho Chi Minh's appeal.

July 23: The PRC embassy protested the banning of overseas Chinese organizations in West Java.

July 23-31: The 1966 Summer Physics Colloquium of the Peking Symposium, held in Peking July 23-31, was attended by 144 scientists from 33 countries and regional academic institutions in Asia, Africa, Latin America, and Oceania.

July 25: The NCNA reported that Mao Tse-tung, 72, had swum nine miles in 65 minutes in the Yangtze River, apparently to dispel rumors that he was in poor health.

A Sino-French air protocol relating to the rendering of technical service by both sides was signed in Peking.

July 26: The PRC embassy protested against alleged anti-Chinese outrages in Atjeh, Indonesia.

July 27: A Sino-Sudan trade protocol for 1967 was signed in Peking.

July 28: Decision of the CPC Peking Municipal Committee concerning the abolition of work groups in various universities, colleges, and schools was issued.

The *Ta-Kung Pao* commentator said that the Japanese Sato government's peremptory refusal of entry permit to Liu Ning-yi, head of the Chinese delegation to the 12th World Conference against Atomic and Hydrogen Bombs, is "further evidence of that government's reactionary character in toeing the U.S. imperialist line, uniting with the Soviet revisionist leading clique, and displaying hostility toward China."

July 29: A Sino-Afghanistan protocol on economic and technical cooperation was signed in Peking.

July 30: The 1966-67 Sino-Korean plan for cooperation between academies of science was signed in Peking.

July 31: The NCNA referred to General Hsiao Wang-tung as acting Minister of Culture.

A Sino-Rumanian protocol in scientific and technical cooperation was signed in Bucharest.

August 1: The removal of General Lo Jui-ching as army chief of staff was indirectly announced when General Yang Cheng-wu was introduced as occupying that post.

The Chinese Foreign Ministry sent a note to the Indonesian embassy in China severely refuting the Indonesian government's notes of May 17 and 25, 1966. The Chinese Foreign Ministry's note pointed out that in these notes the Indonesian government vainly sought to cover up its crimes of damaging, looting, and forcibly occupying premises of Chinese missions in Indonesia.

August 1-5: Mao Tse-tung's call to turn all fields of work into great revolutionary schools, where people take part in both industry and agriculture, and military as well as civilian affairs, has had a great impact all over the country. Reports from various parts of China show that Chinese workers, peasants, soldiers, revolutionary cadres and intellectuals are expressing determination to "read Chairman's Mao's works, follow his teachings, act on his instructions, and become communist people of a new type, people of high political consciousness and all-round development living in the era of Mao Tse-tung."

August 1-12: The 11th plenary session of the 8th Central Committee of the CPC was held in Peking August 1-12. Presided over by Mao Tse-tung, the plenary session stressed that the series of directives by Mao Tse-tung concerning the great proletarian cultural revolution are the guide for action in the present cultural revolution of the country.

August 3: Letters of agreement were exchanged in Colombo under which China undertook to purchase an additional 10,-000 tons of sheet rubber from Ceylon in 1966, apart from the 41,000 tons provided for under the rice-rubber agreement between the two countries.

August 4: It was reported that the Japanese Communist party shifted from a pro-Chinese position to one of neutrality and ordered its members to remove portraits of Mao Tse-tung, to withdraw Chinese books from party bookstores, not to visit China without permission, and not to listen to Radio Peking.

August 7: The "revolutionary teachers and students" of Chengchou University have brought to light the counter-revolutionary "crime" of Wang Pei-wu, former Secretary of the Party Committee and acting President of the university, in suppressing the revolutionary movement of the students. Li Lin, a member of the Party Committee and Vice-President of Changchow University, and Kuo Ksiao-tang were also denounced as "anti-party, anti-socialist elements."

A national conference on the printing and distribution of Mao Tse-tung's works was held in Peking by the Ministry of Culture. Thirty-five million sets of *Selected Works of Mao Tse-tung* were to be printed and distributed this year, according to a decision of the CPC Central Committee.

The PRC issued a statement firmly supporting the statement of the Royal Government of Cambodia on August 3, strong condemning "U.S. imperialism and the South Vietnamese in their new criminal act of aggression" on a Cambodian border village.

August 8: More than 10,000 fully armed militia made a cross-Yangtze swim in Wuhan. Leading members of the local Communist party, government, and army units reviewed the swim.

Sun Yeh-fang, former head of the economics institute of the Chinese Academy of Sciences, was accused of advocation in a revisionist economic policy.

The Central Committee of the CPC adopted a resolution on the cultural revolution, which was reported to have been drafted by Mao Tse-tung himself. The resolution stated that the PRC objective is to struggle against and crush those persons in authority who are taking the capital road; to criticize and repudiate the reactionary bourgeois academic authorities and the ideology of the bourgeoisie and all other exploiting classes; and to transform education, literature, and art, and all other parts of the superstructure that do not correspond to the Socialist economic base. The resolution recommended that elected committees should be set up in colleges, schools, government organizations, industrial enterprises, urban districts, and villages to carry on the cultural revolution. It gave warning, however, against indiscriminate persecution, stating that care should be taken to distinguish carefully between the anti-party, anti-socialist rightists and those who support the party and socialism but have said or done something wrong or have written some bad articles or other works, and also between reactionary bourgeois scholar despots and authorities on the one hand and people who have the ordinary bourgeois academic ideas on the other.

August 9: A Sino-Hungarian protocol on scientific and technical cooperation was signed in Budapest.

August 12: The North Korean Communist party official newspaper, *Rodong Shinmoon,* declared in an editorial that the North Korean was independent of the Chinese and Soviet alike. "Revolution," the editorial said, "can neither be exported nor imported, and outside influence plays only a secondary role."

August 13: Peking Radio broadcast a communique on the work of the 11th plenary session of the CPC Central Committee. The communique stated that "plenary session fully approves the series of brilliant policies of decisive and fundamental importance put forward by Comrade Mao Tse-tung over the past four years." It also implied that China might be on the verge of launching another "Great Leap Forward," although the new policies were described as being of a more gradual nature than those instituted in 1958. The communique placed heavy emphasis on China's split with the Soviet Union. "A clear line of demarcation must be drawn in dealing with modern revisionist groups with the leadership of the Communist party of the Soviet Union as center, and it is imperative to resolutely expose their true feathers as scabs. It is impossible to have united action with them." The plenary session agreed that "our party's comprehensive public criticism of Khrushchev revisions over the last few years have been entirely correct and necessary."

August 13: The PRC and Malagasy signed an agreement on technical aid by the PRC in Tananarive.

August 18-31: The Red Guard is an organization set up by middle-school pupils from the families of workers, farmers, poor and lower-middle peasants, revolutionary cadres, and revolutionary army men. The first mention of the Red Guards was when Mao Tse-tung and Lin Piao received them at a 1,000,000-strong Peking mass rally on August 18 to celebrate the "Great Proletarian Cultural Revolution." The Red Guards have since put up posters and distributed revolutionary leaflets and changed shopsigns and street names in all parts of the country in an attack on old ideas, culture, customs, and habits of "all exploiting classes." Support of the Red Guards has been evinced by editorials and mass meetings. The official list of the party leaders present at the rally on August 18 given by Peking Radio, which apparently denoted their status in the party hierarchy, was considered extremely significant. The first 12 names, after that of Mao Tse-tung, were as follows: Lin Piao, Chou En-lai, Tao Chu, Chen Po-ta, Teng Hsiao-ping, Kang Sheng, Liu Shao-chi, Chu Teh, Li Fu-chum, Chen Yun, Tung Pi-wu, Chen

Yi. The most striking change in the list, apart from the emergence of Lin Piao as Mao's second-in-command, was the downgrading of Liu Shao-chi, who had previously been regarded as Mao's probable successor.

August 20: The Red Guards demonstrated outside the Soviet embassy, carrying portraits of Mao Tse-tung and Stalin, and renamed the street leading to it, "Struggle Against Revisionism Street." A senior Soviet diplomat was prevented by mobs from leaving the embassy for an official appointment.

August 21: A Sino-Vietnamese 1966-67 executive plan for cooperation between academies of science was signed in Peking.

August 22: The PRC embassy in Indonesia protested against alleged illegal occupation of consulate in Medan.

August 22: A Sino-Zambian agreement on cultural cooperation was signed in Peking along with a joint press communique of talks during visit of Vice-President Kamenga.

August 23: Mao Tse-tung has written an inscription comprising the three characters "Hsien Pei Ta" for the new journal of the university.

Reuters reported that thousands of young Chinese had stormed Christian churches in Peking, defacing Biblical paintings, plastering the walls with slogans, and shattering windows. In a Protestant church, a large bust of Mao Tse-tung was erected. The Red Guards attacked stores and private homes containing items considered too bourgeois or extravagant.

August 24: The 20th anniversary on Mao Tse-tung's "Paper Tiger Thesis" was marked with Peking paper editorials and with reports of comments by Chinese workers, peasants, and soldiers who show their contempt for "paper tigers."

August 24-28: The Red Guard demonstrations became increasingly violent. Red Guards broke into private houses and threw into the streets bourgeois possessions such as jewelry and western-style clothes and shoes. Diplomatic sources reported that a number of people had been publicly beaten with ropes, had their heads shaven, or been made to carry placards denouncing themselves. Doctors and nurses were dragged out of a hospital by a gang of adolescents and made to wear togs describing them as reactionary schools or running dogs of the bourgeoisie. Some of those attacked turned on their persecutors, and it was reported on August 28 that violent street clashes had taken place in which eight of the Red Guards had been killed.

August 26: The Soviet government strongly protested to the Chinese embassy in Moscow against the Red Guards' demonstration outside the Soviet embassy in Peking on August 20. The note accused the demonstration of direct breach of generally recognized norms of international law, and demanded the immediate ending of the hooliganism outside the Soviet embassy.

August 28: In Lhasa (capital of Tibet) Red Guards smashed old street signs and denounced reactionary elements in Buddhist monasteries.

The East German embassy had previously made a strong protest after its military attache and his family had been assaulted by Red Guards.

Red Guards are urged in an editorial to conduct themselves as the PLA men—to be always loyal to the party and to Mao Tse-tung and resolutely observe the "Three Cardinal Rules of Discipline" and "Eight Points for Attention" which Mao had laid down for the PLA.

August 29: Thousands of Red Guards marched past the Soviet Union embassy in Peking in an all-day demonstration against "revisionism."

As in Peking, the Red Guards' activities provoked resistance, which in some cities developed into serious riots. At Tsinan (capital of Shantung province) several thousand people, led by a local Communist party secretary, opposed the Red Guards; at Sian many people were injured when a Communist demonstration was attacked; and at Foochow a counter-revolutionary accused of wounding 13 students and others was executed on August 29.

A defecting member of the Chinese Communist commercial mission in Syria, Miao Chen-pai, said upon his arrival in New York that the Chinese leadership was "still very cautious" about confronting the U.S. in Vietnam. On China's current purge, Miao thought that "all those who question the effectiveness of Mao Tse-tung's extreme policies will be deprived of their power and voice."

A Sino-Vietnamese agreement in economic and technical assistance to Vietnam was signed in Peking.

August 31: The Soviet Communist Party's Central Committee adopted a resolution condemning the Chinese Communist leadership for breaking up the international Communist movement and appealed directly to the Chinese people for renewed unity.

Eight foreign nuns from a convent, who were accused of espionage, were taken to the Hong Kong border under armed guard and expelled. The nuns, some of whom had been in China for 40 years, described how they had been escorted throughout their journey by Red Guards, who, however, had not subjected them to physical molestation. Several collapsed from exhaustion after their long journey from Peking and were admitted to the hospital, where one of them died.

"At the demand of Peking's Red Guards and revolutionary masses, and to safeguard China's security and the interests of the people, the Peking municipal people's council announced the banning of the Franciscaines Missionaresse Marie and on August 26 took over L'Eivle Sabe-Coeup run by the mission," an NCNA report said.

The Chinese embassy lodged its strongest protest against alleged persecution of Chinese nationals in Indonesia.

Mao Tse-tung and his close comrades-in-arms received in the afternoon half a million revolutionary teachers and students at a mammoth rally in the Tienanen Square. Chiang Ching, deputy head of the cultural revolution group under the party Central Committee, proclaimed the opening of the rally. Marshal Lin Piao hailed the Red Guards as "the shock fighting force in the great cultural revolution," but he cautioned them to carry on their campaign against counter-revolutionaries "by reasoning and not by coercion or force." The government and the Chinese PLA officials present at the rally were Chou En-lai, Tao Chu, Teng Hsiao-ping, Kan Sheng, Liu Shao-chi, Chu Teh, Li Fu-chun, Chen Yun, Tung Pi-wu, Chen Yi, Ho Lung, Li Hsien-nien, Tan Chen-lin, Nieh Jung-chen, Yeh Chien-ying, Ulanfu, Po I-po, Li Hsueh-feng, and Hsieh Fu-chih.

September 1: Burundi announced it would resume diplomatic relations with Peking, broken off in January, 1965.

September 3: It was announced that the Red Guards would be placed under the leadership of the Cultural Revolutionary Committee, a group controlled by supporters of Mao.

On the first anniversary of the publication of Lin Paio's famous article on "People's War," *People's Daily* carried another article declaring a "People's war of annihilation" on capitalist nations and "Soviet revisionists."

The first rally of Red Guards in Canton was held. (The first rally of Red Guards was held in Chengchou, Honan, on August 28.)

September 4: The Peking Radio announced that Defense Minister Lin Piao had been designated by the Red Guards as their leader. It was reported also that Premier Chou En-lai had been named an adviser to the militant youth groups.

September 5: The NCNA reported that U.S. planes on August 29 had sunk one Chinese ship in the Gulf of Tonkin and damaged another, killing nine Chinese seamen and injuring seven others. U.S. officials said the report would be investigated.

September 7: *People's Daily* urged the Red Guards not to carry the movement into the factories and the rural communes. The movement was seen as possibly threatening the economy of the nation.

September 8: "Provisions of the CPC Central Committee and the State Council concerning the safeguarding of party and state secrets in the Great Cultural Revolution Movement was issued.

September 9: Conference of representatives of industrials and communications, capital construction, urban development, financial and trade workers was held in Canton. The meeting, addressed by Chen Yun, called on the workers of the whole municipality to take the lead in carrying out the 16-point decision and scoring a two-fold victory in both revolution and foundation.

September 11: *People's Daily* published an editorial warning Communist Party officials and government employees not to interfere with the activities of the Red Guards. This was the first official admission that the militant youth group was encountering organized opposition. The editorial acknowledged that the Red Guards had made mistakes, but it was firm in stating that "no matter what the protest, fighting between the students and farmers and laborers must not be permitted."

September 12: A Japanese newspaper's correspondent in Peking reported that units of the Chinese army had been called out to control a crowd of 100,000 people protesting activities of Red Guards in Kwelin, in Southeastern China. The report said that similar clashes had occurred all over the country. "The main cause of resistance put up by local party committees and citizens against the Red Guards," the report said, "is that Red Guards from Peking visit districts suddenly and start propaganda against local party committee members," who defend themselves by attempts to "suppress the activities of Red Guards from Peking through use of the pressure of local people."

A new domestic airline running from Shenyang through Changchun and Harbin to Kiamusze was opened.

The PRC Foreign Ministry demanded that the Indonesian government stop "ob-structing" the return of "persecuted" Chinese nationals.

September 13: It was reported that the Red Guards had seized the party headquarters in Shanghai.

September 14: Provisions concerning the great cultural revolution in rural districts below the *hsien* level were issued.

September 15: The Indian government sent a parliamentary mission to Taiwan to carry out anti-Chinese activities, reported the NCNA.

More than one million Red Guards and soldiers crowded into the Square of Heavenly Peace in Peking to hear Premier Chou En-lai urge them to halt temporarily their anti-bourgeois campaign and join the peasants in the countryside in harvesting crops. Lin Piao also urged the crowd to uphold Chairman Mao's teachings, strengthen the power of the revolution by uniting with workers, peasants, and soldiers, and firmly concentrate on production. *People's Daily* said in an article that the cultural revolution may be "suspended temporarily during the busiest period of the autumn harvest." It added: "It is not necessary for Red Guards and revolutionary teachers and students from colleges and middle schools to go to factories and rural areas to exchange revolutionary experiences and interfere with arrangements there."

September 16: Chou En-lai reportedly ordered the Red Guards to stop their attacks upon Soong Ching-ling, widow of Sun Yet-sen.

A notice gives instructions to "revolutionary teachers and students" who are coming to Peking from other areas or leaving Peking for other areas of China on Red Guard missions, regarding points of embarkation and disembarkation and times of arrival and departure of trains.

The PRC charged that two U.S. planes had attacked across the Chinese border, wounding three peasants. The Chinese asserted that the U.S. planes had been scared away by Chinese air force fighters. On the same day, Secretary of State Dean Rusk said the U.S. would investigate.

Secretary of State Dean Rusk told a news conference that the U.S. would again oppose admission of Communist China to the U.N. He added, however, that the administration's current policy goals centered around the possibility of visitor exchanges with Communist China to help "break through the walls of isolation that Peking built around itself."

September 18: *Red Flag* said that powerful elements within the Communist party were waging a struggle against Mao Tse-tung and Lin Piao. It said that those elements would be crushed.

The China Council for the Promotion of International Trade and the economic friendship delegation from the Japanese Association in the Promotion of International Trade exchanged the minutes of their talks.

The PRC Foreign Ministry refutes in broadcasts Indian government's alleged interference by Chinese frontier guards.

September 19: The scheduled weekly air service between Paris and Shanghai, for which provisions were made by the Franco-Chinese agreement of June 2, was inaugurated by a Boeing-77 of Air France.

September 20: Militant Red Guards in Shanghai ransacked the home of Soong Ching-ling, the widow of Dr. Sun Yet-sen, founder of the Chinese Republic. The 75-year-old Miss Soong, Vice-President of the People's Republic and an older sister of Mme. Chiang Kai-shek, was accused by the youth group of favoring capitalism. It was not known whether Miss Soong was in the house when her possessions were confiscated by the invading youths.

Peking ordered all Soviet students studying in the country to leave because their teachers were preoccupied with the cultural revolution. An unstated reason was that virtually the whole of Red China's educational system was shutting down temporarily. Closing of the upper schools freed millions of students to join the Red Guards and promote the cultural revolution.

September 22: Instruction of the CPC Central Committee concerning the serious study, discussion, comprehension, and application of Comrade Lin Piao's speech by the whole party and the whole army was issued.

September 25: All the six bureaus of the CPC Central Committee have issued circulars calling on its members and all revolutionary masses to emulate the courageous members of the No. 32111 drilling team with their heroism in saving a big gas well from destruction by fire. Editorials praising the drilling team have appeared in Peking papers.

The Soviet government announced that its exports both to the PRC and to North Vietnam have sharply increased in 1965, with the bulk of the increase consisting of industrial machinery, power-generating and road-excavating machines. Soviet imports from China were notably reduced, Moscow said.

September 26: Documents on the talks leading to Chinese help to Algeria in building a daily-use ceramics factory were signed in Algeria.

September 27: A high citation has been conferred on Wang Yu-chang, an air-force quartermaster, for exemplary heroism in risking his life to save his comrades-in-arms. A campaign to emulate Wang Yu-chang was unfolding extensively in the air force of the Chinese PLA.

September 28: China and Afghanistan signed notes on talks for construction of a silkworm feeding station in Afghanistan.

September 29: A Sino-Mongolian 1966 plan for cultural cooperation was signed in Peking.

Chou En-lai, Tao Chu, and other leaders saw Red Guards of the capital perform the famous revolutionary modern Peking operas, "The Red Lantern" and "Sha Chia Pang," on September 28 and the following evening.

Soviet attempted to exclude the PRC from the international Communist movement, for the first time strongly denounced China for disrupting the unity of the Communist nations.

October 1: The 17th anniversary of the People's Republic of China was celebrated in Peking. In the parade, about 5,000 goose-stepping soldiers were followed by an estimated two million Red Guards, taking more than four hours to pass the reviewing stand where Mao, Lin Piao, and other officials were standing. Although the Red Guards made constant requests, Mao refused to speak. At the banquet the night before, it was noted that Head of State Liu Shao-chi was absent, but he attended the National Day ceremonies. Lin Piao hailed Mao, and stressed the importance of the cultural revolution as it was strengthening the dictatorship of the proletariat. Chou En-lai also spoke, giving a favorable report on the state of the nation and praising Mao and the cultural revolution. More than 50 Soviet-bloc diplomats and their wives and families left the reviewing stand during the mammoth ceremonies in Peking. They were protesting a charge by Defense Minister Lin Piao that the Soviet Union was plotting with the U.S. in Vietnam.

The PRC economic and trade exhibition was opened in Kitakyushu, in Japan.

The PRC embassy protested against Ghanaian authorities in "Hatching an anti-Chinese incident."

October 5: Urgent directive of the military commission and the general political department on the Great Proletarian Cultural Revolution in military academies and schools was issued.

Directive of the military commission of the Central Committee was issued on an important criterion for testing the party spirit and revolutionary style, for gauging the success in studying and the effort expended in "applying" Chairman Mao's works.

October 6: The Chinese Foreign Ministry in a statement expressed full endorsement by the Chinese government and people of the just stand enunciated by the Cambodian government in its October 6 statement and expresses firm support for the Cambodian people in their just struggle to defend state sovereignty and territorial integrity.

October 7: The Soviet Union ordered all 65 Communist Chinese students in the U.S.S.R. to leave the country by the end of October.

October 10: Three Sino-Tanzanian contracts on a supply of the PRC equipment and technical aid in construction of textile mill in Tanzania were signed in Dar-es-Salaam.

October 12: The 1967 executive plan of Sino-Vietnamese public health cooperation was signed in Peking.

Soviet Premier Kosygin, in a speech in Svendlovak, accused the PRC of preventing a North Vietnamese victory in the Vietnam war by blocking efforts of Socialist countries to assist North Vietnam.

The Italian Communist party condemned the PRC for the first time, objecting mainly to the cultural revolution.

Over the past few days, extensive activities in the study, discussion, and propagation of Lin Piao's instructions have been going on in all provinces, municipalities, and autonomous regions, from the capital to the remotest parts of the countryside.

October 16: *People's Daily* denounced President Johnson's policies toward East Europe and charged that the Soviet Union had "long ceased to support world revolution." It accused the president of attempting to accelerate capitulation of the Soviet bloc to capitalism and of seeking Soviet cooperation in reducing tension in Europe so that more American troops could be transferred to Vietnam. The article charged that the Soviet Union and the U.S. were trying to create an anti-Communist, anti-people, counter-revolutionary, and anti-China new holy alliance.

October 17: The Taiwan News Agency reported the Nationalists sank two Communist gunboats and damaged two others in a battle near Matsu.

October 18: Mao Tse-tung received and reviewed detachments of the cultural revolution formed by Mao and a half million Red Guards and revolutionary teachers and students from all parts of the country who were in Peking to exchange revolutionary experiences. Mao Tse-tung, Lin Piao, and other responsible comrades of the party Central Committee came right into the midst of the revolutionary masses at Tienanmen Square, riding in nine cars. The other comrades of the CC were: Chou En-lai, Tao Chu, Chen Po-ta, Teng Hsiao-ping, Kang Shen, Liu Shao-chi, Chu Teh, Li Fu-chun, Chen Yun, Tung Pi-wu, Chen Yi, Ho Lung, Li Hsien-nien, Tan Chen-lin, Hsu Hsien-chien, Nieh Jung-chen, Yeh Chien-ying, Li Hsueh-feng, Hsieh Fuchih, Liu Nien-I, Hsiao Hua, Yang Cheng-wu, Chiang Ching, Wang Jen-chung, Liu Cheh-chien, and Chang Chun-chiao.

The PRC Foreign Ministry sends strong protest to Indonesia against illegal detention of Chinese nationals by Medan military authority.

The PRC and Nepal exchanged notes in Katmandu on the PRC economic aid to Nepal.

October 19: The Yugoslav News Agency reported Red Guard demonstrations against the Peking party committee and its leader, Li Hsueh-feng, and Sinkiang party chief Wang En-mao.

Japanese correspondents in Peking reported that Red Guards had plastered the Chinese Foreign Ministry with posters reading: "Bombard the party committee of the Foreign Ministry and burn to death Vice-Premier and concurrently Foreign Minister Chen Yi."

October 20: An "agreement on China's providing a loan for the Albanian petroleum industry" was signed in Peking.

The U.N. Association, an independent, non-partisan organization devoted to support of the U.N., published a study of the problem of China, the U.N., and U.S. policy. The study, prepared by a panel of 27 prominent persons, urged that the U.S. adopt a "two-China policy," permitting representation of both Communist China and Nationalist China in the U.N.

October 21: The PRC Foreign Ministry strongly protested against Indonesia's expelling of Chinese nationals en masse.

A Sino-Pakistan maritime transport agreement was signed in Rawalpindi.

October 22-26: Sayed Sharifuddin Pezoda,

Foreign Minister of Pakistan, and his wife visited China October 22-26.

October 23: The biggest highway bridge spanning the turbulent upper reaches of the Yellow River, on the Tsinghai Plateau 4,100 meters above sea level, was opened to traffic recently.

A note specifying the working conditions for the Chinese experts who are to go to Somalia was signed in Magadishu.

Peking protested the Soviet ouster of Chinese students but the U.S.S.R. refused to accept the note. The Red Guards demonstrated for a second day outside the Soviet embassy in Peking in protest over the Soviet ouster.

Sino-Vietnamese minutes of talks in scientific and technical cooperation were issued in Peking.

October 24: Yu Feng-ying, a woman worker-engineer of the Northeast Machinery Plant, is cited a good worker of Mao Tse-tung.

October 25: Anna Louise Strong, an 80-year-old American who was an honorary member of the PRC's Red Guards, acknowledged in her news-letter from Peking that a minority of the Red Guards attacked Mao Tse-tung, but she said they had not endangered his position. Miss Strong, who lived in Peking, had been a longtime supporter of Mao Tse-tung. She also reported that Chou En-lai was the Red Guards' official adviser and was credited with toning down some of the earlier extreme views. "Flower-shops, goldfish, gay children's clothes and walks in the park are no longer thought bourgeois."

The PRC embassy lodged a serious protest against "preposterous" Indonesian announcement of a take-over of Chinese consulate in Medan.

Surgeons in Shanghai have broken another world medical barrier by re-attaching completely severed fingers, using a new technique of rejoining small blood vessels, an NCNA report says. This new technique involves anastomosing blood vessels less than a millimeter in diameter.

October 26: Chinese students ordered to leave the Soviet Union performed a last act of defiance. After arguing for hours with Soviet guards, the students, all of whom wore Red Guard arm bands, placed two wreaths outside the mausoleum housing the body of Lenin. The second wreath was intended for Stalin's grave, behind the mausoleum, but Soviet guards refused here to let the students approach the area.

October 27: The NCNA announced that the PRC on October 26 had successfully conducted over its own territory a guided missile-nuclear weapons test. This was China's 4th nuclear test, and the first time she had disclosed that she possessed a guided-missile delivering system of nuclear weapons.

The *Toronto Globe and Mail* reported from Peking that Chinese Head of State Liu Shao-chi and General Secretary of the Communist Party Teng Hsiao-ping had been criticized in the latest posters circulated by the Red Guards. Others again criticized included Li Hsueh-feng, chief of the Communist Party's Peking Municipal Committee, and his deputy Wu Teh. They took over the Peking branch following the purge of Peng Chen last June.

October 28: The *People's Daily* observer in an article said that the recent Manila conference was a meeting to dramatize a new peace-talk hoax on the foxing of peace talks through highting, and to plan an expansion of the U.S. aggressive war in Vietnam.

A protocol on Sino-Czechoslovak scientific and technical cooperation was signed.

October 28-November 14: A delegation of the Chinese Communist Party led by Kang Sheng and Li Hsien-nien arrived in Tirana on October 29 to take part in the celebration of the 5th Congress of the Albanian Party of Labor and the 25th anniversary of the founding of the party. The delegation left Albania for home on November 14.

October 29: Peking sent a note to Ghana accusing its government of an anti-Chinese policy and of threatening to break off diplomatic relations.

October 30: Peking announced it was recalling its embassy staff from Ghana.

November 1: The Soviet government allegedly lodged a protest against the "just revolutionary actions" of Chinese youth. The Chinese Foreign Ministry sternly refuted the Soviet side's "absurd protest, unreasonable demands."

November 2: The U.S. Atomic Energy Commission stated that the latest Chinese test seemed to have used enriched uranium, and that preliminary analysis indicated that neither plutonium nor thermonuclear materials were used.

November 3: Mao Tse-tung received revolutionary students, teachers, and Red Guards who had come to Peking to exchange revolutionary experiences, encouraging them to carry the great proletarian cultural revolution through to the end. More than two million pathbreakers in the cultural revolution attended the rally on the Tienanmen Square. In Chairman Mao's company were his close comrade-in-arms, Lin Piao, and other leading comrades of the Party Central Committee and various departments, including Chou En-lai, Tao Chu, Chen Po-ta, Teng Hsiae-ping, Liu Shao-chi, Chu Teh, Li Fu-Chun, Chen Yun, Tung Pi-wu, Chen Yi, Ho Lung, Tan Chen-lin, Hsu Hsiang-chien, Li Hsueh-feng.

November 5: The Chinese ambassador left Ghana following the suspension of diplomatic relations.

November 6: A protocol on Sino-Soviet scientific and technical cooperation was signed in Peking.

Chang Teh-tsuen, acting head of Peking's embassy in Moscow, stormed out of a Kremlin rally during a speech in which the PRC was accused of aiding the American effort in Vietnam by splitting the Communist movement. The speech was delivered by a member of the Soviet Politburo. On the following day, Chang Teh-tsuen and his aides walked away from the diplomatic stand in Moscow's Red Square during festivities celebrating the 49th anniversary of the Bolshevik Revolution. Chang's exit came when Marshal Rodin Y.

Malinovsky, Soviet defense minister, told the crowds: "We regret that the leaders of China oppose the unity of action by the socialist countries in support of the Vietnam people."

Toronto Globe and Mail reported from Peking that Red Guards had demonstrated outside the offices of the Peking branch of the Communist party, demanding an audience with Li Hsueh-feng, head of the party's municipal committee, or his deputy Wu Teh. Posters were circulated criticizing Tao Chu, new head of the Communist party's propaganda department and one of the directors of the cultural revolution.

November 8: The NCNA reported the "thousands upon thousands of the youth were marching throughout the country, spreading the thoughts of Chairman Mao. Stanley Karnow of the *Washington Post* reported: "Chinese Premier Chou En-lai calculated that 30 percent of China's road and rail facilities have lately been devoted to moving the youths in and out of Peking for assorted rallies and other demonstrations. A clue to the magnitude of the movement is suggested by the official claim that a total of six million youngsters attended the five main rallies held in the Chinese capital between August 18 and November 3."

November 10: "The Indonesian reactionaries created a serious new incident on the morning of the 9th in sabotaging the Chinese government's work of repatriating overseas Chinese in Indonesia and beating up victimized Chinese nationals who are assembled in Medan waiting for a ship to return to their motherland," an NCNA report said.

Together with his close comrade-in-arms, Lin Piao, Mao Tse-tung on November 10 and 11 received more than two million Red Guards and other revolutionary students and teachers gathered from other parts of the country to exchange revolutionary experiences.

November 11-16: Guinean government economic delegation arrived in Peking on November 11. An agreement on Sino-Guinean economic and technical coopera-

tion along with a protocol, a Sino-Guinean agreement on the granting of trade loans by China to Guinea, and 1967 trade protocol between the two countries were signed on November 16.

November 12: A letter concerning the coming of Red Guard fighters from other places to Peking and the departure of revolutionary teachers and students from Peking was issued.

A Peking rally of more than ten thousand people was held marking the centennial of Sun Yat-Sen's birthday, during which Chou En-lai attacked the Soviet leaders, causing the U.S.S.R. diplomats to walk out.

November 13: The PRC Foreign Ministry protests most strongly against Indonesian right-wingers' persecution of Chinese nationals.

November 15: "Urgent Circular of the CCP Peking Municipal Committee—a Document of the CCP Peking Municipal Committee" was issued.

People's Daily declared that the PRC would never agree to a treaty banning the spread of nuclear weapons. The treaty plan, the article said, meant that "nuclear weapons should be regarded as a thing to be monopolized by the two clear overlords, the U.S. and the Soviet Union, and that they alone should be allowed to possess such weapons, and not anyone else."

November 16: Supplementary provisions of the CPC Central Committee concerning the handling of the question of archive materials in the great proletarian cultural revolution was issued.

A circular of the CPC Central Committee and the State Council on the question of revolutionary teachers and students exchanging revolutionary experiences was issued.

It was reported that the Standing Committee of the CPC Politburo was enlarged from 7 to 10 members. Ho Hsien-chu was moved to deputy chief of general staff, and Lo Kuei-po was made a full member of the Central Committee.

November 18: The PRC protests Hungary's

not allowing Chinese students to continue their studies.

Alleged Bulgarian revisionist leading clique's discrimination against NCNA correspondent was protested.

"CPC Peking Municipal Committee's Important Notice" was issued to order Red Guards to stop holding unofficial courts and using torture to obtain "confession." The notice was endorsed in the circular of the Central Committee of the CPC issued on November 20. Circular of the Central Committee on transmitting the important notice issued on November 18 was issued by the Peking Municipal Committee.

November 21: Sino-Albanian protocol on exchange of goods and payments in 1967 was signed in Peking along with a protocol for Albania's use of the PRC loans in 1967.

The PRC and Japan signed a protocol in trade in 1967 in accordance with Liao-Takasaki memorandum.

November 22: Chinese delegation protests against the Japanese Sato government for conniving with the rightist organizations in sabotaging the Chinese economic and trade exhibition held in Nagoya, according to an NCNA report.

November 23: *Reuters* reported that the Red Guards Newspaper, *The East Is Red,* had urged members of the youth group to "smash the headquarters of the Red Guards of the capital colleges and universities who are "royalists." The term "royalists" meant reactionary.

November 30: *People's Daily* made clear in a front-page article that Lin Piao was now the only vice-chairman of the CPC. Previously, four other men in addition to Lin Piao had held the title: Liu Shao-chi, Chou En-lai, Chu Teh, and Chen Yun. All four had lost the title of vice-chairman, and Chou alone remained in listings of the party hierarchy, where he continued to hold his place.

December 2: At a Hungarian party congress, leaders of more than twelve Communist parties responded coolly to a Soviet call for a world conference to discuss Chinese leadership.

The CPC Central Committee ordered the country's primary schools to reopen.

December 3: The CPC Central Committee ordered Red Guards remaining in Peking and other cities to return home. The army would be responsible for seeing that the Guards left the cities by the appointed time.

Serious rioting by Chinese Communist sympathizers in Macao on December 3-4, in which eight Chinese were killed, led to a strained situation between the Portuguese and the Chinese Communist authorities, which ended only when the governor of Macao banned Chinese Nationalist authorities in the province and accepted all the other Chinese demands, including a public apology by the local Portuguese authorities.

Sino-North Korean protocol on mutual supply of goods in 1967 was signed in Peking.

December 4: Chiang Ching (Madam Mao Tse-tung) was appointed as a consultant to the general department of the Chinese PLA.

December 5: The governor of Macao, Brigadier Jose Nohe de Carvalho, announced that the officials responsible for the incident on November 15 would be removed, all police truncheons burnt, and compensation paid to those who had been injured. These concessions failed to satisfy the Communist authorities in Peking, however; the NCNA denounced on December 6 the "bloody atrocities organized by the bestial Portuguese imperialists" and in Canton thousands of Red Guards took part in protest demonstrations against the "massacre." Four Chinese gunboats anchored off Macao on December 5, and 10,000 Chinese troops were reported to have been massed on the border.

The PRC National Defense Ministry spokesman protests against alleged U.S. air raids on Chinese fishing boats on high seas.

December 6: Tien Han, well-known dramatist and writer, is denounced by the press for having enthusiastically promoted feudal and capitalist art and suppressed revolutionary modern drama and opposed the thoughts of Mao Tse-tung.

December 7: According to a dispatch from Peking, the Red Guards shouted over loud speakers: "Peng Chen was arrested three days ago."

December 9: "Ten Provisions (Draft) of the CPC Central Committee on Grasping Revolution and Stimulating Production" was issued.

December 10: Hsia Yen, a prominent figure in the literary and film-making world in China, is attacked by the press for his "extreme hostility toward the thoughts of Mao Tse-tung."

The Foreign Affairs Bureau of the Kwangtung Provincial government announced its support for the demands put forward by the Chinese Communists in Macao. These included: (1) The punishment of a number of army and police officers; (2) an official apology for the incidents; (3) a ban on the activities of Chinese Nationalist agents; (4) the surrender to the Chinese government of seven alleged Nationalist agents who had been picked up at sea in 1963 and imprisoned in Macao on a charge of illegal possession of arms. The Macao administration announced its acceptance of these conditions on December 12. Following the Portuguese announcement, the Chinese gunboats were withdrawn. The seven alleged Nationalist agents were handed over to the Communist authorities on December 20.

December 12: Commenting on Soviet Premier Kosygin's trip to France, the NCNA said: "The Soviet Union has further tried to gain French assistance in pushing its peace talk fraud in Vietnam."

December 12-13: The Central Committee of CPSU, at a plenary session, adopted a resolution condemning the policy of "Mao Tse-tung and his group." This was the first time that Mao had been attacked by name in an official statement of the CPSU.

December 14: The Japanese newspaper *Asahi* reported from Peking that Tao Chu,

head of the propaganda department and fourth-ranking member of the Communist hierarchy, had denounced Liu Shao-chi and Teng Hsiao-ping in a Peking speech. It was the first time the two men had been publicly mentioned by a Communist party official.

December 15: "Directive (Draft) of the CPC Central Committee on the Great Proletarian Cultural Revolution in Rural Districts" was issued.

Reuters reported from Peking that Red Guards newspaper confirmed that the former mayor of Peking, Peng Chen, had been presented at a Red Guard rally in a Peking stadium as a leader of the "revisionist clique" in China.

December 16: The PRC charged that American planes had seriously damaged Peking's embassy in Hanoi on December 14.

The NCNA reported that Peking had ordered three of the six Soviet journalists in China to leave the country by Christmas. The dispatch said the action was "in accordance with the principle of reciprocity," for the Chinese had only three correspondents in Moscow.

December 17: Dennis Bloodworth of the *London Observer* reported from Singapore that Communist China had sold "several thousand tons of steel" for use in construction of U.S. military bases in South Vietnam. Bloodworth reported that about $1 million worth of round and flat steel bars were purchased in Singapore and trans-shipped to Saigon early in 1966.

December 18: A Peking rally held by 100,-000 Red Guards, workers, peasants, and other revolutionary people, condemns U.S. bombing of Hanoi and celebrates 6th anniversary of founding of South Vietnam National Liberation Front.

December 19: The Kwangtung Foreign Affairs Bureau put forward a new demand for the prohibition of all Nationalist organizations and activities in Macao, and mass demonstrations by Red Guards took place near the border during the next few days.

December 20: It was reported from London that the PRC diplomats there had denied

Bloodworth's stories, referring to them as "absolute slander."

A quarter of a million commune members have just embarked on the carving out of a 127-kilometer canal on the northern Anhwei Plain in East China, a project that will insure stable and high yields on the rolling farmland, an NCNA report said.

December 21: *Reuters* reported from Peking that new posters there called for dismissal of Liu Shao-chi and Teng Hsiao-ping.

The U.S. embassy in Singapore said it was "skeptical" of reports that the U.S. had been buying steel from Communist China for use in Vietnam.

NCNA reported that Premier Chou En-lai had told a Peking military rally that, although the purge of anti-Maoists was "forging ahead vigorously," it had not been smooth sailing.

Ko Cheng-ping, manager of the Man-kuang Trading Company of Macao, was authorized on December 19 to make a representation to Jose Nohe de Carvalho, the Portuguese governor of Macao, on the handling of the "serious case of the barbarous massacre and persecution of Chinese compatriots in Macao by the Portuguese authorities." "The Portuguese authorities in Macao have been compelled to return to China seven agents of the Chiang Kai-shek gang within the time limit set by the foreign affairs bureau of the Kwangtung Provincial People's Council," an NCNA report said.

A Sino-Nepalese agreement on economic and technical cooperation was signed in Katmandu.

December 22: *Tanjuq*, the Yugoslav news agency, reported that Lo Jui-ching had been arrested.

December 26: Despite pleas from Red Guards for mass demonstrations, Mao Tse-tung's 73rd birthday was officially ignored. With no mention of his age, a full-page article in *People's Daily* was headed: "Chairman is the red sun in the hearts of revolutionary people throughout the world."

Reports from Peking indicated that Chi-nese Head of State Liu Shao-chi had "confessed" to taking an erroneous course. Red Guard newspapers described this as insincere and superficial.

December 27: It was reported from Peking that Mme. Liu Shao-chi had written a 3000-word confession in which she said: "I betrayed the Communist party and Chairman Mao's trust, solicitude, and teachings. This has greatly troubled me." On the same day, a Red Guards rally of 100,000 in Peking denounced him as the "Khrushchev of China" and the "boss of capitalism."

December 28: A circular of the CPC Central Committee and the State Council on Prohibiting the Extensive Promotion of the So-called "Red Ocean" was issued.

Peking announced that the Chinese had exploded their fifth nuclear device, apparently larger than the first four. U.S. experts said the initial evidence indicated that the test constituted a new step toward development of a hydrogen bomb.

Reports from Peking said that Chinese Foreign Minister Chen Yi had been denounced in Red Guard posters. Reuters reported that Peng Teh-huai, a former defense minister, had been arrested by Red Guards.

More than 100,000 Red Guards and revolutionary teachers and students who marched to Peking from all over China met this afternoon at the Peking Workers' Stadium to exchange experiences and celebrate the great victory of their long marches under the guidance of Mao Tse-tung's thought. Present at the rally were leaders of the Chinese Communist party and other departments, including Chou En-lai, Kang Sheng, Li Fu-chun, Yang Cheng-wu, Chiang, Ching, Peng Shao-hui, Lin Chih-chien, Chang Chun-chiao, and Wu Te.

The Soviet SS ZAGORSK, which violated China's harbor regulations and acted contemptuously toward China's sovereignty, was ordered to leave China by the superintendent of the Dairen harbor of the PRC.

A Sino-Afghanistan protocol in exchange of goods in 1966-67 was signed in Kabil.

December 29: Red Guard posters in Peking attacked Tao Chu, who had recently risen from obscurity to fourth place in the Chinese hierarchy. The posters asserted that "Tao Chu is a new bourgeois element."

NCNA reported that the PRC had warned Great Britain it was "courting disaster" by allowing U.S. navy ships to visit Hong Kong. The dispatch said Britain was "toeing the U.S. line and turning Hong Kong into a U.S. military base."

December 30: The PRC and North Korea signed a radio and television broadcasting agreement in Peking.

The U.S. Atomic Energy Commission announced that the recent Chinese nuclear test "involved thermonuclear material" and the "dirtiest" and most powerful type of nuclear weapon.

It was reported from Tokyo that the Red Guards were demanding that the former mayor of Peking, Peng Chen, and three other officials purged during the cultural revolution, Lo Jui-ching, Lu Ting-yi, and Yang Shang-kun (a former member of the Standby Unit of the Chinese Communist Party), be put to death.

Institute of Welding was held in the Dutch capital in July, 1966, when Netherlands officials were allowed to question the eight Chinese inside the legation. After they had made a joint statement that they knew nothing about My Hsu's death, which was officially assured to be a case of suicide, they were allowed to leave for China. On the same day, Mr. Geruit Jonge-jans, the Netherland charge d'affaires in Peking, was granted an exit visa.

December 31: "Circular of the CPC Central Committee and the State Council on Short-Term Military and Political Training for Revolutionary Teachers and Students of Universities and Middle Schools" was issued.

The Peking newspapers devoted entire front pages to a facsimile of the script of a poem written in 1963 by Mao Tse-tung in his own handwriting. The poem was written to the melody of *Man Chiang-hung* in reply to Kuo Mo-jo.

PLA general political department notified the army to carry out "support the government and cherish the people" activities with propaganda of the thought of Mao Tse-tung as the center.

1967

January 3: It was announced that the All-China Trade Union Federation was being reorganized on the ground that it was led by "capitalist elements" who oppose Mao's thought and followed the "revisionist line" of Liu Shao-chi. It was replaced by a new organization, "the Chinese Association of Red Rebels." The "Red Rebels" consist of adult workers who will replace the Red Guards from this time on as the main agents of the cultural revolution.

January 4: The Macao administration announced that the flying of the Nationalist flag and the display of anti-Communist posters had been forbidden.

January 5: An exhibition opened in Hangchow showing how China's young soldier Tsai Yung-hsiang, nurtured by Mao Tse-tung's thought, grew into a Communist, completely devoted to the people.

January 6: The Macao administration issued orders prohibiting the flying of the flag of any country which Communist China considered an "enemy," and on the same day the police closed down the Chinese Nationalist headquarters which had flown the Nationalist flag in defiance of the order. The Chinese Nationalist relief organization, which had helped more than 110,000 refugees from the mainland since 1953, was closed by the Portuguese authorities on January 10.

The regional military commanders in East Java had banned the Chinese from engaging in any kind of business and imposed a special tax on them.

Japanese correspondents in Peking reported that Red Guard posters asserted that Mao Tse-tung's resignation in 1958 as president of the PRC had been forced by pressure from a faction in the CPC headed by the present president, Liu Shao-chi. The posters indicated that Mao had been fighting to regain the position ever since 1958. He was quoted as saying that President Liu Shao-chi and Party General Secretary Teng Hsiao-ping "treated me as if I were their dead parent at a funeral." Mao said Teng had attempted to create his own "independent kingdom."

Japanese correspondents reported that Tao Chu, the propaganda chief who had been raised to prominence during the first stage of the purge, had been denounced by Mao's wife and led through the streets of Peking in disgrace by the Red Guards.

January 7: Reports from Peking said that bloody battles between Red Guards and masses of workers had placed Nanking "in the grip of terror." Japanese news sources reported that 54 people had been killed, 900 wounded, and 6,000 arrested. The report said that the trouble had begun when an estimated 100,000 workers in Nanking, led by the local party secretary, attacked the city's Red Guard headquarters. A huge battle ensued, lasting at least three days.

January 8: Japanese sources reported that uprisings on the Chinese mainland had spread to the Chusan Islands, southeast of Shanghai, where thousands of farmers had attacked Red Guards. On the same day, the Peking Radio announced that anti-Maoist "bourgeois elements" had attempted to cut off Shanghai's water and electricity. Other reports indicated that many workers had walked off their jobs. Much of the urban unrest was attributed to an attempt by Mao Tse-tung and his supporters to organize a mass movement of workers, known as the "Red Rebels Workers," to supplement the Red Guards in their struggle against Mao's enemies.

January 10: Peking Radio and press indicated that strikes were continuing in Shanghai and Foochow. Premier Chou En-lai appealed to the railwaymen to go back to work, and complained that "bourgeois reactionary people have inspired some workers to go to Peking for a revolutionary rampage."

January 11: David Oancia of the *Toronto Globe and Mail* reported that Po I-po, one of Communist China's leading economists, had been jailed by the Red Guards in Peking. The report said Po had been arrested in Canton.

The CPC Central Committee, the State Council, the Military Commission of the Party's Central Committee, and the cultural revolution group under the party's Central Committee have sent a message of greetings to various revolutionary rebel organizations in Shanghai.

"Document of the CPC Central Committee, the State Council, and the Military Commission" was issued to authorize the PLA and the public security departments to be responsible for the protection of the banks in all places.

"Notification by the CPC Central Committee on Opposition to Economism" was issued; "Notification by the CPC Central Committee and the State Council on Prohibiting the Corrosion of the Masses" was also issued; "Notification by the CPC Central Committee Concerning Broadcasting Stations" was issued to cease editing and broadcasting of local programs.

The CPC Central Committee and State Council notified revolutionary teachers and students of universities and middle schools to carry out short-term military and political training.

In the hands of the revolutionary teachers and students of Tsinghua University, Wang Kuang-mei signed a pledge under which she was to make a written statement of her own mistakes and those of her husband every ten days, and to come to Tsinghua whenever she was summoned.

January 12: Chairman Mao Tse-tung and the CPC Central Committee have approved a decision of the military affairs committee of the CPC Central Committee on reorganizing the cultural revolution group of the whole PLA. The reorganization gave Lin Piao and Chen Po-ta, head of the cultural revolution, tighter control. Chiang Ching was appointed as an adviser to the new committee in charge of running the army.

January 13: "Some Provisions Concerning the Strengthening of Public Security Work

in the Great Proletarian Cultural Revolution" was issued.

After an absence of two weeks, the Peking's *People's Daily* resumed publication. The first issue of the reorganized paper devoted its front page to a huge picture of Chairman Mao Tse-tung.

The Nationalist government announced that four of its jet fighters had shot down two Chinese Communist MIG jet fighters over the Taiwan Strait. The Nationalists said their planes all returned safely. However, according to an NCNA report, "an invading U.S.-made F-104 fighter plane of the Chiang Kai-shek gang" was brought down.

January 14: The PRC demanded that the governor of Macao sign a written "apology" for the incidents of December and insisted particularly that the word "murders" should be applied to the incidents and "assassins" to the Portuguese soldiers and policemen involved in them. The governor's proposed counter-version for such an "apology" having been rejected by the Chinese Communist leaders in Macao, the latter were reported to have issued a 24-hour ultimatum threatening that reprisals would be taken if the governor did not accept the wording demanded; and in implementation of this threat the Chinese authorities in Canton announced on January 16 that water supplies to Macao would be cut off every second day, necessitating the rationing of water in the city.

"Notification by the CPC Central Committee Ordering that the Spearhead of Struggle May Not Be Directed Against the Armed Forces" was issued.

Japanese correspondents in Peking reported that President Liu Shao-chi had asked permission of the CPC to retract the "self-criticism" he had made at an October, 1966, party meeting. In that statement, Liu had apologized for building his own support rather than mobilizing the masses in favor of Mao Tse-tung.

January 15: Rene Dabernat, foreign editor of *Paris-Match,* said in an interview in *U.S. News and World Report* that Communist China had informed the U.S.

through Paris, in the spring of 1966, that it would not become involved in the Vietnam war if the U.S. refrained from invading China or North Vietnam and from bombing the latter's Red River dikes. Dabernat said that subsequently statements by President Johnson and other U.S. officials demonstrated that they had "agreed to those conditions." The State Department replied with a "no comment," but other officials acknowledged that the United States had received a number of messages from Communist China through different third parties.

January 17: A Sino-Pakistani protocol on the PRC supply of grain was signed in Rawalpindi.

January 18: "Telegram Dated January 18 of the CPC Central Committee" was issued to endorse the good method taken by the rebel detachment of the Tsientsin Building Construction Material Company in handing over to the bank the sum of more than 3,900 yen which the company had authorized them to use for payment of supplementary wages.

It was reported from Peking that Red Guards and adult Revolutionary Rebels had shut down all stores in Peking in an attempt to force workers who had come to the city to go back to their jobs and get production rolling again.

January 19: "Document of the CPC Central Committee" was issued to dispatch troops to exercise military control over all important granaries and warehouses, prisons, and other important units which must be protected.

January 20: While negotiations between the governor of Macao and the Chinese leaders continued, three Chinese gunboats demonstratively entered the inner harbor of Macao for several hours. On January 22, six gunboats took up positions outside the port, one of them moving close to the wharf; and on January 26, six gunboats sailed into the harbor, followed a few hours after their departure by another eight gunboats.

Hsiao Hua, director of the army's political department and former right-hand man to Defense Minister Lin Piao, was assailed by Chairman Mao's wife and in posters as an opponent of the cultural revolution.

Pravda urged Communists throughout the world to oppose the hard-line policies of Mao Tse-tung and his companions, which, the paper said, were "directly aimed at splitting world communism." Meanwhile, Red Guard newspapers continued to charge that the Soviet Union was acting in collusion with Mao Tse-tung's opponents to oust him from office.

January 21: Peking Radio and the *People's Daily* carried orders to Chinese peasants to remain in their villages and stay away from the cities. The order was believed to be aimed specifically at Shanghai, where reports continued to emphasize clashes between workers and peasants. The Peking broadcast charged that opponents of Mao were sending the peasants into the cities to demand higher wages—a tactic denounced by Maoists as "economism." More than three million peasants were reported to have entered Shanghai alone.

January 23: "Decision of the CPC Central Committee, the State Council, the Military Commission of the Central Committee, and the Cultural Revolution Group under the Central Committee on Resolute Support for the Revolutionary Masses of the Left" was issued.

"Supplementary Notice of the CPC Central Committee Concerning the Question of Broadcasting Stations" was issued.

An NCNA report claims that members of the PLA in various parts of China— Shenyang, Canton, Foochow, Nanking, Kumming, Lanchow, Peking, Chengtu, Tsinan, Tibet, Sinkiang, and Inner Mongolia—have pledged support for Mao Tse-tung in the current power struggle.

January 24: The pro-Peking Chinese in Macao announced a number of "sanctions" to force the Portuguese authorities to sign the "apology" demanded, calling on the Chinese population to refuse to sell food to the Portuguese, to cut off water and electricity supplies, to boycott Portuguese-run bases, and to refuse to pay taxes to the Macao government.

January 25: The U.S. and Chinese ambassadors to Poland met in Warsaw for a secret three and one-half-hour talk. The next meeting was scheduled for June 7, 1967.

"Notification on Safeguarding the Results of the Four Clean-Ups Movement" was issued.

A rally of more than 100,000 people was held in Taiyuan to carry forward the seizure of power in Shansi Province through the great alliance of the proletarian revolutionary rebels.

January 26: "Order of the State Council and the Military Commission of the Central Committee Concerning the Taking Over of the Civil Aviation System by the Army" was issued.

The first Yemeni ambassador to the PRC, Muhammad Abdul Wasse Hameed, arrived in Peking. He presented his credentials to Soong Ching-ling on February 6.

The Chinese tea plantation survey team left Kabul for home after working about three months in Afghanistan.

The PRC embassy in Moscow protested to the Kremlin that 61 Chinese students had been attacked "without provocation" by Russian soldiers when they sought to place a wreath at the Lenin mausoleum in Red Square. The Soviet government answered that the protest was made up of "unpardonable lies." On the same day, huge crowds gathered outside the Soviet embassy in Peking, shouting such slogans as, "Down with the Soviet pigs!"

PRC and Finland exchanged notes on trademark registration in Peking.

January 27: Japanese correspondents in Peking reported that 100 people had been killed and only one of eight army units had remained loyal to Chairman Mao Tse-tung in Sinkiang. The posters accused Wang En-mao, the party and military chief of the area, of being behind the rebellion.

January 28: "Order of the Military Commission of the Central Committee" was issued to allow the armed forces to intervene in the local great proletarian cultural revolution.

"Directive of the Military Commission of the Central Committee Reiterating the Carrying Out of the Great Cultural Revolution Stage by Stage and Group by Group in Military Regions" was issued.

January 29: For the second time, French police clashed with Chinese students demonstrating outside the Soviet embassy in Paris. In the first demonstration, police arrested Chinese students and detained them in a police station overnight for splashing red paint on the embassy.

Peking Radio announced that workers' holiday for the Chinese New Year had been canceled, and that all elementary students had been ordered back to school on February 9. A Peking wall-poster announced that Premier Chou En-lai had ordered all Chinese students studying abroad to return home.

The Portuguese authorities in Macao were compelled to sign an agreement at the Macao Chamber of Commerce (the headquarters of the local Communist Chinese), accepting all the 4-point proposition put forward in the statement by the director of the Foreign Affairs Bureau of the Kwangtung Provincial People's Council and the 6-point demand raised by the Chinese in Macao. They undertook to pay 2,000,000 Hong Kong dollars as compensation for the families of the persons killed in the December riots. The local Chinese leaders thereupon called off their boycott against the Portuguese.

Tsingtao's 23 revolutionary rebel organizations formed a revolutionary rebel committee, seized all powers from the CPC Tsingtao municipal committee and Tsingtao Municipal People's Council.

January 30: "Decision of the CPC Central Committee, the State Council, and Military Commission of the Central Committee Concerning the Recent Incident in Chekiang" was issued.

January 31: Chinese demonstrated outside the French embassy in Peking, protesting the treatment of Chinese students who had been demonstrating against the Soviet embassy in Paris.

The revolutionary rebel committee of Tsingtao has ordered: (1) The CPC

Tsingtao municipal committee and Tsingtao Municipal People's Council be closed and their powers transferred to the Tsingtao revolutionary rebel committee; (2) leaders of the aforesaid committee and council should report to the revolutionary rebel committee and await further instructions, while their staff should carry on work as usual; (3) all directives and documents issued primarily by the CPC Tsingtao municipal committee and Tsingtao Municipal People's Council since May 16, 1966, be considered null and void; (4) all directives concerning the great revolution issued by the CPC Shantung provincial committee and Shantung Provincial People's Council, which continue to follow the bourgeois reactionary line, be ignored.

A Sino-Bulgarian agreement on exchange of goods and payments in 1967 was signed in Peking.

February 1: Peking Radio reported that Maoist forces had reconquered Kweiyang, capital of Kweichow Province in southern China.

PRC Vice-Foreign Minister Lo Kuei-po lodged a serious protest with the French ambassador to China and demanded that Robert Richard, commercial counsellor of the French embassy, and his wife admit their fault and apologize to the Chinese injured when the counsellor was backing his car.

Chiang Ching met representatives of two film studios and spoke to them. She wanted all shots of Liu Shao-chi, Teng Hsiao-ping, and Tao Chu cut from the film.

February 2: The PRC embassy in the Soviet Union lodged stern protest with Soviet Foreign Ministry against "unreasonable refusal of the Chinese students' request to lay wreaths before Lenin's mausoleum and Stalin's tomb." Meanwhile, the nine injured Chinese students returned to Peking. The Chinese staff working in the Soviet embassy in Peking declared a 3-day strike on January 27 in protest against the Soviet revisionist-leading clique for the beating

up of Chinese students on Red Square in Moscow.

February 3: "Notification by the CPC Central Committee and the State Council Concerning the Question of Exchange of Revolutionary Experience on Foot by Revolutionary Teachers and Students and Red Guards" was issued.

The PRC embassy in Kenya protested against "hooligans" smashing embassy's information windows.

A mass rally of 100,000 "red rebels" and PLA men was held in Harbin on January 31 to declare the inauguration of a "Heilun-kiang Provincial Red Rebels Revolutionary Committee."

Chairman Mao Tse-tung in the afternoon received Albanian delegation, headed by Hysni Kapo, member of the political bureau and of the secretariat of the Central Committee of the Albanian Party of Labor.

February 4: "Notification by the State Council and the Military Commission of the Central Committee Forbidding Exchange of Revolutionary Experience in Industrial and Mining Units, Scientific Research Organs, Designing Units and Capital Construction Units under the Industrial System for National Defense" was issued.

"CPC Central Committee's Notification (draft) Concerning the Great Proletarian Cultural Revolution in Primary Schools" was issued.

The PRC embassy in Moscow issued a statement sternly protesting the Soviet policemen's action in tearing down a photographic display in front of the Chinese embassy. In the meantime, in an official note to Peking, Moscow demanded that China stop villifying the Soviet Union and humiliating Soviet citizens in Peking. Retaliatory measures were threatened if such actions continued.

February 5: The PRC government issued a statement demanding the Soviet government admit publicly its mistakes, apologize to all the victims in the Chinese embassy, severely punish all the culprits, restore the six display cases of the Chinese embassy, and guarantee against any recurrence of similar incidents in the future.

February 6: In the evening of February 6, the Chinese Foreign Ministry notified the Soviet embassy that its officials were forbidden to leave the embassy compound, as otherwise their security could not be guaranteed, and for some days the embassy was under a virtual state of siege.

"Proclamation of the Armed Force Units on the Fukien Front Transmitted by the Military Commission of the Central Committee" was issued.

Taiyuan municipal revolutionary committee was inaugurated.

Liang Keng, Chinese secretary at the permanent secretariat of the Afro-Asian People's Solidarity Organization, reaffirmed China's stand in refusing to participate in the 8th council session of that organization in Cyprus, because it was engineered by the Soviet revisionists.

February 8: "Notification by the Military Commission of the Central Committee Setting a Time Limit for Those Who Have Gone to Other Places to Exchange Revolutionary Experience to Return to Own Units" was issued.

"Order of the Military Commission of the Central Committee" was issued to the navy, the air force and various military districts to carry out education by positive example without promoting full and frank airing of views, wall posters, and debates for the time being.

February 9: The Soviet government unilaterally cancelled the agreement allowing Chinese and Soviet citizens to visit each other's countries without a visa. Similar action was taken by the PRC government on February 10.

February 10: The joint investigation team on Liu Shao-chi's crimes published its first report denouncing his bourgeois stand in dealing with the peasant problem and land reform.

February 11: As ordered by the State Council and the military commission of the Central Committee, the Peking garrison headquarters of the PLA has taken over the control of the Peking Municipal Public Security Bureau.

"Regulations of the CPC Central Committee, the State Council, and the Military Commission of the CPC Central Committee" was issued to exercise military control over the production and construction corps of the Sinkiang Military Region during the period of the cultural revolution.

"Some Provisions of the Military Commission of the CPC Central Committee Concerning the Great Cultural Revolution in Leading Organs Above the Army Level" was issued.

Construction was started on the railway to Mao Tse-tung's birthplace.

February 11-12: At a public meeting in Peking, Premier Chou En-lai violently denounced the Soviet "revisionists" but said that no reprisals should be taken against Soviet diplomats. His speech was broadcasted but was not published in the press. On February 12 the Soviet embassy staff was informed that they could now leave the building, "provided they did not provoke incidents," and the demonstrations outside the embassy came to an end.

February 12: In a notice, the CPC Central Committee and the State Council ordered the immediate dissolution of all "national organizations" formed in Peking and elsewhere during the early period of the great cultural revolution. Members of these organizations were ordered to return to their respective units. These groups were also ordered to return the funds they have taken from the state treasury.

"Notice of the CPC Central Committee on the Question of Handling the Party Membership of Party Members" was issued.

"Provisions Governing the Return of Armed Force Work Groups Participating in the Local Great Cultural Revolution to Schools and Organs to Make Self-Examination" was issued.

February 12-16: A 7-member government delegation from the Islamic Republic of Mauritania arrived in Peking on February 12 and were received by Chairman Mao

Tse-tung on February 15. Agreements on trade, economic and technical cooperation and cultural cooperation between the two nations were signed on February 16. A joint press communique of talks was also issued in the same day.

February 13-March 16: Mao Tse-tung's policy of leniency toward cadres who have made mistakes was widely acclaimed. The revolutionary rebels are urged to distinguish good leading cadres from bad ones by the method of class analysis. Those who have made mistakes and repented are to be received back into the revolutionary ranks.

February 14: The Sino-Rumanian agreement on 1967 commodity exchange and payments was signed in Bucharest.

February 15: Japanese correspondents in Peking reported that anti-Mao forces had gained control of Lhasa, capital of Tibet. Army units opposed to Mao Tse-tung were said to be in command of the police department and of party headquarters in that city.

February 16: "Notification of the State Council and the Military Commission of the Central Committee Concerning the Carrying Out of the Great Cultural Revolution in the Capital Constructions Engineering Corps" was issued.

"Regulations of the Military Commission of the Central Committee Governing Seizure of Power Within the Party" was issued.

The PRC embassy in Tunisia issued a protest note to Tunisian Foreign Ministry against "openly advertising and trying to create two Chinas."

February 17: "Notice of the CPC Central Committee on the Question of Dealing with Work Group in the Great Proletarian Cultural Revolution" was issued.

"Regulations of the CPC Central Committee Concerning the Great Proletarian Cultural Revolution in Literacy and Art Bodies" was issued.

"Notice of the CPC Central Committee and the State Council Concerning Urban Educated Youths Working in Rural and Mountain Areas Who Go Out to Exchange Revolutionary Experience, Make Petitions, or Call on People at Higher Levels" was issued.

"Some Decisions of the CPC Central Committee and the State Council on Insuring Security of Confidential Documents and Files" was issued.

"Urgent Notice of the CPC Central Committee and the State Council on the Need for Workers Aiding Construction in the Hinterland and Frontierland to Participate in the Great Proletarian Cultural Revolution in Their Own Localities" was issued.

The dissolution of the National Rebel General Corps of Red Laborers was ordered.

February 18: "Notification Concerning the Free Distribution of Quotations from Chairman Mao Tse-tung to Foreigners" was issued.

Teng Hsiao-ping is accused of having built a clubhouse for high-ranking cadres with state funds and gathered there a number of "capitulationists and renegades" as well as "demons and monsters" —by an article in *Peking Tung Fang Hung*, No. 20, a tabloid published by the revolutionary rebel liaison center of Red Guards of universities and colleges of Peking.

February 19: "CPC Central Committee's Notification on the Question of Propagandizing and Reporting on the Struggle to Seize Power" was issued.

February 20: "CPC Central Committee's Letter to Poor and Lower-Middle Peasants and Cadres at All Levels in Rural People's Communes Throughout the Country" was issued.

February 21: "Notification of the CPC Central Committee" was issued to forbid storming and attacking military leadership organs by any person.

According to an NCNA report, U.S. military planes made repeated intrusions into China's territorial air space over the western part of Hainan Island on February 20 and 21.

February 22: More than 10,000 Red Guards held a rally to celebrate the formation of the Congress of Red Guards of Universities and Colleges in Peking.

February 23: "State Council's Notice on Adoption of Arm Bands and Badges in Making New Insignia for Red Guards in Future" was issued.

February 24: An impressive rally was held by the Shanghai revolutionary committee to hail Mao's latest directive on "Three-in-one Combination" of revolutionary masses, revolutionary leading cadres, and the PLA in seizing power.

February 25: "Notice of the PLA Military Control Committee of Peking Municipal Public Security Bureau" was issued.

The PRC Foreign Ministry in a statement strongly condemned "U.S. imperialism and its vassals" for their "recent series of intrusions into the Kingdom of Cambodia." It expressed its resolute support for the just stand taken by the royal government of Cambodia.

February 26: The Military Committee calls upon all cadres and fighters to support spring plowing and production.

February 27: A Sino-Bulgarian protocol in scientific and technical cooperation was signed in Peking.

March 1: Peking Radio reported a Maoist victory in Shantung Province. The broadcast said "the ruling clique" was deposed by army units and a new Shantung revolutionary council was set up.

March 6: The PRC embassy strongly protests alleged Indonesian Congress insults against China.

March 7: "CPC Central Committee's Notice on No Seizure of Power in Production Brigades and Production Teams During the Spring Farming Period" was issued.

"CPC Central Committee's Regulations (Draft) Governing the Great Proletarian Cultural Revolution Currently Under Way in Universities, Colleges and Schools" was issued.

"Document of the CPC Central Committee" was issued to give military training group by group and stage by stage in universities, middle schools and to senior classes in primary schools. Military and primary schools were reopened.

March 8-16: V. G. Wilcox, general secretary of the Communist Party of New Zealand, arrived in Peking on March 8. Welcomed at the airport by Premier Chou En-lai and Kang Sheng. Chairman Mao Tse-tung met Wilcox on March 12. Wilcox left Canton for home on March 16.

March 11: The PRC Foreign Ministry declared two second secretaries of the Soviet embassy persona non grata, on the ground that they had dismissed Chinese employees of the embassy who had gone on strike in protest against the Moscow incident of January 25; this "political persecution" was described as "extreme contempt of Chinese law and a gross insult to the working class of China." The Soviet government expelled a first secretary and a third secretary of the Chinese embassy on March 18, accusing them of having organized the embassy's anti-Soviet activities.

March 12: The Shansi Provincial Revolutionary Committee was inaugurated.

The PRC protests alleged Indonesian right-wing authorities' anti-China and anti-Chinese activities in East Java.

March 14: "Notification Concerning the Question of the New China News Agency" was issued.

A Sino-Nepalese contract on the PRC supply of rice to Nepal was signed in Katmandu.

March 15: The Danish Industrial Exhibition, opened on February 28 under the sponsorship of the Danish Government Committee on Exhibitions Abroad, closed in Peking.

March 16: "Notice by the CPC Central Committee, the State Council, and the Military Commission of the CPC Central Committee on the Protection of State Property and the Practice of Economy While Making Revolution" was issued.

March 17: A Chinese international trade organization and a Japanese trade delegation signed a joint statement. The statement declared that both sides agreed it was necessary to adhere to the three principles concerning relations between China and Japan, the three principles on Sino-

Japanese trade, and the principle on indivisibility of politics and economics, and to stand in the forefront of the Sino-Japanese friendship and trade movement to promote them.

March 18: "Notice of the Military Control Committee of the Peking Municipal Public Security Bureau" was issued.

"Measures for Dealing with Persons Back in Peking after Having Been Sent Away in the Great Cultural Revolution" was issued.

"CPC Central Committee's Letter to Revolutionary Workers and Staff Members and Revolutionary Cadres of Factories and Mining Enterprise All Over the Country" was issued.

March 19: "CPC Central Committee's Notice on Suspension of the Establishment of Revolutionary Ties All Over the Country" was issued.

March 20: On the 17th anniversary of the Vietnam Day, people of all circles in Peking held a rally condemning "latest U.S. imperialist war escalation" in Vietnam.

At a meeting of former poor and lower-middle peasants of Peking, attended by more than 2,500 people, Premier Chou En-lai urged the peasants to carry out spring farming successfully so as to win good summer and autumn harvests. He also warned them not to seize power in production brigades and teams during the spring farming season, even though such seizure of power might be necessary. At the meeting, Lin Piao gave important instructions. Among those present were Chen Po-ta, Kang Sheng, Hsieh Fu-chih, Chiang Ching, Wang Li, Kuan Feng, and Chi Pen-yu. A letter of salute to Mao Tse-tung was adopted.

The PRC protested to Britain over alleged U.S. use of Hong Kong as "Vietnam war base."

France returned two Chinese buildings in Paris to the PRC.

March 21: The PRC Foreign Ministry protested alleged Indian government use of Chinese Tibetan traitors for anti-China activity.

The 1967 Sino-Cuba trade protocol was signed in Peking.

March 22: A conference of representatives of Peking revolutionary workers and staff was held in the Great Hall of the People in Peking. At the conference the 10,000 present celebrated the coming together of the proletarian revolutionary forces in Peking's industrial and mining enterprises under the great red banner of Mao Tse-tung's thought.

March 23: Pierre M'vouama, minister of information of the Congo (B), received all the members of the Chinese mission of broadcasting experts who have set up a broadcasting station in the country.

"China News Agency" was set up in Japan.

March 24: "Decision of the CPC Central Committee, the State Council, the Military Commission of the Central Committee, and the Cultural Revolution Group under the Central Committee Concerning the Question of Tsinghai" was issued.

March 25: More than 10,000 representatives of middle school Red Guards of Peking met to inaugurate the Congress of Middle School Red Guards of Peking.

March 27: "Decision of the CPC Central Committee on the Question of Anhwei" was issued.

March 29: A 6-member Chinese-Rumanian friendship delegation arrived in Rumania.

The Indonesian government is condemned for "obstructing the Chinese government in sending a ship on the fourth occasion to bring back victimized overseas Chinese in Indonesia who wish to return to their motherland."

March 30: The Indonesian army announced that a number of Chinese nationals had been arrested in Jakarta for circulating pamphlets protesting the restrictive measures imposed upon the Chinese community, and on the following day three Chinese-owned factories, alleged to have been used as centers for disseminating subversive propaganda, were confiscated.

April 1: "Document of the CPC Central Committee" on the decision in respect to the Anhwei problem was issued.

April 2: Under the banner headline "Thoroughly Criticize and Repudiate the Top Party Person in Authority Taking the Capitalist Road," the *People's Daily* carried on its front page a report on the exposure and condemnation of the harm done by the book on *Self-Cultivation*, written by that top party person (Liu Shao-chi).

April 3: A mass rally was held by the Congress of Red Guards of Universities and Colleges in Peking criticizing and repudiating the reactionary book on Communist self-cultivation.

April 6: Harvard Professor Edwin O. Reischauer, former ambassador to Japan, suggested to the Joint Economic Committee of Congress that the United States lift its total embargo on trade with mainland China. Reischauer said the policy "has had no effect at all on China's economy, but has put a strain on U.S. relations with its allies, particularly Japan." He asserted that, in fact, "a rich and strong China might serve American interests and the cause of world peace better than an unstable and sick one."

In the "Order of the Military Commission of the CPC Central Committee," Chairman Mao Tse-tung directed the Chinese PLA to intervene in local great cultural revolutions and gave the Left vigorous support.

April 7: "Notification of the CPC Central Committee Concerning the Broadcasting of Comrade Lin Piao's Speech" was issued.

The "docile tool" theory attributed to Liu Shao-chi is said to be in opposition to the "thought of Mao Tse-tung" and the party's general line for building socialism, says *Peking Jih-Pao*.

April 9: The new Vietnamese ambassador to the PRC, Ngo Minh Loan, arrived in Peking on April 9 and presented his credentials to Soong Ching-lin on April 11.

April 10: *Reuters* reported that Branko Bogunovic, the Yugoslav news agency's chief correspondent in China, had been asked to leave China. Bogunovic, who had been reporting from China for several years,

was accused of "distorting and slandering the cultural revolution."

A Red Guard newspaper reported that at a meeting of the Standing Committee of the Party's Politburo at the end of March a resolution condemning Liu Shao-chi and Teng Hsiao-ping for "revisionism" had been carried by only six votes to five; the resolution had been supported by Mao Tse-tung, Lin Piao, Chou En-lai, Kang Sheng, Chen Po-ta, and Li Fu-chun, and opposed by Liu Shao-chi, Teng Hsiao-ping, Tao Chu, Chu Teh, and Chen Yun.

April 11: The PRC Foreign Ministry protests against alleged bloody anti-Chinese incident in East Java.

April 12: One of China's leading musicians, the concert violinist and composer Mao Szu-tsung, had been given asylum in the U.S. with his family at his own request after escaping from Communist China. The 46-year-old musician had been director of the Central Academy of Music in Peking and a delegate to the NPC, although he had never joined the CPC.

The PRC issued a protest note against "the fresh aggression and provocation against China recently committed by Indian troops on the China-Sikkim boundary."

April 13: "Decision of the CPC Central Committee on the Handling of the Inner Mongolia Question" was issued.

The PRC and Syria exchanged letters on the PRC technical aid in construction of a cotton-spinning mill in Damascus.

April 14: A Sino-East German agreement on exchange of goods and payments for 1967 was signed in Peking.

April 15: 1967 spring export commodities fair opens in Canton.

The Investigators of *People's Daily* editorial department issued a report on an investigation into the visit of the No. 1 party person in authority taking the capitalist road in April, 1949, to the privately owned Tungya Woolen Mill in Tientsin (now the No. 3 Woolen Textile Mill of the Tientsin Municipality).

April 16: According to posters which appeared in Peking, Marshal Hsu Hsiang-chien had been removed from his post as director of the cultural revolution in the Army and replaced by General Hsiao Hua (the head of the Army's political department), General Yang Cheng-wu (the acting chief of staff), and General Hsieh Fu-chih (the security minister). Marshal Hsu was accused of opposing Marshal Lin Piao at a recent meeting of the Party's military commission, and of ignoring Chiang Ching in her role as adviser to the army on cultural revolution.

April 17: "Notification Reiterating Suspension of Exchange of Revolutionary Experience in Other Places" was issued.

Posters which appeared throughout Peking asserted that Liu Shao-chi had collaborated in Peng Chen's alleged plan for a military coup, which was to have taken place in February, 1966; accused the Soviet Union of being implicated in the plot; and demanded the trial of the conspirators and harsh punishment for them. On April 28, Chou En-lai and Kang Sheng declared that there had been no such plan.

April 18: Following protest demonstrations by the Chinese community in Situbondo, Indonesian gangs of youths attacked Chinese, ransacked their homes, and burned down a Chinese-owned factory, while similar rioting occurred on the following day in the nearby towns of Besuki and Panarukan.

April 19: "Decision of the Military Commission of the CPC Central Committee Concerning the Enforcement of Military Control in Higher Military Academies and Schools" was issued.

The PRC embassy in Djakarta protests against alleged torturing of Chinese nationals.

April 20: A municipal revolutionary committee was established in Peking to act as a provisional municipal council, with General Hsieh Fu-chih as its chairman.

"Notice of the CPC Central Committee, the State Council, the Military Commission, and the Cultural Revolution Group on Exchange of Revolutionary Experience by Students" was issued.

The U.S. Department of Commerce an-

nounced its willingness to license exports of drugs to combat reported epidemics of meningitis, cholera, and contagious hepatitis in China. Nine days later, China rejected the offer, calling it a "dirty trick."

April 21: A special group headed by Chou En-lai had been formed inside the party's Central Committee, consisting of Chen Po-ta, Li Hsien-nien, Li Fu-chun, and Liu Po-cheng, who would be responsible for foreign policy, finance, industry, and defense, respectively. The functions of this committee were not defined but it was suggested that it might be intended to replace the Standing Committee of the Politburo.

The PRC embassy in Indonesia in a note to the Indonesian Foreign Ministry lodged the most urgent and strongest protest against the Indonesian government's suppression of Chinese nationals in Djakarta.

April 22: The PRC Foreign Ministry lodged the strongest protest with Indonesian government against new provocation.

April 23: It was reported that in Borneo 350,000 Chinese were being moved into controlled areas to await deportation.

April 24: The Sino-Albanian 1967-68 plan for cultural cooperation was signed in Tirana.

Chairman Mao Tse-tung received members of the revolutionary committees of the Shanghai Municipality, Shansi, Kweichow, Heilungkiang, and Shantung Provinces, and the Peking Municipality. Lin Piao, Chou En-lai, Chen Po-ta, Kang Sheng, and Li Fu-chun were among those present.

Chairman Mao Tse-tung attended a performance of "The White-Haired Girl" by the Shanghai School of Dancing, accompanied by Lin Piao and Chou En-lai.

The PLA air force allegedly brought down two U.S. planes over Kwangsi.

The Indonesian government ordered the Chinese charge d'affaires and the consul general to leave the country within five days. On the same day, the PRC gave similar instructions to the Indonesian charge d'affaires and information chief in

Peking. The expulsions followed several days of violent anti-Chinese demonstrations in Indonesia. Indonesian Foreign Minister Adam Malik accused the two Chinese diplomats of promoting Communist subversion in the country. In Peking, protest demonstrations against the persecution of the Chinese community began outside the Indonesian embassy, and continued for several days.

April 25: A trade agreement was signed in Helsinki between the PRC and Finland for the current year along with exchange of letters on revision of 1953 payments agreement to convert clearing currency from rule to Finnish mark.

The 1967 executive plan for Sino-North Vietnam cultural cooperation agreement was signed in Peking.

April 26: The Chinese Foreign Ministry in a statement indignantly condemned "U.S. imperialism" for "once again wantonly bombing the city of Haiphong on a big scale."

April 27: Wall posters in Peking reported fighting between Maoist and Chinese army units in the western province of Tsinghai. According to the posters, several hundred Maoist supporters were injured.

April 28: A Sino-Zambia trade agreement was signed in Peking.

April 29: U.S. pilotless aircraft was shot down "somewhere over Kwangsi."

April 30: The PRC rejected a plea by Leonid I. Brezhnev for unity of action in aiding North Vietnam. The *People's Daily* said the Chinese never would cooperate with the Russians—"a pack of rank traitors to the Vietnam revolution, shameless scabs serving as advisers to United States imperialism."

May 1: The PLA claimed the shooting down of two U.S. A-4B attack planes "somewhere over Kwangsi."

The change of policy became apparent at the May Day celebrations in Peking on May 1, when several leaders who had recently been denounced appeared in places of honor. The *People's Daily*, on April 30, called for unity with all cadres who did not belong to the "handful of bourgeois reactionaries." The several leaders concerned included Marshal Chu Teh; Chen Yun, a vice-premier who had frequently been accused of "economism"; Mr. Li Hsueh-feng, the former first secretary of the Peking Communist Party; Mr. Tan Chen-lin, the vice-premier responsible for agriculture; Marshal Hsu Hsiang-chien; and General Chang Kuo-huo, who was previously reported to be leading the armed opposition to the cultural revolution in Tibet. The official list of persons accompanying Mao Tse-tung at the celebrations apparently denoted the new order of precedence in the party hierarchy. The first 12 names after that of Mao were as follows: Lin Piao, Chou En-lai, Chen Po-ta, Kang Sheng, Chu Teh, Li Fu-chun, Chen Yun, Tung Pi-wu, Chen-Yi, Li Hsien-nien, Tang Chen-lin, and Hsu Hsiang-chien.

May 2: A spokesman of the PRC Ministry of Defense protested against the intrusion of 4 U.S. F-105 fighters into Kwangsi and their dropping of several bombs over Ningming Hsien. On May 3 the Defense Department in Washington asserted that "reports failed to show any evidence that these propaganda allegations are true."

The Kowloon disturbances began outside one of two artificial-flower factories.

Wall posters in Peking reported disunity among Maoist supporters. Thousands were involved in bloody fighting in Chengtu, Szechuan province. Similar incidents were reported from Chungking, from Manchuria and Inner Mongolia, and from Kansu and Kweichow provinces.

May 7: "Decision of the CPC Central Committee Concerning the Question of Szechwan" was issued.

May 8: *Red Flag* and *People's Daily* published jointly an article, "Betrayal of the Dictatorship of the Proletariat Is the Essential Element in the Book on Self-Cultivation," to denounce Liu Shao-chi.

May 12: Thousands of workers rioted in the Hong Kong industrial area of Kowloon. Cars were burned, and police were struck with stones and bottles as they threw tear gas into the crowd and arrested 200 rioters. The Hong Kong disturbances' were reflected in sympathetic demonstrations in the Portuguese colony of Macao. A crowd of Chinese invaded the grounds of the British consulate protesting against the "bloody suppression" of workers in Hong Kong.

May 14: The rioting in Kowloon temporarily subsided. The police lifted the curfew and withdrew all riot squads from the affected areas, but rioting flared up again on May 15, when gangs of Chinese youths smashed windows of an office of the American Express Company and of a post office.

The Peking municipal revolutionary committee issued a notice reiterating the banning of "struggle for force" and saying that PLA units are empowered to enforce this ban.

May 15: The British charge d'affaires in Peking, Mr. D. C. Hopson, was summoned to the Chinese Foreign Ministry and handed a statement by the vice-minister of foreign affairs, Mr. Lo Kuei-po, protesting against the recent actions of the Hong Kong government. The Chinese government demands in all seriousness that the British government instruct the British authorities in Hong Kong as follows: (1) Immediately accept all the just demands put forward by workers and residents in Hong Kong; (2) immediately stop all fascist measures; (3) immediately set free all the arrested persons, including workers, journalists, and cameramen; (4) punish the culprits responsible for these sanguinary atrocities, offer apologies to the victims, and compensate them for all their losses, and (5) guarantee against the recurrence of similar incidents. In Peking, the office of the British charge d'affaires was surrounded by Red Guards.

May 16: A circular of the CPC Central Committee, dated May 16, 1966, was published. The circular revoked the "Outline Report on the Cultural Academic Discussion Made by the Group of Five in Charge of the Cultural Revolution," allegedly prepared by Peng Chen (also known as the "February Outline"), and

enumerated the main errors of the report.

In Shanghai, a serious incident occurred when Red Guards invaded the home of Mr. Peter Hewitt, first secretary at the charge d'affaires' office in Peking and British diplomatic representative in Shanghai. Immediately on receipt of this news, Mr. Hopson lodged a strong protest with the Chinese Foreign Ministry, while in London the Chinese charge d'affaires, Mr. Shen Ping, was summoned to the Foreign Office to receive a similar protest, demanding guarantees for the future protection and safety of British citizens and property in China. On the same day, the crowd in front of the British charge d'affaires grew to hundreds of thousands to protest alleged "fascist outrages" by the British in Hong Kong.

The Commonwealth Office in London issued a statement attributing the Kowloon disturbance to a "comparatively small industrial conflict which it should be possible to settle soon if the management and trade unions would sit down together to discuss in reason and good will."

May 17: The Peking Revolutionary Committee forbade the movement of students and "revolutionary workers" from place to place.

The worst violence yet in Kowloon erupted. The police reported 42 arrests and injuries to 32 policemen and two civilians.

May 18: While in Kowloon 70 persons were sentenced to terms of imprisonment of between three months and two years for rioting, several hundred Communist demonstrators, organized by a recently formed 17-man committee "for resisting British oppression," stood all day outside the closed doors of government house reciting passages from Mao Tse-tung's Red Books and shouting abuse at the governor, Sir David Trench. The following day, between 2,000 and 3,000 demonstrators marched through the business quarter of Victoria to Government House, where they unsuccessfully demanded to see the governor.

May 19: Shen Ping was summoned to the

British Foreign Office, this time by Mr. George Brown, the foreign secretary, and was strongly rebuked for failing to transmit the previous British protests to Peking.

May 21: A delegation of the Albanian Ministry of Communications arrived in Peking after attending the 6th meeting of the administrative council of the Sino-Albania Joint Stock Shipping Company in Canton.

The PRC delegation led by Lin Haiyun, acting minister of foreign trade, arrived in Katmandu, Nepal, to take part in ceremony of opening of Katmandu-Kodari highway to traffic.

Mongolia expelled three Chinese teachers on the ground of "anti-Mongolian activities." The PRC Foreign Ministry alleged that the Chinese who had gone to the station to see the three teachers off, and who included five officials from the Chinese embassy and a photographer of the NCNA, had been "savagely attacked" by a number of Mongolian police and secret service agents; that many had been injured; and that more than 20 Chinese had been detained after being brutally beaten, including the diplomats and the NCNA photographer, whose camera was seized. The Mongolian government subsequently protested to the Chinese government against the demonstration by the Chinese nationals at the railway station.

Thousands of Chinese staged an anti-British demonstration in the Colony's business district. At least 44 persons were arrested. The disturbances continued on May 22, and for the first time shots were fired by the police when a group of demonstrators started throwing "Molotov cocktails" in Statute Square, in the center of Hong Kong. Altogether 150 demonstrators were arrested, and the police imposed a dusk curfew on the island's most heavily populated area. Disturbances also flared up again in Kowloon where a group of 70 bus conductors attacked a police station. Sir Arthur Galsworthy, deputy undersecretary of state at the Commonwealth office, arrived in Hong Kong together with two other British officials for talks with the governor.

Mr. Hopson was called to the Chinese Foreign Ministry and informed by the vice-minister of foreign affairs that "in view of events in Hong Kong" his government had decided to close the British office in Shanghai and had ordered Mr. Hewitt to leave China within 48 hours. Mr. Brown, in a note on May 22 to the Chinese foreign minister, said that the Chinese government was not entitled unilaterally to abrogate the agreement of 1954 establishing a British diplomatic office in Shanghai, but that if Marshal Chen Yi wished to propose discussions about the agreement, whether in Peking or London, the British government "would be happy to agree." The note added that a decision had already been taken to withdraw Mr. Hewitt because of the treatment he had received, and that the foreign secretary would be pleased to receive the acceptance of the Chinese government to the appointment in his place of Mr. R. W. Whitney, at present serving in Peking.

May 22: Following the U.S. offensive in the demilitarized zone, PRC Foreign Minister Chen Yi assured the North Vietnamese charge d'affaires in Peking that "the Chinese government will be ready at all times to take the necessary action, according to the need of the Vietnamese government and people, to give all-out support to the Vietnamese people's war against U.S. aggression."

May 23: The Hong Kong government issued an emergency ordinance announcing penalties of up to 10 years' imprisonment for those found guilty of permitting the use of loudspeakers in order to incite riots.

May 24: Two British diplomats were physically harassed by demonstrating Chinese as they left Shanghai. Peter Hewitt and Raymond Whitney arrived in Peking with torn jackets and glue on their clothing.

May 25: "Comment of the Military Commission of the Central Committee on the May 24 Order of the Inner Mongolia Military District" was issued.

A rally was held in Peking in support of the struggle by the Palestinian and other Arab peoples against the U.S. and Israel.

Kuo Mo-jo was principal speaker at the rally.

A Sino-UAR 1967 trade protocol was signed in Peking.

The PRC and Nepal signed a protocol for the construction of a power station over Sun Kosi River with Chinese help.

May 26: All British-employed Chinese in Peking began a four-day strike, culminating on May 29 in a sit-down demonstration on the threshold of the charge d'affaires' office. Mr. Hopson on May 27 walked out of a reception given by the Afghan ambassador to celebrate his country's National Day when Chen Yi accused Britain of continuing the "atrocious suppression" of Chinese in Hong Kong.

A rally of 15,000 was held in Peking to welcome home the three Chinese expelled from Mongolia. Main speaker at the rally was Wu Te.

People's Daily published Mao's article, "Give Serious Attention to the Discussion of the Film *The Life of Wu Hsun*," which was really part of an editorial which Mao wrote for *People's Daily* on May 20, 1951.

May 27: *People's Daily* published Mao's letter (dated October 16, 1954) to members of the political bureau, CPC Central Committee, concerning studies of the *Dream of the Red Chamber*.

The PRC Foreign Ministry protested a "barbarous anti-Chinese incident of bloodshed" at Ulan Bator railway station on May 21, which was "engineered" by the Mongolian government, and demanded that Mongolia: (1) Publicly admit its "crime" of beating and detaining Chinese diplomatic personnel; (2) immediately set free all Chinese who had been arrested; (3) severely punish the culprits and compensate the Chinese for their losses.

The PRC embassy in Indonesia lodged a protest with Indonesian government against massive eviction of Chinese nationals engaged in farming in Pontianak county and their being put in concentration camps.

May 28: Sino-Nepalese agreement on the PRC aid in extension of Kordari highway

to Katmandu was signed in Katmandu.

People's Daily published Mao's "two instructions concerning literature and art (dated respectively December 12, 1963, and June 27, 1964), while NCNA released a "Summary of the Forum on Literature and Art in the Armed Forces with Which Comrade Lin Piao Entrusted Comrade Chiang Ching."

May 28: Sino-Albanian protocol on shipping was signed in Peking.

May 31: Chingkangshan Fighting Corp of the Fourth Hospital, Peking, reprinted a chronicle of events in the life of Liu Shao-chi.

June 1: In Hong Kong, a new phase of the disturbances began after the enactment on June 1 of a government ordinance temporarily banning "the inflammatory" posters. The same night, workers at a government shipyard in Kowloon went on strike against the removal of offending posters and their replacement by official ones, as a result of which 300 workers were immediately suspended by the administration.

June 2: A *Reuters* dispatch said that Peking wall posters reported a wave of "white terror" throughout China. In Honan, Inner Mongolia, Szechwan, and particularly in Sinkiang, large forces were reported to be fighting white terorists or anti-Maoists.

June 5: The PRC embassy in Djakarta protested to the Indonesian Foreign Ministry against atrocities committed by Indonesian army and police against Chinese nationals in Lumadjang, East Java.

June 6: A CPC Central Committee directive ordered railwaymen to remain at their posts, and forbade Red Guards and other "revolutionaries" to seize transport by force, stop trains by lying on the rails, or travel without tickets.

The PRC government issued a statement on the Middle East war, accusing the U.S. of "Instigating Israelite aggression against the Arab countries" and the Soviet Union of conniving in such aggression. Premier Chou En-lai sent messages to President Nasser of UAR, pledging Chinese support for the Arab countries against U.S. and Israeli "aggression."

June 7: Tens of thousands of Red Guards, workers, students, etc., demonstrated in Peking against U.S. and Israeli "aggression" against the Arab countries.

A campaign of "rectification and self-criticism" was launched in June in order to eliminate the differences which had led to clashes between rival groups of Maoists. This took as its starting-point a series of "Regulations on Seriously Improving Style of Work," which had been adopted by the Shantung Revolutionary Committee on June 7. After being endorsed by *Red Flag*, those regulations were adopted by other revolutionary committees.

The CPC Central Committee issued an order forbidding the use of violence, arbitrary arrests, and the searching of houses and government offices, and making the army and the police responsible for the endorsement of the order.

June 9: Chairman Mao Tse-tung and Lin Piao received Afro-Asian writers who went to Peking to attend a seminar sponsored by the Afro-Asian Writers' Bureau and held in commemoration of the 25th anniversary of the publication of Mao's "Talks at Yenan Forum on Literature and Art."

June 10: The PRC Foreign Ministry sent a protest note to Bulgarian embassy in Peking protesting Bulgaria's declaring of three Chinese students as persona non grata.

A rally of 14,000 representatives of literary and art units all over the country was held in Peking to mark a great alliance of literary and art workers.

June 12: A pilotless reconnaissance plane, said to be American, was brought down by an air force plane of the PLA over Kwangsi.

June 13: The Peking's Municipal Higher People's Court held a "public trial" of K. Raghunath, 2nd secretary of the Indian embassy in Peking, for his espionage activities. Raghunath was convicted and ordered to be expelled from China at once, and P. Vijai was declared persona non

grata and ordered to leave China within three days.

June 15: The PRC Foreign Ministry handed to D. Sathe, charge d'affaires ad interim of the Indian embassy in China, a note of protest against the Indian government's forcing Chen Lu-chih, first secretary of the Chinese embassy in India, to leave India at once, and declaring Third Secretary Hsieh Chen-hao persona non grata and ordering him to leave within 72 hours.

A PRC Foreign Ministry spokesman stated that all foreigners, including diplomats, found photographing or copying posters would be prosecuted for espionage.

The PRC embassy in Indonesia protested against persecution of Chinese nationals in Pasuran by the military and administrative authorities of East Java.

June 16: Mao Tse-tung and Lin Piao saw Peking opera, "Taking the Bandits' Stronghold," in Peking.

Eight Chinese embassy officials in New Delhi were assaulted and injured by a crowd of Indian students. The students forcibly entered the embassy, ransacked Maoist exhibits, and broke windows. The action apparently was in retaliation for massive protests outside the Indian embassy in Peking and harsh treatment of the two Indian diplomats expelled from China June 14.

June 17: The PRC successfully exploded her first hydrogen bomb over the western region of the country.

The PRC Foreign Ministry informed the Indian charge d'affaires in Peking, Mr. Ram Sathe, that unless the entire Indian embassy staff and their families were taken to the embassy within two hours their safety could not be guaranteed. Demonstrators smashed the embassy windows and broke down the door of Mr. Sathe's residence.

June 18: An Indian note of June 18 protesting the seizure of the embassy gave warning that unless it were lifted within 24 hours India would be obliged to take "appropriate counter-measures," and on the following day armed sentries were posted around the Chinese embassy in

New Delhi to prevent members of the staff from leaving the building. The demonstrations outside the Indian embassy in Peking ceased after June 19 and on the following day Mr. Sathe was informed that the embassy staff were free to return to their flats; as a reciprocal gesture the Indian government lifted the restrictions on Chinese embassy personnel in New Delhi on June 21.

The PRC Foreign Ministry asked the Indian government to provide facilities for an aircraft which would be sent to New Delhi to bring home the Chinese diplomats injured in the attack on the embassy. The Indian government replied on June 20 that such facilities could be granted only if an Indian aircraft were allowed to remove some of the Indian embassy personnel from Peking. The Chinese government, however, refused the Indian request on June 21, and the Indian government accordingly refused on the following day to provide facilities for a Chinese aircraft.

June 21: President Kenneth Kaunda of Zambia arrived in Peking. Premier Chou En-lai called for high vigilance against Soviet revisionism's big global gang-up with U.S. imperialism, through the United Nations, at the banquet given in honor of President Kaunda on June 24.

The PRC embassy in Indonesia protested the incident which resulted in the wounding of 80 Chinese nationals created by the East Java military and government authorities in Medan on June 13.

June 22: Mao Tse-tung and Lin Piao saw "On the Docks," a revolutionary Peking opera on contemporary theme.

Chinese pupils refused to remove their Mao Tse-tung badges, and despite a protest from the Chinese embassy, the Burmese government closed two schools on the following day.

June 23: The PRC and Zambia signed an agreement on economic and technical cooperation in Peking.

The most serious disturbance to date occurred at the headquarters of the Communist-dominated Rubber and Plastic Workers' Union in Kowloon. Police used tear-gas to storm the building and made 40 arrests. During the fighting, one Chinese was shot dead by a detective, and 12 policemen, including three British inspectors, injured.

June 24: Mao Tse-tung and Lin Piao received Zambia President Kaunda in Peking.

A Tanzanian military delegation led by Lt. Col. S. M. S. Kashmiri, chief of logistics and engineering of the People's Defense Armed Forces of Tanzania, arrived in Peking.

June 25: The NCNA denounced the meeting of Soviet Premier Kosygin and President Johnson at Glassboro, N.J., on June 23 and 25. The Chinese contended that the purpose of the summit talks was to establish "a global American-Soviet deal intended to enhance the anti-China, anti-Communist, anti-people, and counter-revolutionary Washington-Moscow alliance."

A joint communique of the PRC and Zambia was issued on talks during President Kaunda's visit.

June 26: An air unit of the navy of the PLA shot down an F-4C plane of the U.S. over the southeastern area of Hainan Island.

People's Daily observer repudiated the resolution of the CPSU Central Committee on the Soviet Union's policy in connection with Israel's aggression in the Middle East as "a vile declaration of the Soviet revisionists to persist in their treacherous policy."

In its official note of protest, the Chinese government accused Britain of "frenzied provocations" and "fascist atrocities" against Chinese workers, and called on Britain to satisfy the five-point demand made by the Chinese government on May 15 and to instruct the Hong Kong authorities to accept the "just demands" of the demonstrators. The note was read by Mr. Lo Kuei-po, vice-foreign minister, to Mr. Hopson, who refused to accept it on account of its "grossly undiplomatic language."

Some 2,000 Burmese massed outside

two Chinese schools. When Chinese arrived in a diplomatic car and distributed Mao badges to the pupils, the mob destroyed the national emblem over the gate of the Chinese embassy, tried to break into the office of the NCNA, attacked Chinese houses and shops, and set fire to cars. The rioting continued from June 27 to June 30.

June 28: A new offer by the PRC government to build the proposed railway linking Dar-es-Salaam and the Zambia copperbelt, and to finance it to the extent of £100,000,000, was announced by President Kaunda of Zambia after his return from a visit to Peking.

PRC Deputy Foreign Minister Han Nien-lung handed Sinwa Nawng, Burmese ambassador to Peking, a note of protest against the Burmese government's instigation of and connivance in the Burmese ruffians' outrages in assaulting the Chinese embassy and other Chinese agencies on June 26 and 27, and killing a Chinese expert, Liu I, on June 28. In Rangoon, the Chinese charge d'affaires lodged a strong protest and demanded the punishment of the rioters, relief for the victims' families, a public apology, a guarantee of the safety of the Chinese embassy and an immediate end to the Fascist atrocities against overseas Chinese.

June 29: Towards the end of June the Communists in Hong Kong mounted two large-scale strikes, both lasting four days. The first (June 25-28), involving transport and other public utility workers, failed in its attempt to paralyze the Colony's commercial life, and was immediately followed by a strike of food importers (from June 29 to July 2). The Hong Kong government rationed water consumption to four hours' supply on alternate days following China's decision on June 25 to stop pumping operation from Kwantung Province.

Mr. Hopson received a second note protesting alleged violation of Chinese airspace off Kwangtung Province both on June 5 by three groups of British military helicopters and on June 26 by a single military aircraft on a reconnaissance mission. Replying on July 7, the British gov-

ernment apologized for the violations of June 5, which had been caused by navigational errors of the helicopter pilots concerned, but rejected the second Chinese allegation.

The PRC Foreign Ministry protested the blockade of Chinese embassy in Burma by Burmese troops. In Peking, 200,000 revolutionaries held a tumultuous demonstration in front of the Burmese embassy. The PRC government also announced that it had decided not to send its ambassador back to Rangoon.

The PRC embassy in Indonesia sent a note of protest to the Indonesian Foreign Ministry against the latest persecution of Chinese nationals at Lumadjang.

Kenya ordered expulsion of the Chinese ambassador and recalled its ambassador from Peking. As a reprisal the acting Kenyan charge d'affaires was ordered on July 1 to leave China within 48 hours.

June 29: Sino-Hungarian protocol on exchange of goods and payments in 1967 was signed in Budapest.

June 30: The PRC and Poland signed a goods exchange and payments agreement for 1967 in Warsaw.

A demonstration was staged by the Chinese embassy staff in East Berlin to protest the death of three Chinese diplomats in an automobile accident in East Germany.

July 1: The PRC Foreign Ministry handed to Sinwa Nwang, Burmese ambassador to Peking, a memorandum of the Chinese government rejecting the demand of the Burmese government. The note also reiterated the Chinese government's demands.

Nepalese students staged a demonstration outside the Chinese pavilion at an international exhibition in Katmandu, demanding the withdrawal of portraits of Mao Tse-tung and the Chinese flag. Pro-Chinese students began a counter-demonstration, whereupon the police intervened to prevent clashes between them.

July 3: During July the universities and other centers of higher education were reopened after being closed for the past year, beginning with the Peking Aeronautical Engineering Institute on July 3.

The PRC Foreign Ministry summoned Rezduhov, charge d'affaires ad interim of the Soviet embassy in Peking, and lodged a strong verbal protest with him against the stealing of information by staff members of the Soviet Commercial Representative's Office in Peking.

July 4: Hsiao Ming, charge d'affaires ad interim of the PRC embassy in Burma, protested against the arrest and detention of overseas Chinese students by the Burmese government and demanded that permission be given to Chinese diplomats to visit the persecuted Chinese students in Burmese military detention camps.

The PRC embassy in Indonesia lodged a note of protest with the Indonesian Foreign Ministry against the looting of Chinese shops and the assault on Chinese nationals in Djember and Banjuwangi, East Java.

PRC Ambassador to Nepal Yang Kung-su lodged a serious protest with the Nepalese government against anti-China outrages in Nepal.

July 5: The PRC Foreign Ministry sent a note to the Indonesian embassy in Peking warning against "the outrages of the Indonesian government in its anti-China and anti-Chinese campaign and in persecuting Chinese nationals."

The PRC Foreign Ministry handed a note to Sinwa Nawng demanding the Burmese government guarantee the safety of the personnel sent by the Chinese embassy in Burma to the overseas Chinese quarters in Rangoon to investigate "the persecution and losses suffered by the overseas Chinese."

July 7: Mao Tse-tung, Lin Piao, Chou En-lai, and other leaders received the delegates to the Conference of the Chinese PLA on Military Training.

A rally was held in Peking to commemorate the 46th anniversary of the founding of the Chinese Communist Party.

July 8: A serious incident took place at the village of Sha Tau Koi, on the border of China, during which five Hong Kong policemen—two Pakistanis and three Chinese—were shot dead by Communist rifle and machine-gun fire, and 12 persons, including a British police inspector, wounded. The following day protests, neither of which was accepted, were exchanged between Mr. Hopson and Mr. Lo Kuei-po.

July 9: Liu Shao-chi was reported to have made a new self-criticism which had been rejected by the Central Committee as "an attempted counteroffensive under the disguise of an admission of guilt." It was reported on August 2 that he had submitted yet another self-criticism in which, while admitting some errors, he had laid the responsibility for others on certain former ministers and on the Central Committee.

July 11: The PRC Foreign Ministry protested the arrest by the British authorities in Hong Kong of Hsueh Ping, correspondent of the Hong Kong branch of the NCNA, and their repeated provocations and persecution of NCNA personnel.

July 12: For the first time since rioting began in May, troops were used in an internal security role when a company of the Welsh Regiment barricaded buildings in the Wanchai and North points area of Hong Kong, while police raided the premises of the Motor Transport Workers' Union, arresting over 40 men and seizing large quantities of home-made weapons, including a number of sharpened iron crowbars.

July 14: "Notification of the CPC Central Committee Banning the Instigation of Peasants to Carry Out Armed Struggle in Cities—A Document of the CPC Central Committee" was issued.

July 16: The PRC embassy in Burma protested the expulsion of NCNA correspondent Yu Min-Sheng by the Burmese government.

The NCNA protested the arrest of correspondents Chen Feng-ying and Chen Te-mu of its Hong Kong branch and five other Chinese correspondents by the British authorities in Hong Kong.

July 18: NCNA reported that a new modern workshop had recently been commissioned for production in the nitrogenous fertilizer plant in Tsinghai province, which would increase the output of liquid ammonia and ammonium bicarbonate in this plant by two and a half times.

July 19: Mr. Hsueh Ping, a correspondent in Hong Kong of the NCNA, was sentenced to two years' imprisonment on charges of unlawful assembly and intimidation. Mr. Hsueh had been arrested on July 11 during disturbances in the Wanchai district of Hong Kong.

The PRC Foreign Ministry lodged a protest with the Indian government against the intrusions of Indian military aircraft into China's air-space between July 12 and 17.

July 20: NCNA demanded that the British authorities in Hong Kong immediately cancel their sentence on correspondent Hsueh Ping, stop the trial of other Chinese correspondents, and promptly and unconditionally release all correspondents.

July 21: The information department of the PRC Foreign Ministry summoned the resident *Reuters* correspondent in Peking, Anthony Grey, and announced that in view of the British "persecution" of correspondents of the Hong Kong branch of the NCNA and other reporters, the Chinese government had decided to restrict Grey's freedom of movement.

The crew of a Chinese ship which arrived at Venice, Italy, were refused permission to land until they had removed the political slogans with which the ship was covered, on the ground that political propaganda by foreign sailors was forbidden by Italian law. A settlement was reached two days later whereby all the slogans were removed except one reading "Long live the Italian workers."

In an attempt to hasten the formation of the triple alliance and end the conflict between the pro-Mao groups, the military, and communist leaders, Hsieh Fu-chih and Wang Li arrived in Wuhan, but were arrested and detained for a few hours. They were released as the result of the personal intervention of Chou En-lai, who flew to Wuhan. They returned to Peking

on July 22 and were welcomed at the airport by great crowds. Mass demonstrations against General Chen Tsai-tao took place in Peking on July 21 and posters appeared accusing him of being a counter-revolutionary who had massacred many Maoists. About 1,000,000 soldiers took part in another demonstration on July 25, presided over by Marshal Lin Piao, at which the slogan was raised, "Down with the military leaders taking the capitalist road."

July 26: The leading organ of the PLA units in Wuhan was issued notice to review its mistakes in the Wuhan incident.

Japanese "Haguruma" theater arrived in Peking.

July 27: The PRC Foreign Ministry lodged protest against the Czechoslovak government's breach of the Sino-Czechoslovak agreement for cultural cooperation, its aggravation of the relations between the two countries, its refusal to receive Chinese students to study in Czechoslovakia, and its verbal attack on Mao Tse-tung. Red Guards demonstrated outside the Czechoslovak embassy on the same day.

A Sino-Soviet protocol on the exchange of goods in 1967 was signed in Moscow.

July 28: Peking Radio claimed that the Wuhan military leaders had "admitted the errors" and promised to "follow Chairman Mao's revolutionary line and cooperate closely with the masses."

The PRC embassy in Burma lodged a protest against the Burmese government for violating international practice, infringing upon the diplomatic immunities of the Chinese embassy and worsening diplomatic relations between the two countries.

July 30: The PLA General Political Department issued a notice calling on all PLA units to commemorate the 40th anniversary of the Army Day on August 1 by studying Mao Tse-tung's articles on people's war and Lin Piao's "Long Live the Victory of People's War," criticizing and repudiating the "bourgeois reactionary military line" of Peng Teh-huai and Lo Jui-ching, and discussing Mao Tse-tung's "proletarian revolutionary line."

August 1: Peking Radio claimed that the rebellion in Wuhan had been stamped out, and the following day Wuhan Radio broadcast a statement of support for the Maoist Red Guard organizations opposed to the "Million Heroes." Japanese sources reported that General Chen was being held a prisoner in Peking; the *Liberation Army Daily,* however, while claiming that the leaders of the rebellion had been overthrown, admitted on the same day that rebellious elements were still inciting workers to strike and peasants to storm into the cities to disrupt production and public order. It was announced on August 5 that the responsibility for the defense of the Wuhan area had been transferred from the army to the air force.

August 2: The U.S. Government Congressional Committee on Atomic Energy issued a report stating that Communist China was making "rapid progress" in developing thermonuclear warheads, and predicted that it would be capable of launching a missile attack on the U.S. by the early 1970s.

August 3: A revolutionary committee at the Chinese Academy of Sciences was established.

A Sino-North Vietnamese protocol on scientific and technical cooperation was signed in Peking.

August 4: The NCNA released the text of "Bombard the Headquarters—My Big Character Poster," written by Mao Tse-tung on August 5, 1966.

The PRC embassy in Sweden addressed a note to the Swedish Foreign Ministry categorically rejecting the groundless charge against China over the Sigurdson-Munthe-Kaas incident.

August 5: A mob attacked the Chinese embassy in Djakarta, used a lorry to ram its gates, burned down a building within the embassy compound, and assaulted and injured four of its staff; the rioters were finally dispersed after troops fired into the air. An Indonesian note of August 9 alleged that four Indonesians had been wounded by shots fired from the embassy; the Chinese charge d'affaires, however,

denied that any of his staff had opened fire. The Chinese Foreign Ministry announced that Indonesian diplomats in Peking would not be allowed to leave the embassy until the security of the Chinese embassy in Djakarta and its personnel was assured. The Indonesian government retaliated on the following day by posting troops outside the Chinese embassy, with orders not to allow Chinese diplomats to leave without official permits. Demonstrations took place outside the Indonesian embassy in Peking on August 5-7, culminating in a rally in which 400,000 people were reported to have taken part.

A Sino-North Vietnamese agreement on the PRC economic and technical aid was signed in Peking.

August 9: Red Guards threw a portrait of Mao Tse-tung into the Mongolian ambassador's car in Peking, and when the chauffeur refused to accept it they dragged him out, handed him over to the police, and set fire to the car. Later the same day Red Guards forced their way into the Mongolian embassy and assaulted five of the staff. A Chinese note of August 10 asserted that the chauffeur's "grave crime" was proof of the "reactionary-class nature of the Mongolian revisionist-leading clique." A Mongolian protest note of the same date retorted that neither Mao Tse-tung nor his supporters had "any idea of the norms of human morals," and that China had sabotaged the friendly relations between the two peoples by its "policy of big-nation chauvinism and expansionism." A Chinese verbal note of August 18 declared in reply that this "vicious" attack on Mao Tse-tung showed that the chauffeur's "crime" had been "deliberately plotted and instigated by the Mongolian revisionist authorities."

Lin Piao's August 9, 1967, directive concerning the cultural revolution and the PLA was published.

August 10: A serious incident occurred when the port authorities at Dairen alleged that the second officer of a Soviet merchant ship, the Svirsk, had not only refused to accept a badge bearing a portrait of Mao

261

Tse-tung but had thrown it into the sea. The ship was prevented from sailing, and when the captain went ashore for clearance papers on the following day he was arrested, while Red Guards over-ran the ship and painted anti-Soviet slogans. Although a Soviet note demanded the captain's immediate release and the ship's unhindered departure, the captain was paraded through the streets in a lorry on August 12, and a mob again invaded the ship, blocking the funnel, tearing down the aerial, and breaking other equipment. After the Soviet prime minister, Mr. Kosygin, had sent a telegram to Mr. Chou En-lai, warning him that these "arbitrary and lawless acts" were "placing in doubt the fulfillment of existing trade relations between the Soviet Union and China," the Svirsk was allowed to sail on August 13. A Chinese note of the same date asserted that its crew had been instructed to insult Mao Tse-tung while in port, and that it had therefore been decided to "deport" the captain and conduct the ship out of Chinese waters.

Two Chinese notes alleged that Burmese troops had killed seven civilians in the Chinese Province of Yunnan in recent months, and that Burmese aircraft had repeatedly flown over the province.

August 13: The PRC Foreign Ministry lodged a protest with the British government against the British authorities in Hong Kong for "repeatedly engineering provocations at Man Kam To and other places in the border area." Mr. Hopson rejected the note because of its references to "fascist white terror" in Hong Kong.

At Genoa, Italy, the Chinese ship *Li Ming* was refused permission for the cargo to be unloaded or the ship to take on supplies or water until the offending slogans with which it was covered had been removed. In Peking, about 100 Red Guards broke into the Italian trade mission on August 16 and staged a "trial" of the head of the mission, who was afterwards released unharmed, a protest being subsequently lodged by the Italian government. After long negotiations between the captain of the *Li Ming* and the port authorities, it was agreed on September 5 to remove those slogans to which exception had been taken, while allowing the rest to remain.

August 14: Protest demonstrations against the Svirsk incident began outside the Soviet embassy in Peking and culminated in an attack on the building on August 17, when Red Guards smashed windows, destroyed furniture and documents, beat up a Soviet diplomat, and set fire to an embassy car. A Soviet note of August 18 denounced the attack as "a great provocation, premeditated, organized, and carried out by the Mao Tse-tung group," and as a criminal act "incompatible with normal relations between states."

Sino-Mali agreements on the PRC economic aid to Mali were signed in Peking.

August 15: A Chinese note to the Ceylonese External Affairs Ministry alleged that "ruffians" had looted· the cargo of a Chinese ship in Colombo harbor, destroying many copies of Mao Tse-tung's works, and asserted that "such acts of robbery and sabotage were perpetrated with the connivance and at the instruction of the Ceylon government." The Chinese protest was rejected on August 19 in a note handed to the Chinese charge d'affaires in Colombo.

August 15-16: The NCNA released excerpts from the resolution concerning the "anti-party clique headed by Peng Teh-huai," adopted on August 16, 1959, at the 8th plenum of the 8th Central Committee.

August 16: Sino-Somalian minutes of talks on rice and tobacco experiment station built by the PRC experts was issued in Mogadishu.

August 17: The PRC Foreign Ministry lodged protest with the Swiss embassy in China against the Swiss government for "supporting and encouraging the anti-China activities carried out by the Tibetan bandits in Switzerland."

The PRC embassy in Burma demanded the immediate, unconditional release of all arrested or detained Chinese nationals.

August 19: The Sino-Somalian 1967-68 plan for cultural cooperation was signed in Mogadishu.

August 20: The PRC Foreign Ministry handed D. C. Hopson a note of protest giving the British government and the British authorities in Hong Kong 48 hours to cancel the ban on *Hong Kong Wan Pao, Tien-feng Jih Pao*, and *Hsin Wu Pao,* set free the 19 Chinese journalists and 34 staff members of the three publications, call off the lawsuits against *Ta-Kung Pao* and *Ching Pao,* and the Nam Cheung Printing Co., Ltd., and the Hong Kong Press Enterprise Ltd., and make it possible for the above papers and printing companies to resume their normal operation. Mr. Hopson immediately rejected the Chinese note, while in London Mr. Shen Ping was summoned to the foreign office on August 21 and reminded that the British government held the Chinese government responsible for the safety both of the British mission in Peking and all British subjects in China, particularly Mr. Anthony Grey, whose telephone had been cut off on August 18. Meanwhile, in Peking about 200 Chinese soldiers surrounded the two villas housing the British diplomatic mission, while Red Guards covered the walls with "anti-imperialist" slogans. At the same time, groups of Chinese journalists and broadcasters paraded outside the compound and demanded the release of their Hong Kong colleagues and the lifting of the ban on the three Communist newspapers.

August 22: The Mission's Chinese office and domestic staff assembled on the terrace and called on Mr. Hopson to receive their protest in person. When Mr. Hopson appeared, he was engaged in argument for 2½ hours, while the demonstrators demanded that he should "bow his head and admit his guilt." Eventually they withdrew this demand when Mr. Hopson agreed to accept a written protest against British rule in Hong Kong. At 10:45 P.M. (Peking time), immediately after the expiration of the Chinese "ultimatum," a mob of Red Guards broke into the British mission, burnt down the main chancellery building, and smashed furniture from Mr. Hopson's official residence. Radio contact with the foreign office was lost after the operator had interrupted a routine message with the words "mob breaking in." Meanwhile the British foreign office had informed Mr. Shen Ping on August 22 that all Chinese diplomats and members of official Chinese agencies in Britain would be forbidden to leave the country without express permission, and later summoned him to receive a strong protest over the sacking of the British mission from Mr. George Thompson, then minister of state for foreign affairs.

The PRC embassy in Ceylon lodged protest with the Ceylon government against "its grave steps in bare-facedly trailing behind U.S. imperialism in creating 'two Chinas' by continuously keeping unseemly connections with the Chiang Kai-shek gang and deliberately undermining the normal relations between China and Ceylon." The Ceylon government rejected this note, emphasizing that Ceylon recognized only the PRC.

August 23: The PRC embassy in Burma lodged protest with the Burmese Foreign Ministry against the murder of Liu Yingchao, a leader of Chinese nationals in Burma.

The Kenya government protested to the new Chinese charge d'affaires concerning a recent incident in Peking, when, after a Kenyan diplomat had been involved in a motor accident, a mob had attacked the embassy, smashing windows and damaging property. The Chinese charge d'affaires rejected the protest and tried to hand over a note protesting against a statement by the vice-president of Kenya, Mr. Daniel Moi, who had accused the embassy of interfering in Kenya's internal affairs by attempting to distribute Mao Tse-tung badges and copies of Mao's thought in a Kenyan school.

August 24: The NCNA released a report on denunciation of Lo Jui-ching by PLA men.

August 26: The PRC embassy in Indonesia

lodged a protest with the Indonesian Foreign Ministry against "the unwarranted arrest and persecution of Chinese nationals in Indonesian government."

August 30: Vice-Foreign Minister Lo Kuei-po lodged a protest with the British government "for making provocations against the office of the Chinese charge d'affaires and other offices of the PRC, and for beating up the personnel of the office of the charge d'affaires."

The PRC Foreign Ministry issued statement condemning the United States for its repeated large-scale bombing of North Vietnam and its "collusion with the Soviet revisionist ruling clique in its scheme of forcing peace talks through bombing."

September 2: The PRC embassy in Ceylon protested "the serious political provocation by the Ceylon government in unwarrantedly holding up and refusing to return to the Chinese embassy" a consignment of badges with a profile of Mao Tse-tung.

September 3: Premier Chou En-lai was reported to have issued an order that Red Guards must not intrude into the compounds of foreign embassies or missions or indulge in acts of violence and destruction.

The PRC embassy in Burma protested the murder of Liu Hung-chu, an overseas Chinese in Bassein, Burma.

September 5: The CPC Central Committee, State Council, and Military Commission and Cultural Revolution Group under the CPC Central Committee issued an order forbidding a seizure of "arms, equipment, and other military supplies from the PLA."

Premier Chou En-lai received the members of the Tanzanian-Zambian joint economic delegation in Peking and attended the signing ceremony relating to an agreement between the PRC and the United Republic of Tanzania and the Republic of Zambia on the construction of the Tanzania-Zambia railway.

The PRC embassy in Mongolia protested the Mongolian authorities' undermining of the agreement for cultural cooperation between China and Mongolia,

cutting off cultural exchange between the two countries, and further worsening relations between them.

Nguyen Minh Phuong, acting head of the permanent mission of the South Vietnam National Front for Liberation to China, gave a press conference in Peking to introduce to the press the political program adopted by the National Front at its recent extraordinary congress.

The PRC, Tanzania, and Zambia signed an agreement in Peking on the PRC economic and technical aid in construction of Tanzania-Zambia railway.

September 6: The PRC embassy in Burma lodged a protest with the Burmese Foreign Ministry against the arrest of 13 overseas Chinese in Rangoon, Bogale, and Kyaiklat.

September 8: PLA air force shot down a U.S.-made U-2 high altitude plane of the "Chiang Kai-shek bandit gang" over East China.

September 9: The administrative office of the CPC Central Committee issued a notice calling on proletarian revolutionaries to earnestly study Chiang Ching's statement of September 5.

September 10: The PRC Foreign Ministry ordered that the three correspondents of *Mainichi Shimbun, Sankei Shimbun,* and *Tokyo Shimbun* must leave China within a specified time.

A. Q. Shabab, secretary of the Ministry of Education of Pakistan, arrived in Peking to sign the 1967-68 executive plan for the Sino-Pakistan cultural cooperation agreement.

September 11: The PRC government made a strong protest at the action of the "Indonesian fascist military regime" in inviting a trade mission from Taiwan to visit Indonesia.

September 12: The Shanghai office of the British diplomatic mission in China, vacant since the withdrawal on May 24 of Mr. Hewitt, first secretary in charge, was taken over, after the formal raising of the Chinese flag, by the Shanghai revolutionary committee.

September 14: Two officials of the Chinese

embassy in Djakarta, the interim charge d'affaires (Li Tshiu-koh), and the second secretary (Sin Sang), were declared persona non grata and ordered to leave Indonesia by September 18, for having allegedly shot at four Indonesian youths during the raid on the Chinese embassy in August.

Prince Sihanouk stated that the government would recall the entire staff of the Cambodian embassy in Peking, except one secretary, "to avoid incidents if there are Chinese demonstrations against our embassy." He added: "We shall not break off diplomatic relations with China, which remains our friend, if China does not try to interfere in our internal affairs." Premier Chou En-lai subsequently sent Prince Sihanouk a conciliatory message in which he asked him to reconsider his decision. In view to Mr. Chou's message, Prince Sihanouk decided not to recall the embassy staff.

Tokyo liaison office of the Liao Cheng-chih office and Chinese correspondents in Japan issued a statement at a press conference roundly refuting the reactionary Sato government's allegations concerning its outrages against Chinese personnel in Japan.

The PRC embassy in Tunisia protested Tunisian President Bourguiba's vilification of Mao Tse-tung, and the Tunisian government's creation of a series of "grave anti-China incidents." On the same day, the authorities in Peking recalled all four table-tennis instructors, who had been sent to Tunisia for one year as "technical advisers." President Bourguiba rejected the Chinese protest on September 17 on the ground that it contained "inadmissible statements on the Tunisian government," and demanded a retraction and an apology.

A Sino-Pakistani 1967-68 plan for cultural cooperation was signed in Peking.

September 15: The Indonesian foreign minister, Mr. Adam Malik, announced that he had ordered the recall of the entire Indonesian embassy staff in Peking, as the embassy could no longer carry out its functions because of lack of protection by the Chinese authorities, but that the latter had so far refused to grant exit permits to the diplomats. Mr. Malik added that the Indonesian government did not intend to break off relations with China. In retaliation for the expulsion by Indonesia, the Chinese government on September 25 declared the Indonesian charge d'affaires and the second secretary persona non grata and ordered them to leave China by September 29.

All-China Journalists' Association, *People's Daily,* and the NCNA issued a joint statement against the British authorities in Hong Kong for sentencing Lo Yu-ho, correspondent of the NCNA Hong Kong branch, and four other reporters from the *Wen-hui Pao,* and *Ching Pao* to three years imprisonment.

September 17: Chou En-lai, Chiang Ching, Chen Po-ta, Kang Sheng, and Hsieh Fu-chih spoke in Peking to 53 work units and more than 300 delegates from universities, colleges, and schools. Chou En-lai predicted in the speech that power would be seized in 20 or as many as 25 out of the 29 provinces and municipalities before the end of the year.

September 19: David Joseph Steele, an American, was expelled from China after a month of detention for intrusion into China's territorial waters south of Hainan Island on August 17.

September 21: The PRC issued a warning against the intrusion of a U.S. military plane into China's territorial air-space over the area of Tung Island and Yunghsing Island of the Hsisha group.

September 24: The NCNA reported that Mao Tse-tung recently inspected parts of North China, Central-South China, and East China and investigated the state of the cultural revolution in Honan, Hupeh, Hunan, Kiangsi, Chekiang, and Shanghai.

A Tunisian announcement said that a fair period had been granted to the Chinese government for instructing its representatives in Tunis to comply with the Tunisian demand of September 17, failing which "it would appear that the entire embassy personnel would be declared persona non grata and become liable to expulsion." On the following day, the PRC Foreign Ministry announced that the PRC had decided to close her embassy in Tunisia and to recall its personnel. The 10 members of the Chinese embassy staff left Tunis by air for Algiers on September 27. On the same day, Tunisian officials pointed out that the withdrawal of the Chinese diplomatic staff did not mean a formal break of relations between China and Tunisia.

September 25: The PRC Foreign Ministry protested the expulsion of Lu Tze-po, charge d'affaires ad interim, and Su Sheng, second secretary and consul, both of the Chinese embassy in Indonesia, by the Indonesian government.

September 27: The Peking Municipal Revolutionary Committee called a mass rally to announce the sentence of five U.S. special agents and 12 other counter-revolutionaries and criminals guilty of grave crimes.

September 28: Wu Shu-tung, representative of the Tokyo liaison office of the Liao Cheng-chih office, warned and denounced the *Yumiuri Shimbun* for having invited the Dalai Lama to Japan.

September 29: At the banquet given in honor of the DRV party and government delegation and the delegation of the South Vietnam National Front for Liberation, Premier Chou En-lai condemned "U.S. imperialism and Soviet revisionism for plotting a new hoax to induce peace talks through a bombing pause in a vain attempt to involve the United Nations in the Vietnam question."

October 1: A Canton tabloid carried the text of the August 14, 1967, notification of the Central Committee concerning criticism and repudiation by name in publications.

The PRC Foreign Ministry protested "fresh fascist atrocities committed by Indonesian troops and ruffians in attacking and wrecking the Chinese embassy and injuring Chinese diplomatic personnel."

The PRC Foreign Ministry lodged protest against military provocations by In-

dian troops across the China-Sikkim border.

October 4: The PRC Foreign Ministry accused the Ne Win government of Burma of tearing up the agreement on economic and technical cooperation between China and Burma.

October 5: The PRC Foreign Ministry protested the Indonesian government for organizing troops, police, and ruffians to launch attack on the Chinese embassy in Indonesia, and notified Djakarta of its decision to send a special plane to bring back the wounded Chinese diplomatic personnel.

An agreement on mutual goods supply and payment in 1968 between the PRC and the DRV was signed in Peking.

October 9: Indonesia suspended diplomatic relations with the PRC and ordered all Chinese diplomats to leave the country immediately, after the Chinese authorities had refused to allow exit permits for the eight remaining Indonesian diplomats in Peking.

October 12: Liao Cheng-chih office of Peking announced the cancellation of the right of the Japanese newspaper *Yomiuri Shimbun* to accredit a correspondent to Peking.

October 13: The PRC embassy in Burma demanded that the Burmese government release all Chinese residents "unwarrantedly arrested."

October 14: The PRC and Mauritania signed a protocol for the agreement of economic and technical cooperation in Nousakchott, capital of Mauritania.

October 17: The CPC Central Committee, State Council, Military Commission, and Cultural Revolution Group issued a notice carrying out the "revolutionary great alliance" according to systems.

The CPC Central Committee and its related agencies issued a four-point directive concerning propaganda work.

The Military commission of the Central Committee issued notification calling on the whole army to stir up a great wave of studying the latest directives of Mao Tsetung.

October 18: The Peking Municipal committee and other provincial committees called for extensive propaganda and study of Mao Tse-tung's latest instructions.

An agreement on Sino-Polish scientific cooperation was signed in Peking.

October 19-27: President Moktar Ould Daddah of Mauritania visited China.

October 20: The PRC Foreign Ministry protested provocations on the part of the British authorities in Hong Kong at the Shumohun border area.

The PRC embassy in Burma protested "the unlawful trial of the unwarrantedly arrested patriotic Chinese nationals by the reactionary Burmese government."

October 25: Sino-Rumanian scientific and technical cooperation protocol was signed in Peking.

October 27: The PRC announced the closing of its embassy in Djakarta and the withdrawing of its diplomats. On October 31 the eight Indonesian diplomats in Peking were flown to Djakarta; the same plane picked up the Chinese diplomats, two of whom were on stretchers.

October 31: Chinese and American ambassadors agreed to postpone the 134th meeting of the Sino-American ambassadorial talks from November 8, 1967, to January 8, 1968.

The PRC government issued a statement on bringing back all Chinese experts and technicians from Burma.

November 1: The Revolutionary committee of the Inner Mongolia Autonomous Region was set up.

November 4: The PRC Foreign Ministry informed Indonesia that the Rumanian embassy in Indonesia had been asked to look after China's rights and interests in that country.

November 7: The latest edition of the UN Demographic Yearbook contained this information on Chinese population: "China, with an estimated population of 710,000,-000 in mid-1966, was expected to double its population in 46 years."

A new five-year trade agreement, the fourth of its kind since 1952, was signed by Ceylon and the PRC, together with a protocol covering trade exchange in 1968.

November 10: China Council for Promotion of International Trade and Japanese Trade Promotion Association delegation issued a joint statement.

November 14: Mao Tse-tung, Lin Piao, Chou En-lai, and other leaders received PLA cadres and representatives of the revolutionary masses studying Mao Tse-tung's thought in Peking, delegates of revolutionary mass organizations and PLA and provincial cadres attending conferences in Peking, and Red diplomat and experts recalled from Indonesia and Burma.

November 14-25: Chinese Song and Dance Ensemble arrived in Baghdad for a performance tour in Iraq.

November 15-December 15: China's 1967 Autumn Export Commodities Fair opened in Canton.

November 20: A fossil skull cap of "Peking man" (Sinathroups) was unearthed at Chowkow-tien, the home of "Peking man," a little over 50 kilometers southwest of Peking.

November 21: It was announced by the British Foreign Office that the staff of the Chinese legation in London had been freed from the restrictions imposed upon them after the sacking of the British mission in Peking in August and the maltreatment of the charge d'affaires, Mr. Hopson, and his staff. As a result, Chinese diplomats would be able to travel up to 35 miles from London, instead of being restricted to within five miles of Marble Arch, and to make use of their diplomatic radio. A further announcement by the Foreign Office on November 29 stated that all restrictions on the movement of British diplomatic staff in Peking, imposed by the Chinese government in August, had likewise been removed and that exist visas would be issued for members of the mission and their dependents wishing to leave China.

November 23: The PRC embassy in Kenya protested against the Kenyan government's participation in the activities of creating "two Chinas."

The First Chinese medical team to Somali left for home after completing their term of service lasting two years and four months.

November 25: *People's Daily* commentator attacked the British resolution adopted by the U.N. Security Council on November 22 on the Middle East situation as "the product of a new U.S.-Soviet deal and another act of betrayal by the Soviet revisionist ruling clique against the Arab people."

November 26: *People's Daily* commentator said that the U.N. resolution on Korea "is null and void."

The PRC Foreign Ministry issued a statement in support of the November 23 communication of the Cambodian government.

November 27: The NCNA released a report on the recent plenary meeting of the CPC Committee attached to the PLA air force.

November 30: The NCNA reported that the Peking Observatory of the Chinese academy of sciences completed China's largest solar radio telescope.

The PRC recognized the People's Republic of Southern Yemen.

December 2: The PRC Foreign Ministry protested the attack by U.S. military aircraft on a Chinese freighter at the port of Hong Gai in Vietnam.

December 6: The PRC Foreign Ministry protested the recent "atrocities" committed by the British authorities in Hong Kong.

The PRC and Afghanistan exchanged letters of agreement on technical cooperation in experimental tea planting in Konar Province of Afghanistan with Chinese assistance.

December 9: A Sino-Albanian protocol on goods exchange and payments for 1968 was signed in Tirana.

December 11-21: Syrian "Omaya" Folk Song and Dance Ensemble was feted in Peking.

December 18: A Sino-Rumanian scientific cooperation plan for 1968-69 was signed in Peking.

December 19: Mao Tse-tung greeted the 7th anniversary of the founding of the South Vietnam National Front for Liberation. The *People's Daily* editorially reaffirmed the Chinese people's pledge to provide solid backing to the Vietnamese people in their struggle for national salvation.

December 24: The PRC issued a warning against the intrusion of U.S. warships and aircraft into China's territorial waters and air-space off Fukien Province and Hainan Island.

December 25: The U.S. Atomic Energy Commission announced that Communist China had carried out a nuclear test the previous day in the Lop Nor area of Sinkiang, described as of fairly low power with a yield of about 20 kilotons (equal to 20,000 tons of TNT, about the power of the bomb dropped on Hiroshima in 1945). No statement was issued in Peking, but a sudden threefold increase in radioactivity in the atmosphere was reported by Japanese scientists, confirming U.S. announcement of a nuclear detonation in China. The fact that the test was not announced by Peking led to speculation abroad that something might have gone wrong.

The NCNA reported that 86.4 million sets of *Selected Works of Mao Tse-tung* had been published in 1967.

A Congress of Revolutionary Workers was held in Lanchow from December 25-30.

December 26: A consultative conference of Revolutionary Great Alliance of Shensi was inaugurated.

December 31: A Sino-Rumanian goods exchange and payments agreement for 1968 was signed in Peking.

A 1967-68 executive plan of the Sino-Korean agreement of sanitary cooperation was signed in Peking.

1968

January 1: *People's Daily, Red Flag* and *Liberation Army Daily* jointly carried 1968 New Year Day editorial entitled "Ushering in the All-Round Victory of the Great Proletarian Cultural Revolution." The editorial outlined these basic "fighting tasks for 1968": (1) To develop the great mass movement of the creative study and application of Mao Tse-tung's thought still more extensively and deeply; (2) to continue to develop the revolutionary mass criticism in depth, promote and consolidate the revolutionary great alliance and revolutionary "3-in-one" combination and penetratingly carry out the struggle-criticism-transformation in each unit and department; (3) to rectify the party organization and strengthen the party building; (4) to implement still further Chairman Mao's great call, "support the army and cherish the people," and greatly strengthen the unity between army men and civilians; (5) to grasp revolution and promote production and other work and promote preparations against war.

Peking Radio reported that Chairman Mao Tse-tung has been greeted by more than 20,000 "revolutionary fighters" at a rally in Peking New Year's Eve. The broadcast said Mao, 74, was "in excellent health and high spirits."

January 2: Peking issued a warning against the intrusion of U.S. warships into China's territorial waters south of Hainan Island and east of Fukien Province.

January 3: The U.S. Atomic Energy Commission reported that "preliminary analysis of the fallout of the 7th Chinese Communist nuclear test conducted December 24, 1967, indicates that it contained uranium-235, uranium-238, and lithiul-6, and did not employ "plutonium." The AEC reaffirmed its previous assessment that the test had been in the "low-yield range."

The PRC Foreign Ministry issued a statement pledging firm support for the royal government of Cambodia and the Cambodian people in their just struggle against U.S. "imperialist aggression."

January 4: It was reported that the Ceylonese government had lifted its ban on the import of Communist Chinese publications and that there had been an easing of tension between the two countries.

Cambodia received from Communist China planes and anti-aircraft guns. In accepting the equipment, Cambodian Premier Son Sann said the shipment from "our friend China has a great significance" in view of the "growing threat of American intervention against our independence, our neutrality, and our territorial integrity."

January 5: A revolutionary committee for Kiangsi Province was established in Nanchang, the capital.

January 6: A Finnish government trade delegation arrived in Peking.

January 7-11: The PRC Foreign Ministry and other agencies protested U.S. bombing of Chinese freighter anchored at Cam Pha in Vietnam.

January 8: The 134th meeting of the Sino-American ambassadorial talks was held in Warsaw for 2½ hours after a break of 7 months—the longest gap for more than four years in their periodic contacts.

Shanghai Radio had reported that "revolutionary organizations at a number of townships of the city are still engaged in armed clashes among themselves instead of fighting the enemy of the proletarian class." The radio added: "The Maoist revolutionaries, to our disappointment, care nothing about the cultural revolution. What they care about is their personal grievances, thus leaving no time or energy for the revolutionary task confronting them."

January 9: The NCNA released a report on China's first big ocean-going freighter of 11,700 tons.

January 10: *Wen Hui Pao,* the main Shanghai newspaper, was reported to have listed 10 high government and party officials who had been vanquished by the cultural revolution. They were: Liu Shao-chi, Teng Hsiao-ping, Li Ching-chuan, Peng Chen, Tang Chen-lin, Po I-po, Lu Ting-yi, Lo Jui-ching, Yang Shang-kun, and An Tzu-Wen.

January 12: Peking charged that three American-Laotian planes had intruded into Chinese territory in Yunnan Province on January 6 and had bombed villages, causing loss of life and property damage. Peking described the incident as a "war provocation against the Chinese people" and warned that China would take "all necessary measures to support the just struggle of the Laotian people" if the U.S. extended the Vietnamese war into Laos. The U.S. Defense Department on January 12 said it had no confirmation of the alleged raid on Chinese territory.

January 15: Representative Charles F. Chamberlain (R. Mich.) reported to the U.S. House of Representatives, on the basis of U.S. Defense Department figures, that the number of Communist Chinese ships arriving in North Vietnam dropped from 138 in 1966 to 93 in 1967.

January 20: Talking to a Japanese group which had come to Peking at the invitation of the People's Institute of Foreign Affairs, in the third week of January, Prime Minister Chou En-lai indicated China's willingness to discuss trade with Japanese representatives. In Tokyo, a government spokesman on January 20 welcomed Mr. Chou's statement. However, he made it known that Japan would conduct negotiations along the government set policy of separating policies from economics.

January 22: Kuo Mo-jo received Bernardo Kordon, Argentine writer, and his wife.

January 23: *People's Daily* commentator described the annual State of Union message delivered by President Johnson as "a virtual admission of the agonizing difficulties of U.S. imperialism at home and abroad."

The Chinese embassy in Burma protested the "arbitrary expulsion and perse-cution of the personnel of the Rangoon branch of the NCNA" by the Burmese government.

The U.S. Navy intelligence ship *Pueblo* and its 83 crew members were captured by four North Korean patrol boats in the sea of Japan off North Korean's eastern coast and taken to the port of Wonsan.

January 24: *People's Daily* described in a commentary the complete text of the "nuclear non-proliferation draft treaty" as a new move in "U.S.-Soviet counter-revolutionary collusion against China, Communism, and the people."

January 25: A revolutionary committee of Kansu Province was set up.

A Chiangmen (Kwantung) tabloid reported that preparations were being made for the convention of the 9th Party Congress, according to Chiu Hui-tso, director of the logistics department.

January 26: Mao Tse-tung, Lin Piao, Chou En-lai, Chen Po-ta, Kang Sheng, Li Fu-chun, Chiang Ching, and Yao Wen-Yuan received activists of the PLA in the study of Mao Tse-tung's work.

January 27: Honan Provincial Revolutionary Committee was set up.

Chinese economic and trade exhibition opened in Bamako, Mali.

January 28: The Chinese government issued a statement on the seizure of U.S. "spy" ship *Pueblo* by the naval units of the Korean People's Army in Korea's territorial waters for espionage activities.

January 31: Peking claimed that a U.S. plane had violated China's air-space over Hainan Island and Kwanatung Province, near North Vietnam. The U.S. State Department January 31 conceded that a U.S. navy plane had inadvertently flown within seven miles of Hainan.

Lin Piao, Chou En-lai, Chen Po-ta, Kang Sheng, Chiang Ching, Yao Wen-Yuan, and other dignitaries saw a performance by the National Peking Opera Theater of the revolutionary model Peking opera, "The Red Lantern."

February 1: Chinese Foreign Ministry issued a statement on the bombing by U.S. aircraft of Chinese freighters anchored at a Vietnamese port.

The Syrian Song and Dance Ensemble left Shanghai for home.

February 2: Chou En-lai delivered a speech at a 10,000-man rally of representatives of various factions of the industrial-communications, finance-trade, agricultural-forestry systems under the State Council on the domestic situation, the *Pueblo* incident and the Vietnam war.

Chou En-lai sent a message to Nguyen Huu Tho, president of the presidium of the Central Committee of the South Vietnam National Front for Liberation, extending congratulations to South Vietnam for its "victories" in launching surprise attacks on more than 50 cities and towns.

Kaheita Okazaki, Yoshini Furui, Seiichi Tagawa, and two other leading members of the Tatsunosuke Takasaki office arrived in Peking.

February 3: The Hopei provincial revolutionary committee was set up.

People's Daily editorially hailed the establishment of diplomatic relations between China and South Yemen.

Chou En-lai and Chen Yi received Ngo Minh Loan, ambassador of the DRU, and Nguen Minh Phuong, acting leader of the permanent mission of the South Vietnam National Front for Liberation in China.

February 4: *People's Daily* commentator attacked Indonesian "reactionaries."

February 5: The Hupeh provisional revolutionary committee was set up.

February 5-6: Shanghai municipal revolutionary committee held an enlarged meeting to review its experience in exercise of power over the past year.

February 6: Chen Yi received Bossina Georges and eight other visiting friends from the Congo (Brazzaville).

February 9: 10,000 "revolutionary" workers held a rally in Peking pledging implementation of Mao Tse-tung's instructions.

Photo exhibition on Albania opened in Harbin.

February 10: *People's Daily* carried an arti-

cle entitled "Victory of the People's Commune." Article dealt with bankruptcy of fallacy about "going beyond the proper stage of development" to refute the fallacy of another top capitalist roader in addition to China's Khrushchev.

The Albanian government scientific and technical delegation arrived in China.

China sent medical team to Mali.

February 11: *People's Daily* commentator hailed the "Laotian people's new victories."

February 12: The NCNA reported that the Kian Administrative Region of Kiangsi province had been renamed the Chingkang Mountains Administrative Region.

February 13: The PLA naval air force shot down a carrier-borne plane of the U.S. Navy and damaged another over Hainan Island. The Defense Department in Washington admitted that a Chinese fighter had shot down an unarmed U.S. navy plane off Hainan Island on February 13. The Defense Department said that the planes had inadvertently strayed into Chinese air-space because of navigational difficulties.

February 14: Lin Piao greeted the 7th anniversary of the unification of the People's Liberation Armed Forces of South Vietnam.

February 14-26: Peking Red Guard organizations denounced Chi Pen-Yu's crimes.

February 15: The Albanian plastic arts exhibition opened in Hangchow.

February 16: Hsieh Fu-chih delivered talk at the Supreme People's Court on decision of the Central Committee to impose military control on all organs of dictatorship.

The NCNA denounced the Soviet "revisionist renegade clique" for trying to instill various kinds of revisionist ideas into the minds of children and youth.

February 17: Posters appearing in Peking denounced Chi Pen-yu, the only remaining editor of the CPC theoretical journal *Hung Chi*. The posters branded Chi as a "counter revolutionary" who had committed "crimes in literary and artistic areas."

February 19: The anniversary of China-Tanzania friendship treaty marked in Peking.

February 21-23: The Kwangtung provincial revolutionary committee was set up.

February 21-25: The NCNA released reports on congresses of activists in the study of Mao Tse-tung's work convened by the PLA.

February 22: The PRC embassy in Burma protested the "political persecution" of Chen Po-fu and ten other overseas Chinese by the Burmese government.

February 23: The NCNA answered the Soviet charge that "Chinese authorities refused permission to staff members of the Soviet embassy to lay wreaths on the graves of Soviet soldiers in China."

The Afro-Asian Writers' Bureau in Peking commemorated the centennial of the birth of Dr. W. E. B. Du Bois, noted Afro-American leader.

February 24: Chinese "East Is Red" song and dance ensemble left Dacca, Pakistan, for home.

February 25: The Overseas Chinese Affairs Commission lodged protest with the Burmese government against its arrest of three groups of overseas Chinese.

February 26: The PRC and Albania signed protocol on scientific and technical cooperation.

February 27: The PRC issued a warning against the intrusion of U.S. military planes over China's territorial waters east of Namoa Island and into China's territorial air-space over the Yunghsing Island of the Hsisha group in Kwangtung province.

March 1: The PRC government issued statement condemning the "monstrous crimes recently committed by U.S. imperialism and its South Vietnamese lackeys" in South Vietnam.

March 2: Chen Yi received Fujio Suganuma and three other Japanese guests.

China presented Yemen with 283 cases of educational equipment.

March 4: Posters appearing in Peking accused Chi Pen-yu of being a member of an "extreme left-wing" group that opposed Premier Chou En-lai. They also announced the "overthrow" of Cheng Chin, a member of the revolutionary committee of the Peking School of Art. They also denounced Liu Ning-yi, head of the All-China Federation of Trade Unions.

March 5: Chou En-lai issued a three-point directive to the Foreign Ministry.

A Sino-North Korean protocol on goods exchange for 1968 was signed in Pyongyang.

March 6: The Kirin provincial revolutionary committee and Changchun municipal revolutionary committee were established.

Chou En-lai received Yoshini Furui, Kaheita Okazaki, Seiichi Tagawa, Juzo Sugimoto, Teiji Hagihara, Ichizo Kimura, and other Japanese guests.

Chinese representatives of the China-Japan memorandum trade office and Japanese representatives of the Japan memorandum trade office issued a communique on their talks. The communique accompanied the signing of a new one-year, $100 million trade pact. It asserted that "all obstacles now existing in Japan-China relations have been brought on by U.S. imperialism and the hostile policy toward China pushed by the Japanese authorities. The communique was repudiated March 7 by Japanese Foreign Ministry officials who assailed it as "a regrettable attack on a friendly power" and emphasized that the delegation in Peking did not represent the Japanese government.

March 7: Mao Tse-tung, Lin Piao, Chou En-lai, Chen Po-ta, Kang Sheng, Li Fu-chun, Chiang Ching, and Yao Wen-Yuan received PLA activists in the study of Mao Tse-tung's thought.

NCNA released text of Mao Tse-tung's "March 7 (1967)" directive concerning the great strategic plan for the cultural revolution.

Pilotless high-altitude U.S. military reconnaissance plane was shot down over Southwest China.

March 9: *People's Daily* carried a signed article on degeneration of trade unions in the Soviet Union.

March 10: The PRC Foreign Ministry lodged protest against "intrusion into the Chinese embassy in India and violation of diplomatic immunity by Indian policemen on March 6."

March 11: *People's Daily* devoted a special page to articles repudiating the "counter-revolutionary revisionist line" on the women's movement pushed by "China's Khrushchev."

March 11-April 18: Seimin Miyazake and Masao Shimada of the headquarters of the Japan-China Friendship Association (Orthodox) arrived in Peking at the invitation of the China-Japan Friendship Association.

March 11-12: Chou En-lai greeted the independence of Mauritius.

March 12-15: The NCNA released a report on the charges against George Watt and Peter Deckart of the British Vickers Zimmer Ltd. for conducting espionage activities in Lanchow, Kansu.

March 13: *People's Daily* carried an article by a commentator declaring the "U.S. imperialists and Soviet modern revisionists have taken another grave step toward an open nuclear-military alliance to increase their global counter-revolutionary collaboration in opposing China, Communism, and the people."

Milan Honusek, head of the Czechoslovak government trade delegation and vice-minister of foreign trade, arrived in Peking for talks on Sino-Czechoslovak trade in 1968.

March 13-26: V. G. Wilcox, general secretary of the Communist party of New Zealand, arrived in Peking at the invitation of the CPC Central Committee.

March 15: The NCNA denounced the Soviet Union for selling out the interests of the Vietnamese people by working in collaboration with the U.S. to peddle Johnson's "peace talks."

March 16: Candito da Costa Aragab, a Brazilian guest, arrived in Peking for a visit at the invitation of the China-Latin America Friendship Association.

March 18-April 2: South Vietnam delegation of youth, led by Vo Cong Trung, member of the executive committee of the Central Committee of the South Vietnam Liberation Youth Federation, arrived in Peking at the invitation of the China-Vietnam Friendship Association.

March 18: *People's Daily* commentator described the Budapest consultative meeting of Communist and workers parties as a "foul counter-revolutionary performance by a handful of renegades and scabs."

People's Daily published an article by a commentator entitled "International Olympic Committee Is a Tool Controlled by U.S. Imperialism and in the Latter's Pay."

March 19: *People's Daily* commentator warned that members of the newly established revolutionary committees must not regard themselves as government officials and place themselves above the masses.

Peking held a mass rally in support of the Vietnamese struggle against "U.S. aggression" and for national salvation.

Minutes of talks between the China Council for the Promotion of International Trade and the Japanese Association for the Promotion of International Trade and five other Japanese organizations were signed in Peking.

March 20: China issued a warning against the intrusion of a U.S. warship into China's territorial waters off Fukien Province and of a U.S. military plane into China's air-space over the Hsisha Islands.

Joint China-Vietnam boundary railway commission signed a protocol on joint transport at its 11th meeting in Hanoi.

March 21: The Chinese Foreign Ministry protested against "the new grave crime committed by the Soviet revisionist ruling clique in actively collaborating with U.S. imperialism in its criminal plot for the creation of two Chinas."

People's Daily commentator denounced the Sato government of Japan as U.S. accomplice in aggression against Vietnam.

March 22: A pilotless high-altitude U.S. military reconnaissance plane was shot down over South China by a PLA air force unit.

People's Daily condemned in a commentary the Soviet Union for its "new crime of boosting the Chiang Kai-shek gang in collaboration with U.S. imperialism."

China-Pakistan Friendship Association gave a reception in honor of the 12th anniversary of the founding of the Islamic Republic of Pakistan.

March 23: Kiangsu provincial revolutionary committee and Nanking municipal revolutionary committee were established.

The NCNA reported that the third stage in the massive battle to harness the unruly Haiho River, one of the biggest river systems in China, is now underway.

Speaking at a Pakistan Day reception at the Pakistan embassy in Peking, Chen Yi reiterated China's "firm support to the Pakistan government and people in their just struggle in opposing foreign aggression."

People's Daily commentator hailed the armed struggle in Thailand.

March 24: *People's Daily* and the NCNA commented on the dollar crisis.

March 26: The NCNA reported that Mao Tse-tung and Lin Piao recently received more than 10,000 PLA cadres.

The PRC and Czechoslovakia signed barter and payments agreement for 1968 in Peking.

March 27: Chekiang provincial revolutionary committee was established.

Chinese-African People's Friendship Association condemned the "atrocities of the white colonialist authorities in South Rhodesia for killing Zimbabwe freedom fighters."

People's Daily commentator hailed the victories won by the people of Laos in their "war against U.S. aggression and for national salvation."

March 28: The CPC Central Committee greeted the 20th anniversary of the revolutionary armed struggle led by the Communist Party of Burma.

March 29: Prime Minister Pierre Elliot Trudeau of Canada issued a 3,500-word foreign policy statement that would serve as a guideline for his government if it won the June 25 elections. He said: "We shall

be looking at our policy in relation to China in the context of a new interest in Pacific affairs generally." "Our aim will be to recognize the People's Republic of China government as soon as possible and to enable that government to occupy the seat of China in the U.N., taking into account that there is a separate government (Nationalist China) in Taiwan."

The PRC Foreign Ministry protested against U.S. bombing of premises of Chinese economic and cultural mission in Laos.

March 31: *People's Daily* commentator in an article described the struggle of Afro-Americans in Memphis, Tennessee, as the roar of spring thunder portending an approaching violent and irresistible revolutionary storm in the U.S.

April 2: The PRC and Bulgaria signed 1968 agreement for goods exchange and payments in Peking.

April 3: The Soviet Union protested to Communist China March 31 and April 3 over detention of a Soviet tanker carrying supplies to North Vietnam. The Soviet news agency Tass reported April 3 that Moscow had assailed "the unlawful detention starting March 27 in port of Whampoa, near Canton, of the Soviet tanker KOMSOMOL UKRAINY carrying a cargo for embattled Vietnam."

April 4: The PRC Foreign Ministry protested the "crime committed by Ponomarchuk, second mate of the Soviet ship KOMSOMOL, in carrying out espionage activities encroaching on China's sovereignty and the serious violation of law by Kosyakov, captain of the ship."

The Chinese embassy in Burma protested the new wave of arrests of overseas Chinese by the Burmese government.

Chen Yi received Seimin Miyazake and Masao Shimada of the headquarters of the Japan-China Friendship Association.

April 5: The NCNA released an article against the U.S. entitled "Lyndon Johnson Plays New Trick of Partial Stop of Bombing to Induce 'Peace Talks'." The article charged that the partial U.S. bombing halt was a cover-up for further intensified U.S.

military action. "Peace will return to Vietnam only after the Vietnamese people win victories in the battlefield and drive the U.S. aggressor out," the article asserted.

People's Daily carried an article by a commentator entitled "No Nuclear Armament by Japanese Militarism Is Permissible."

April 6: NCNA declared Martin Luther King's assassination prompted a "large-scale Afro-American struggle against racial aggression." The agency cited the outbreak of violence in Washington and asserted that President Johnson was "panic-stricken in the face of the violent storm of the black American struggle."

Shanghai held televised political meeting directed against Chen Pei-hsien, Tsao Ti-chiu, and Yang Hsi-kuang.

An agreement on news coperation between NCNA and the Syrian Arab News Agency was signed in Peking.

April 8: Representatives of Zambia, Tanzania, and the PRC met in Dar-es-Salaam, Tanzania, and signed protocols providing for surveys and design of the projected "Tanzam" railroad, construction to begin in 1970.

The PRC presented sports equipment to Somalia.

M. Dmochowski, head of the Polish government delegation and vice-minister of foreign trade, arrived in Peking for talks on Sino-Polish trade for 1968.

Chou En-lai received Seimen Miyazaki and Masao Shimada of the headquarters of Japan-China Friendship Association.

The Chinese Foreign Ministry lodged a strong protest with the Indian government against its "Provocation against the Chinese embassy in India by unjustifiably arresting two Indian employees of the embassy on April 3."

April 9: Hunan provincial revolutionary committee was set up.

The PRC Foreign Ministry protested against the "Soviet revisionist authorities' unjustifiable expulsion from the Soviet Union of Chen Chi-hsien member of the Chinese experts team, in Russia to check up and take over aircraft."

People's Daily commentator warned the Sukarno government of Indonesia against "hatching the two Chinas" scheme in opposition to the Chinese people.

April 10: The Revolutionary committee of the Ninghsia Hui Autonomous Region was established.

Representatives of the China-Japan Friendship Association and the headquarters of that body issued the minutes of their talks.

The PRC and Poland signed goods exchange and payments agreement for 1968.

April 11: *People's Daily* commentator hailed the recent demonstrations by thousands of "patriotic" Japanese workers and students in Tokyo opposing the setting up of a field hospital in Japan by the U.S. armed forces.

April 13: The PRC presented 30 Chinese-made jeeps to the Malian government in Bamako.

April 14: The NCNA released a report on the second year's work on a 127-kilometer man-made waterway called the "new Pienho River," which will run east from a point on the Pienho tributary of the Huai River into the Hungtse Lake on the Northern Anhwei Plain, East China.

April 15: 1968 Spring Chinese Export Commodities Fair opened in Canton.

People's Daily commentator described Lyndon Johnson's March 31 program of partial stop of bombardment of North Vietnam as an "out-and-out big fraud."

April 15-18: *Kuan-Ming Jib Pao* and *People's Daily* published articles attacking the film, "Mad Torrents of the Red River," as an attempt to rehabilitate "anti-party element" Kao Kang and the Kao-Kang-Jao Shu-shih clique.

April 16: The PRC announced the deportation of the captain and second mate of the Russian tanker KOMSOMOL UKRAINY. The NCNA said that the commander, Captain Kosyakov, had violated Chinese law, while the second mate, Ponomarchuk, had carried out espionage activity and "encroached on China's sovereignty."

Mao Tse-tung issued statement in support of the Afro-American "struggle against violent repression."

April 17: Kuo Mo-jo received the 9-member delegation of rural activists of the Japanese Socialist Party from Niigata prefecture of Japan, headed by Yagi Ichiro.

April 18: Anhwei provincial revolutionary committee and Hopei municipal revolutionary committee were set up.

The PRC issued a warning against intrusion of U.S. military planes into China territorial air-space over Hsisha Island on April 17 and 18.

Anna Louise Strong hailed Mao Tse-tung's statement in support of the "Afro-American struggle against violent repression in the U.S."

April 21: According to Richard Hughes of the *London Sunday Times* (reported by the Washington Post, April 21), the army had taken over the Supreme People's Court, China's highest judicial body. The court, a party-state organ, previously had been technically free from military control. According to the report, Public Security Minister Hsieh Fu-chih had announced that a 5-man military committee would administer the court and carry out whatever purges were necessary.

A Shanghai municipal revolutionary committee urged the masses to join in a patriotic health movement with emphasis on the extermination of the four pests, as well as a mass movement for family planning and against early marriage.

April 22: Speaking before the Overseas Press Club in New York, Vice-President H. H. Humphrey said there was a need to replace the "iron curtains" in the world with "open doors." "I look forward to the day when the great Chinese people, no longer victimized from within, take their place in the modern world," he declared.

In parallel ceremonies in Washington, London, and Moscow the U.S., Britain, and U.S.S.R. signed a treaty pledging international cooperation in the rescue and return of astronauts in danger on the earth, in space, or on the moon. 41 other nations joined in the signing ceremonies.

France and Communist China were among the countries that neither signed nor indicated an intention to sign the pact.

April 23: An agreement was signed in Peking replacing sterling with French francs for all future trade transactions between Communist China and Japan. The switch-over became effective immediately. The agreement was expected to have much larger implications than its effect on direct Sino-Japanese trade. For one thing, other Asian Communist countries with whom Japan trades, namely North Korea and North Vietnam, were expected to follow the Chinese example and shift to franc sterling. Second, some East European countries which had switched from sterling to dollar in 1967 were now suggesting in increasing numbers to Japanese trading houses to settle future deals in francs, and if they were implemented as expected, the international role of sterling would shrink further.

A Guinean government economic delegation headed by Israel Toure, minister of economic development, arrived in Peking.

The PRC issued a warning against the intrusion of a U.S. warship into China's territorial waters off Fukien Province, and of a U.S. military plane into China's airspace over the Hsisha Islands.

April 25: A televised political meeting was held in Shanghai against Ho Lu-ting, formerly president of Shanghai Conservatory of Music.

The NCNA released a report accusing Moscow as being Washington's No. 1 accomplice in suppressing Afro-American struggle.

Chinese-African People's Friendship Association marked 4th anniversary of the founding of the United Republic of Tanzania.

April 27: Protocol on basic technical principles for the construction of the Tanzania-Zambia railway and agreement on accounting procedures for loans for the railway were signed in Dar-es-Salaam by delegations of the PRC, Tanzania, and Zambia.

Tordoi Jeno, head of the Hungarian

government trade delegation and vice-minister of foreign trade, arrived in Peking for talks on Sino-Hungarian trade for 1968.

April 27-June 28: Albanian Vaut I Denies Hydro-Electric power station delegation, headed by Petrit Radiovicka, vice-president of Tirana University, arrived in Peking.

April 27: A trade protocol for 1968 was signed in Rawalpindi between the Chinese and Pakistani governments.

The China-Nepal Friendship Association marked the 8th anniversary of the signing of the Sino-Nepalese treaty of peace and friendship.

April 28: Chou En-lai sent a message to the Kwangtung provincial revolutionary committee objecting to the use of his name in a "rally to celebrate the first anniversary of Premier Chou's rehabilitation of the 'East Is Red' of the Pearl River Film Studio" held in Canton and to some of the slogans used at the rally.

April 29: A Revolutionary committee was set up on Hainan Island.

The 4th anniversary of the inauguration of direct China-Pakistan air service was marked in Peking.

People's Daily commentator denounced Soviet "revisionists" for stirring up another anti-China campaign over the expulsion of the captain and second mate of the Soviet ship KOMSOMOL UKRAINY and over the expulsion of the ship from a Chinese port under armed escort.

April 30-May 18: Chou Hua-min, head of the Chinese government trade delegation and vice-minister of foreign trade, left for the Republic of Guinea and the German Democratic Republic on a visit.

May 1: May Day was celebrated in Peking, Shanghai, and Tientsin.

Shenoi provincial revolutionary committee and Sian municipal revolutionary committee were set up.

The NCNA reported phenomenal growth in China's low-alloy steel output.

May 2: Chiang Ching, wife of Chairman Mao, was listed by Peking Radio as 9th among the leaders appearing in the rostrum with Mao and Defense Minister Lin Piao for the annual May Day celebration. On May Day, 1967, she had been listed 22nd and last among the leaders on the rostrum; she ranked 19th in the listing for National Day, October 1, 1967. The May Day listing, as reported by *Peking Review* May 3, 1968, was as follows: Mao Tse-tung, Lin Piao, Chou En-lai, Chen Po-ta, Kang Sheng, Chu Teh, Li-Fu-Chun, Chen Yun, Chiang Ching, Chang Chun-Chiao, Yao Wen-Yuan, Tung Pi-wu, Chen Yi, Liu Po-Cheng, Li Hsien-nien, Hsu Hsiang-chien, Nieh Jung-chen, Yeh Chien-ying, Li Hsueh-feng, Hsieh Fu-chih, Huang Yung-Sheng, Wu Fa-hsien, Yeh Chun, Li Tso-Peng, Chiu Hui-tso, Liu Hsien-Chuan, and Wang Tung-hsing.

May 4: *People's Daily* published a commentary entitled, "Loss of Political Power Means Loss of Everything," denouncing the Soviet "revisionist renegade clique as a bunch of new blood suckers."

Ali Lotf Athawr, vice-chairman of the directors of the Yemen Bank for Reconstruction and Development, arrived in Peking.

An agreement on goods exchanges and payments for 1968 between the PRC and the German Democratic Republic was signed in Berlin.

An agreement on goods exchanges and payments for 1968 between the PRC and Hungary was signed in Peking.

May 6: The PRC and Tanzania signed a protocol on sending of Chinese medical team to Tanganyika.

People's Daily devoted a full page to peasants' articles repudiating the "counter-revolutionary revisionist line" pushed by "China's Khrushchev" in the countryside.

May 7: Chengtu municipal revolutionary committee was set up in Szechwan.

Jean Vincent, resident correspondent of the Agence France-presse in Peking, was declared persona non grata on May 7 and ordered to leave China within three days.

May 8: Mao Tse-tung, Lin Piao, Chou En-lai, Chen Po-ta, Kang Sheng, Li Fu-chun, Chiang Ching, Chang Chun-chiao, Yao

Wen-Yuan, Hsieh Fu-chih, Huang, Yung-sheng, Wu Fa-hsien, Yeh Chun, and Wang Tung-hsing received commanders and fighters of the PLA, party and government cadres, and representatives of the revolutionary masses from different parts of the country attending study courses in Mao Tse-tung's thought in Peking.

China marked the 2nd anniversary of Mao Tse-tung's May 7 directive.

The NCNA accused Soviet televised chronicle of distorting history.

"Proletarian revolutionaries" of Shanghai and Kiangsu held a televised struggle meeting against the Li Shun-Chin and Chi Cheng "counter-revolutionary clique."

May 9: *People's Daily* devoted a page and a half to a report on a "model company"—the Red 9th Company of a PLA unit stationed in Shenyang—in making living study and application of Mao Tse-tung's thought.

The PRC issued a warning against the intrusion of U.S. military planes into China's territorial air-space over Hainan Island and Hsisha Islands on May 5 and 6.

May 10: Revolutionary committees of Liaoning Province and Shenyang municipality were inaugurated.

Yu Li-huan, charge d'affaires ad interim of the Chinese embassy in Yugoslavia, protested against Tito's "vicious attacks on Chinese domestic and foreign policies."

Prime Minister Trudeau said that Canada should increase its contacts with Communist China for its own economic advantage and for the good of world order.

The *New York Times* reported that a Canton newspaper, the *Cultural Revolution Bulletin,* identified Chairman Mao Tse-tung as the target of an attempted coup in Wuhan, Hupeh Province, in July, 1969. The report said that Mao and Defense Minister Lin Piao had gone to Wuhan July 15, 1967, after having been informed of the plot, allegedly led by Chen Tsai-tao, the regional military commander, and Chung Han-hua, the political commissar of Hupeh. According to the

paper, the personal threat to Mao had occurred July 20, 1967, when he escaped from the military regional command headquarters only 20 minutes before Chen's "counter-revolutionary" forces surrounded the building.

May 11: The NCNA reported that the Kiangsi motor vehicle plant successfully produced a first batch of 12 trucks in a matter of four months.

People's Daily gave front-page prominence to a report on the experience of the militiamen of an East China commune in mounting vigorous attacks on the "class enemy through sustained revolutionary mass repudiation."

May 13: A Sino-Mongolian trade protocol for 1968 was signed in Peking.

The Chinese embassy in Sanaa held a memorial meeting to mourn the death of Tu Chiu-ching, a technician of the Chinese technical work group for assisting Yemen to build the Sanaa-Sada highway project, who died on duty May 11.

May 14: The NCNA announced the successful completion of another ocean-going cargo ship, "Chao Yang," with a displacement of 19,000 tons and a cargo capacity of 13,000 tons.

The PRC and Guinea signed a commercial protocol for 1968 in Conakry.

May 15: National railway and communications conference was concluded in Peking.

Afro-Asian Writers' Bureau and Afro-Asian Journalists' Association held a joint meeting in Peking supporting the armed struggle of the Palestine Arab people to liberate their motherland.

The PRC government lodged strong protest against provocations by French "reactionaries" in front of the Chinese embassy in France.

May 16: The editorial department of *People's Daily, Red Flag* and *Liberation Army Daily* wrote an article in commemoration of the May 16, 1966, circular of the Central Committee of the CPC. In the editorial, "the top ten" of "the handful of the top party persons in authority taking the capitalist road" were identified as Liu Shao-chi, Teng Hsiao-Ping, Tao

Chu, Peng Teh-huai, Peng Chen, Tan Chen-lin, Lo Jui-ching, Lu Ting-Yi, Yang Shang-kun, An Tzu-Wen.

Vice-Premier Chen Yi received Brazilian guest Candido da Costa Aragao.

Tung Hua-min, member of a Chinese communications delegation, arrived in Tirana to attend the 7th meeting of the administrative council of the Sino-Albanian Joint Stock Shipping Company.

May 17: *People's Daily* published an article refuting the Soviet "revisionist renegade clique for shamelessly slandering" the revolutionary committees of China.

May 18: Guinean-Malian joint delegation of friendship to China, led by Ousman Ba, Malian foreign minister, and Lansana Beavogui, Guinean foreign minister, arrived in Peking.

The PRC proposed that the 135th meeting of the Sino-American ambassadorial talks scheduled on May 29, 1968, be postponed till the middle of or late November.

May 20: Mao Tse-tung, Lin Piao, Chou En-lai, Chen Po-ta, Kang Sheng, Li Fu-Chun, Chiang Ching, Yao Wen-Yuan, Hsieh Fu-chih, Huang Yung-Sheng, Wu Fa-hsien, Yeh Chur, and Wang Tung-hsing received more than 20,000 revolutionary fighters from all parts of China.

The NCNA reported revolutionary committees had been set up in all the administrative areas of Tsinghai Province—the provincial capital, six antonomous *Chou* and 37 *hsien*—following the establishment of the Tsinghai provincial revolutionary committee in August last year.

May 20-June 3: Swiss instrument and watch exhibition was opened in Peking.

May 21: U.S. Undersecretary of State Nicholas de B. Katzenbach and Eugene V. Rostow, undersecretary for political affairs, urged in separate speeches that Communist China reconsider its policy of isolation and accept U.S. offers of new contacts and exchange. Rostow said, "We have made clear our willingness to welcome Chinese scientists, scholars, and journalists to the U.S. and have encouraged our own academies to establish contacts with their counterparts on the mainland of China." Katzenbach hinted that U.S. was ready to reconsider its policy of no trade with China.

May 21-24: Workers, Red Guards, "revolutionary" teachers, students and cadres staged mammoth demonstrations in Peking and other parts of China in support of the "just struggle of the workers and students of Paris, the revolutionary people of the whole of France, and the people of Europe and North America."

May 23: The Nepalese deputy prime minister, Mr. Kirtinidhi Bista, arrived in Peking on a seven-day visit during which a trade agreement and a protocol to the trade agreement between the PRC and Nepal were signed. (May 28)

May 24: The PRC signed agreement on the construction of the Guinea-Mali Railway with Guinea and Mali in Peking.

May 25: The China-Afghanistan Friendship Association marked the Independence Day of Afghanistan.

The PRC issued a warning against the intrusion of U.S. military planes into China's air-space over the Hsisha Islands in Kwangtung and Kiangsu Province on May 24 and 25, respectively.

May 26: *People's Daily* devoted a full page to articles written in commemoration of the 26th anniversary of Mao Tse-tung's "Talks at the Yenan Forum on Literature and Art."

May 27: The PRC lodged a strong protest with the British government against the entry of the U.S. nuclear-powered aircraft carrier *Enterprise* into Hong Kong and against the British government's "abetting U.S. imperialism, using Hong Kong as a base of operations for its war of aggression against Vietnam."

May 30: The CPC Central Committee, State Council, Military Commission, and cultural revolution group issued instructions concerning the formation of the Szechwan provincial revolutionary committee.

The NCNA released a report on the successful operation of the first methanol-producing project designed, built, and equipped by China.

A trade agreement and a protocol to the trade agreement between the PRC and Nepal were signed in Peking.

May 31: Szechwan Province revolutionary committee was established.

The NCNA claimed that 47 officers and men of "remnant Chiang Kai-shek bandit troops," who had fled beyond the Chinese border from Yunnan province, recently crossed over to frontier defense units of the PLA in Yunnan Province.

Governments of the PRC, Guinea, and Mali issued a joint communique in Peking in which the PRC agreed to help build a railroad from Bamako, capital of Mali, to the Guinean rail line at Kouroussa. Bamako would thus be linked with Conakry on the Atlantic Ocean.

June 1: Official Peking news sources confirmed in June that General Huang Yung-Sheng had succeeded Yang Cheng-wu as chief-of-staff of the PRC's armed forces. Huang was commander of the Kwangtung provincial revolutionary committee, which was established February 21. Yang had been dismissed March 29 along with two other high military leaders—Yu Li-Chin, political commissar of the air force, and Fu Chung-pi, commander of the Peking garrison.

The NCNA accused the Soviet Union of stepping up over-all collaboration with India.

A Malian military delegation, led by Mamadou Diakite, minister delegate for defense and security to the presidency, arrived in Peking.

June 2: Chungking municipal revolutionary committee was established.

The PRC issued a warning against the intrusion of a U.S. warship and U.S. military planes into China's territorial waters and air-space on June 1 and 2.

June 3: Mao Tse-tung, Lin Piao, Chou En-lai, Chen Po-ta, Kang Sheng, Chiang Ching, Chang Chun-chiao, Yao Wen-Yuan, Hsieh Fu-chih, Huang Yung-sheng, Wu Fa-hsien, Ye Chun, and Wang Tung-hsing received more than 20,000 PLA cadres.

June 4: The NCNA released quotations from Mao Tse-tung on the youth movement.

June 6: *People's Daily* devoted the whole of its front page to an article by its commentator denouncing the "betrayal of the French revolutionary mass movement by the French revisionist renegade clique."

June 7: The NCNA released a report on the successful manufacture of a laser machine for drilling micro-holes in diamonds and hard metals in China.

June 8: The NCNA accused Indonesia of stepping up its "collusion with the bandit gang of Chiang Kai-shek."

June 9: A Guinean trade delegation, led by Fofana Sekou, director of the home trade bureau of the Ministry of Trade, Communications, and Posts and Tele-Communications, arrived in Peking.

June 10: The NCNA authorized the issue of a warning concerning the intrusion of Indian military planes into the air-space over Yatung area in Tibet on nine occasions. However, India denied that there were any such intrusions by Indian planes.

June 11: Vice-Premier Chen Yi declared that the Chinese government opposed the resolution "peddling the so-called treaty on non-proliferation of nuclear weapons" adopted by the political committee of the U.N. General Assembly.

Protocol of the 7th meeting of the administrative council of the Sino-Albanian Joint Stock Shipping Company was signed in Tirana.

June 12: The U.N. General Assembly adopted a resolution commending the draft of nuclear non-proliferation treaty submitted to it March 15 by the U.N.-18-Nation Disarmament Committee (HNDC). The vote was 95-4 with 21 abstentions and 4 absent. On June 16, NCNA charged that the treaty was "fraudulent" and was "aimed at enslaving others."

June 13: The NCNA reported the introduction of a new technique in iron-smelting—combining industrial television with carrier-wave remote control—by the Penki Iron and Steel Company in Northeast China.

The NCNA signed an agreement on exchange of news with the National News Agency of Nepal.

The CPC Central Committee, State Council, Military Commission, and Cultural Revolution Group issued a joint directive ordering the rival factions in Kwangsi to stop their armed fights, restore railway traffic, and return the stolen goods.

June 14: The Chinese embassy in Burma protested the expulsion of "patriotic" overseas Chinese.

June 15: The CPC Central Committee issued instructions concerning assignment of work to school dropouts, according to a Canton tabloid.

June 18: President Julius K. Nyerere of the United Republic of Tanzania arrived in Peking.

June 19: The PRC issued a warning against the intrusion of a U.S. military plane and a U.S. warship into China's air-space and territorial waters off Kwangtung Province.

June 20: The CPC Central Committee sent a message to the Central Committee of the Malayan Communist party greeting the 20th anniversary of the Malayan people's "Anti-British rational liberation war."

Trade protocol for 1968 was signed between the PRC and the Sudan at Khartoum.

June 21: Mao Tse-tung and Lin Piao received President Nyerere of Tanzania.

June 22: A Canton tabloid reproduced from NCNA's Trend of Cultural Revolution No. 1220 a report telling how the "military control committee" of a large printing plant in Peking carried out a purge of followers of "China's Khrushchev" and "remnants of Kuomintang reactionaries."

The NCNA reported production of two new precision instruments—Model DMJ-2 electronic analog computer and Model 2HL-01 quadruple spectrometer—by Peking workers.

June 23: In an interview with editors of the *New York Times* (on June 21, reported on June 23), Vice-President Humphrey said that U.S. embargo on trade with Communist China should be lifted except for strategic materials.

June 24: Exhibition in commemoration of Norman Bethune closed in Peking.

June 25: The PRC issued a warning against the intrusion of U.S. warships and a U.S. military plane into China's territorial waters and air-space off Kwantung province.

The *New York Times*, attributing its information to tabulations by western analysts of Chinese affairs, reported that 34 or 63 active members of the CPC's 1965 Central Committee had been purged and nine members had been publicly criticized by leaders of the Maoist cultural revolution. Of 72 active alternate members of the Central Committee, 27 had been purged and 29 had been publicly criticized. Of the 45 first and second secretaries of regional party organizations in office in China before the outbreak of the cultural revolution in 1966, only nine were known to be still active by June of 1968. With respect to the highest level of Communist China's leadership, the following changes were noted: (a) Politburo current members (8): Mao Tse-tung, Lin Piao, Chou En-lai, Chen Yi, Li Fu-Chun, Li Hsien-Nien, Chen Po-ta (new), and Kang Sheng (new). Members purged from the old 13-member politburo (7): Liu Shao-Chi, Teng Hsiao-Ping, Peng Chen, Peng Teh-huai, Ho Lung, Li Ching-Chuan, and Tan Chen-lin; (b) Cultural revolution group (formerly secretariat of the CPC Central Committee), present members (5): Chiang Ching, Kang Sheng, Chen Po-ta, Chang Chun-Chiao, and Yao Wen-Yuan. Members purged from the old 10-member secretariat (6): Teng Hsiao-ping, Peng Chen, Wang Chia-hsiang, Ten Chen-lin, Lu Ting-yi, and Lo Jui-ching; (c) State Council: Present members (premier and six deputy premiers): Chou En-lai (premier) Lin Piao, Chen Yi, Li Fu-chun, Li Hsien-nien, Nieh Jung-Chen, and Hsieh Fu-Chih. Members purged from the old State Council, which consisted of the premier and 14 deputy premiers (8): Teng Hsiao-ping, Ho Lung, Ulanfu, Tan Chen-lin, Po I-Po, Lu Ting-yi, Lo Jui-Ching, and Tao Chu; (d) Military Affairs

Committee; present members (7): Lin Piao, Nieh Jung-Chen, Hsu Hsiang, Chien, Yeh Chien-ying, Huang Yung-sheng (new), Hsieh Fu-chih (new), and Su Yu (new). Members purged from the old-member Military Affairs Committee (3): Ho Lung, Lo Jui-ching, and Hsiao Hua.

June 26: The NCNA reported that 11 big and small synthetic ammonia chemical fertilizer plants had been built in Shantung Province since the beginning of 1967.

Guinea trade delegation led by Fofana Sekon left Peking for home after signing a trade protocol for 1968 between the two countries.

June 27: Vaclav Kristek, ambassador of Czechoslovakia to China, left Peking for home.

June 28: A second conference of representatives of "Four Good" Companies of the navy of the PLA opened in Peking.

A *New York Times* report from Washington quoted U.S. officials as saying that Communist China in recent days had barred use of its rail lines to ship war supplies to North Vietnam. The last train carrying military equipment to Hanoi via China, largely from the Soviet Union, was said to have entered North Vietnam June 14. U.S. officials were said to have speculated that the interruption of North Vietnam-bound supplies was the result of clashes between Red Guard factions in the three provinces bordering North Vietnam (Yunnan, Kwangsi and Kwangtung), or represented a deliberate move by Peking to penalize Hanoi for its participation in peace talks with the U.S.

June 29: Abdolwahed Al-Kherbash, new ambassador of the Arab Republic of Yemen to China, arrived in Peking.

June 30: The NCNA released the full text of the joint editorial of *People's Daily, Red Flag* and *Liberation Army Daily*—"develop the party's working style of forging close links with the masses"—in commemoration of the 47th anniversary of the founding of the Chinese Communist party.

Mao Tse-tung, Lin Piao, Chou En-lai, Chen Po-ta, Kang Sheng, Li Fu-Chun, Chiang Ching, Chang Chun-Chiao, Yao Wen-Yuan, Hsieh Fu-chih, Huang Yung-Sheng, Wu Fa-hsien, Yeh Chun, and Wang Tung-hsing received more than 20,000 PLA cadres from units stationed in the Tsinan, Canton, and Lanchow areas, representatives of "revolutionary staff members and workers," leading comrades of military control committees, and "revolutionary fighters" from other fronts.

July 1: It was reported that the PRC had refused on June 27 to accept an invitation by U.N. Secretary General U. Thant to attend, as an observer, a planned conference in Geneva August 29-September 28 of the world's non-nuclear-weapon states. It was the first time that China had been invited to attend a U.N.-sponsored conference.

Red Flag No. 1 carried an article by commentator entitled "Make Class Analysis of Factionalism."

Mao Tse-tung and Lin Piao attended a theatrical performance sponsored by the cultural revolution group in celebration of the 47th anniversary of the founding of the party.

July 3: Peking Municipal Intermediate People's Court pronounced at a mass meeting its verdict on the "fraud" case of the British Vickers-Zimmer Ltd.

July 4: Abdolwahed Al-Kherbash, new ambassador of the Arab Republic of Yemen to the PRC, presented his credentials to Tung Pi-wu, vice-chairman of the PRC.

The PRC and United Arab Republic signed in Cairo a trade protocol for 1968 and exchanged letters for the extention of the validity of the trade and payments agreements between the two countries.

July 5: Two British merchant naval officers, Captain R. V. Pope and first officer D. V. Jones, were sentenced by the PRC to be deported for alleged spying and crossed the frontier into Hong Kong.

Moscow Radio charged that rail traffic from Kwangsi into North Vietnam had been held up for several weeks because of armed strife in the province.

July 6: Soviet trade with Communist China reached an all-time low in 1967. Figures released by the Soviet Ministry of Foreign Trade and reported by the Washington Post showed that total Sino-Soviet trade in 1967 was $107 million, compared with $318.4 million in 1966 and $2.2 billion in 1959. Soviet exports to China were $49.2 million in 1967, compared with $173.5 million in 1966; imports from China fell to $5.6 million, compared with more than $141.6 million in 1966.

July 7: The PRC issued warning against the intrusion of U.S. warship into China's territorial waters off Fukien and Kwangtung Provinces, and of a U.S. military plane into her air-space over the Hsisha Islands in Kwangtung Province.

A three-member delegation from the West Pakistan Industrial Development Corporation, led by M. A. Basith, arrived in Peking.

July 9: A North Vietnamese government economic delegation, headed by Le Thanh Nghi, arrived in Peking.

July 10: A decline in Chinese trade with Communist countries in 1967 had been matched by an increase in its trade with Western Europe and Japan, countries that supplied China with machinery, chemicals, iron, and steel and other items previously provided by the Soviet Union and Eastern Europe. But figures for the first quarter of 1968 indicated a substantial drop in trade with the West and Japan. The *Washington Post* reported that total Chinese trade with Japan during the first quarter of 1968 was 26% below that of the first quarter of 1967. For the same period, China's trade with Great Britain declined by 30% and with West Germany by 19%.

The Chinese Foreign Ministry issued a statement strongly condemning "U.S. imperialism for its fresh crime of aggression against Cambodia on June 29 and expressing resolute support for the just stand of the Royal Government of Cambodia."

July 11: *People's Daily* gave front-page prominence to the experience of a *hsien* revolutionary committee in organizing a

revolutionized leading group which linked itself with the masses.

July 12: Kwangtung provincial revolutionary committee issued proclamation ordering immediate cessation of armed struggle, restoration of traffic and communications, surrender of all arms to the PLA, return of all stolen goods, and release of captives.

Kwangtung provincial revolutionary committee and Canton municipal revolutionary committee asked all persons from other provinces or *hsien* to leave Canton at once, and to surrender their arms and stolen state property to the Canton garrison command.

The NCNA released a report on the successful production of high-grade histotomes, precision cutting instrument used in microtomy, by a factory in Liaoning Province.

July 14: China's industrial production for the first part of 1968, though slightly above 1967 level, was still substantially below level reached before the start of the cultural revolution, according to the *New York Times*. The production of coal, the source of 90% of all energy utilized in China, was estimated to be 20-25% below the normal 1966 output of 240 million tons. Similar cutbacks were noted in railway mile-tonnage.

The *New York Times* reported that statistics from countries trading with Communist China placed its total 1967 trade at $4.2 billion, down 1.4% from 1966. Chinese imports increased in 1967 to approximately $2.2 billion, but exports dropped about 9% to $1.96 billion.

People's Daily reported the experience of *hsien* revolutionary committees in simplifying their administrative structures, forging close links with the masses, and leading them in the attack against the class enemy.

The PRC issued a warning against the intrusion of a U.S. warship into China's territorial waters off Fukien Province and of a U.S. military plane into China's airspace over the Hsisha Islands in Kwangtung province.

July 16: The 4th assembly of the World

Council of Churches, meeting in Uppsala, Sweden, July 4-19, adopted a 4,000-word statement which urged Communist China's admission to the U.N. and urged all governments, including France and Communist China, to sign the nuclear-weapon non-proliferation treaty.

The PRC marked the anniversary of Mao Tse-tung's swim in the Yangtze River on July 16, 1966.

July 17: Accounts of intense fighting in Kwangtung reached Hong Kong almost daily during June and July according to the *Washington Post*.

July 19: The delegation of the Central Committee of the Communist party of Indonesia published an article entitled, "Comrade Mao Tse-tung's teaching on People's War is the Indonesian people's powerful weapon for smashing the Suharto-Nasution Fascist military regime and establishing the people's democratic power in Indonesia," to hail the publication of the Indonesian version of the *Selected Military Writings of Mao Tse-tung*.

The China-Japan Friendship Association and Chinese People's Association for Cultural Relations and Friendship with Foreign Countries greeted the opening of the 17th national conference of the Japan-China Friendship Association (orthodox).

The Chinese Red Cross Society donated 100,000 rupees for the relief of flood victims in East Pakistan.

July 20: Vice-Premier Chen Yi welcomed Ngo Minh Loan, ambassador of the DRV (the Democratic Republic of Vietnam), to China.

July 21: The *New York Times* reported that the Peking Revolutionary Committee had forbidden wall posters, unofficial newspapers, and news sheets to publish government documents, reports of meetings, and speeches of Communist leaders. Official policy and decisions, the committee decreed, were to be followed only as reported in one of three official publications—*Liberation Army Daily*, the army newspaper; *People's Daily*, the Communist party paper, and *Red Flag*, the party's ideological journal.

People's Daily published an article denouncing the Sato government of Japan for its frantic efforts in reviving Japanese militarism.

July 22-23: Mao Tse-tung's latest instruction on revolution in education was issued.

July 23: A Guinean military delegation led by Colonel Kaman Diabi, deputy chief of the general staff of the people's army of the Republic of Guinea, arrived in Peking at the invitation of the Chinese Ministry of National Defense.

Agreement in Chinese economic and technical aid to North Vietnam and protocols were signed in Peking.

July 24: The CPC Central Committee, State Council, military commissions, and cultural revolution group issued notice denouncing the "agents of top capitalist roaders within the party" in Shanghai for robbery, arson, seizure of arms, and other crimes, and ordering the immediate cessation of armed struggle, return of all stolen goods, and restoration of traffic.

July 25: Reports from Canton appearing in the *New York Times* indicated that the army had actively intervened in recent clashes between the Red Flag and East Wind revolutionaries.

Chou En-lai received Mamadou Talla, envoy of the president of the Republic of Mali.

July 26: Lin Piao gave weight to the Army's strengthened role in an inscription for a special set of stamps issued July 26 commemorating the 41st PLA anniversary. The inscription read: "The PLA is a force armed with Mao Tse-tung's thought, a force that serves the people wholeheartedly, and therefore a force that is invincible."

July 29-August 5: Army Day was celebrated in China.

July 31: *Liberation Army Daily* carried an article entitled "The Gun Under the Command of Mao Tse-tung's Thought Is the Pillar of the Dictatorship of the Proletariat," to mark the August 1 Army Day.

Chinese embassy in the Arab Republic of Yemen issued a statement condemning the "grave anti-Chinese crime of the reactionary armed forces in Yemen supported by U.S. imperialism in brazenly bombarding the living quarters of the Chinese technical personnel working in Yemen and the textile plant which China has helped Yemen to build."

August 1: The celebration of the 41st anniversary of the PLA reflected the general trend toward moderation. The anniversary reception held in Peking by top military officials was not attended by senior officials with radical leanings or by leaders of the cultural revolution group; both had been honored guests at the 1967 celebration. In a joint editorial published by *People's Daily, Red Flag* and *Liberation Army Daily*, the army was directed to support revolutionary committees at all levels and to defend them from enemies of the "right" and the "extreme left." The editorial, in effect, appeared to give the army a green light to deal with China's disturbances and called upon the masses to obey its dictates.

August 3: The NCNA reported the discovery of teeth fossils of giant by young revolutionary scientific workers in Hupeh Province.

Pakistan Foreign Minister Arshad Husain arrived in Peking on a friendly visit at the invitation of the PRC government.

People's Daily published an article by the PLA People's Arms Department of Tzukung municipality, Szechwan Province, about factional struggles in Tzukung last year and how the revolutionary committee there was streamlined.

August 5: Mao Tse-tung sent mangoes to the worker-peasant propaganda team publicizing the thought of Mao Tse-tung in Tsinghua University, Peking.

August 5-15: *People's Daily* published editorials and articles in commemoration of the publication of Mao Tse-tung's big-character poster, "Bombard the Headquarters," two years ago. The editorial and articles proclaimed the absolute primacy of centralized power.

August 6: The PRC issued warning against intrusion of U.S. military planes into China's air-space over the Hsisha Islands in Kwangtung Province and over China's territorial waters off Kiangsu Province.

August 7: The 1968 Republican Party Platform, adopted at the Republican Party National Convention in Miami, said that, "Under existing conditions, we cannot favor recognition of Communist China or its admission to the U.N."

Concurrent with the apparent crackdown on factional fighting in China was the appearance of newly formed groups called "Mao Tse-tung's Thought Propaganda Teams." Composed of workers, peasants, and soldiers (with publicity centering on the workers), the teams were sent to universities and were charged with carrying out Mao's latest instructions and countering "erroneous tendencies." The campaign was launched with a flurry of publicity over "a precious gift of mangoes" sent by Mao to a propaganda team at Peking's Tsinghua University. A *People's Daily* editorial praised the formation of the teams August 7 and emphasized the necessity of "strengthening the sense of organization and revolutionary discipline . . ." Subsequently, Peking statements were reported by the *Washington Post* August 11 to have ordered *Red Guards* to integrate with the propaganda teams and obey their directions.

August 8: The second anniversary of the publication of the "sixteen-point decision" was hailed.

August 9: Bhayome Chulanond, representative of the "Patriotic Front of Thailand," gave a press conference in Peking.

August 11: Mao Tse-tung and Lin Piao received PLA cadres and other revolutionary fighters in Peking.

August 12: Sir Donald Hopson, British charge d'affaires in Peking, was granted an exit visa August 12 and left for London August 13. Sir Donald had been in Peking since May 1965 as head of the British mission. He was to have left last year but delayed his departure after the British mission building was sacked by Red Guards and set on fire on August 22, 1967. Other British officials were allowed to leave in September. L. V. Applegard, second secretary of the mission, and his family left China September 15; Alister Hunter, acting trade missioner, and his family were granted exit visas September 13.

August 12-September 25: Workers' propaganda teams entered colleges and schools.

August 13: Mao Tse-tung and other leaders received the delegation of the Italian Communist party (Marxist-Leninist).

Yunnan provincial revolutionary committee was set up.

Huang Hua, head of the Chinese government delegation and China's ambassador to the United Arab Republic, arrived at Brazzaville to attend the celebration of the 5th anniversary of the August Revolution of the Congo (B).

August 14: China-Afghanistan Friendship Association gave a film reception to mark the 5th anniversary of the founding of the association.

The PRC sent anti-cholera vaccines to Cambodia.

Washington Post reported that Mao Tse-tung had become disillusioned with the Red Guards and had bitterly condemned five Peking leaders at an all-night meeting July 28. The report said that Red Guard groups in Kirin, Liaoning, and Honan provinces had been dissolved. (The February 7 Commune, a leftist youth group that had been blessed publicly by Mao in 1967, was among the disbanded groups in Honan.)

August 15: Mao Tse-tung and Lin Piao received representatives of Peking working class and PLA commanders and fighters.

Mao Tse-tung followed the establishment of the propaganda teams with a directive issued August 15 in which he said: "Our country has 700 million people and the working class is the leading class. Its leading role in the great cultural revolution and in all fields of work should be brought into full play. The working class also should continuously enhance its political consciousness in the course of the struggle."

August 18: The celebration of the second anniversary of the Red Guard movement

August 18 indicated that the movement's powers were being curbed. An editorial in *People's Daily* that day said that the "Red Guards can have a sound future and carry the current great proletarian cultural revolution through to the end only by integrating themselves with the main force, the workers, peasants, and soldiers, armed with Mao Tse-tung's thought."

Chou En-lai received a shipping delegation from Tanzania, led by H. A. Ngirenda.

August 19: The NCNA accused the Indian government of toeing the U.S. line of creating two Chinas.

A Chinese survey team to help in the construction of the Guinea-Mali railway arrived at Conakry.

August 20: Fukien provincial revolutionary committee was set up.

Kuo Mo-jo received Chojuro Kawarazaki, standing director of the Japan-China Cultural Exchange Association.

August 21: The U.S. House of Representatives' Armed Services Sub-committee on National Defense, headed by Mr. Porter Hardy, Jr., told the U.S. Congress in a report that China would have operational deployment of a medium-range ballistic missile this year and would be able to deploy a long-range intercontinental ballistic missile by 1970.

Chen Yi received the delegation of Royal Council of Cambodia, headed by its president, Keuk Ky Heang.

August 23: Chou En-lai condemned the Soviet Union for armed occupation of Czechoslovakia in a speech at the Rumanian National Day reception in Peking.

An article in *People's Daily* denounced the Russian invasion of Czechoslovakia as "a shameless act." The article said the invasion pointed up the "total bankruptcy of Soviet revisionism." Deriding the Soviet contention that the invasion was designed to protect the fruits of socialism, the article asked: "Who capitulated to U.S. imperialism and so lost the fruits of Soviet socialism? Who was it who peddled Soviet revisionism to Europe?" The Chinese statement accused Soviet leaders of working "hand-in-glove" with the U.S. and said that "Czechoslovak revisionists" had hoped to work out similar cooperation with the U.S. and West Germany.

August 25: *Red Flag* No. 2 carried instructions by Mao Tse-tung to workers and peasants to take over and run the schools and universities. According to the instructions, it was essential for the proletarian revolution in education to be carried out by the working class. Workers' teams, recently formed to ensure diffusion of the thoughts of Mao Tse-tung, should head the country's schools. Peasants, "the surest allies of the working class," should run schools in the countryside.

Another article reported that the workers' teams had begun to take control of newspapers and press organs. The article reviewed the history of the Communist Chinese press and called for increased "class struggle" to get rid of the "reactionary revisionist line of the journalistic front." It condemned the publication of unauthorized and classified news, apparently in criticism of the numerous Red Guard tabloids that had published secret documents and reports of conferences.

August 26-September 5: The PRC Foreign Ministry lodged a protest with the Soviet government against the intrusion of Soviet occupation troops into the Chinese embassy in Czechoslovakia.

The PRC Foreign Ministry lodged a protest with the British government against Hong Kong's cancelling the registration of Chung Wah Middle School.

August 27: The 80 non-aligned nations at the Geneva Conference of the 18-nation U.N. Disarmament Committee denounced France and Communist China for carrying out atmospheric nuclear tests.

Kwangsi autonomous regional revolutionary committee was set up.

August 28: A Canton Red Guard bulletin quoted by the *New York Times* provided evidence that the cultural revolution had slowed China's nuclear weapon progress. The bulletin said that Nieh Jung-chen, director of the scientific and technological commission for national defense, had been

forced to submit a written self-criticism to Chairman Mao and was assigned to the personal charge of Premier Chou En-lai for a period of self-examination.

August 29: 1968 Democratic Party platform, adopted at the Democratic Party National Convention in Chicago, said that "the immediate prospects that China will emerge from its self-imposed isolation are dim. But both Asians and Americans will have to coexist with the 750 million Chinese on the mainland. We shall continue to make it clear that we are prepared to cooperate with China whenever it is ready to become a responsible member of the international community. We would actively encourage economic, social, and cultural exchange with mainland China as a means of freeing that nation and her people from their unhealthy isolation."

August 29-31: The tenth anniversary of the publication of Mao Tse-tung's instruction, "people's communes are fine," commemorated.

August 30: In a statement published in the August 30 *Peking Review*, Mao stated that "the workers' propaganda teams should stay permanently in the schools and take part in fulfilling all the tasks of struggle-criticism-transformation in the schools, and they will always lead in those institutions. In the countryside, the schools should be managed by the poor and lower-middle peasants—the most reliable ally of the working class."

The *Red Flag* article written by Yao Wen-yhan (published in *Peking Review* August 30) accused Red Guard elements of undermining national unity. Certain Red Guards, he said, ". . . incited the masses to struggle against each other, and set themselves to sabotage the great cultural revolution, disrupt struggle-criticism-transformation, undermine the great alliance and the revolutionary 'three-in-one' combination and obstruct the work of purifying the class rank and of party rectification." He ordered the Red Guards and all "intellectuals" to obey the workers' propaganda teams.

August 31: The head of the Chinese pavillion at the 15th Damascus International Fair gave a reception on the occasion of the "Chinese Pavillion Day."

The 23rd anniversary of the proclamation of independence by the Democratic Republic of Vietnam was greeted.

September 1-18: *People's Daily* published articles against "China's Khrushchev."

September 2: Chou En-lai spoke at the National Day reception in Peking given by Ngo Minh Loon, Vietnamese ambassador to China. In the speech, he devoted most of his remarks to an attack on the Soviet Union and only perfunctorily referred to North Vietnam. He predicted that the Soviet Union would betray North Vietnam by recognizing the Middle East and Southeast Asia as a U.S. sphere of influence in return for U.S. recognition of Eastern Europe as a Soviet sphere of influence. He cited the invasion of Czechoslovakia as an example of the U.S.-Soviet division of the world.

September 3: The NCNA reported the establishment of revolutionary committees in all the 15 administrative districts and municipalities and the 75 *hsien* in Anhwei province.

September 5: Peking Radio announced that revolutionary committees loyal to Mao Tse-tung had been set up in Tibet Autonomous Region and Sinkiang Uighur Autonomous Region, thus bringing all 29 of China's administrative regions under its control.

Another Peking note, delivered to the Soviet charge d'affaires, charged that Soviet troops in Prague had distributed anti-Chinese literature outside the embassy, threatened the safety of its members, and intercepted its foreign visitors. The strong protest demanded the removal of Soviet troops outside the Chinese embassy in Prague and a halt to all "provocative activities."

The Pakistan government presented mangoes and mango saplings in China as a token of Sino-Pakistani friendship.

September 7: *People's Daily, Red Flag* and *Liberation Army Daily* published a joint editorial entitled "Long Live All-Round Victory of the Great Proletarian Cultural Revolution," hailing the establishment of revolutionary committees in every province, municipality, and autonomous region in China.

The NCNA reported the establishment of revolutionary committees in all administrative districts, cities and *hsien* in the Ninghsia Hui Autonomous Region.

The *London Times* reported that 13 British subjects were thought to be detained in China. David C. Johnson, branch manager of the Chartered Bank in Shanghai, reportedly had been arrested August 25. Other British citizens under detention included Anthony Grey, a *Reuters* correspondent, several seamen, an engineer, and a woman married to a Chinese. The foreign office in London on September 6 protested to Sheng Ping, Chinese charge d'affaires, about the unexplained detentions.

Chou En-lai and Chiang Ching spoke at a Peking rally celebrating the establishment of revolutionary committees all over China. Both stressed the leading role of the working class in China's future. Miss Chiang called on Red Guards to accept the leadership of the working class, but urged workers to "protect young Red Guard fighters, help them, and educate them." Chou's speech did not mention the Red Guards except in greeting. He stressed that "young people should respond to the call of our great leader, Chairman Mao, go to the grassroot levels, to the masses and to production, settle in mountainous areas and the countryside, and take part in physical work in factories, mines, and villages." "We should call on the revolutionary people all over the country to accept working class leadership," he said.

September 8: Western news agency reports from Hong Kong quoted a Red Guard science bulletin published in Peking as saying that five scientists had been jailed for treason and spying for the Soviet Union. The Red Guards Scientific Technological War News Bulletin said that the five men were headed by a nuclear physicist, Mr. Wang Kan-chang, who was either director or deputy director of the Physics Research Institute of the Chinese academy of science, and followed by Hua Lo-kenk (former Illinois professor), Chien San-Chiang, per L-Seng, and Tu Jun-Sheng.

The new Chinese provincial committees are ruled by men whose primary ties were with the military. According to the *Washington Post*, 19 of the 29 revolutionary committees were controlled by army commanders, though most of them were men with long service in Communist party posts. Except for seven committees established by Red Guard and radical elements early in the cultural revolution, the group generally were created only after lengthy negotiations between local officials and the party leadership in Peking.

September 9: Chen Yi spoke at a reception given by Kim Jai Sook, charge d'affaires ad interim of the Korean embassy in China, celebrating the 20th anniversary of the founding of the Democratic People's Republic of Korea.

September 10: *Red Flag* No. 3 published an article entitled, "The revolution in education in colleges of science and engineering as reflected in the struggle between the two lines at the Shanghai Institute of mechanical engineering."

Red Flag No. 3 carried an investigation report entitled, "The orientation of revolution in medical education as seen from the 'barefoot doctors.'"

Red Flag No. 3 carried two articles by workers about the grasping of leadership and technical power by workers.

The NCNA reported the establishment of revolutionary committees at various levels in Kirin Province.

Hoxha and Shehu of Albania greeted the establishment of revolutionary committees in all provinces, municipalities, and autonomous regions in China.

Assane Guindo, new ambassador of the Republic of Mali to the PRC, arrived in Peking.

September 11: The NCNA released the text of a joint commentators' article of the *People's Daily* and *Red Flag* entitled, "On the Question of Re-educating Intellectuals."

September 12: A delegation of the Central Committee of the Communist party of Burma issued a statement greeting the victory of China's cultural revolution.

September 13: Chen Yi received S. M. Yusuf, foreign secretary of the Ministry of Foreign Affairs of Pakistan.

Lin Ping-nan, charge d'affaires ad interim of the Chinese embassy in Guinea, gave a reception in celebration of the 8th anniversary of the Sino-Guinean friendship treaty.

September 14: Mao Tse-tung's latest instruction on re-educating the intellectuals acclaimed all over China.

The NCNA reported the establishment of revolutionary committees at all levels in Kwangtung province.

September 15: The PRC issued a warning against the intrusion of a U.S. warship into China's territorial waters east of Fukien Province.

Malayan Communist party greeted the establishment of revolutionary committees throughout China.

September 15-21: Chen Yi received Mohamed Scek Yusuf Perbi, minister of state of the Somali Republic.

September 16: The PRC charged formally that Soviet aircraft had violated its northeastern borders. A note presented to the Soviet charge d'affaires in Peking, Y. N. Razdukhov, listed 29 intrusions over Heilungkiang Province August 9-29 and 119 intrusions during the past year. The protest was the first publicized complaint against the alleged border violations; it accused Moscow of engineering "reconnaissance, harassment, and provocation" flights to support its "aggression against Czechoslovakia." The Soviet government newspaper *Izvestia* November 2 denied the Chinese allegations and asserted that Soviet aircraft were prohibited from flying in certain border areas.

The NCNA reported the establishment of revolutionary committees in all eight administrative districts, three municipalities and 93 *hsien* in Shensi Province.

People's Daily and *Red Flag* jointly published a report of an investigation into the experience gained by a commoner in Liaoning province, entitled, "It Is Essential to Rely on the Poor and Lower-Middle Peasants in Revolutionizing Education in the Countryside."

Joern Stenbach Hansen, new ambassador extraordinary and plenipotentiary of the Kingdom of Denmark to the PRC, arrived in Peking.

September 17: The NCNA reported the establishment of revolutionary committees in all the 10 administrative districts and 126 *hsien* and municipalities in Honan Province.

A televised "struggle" meeting was held in Shanghai against Chen Pei-hsien and Tsao Ti-Chiu under the sponsorship of the "Attack with Words, Defend with Arms" command.

September 18: The *Washington Post* reported that Wu Chuan-pin, head of the Red Flag, a large Red Guard organization at Chungshan University in Canton, had been arrested. He was accused of being a "counter-revolutionary double-dealer" who had opposed the Canton military leaders and provoked "numerous derived clashes" at Chungshan University. He was also charged with espionage, sexual promiscuity, and instigating a handful of hooligans in the killing of a student who was "the son of poor peasants."

Chen Yi gave a banquet in honor of Southern Yemeni Foreign Minister Saif Ahmad Dhalai and the delegation of the People's Republic of Southern Yemen.

September 18-26: The Chinese embassy in Burma lodged a protest with the Burmese government against the persecution of "patriotic" overseas Chinese.

September 19: The NCNA reported the establishment of revolutionary committees in all the 10 administrative districts and 95 *hsien* and municipalities in Hunan Province.

Amoy municipal revolutionary committee was established at a meeting of more than 10,000 representatives of workers' Mao Tse-tung's thought propaganda teams held in Shanghai; Chang Chun Chiao and Yao Wen-Yuan attended and spoke at the meeting.

The NCNA reported the arrival of about 60 Chinese technicians at Katmandu to work on the construction project of the Sunkosi hydraulic power station.

Chen Yi received Cambodian Foreign Minister Norodom Phurissara.

September 20: The NCNA reported the establishment of revolutionary committees in all the nine administrative districts, four municipalities and 112 *hsien* of Shantung Province.

September 21: Delegation from the Ministry of Culture of the Vietnam Democratic Republic, led by Vice-Minister Co. Huycan, arrived in Peking.

Chinese-African People's Friendship Association gave a reception to mark the 8th anniversary of the founding of the Republic of Mali.

September 22: Chinese Survey, design group for Tanzania-Zambia Railway, arrived in Lusaka.

A *Washington Post* report said that key Red Guard leaders in Peking had been arrested. The most prominent of them, arrested by the propaganda team at Tsinghua University, was Kuai Ta-fu, head of one of the first youth units of the cultural revolution. At least eight Red Guard units in Peking were reported to have been disbanded or purged of extremist elements.

September 24: The general secretary of the Ceylon Communist party greeted the establishment of revolutionary committees throughout China.

September 25: *People's Daily* and *Liberation Army Daily* published joint editorial to celebrate the first anniversary of Mao Tse-tung's inspection tour of North, Central-South, and East China.

The NCNA reported the establishment of revolutionary committees in all cities, administrative regions, and *hsien* of Hupeh Province.

Delegation of New Zealand Communist

party led by Joy Foulds arrived at Peking to attend China's National Day celebrations.

The NCNA reported that China had attained an "all-around leap forward" in industrial production in 1968. The dispatch claimed that workers throughout the country had pushed production "to new levels of quantity, quality, and variety." The report cited figures from industrial cities and plants and compared relatively short periods of time; it did not list any nation-wide statistics or make any comparisons with 1967.

Stanley Karnow reported in *Washington Post* that illegal private enterprises had sprung up throughout China due to the breakdown in central political and economic controls resulting from the cultural revolution. The businesses apparently included small- and medium-sized factories producing glassware, leather goods, textiles, hardware, mechanical devices, and other consumer merchandise. In addition, some peasants were said to be selling rice, wheat, edible oils, cotton, and other agricultural products to free-lance intermediaries rather than to the prescribed state purchasing agents.

September 26: The NCNA reported the establishment of revolutionary committees in all administrative districts, cities, and *hsien* of Kansu Province.

September 26-30: The PRC government and military delegation headed by Chang Ting left Peking for Conakry to attend the 10th anniversary of the independence of the Republic of Guinea.

September 27: The PRC and Nepal signed an agreement on the construction of the Katmandu-Bhaktapur highway.

The *London Times* reported that propaganda teams had been sent into finance and trade units, hospitals, and local government offices.

September 28: The first all-weather road linking Gilgit in Azad Kashmir with Skardu in Chinese Sinkiang was opened by the Pakistan minister for Kashmir affairs, Vice-Admiral A. R. Khan.

Pakistan government goodwill delegation headed by Syek Fida Hassan, adviser to President Mohammed Ayub Khan, arrived in Peking. The *New York Times* reported that Communist China had agreed to finance a $29-million foundry at Texila as an adjunct to their $31-million mechanical complex already under construction in that city. Since 1960, China had granted $100 million to Pakistan.

Albanian party and government delegation arrived in Peking.

Chen Yi received Ho Hue Bo, member of the Central Committee of the South Vietnam National Front for Liberation and South Vietnamese combat hero Hoang Thuc Ba.

Chen Yi received Sithon Khommadam, vice-chairman of the Central Committee of Neo Lao Haksat, and Thimouan and Nhia Vu, members of the Standing Committee of the Central Committee of Neo Lao Haksat.

Chinese-African People's Friendship Association gave a reception to mark the 10th anniversary of the founding of the Republic of Guinea.

September 29: The NCNA announced publication of a deluxe single volume pocket size edition of the *Selected Works of Mao Tse-tung* on the eve of China's National Day.

A ten-member delegation sent jointly by the Japan-China Friendship Association (Orthodox) and the Japan-China Cultural Exchange Association, headed by Hisao Kuroda, arrived in Peking.

September 29-30: National Day greetings received from Albania, Neo Lao Haksat, Pakistan, Rumania, South Vietnam National Front for Liberation, Southwest African National Union, and Democratic Republic of Vietnam.

September 30: China's National Day was celebrated in Tirana and Hanoi.

Agreement on mutual commodity supply and payment in 1969 between the PRC and the DRV was signed in Peking.

October 1: The 19th anniversary of the founding of the PRC was celebrated. As usual, the main highlight of the celebrations was the parade at Tienanmen Square in Peking. The keynote speech was made by Defense Minister Lin Piao. He praised Mr. Mao Tse-tung for leading China for 19 years, the great cultural revolution, and the working class. He briefly referred to the work of building the party, but did not dwell on it. He said that China should step up war preparedness and help smash the "conspiracy of the U.S. and Russia" to divide the world. The full official list of Chinese leaders was as follows: Mao Tse-tung (chairman), Lin Piao (vice-chairman), Chou En-lai (premier), Chen Po-ta (Mao's secretary), Kang Sheng (ex-secret police chief), Chiang Ching (Mao's wife), Chang Chun Chiao (chairman of the Shanghai revolutionary committee), Yao Wen-Yuan (Chiang Ching's spokesman), Hsieh Fu-chih (public security minister and chairman of the Peking revolutionary committee), Huang Yung-Sheng (PLA chief of staff and chairman of Kwangtung revolutionary committee), Wu Fa-hsien (PLA deputy chief of staff), Mrs. Yeh Chun (Lin Piao's wife), Wang Tung-hsing (director of the central committee's general office), Wen Nu-cheng (deputy minister of public security).

The 20,100-foot Nanking bridge on the Yangtze River was opened to traffic.

The PRC's celebration of its 19th National Day gave evidence that Peking's tie with North Vietnam had further deteriorated. Relations between the two countries had been strained due to the interruption of Vietnam-bound war supplies as a result of the factional political clashes sweeping China. The Vietnamese war had been a major focus of previous National Day celebrations, but the 1968 Peking ceremonies contained only perfunctory reference to the war.

Soviet-bloc diplomats walked out of four recent Peking receptions at which Chinese officials attacked the U.S.S.R. for the invasion of Czechoslovakia and collusion with the U.S. The receptions were in honor of the Rumanian National Day, August 24; the Mali National Day, September 23; the visiting Albanian deputy minister, September 29, and the PRC's National Day, October 1.

Writing in the *Washington Post*, Stanley Karrow said that the cultural revolution, launched to rid the party of "revisionists," had shattered the party bureaucracy, the only national political machinery in China. The 29 provincial revolutionary committees apparently possessed more power over local matters than the six regional party bureaus they replaced. Further, the committee chairmen often appeared to be more responsive to local conditions than to orders from Peking.

A National Day editorial published jointly by *People's Daily, Red Flag,* and *Liberation Army Daily* stressed the need to rebuild the Communist party. The editorial said that it was necessary to "admit into the party a number of outstanding proletarian revolutionary rebel fighters who have been tempered and tested in the cultural revolution, and primarily advanced elements among industrial workers, thereby impressing the party with new blood and strengthening its fighting force." "We must give a very important position to the work of consolidating and building the party."

October 2: Lin Piao met Begir Balluku, head of the Albanian party and government delegation; Chou En-lai, Huang Yung-Sheng, and Wen Yu-Cheng held talks with the group.

October 4: Hong Kong branch of the New China News Agency lodged a protest with the British authorities in Hong Kong against their unwarranted searching and beating of NCNA reporters engaging in normal reporting activities.

October 5: Mao Tse-tung, Lin Piao, Chou En-lai, Chen Po-ta, Kang Sheng, Chiang Ching, Chang Chun-Chiao, Yao Wen-Yuan, Hsieh Fu-chih, Huang Yung-Sheng, Wa Fa-hsien, Yeh Chun, Wang Tung-hsing, and Wen Yu-Cheng received leading members of revolutionary committees and works' representatives from various provinces, autonomous regions, and municipalities who had attended National Day celebrations in the capital.

Mao Tse-tung and Lin Piao received the Albanian party and government delegation.

Shanghai municipal revolutionary committee held an enlarged meeting to discuss Mao Tse-tung's latest instruction on sending cadres to the lower level to do manual labor.

The NCNA released a report on new contributions by members of the Chinese academy of agriculture sciences.

A document was signed turning over to Cambodia the Cambodian Siem Reap airport built with Chinese aid.

October 5-7: Chen Yi received Co Hug Can, vice-minister of culture of the DRV, and other members of the delegation of the DRV Ministry of Culture.

October 8: A report by the CPC Central Committee's special panel on "renegade, traitor and scab" Liu Shao-chi published, according to a Foochow tabloid.

Chen Yi received members of the delegation sent jointly by the Japan-China Friendship Association (Orthodox) and the Japan-China Cultural Exchange Association.

The PRC government and military delegation headed by Chang Ting left Conakry for home.

October 9-11: Delegation of Albanian State University of Tirana, led by Fehmi Shehu, vice-director of the University, arrived in Peking.

October 11-23: Albanian government economic delegation arrived in Peking.

October 11: Chou En-lai sent a message to Prince Souphanouvong, Chairman of the Central Committee of the Neo Lao Haksat, greeting the 23rd anniversary of the Laotian Revolutionary Day.

October 13: A *New York Times* report said that the government offices in Shanghai had sent "40% of the cadres to do manual work." In addition, the ruling revolutionary committee of the city had declared "that no one could dodge doing manual work on any pretext."

Another *New York Times* report indicated that the establishment of worker-soldier-peasant propaganda teams had affected industrial production, though there had not been any definite evidence of widespread economic dislocation. Shanghai Radio reported that 80% of the city's factories and other enterprises had "simplified" their administration or were "streamlining the management" through reduction of "non-productive personnel." Peking Radio reported October 9 that the Tientsin steel mill had lost 87% of its 1,100 workers to agriculture.

Exhibition on class struggle opened in the Santiooshin Historical Museum in Tientsin.

October 14: *Red Flag* No. 4 carried an editorial entitled, "Take in fresh blood from the proletariat—an important question in the party rectification."

Red Flag No. 4 published two articles on "better troops and simpler administration."

Red Flag No. 4 carried an article by Chang Hsing-pei concerning a certain air force unit of the Lanchou units about how the PLA Mao-tung's thought propaganda teams propagated Mao's thought among and served the peasants in the Chienho mountainous area.

Red Flag No. 4 carried an article by Keng Chang-so, a farm labor model of Hopei, entitled, "Always Follow Chairman Mao in Making Revolution."

Red Flag No. 4 published an alleged leaflet by the "Stalin group" entitled "Take the Road of Stalin."

October 15: Peking Radio reported that Mr. Liu Shao-chi had been deprived of all party posts. Mr. Liu, who is 70, had not been seen in public since early 1967 when a campaign was mounted against him by followers of Mao Tse-tung. The broadcast did not say whether Mr. Liu was still holding his government post of chairman of the republic.

According to the *Toronto Globe and Mail*, the fall harvest in China indicated that the 1968 production of rice and wheat would top the record 1967 level. China's 20 major wheat-producing areas had reportedly exceeded their quota by the beginning of October in spite of floods and drought in parts of the country. By September 10, winter wheat and early rice harvest were said to have exceeded the 1967 total by 16.7%. (However, Stanley Karnow, writing in the *Washington Post* November 23, said that specialists had estimated a 5% drop in Chinese grain products in 1968; his article also speculated that rural bureaucratic breakdowns, resulting from the cultural revolution, had hampered government control over agricultural production.)

Mao Tse-tung greeted Enver Hoxha's 60th birthday.

October 15-November 15: China's 1968 autumn export commodities fair opened in Canton.

October 17-21: *People's Daily* published articles by workers, peasants, and soldiers acclaiming Mao Tse-tung's latest instruction on building the party by getting rid of the waste and letting in the fresh.

October 19: Stanislav Kohousek, new ambassador of the Czechoslovak Socialist Republic to the PRC, arrived in Peking.

October 21: The NCNA denounced the Soviet-Czechoslovak treaty for long-term Soviet military occupation of Czechoslovakia.

October 23: The PRC issued a warning against the intrusion of a U.S. warship into China's territorial waters east of the Matsu Islands in Fukien Province, and of a U.S. military plane into China's airspace over the Hsisha Islands in Kwangtung Province.

Chinese-African People's Friendship Association gave a reception to mark the 4th anniversary of the independence of the Republic of Zambia.

October 24: The Chinese embassy in Burma sent memorandum to the Burmese government demanding that it take measures to cut all "sinister activities of the Chiang Kai-shek bandit clique's elements in Burma."

October 27: The Central Committee of the Communist Party of Italy (Marxist-Leninist) greeted the establishment of revolutionary committees in all provinces,

municipalities, and autonomous regions throughout China.

The *New York Times* reported that the number of Red Guard publications regularly reaching the West via Hong Kong had dropped from 98 in July to 18 in September.

October 30: The PRC issued a warning against the intrusion of U.S. warships and military planes into China's territorial waters and air-space off and over Fukien and Kwangtung provinces.

October 31: The CPC Central Committee announced that Chief of State Liu Shao-chi was formally stripped of "all posts both inside and outside the party" and had been expelled from the party "once and for all". The announcement was made in a communique issued at the close of the Central Committee's 12th plenary session, held secretly in Peking October 13-31. Labeling Liu a "renegade, traitor, and scab" and a "lackey of imperialism, modern revisionism, and Kuomintang reactionaries," the committee pledged to "settle accounts with him and his accomplices for their crimes." Liu's official positions at the time of the announcement were: Chairman of the republic and the National Defense Council; first of the five vice-chairmen of the CPC Central Committee and a vice-chairman of the party's politburo.

The communique issued October 31 on the "Enlarged 12th plenary session of the 8th Central Committee" also affirmed the success of the cultural revolution and stated that Mao Tse-tung's plans for carrying out the revolution, along with Defense Minister Lin Piao's views, "are all correct." The communique called for re-education of China's intellectuals by the "workers, peasants and soldiers," and stated that plans were under way for convening the 9th National Party Congress, which was to be held at "an appropriate time." The "enlarged" plenary session included members and alternate members of the Central Committee (a total of almost 200 persons), "all members" of the cultural revolution group, and "principal responsible comrades" of the 29 revolutionary committees and the people's Liberation Army.

Decision on the "(Draft) Constitution of the Communist party of China" was adopted by the enlarged 12th plenum of the 8th Central Committee of the CPC, according to a Foochow tabloid.

November 2: *People's Daily* reported the setting up in September of a communication network called the "Red line" for relaying Mao's latest instructions to the rural populace in Huaiyin *hsien* in Chekiang Province.

November 5: Stanislav Kohousk, new ambassador and plenipotentiary of the Czechoslovak Socialist Republic to the PRC, presented his credentials to Tung pi-wu, vice-chairman of the PRC.

November 8-15: Pakistan armed forces goodwill delegation arrived in Peking.

November 11: The NCNA reported that revolutionary committees had been set up in all parts of Fukien Province, excepting Quemoy.

November 11-12: The NCNA and *People's Daily* published reports on mass criticism and repudiation against Liu Shao-chi.

November 12: The PRC Foreign Ministry lodged a protest with the Indian government against its "intensified efforts to create 'two Chinas'."

November 12-21: B. F. Hill, chairman of the Australian Communist party (Marxist-Leninist) arrived in Peking on a visit at the invitation of the CPC Central Committee.

November 14: The NCNA accused Indonesia of attempting to tear up the Sino-Indonesian dual nationality treaty.

People's Daily published a report on the activities of a Mao Tse-tung's thought spare-time literary and art propaganda team in Erhlangmiao Commune, Lu Shan *hsien*, Honan Province.

November 15: The sale of 58½ million bushels of wheat to Communist China was announced by Commerce of Trade Minister Jean-Lnc Pepin. The contract, signed in Canton by a mission of the Canadian Wheat Board, was the 5th

negotiated under a long-term agreement running from August 1, 1966, to July 31, 1969. The current sale at about $115 million brought the total amount purchased by China under the 3-year arrangement to 235 million bushels, worth about $470 million. Under the long-term contract, China had pledged to buy 168-280 million bushels. Pepin said that the 45 million bushels still available to China would allow time for negotiations toward a new agreement. Deliveries for the current sale would take place between December 1968 and July 1969.

Chou En-lai sent a message to Pakistan President Ayub Khan expressing cordial regards to him on his escape from an attempt on his life.

November 16: British officials in Hong Kong released Hsieh Ping, a Chinese Communist journalist imprisoned in 1967; he had been convicted for taking part in the Communist uprisings against the Colony's government. Another Chinese journalist convicted on similar charges was not released and 13 others were being held indefinitely. Officials hoped that the Chinese would reciprocate by freeing Grey, but Hong Kong Communist newspapers reported November 17 that he would not be released until all the Chinese journalists had been freed.

November 16-20: J. W. Kihampa, junior minister of agriculture and cooperatives and chairman of Lint and Seed Marketing Board of Tanzania, arrived in Peking.

November 19: The U.N. General Assembly rejected a resolution calling on the U.N. to seat Communist China and expel Nationalist China by 58-44-23 (Indonesia was absent). The Assembly earlier had adopted by 73-47-5 a resolution declaring the issue of Communist China's membership to be an "important question" under Article 18 of the U.N. Charter, one requiring a 2/3 majority of members present and voting for adoption of a resolution. The Assembly also rejected, by 30-67-27, an Italian proposal for appointment of a special committee to investigate Communist China's position with regard to U.N. membership and to recommend "an equitable and practical solution to the question of the representation of China" at the next Assembly session. The Italian resolution was also made by 63-32-29 an "important question" under Article 18. The Assembly's debate on the matter had begun November 11.

November 20: Memorial Hall, built in honor of Lei Feng, was completed in the Lei Feng production brigade of the Lei Feng People's Commune in Changshe *hsien*, Hunan Province.

An economic agreement and two protocols were signed by the PRC and Albania in Peking.

The *Wall Street Journal* reported that Communist China had cut the only remaining telephone cable to the U.S. The cable, which linked Oakland, Cal., and Shanghai, handled about 20 calls per year; it was opened in 1937. The circuit had operated continuously except during World War II.

November 22: The NCNA released a report on the recent launching of a new 10,000-ton ocean-going vessel named "Kaoyang" which was designed and built by Chinese workers and technicians.

The 5th anniversary of the signing of the Sino-Afghan boundary treaty was marked in Peking.

The PRC embassy in Tirana gave a reception marking the 19th anniversary of the establishment of diplomatic relations between the PRC and Albania.

November 24: *People's Daily*, *Red Flag*, and *Liberation Army Daily* published a joint editorial entitled, "Study of the History of the Struggle Between the Two Lines Conscientiously."

The NCNA released once again the full text of Mao Tse-tung's report to the second plenum of the 7th CPC Central Committee on March 5, 1949.

Red Flag No. 5 published a series of articles against Liu Shao-chi.

Red Flag No. 5 carried an article entitled, "Indigenous Experts and the Revolution in Agricultural Education."

It also published an investigation re-

port of Liaoning Province entitled, "A Primary School Where Poor and Lower-Middle Peasants Hold Power." Also published was an article by a member of the workers' Mao Tse-tung's thought propaganda team stationed at the Shanghai Foreign Languages Institute, making a concrete analysis of the specific problems he faced.

November 26: Peking proposed that its representatives meet with those of the Nixon administration February 20, 1969, in Warsaw. The statement, issued by the Foreign Ministry, called on the U.S. to join "an agreement on the five principles of peaceful co-existence" and "to immediately withdraw all its armed forces from China's Taiwan Province and the Taiwan Straits and dismantle all its military installations in Taiwan Province."

Acting British charge d'affaires in Peking, Percy Craddock, and a British mission staff member, R. R. Garside, were allowed a 25-minute visit with Grey. They were the correspondent's first visitors since April. Grey, confined in a 12-foot by 12-foot room and denied books since August, was said to be suffering from his isolation.

Chinese party, government, and army delegation headed by Huang Yung-Sheng left for Albania.

Chinese-African People's Friendship Association gave a reception in celebration of the 8th anniversary of the Islamic Republic of Mauritania.

November 28: Mao Tse-tung, Lin Piao, and Chou En-lai greeted the 24th anniversary of the liberation of Albania.

November 29: Washington officials reported that the U.S. had decided to accept Peking's proposal that their ambassadors meet in Warsaw February 20, 1969, and renew the suspended U.S. Communist Chinese ambassadorial talks.

Prime Minister Elliot Trudeau said that Canada should recognize Communist China but that difficulty would evolve in relations with Nationalist China.

December 2: *People's Daily* published an article by its commentator entitled, "Insurmountable Contradictions, Inextricable

Crisis," dealing with "the financial crisis in the capitalist world."

December 3: *People's Daily* published an article entitled, "Let us Take Vice-Chairman Lin Piao as Our Brilliant Example of Boundless Loyalty to Chairman Mao's Revolutionary Line," about "the struggle between the two lines in the northeast region after the victory of the anti-Japanese war."

December 10: Ex-U.S. Ambassador to the U.N. Arthur J. Goldberg said, in a televised interview, that he favored seating both Communist China and Nationalist China in the U.N. He said that the "U.N. should be a place where all nations of the world gather" and that the U.S. "ought not to be a barrier to the admission of mainland China." He said that a change in the U.S. policy "would revolutionize the attitude of the world community toward the U.S., and I think would have profound effects in helping liberalize developments on mainland China."

Spokesman for the Chinese department concerned lodged a strong protest against a U.S. military helicopter strafing Chinese fishing boats on the high seas off Hainan Island on December 5.

December 14: Chinese water conservation and agriculture study group led by Lu Teh arrived in Dar-es-Salaam.

Albanian leaders sent a message to Chinese leaders thanking the latter for greetings on the occasion of the 24th anniversary of the liberation of Albania.

Pakistan Ambassador to the PRC Sultan M. Khan left Peking for home.

December 16: The British government named John P. Derson, 42, as acting charge d'affairs in Peking.

The PRC Foreign Ministry lodged a strong protest with the Burmese government against its "illegal arrest and brutal killing of overseas Chinese, and persecution of Chinese border inhabitants."

The NCNA accused the "Rahmen-Lee Kuan Yew puppet clique of frenziedly expanding arms and preparing for war in Singapore in the service of the U.S.

and British imperialist policy of aggression in Southeast Asia."

December 17: The NCNA reported that revolutionary committees had been established at all levels in Yunnan Province.

December 18: Chinese People's association for cultural relations and friendship with foreign countries and China-Vietnam Friendship Association gave a film reception to mark the 8th anniversary of the founding of the South Vietnam National Front for Liberation.

The 8th anniversary of both the founding of the China-Cambodian Friendship Association and the signing of the Sino-Cambodian treaty of friendship and mutual non-aggression was marked in Peking.

December 19: Mao Tse-tung, Lin Piao, and Chou En-lai sent message of greetings to President Nguyen Hun tho on 8th anniversary of the founding of the South Vietnam National Front for Liberation.

The *New York Times* reported that a major administrative reorganization of rural communes was underway in some areas of Communist China. Communes were reported to have been merged into larger collective units and farming teams absorbed by larger brigades. The recent moves appeared to be a step in returning to the type of controlled administrative set-up that existed during the beginning of the "Great Leap Forward" in 1958. In many rural areas of mainland China the cultural revolution had resulted in breakdown of central political and economic controls.

December 20: Photographic exhibition on the South Vietnamese people's "war against U.S. aggression and for national salvation" opened in Peking.

December 21: Lin Piao sent a message of greetings to Vo Nguyen Giap on the occasion of the 24th anniversary of the founding of the Vietnamese people's army.

December 22: Moslems in Peking celebrated the annual Bairam Festival at the Tungszu Mosque.

December 24-29. The PRC government trade delegation, led by Lin Hai-yun, acting minister of foreign trade, arrived in Rawalpindi.

December 25: Delegation of the Communist party of New Zealand, composed of Jack Manson and Ralph Hegman, arrived in Peking.

December 26: Agreement on economic and technical cooperation between the PRC and Pakistan was signed in Rawalpindi, providing for an interest-free loan to Pakistan of 100,000,000 yuan.

December 27: The NCNA denounced the British government for using the case of Anthony Grey to "fan up an anti-China outcry."

The U.S. Atomic Energy Commission announced that Communist China carried out an atmospheric nuclear-weapon test earlier the same day in the Lop Nor area of Sinkiang, and that it had a yield of three megatons (about 3,000,000 tons of TNT). The test—the eighth held to date by Communist China—took place on the day following the 75th birthday of Mao Tse-tung. The NCNA confirmed December 28 that China had conducted a hydrogen-bomb test in the western region of China on December 27 and described it as "another great victory for the invincible thought of Mao Tse-tung and another fruitful result of the great proletarian cultural revolution."

December 29: The whole of the double-decker, double-track Yangtze River bridge was completed and opened to traffic ahead of schedule.

December 30: Chou En-lai, Chen Po-ta, Hsien Fu-chih, Huang Yung-Sheng, and Wu Fa-hsien gave a farewell banquet to Albanian ambassador to the PRC, Vasil Nathanacti

Spokesman of the PLA headquarters on the Fukien front announced that the artillery forces had been ordered to suspend shelling for two days on December 31 and January 31 (against Quemoy and Matsu).

China-Cuba Friendship Association gave a film reception to mark the 10th anniversary of the liberation of Cuba.

December 31: The NCNA released the full text of the 1969 New Year Day editorial of the *People's Daily, Red Flag,* and *Liberation Army Daily* entitled, "Place Mao Tse-tung's thought in command of everything."

The NCNA released excerpts from a letter sent by the Marxist-Leninist Communist party of France to the CPC Central Committee hailing the publication of the communique of the enlarged 12th plenum of the 8th Central Committee of the CPC.

1969

January 1: The *People's Daily* carried a New Year's Day editorial of *People's Daily*, *Red Flag* and *Liberation Army Daily* entitled "Place Mao Tse-tung's Thought in Command of Everything." The editorial was devoted almost entirely to the necessity for order and unity and called on the Chinese people to establish "democratic centralism" and to "consciously use Mao Tse-tung's thought to achieve unified thinking, policies, plans, command and actions." In addition, the editorial officially announced that the Chinese Communist Party would hold its Ninth National Party Congress this year.

The year's first issue of *Red Flag* carried an article about sending educated youth to the countryside for re-education.

January 2: The NCNA reported that 150 million sets of *Selected Works of Mao Tse-tung* had been published in China in the past three years.

Khwaja Mohammad Kaiser, new Ambassador Extraordinary and Plenipotentiary of Pakistan to China, arrived in Peking.

January 3: In a written interview published January 3 by the Japanese newspaper *Mainichi* and January 5 by *Pravda*, Premier Kosygin expressed his conviction that Sino-Soviet friendship would "triumph sooner or later." He asserted that "no matter how difficult the adjustment of our relations may seem, we are optimistic over this process."

The Chinese Foreign Ministry lodged a protest with the Indian government against its "instigating Indian ruffians and Tibetan traitor bandits to raid" the Chinese Embassy in India on December 30, 1968.

The NCNA announced the completion of China's largest modern bridge, a double-decker rail and highway bridge over the Yangtze River at Nanking, capital of Kiangsu Province. The bridge consisted of a 7,300-yard railroad line on the bottom deck and a 4,900-yard, four-lane highway on the upper deck.

January 4: The PRC issued a warning against the intrusion of a U.S. military aircraft into the air space over China's territorial waters east of Kiangsu province.

January 5–26: The NCNA released reports on the re-education of urban educated youths by poor and lower-middle class peasants. Other articles discussed the management of primary schools by poor and lower-middle class peasants in the countryside.

January 8: A protocol for the exchange of commodities between the PRC and Ceylon for 1969 signed in Colombo.

The draft of a new Chinese Communist Party constitution, which became available outside China early in January, formally designated Defense Minister Lin Piao, Mao Tse-tung's "close comrade-in-arms and successor," as CPC Chairman. The proposed constitution, which, together with a report on the "crimes" of former chief of state Liu Shao-chi, was circulating among Chinese provincial officials. It was expected to be approved at the CPC's Ninth Congress, scheduled to be held later in the year. A text of the draft was published January 8 by the *New York Times*.

January 11: The PRC refused to accept payment of about $600,000 from the Radio Corporation of America and three other U.S. communications companies in June, 1968, according to a U.S. State Department disclosure.

Pravda published a statement accusing Chairman Mao and his associates of virtually destroying the accepted principles of Communism and replacing them with a dictatorship devoted to Mao personally and not to Communism. The article charged that "a prolonged reactionary campaign is being conducted in China, camouflaged by 'left-revolutionary' phrases, but in fact directed at establishing a military-bureaucratic regime that has nothing in common with the dictatorship of the proletariat, the true ideas of socialism and democracy and the vital interests of the working people of China."

January 13–28: The NCNA published reports on mass criticism and repudiation of Liu Shao-chi.

January 16: Tillman Durdin of the *New York Times* reported that a massive migration from urban areas to the countryside had taken place in China. The main reason behind the exodus, which reportedly involved 15 to 20 million persons, was believed to be the desire to clear the cities not only of intellectuals and undisciplined youths, but also persons who had been disruptive during the Cultural Revolution.

January 18: In his final report to Congress, U.S. Defense Secretary Clark M. Clifford asserted that the PRC's nuclear weapons program had slowed during 1968, but that Peking was expected to have a "moderate" ICBM force by 1975.

Chou En-lai and Kang Sheng held a talk with and gave a banquet for the delegation of the Communist Party of New Zealand—Jack Manson and Ralph Hegman.

January 19: Lin Piao greeted the 20th anniversary of the founding of the Laotian People's Liberation Army.

January 22: Canadian External Affairs Minister Mitchell Sharp told reporters that the Canadian government had decided to open discussions with the PRC at a future date on the possible establishment of diplomatic relations.

The NCNA released a report on activities of art propaganda teams, promoting Mao Tse-tung's thought, composed of poor and lower-middle class peasants in Anhwei province. Publicity was also given to a senior middle school run by a factory in Hupeh province.

January 23: Chou En-lai received Khwaja Mohammad Kaiser, new Ambassador from Pakistan to the PRC.

The NCNA released reports on China's successful observation of a total solar eclipse.

January 24: A 1969 goods exchange protocol between the PRC and North Korea was signed in Peking.

The Chinese charge d'affaires in The Hague, Mr. Laio Ho-Shu, was given asylum in the Netherlands at his own request after he had informed the Dutch authorities that he did not wish to continue in his post or to return to China.

Italian Foreign Minister Pietro Nenni announced that his government had decided to recognize the PRC. A Chinese Nationalist government spokesman in Rome said on January 26 that his government would sever relations with Italy if Rome recognized the PRC. "We do not believe in a two-China policy," the Nationalist representative said.

Canadian Prime Minister Pierre Elliot Trudeau told the House of Commons that his government would take no position on its future relations with Nationalist China before the start of talks with Chinese Communists. Trudeau added: "There is no question of sacrificing the people of Formosa. The position of the government is that the fate of the people of Formosa should be determined by those people themselves."

January 25: The NCNA released a report on the students' "struggle" in San Francisco State College. Another report described how the workers' Mao Tse-tung's thought propaganda team at Central China Normal College helped the teachers and students to revolutionize themselves ideologically.

After two months of seclusion, Mao Tse-tung attended a massive 40,000-person reception in Peking with Lin Piao. Mao's appearance ended Western Press speculation about his ill health. Mao was described as in "excellent health and high spirits."

January 26: A 1969 protocol on exchange of goods between the PRC and Afghanistan was signed in Kabul.

NCNA articles marked the 5th anniversary of the publication of Mao Tse-tung's "statement supporting the Japanese people's Just Patriotic Struggle Against U.S. Imperialism."

January 27: President Nixon, in his first news conference, told newsmen that "the policy of this country and this administration at this time will be to continue to oppose the PRC's admission to the U.N." But his administration looked forward to the scheduled February 20 meeting with Peking's negotiators in Warsaw: "we will be interested to see what the Chinese Communist representatives may have to say at the meeting, whether any changes of attitudes on their part on major substantive issues may have occurred. Until some changes occur on their side, however, I see no immediate prospect of any change in our policy."

January 28: The PRC launched personal attacks on President Nixon in two Communist Party publications—*People's Daily* and *Red Flag*. The articles characterized Nixon as a frightened man taking over the reins of a government threatened by economic catastrophe and revolt, and denounced his inaugural address as "utter nonsense."

Red Flag (No. 2, 1969) published an article on who has the final say in work of cleaning up the class ranks and an article on how to correctly deal with the intellectuals.

The NCNA reported the publication of Mongolian, Tibetan and Korean translations of "Mao Tse-tung's poems."

The Australian Wheat Board announced that the PRC had agreed to buy 2.2 million long tons of wheat from Australia's 1968-1969 crop. The wheat was valued at $140 million.

Philemon Ngoma, first Ambassador Extraordinary and Plenipotentiary of the Republic of Zambia to the PRC, arrived in Peking.

January 29: The NCNA reported establishment of the Tsinghua University Revolutionary Committee.

The NCNA reported that Nixon again admitted a "U.S. imperialist impasse" at a press conference.

January 30: Li Tsung-jen, former Vice-President of Nationalist China, died of illness in Peking at age of 78.

The NCNA released a report on how doctors and nurses of a Shanghai hospital saved the life of a worker who had received a high-tension electric shock and whose heart had stopped beating for 23 minutes.

January 31: The NCNA released an article entitled "Soviet Revisionist Renegade Clique Finds Going Tougher and Tougher."

A new steel rolling mill in the Paotou industrial center northwest of Peking was completed a year ahead of schedule, according to the NCNA.

February 2: *People's Daily* published reports on the re-education of intellectuals and educated youths by poor and lower-middle class peasants, workers and soldiers.

The NCNA reported completion of the Linchow bridge in Linchow, Kwangsi.

February 4: The NCNA reported the completion in 48 days of a 32-kilometer railway connecting Kowpantze with Panshan in Liasoning province.

It was announced in Washington that Mr. Liao Ho-shu (46) the Chinese charge d'affaires in The Hague who had been given political asylum by the Dutch authorities in January, had arrived in the United States requesting asylum there.

Canadian External Affairs Minister Sharp told the Commons that Trudeau might allow the Chinese Nationalists to decide their relations with Canada if and when Canada established ties with Peking. He denied that the PRC had given any response to the Canadian announcement of willingness to start negotiations. A Japanese government source was reported by the Associated Press to have said Canada had indicated to the Japanese government that it was prepared to break relations with Nationalist China as a price for ties with Peking. The Japanese source said the PRC had refused any offers by Canada as long as Canada maintained ties with Formosa.

February 5: Chou En-lai received Paul Mwaluko, Ambassador of the United Republic of Tanzania to the PRC.

February 6: The NCNA accused the U.S. of stepping up chemical-biological warfare research.

February 9: *People's Daily* published an article about the achievements scored by a Peking commune after having formed a revolutionary committee.

The NCNA reported that poor and lower-middle class peasants in many parts of China had set up their own broadcasting services for relaying instructions from Mao Tse-tung and the CPC Central Committee.

Chou En-lai received Sekou Camara, Guinean Ambassador to the PRC.

An exhibition of modern Chinese porcelain and ceramics jointly held by the Chinese Embassy in Norway and the Norway-China Friendship Association closed in Oslo.

February 10: Canadian External Affairs Minister Sharp told the Commons that the Canadian Embassy in Stockholm had been instructed to try to start negotiations with the PRC mission there in the possible establishment of diplomatic relations. Sharp said Canada would propose that "talks concerning relations between the two countries be held at a mutually convenient time and place in the near future."

The NCNA told how the revolutionary committee of a commune on the outskirts of Peking had reaped big gains by placing Mao Tse-tung's thought in command.

February 11: The U.S. State Department said that it had informed Ottawa of U.S. concern at the Canadian move to recognize the PRC.

February 12: The NCNA released reports of mass criticism and repudiation of Liu Shao-chi.

The NCNA reported how an old steam locomotive had been remodeled so that heat could be recovered from the steam discharged.

Canadian External Affairs Minister Sharp told the Commons that Canadian recognition of the PRC would not necessarily mean that "the Canadian govern-

ment would recognize the sovereignty of Peking over Taiwan."

Wang Hsin-ting, Deputy Chief of the General Staff of the PLA, and Chang Hsien-yueh, Deputy Director of the General Logistics Department of the PLA, attended the film reception given by Nguyen Van Quang, head of the permanent mission to China of the South Vietnam National Front for Liberation, to celebrate the 8th anniversary of the unification of the "people's liberation armed forces" of South Vietnam.

February 13: The NCNA cited the successes of a commune on Hainan Island.

February 14: The Japanese External Trade Organization announced that Japan's trade with the PRC had totaled $549 million in 1968, a decrease of 1.4% compared with 1967. Although Japanese exports to China had increased by 12.9% in 1968 to $325 million, imports from the mainland had fallen 16.8% to $224 million. The main Japanese product had been steel, which represented 32.7% of the total imported by Peking. Machinery exports had dropped 25.2%. Japanese imports of Chinese textiles had risen 58% during 1968, but imports of iron ore, coal and foodstuffs had been greatly reduced.

A delegation of the Ministry of Labor and the State Planning Board of the Democratic Republic of Vietnam led by Bui Quy, Vice Minister of Labor, arrived in Peking.

The PRC and Cuba signed a 1969 trade protocol in Peking.

February 15: A Chinese Ministry of National Defense meeting celebrated the 8th anniversary of the unification of the People's Liberation Armed Forces of South Vietnam.

The NCNA described a new aviation agreement between the Soviet Union and Japan as a collusion against China.

February 16: Three pleasure yachts, en route from Hong Kong to Macao, were captured by Communist Chinese patrol boats and towed to the mainland. Among the 15 persons aboard the yachts were four

Americans, three Swedes, two Britons, a Frenchman, an Australian and four Chinese crewmen. Although Peking refused to reply to an inquiry made by Hong Kong officials February 17, a dispatch from Peking to the Hungarian Press Agency MTI February 18 hinted that the fate of the U.S. captives might be linked with the defection of Liao Ho-shu to the U.S. The Hong Kong *Star* reported March 2 that Peking had told the Macao government it would release the 15 yachtsmen.

A spokesman for the headquarters of the Chinese People's Liberation Army on the Fukien front announced no shelling of the Quemoys during the Spring Festival.

A delegation from the Japanese-Chinese memorandum trade office in Japan, including Yoshimi Furui, Seiichi Tagawa, and five others, arrived in Peking.

February 19: The Foreign Ministry in Peking issued a statement alleging that Mr. Liao Ho-shu had been "incited to betray his country and carried off to the U.S. by the U.S. Central Intelligence Agency." It added that "in the current anti-China atmosphere which is solely created by the U.S. government," it would be "obviously most unsuitable" to hold the 135th meeting of the Sino-U.S. ambassadorial talks scheduled to take place on February 20 in Warsaw.

February 20: Canadian External Affairs Minister Sharp revealed that formal contact had been made by the Canadian and PRC embassies in Stockholm on February 12 on the question of establishing diplomatic relations.

February 21: An editorial in *People's Daily* announced a new economic drive for 1969. The editorial, entitled "Grasp Revolution, Promote Production and Win New Victories on the Industrial Front," reviewed 1968 achievements. It asserted that "many industrial and mining enterprises had set one new production record after another and outstripped their past peak production figures." It said that industrial production had increased substantially during the second half of 1968, compared with the first six months of the

year, that prices were stable and that all national bonds had been paid. For the current year, the editorial continued, "We will continue" to "give energetic leadership to the great mass movement on the industrial front, carry the great proletarian cultural revolution through to the end and seize still greater victories in both revolution and production." In order to achieve the goal of greater production, stressed the editorial, the need continued for "struggle-criticism-transformation" within the revolution, for consolidation of the Communist Party, for purification of class ranks and increased efforts "to push ahead the vigorous revolutionary mass movement."

February 22: A Guinean government delegation led by Keita Nfamara, Minister of Commerce, Transport and Telecommunications, arrived in Peking at the invitation of the Chinese government.

Xhorxhi Robo, new Ambassador of Albania to the PRC, arrived in Peking.

Chou Po-ping, charge d'affaires ad interim of the Chinese Embassy in Tanzania, gave a reception to celebrate the 4th anniversary of the signing of the Sino-Tanzanian Friendship Treaty.

Li Chen-kuang, charge d'affaires ad interim of the Chinese Embassy in the Congo (B), gave a film reception at Brazzaville to mark the 5th anniversary of the establishment of diplomatic relations between the PRC and Congo.

February 23: Chou En-lai received Philemon Ngoma, Ambassador of Zambia to the PRC.

February 26: A UAR government trade delegation, headed by Khalil Jemal El-bin, Under-secretary of State for the Ministry of Economy and Foreign Trade, arrived in Peking.

February 28: Mao Tse-tung and Chou En-lai received the Guinean government delegation.

Chou En-lai received Lennart Petri, ambassador of Sweden to the PRC.

A trade protocol for 1969 between the PRC and Guinea and an agreement on a

Chinese loan in commodities to Guinea were signed in Peking.

March 1: N'famara Keita, head of the Guinean government delegation and Minister of Commerce, Transport and Telecommunications, left Peking for home.

Lennart Petri, ambassador of Sweden to the PRC, left for home.

The Afro-Asian Journalists Association issued a statement denouncing the "aggressive acts" of Israel and supporting the Arab people's armed struggle.

March 2: Armed clashes between Soviet and Chinese frontier guards, causing considerable loss of life, occurred on March 2 on the River Ussuri, the border between the Chinese province of Heilungkiang and the Soviet Far East. The scene of the fighting was a small uninhabited island 1½ miles long by half a mile wide, known to the Russians as Damansky Island and to the Chinese as Chenpao Island, which lies about 110 miles South of Khabarovsk and 250 miles north of Vladivostok. Each government sent strongly worded protest notes to the other on March 2. The Soviet note demanded an immediate investigation, the punishment of those responsible for the incident, and immediate steps to preclude any further violation of the frontier, and declared that "reckless and provocative actions by the Chinese authorities" would be " met on our side by a rebuff." The Chinese note similarly demanded the punishment of the culprits, reserved the right to demand compensation, and declared that if the Soviet government continued to "provoke armed conflicts" it would receive "resolute counter-blows."

March 3: Mass protest demonstrations began outside the Soviet Embassy in Peking, which for four days was virtually besieged by thousands of Chinese servicemen and civilians shouting such slogans as "Hang Kosygin" and "Fry Brezhnev." Similar demonstrations, in which (according to the NCNA) 260,000,000 people took part, were held in the next few days throughout China.

Vice Premier Li Fu-chun attended the National Day reception given by Abdellatif Lakhmiri, charge d'affaires ad interim of the Embassy of the Kingdom of Morocco in China.

March 4–23: The NCNA released articles and reports written against the Soviet Union.

March 5: *People's Daily* carried reports about the re-education and "liberation" of "errant" cadres by the workers' propaganda teams in institutions of higher learning.

The PRC and the UAR signed a trade protocol for 1969 in Peking.

March 6: The NCNA released a report of progress made in the Chingkiang water diversion project in the middle reaches of the Yangtze River.

The NCNA accused the Soviet Union of stepping up "counterrevolutionary collusion with the Chiang Kai-shek bandit gang."

March 7: The NCNA released an article entitled "Nixon's Aggressive Policy in Middle East Cannot Save U.S. Imperialism from Defeat."

People's Daily published articles on the operation of urban schools.

In Moscow, over 50,000 people marched past the Chinese Embassy in the largest organized protest seen in the city for many years; some of the crowd threw stones, lumps of ice, ink bottles, and paint bombs at the building and many windows were broken. On the following day (March 8), over 100,000 people took part in an even larger demonstration in Moscow, although on this occasion there were no disorders.

The Chinese Embassy in the Soviet Union sent a note to the Soviet Foreign Ministry protesting the "despicable provocative anti-China incident created by the Soviet revisionist renegade clique" on the afternoon of March 7, before the Chinese Embassy.

The NCNA released a report on the installation of electrical equipment for controlling signals and switches in a shunting yard at the North Station, Dairen.

March 8: *People's Daily* published a report on how 10,000 PLA men and civilians built a seawall 9 *li* long on the shores of Po Hai to make available 36,000 *mow* for cultivation.

The NCNA reported fulfillment of a 1968 state cotton purchase plan.

Gustav Hertzfeldt, new Ambassador of the German Democratic Republic to the PRC, arrived in Peking.

March 9: A Chinese engineering and technical team on fishing industry and the Afghan Ministry of Agriculture and Water Conservation signed notes of talks on China's helping Afghanistan in artificial breeding of fish at the Darunta Experimental Fish-breeding Center.

March 10: The information department of the Chinese Foreign Ministry released an article entitled "Chenpao Island Has Always Been Chinese Territory." The statement contended that under international law the central line of the main channel of the Ussuri formed the boundary line, that Chenpao Island was situated on the Chinese side of this line, and that it had always been under Chinese jurisdiction and had been admitted to be Chinese by the Soviet delegation at boundary negotiations in 1964. However, on the other hand, a Soviet note of March 29 maintained that a map approved by both governments in 1861 showed the Chinese bank of the Ussuri as the boundary line in this area.

March 10–24: Articles in *People's Daily* described rural commerce conducted by poor and lower-middle class peasants.

March 11: In Peking, three days of protest demonstrations against the stoning of the Russian Embassy were begun.

The Chinese Embassy in the Soviet Union delivered a note to the Soviet Foreign Ministry protesting the "provocative anti-China incident caused by the Soviet revisionist renegade clique directing ruffians to violate a diplomatic car of the Chinese Embassy and brazenly remove letters and material by force.

An exhibition of Chinese clay sculpture, "Rent Collection Courtyard," opened in Elbajan, Central Albania.

March 12: The Chinese Embassy in the Soviet Union delivered a note to the Soviet Foreign Ministry protesting "the Soviet revisionist renegade clique directing ruffians to insult and beat up the working personnel of the Chinese Embassy going out on an official mission."

A Nepalese brick and tile factory, built with Chinese assistance, was inaugurated at Katmandu.

March 13: The Chinese Foreign Ministry sent a note to the Soviet Embassy in Peking protesting the "repeated grave encroachments on Chinese territory and a series of military provocations made by Soviet frontier troops after provoking the armed border conflict on March 2." The note alleged that between March 4 and March 12 Soviet armored vehicles had "intruded into China's territory, Chenpao Island," on six occasions and that Soviet helicopters had twice flown over it during this period. The Soviet Embassy refused to accept the note.

Sekou Camara, Ambassador of the Guinean Republic to the PRC, left Peking for home.

The NCNA accused India of using "Tibetan rebels" to carry out anti-China activities.

March 14: Lucien Page, French Ambassador to China, left Peking for home.

A *People's Daily* article stressed the importance of investigation and fact-finding as a basis for implementing Mao Tsetung's policies, particularly those concerning "purification of the class ranks."

March 15: The Chinese Foreign Ministry sent a note to the Soviet Embassy in China protesting the "fresh incident of bloodshed created by the Soviet government which, beginning in the early morning of March 15, sent large numbers of armored vehicles, tanks and armed troops to intrude once again into China's territory, Chenpao Island, and the Chinese waterway to the west of the island."

A Soviet note of March 15 maintained that "Damansky Island is an inalienable part of Soviet territory," and declared that "if further attempts are made to violate the inviolability of Soviet territory, the U.S.S.R. and all of its peoples will resolutely defend it and will deliver a crushing rebuff to such violations."

March 16: The CCP Central Committee sent a message of condolence to the Central Committee of the Communist Party of Burma on the death of Thakin Than Tun, chairman of the Communist Party of Burma.

March 16–17: Publication of Mao Tse-tung's latest instructions and the important *Red Flag* editorial entitled, "On Summing Up Experience," was hailed by military men and civilians throughout China, according to an NCNA report.

March 17: A Sino-Yugoslav trade and payments agreement was signed in Peking.

The NCNA released a report entitled, "Nixon Coordinates U.S. Anti-Ballistic Missile System, Soviet Revisionist Opposition to China."

March 18: Minutes of talks on well-drilling in Belet Uen and hydro-geological prospecting and surveying in Hargeisa in Somalia with Chinese assistance were signed in Mogadishu by Chang Ching-jang, charge d'affaires ad interim of the Chinese Embassy, and Ali Alio, Somali Minister of Public Works.

March 19: The NCNA reported that the Sinankiang hydro-electric power plant, China's largest, had fulfilled the first quarter's state plan for power generation 25 days ahead of schedule.

March 20: Senator Edward M. Kennedy (D. Mass.) urged the Nixon administration to seize its opportunity "to rectify the errors of the past" and engage in "new initiatives" toward better relations between the U.S. and the PRC. Peking should be offered a "clear and attractive alternative to the existing impasse in our relations," he said. Kennedy made the remarks in New York at a conference sponsored by the National Committee on U.S.-China Relations. Kennedy urged the elimination of U.S. military bases in Taiwan and announcement by the U.S. of its "willingness to re-establish the consular offices we maintained in the People's Republic during the earliest period of Communist rule." The "demilitarization of Taiwan could take place at no cost to our treaty commitments, or to the security of the island," he said.

The NCNA reported that Chou En-lai and Kang Sheng recently met Thakin B. Thein, vice chairman of the Communist Party of Burma and head of the delegation of its Central Committee, Thakin Pe Tint, member of the Central Committee of the Burmese Communist Party and member of the delegation, and other Burmese.

The NCNA released the December 15, 1968 statement of the Central Committee of the Communist Party of Burma on the assassination of Thakin Than Tun. Also released was the full text of a radio speech made by Thakin Ba Thien Tin, vice chairman of the Central Committee of the Communist Party of Burma, on the Thakin Than Tun assassination.

March 22: The official Soviet news agency Tass announced that the long-heralded World Conference of Communist and Workers' parties would begin in Moscow June 5. The announcement also said that the preparatory committee for the conference, which had met in Moscow March 18–22, would hold its final meeting there May 23. The Moscow preparatory committee meetings had been boycotted by Albania, Communist China, Cuba, North Korea, North Vietnam and Yugoslavia.

A Japanese industrial exhibition opened in Peking.

The China-Pakistan Friendship Association gave a reception to mark the National Day of the Islamic Republic of Pakistan.

March 23: Chou En-lai and Hsieh Fu-chih received Xhorxhi Robo, new Ambassador of Albania to China.

Vice Premier Li Hsien-nien received Bui Quy, Vice Minister of Labor of the DRV and other members of the delegation of the Ministry of Labor and State Planning Board of Vietnam.

March 24: After his talks with President Nixon in Washington, Canadian Prime Minister Trudeau said at a news conference at the National Press Club that Canada's policy differences with the U.S. such as trade with Cuba and recognition of the PRC, gave "evidence of your [i.e., of American] basic qualities of understanding and tolerance." Trudeau also said that "Canada was not distressed over Communist China's delay in responding to Canadian overtures for recognition."

A delegation of the Ministry of Labor and State Planning Board of the DRV, led by Bui Quy, left Peking for home.

A PRC trade delegation arrived in Helsinki to negotiate the 1969 trade agreement between China and Finland.

March 27: The Cambodian government appointed Nay Valentin Ambassador Extraordinary and Plenipotentiary of Cambodia to the PRC.

The PRC issued a warning against the intrusion of any U.S. military plane or warship over and into China's territorial waters off Kiangsu and Kwangtung provinces.

March 29: The NCNA made accusations against the Indonesian "fascist military regime" for "stepping up collaboration with the Chiang Kai-shek bandit gang."

In a long and moderately worded note, the Soviet government reaffirmed in detail its claim to sovereignty over Damansky Island, and proposed that the boundary negotiations broken off in 1964 should be resumed as soon as possible. An official at the Chinese Embassy denounced the note as "slander," though the Peking government made no comment.

March 31: The NCNA reported that well-printed copies of Mao Tse-tung's works were being turned out and distributed quickly in Tientsin and Hupeh province to greet the 9th National Congress of the CPC.

April 1: The Ninth Congress of the Chinese Communist Party, the first held since 1958, took place in Peking from April 1 to April 24, and was attended by 1,512 delegates. It was held under conditions of strict secrecy, no journalists or foreign observers being admitted, and the only

information on the proceedings published was contained in three communiques issued on April 1, 14, and 24. The agenda consisted of three items: (1) the Central Committee's report, presented by Marshal Lin Piao, Vice-Chairman of the party; (2) revision of the party's constitution; (3) election of the Central Committee. Mao Tse-tung presided over the first session on April 1, and according to the official communique made "a most important speech," although this was not published. After the congress had elected a presidium of 176 members, Marshal Lin Piao presented a 24,000-word report on the Cultural Revolution and China's foreign policy, which was published on April 27. The congress also approved on April 14 the new party constitution, which replaced that adopted in 1956 and specifically laid down that "Comrade Lin Piao is Comrade Mao Tse-tung's close comrade-in-arms and successor." From April 15 to its close on April 24 the congress was occupied with the election of a new Central Committee of 170 full members and 109 alternate members.

The PRC and Sudan signed a trade protocol for 1969 in Khartoum.

April 2: The Soviet Union denounced the ninth congress as a "Maoist farce." *Izvestia* charged that the real leaders of the Chinese Communist Party had been "routed" by Mao during the Cultural Revolution, and it claimed that the delegates to the congress "were not elected, of course, but appointed by Mao's emissaries from among specially picked people." *Izvestia* also charged that Mao still had difficulties with the army: "The army, which wields real power in the country, does not want, and is scarcely likely to want, to share power with other organizations. But Mao did not destroy the Chinese Communist Party with the help of the army in order to transfer power to the army."

April 4: After six weeks of talks, a communique between the Chinese representatives of the China-Japan Memorandum Trade Office and the Japanese representatives of the Japan-China Memorandum Trade Office was signed in Peking. The agreement provided for the exchange of $78 million worth of goods during the remaining nine months of 1969; this was a drop of 30% from 1968. The decrease in trade reportedly was due to the Japanese refusal to import rice from China and China's unwillingness to accept meat processed aboard a Japanese factory ship.

April 6: A record number of Mao Tse-tung's works and portraits of him were printed and distributed in China, according to NCNA reports.

April 7: The Presidium of the 9th National Congress of the CPC sent a message to the Central Committee of the Albanian Party of Labor and Enver Hoxha, expressing sympathy to the people of six regions in the southwestern part of Albania struck by a strong earthquake.

The Chinese Red Cross Society sent a message and a donation of 500,000 *yuan* to the Albanian Red Cross Society, extending sympathy to the people of the earthquake-stricken areas.

April 8: The Revolutionary Committee of the Tuyun branch of the Liuchow Railway Bureau was established.

April 9: Tung Pi-wu, Vice Chairman of the PRC, accepted the credentials presented by Bernt Arne Bjornberg, new Ambassador Extraordinary and Plenipotentiary of the Kingdom of Sweden.

Vice Premier Li Hsien-nien visited the Japanese Industrial Exhibition in Peking which ended on April 17.

April 10: Canadian External Affairs Minister Mitchell Sharp announced that the PRC had responded favorably to Canada's bid for the start of talks on diplomatic recognition and that negotiations were scheduled to begin in Stockholm in May.

April 11: A second Soviet note was sent to Peking proposing that boundary negotiations be resumed in Moscow on April 15 or at any other early date convenient for the Chinese. Peking had not responded to the earlier note and it did not immediately reply to the second one.

The NCNA released a report on PLA units sending propaganda teams and personnel to help people's communes with spring farming.

The NCNA reported completion of a documentary film on the second congress of activists in the study of Mao Tse-tung's works under the auspices of the Central Logistics Department of the PLA. Also released was a report on the production of new portable film projectors for remote mountain areas.

April 14: Lin Piao delivered a report to the 9th National Congress of the CPC. The Secretariat of the Presidium of the 9th National Congress of the CPC issued a press communique.

April 15: China's 1969 Spring Export Commodities Fair opened in Canton.

April 17: The NCNA released reports on the Afro-American struggle. *People's Daily* carried an editorial commemorating the anniversary of Mao Tse-tung's statement in support of the Afro-American struggle against violent repression.

April 19: The NCNA reported that the U.S. had dispatched another airlift squadron to Formosa.

April 20: *Kung-ming Jih-pao* carried a report on the launching of a "four good" movement (good in political thinking, good in the "three-eight" work style, good in education reform and study, and good in livelihood management) in a Canton middle school.

April 21: Karely Patak, correspondent for the Hungarian press agency MTI, was ordered to leave China within three days. Patak was accused of writing false information during his one-year stay.

People's Daily published articles on schools run by poor and lower-middle class peasants.

April 22: Nay Valentin, new Ambassador Extraordinary and Plenipotentiary of the Kingdom of Cambodia, arrived in Peking.

Salim Ahmed Salim, new Ambassador Extraordinary and Plenipotentiary of the United Republic of Tanzania, arrived in Peking.

Claude-Ernest Ndalla, new Ambassador Extraordinary and Plenipotentiary of the Republic of the Congo (B), arrived in Peking.

A trade agreement between the PRC and Finland for 1969 was signed in Helsinki.

April 24: The Secretariat of the Presidium of the 9th National Congress of the CPC issued a press communique and released a list of the 279 members and alternate members of the 9th Central Committee of the CPC.

The NCNA told how a Navy diving team of the PLA made it possible to complete construction of the hydro-electric power station before the onset of the high-water season.

The Afro-Asian Journalists Association held a meeting in Peking to celebrate Afro-Asian Journalists Day.

April 25: The Yugoslav press agency reported that of the 99 members of the Central Committee elected in 1956, only 32 were re-elected to the new committee, and two others were elected as alternates. Of the 99 alternates elected in 1956, only one remained as a candidate member, 13 were promoted to full membership, and 85 were dropped entirely.

The NCNA released reports on rallies and celebrations hailing the closing of the 9th National Congress of the CPC and the birth of the 9th Central Committee of the CPC.

A documentary film in color, "The Ceremonial Opening of the 9th National Congress of the CPC in Peking" would be shown in Peking and other parts of China beginning April 26, according to the NCNA.

Tung Pi-wu, Vice-Chairman of the PRC, accepted the credentials presented by Nay Valentin, new Ambassador of Cambodia, Claude-Ernest Ndalla, new Ambassador of the Congo (B), and Salim Ahmed Salim, new Ambassador of Tanzania.

On the final communique of the 9th National Congress of the CPC, the Soviet press agency Tass said the communique showed that "repressions and purges in the party and the country will be intensi-

fied." It also added: "The communique shows that the consolidation of the military bureaucratic regime is far from completed. . . . The army remains the main support of the Mao group."

April 26: On the newly elected 9th Central Committee of the CPC, the *New York Times* commented that the list of committee members revealed that the army, "propagandists," and "moderates" had emerged from the congress slightly strengthened. But it noted that confirmed Maoists associated with the purported excesses of the Cultural Revolution remained numerous.

April 27: The NCNA released the full text of Lin Piao's report to the 9th National Congress of the CPC.

The 5th anniversary of the inauguration of the direct China-Pakistan air service was marked in Peking.

Kamano Ansou, new Ambassador Extraordinary and Plenipotentiary of Guinea to China, arrived in Peking.

April 28: The First Plenum of the 9th CPC Central Committee issued a press communique, naming the Chairman and Vice Chairman of the Central Committee, members of the Standing Committee of the Political Bureau, and members and alternate members of the Political Bureau.

The NCNA released the text of the constitution of the Communist Party of China adopted by the 9th National Congress of the CPC on April 14.

The Chinese Embassy in Nepal held a reception at Katmandu to mark the 9th anniversary of the signing of the Sino-Nepalese Treaty of Peace and Friendship.

April 29: The election of Mao Tse-tung and Lin Paio respectively as Chairman and Vice Chairman of the 9th CPC Central Committee and publication of the new party constitution were hailed in all parts of China.

Tung Pi-wu accepted the credentials presented by Kamano Ansou, the newly appointed Ambassador from Guinea.

A gift of 3,000 tons of cereal grains to the Mauritanian government by the Chinese government arrived in Nouakchott.

April 30: A spokesman for the PLA command at the Fukien front announced the suspension of shelling on May 1.

May 1: Mao Tse-tung and Lin Piao celebrated May Day together with delegates to the Party Congress and half a million people in Peking. They also received Xhorxhi Robo, new Ambassador of Albania; Nay Valentin, new Ambassador of Cambodia; K. M. Kaiser, new Ambassador of Pakistan; Kamano Ansou, new Ambassador of Guinea; Claude-Ernest Ndalla, new Ambassador of the Congo (B); Salim Ahmed Salim, new Ambassador of Tanzania; P. N'goma, new Ambassador of Zambia, and Bernt Arne Bjornberg, new Ambassador of Sweden.

The NCNA released messages of greeting from foreign countries to the 9th National Congress of the CPC.

The Shanghai administration of the Chinese Civil Airlines and Sultan Hyder, manager of the Pakistan International Airlines Corporation in China, gave banquets in Shanghai in honor of the 5th anniversary of the inauguration of the China-Pakistan air service.

May 2: Mao Tse-tung received a message of congratulations from Marien Ngouabi of the Congo (B) on the occasion of his re-election to the Chairmanship of the CPC.

Samdech Sihanouk, head of state of Cambodia, wrote to Chou En-lai expressing his gratitude for China's assistance to Cambodia in completing the work of transforming the Cambodian-Chinese People's Paper Mill.

The NCNA reported that *People's Daily* in the past few days gave wide coverage to articles by workers, peasants and soldiers hailing Lin Piao's political report to the 9th National Congress of the CPC.

May 3: The Soviet Union disclosed that it had again called on the Peking government to resume their border negotiations, broken off in 1964. The latest offer, transmitted to China April 26, called for a meeting of the Soviet-Chinese Commission on Borderline.

May 4: Representatives of seven French firms reached an agreement with Chinese officials on a contract to deliver 800,000 tons of wheat to the PRC early in 1970. The French businessmen had been attending a trade fair in Canton. Payment was reportedly to be in French francs.

A new campaign to strengthen control over China's youth emerged May 4. In a joint editorial published by *People's Daily, Red Flag* and *Liberation Army Daily*, the Peking government emphasized that "young intellectuals must integrate themselves with the masses of workers and peasants."

May 5: The 24th anniversary of the defeat of the Nazi government was celebrated in Moscow. Defense Minister Andrei A. Grechko expressed concern over the PRC's foreign policy. He wrote in *Pravda*: "The adventurist policy of the Mao Tse-tung group, which proclaims its chauvinistic-hegemmistic desires and makes anti-Sovietism the official line of its policy, cannot but give rise to concern."

May 6: The NCNA alleged that Singapore authorities had stepped up the political persecution of the Singapore branch of the Bank of China.

Moscow Radio attacked Mao Tse-tung as a killer of thousands of Chinese. The broadcast, in Chinese, said: "Mao's road to seize power is one stained with the fresh blood of thousands of real Communists, his old comrades-in-arms and 10,000 patriots." The broadcast said that "millions of lives will be lost if Mao tries to consolidate his political power."

May 7: The Soviet Defense Ministry newspaper, *Krasnaya Zvesda (Red Star)*, said that Soviet artillery destined for North Vietnam had been seized in China for use by Mao's supporters in civil warfare. The newspaper claimed that the Chinese army was in complete control of the country.

May 8: *People's Daily* published articles containing suggestions for compiling new school textbooks.

The State Council of the PRC extended greetings to and expressed admiration for the unyielding Czechoslovak people on the occasion of the National Day of the Czechoslovak Socialist Republic.

An official of Canadian Pacific Airlines, a government-owned corporation, announced that Canadian Pacific was negotiating to establish the first commercial air route between the PRC and North America. The proposed route, if China agreed, would run from Vancouver through Hawaii, Tokyo and Hong Kong to Shanghai or Peking or both.

May 10: Sources in Moscow reported that Chinese and Soviet troops had clashed several times during the week along the border separating Soviet Kazakhstan and China's Sinkiang region.

The NCNA released reports on labor schools, farms, factories, and mines run by the PLA in accordance with Mao Tsetung's May 7 directive for the revolutionization of army cadres.

The NCNA accused the U.S., the U.S.S.R., France and Britain of plotting a "Middle East Munich."

The Chinese Foreign Ministry lodged a strong protest with the Indian government on its vilification against China and its acts of provocation along the China-Sikkim boundary and the Sino-Indian border.

May 11: The Chinese government issued a warning against the intrusion of a U.S. military plane and a U.S. warship respectively over the Hsisha Islands and off Fukien province.

The *New York Times* reported that a Shanghai study team had proposed reducing Chinese basic schooling to nine years: primary school would be reduced from six to five years, and middle school from six to four years. There was no mention of university education. The report also proposed that the curriculum be revised because it "occupied too many hours per week."

The NCNA reported that Peking had agreed to a meeting of the Soviet-Chinese Border Navigation Committee to be held in Khabarovsk in mid-June, "the exact date to be agreed upon by the two sides." The note was sent by Chen Fa-ping, senior

Chinese delegate on the Committee. The note was in reply to a Soviet proposal April 26 to convene the committee in May. The Chinese, however, argued that "both sides must make preparations," and the meeting should be delayed until mid-June. There was no indication in the note that Peking was willing to resume border negotiations with the Soviet Union, broken off in 1964.

May 13: A military delegation of the Syrian Arab Republic led by Major General Moustapha Tlass, Chief of the General Staff of the Army and Armed Forces and First Deputy Minister of Defense of the Syrian Arab Republic, arrived in Peking.

May 14: The NCNA released a report on the 1969 Spring Export Commodities Fair in Canton.

Malaysian Prime Minister Rahman suspended the constitution due to fighting between Malay and Chinese ethnic groups in Kuala Lumpur (May 13–16). In his announcement, he charged that Communist China had sent funds to anti-government groups in Malaysia to foment unrest.

May 15: Keng Piao, newly appointed Ambassador Extraordinary and Plenipotentiary of the PRC to Albania, left Peking for Tirana. It was China's first ambassadorial appointment since 1966, despite the recall to Peking of 91 ambassadors and diplomats from China's 47 legations during the Cultural Revolution.

The executive secretariat of the Afro-Asian Writers' Bureau issued a statement condemning the "sinister maneuvers of U.S. imperialism, Soviet revisionism and Israeli reactionaries" in the Middle East and supporting the Palestinian and other Arab people in their struggle for "national liberation."

The secretariat of the Afro-Asian Journalists Association issued a statement condemning the "sinister plots of U.S.-led imperialism, Soviet-led revisionism and the Zionists" in the Middle East and reiterating its support to the "just struggle" of the Palestinian people.

Minutes of talks between representatives of the China National Cereals, Oils, and Foodstuffs Import and Export Corporation and Japanese commercial firms on the question of Japan's importing meat from China were signed in Canton.

May 16: The third anniversary of the May 16, 1966 circular of the CPC Central Committee was hailed.

May 19: Mao Tse-tung and Lin Piao received "10,000 revolutionary fighters" from various parts of China.

The NCNA accused the United States of sending Chiang Ching-kuo, Defense Minister of Nationalist China, to Bangkok to stage an "anti-China farce" on the eve of the Bangkok meeting of the SEATO.

A study prepared by the Japanese Foreign Ministry reported that the PRC's economic growth rate had been stunted since the beginning of the Cultural Revolution in 1966. During China's first five-year plan (1953–57), the economic growth rate had been 8.9% annually, but the rate in the forseeable future would be no more than 4% a year, the study forecast. In 1968, the report said, industrial and agricultural production was only slightly higher than 1965 levels. According to the report, 400,000 specialists were lost to the economy when schools and technical institutes were closed in 1967–68 to allow students to take part in the Cultural Revolution. An estimated 90,000 potential teachers, 140,000 potential industrial technicians and 50,000 potential doctors were among those lost. "The slighting of basic research," the report said, "will have particularly great effects in matters of military technology." The study noted what it considered to be two basic problems of the Chinese economy: (1) Low productivity of agriculture, limiting the development of industry, and (2) Increasing size of the work force, keeping the problem of unemployment constantly unsolved.

May 20: General Huang Chen, Ambassador of the PRC to France, left Peking for Paris to resume his post. Huang had been recalled to Peking in January, 1967.

M. Etienne Manac'h, new Ambassador of France to China, arrived in Peking.

May 23: French Machine Tools and Public Works Equipment Exhibition opened in Peking.

A Soviet note proposed June 18 as the starting date for resumption of talks by the Soviet-Chinese Border Navigation Committee. The note, which suggested Khabarovsk (called Poli by the Chinese), near the Chinese Manchurian border, as the site for talks, was in response to Peking's offer May 11 to renew discussions with the Soviet Union. On June 7 NCNA announced China's acceptance of the Soviet proposal and reported that Peking would send a 10-man delegation led by Chang Chan-teh.

May 24: The NCNA published the full text of the statement of the Soviet government of March 29 on the Sino-Soviet boundary question.

The PRC, in a statement issued through the NCNA, expressed readiness to reopen general talks with the Soviet Union on Sino-Soviet frontier problems and suggested diplomatic contacts in fixing a date and a place for the talks. Responding to a March 29 Soviet proposal, China stipulated that Russia first had to halt "heavy artillery and machine-gun fire on China's Chenpao Island [which the Russians called Damansky] and other areas deep within Chinese territory." China also urged that border guards refrain from crossing into disputed territory and proposed a cease-fire along the border pending a settlement of the dispute. In reference to the islands in the Ussuri River along the border, the NCNA statement said that China's ownership was based on the fact that, "according to established principles of international law in the case of navigable boundary rivers, the central line in the main channel shall form the boundary line and determine the ownership of the islands." In the case of disputed Chenpao Island, China noted that the island lay on the Chinese side of the central line and therefore "indisputedly belonged to China."

May 26: Taiwan airmen crossed over to the Chinese mainland in a U.S.-made T-33 training jet plane, according to an NCNA report.

May 27: *People's Daily* published articles in commemoration of the 27th anniversary of the publication of Mao Tse-tung's "Talks at the Yenan Forum on Literature and Art."

Chou En-lai greeted the opening of the 14th Congress of the Tanganyika African National Union.

Chou En-lai, Li Hsien-nien, and Kuo Mo-jo attended a National Day reception given by the Afghan Ambassador to China.

Senator Alan Cranston (D. Calif.) proposed in the U.S. Senate a resolution calling for diplomatic recognition of other governments without the implication that the U.S. "necessarily approves of the form, ideology or policy of that foreign government." The resolution was considered a new approach to the China problem in that it would eliminate the concept of "democratic legitimacy" associated with extension of recognition, and that the resolution would not settle the question of U.S. recognition of the PRC, but would remove a barrier in the event "a time comes when recognition would otherwise be negotiable and would clearly serve our national interests." The resolution had support in the Senate Foreign Relations Committee. Chairman J. W. Fulbright (D. Ark.) praised Cranston "for his initiative and foresight" in devising the measure; the Committee's ranking Republican, Vermont Senator George D. Aiken, was co-sponsor.

May 28: The NCNA released a report on U.S.-Soviet cooperation entitled "Nixon-Dobrynin Performance in White House Rose Garden."

May 30: The NCNA and *People's Daily* commented on U.S. Secretary William Rogers' recent tour of Southeast Asia.

May 31: Chou Hua-min, head of the PRC Trade Delegation and Vice Minister of Foreign Trade, left Peking for Rumania and Czechoslovakia.

June 1: An NCNA report told of a new-type engineering university set up by teachers and students of Tungchi University on a construction site in suburban Shanghai.

The NCNA released more reports on the sending of educated youths to rural areas for re-education by poor and lower-middle class peasants.

June 3: A Radio Peking dispatch claimed that the U.S.S.R. had installed launching pads for nuclear-tipped missiles along China's Soviet and Mongolian borders "for use against China."

The PRC and Rumania signed a 1969 trade agreement in Bucharest providing for a 13% increase over their 1968 trade.

A spokesman for the Information Department of the Chinese Foreign Ministry made a statement against the "extremely grave political incident engineered by the Bulgarian government in trailing after U.S. imperialism and Soviet revisionism in their plot to create two Chinas" by openly inviting "a government delegation of the Chiang Kai-shek bandit gang" to attend the World Inter-Governmental Conference on Tourism held in Sofia.

June 4: The NCNA claimed medical workers in a PLA hospital had succeeded in curing the after-effects of infantile paralysis.

June 5–17: The long-postponed World Conference of Communist and Workers' parties was held June 5–17 at the Kremlin in Moscow. The Congress, attended by representatives of 75 Communist parties, was the first international Communist conference since November 1960 and climaxed three years of intensive diplomatic activity and planning by the Soviet Union. Called to discuss the "urgent tasks of the struggle against imperialism and problems of united action by Communists," the meeting was marked by dissension over the question of policy toward the PRC (not represented at the conference), the Soviet-led invasion of Czechoslovakia, and the independence of national Communist parties. A final declaration was signed June 17, entitled, "The Tasks of the Struggle Against Imperialism at the Present Stage, and the Unity of Action of the Communist and Workers' Parties and of All Anti-Imperialistic Forces." During the conference it was agreed to set up a preparatory commission of 13 parties to prepare an agenda and set a date for a future World Anti-Imperialist Congress. In addition to the Chinese party, four ruling parties did not attend the conference: Albania, North Vietnam, North Korea and Yugoslavia. The Japanese and Dutch parties also did not attend.

Wang Yu-ping, newly appointed Ambassador Extraordinary and Plenipotentiary of the PRC to the Democratic Republic of Vietnam, left Peking for Hanoi.

June 6: In a note delivered to the Soviet Embassy in Peking, the PRC protested what it called "intensified" and "deliberate" border provocations, including the slaying of a Chinese border guard May 15, the kidnapping of two other guards and 16 civilians, and the repeated shelling of Chenpao Island. The incidents were said to have occurred during April and May. But the *London Times* on June 7 reported that a senior official at the Soviet Foreign Ministry in Moscow had told a press conference that "according to our information, the situation on the Soviet-Chinese border is absolutely quiet."

Kang Mao-chao, newly appointed Ambassador Extraordinary and Plenipotentiary of the PRC to Cambodia, left Peking for Cambodia.

The chairman of the Chinese side of the Sino-Soviet Joint Commission for Navigation on the Boundary River sent a reply to the chairman of the Soviet side agreeing to hold the 15th regular meeting in Poli on June 18.

June 7: Chang Tung, newly appointed Ambassador Extraordinary and Plenipotentiary of the PRC to Pakistan, left Peking for Pakistan.

Radio Peking began its Albanian language program.

The NCNA released a report on the visit of Japanese Foreign Minister Kiichi Aichi to the United States and Japan-U.S. "military collaboration."

The NCNA relayed the June 1 statement by a spokesman of the Communist Party of Thailand and broadcasts by the "Voice of the People of Thailand."

Despite Rumania's appeal for avoidance of criticism of other parties, Brezhnev's major address to the meeting of the World Conference of Communist and Workers' Parties was dominated by what was said to have been the longest and sharpest attack on the PRC ever publicly made by the Soviet leaders. Taking note of previous Soviet assurances that the conference would not become an anti-China forum, Brezhnev said his remarks were in response to the decisions of the Chinese Party's Ninth Congress, which, he said, had consecrated a "merciless struggle" against "the overwhelming majority of the socialist countries and Communist parties." Brezhnev charged Chairman Mao Tse-tung with proclaiming his own thoughts as "the Marxism-Leninism of the modern epoch," attempting to mislead other Communists and split their parties, and indoctrinating the Chinese people with hatred for the U.S.S.R. Brezhnev declared: "We do not consider it possible to remain silent about the anti-Leninist, anti-popular essence of the political and ideological principles of the present leaders of China. We shall carry on a resolute struggle against its great-power foreign policy line."

June 8: The NCNA commented on Richard Nixon's call for "a resurgence of American idealism" in his June 4 speech at the U.S. Air Force Academy.

June 9: In a joint editorial published by *People's Daily*, *Red Flag*, and *Liberation Army Daily*, the Peking government announced a new drive to unite the Chinese people. Entitled "Hold Aloft the Banner of Unity of the Party's Ninth Congress and Win Still Greater Victories," the editorial stressed the need for the working class to unite its own ranks and with its allies and also with those "who committed serious mistakes but are not incorrigible."

According to the editorial, the unity drive was begun on instructions given by Chairman Mao Tse-tung during the Ninth Party Congress (April 1–24). Mao was reported to have said: "Unite for the single purpose of consolidating the dictatorship of the proletariat. This must be realized in every factory, village, office and school." In offering a reprieve for those who had committed mistakes during the Cultural Revolution, the editorial quoted another teaching of Mao: "We have come together from every corner of the country and should be good at uniting in our work not only with comrades who hold the same view as we but also with those who hold different views. There are some among us who have made very serious mistakes: we should not be prejudiced against them but should be ready to work with them."

June 10: The NCNA announced the recent publication of a Spanish translation of the *Selected Works of Mao Tse-tung*, Vol. III.

The National Liberation Front (NLF) announced the formation of a Provisional Revolutionary Government of the Republic of South Vietnam (PRG). The PRC was recognized by 16 governments June 12–15. On June 14, Chou En-lai sent a message to Huyan Tan Phat, President of the PRG, congratulating him on the proclamation establishing that government.

June 11: The PRC Foreign Ministry, in a note to the Soviet Embassy in Peking, charged that Soviet troops, tanks and armored cars had crossed China's northwestern border into Sinkiang the previous day. The protest said the Russian troops had killed one herdsman and had kidnapped another. It said that Chinese frontier guards had fought back "in self-defense." China threatened "severe punishment" unless the U.S.S.R. ceased its encroachment and armed provocation on Chinese territory and returned the kidnapped herdsman. However, a Soviet note delivered to the Chinese Embassy in Moscow denied the charges and reversed the blame.

Chou En-lai, Li Hsien-nien, and Kuo

Mo-jo attended a reception given by Nepalese Ambassador to China Ranadhir Subba to mark the 50th birthday of King Mahendra of Nepal.

June 12: Chung Hsi-tung, newly appointed Ambassador Extraordinary and Plenipotentiary of the PRC to Tanzania, left Peking for Tanzania.

Han Ko-hua, newly appointed Ambassador Extraordinary and Plenipotentiary of the PRC to Guinea, left Peking for Guinea.

Chin Li-chen, Ambassador Extraordinary and Plenipotentiary of the PRC to Zambia, left Peking to return to his post.

The NCNA condemned the "4th Ministerial Meeting of the Asian and Pacific Council" in Tokyo as another grave step taken by the United States in its "plot to rig up a new anti-China military alliance headed by Japanese reactionaries."

June 13: The Soviet News Agency Tass reported that the U.S.S.R. had offered to resume talks with China on border problems "within the next two or three weeks." The note was apparently in response to a May 24 Chinese offer.

The NCNA released reports on the students' movement in the U.S.

June 14: China's Photo and Products Exhibition was opened in Sapporo, Hokkaido, Japan.

June 15: Peking Radio charged that the U.S.S.R. had provoked 4,189 border incidents between October 15, 1964 and March 15, 1969.

People's Daily published an article urging revolutionary committees to deal seriously with matters that concern Mao Tse-tung's thought and the Party's policies and principles, and to ignore personal grievances and the interests of small groups or factions.

June 16: The PRC and Czechoslovakia signed a 1969 trade agreement in Prague providing for an 11% increase over 1968 trade.

Nguyen Van Quang, head of the South Vietnam National Front for Liberation's Permanent Mission to the PRC, held a press conference for Chinese and foreign correspondents in Peking.

June 17–28: Chang Hsi-feng, newly appointed Ambassador Extraordinary and Plenipotentiary of the PRC to Rumania, and Wang Tung, newly appointed Ambassador Extraordinary and Plenipotentiary of the PRC to Sweden, left Peking for their posts.

June 18: Sino-Soviet river navigation talks began in Khabarovsk.

The NCNA reported defection of airmen from Formosa on May 26.

June 19–24: Wang Yu-tien, newly appointed Ambassador Extraordinary and Plenipotentiary of the PRC to the Congo (B), and Chin Chia-lin, newly appointed Ambassador Extraordinary and Plenipotentiary of the PRC to the Syrian Arab Republic, left Peking for their posts.

June 20: The *London Times* reported that 12,000 Chinese workers had moved into Kashmir to open a second strategic route between China and the Pakistan side of Kashmir. The routes reportedly would give the Chinese direct access into Kashmir's western districts. The *Times* also reported that the PRC had constructed a 118-mile highway between the Khunjerab Pass and Qualanadi, on the main road to Lhasa.

June 21: Radio Shanghai reported that a Communist party branch office had been established in Shanghai. It was the first party office set up in the city since all local party branches were disbanded during the Cultural Revolution. The broadcast said the action was in conformity to the New Communist Party Constitution.

June 22: The *Hong Kong Star* reported that General Wang En-mao, commander of the Sinkiang Military Region and Vice-Chairman of the Province's Revolutionary Committee, had resigned from the Committee because Chairman Mao had appointed three co-commissars to direct the province's political affairs. According to the newspaper, Mao and Lin Piao were attempting to conceal Wang's resignation because of difficulties with the U.S.S.R. along the Sinkiang border.

June 23: The PRC issued a warning against the intrusion of a U.S. warship and two U.S. military planes.

June 24: The minutes of Sino-Tanzanian talks concerning the expansion of the national stadium in Dar-es-Salaam with Chinese assistance were signed in that city.

June 27: The NCNA told how hundreds of thousands of armymen and civilians from Peking went to the outskirts of the city to help gather the summer crop.

June 28: The NCNA accused Indira Gandhi of collaborating more closely with Sato to serve "American-Soviet scheme against the PRC."

June 29: The NCNA described Nixon's withdrawal plan as an "out-and-out swindle."

People's Daily published an article entitled, "India Is a Vivid Example of Soviet Revisionists' Pushing of Socialism-Imperialism."

June 30: The NCNA announced the release of the full-length color documentary film, "The 9th National Congress of the Communist Party of China" on July 1 in Peking and other parts of China in honor of the 48th anniversary of the founding of the Communist Party of China.

July 1: In a joint editorial published in *People's Daily*, *Red Flag* and *Liberation Army Daily*, the Peking government called for rebuilding the Communist Party's structure and leadership. The editorial, marking the 48th anniversary of the "Long Live the Communist Party," called for total obedience to the party's policies and leadership. It said that the Central Committee "is the only center of leadership for the whole party, the whole army and the people throughout the country. The whole party must observe unified discipline and be subordinated to the Central Committee." The editorial apparently was aimed at the Revolutionary Committees, which had gained power and control during the Cultural Revolution at the expense of the party. The editorial quoted Mao as saying that "the tasks of struggle-criticism-transformation" had not yet been fulfilled by the Cultural Revolution.

Tung Pi-wu accepted the letter of credence presented by Nguyen Van Quang, first Ambassador Extraordinary and Plenipotentiary to the PRC of the Provisional Revolutionary Government of the Republic of South Vietnam.

July 3: The NCNA reported the completion of the project to enlarge the capacity of the Tulichien Channel—the first stage in a massive effort to tame the Taching River in Hopei province.

July 5: A 1969 trade agreement between the PRC and Bulgaria was signed in Peking.

July 7: An agreement on exchange of goods and payments for 1969 between the PRC and the German Democratic Republic was signed in Peking.

July 8: Han Ke-hua, new Ambassador Extraordinary and Plenipotentiary of the PRC to Guinea, presented his credentials to President Sekou Toure of Guinea.

The PRC Foreign Ministry lodged a protest with the Soviet government against its directing Soviet frontier troops to intrude on July 8 into China's territory— the Pacha Island area of the Heilung River in Fuyuan hsein, Heilunkiang province.

July 9: A Soviet statement asserted that Chinese hiding on the Soviet part of Pacha Island had opened fire on workers repairing navigation markers on the island, killing one worker and wounding three. The Soviet note to the Chinese Embassy called the incident "a malicious provocation" aimed at frustrating the talks in Khabarovsk.

Chou En-lai, Huang Yung-sheng, Li Hsien-nien, Kuo Mo-jo, and Wen Yu-cheng attended the reception given by Nguyen Van Quang, Ambassador to the PRC of the Provisional Revolutionary Government of the Republic of South Vietnam in honor of the establishment of that government.

July 10: Soviet Foreign Minister Andrei A. Gromyko delivered a wide-ranging foreign policy address before the Supreme Soviet in Moscow. He charged that the PRC had done everything to break good relations between the two Communist powers. He noted that (1) Sino-Soviet trade had dropped to less than half of its 1959 level; (2) scientific, technical, and cultural exchanges had stopped almost completely; (3) economic agreements had been annulled or suspended. He condemned the "anti-Soviet statements of the Chinese leaders that show hostile intentions against our country." He charged China with obstructing the Khabarovsk border navigation talks by its attitude at the negotiating table and by its recent provocation on the Amur River.

July 11: *People's Daily* published reports on storing up grain for preparedness against war and natural calamities.

The NCNA reported the completion of a shipping lock between the Yangtze River and Tsaohu Lake in Anhwei province.

An exhibition of China's modern porcelain and ceramics, jointly arranged by the Embassy of the PRC in Denmark and the Danish Association of Cultural Relations with China, opened in Copenhagen.

The NCNA accused "U.S. imperialists and Soviet revisionists of taking new steps to promote their Middle East Munich Plot."

July 12: Air Marshal Nur Khan, member of the Pakistan President's Council of Administration, and the Goodwill and Friendship Delegation of Pakistan led by him, arrived in Peking on a friendly visit to China at the invitation of the PRC government. He and the group left China on July 17.

Wang Yu-tien, newly appointed Ambassador Extraordinary and Plenipotentiary of the PRC to the Republic of Congo (Brazzaville), presented his credentials to Marien Ngouabi, President of the National Council of the Revolution and Head of State of Congo (B).

Wang Tse, newly appointed Ambassador Extraordinary and Plenipotentiary of the PRC to the Kingdom of Nepal, left Peking for Nepal.

The NCNA released a report on protests by Chinese residents in Japan against the Sato government's anti-China move.

July 14: Li Hsien-nien, Lin Hai-yun, and Lo Kuei-po attended a reception given by M. Etienne Manac'h, French Ambassador to the PRC, to celebrate the National Day of the Republic of France.

Minutes of the Chinese-Yemeni talks concerning the PRC government's assistance in building a secondary technical school for the Yemeni government were signed in Sanaa.

July 15: Feng Yu-chiu, newly appointed Ambassador Extraordinary and Plenipotentiary of the PRC to the Islamic Republic of Mauritania, left Peking for Mauritania.

July 16: Rallies were held in Peking in celebration of the third anniversary of Mao Tse-tung's swim in the Yangtze River three years ago.

July 17: Hsieh Pang-chih, newly appointed Ambassador Extraordinary and Plenipotentiary of the PRC to Afghanistan, left Peking by air.

Li Chiang-fen, charge d'affaires ad interim of the Chinese Embassy in the People's Republic of Southern Yeman, left Peking for his post.

July 18: The NCNA released a report on the dredging of the Toho River in Honan and Anhwei Provinces and the excavation of the new Pienho River in Anhwei and Kiangsu Provinces.

July 19: Yang Chi-liang, newly appointed Ambassador Extraordinary and Plenipotentiary of the PRC to the Democratic People's Republic of Algeria, left Peking for his post.

Wang Jo-chieh, Ambassador Extraordinary and Plenipotentiary of the PRC to the Arab Republic of Yemen, left Peking for his post.

Youssef Chakra, newly appointed Ambassador Extraordinary and Plenipotentiary of the Syrian Arab Republic, arrived in Peking.

July 21: The Nixon administration announced steps to relax travel and trade restrictions that had been applied to the PRC since 1950. Beginning July 23, U.S. citizens traveling abroad would be allowed to bring back $100 worth of goods produced in the PRC, the State Department announced. The department also announced that certain categories of U.S. citizens would be allowed to travel to China, although a general travel ban would remain in effect. Six categories of citizens to be automatically cleared for travel to China by the State Department were: Congressmen, journalists, teachers, scholars with post-graduate degrees and undergraduates enrolled in a college or university, scientists, medical doctors, and American Red Cross representatives. The department noted, however, that travelers would still have to obtain entry visas from Peking.

July 24: Housni Younes, new representative of the Palestine Liberation Organization in the PRC and head of the Palestine Liberation Organization Mission in Peking, arrived in Peking.

A 1969 protocol for the mutual delivery of goods between the PRC and Mongolia was signed in Ulan Bator.

July 26: An NCNA report marked the anniversary of the entry of the first workers-PLA Mao Tse-tung thought propaganda team into Tsinghua University.

July 28–August 8: Secretary of State William P. Rogers visited Japan, South Korea, Formosa, Indonesia, New Zealand, and Australia. In his public statement during the tour, Rogers expressed the desire of the U.S. to renew diplomatic talks with the PRC.

An NCNA statement refuted the rumor that China had issued stamps featuring revolutionary leaders and groups in Africa, Asia, and Latin America.

July 29: Fan Wen-lan, member of the CCP Central Committee and the Standing Committee of the National People's Congress, and director of modern history of the department of philosophy and social sciences of the Chinese Academy of Sciences died of illness in Peking at the age of 76.

July 31: The Ministry of National Defense gave a party of diplomatic envoys and military attaches of various countries stationed in China in honor of the 42nd anniversary of the founding of the Chinese People's Liberation Army.

Albania sent greetings and held celebrations on the occasion of China's Army Day.

August 1: The Ministry of National Defense gave a reception celebrating the 42nd anniversary of the founding of the Chinese People's Liberation Army. The NCNA released the full text of a speech delivered by Huang Yung-sheng, Chief of the General Staff of the Chinese People's Liberation Army at the reception given by the Ministry of National Defense.

An NCNA report told of the conscientious study of Mao Tse-tung's latest instructions by armymen and civilians on the 42nd anniversary of the founding of the Chinese People's Liberation Army.

August 5: A Sino-Hungarian goods exchange and payment agreement for 1969 was signed in Budapest.

Chinese residents in Japan held a protest meeting in Tokyo against Soviet armed intrusions into China.

August 6: The Canadian government announced that Miss Margaret Meagher, former Canadian High Commissioner to Kenya, would replace Arthur Andrew as the Canadian envoy at the Stockholm, Sweden talks with the PRC regarding recognition of Peking. The announcement came at a time of an apparent impasse in the talks.

August 7: The NCNA reported the discovery of huge coal reserves beneath the old pits at the Fanti colliery of the Liaoyuan Mining Administration in Kirin Province.

The PRC issued a warning against the intrusion of a U.S. warship into China's territorial waters off Kwangtung and Fukien.

August 8: Talks between the U.S.S.R. and the PRC on border river navigation, begun June 18 in Khabarovsk, ended August 8 with the signing of an agreement to hold further talks in China in 1970. A com-munique said the two nations had agreed to "improve the shipping situation" during 1969 along the Amur and Ussuri.

A Sino-Polish goods exchange and payment agreement for 1969 was signed in Warsaw

August 9: The NCNA released a statement issued by the Central Committee of the Communist Party of Malaya, calling on people of all nationalities of Malaya to unite, oppose "counterrevolutionary" violence with "revolutionary" violence, and smash the policy of "national massacre" of the Rahman-Razak "puppet clique."

August 10: The Chinese Embassy in Yemen gave a reception in honor of a group of Chinese water-sources technical personnel about to leave Yemen for home.

August 11: The PRC delegation to a Sino-Soviet Joint Commission for Navigation on Boundary Rivers returned to Harbin.

August 12: Kuo Mo-jo received Sunao Ohiro, Yoshitomi Takemoto, Kiyoshi Kanaii, and other members of the visiting friendship delegation of Japanese teachers.

A textile combine built with Chinese assistance was transferred to the Congolese (B) government.

August 13: In a protest note delivered to the Soviet Embassy in Peking, the PRC charged that the U.S.S.R. had sent "helicopters, tanks, armored vehicles, and several hundred armed troops to deliberately intrude into the Tiehliekti area in Yumin County of the Sinkiang Uighur Autonomous Region, China, creating a fresh incident of bloodshed in which many Chinese frontier guards were killed and wounded." The Soviet protest note charged that "several groups of Chinese armymen violated the Soviet state border . . . and entered Soviet territory."

August 14: An NCNA report described China's success in coping with shifting sand along her first cross-desert railway.

Chung Hsi-tung, Chinese Ambassador to Tanzania, gave a reception to welcome Pu ke, leader of the Chinese working team helping in the building of the Tanzania-Zambia Railway, and Wang Tsung-min, newly appointed Chinese economic representative in Tanzania, and to bid farewell to Chiang Ta, outgoing Chinese economic representative in Tanzania.

August 15: Peking charged that the U.S.S.R. was mobilizing for war, and it warned people to prepare for the eventual conflict. A Radio Peking broadcast charged that the U.S.S.R. had constructed a 12-mile-wide "no man zone" at the border, and was also building military roads and railroads along the border.

August 16: *People's Daily* published an article discussing the system of examination in rural schools.

A group of Chinese engineering and technical personnel arrived at Dar-es-Salaam to help in the building of the Tanzania-Zambia railway.

August 19: The Chinese Foreign Ministry lodged a strong protest with the Soviet Government against Soviet troops making repeated intrusions into China's territory, territorial waters, and airspace at many points along the Sino-Soviet border in June and July.

A full-length color documentary, "The 9th National Congress of the Communist Party of China," was shown at a film reception and cocktail party given by Chang Hai-feng, PRC Ambassador to Rumania, at Bucharest.

August 20: Abdulla Abodah Hamam, charge d'affaires ad interim of the Embassy of the People's Republic of Southern Yemen in the PRC, arrived in Peking.

The Red Cross Society of China condemned the Standing Commission of the International Red Cross for "serving the U.S. imperialist scheme to create Two Chinas."

The showing of a documentary film entitled, "Chenpao Island Brooks No Violation," began in Peking and other parts of the country. Showing of the new documentary, "The Czechoslovak People Will Never Submit," also began.

August 21: The historic Silk Route between China and the Indian subcontinent (now West Pakistan) was reopened in mid-August after being closed for 20 years. A Chinese caravan of 50 camels left Lupgaz

in Sinkiang Province August 21, crossed at Mintaka Pass in the Himalayas into Pakistan, and arrived August 24 at Misgar, 135 miles from Gilgit. Some $60,000 worth of goods were bartered on each side.

August 22: A documentary, "Anti-China Atrocities of the New Tsars," was shown at a film reception given by the PRC Embassy in Norway.

August 24–31: E. F. Hill, chairman of the Australian Communist Party (Marxist-Leninist), visited Peking at the invitation of the Central Committee of the Chinese Communist Party.

August 24: The NCNA released a report of the construction of the Kinsoundi Textile Combine in the Congo (B) with Chinese technical assistance.

August 25: An NCNA report described the showing of two documentaries—"Anti-China Atrocities of the New Tsars" and "Down with the New Tsars"—at two film receptions held recently by the PRC Embassy in the United Arab Republic.

August 26: The trial production of creosote from coconut shells by a small pharmacy on Haian Island was reported by the NCNA.

August 26–September 8: A Zambian government goodwill mission, headed by Sikota Wina, arrived in Peking at the invitation of the PRC government.

August 28: The U.S.S.R. warned the PRC that atomic weapons would be used if war broke out. In a long, unsigned article in *Pravda,* "Peking's Adventurist Course," the Soviet Union charged that China's "adventurist" and reckless policy was endangering the whole world. The article reiterated Soviet suggestions for talks to settle differences between the two countries, but warned: "Any attempt to talk with the Soviet Union in the language of guns, to encroach on the interests of the Soviet peoples who are building Communism, will be firmly rebuffed."

August 29: Japanese geologists reported the discovery of huge oil deposits in the Senkaku Island area in the East China Sea during a survey conducted June 4 to July 13. The islands, currently administered by the U.S. as part of the Ryukyu Island Chain, are about 100 miles northeast of Formosa and 50 miles from the Chinese mainland. Dr. Hiroshi Niino of Tokai University said the underwater oil field could be one of the 10 largest in the world. The government announced that $280,000 would be allocated in next year's budget for exploration and development of the oil fields.

A *People's Daily* article charged that Soviet troops had tried unsuccessfully to destroy evidence that they had invaded Chenpao (Damansky) Island March 15.

August 31: *People's Daily* called for destruction of old customs and habits and for the practice of frugality in weddings.

The NCNA announced that a former first lieutenant platoon leader of the army under Chiang Kai-shek crossed over on August 3 from Greater Quemoy to a PLA unit of the Fukien front.

The PRC government made a gift to Ceylon of a quantity of anti-malaria drugs.

September 1: Mao Tse-tung, Lin Piao, and Chou En-lai sent a message to Ho Chi-Minh and other Vietnamese Party and government leaders extending congratulations on the 24th anniversary of the proclamation of independence of the Democratic Republic of Vietnam.

September 2: Chou En-lai, Huang Yung-sheng, Li Hsien-nien, and Kuo Mo-jo attended the reception given by Ngo Minh Loan, North Vietnamese Ambassador to the PRC, marking the 24th anniversary of the proclamation of independence of the Democratic Republic of Vietnam.

September 3: North Vietnamese President Ho Chi-Minh died on September 3 at the age of 79. The NCNA published Ho's will on September 11.

September 4: The CPC Central Committee sent a message of condolence to the Central Committee of the North Vietnam Workers' Party on the passing away of President Ho Chi-Minh.

A CPC delegation headed by Chou En-lai left by special plane for Hanoi to tender condolences on the death of President Ho Chi-Minh. Chou and his group

returned to Peking the following morning, avoiding a possible face-to-face meeting with Premier Kosygin, who arrived in Hanoi September 6. A new PRC delegation led by Vice-Premier Li Hsien-nien flew to Hanoi on September 8. Peking did not explain its reason for changing the delegations. During his brief stay in Hanoi, Chou had conferred with Communist Party Secretary General Le Duan and members of the Politburo. Chou assured the North Vietnamese leadership of continued support in the war .

September 6: Chou En-lai, Chen Po-ta, Kang Sheng, and other members of the Political Bureau of the CPC Central Committee called at the DRV Embassy to tender condolences on the death of President Ho Chi-Minh.

September 7: A U.S.-made jet trainer brought back by former Chiang airmen was now on display in Peking, according to an NCNA report.

A Rumanian Party and government delegation led by I. G. Maure arrived in Peking on its way to Hanoi to attend the funeral of President Ho Chi-Minh.

An agreement on a plan to construct a small-sized wooden boat-building yard in the Congo (B) with the assistance of and the supply of the required equipment and materials by China was signed between China and the Congo (B) in Brazzaville.

A four-day conference of the Japanese-American Assembly held in Shimoda agreed that Japan and the U.S. should "normalize" relations with the PRC and seek to end Chinese isolation.

September 8: Hsieh Fu-chih, Chiu Hui-tso, and Kuo Mo-jo attended the reception given by Kim Jai Sook, charge d'affaires ad interim of the Korean Embassy in China, marking the 21st anniversary of the founding of the Democratic People's Republic of Korea.

September 9: Bulgaria celebrated the 25th anniversary of the overthrow of its wartime pro-Nazi regime. The PRC delegation walked out of the ceremonies to protest a statement by Defense Minister

General Dobri Dzhuriv that "contemporary left and right revisionists are objecting at the service of imperialism." (The term "left revisionism" has been used to denounce Peking.)

September 10: The U.S.S.R. charged that the PRC had instigated 488 border incidents between June and mid-August. The Tass statement said 2,500 Chinese soldiers had participated in the clashes.

September 10–16: Rita Marko, head of the Albanian Party and government delegation, and Tonin Jakova and Dilaver Poci, members of the delegation, arrived in Peking after attending the funeral of President Ho Chi-Minh.

September 11: A Rumanian Party and government delegation passed through Peking on its way home from Hanoi after attending the funeral of President Ho Chi-Minh.

Chou En-lai met at Peking airport, and had a frank conversation with, Soviet Premier Kosygin who was passing through Peking on his way home from Hanoi after attending the funeral of President Ho Chi-Minh. This was the first time the two leaders had met since February 10, 1965. In a brief announcement of the meeting September 11, Tass said Kosygin and Chou "frankly made known their positions and had a conversation useful for both sides." The report said only that the two had met by "mutual agreement." Six hours after the Tass report, the NCNA reported the two leaders had had a "frank conversation."

September 13: The Red Cross Society of China presented one million doses each of smallpox vaccines and tabc vaccines as a gift to the Red Cross Society of Nepal.

September 14: In a *People's Daily* editorial, the Peking government called the PRC's recently inaugurated steel production campaign "a concrete action taken to support national defense, safeguard the motherland and smash all aggressive plots of U.S. imperialism and Soviet revisionism."

September 16: Peking issued a list of 22 slogans to mark the 20th anniversary of the founding of the PRC October 1. Two of the slogans denounced the U.S.S.R. The 16th said: "Down with U.S. imperialism! Down with Soviet revisionist socialist-imperialism! Down with the reactionaries of all countries!" The 22nd slogan warned against a nuclear war.

Canadian Foreign Minister Mitchell W. Sharp said that he and U.N. Secretary General Thant both believed that the PRC had changed its attitude and currently wanted to become a member of the U.N. Sharp said his conviction came out of the talks between Canadian and Chinese representatives in Stockholm on Canadian recognition of the Peking government.

September 18: Sources in Moscow said that border incidents along the Sino-Soviet frontier had ceased since the September 11 meeting in Peking between Chou En-lai and Kosygin.

September 19: The NCNA reported that the discovery of new oil deposits and the development of refining facilities and production had enabled China to become self-sufficient in oil. The NCNA said 1969 output had "already gone up several times over that of 1965," but it gave no production figure. Sources in Hong Kong estimated China's 1965 oil production at 10 million tons.

September 20: The NCNA reported that Mao Tse-tung approved the order by the Military Commission conferring the title of "combat hero" on Sun Yo-kuo and nine other comrades.

September 21: The PRC successfully conducted its first underground nuclear test.

The Chinese Red Cross Society donated foodstuffs and medicine valued at Renminbi 40,000 *yuan* as a token of the Chinese people's sympathy with and aid for the drought victims of Somalia.

September 25: The Canadian Wheat Board announced in Ottawa the sale of 86.2 million bushels of Canadian wheat to the PRC. The sale, totaling $135 million, represented a quarter of Canada's total wheat exports in 1968.

September 25–30: A delegation of the National Council of Revolution and the Government of the Republic of Congo

(B) led by Major Alfred Raoul, Prime Minister and President of the Government Council, arrived in Shanghai on the way to Peking to attend the celebrations of the 20th anniversary of the founding of the PRC.

September 26: An agreement and protocol on China's assistance to North Vietnam between the governments of the PRC and the DRV were signed in Peking.

A national delegation from Cambodia led by Lieutenant-General Lon Nol, Premier of Cambodia, arrived in Canton on the way to Peking to attend the celebrations of the 20th anniversary of the founding of the PRC.

September 27: China's second 15,000-ton oil tanker, "Taching No. 28," was launched at the Hungchi Shipyard.

(1) Haki Toska, member of the Political Bureau of the Central Committee of the Albanian Party of Labour and Vice-Chairman of the Council of Ministers of the People's Republic of Albania, (2) Pham Van Dong, Premier of the DRV, (3) R. P. Giri, Minister of Transport, Communications and Public Works of Nepal, (4) Hamid Ould Mouknass, Minister of External Affairs of Mauritania, (5) Abu Kasem, leading member of the Palestine National Liberation Movement, and (6) G. Bylin, Chairman of the Communist League (Marxist-Leninist) of Sweden arrived in Peking to attend the celebrations of the 20th anniversary of the founding of the PRC.

September 29: The PRC successfully conducted a new hydrogen bomb explosion.

(1) Nguyen Nuu Tho, delegate of the South Vietnam National Front for Liberation and the Provisional Revolutionary Government of the Republic of South Vietnam, (2) N. Sanmugathasan, General Secretary of the Communist party of Ceylon, (3) Lansana Diane, Minister of Interior of Guinea, arrived in Peking to attend the celebration of the 20th anniversary of the founding of the PRC.

September 30: Premier Chou En-lai gave a reception celebrating the 20th anniversary of the founding of the PRC.

(1) Choi Yong Kun, Korean Party and Government delegation, (2) Mohamed Said Mazouzi, Minister of Labor and Social Affairs of Algeria, (3) Joseph-Andre Marchisio, delegate of the France-China Friendship Association, and (4) Clive Sandy, Chairman of the Australian-China Society, arrived in Peking to attend the celebration of the 20th anniversary of the founding of the PRC.

A spokesman of the PLA headquarters at the Fukien front announced suspension of shelling of offshore islands on October 1 and 3.

October 1: The PRC celebrated its 20th National Day with a massive rally in Peking's Tienanmen Square. CPC Chairman Mao Tse-tung and Vice-Chairman Lin Piao presided over the rally in their first public appearance since May 19. Mao's appearance silenced speculation that he was dead or had suffered a stroke.

October 4: Anthony Grey, a Reuters correspondent under house arrest in Peking since July 21, 1967, was released by the PRC. This followed the release October 3 of the last of the 13 Chinese journalists imprisoned in Hong Kong during the 1967 disturbances. Grey left Peking on October 9.

The NCNA announced the success of the PRC's first underground nuclear test on September 23 and the successful explosion of a new hydrogen bomb on September 29.

Tang Pi-wu congratulated Ton Duc Thang and Nguyen Luong Bang on their being elected President and Vice-President of the Democratic Republic of Vietnam.

The Chinese Foreign Ministry sponsored a meeting welcoming a delegation of South Vietnam Youth, Heroes and Intrepid Fighters Against U.S. Aggressors.

October 5: The *New York Times* reported that Peking continued to detain 8 Americans, 8 Britons, 14 Japanese, 8 West Germans, 1 Bulgarian, and 1 Italian.

People's Daily published articles on the sending of office cadres to the lower level to perform manual labor.

October 6: The NCNA released a report on the establishment of the revolutionary committee of Peking University.

Chen Po-ta, Yeh Chien-ying, and Li Hsien-nien received "patriotic compatriots" from Hong Kong and Macao, and patriotic overseas Chinese.

October 6–7: Chinese officials attended the various receptions given by the Embassies of North Korea, Rumania, and East Germany to mark the 20th anniversary of the establishment of diplomatic relations between the PRC and these countries.

October 7: The PRC announced that Peking and the U.S.S.R. had agreed to begin negotiations to end their border dispute. The NCNA statement said talks would be held in Peking at the deputy foreign ministers level at a date "now under discussion." The NCNA statement also contended that it had been Chinese Premier Chou En-lai who proposed at his meeting with Soviet Premier Kosygin on September 11 steps to reduce tensions along the border.

October 8: The NCNA released critical reports of capitalist tendencies in production brigades.

Chou En-lai gave a banquet in honor of President Nguyen Huu Tho, President of the Presidium of the Central Committee of the South Vietnam National Front for Liberation and President of the Advisory Council of the Provisional Revolutionary Government of the Republic of South Vietnam.

The NCNA released a Chinese Foreign Ministry document in refutation of the Soviet Government's statement of June 13, 1969. The document contained a five-point proposal for an overall settlement of the Sino-Soviet boundary question: (1) Both sides should confirm that the treaties relating to the present Sino-Soviet boundary are unequal treaties imposed on China by Tsarist Russian imperialism; (2) these treaties should be taken as the basis for an overall settlement through peaceful negotiations and for determining the entire alignment of the boundary line; it added that China did not demand the return of annexed territory; (3) any territory occupied in violation of the treaties must be returned unconditionally to the other side, but adjustments to the frontier could be made based on mutual understanding and mutual accommodation; (4) a new and equal Sino-Soviet treaty must be concluded to replace the old treaties and to carry out a boundary survey and erect boundary markers; and (5) pending a settlement, the two sides should maintain the status quo of the border, avert armed conflicts and disengage armed forces of both sides by withdrawing them from, or refraining from sending them into, all the disputed areas along the Sino-Soviet border.

October 9: The NCNA reported the launching of a 10,000-ton freighter, "Tientsin," designed and built entirely by the Tientsin New Harbor Shipyard.

A Sino-Guinea economic and technical cooperation agreement was signed in Peking.

Juan Bosch Gavino, former President of the Dominican Republic and leader of the Dominican Revolutionary Party, and Hector Aristy, ex-Minister to the President of the Revolutionary Government of 1965 and leader of the movement of April 24, arrived in Peking.

October 10: A Sino-Congo (B) agreement on economic and technical cooperation was signed in Peking.

A spokesman of the Chinese Foreign Ministry denounced the U.S. for "sending military aircraft and warships to carry out unbridled armed provocations for many days against Chinese fishing fleets on the high seas in the Bac Bo Gulf."

Completion of water supply works built with Chinese aid was marked at Dar-es-Salaam in Zanzibar.

October 11: Norman Barrymaine, a British free-lance journalist, was released by the PRC after he served a 19-month prison term in Shanghai. Barrymaine, 69, who had been arrested in 1968, was charged with espionage but was never sentenced.

Mao Tse-tung and Lin Piao received 10,000 representatives of workers, poor and lower-middle class peasants, the PLA, Red Guards, revolutionary cadres and revolutionary intellectuals and of "May 7" cadre schools who had come from all parts of China to attend the National Day celebrations.

Chou En-lai sent a message of greetings to Prince Souphanouvong on the occasion of the 24th anniversary of the Laotian Revolution Day.

Kang Sheng and Yao Wen-yuan met Fosco Dinucci, General Secretary of the Communist Party of Italy (Marxist-Leninist).

October 13: In a *Red Flag* editorial the PRC announced a new economic policy, the first overall economic policy statement issued since the start of the Cultural Revolution in 1966. The editorial, entitled "The Road of Socialist Industrialization in China," called for a balanced approach to development of heavy and light industry and agriculture.

The Chinese People's Association for Friendship with Foreign Countries and China-Latin American Friendship Association gave a dinner in honor of Juan Bosch Gavino and Hector Aristy.

The Chinese Red Cross Society donated woolen blankets and canned food for flood victims in Algeria.

October 14: Mao Tse-tung and Lin Piao received commanders and fighters from the headquarters of the General Staff and the General Logistics Department of the PLA and commanders and fighters of various services and arms of the PLA in Peking.

October 15: China's 1969 Autumn Export Commodities Fair opened in Canton.

The NCNA accused the Indian government of manipulating Dalai into conducting anti-China activities.

October 16: Captain Peter M. Will, a Scottish sea captain, was released after having been detained near Tientsin for nearly 17 months. Will had been arrested May 28, 1968, and charged with insulting Mao when his ship was anchored at Taku.

The NCNA released the full text of a communique on talks between Premier

Chou En-lai and President Nguyen Huu Tho.

Kuang-ming Jih-pao published an article condemning Stanislavsky's system of stage acting and praising Chiang Ching for her part in the creation of "model revolutionary plays."

October 17: The Peking Municipal Revolutionary Committee invited more than 2,000 foreign friends in Peking to sports performances given by outstanding Chinese athletes.

The Chinese charge d'affaires office in Britain held a photo exhibition in celebration of the 20th anniversary of the founding of the PRC.

October 17–30: A delegation of the Laotian Patriotic Front, headed by Tiaosouk Vongsak and Nhia Vu, arrived in Peking.

October 18: The NCNA released reports on Sino-Soviet negotiations on the boundary question.

A Tanzania acrobatics study group left Peking for home.

October 19: The Soviet news agency Tass made public excerpts from a forthcoming article in the Communist Party journal *Kommunist* by Mikhail A. Suslov, the Communist Party's leading ideologist. Suslov charged that Peking was following an "adventuristic, chauvinistic policy" that was damaging to the international Communist movement. The timing of the article was regarded as a confirmation that the two countries were still not able to reconcile their ideological views.

Chou En-lai sent a message of condolence to Somali President Ad Interim Hussein and Prime Minister Egal on the death by assassination of President Shermarke.

October 20: The PRC and the U.S.S.R. opened border negotiations in Peking. Except for listing the delegate on both sides, no official announcement on details of the talks was given through November 11. The Soviet delegation was led by First Deputy Foreign Minister Vaily V. Kuznesov. The Chinese delegation was led by Deputy Foreign Minister Chiao Kuan-hus.

October 22: Chou En-lai held talks with and

gave a banquet for Premier Pham Van Dong who arrived in Peking as the head of the DRVN party and government delegation.

The NCNA reported that Trutz Von Xylander, 34, a West German, had been sentenced to 10 years in jail in Lanchow, Kansu, as a "U.S. imperialist spy." The NCNA said Von Xylander had photographed restricted areas "rendering active service to the U.S. policies of war and aggression and seriously endangering China's security."

A protocol relating to the exchange of commodities between the PRC and Ceylon for 1970 was signed in Peking.

The NCNA released a report on the U.S.-Soviet draft treaty on the prohibition of the emplacement of nuclear weapons on the seabed and the ocean floor.

October 24: Kang Sheng held talks with N. Sanmugathasan, General Secretary and member of the Political Bureau of the Central Committee of the Communist Party of Ceylon.

October 25: The NCNA released a communique on talks between Chou En-lai and Pham Van Dong.

October 28: Seven West Germans were freed by the PRC after 14 months of house arrest. They had not been charged with any crime but were held in connection with customs formalities.

A Chinese government and military delegation headed by Chen Shih-chu, commander of the Engineering Corps of the Chinese PLA, left Peking for Algeria to attend the celebrations of the National Day of the Democratic People's Republic of Algeria. The group returned to Peking on November 13.

October 30: The NCNA released a report on the trial production by a Peking hospital of an effective drug for treating psoriasis.

October 31: Executive secretaries of the Afro-Asian Writers' Bureau issued a statement condemning "U.S. imperialism for colluding with the Lebanese authorities in suppressing the Palestinian guerrillas."

November 1: The NCNA released reports on the launching of the socialist revolutionary emulation drive.

A PRC railway delegation led by Kuo Lu, Vice Minister of Railways, arrived in Dar-es-Salaam.

The NCNA released reports criticizing the U.S., Malaysia, and Thailand.

November 2: Chinese Communist activities within Burma were expanding and intensifying, according to a *Washington Post* report. The *Post* reported that Chinese soldiers were serving as military advisers to a 4,000-man guerrilla band opposed to General Ne Win's regime. The insurgents, an indigenous Communist group, were in control of the state of Kokang and other regions near the Chinese border. The report said the group had staged battalion-force attacks along the Burma Road. Other Chinese army units were reported patrolling east of the Salween River in an effort to flush out Chinese Nationalist irregulars. Chinese civilian cadres were reported to be helping the insurgent group administer "liberated" areas near the Chinese border, the *Post* report said.

The NCNA released reports on agricultural production, animal husbandry, water conservation, agricultural mechanization, rural electrification, and land reclamation.

November 3: The PRC issued a warning against the intrusion of a U.S. warship into China's territorial waters in the area south of Pinghai in Kwangtung province.

November 4: The NCNA released a report on trial production of medical equipment for the countryside.

November 5: The NCNA released a report on preliminary discussions of strategic arms limitation talks by the United States and the Soviet Union. It accused the two countries of using the Helsinki talks to maintain their "nuclear collusion." It said they were cooperating with each other "in their big conspiracy to further the nuclear military alliance between the two countries so as to maintain their already bankrupt nuclear monopoly."

November 6: The NPC Standing Committee and the State Council sent a message of greetings, and the Chinese People's Association for Friendship with Foreign Countries and the Sino-Soviet Friendship Association held a film reception on the occasion of the 52nd anniversary of the October Revolution.

The NCNA claimed that a Chinese medical team had cured deaf-mutes in Yemen.

November 7: The Political Bureau of the CPC Central Committee gave a banquet in honor of Xhorxhi Robo, Albanian Ambassador to the PRC, and his wife.

A Sino-Iraqi agreement on air transport was signed in Peking.

Seimin Miyazaki, Director-General of the Japan-China Friendship Association (Orthodox) Headquarters, and four other Japanese arrived in Peking on a friendly visit to China at the invitation of the China-Japan Friendship Association.

November 9: Chou En-lai, Li Hsien-nien, and Kuo Mo-jo attended a reception given by the Cambodian Ambassador to the PRC to celebrate the 16th anniversary of the independence of the Kingdom of Cambodia.

November 10: The NCNA released a report on maiden voyages to Japanese ports made by two 10,000-ton ocean-going freighters, "Xieng Yang" and "Chao Yang," designed and built by China.

November 11: The NCNA reported completion of the 800-meter "Yukung" tunnel on the Taihang Mountain highway in the northern part of Hwiehsien in Honan Province.

The U.N. General Assembly rejected a 17-power draft resolution to seat Communist China and expel Nationalist China. The vote was 48 in favor of the resolution, 56 against and 21 abstentions. Earlier, the Assembly had approved an 18-power draft resolution declaring the issue of Communist Chinese membership to be "an important question" requiring a two-thirds majority of those present and voting to reallocate the seat held by Nationalist China. The vote on this resolution was 71 in favor to 48 opposed with four abstentions. The motion to seat Peking

picked up four votes over 1968. Four Afro-Asian countries—Ghana, Libya, Mauritius and Nigeria—switched from abstentions to vote in favor of the resolution. Belgium, Chile, and Italy switched from opposition to abstentions. Senegal moved from abstention to opposition. The *New York Times* reported that the Soviet Union had exerted no noticeable pressure in favor of the resolution, which had come to a vote annually since 1950. The U.S.S.R. did not speak in the debate on the resolution. Representatives of 44 countries had made statements in the debate on the resolution, which began November 3. The *Times* noted the U.S. had also done less active canvassing against Peking than in the past.

November 14: The NCNA reported the opening of the Shaoshan-Chingkang Mountain highway to traffic.

Eric Gordon, 31, his wife, and son were released after almost two years of confinement in Peking. Gordon was arrested on November 5, 1967.

A supplementary agreement between the PRC, Tanzania, and Zambia on the construction of the Tanzania-Zambia Railway was signed in Lusaka.

November 14–27: An Albanian People's Army art troup led by Nane Kutra, Deputy Chief of the Political Department of the Albanian People's Army, arrived in Peking.

November 15: The 1969 Autumn Chinese Export Commodities Fair closed.

November 15–23: Hisao Kuroda, chairman of the Japan-China Friendship Association (Orthodox) Headquarters, and four other Japanese, arrived in Peking on a friendly visit to China at the invitation of the China-Japan Friendship Association.

November 17: The PRC's 1968 trade with the U.S.S.R., Czechoslovakia, Hungary, Poland, Rumania, and Yugoslavia was reported in a Radio Free Europe research report. Peking's trade with the six countries amounted to about $282 million. Rumania was the only country whose trade with Peking had increased above the 1969 level.

November 18: *People's Daily* published a signed article stating that the PRC must rely on her own effort in developing her light industry and must not rely on imported machine tools or foreign aid.

November 20: In a *People's Daily* editorial the Peking government called on officials and cadres to participate in manual labor. The editorial, entitled "Cadres Should Persist in Taking Part in Collective Labor," said the best way for officials to keep in contact with the masses would be to follow the instructions of Chairman Mao Tse-tung. "This is the most basic requirement of a fighter in continuing the revolution under the dictatorship of the proletariat," it said.

November 21: Following three days of meetings in Washington (November 19–21), President Nixon and Japanese Premier Eisaku Sato issued a 15-point communique announcing the return of Okinawa and other U.S.-held Ryukyu Islands to Japan in 1972. On security in the Far East, Sato acknowledged "the security of the Republic of Korea was essential to Japan's own security . . . and the maintenance of peace and security in the Taiwan area was also a most important factor in the security of Japan." In his comments on November 21, Sato pledged that if the U.S. needed to use bases in Japan and against South Korea or Taiwan, "the policy of the government of Japan towards prior consultation would be to decide its position positively and promptly." He also added that the decision on the use of the bases would be made in context with U.S. treaty commitments to Nationalist China. Mr. Nixon said the U.S. would continue to honor its treaty obligations in the Far East.

November 22: Li Hsien-nien, Hsieh Fu-chih, and other Chinese officials attended the reception given by Xhorxhi Robo, Albanian Ambassador to the PRC, in celebration of the 20th anniversary of the establishment of diplomatic relations between Albania and the PRC.

November 23: Chou En-lai and Li Hsien-nien received Ngo Minh Loan, Ambassador of the DRVN to the PRC.

An agreement on mutual goods supply and payments in 1970 between the PRC and the DRVN was signed in Peking.

November 23–24: Chou En-lai met Le Thanh Nghi, Vice-Premier of the DRVN government, and Ly Ban, Vice-Minister of Foreign Trade of the DRVN, who were on their way home via Peking.

November 25–December 6: A Chinese party and government delegation, with Li Hsien-nien as head and Li Teh-sheng as deputy head, left Peking for Tirana to attend the celebrations of the 25th anniversary of the liberation of Albania.

November 26: The NCNA released a report on the successful treatment of scalds over a large area of the body by mainly using traditional Chinese medicinal herbs combined with Western medicine.

The Chinese Foreign Ministry issued a statement expressing firm support for the just statement of Samdech Sihanouk on the "barbarous crime of aggression perpetrated by U.S. imperialism against Cambodia."

A Chinese party and government delegation stopped over at Kabul en route to Albania.

November 28: The NCNA claimed that more than 80 blind people had regained their sight when treated with new methods of acupuncture.

Mao Tse-tung, Lin Piao, and Chou En-lai sent messages of greeting to the Albania Party and government leaders on the occasion of the 25th anniversary of the liberation of Albania.

Chou En-lai, Hsieh Fu-chih, and Kuo Mo-jo attended a reception given by the Mauritanian Ambassador to the PRC celebrating the 9th anniversary of the independence of the Islamic Republic of Mauritania.

November 29: A contract on a well-sinking project in Mauritania with Chinese assistance was signed in Nouakchott, capital of Mauritania.

December 2: The Chinese Embassy in Zambia held a memorial meeting for Chinese engineers and technicians who died in November while helping Zambia in construction work.

December 2–4: The NCNA released a series of *People's Daily* articles criticizing the "counterrevolutionary revisionist line in medical and health work" pushed by Liu Shao-chi.

December 3: The NCNA released a report of the first large salt mine in Hunan province, which went into production ahead of schedule.

December 6: A protocol between the PRC and Southern Yemen on the dispatching of a Chinese medical team to Southern Yemen was signed in Aden.

December 7: Two Americans, Simeon Daldivin, 56, of California, and Mrs. Bessie Hope Donald, 46, of Virginia, were released by Peking after being held since February 16, when their pleasure yacht was seized by a patrol boat en route from Hong Kong to Macao. The detainees said they had been treated well but had been forced to sign confessions for alleged crimes, including illegal intrusion into Chinese territorial waters.

A delegation of Marxist-Leninist Communists of France, led by Jacques Jurquet, arrived in Peking at the invitation of the CPC Central Committee.

December 9: The NCNA released a report on the fulfillment of a 1969 state plan for repair of locomotives and freight cars by a Peking rolling stock plant.

December 11: For the first time in nearly two years, U.S. and the PRC diplomats held a formal meeting in Warsaw to discuss the resumption of ambassadorial talks. U.S. Ambassador to Poland Walter Stoessel met with Charge D'affaires Lei Yang at the Chinese Embassy for 75 minutes. State Department spokesman Robert J. McClosky said on December 12 that the meeting had taken place in a "cordial" atmosphere and the diplomats had discussed "matters of common interest." Plans to resume diplomatic talks reportedly had been proposed by Stoessel in a brief encounter with Lei on December 3 at a fashion show in Warsaw.

A full-length color documentary, "Celebration of 20th Anniversary of Founding of Great People's Republic of China," began showing in Peking and other parts of the country.

Moslems in Peking observed the annual Corban Festival at the Tungssu Mosque.

December 12–29: E. F. Hill, Chairman of the Australian Communist Party (Marxist-Leninist), and C. J. McCaffrey arrived in Peking at the invitation of the CPC Central Committee.

December 14: The NCNA reported that negotiations on the Sino-Soviet boundary question adjourned temporarily due to the departure of V. V. Kuznetsov and V. A. Matrosov for home to attend the session of the U.S.S.R. Supreme Soviet, scheduled to open in December in Moscow. The negotiators would be gone for about one week. According to diplomats in Moscow, the conferees had been recalled for consultations on the progress of the talks.

December 15: Stanley Karnow of the *Washington Post* reported that during the past months measures had been intensified to prepare the Chinese people for war. These included mobilization of the civilian militia, construction of air raid shelters, and evacuation of children from major cities.

December 17–22: The 9th anniversary of the signing of the Sino-Cambodian Treaty of Friendship and Mutual Non-Aggression was marked.

December 18–19: A Chinese scientific and technical cooperation delegation led by Sun Hsiao-feng left Peking for Tirana to attend the regular meeting of the Joint China-Albania Committee for Cooperation in Technology and Technical Science.

December 19: Mao Tse-tung, Lin Piao, and Chou En-lai sent a message to President Nguyen Huu Tho of the Presidium of the Central Committee of the South Vietnam National Front for Liberation greeting the 9th anniversary of the founding of that front.

December 20: Keiji Samejima, Japanese correspondent of "Nihon Keizai Shimbun," departed from China.

December 21: Lin Piao sent a message to Vo Nguyen Giap greeting the 25th anniversary of the founding of the Vietnamese People's Army.

December 22: Hao Hsiang-chien, head of the Chinese agricultural technical team working in Somalia, presented samples of "Somali cigarettes" to the Supreme Revolutionary Council of the Somali Democratic Republic.

December 23: The minutes of talks on experimental tea planting in Afghanistan with Chinese aid were signed in Kabul.

December 24: Chou En-lai sent a message to President Obote of Uganda expressing sympathy for an attempt on his life "made by the imperialists and reactionaries."

December 26: The first ice-breaker designed and built in China, the 3,200-ton "Haiping 101," was successfully launched by Shanghai's Chiu Hsin shipyard.

Chinese medical personnel arrived in Mogadishu, capital of Somalia.

December 27: A Chinese government railway delegation headed by Kuo Lu returned to Peking after taking part in the China-Tanzania-Zambia negotiations on the construction of the Tanzania-Zambia railway and paying friendly visits to those countries.

December 30: A spokesman of the headquarters of PLA units in the Fukien front announced the suspension of shelling on December 31 and January 1.

The China-Cuba Friendship Association gave a film reception to mark the 11th anniversary of the liberation of Cuba.

December 31: The PRC and Zambia signed and exchanged letters concerning China's gratis provision of broadcast transmitters for Zambia.

The NCNA announced the staging of "model revolutionary theatrical works" in Peking and Shanghai beginning New Year's Day of 1970.

INDEX

DOMESTIC AFFAIRS

AGRICULTURE:

1950: 2-24; 3-10; 3-24; 4-10; 6-14; 7-14
1951: 2-3
1952: 2-15; 8-29
1953: 2-4; 2-13; 3-26; 7-19; 10-12; 12-16; 12-17
1954: 1-1; 1-11; 2-6; 2-28; 3-15; 3-18; 5-13
1955: 2-16; 3-23; 4-28; 7-31; 8-25; 10-15; 11-9; 11-20; 12-17
1956: 1-12; 1-25; 3-9; 3-17; 4-4; 6-15
1957: 3-19; 9-14; 9-20
1958: 1-6; 4-29; 6-3; 8-29; 9-30; 11-28; 12-18
1959: 1-28; 6-18; 10:15
1960: 3-29; 4-6; 4-11; 4-13; 6-21; 7-19; 12-29
1961: 1-20
1962: 3-27; 9-28
1963: 5-20
1964: 10-15
1965: 5-23
1966: 3-3; 6-16; 12-20
1967: 1-21; 2-26; 3-20
1968: 5-1; 5-6; 5-11; 12-19
1969: 2-9; 2-10; 2-13; 3-8; 4-11; 6-27; 7-11; 7-18; 10-8; 11-2

CPC:

1950: 6-6; 7-1
1951: 7-1
1952:
1953: 2-13; 4-23; 6-27; 7-1; 7-30; 12-16; 12-24
1954: 1-11; 1-22; 2-6; 8-31; 11-15
1955: 3-8; 4-4; 4-28
1956: 1-14; 4-5; 6-6; 9-7; 11-10
1957: 2-27; 3-18; 3-19; 4-27; 5-25; 6-20; 6-25; 6-26; 7-5; 8-8; 9-12; 9-14; 9-20; 9-23; 12-18
1958: 3-3; 4-7; 5-25; 6-1; 6-16; 8-17; 8-29; 9-25; 12-9; 12-20
1959: 6-18; 9-25; 11-15
1960: 7-19; 9-29
1961: 1-20; 1-21; 7-1; 8-13; 11-8; 12-14
1962: 9-28
1963: 7-1; 7-5; 7-10
1964: 2-29; 8-30
1965: 5-29; 11-10
1966: 1-17; 3-23; 5-16; 6-3; 6-13; 6-15; 7-28; 8-1; 8-8; 8-13; 9-8; 9-22; 9-25; 10-5; 11-15; 11-16; 12-2; 12-3; 12-9; 12-15; 12-26; 12-28; 12-31

1967: 1-11; 1-12; 1-13; 1-14; 1-19; 1-23; 1-26; 1-28; 1-30; 2-3; 2-4; 2-6; 2-8; 2-11; 2-12; 2-16; 2-17; 2-18; 2-19; 2-20; 2-21; 2-23; 2-25; 3-7; 3-16; 3-18; 3-19; 3-24; 3-27; 4-1; 4-6; 4-7; 4-13; 4-17; 4-19; 4-20; 4-21; 5-8; 5-16; 5-25; 6-6; 6-7; 7-14; 9-5; 9-9; 10-17; 11-27
1968: 5-16; 6-13; 6-15; 6-30; 7-24; 10-1; 10-17; 10-31; 11-24
1969: 1-8; 2-9; 2-21; 3-5; 3-31; 4-1; 4-7; 4-14; 4-24; 4-25; 4-26; 4-27; 4-28; 4-29; 5-2; 6-9; 6-15; 6-21; 6-30; 7-1; 7-29; 8-19; 9-4

CONSTRUCTION:

1950: 6-16
1951:
1952: 6-20; 7-1; 7-2; 8-2; 8-25; 11-20
1953: 5-5; 7-10; 7-15
1954: 1-1; 1-8; 11-27; 12-2; 12-25
1955: 2-8; 2-9; 2-20; 3-2; 6-23; 7-20; 7-23; 8-1; 10-12; 11-5; 12-27
1956: 3-25; 3-26; 3-29; 4-27; 5-10; 5-11; 6-16; 7-3; 7-11; 7-13; 11-16; 12-9
1957: 1-5; 1-9; 4-13; 5-23; 6-11; 9-25; 10-5
1958: 1-1; 6-15; 6-30; 7-30; 9-27; 10-18; 11-26; 11-27; 12-26
1959: 1-2; 2-7; 4-11; 6-23; 9-25; 10-1; 10-18; 12-10
1960: 1-20; 3-5; 3-27; 4-1; 6-10
1961: 5-25; 10-19
1962: 4-12; 6-19; 9-9
1963: 1-29; 2-8; 4-1; 5-6; 9-25; 12-20
1964: 7-7; 10-11; 10-31
1965:
1966: 1-1; 1-2; 5-26; 7-18; 9-12; 10-23; 12-20
1967: 1-18; 2-11; 7-18; 11-30
1968: 1-9; 3-23; 4-14; 5-14; 5-15; 5-30; 6-7; 6-13; 6-22; 6-26; 7-12; 8-3; 10-1; 11-2; 11-22; 12-29
1969: 1-3; 1-23; 1-31; 2-2; 2-4; 2-12; 3-6; 3-7; 3-8; 3-19; 4-8; 4-24; 7-3; 7-11; 8-14; 8-21; 8-26; 9-14; 9-19; 9-27; 10-9; 11-1; 11-10; 11-11; 11-14; 12-2; 12-26

CULTURAL REVOLUTION:

1965: 5-29; 11-10
1966: 1-2; 1-17; 1-18; 1-25; 2-1; 2-7; 2-27; 3-5; 3-11; 4-2; 4-14; 4-16; 4-18; 5-1; 5-4; 5-9; 5-16; 5-25; 6-1; 6-3; 6-6; 6-13; 6-14; 6-15; 6-16; 6-17; 6-19; 6-24; 6-25; 6-27; 6-30; 7-3; 7-5; 7-10; 7-11; 7-13; 7-25; 7-28;

334 INDEX

CULTURAL REVOLUTION — *Continued*

1966: 7-31; 8-1; 8-7; 8-8; 8-13; 8-18; 8-20; 8-23;
8-24; 8-26; 8-28; 8-29; 8-31; 9-3; 9-4; 9-7;
9-8; 9-9; 9-11; 9-12; 9-13; 9-14; 9-15; 9-16;
9-18; 9-20; 9-22; 9-25; 9-27; 9-29; 10-1;
10-5; 10-12; 10-18; 10-19; 10-23; 10-24;
10-25; 10-27; 11-3; 11-6; 11-8; 11-10; 11-12;
11-15; 11-16; 11-18; 11-23; 11-30; 12-2;
12-3; 12-4; 12-6; 12-7; 12-8; 12-10; 12-14;
12-15; 12-18; 12-20; 12-21; 12-22; 12-26;
12-27; 12-28; 12-29; 12-30; 12-31

1967: 1-3; 1-5; 1-6; 1-7; 1-8; 1-10; 1-11; 1-12;
1-13; 1-14; 1-17; 1-20; 1-21; 1-23; 1-25;
1-27; 1-28; 1-29; 1-30; 1-31; 2-1; 2-3; 2-4;
2-6; 2-8; 2-10; 2-11; 2-12; 2-13; 2-15; 2-16;
2-17; 2-18; 2-19; 2-20; 2-21; 2-22; 2-23;
2-24; 2-26; 3-1; 3-7; 3-12; 3-14; 3-16; 3-18;
3-19; 3-20; 3-22; 3-24; 3-25; 3-27; 4-1; 4-2;
4-3; 4-6; 4-7; 4-10; 4-13; 4-14; 4-16; 4-17;
4-19; 4-20; 4-21; 4-24; 4-27; 5-1; 5-2; 5-7;
5-8; 5-14; 5-16; 5-17; 5-18; 5-25; 5-26; 5-27;
5-28; 5-31; 6-2; 6-6; 6-7; 6-10; 6-16; 6-22;
7-3; 7-7; 7-9; 7-14; 7-21; 7-26; 7-28; 7-30;
8-1; 8-3; 8-4; 8-9; 8-10; 8-14; 8-15; 8-24;
9-3; 9-5; 9-9; 9-17; 9-24; 10-1; 10-17; 10-18;
11-1; 11-14; 11-27; 12-25; 12-26

1968: 1-1; 1-5; 1-8; 1-10; 1-25; 1-26; 1-27; 1-31;
2-3; 2-5; 2-6; 2-9; 2-10; 2-12; 2-14; 2-16;
2-17; 2-21; 3-4; 3-6; 3-7; 3-11; 3-19; 3-23;
3-26; 3-27; 4-6; 4-9; 4-10; 4-15; 4-18; 4-21;
4-25; 4-28; 4-29; 5-1; 5-2; 5-6; 5-7; 5-8; 5-9;
5-10; 5-11; 5-16; 5-20; 5-21; 5-26; 5-30;
5-31; 6-1; 6-2; 6-3; 6-4; 6-13; 6-15; 6-22;
6-25; 6-28; 6-30; 7-1; 7-11; 7-12; 7-14;
7-16; 7-17; 7-21; 7-22; 7-24; 7-25; 7-26;
7-31; 8-3; 8-5; 8-7; 8-8; 8-11; 8-12; 8-13;
8-14; 8-15; 8-18; 8-20; 8-25; 8-27; 8-28;
8-29; 8-30; 9-1; 9-3; 9-5; 9-7; 9-8; 9-10;
9-11; 9-14; 9-16; 9-17; 9-18; 9-19; 9-20;
9-22; 9-25; 9-26; 9-27; 9-29; 10-1; 10-5;
10-8; 10-13; 10-14; 10-15; 10-17; 10-27;
10-31; 11-2; 11-11; 11-14; 11-20; 11-24;
12-3; 12-17; 12-19; 12-31

1969: 1-1; 1-5; 1-8; 1-13; 1-16; 1-22; 1-25; 1-28;
1-29; 2-9; 2-10; 2-12; 2-13; 2-21; 3-5; 3-7;
3-8; 3-10; 3-14; 3-16; 3-31; 4-1; 4-6; 4-7;
4-11; 4-14; 4-20; 4-21; 4-24; 4-25; 4-26;
4-27; 4-28; 4-29; 5-1; 5-2; 5-8; 5-10; 5-11;
5-16; 5-19; 5-27; 6-1; 6-4; 6-9; 6-10; 6-15;
6-21; 6-22; 6-27; 6-30; 7-1; 7-11; 7-16; 7-26;
8-1; 8-16; 8-19; 8-31; 9-16; 9-20; 10-5; 10-6;
10-8; 10-11; 10-14; 10-16; 11-1; 11-8; 11-20;
12-2; 12-11; 12-15; 12-31

ECONOMY:

1950: 1-10; 1-27; 3-3; 3-10; 3-24; 12-1; 12-3;
12-8; 12-15
1951: 3-24
1952: 11-1; 12-24
1953: 1-13; 1-14; 2-20; 4-1; 7-7; 7-10; 8-5; 12-9
1954: 2-6; 2-28; 3-21; 3-23; 7-13; 8-7; 9-2; 9-14
1955: 2-2; 2-21; 3-1; 3-23; 3-26; 6-10; 6-20; 8-13;
8-31; 11-1
1956: 1-21; 2-8; 6-18; 7-28
1957: 2-28; 3-19; 4-12; 4-29; 8-1; 8-4; 8-9; 9-30;
10-25; 11-8; 11-13; 11-20; 12-9

1958: 1-6; 3-29; 4-7; 4-29; 5-12; 6-5; 6-9; 8-5;
8-17; 9-17; 10-12; 12-20
1959: 4-28; 5-6; 6-8; 6-25; 7-17; 8-2; 8-26;
9-23; 9-25
1960: 3-30
1961: 4-15; 8-13;
1962: 4-15; 7-20; 9-28; 9-30; 11-17; 12-1
1963: 3-31
1964: 7-7; 12-21
1965: 5-1; 7-10; 12-19
1966: 1-2; 4-2; 6-9; 9-9
1967: 1-10; 1-11; 4-15; 11-15
1968: 4-15; 6-13; 7-10; 7-12; 7-14; 9-25; 10-13;
10-15; 12-19
1969: 4-15; 5-14; 5-19; 8-26; 9-14; 9-19; 10-8;
10-13; 10-15; 11-15; 11-18; 12-2; 12-9

POLITICAL REFORMS:

1949: 10-1; 10-9; 10-15; 10-19; 10-25; 10-28; 12-2;
12-4; 12-9; 12-16
1950: 1-6; 1-27; 4-23; 5-19; 6-14; 7-14; 12-8
1951: 6-1; 8-3; 9-14; 10-23
1952: 2-7; 2-22; 6-27; 8-6; 8-9; 8-12; 10-10;
11-15; 12-24
1953: 1-13; 1-14; 1-23; 2-4; 2-7; 2-11; 3-1; 4-3;
4-7; 5-21; 6-15; 6-25; 7-24; 8-31; 10-1; 11-1;
12-8; 12-31
1954: 1-1; 2-27; 3-23; 3-29; 4-15; 5-3; 6-14; 6-19;
7-5; 8-1; 8-29; 11-8; 12-20; 12-25
1955: 5-13; 6-22; 7-5; 7-16; 7-30; 7-31; 8-1; 8-23;
9-27; 10-15; 11-11
1956: 1-1; 3-14; 5-12; 5-28; 5-29; 6-15; 6-22;
7-11; 11-13
1957: 2-27; 3-5; 3-12; 6-7; 6-18; 6-20; 6-25; 6-26;
7-15; 7-26; 10-13; 10-15; 10-23; 11-25;
11-29; 12-5
1958: 1-6; 1-13; 1-17; 1-18; 1-29; 2-11; 3-7; 4-24;
5-5; 6-3; 6-29; 7-3; 8-4; 9-5; 9-7; 9-9; 9-10;
10-20; 11-23; 11-28; 11-30; 12-17
1959: 1-23; 3-11; 3-24; 4-2; 4-11; 4-15; 4-17; 4-18;
4-24; 4-27; 8-24; 8-26; 9-17; 11-27;
12-4; 12-8
1960 1-25; 3-29; 3-30; 11-28
1961: 9-17; 10-1; 11-8; 12-17
1962: 3-23; 3-27; 8-4; 9-30; 10-20; 11-20; 12-18
1963: 1-17; 2-2; 3-30; 4-14; 7-8; 10-10; 11-17;
11-18; 11-28
1964: 4-27; 6-5; 7-22; 8-31; 9-12; 10-1; 10-16;
12-12; 12-18; 12-20; 12-21; 12-28; 12-30
1965: 1-3; 1-4; 1-19; 3-8; 4-30; 5-14; 5-24; 6-18;
7-20; 9-2; 9-20; 10-1; 10-22; 11-26
1966: 1-17; 1-18; 1-25; 3-9; 3-22; 4-16; 5-9; 7-25;
7-31; 8-1; 8-8; 9-4; 9-11; 10-1; 10-27; 11-30;
12-4; 12-7; 12-22; 12-26; 12-27; 12-28
1967: 1-23; 1-29; 1-31; 2-1; 2-3; 2-6; 2-7; 2-18;
2-23; 3-1; 3-12; 3-22; 4-2; 4-20; 5-14; 5-31;
6-7; 6-10; 6-17; 7-7; 7-9; 7-21; 7-28; 7-30;
8-1; 8-3; 8-9; 8-15; 8-24; 9-24; 10-18; 11-1;
11-14; 12-25; 12-26
1968: 1-1; 1-5; 1-10; 1-25; 1-27; 2-1; 2-3; 2-5; 2-6;
2-12; 2-16; 2-21; 3-6; 3-23; 3-27; 4-9; 4-10;
4-18; 4-29; 5-1; 5-2; 5-7; 5-10; 5-11; 5-20;
5-26; 5-30; 5-31; 6-1; 6-2; 6-13; 6-25; 6-28;

POLITICAL REFORMS — *Continued*

1968: 7-11; 7-14; 7-16; 7-29; 7-31; 8-1; 8-5; 8-13;
8-20; 8-25; 8-27; 9-1; 9-3; 9-5; 9-7; 9-8;
9-10; 9-14; 9-16; 9-17; 9-18; 9-19; 9-20;
9-22; 9-25; 9-26; 9-29; 10-1; 10-5; 10-8;
10-13; 10-14; 10-15; 10-31; 11-11; 11-24;
12-2; 12-3; 12-17; 12-19; 12-27; 12-31

1969: 1-1; 1-13; 1-22; 1-25; 1-29; 1-30; 2-12; 3-16;
3-31; 4-6; 4-14; 4-17; 4-24; 4-26; 4-27; 4-28;
4-29; 5-1; 5-2; 5-10; 5-16; 5-27; 6-9; 6-15;
6-21; 6-22; 7-16; 7-29; 8-1; 9-16; 9-20; 9-21;
9-29; 10-1; 10-4; 10-6; 10-11; 10-14; 11-18;
12-2; 12-11; 12-15

SOCIAL, CULTURAL, AND MILITARY
REFORMS:

1950: 2-24; 4-21; 4-30; 5-19; 6-29; 7-21

1951: 1-2; 2-23; 2-26; 4-20; 5-1; 5-25; 6-1; 7-13;
8-1; 10-12; 12-21

1952: 1-1; 2-1; 3-27; 4-10; 6-14; 7-27; 9-2

1953: 4-6; 4-10; 5-21; 5-29; 6-3; 7-15; 8-5;
10-6; 12-8

1954: 1-22; 3-15; 3-23; 4-27; 6-11; 7-14; 8-10;
9-14; 9-15; 10-28; 12-18; 12-20

1955: 1-31; 2-3; 2-9; 2-15; 5-1; 5-2; 5-25; 5-30;
6-6; 7-2; 7-13; 7-16; 7-23; 9-1; 9-27; 10-12;
11-1; 12-27

1956: 1-1; 1-14; 1-15; 1-18; 1-21; 1-25; 2-10; 3-30;
4-1; 5-26; 6-12; 7-25; 11-5; 11-16

1957: 2-27; 3-25; 7-15; 7-19; 8-3; 8-8; 9-6; 9-12;
10-20; 10-29; 12-5; 12-11

1958: 1-9; 3-4; 3-13; 4-7; 6-21; 8-17; 8-29

1959: 5-31; 10-1

1960: 9-29

1961: 11-22

1962: 5-12; 6-17; 8-21

1963: 9-28

1964: 2-6; 6-5

1965: 1-23; 5-29; 5-30

1966: 3-8; 3-23; 3-30; 5-25; 6-6; 6-13; 7-13; 9-27;
10-24; 10-25; 12-10

1967: 1-3; 1-5; 1-13; 1-29; 3-14; 4-24; 6-16; 6-22;
7-3; 11-20; 12-25

1968: 1-31; 4-21; 4-28; 6-4; 6-24; 7-1; 7-22; 8-5;
8-12; 8-29; 8-30; 9-11; 9-29; 10-5; 10-13;
11-14; 11-20; 12-22

1969: 1-1; 1-2; 1-5; 1-6; 1-28; 1-30; 2-2; 2-21; 3-7;
3-14; 4-11; 4-20; 4-21; 5-4; 5-8; 5-10; 5-11;
5-27; 6-1; 6-4; 6-10; 7-26; 8-1; 8-16; 8-31;
10-5; 10-6; 10-16; 10-30; 11-4; 11-20;
11-26; 11-28; 12-11; 12-15; 12-31

TIBET:

1950: 9-30; 10-24; 10-30; 11-24

1951: 5-23

1953: 2-24; 12-31

1954: 1-8; 4-29

1955: 3-12; 4-1; 6-29; 10-7

1956: 4-22; 5-26

1957: 3-18; 10-5

1959: 3-10; 3-28; 3-30; 3-31; 4-2; 4-5; 4-12; 4-15;
4-18; 4-21; 4-22; 4-23; 4-28; 6-20; 7-8;
8-20; 9-9; 9-25; 10-21; 10-23

1961: 5-7; 9-22; 10-5

1963: 3-1; 3-30

1964: 12-17

1965: 7-14; 8-25; 9-1; 9-9

1966: 5-26; 8-28

1967: 2-15

1968: 6-10; 9-5

1969: 3-13

FOREIGN AFFAIRS

A. International Conferences and Multilateral Agreements:

INDOCHINA CONFERENCE:

1954: 2-18; 3-3; 3-29; 4-26; 5-3; 5-5; 5-7; 6-1; 6-9;
6-19; 6-23; 6-24; 7-12; 7-21

1959: 2-18; 5-18; 5-25

1960: 1-31; 12-28

1961: 3-19; 5-4; 5-11; 5-17; 5-24; 6-12; 9-7

1962: 1-5; 8-4

1963: 4-16; 8-30

1964: 2-25; 5-13; 5-21; 5-26

1965: 1-13; 1-20

1966: 1-28

KOREAN WAR:

1950: 6-25; 6-27; 6-28; 7-6; 7-31; 8-1; 8-20; 8-31;
10-10; 10-25; 11-4; 11-6; 11-8; 11-10;
11-30; 12-4; 12-13; 12-22

1951: 1-13; 1-24; 1-29; 4-10; 6-23; 6-29; 7-1;
7-10; 8-23; 9-6; 10-25; 11-13

1952: 1-9; 2-7; 2-24; 12-3; 12-5; 12-14

1953: 2-4; 2-7; 2-22; 3-28; 3-30; 4-6; 4-11; 4-20;
4-26; 6-8; 7-20; 7-27; 8-24; 9-13; 10-10; 12-7

1954: 1-23; 1-25; 2-18; 3-3; 4-26; 5-3; 5-5; 6-15;
6-21; 9-5

1956: 4-9; 6-1

1958: 2-7; 2-19; 5-6; 7-2; 7-11; 10-17; 10-26

MULTILATERAL RELATIONS AND
AGREEMENTS:

1950: 12-5
1951: 6-3; 9-5
1952: 1-9; 2-4; 7-13; 10-10
1953: 8-3
1954: 3-3; 4-26; 5-3; 5-5; 8-9; 8-10
1955: 4-11; 4-18; 4-24
1956: 6-28; 7-3; 9-24; 10-3; 10-5; 10-31;
11-17; 12-28
1957: 5-24; 10-23; 11-2; 11-25; 12-12; 12-16; 12-23
1958: 3-24; 5-20; 6-5; 6-30; 8-14; 8-20; 11-6;
11-28; 12-1; 12-9
1959: 1-21; 1-22; 10-6; 12-5; 12-11
1960: 1-21; 2-4; 3-7; 3-17; 3-22; 4-10; 5-3; 5-8;
5-14; 5-20; 6-5; 8-26; 11-21
1961: 3-23; 5-17; 5-24; 6-12; 12-31
1962: 4-22; 6-22; 6-30
1963: 1-1; 2-8; 6-29; 7-14; 8-3; 12-4; 12-13; 12-30
1964: 2-5; 3-3; 8-31; 9-10; 9-16; 10-5; 10-20;
10-27; 11-6; 11-9
1965: 3-1; 3-15; 3-29; 4-6; 6-28; 7-14; 9-23; 9-26;
10-27; 11-14
1966: 1-22; 1-26; 4-19; 5-12; 6-9; 6-20; 6-27;
7-11; 7-23; 11-15
1967: 2-6; 5-25; 6-9; 6-15; 11-10; 11-25
1968: 1-24; 2-23; 3-5; 3-18; 3-27; 3-31; 4-16;
4-22; 5-15; 6-11; 7-1; 7-10; 9-22; 12-2
1969: 1-25; 2-16; 3-1; 3-22; 4-17; 4-24; 5-1; 5-10;
5-15; 5-27; 5-28; 6-5; 6-12; 7-11; 7-24;
7-28; 7-31; 8-20; 9-27; 9-30; 10-13;
10-17; 10-20; 10-31

UNITED NATIONS:

1949: 11-18; 12-8; 12-29
1950: 1-8; 1-10; 1-13; 2-3; 3-8; 4-5; 6-6; 8-1; 8-20;
8-24; 8-27; 9-11; 9-16; 9-19; 9-27; 9-29;
10-10; 10-17; 10-24; 11-8; 11-10; 11-15;
11-25; 11-28; 12-1; 12-16
1951: 1-13; 1-20; 1-29; 2-1; 5-3; 10-16
1952: 2-1; 10-25; 10-27
1953: 9-13; 9-15; 10-8; 12-7
1954: 9-21; 10-7; 10-10; 12-7
1955: 1-5; 1-24; 1-31; 2-3; 9-20
1956: 11-6
1957: 9-24
1958: 9-18; 9-23
1959: 9-22
1960: 10-8
1961: 4-8; 6-27; 9-21; 12-15
1962: 10-30
1963: 10-21; 12-12; 12-17
1964: 11-22
1965: 4-12; 9-1; 9-21; 9-23; 9-29; 11-17; 11-19;
11-29; 12-1
1966: 3-21; 3-28; 4-19; 9-16; 10-20
1967: 11-7; 11-25; 11-26
1968: 6-12; 7-1; 7-16; 8-27; 11-19; 12-10
1969: 1-27; 9-16; 11-11

VIETNAM WAR:

1965: 2-5; 2-7; 2-8; 2-10; 2-13; 2-15; 2-18; 2-27;
3-4; 3-12; 3-13; 3-17; 3-18; 3-20; 3-21;
3-25; 4-6; 4-7; 4-9; 4-12; 4-18; 4-22; 5-1;
5-5; 5-9; 5-13; 6-11; 6-16; 6-25; 8-5; 8-9;
8-16; 9-1; 9-15; 9-16 11-13; 11-28; 12-3;
12-5; 12-20
1966: 1-3; 1-4; 1-7; 1-8; 1-28; 1-30; 2-1; 2-2;
2-12; 3-3; 3-4; 4-21; 7-3; 10-28
1967: 1-15; 3-20; 4-26; 5-22; 8-30; 9-29; 12-19
1968 1-7; 2-2; 3-1; 3-19; 4-5; 12-19; 12-21
1969: 2-12; 2-15; 6-10; 6-16; 7-9; 10-4; 10-8;
10-16; 12-19

B. Bilateral Relations:

AFGHANISTAN:

1955: 1-20
1957: 1-19; 7-28; 10-22
1959: 9-5
1960: 8-26; 12-12
1961: 9-21
1962: 7-18
1963: 3-2; 8-3; 10-9; 11-22; 12-11; 12-30
1964: 4-10; 10-24; 10-30
1965: 3-24; 9-4; 11-6
1966: 4-4; 5-24; 7-29; 9-28; 12-28
1967: 1-26; 12-6
1968: 5-25; 8-14; 11-22
1969: 1-26; 3-9; 5-27; 7-17; 11-26; 12-23

ALBANIA:

1949: 11-23
1953: 7-31
1954: 1-1; 10-12; 10-14; 12-3; 12-6
1955: 3-2; 8-17; 9-28
1956: 3-11; 3-13; 6-28; 9-24; 10-22
1957: 3-8; 5-31; 11-2
1958: 3-12; 4-28; 6-4; 12-27
1959: 1-16; 4-20; 7-11; 12-11
1960: 3-4; 3-15; 10-18; 10-24
1961: 2-2; 4-12; 7-22; 12-26
1962: 1-13; 1-15; 4-11; 4-13; 5-7; 12-11; 12-12
1963: 1-17; 2-8; 2-19; 5-2; 6-29; 10-15; 12-6
1964: 1-2; 1-8; 3-5; 3-25; 5-23; 10-10; 11-28
1965: 3-12; 3-22; 3-27; 5-6; 6-3; 10-6; 11-12

ALBENIA — *Continued*

1966: 3-14; 4-26; 5-4; 5-10; 5-24; 6-24; 10-20;
       10-28; 11-21
1967: 3-2; 4-24; 5-21; 5-28; 12-9
1968: 2-9; 2-10; 2-15; 2-26; 4-27; 5-16; 6-11; 9-10;
       9-28; 9-29; 9-30; 10-2; 10-5; 10-9; 10-11;
       10-15; 11-20; 11-22; 11-26; 11-28;
       12-14; 12-30
1969: 2-22; 3-11; 3-22; 3-23; 4-7; 5-1; 5-15; 6-5;
       6-7; 7-1; 9-10; 9-27; 11-7; 11-14; 11-22;
       11-25; 11-28; 12-18

ALGERIA:

1958: 9-22; 12-3; 12-20
1959: 3-29
1960: 5-13; 10-5
1962: 7-3; 8-21
1963: 9-11; 10-11; 10-28; 12-21; 12-30
1964: 4-10; 4-14; 7-15; 9-14; 12-25
1965: 1-14; 2-11; 3-27; 3-30; 6-26; 8-28; 9-4; 12-8
1966: 6-20; 9-26
1969: 7-19; 9-30; 10-13; 10-28

ARGENTINA:

1954: 11-12
1964: 2-19
1968: 1-22

AUSTRALIA:

1956: 8-5
1957: 6-21
1961: 2-6
1962: 10-10; 12-28
1963: 5-31
1964: 4-5
1965: 11-8
1968: 11-12
1969: 1-28; 2-16; 8-24; 9-30; 12-12

AUSTRIA:

1956: 9-13
1964: 12-7
1965: 12-10

BELGIUM:

1956: 2-10
1957: 10-11
1961: 9-25

BRAZIL:

1961: 5-10; 8-21
1964: 5-6; 12-9; 12-22
1965: 4-7
1968: 3-16; 5-16

BULGARIA:

1949: 10-3
1952: 7-14; 12-3
1953: 7-31; 10-15
1954: 1-1; 3-25; 5-4
1955: 1-27; 2-17; 3-23; 7-11; 9-14; 11-15
1956: 1-21; 3-27; 6-28; 9-16; 9-24
1957: 1-28; 2-20; 9-14; 11-2
1958: 3-13; 3-19; 9-22; 11-13; 11-27; 12-18
1959: 4-23; 8-6; 8-28; 12-5; 12-11
1960: 3-15; 11-5
1961: 3-8; 4-20; 5-25
1962: 3-30; 4-18; 6-22; 9-13
1963: 2-8; 3-5; 3-20; 6-19; 11-26
1964: 3-21; 4-14; 9-24; 11-30; 12-12
1965: 5-13; 11-9
1966: 6-16; 7-1; 11-18
1967: 1-31; 2-27; 6-10
1968: 4-2
1969: 6-3; 7-5; 9-9; 10-5

BURMA:

1949: 12-17
1954: 4-22; 5-5; 6-28; 11-3; 12-1
1955: 3-28; 4-14; 11-8; 12-29
1956: 1-2; 1-19; 4-11; 7-31; 8-7; 10-2; 10-22; 12-10
1957: 3-22; 11-1
1958: 1-31
1960: 1-28; 4-15; 5-14; 6-27; 7-25; 9-5; 9-24;
       10-6; 10-24; 12-24
1961: 1-2; 4-16; 5-9; 6-4; 12-7
1962: 3-6; 12-31
1963: 4-20; 8-1; 8-28; 10-23
1964: 2-14; 7-10
1965: 1-26; 4-3; 7-14; 7-24; 8-1
1966: 4-17
1967: 6-22; 6-26; 6-28; 6-29; 7-1; 7-4; 7-5; 7-16;
       7-28; 8-10; 8-17; 8-22; 9-3; 9-6; 10-4;
       10-13; 10-20; 10-31
1968: 1-23; 2-22; 2-25; 3-28; 4-4; 6-14; 9-12;
       9-18; 10-24
1969: 3-16; 3-20; 11-2

BURUNDI:

1962: 7-1
1963: 3-20
1964: 2-6; 5-29; 10-22
1965: 1-30
1966: 9-1

CAMBODIA:

1954: 6-1; 6-16; 6-19; 6-23
1955: 4-23
1956: 2-13; 4-24; 4-29; 6-21; 11-22
1957: 6-2; 6-22
1958: 3-26; 6-28; 7-24; 8-15
1959: 5-30; 11-21

CAMBODIA — *Continued*

1960: 5-5; 5-8; 12-19
1961: 1-14; 8-3
1962: 5-23; 7-5; 7-31; 8-27
1963: 2-8; 5-1; 6-15; 11-20; 11-25; 11-26
1964: 1-6; 3-15; 4-10; 5-12; 6-15; 9-27; 10-8;
      12-1; 12-29
1965: 3-22; 5-2; 6-26; 9-16; 9-22; 12-28
1966: 3-31; 4-9; 6-3; 8-7; 10-6
1967: 2-25; 9-14; 11-26
1968: 1-3; 1-4; 7-10; 8-14; 8-21; 9-19; 10-5; 12-18
1969: 3-27; 4-22; 4-25; 5-1; 5-2; 6-6; 9-26; 11-9;
      11-26; 12-17

CAMEROON:

1960: 7-3
1964: 4-10
1965: 8-28

CANADA:

1958: 3-31; 11-1
1961: 2-2; 8-7; 12-21
1962: 3-28; 12-8
1963: 7-26; 8-2; 12-4
1964: 3-3
1965: 1-25; 10-28
1968: 3-29; 5-10; 11-15; 11-29
1969: 1-22; 1-24; 2-4; 2-10; 2-12; 2-20; 3-24;
      4-10; 5-8; 8-6; 9-16; 9-25

CENTRAL AFRICA:

1960: 8-15
1964: 9-29
1965: 1-14; 3-15
1966: 1-6

CEYLON:

1950: 1-6
1952: 10-4; 12-16
1953: 9-21
1954: 5-5; 10-6; 10-8
1955: 10-14; 10-16
1956: 9-6; 9-8; 12-29
1957: 1-31; 9-19
1958: 9-17
1959: 3-26; 6-13
1960: 1-3; 2-8
1961: 4-4; 5-4; 8-7; 10-7; 12-3
1962: 2-17; 5-28; 8-1; 9-15; 10-3; 12-10; 12-31
1963: 1-7; 1-19; 7-25; 10-10
1964: 2-26; 4-10; 6-15; 7-7; 10-24; 11-25
1965: 3-15; 7-13; 10-12
1966: 8-3
1967: 8-15; 8-22; 9-2; 11-7
1968: 1-4; 9-24
1969: 1-8; 8-31; 9-29; 10-20; 10-24

CHAD:

1960: 8-10

CHILE:

1952: 10-23
1963: 11-27
1964: 5-13
1965: 5-24

CONGO (BRAZZAVILLE):

1960: 6-26; 7-3; 7-19; 9-14
1961: 2-14; 9-28
1964: 2-22; 7-11; 7-23; 9-28; 10-11; 11-28
1965: 1-9; 2-6; 3-15; 5-12; 6-13; 8-13
1966: 4-14
1967: 3-23
1968: 2-6
1969: 2-22; 4-22; 4-25; 5-1; 5-2; 6-19; 7-12; 8-12;
      8-24; 9-7; 9-25; 10-10

CUBA:

1959: 12-31
1960: 7-23; 9-2; 11-30
1961: 1-21; 2-15; 3-8; 3-15; 4-20; 9-11; 10-2; 10-21
1962: 1-27; 4-25; 7-20; 8-23; 10-22; 11-4; 11-5
1963: 1-21; 2-22; 2-26; 2-28; 6-25; 7-24;
      11-14; 11-15
1964: 1-14; 1-15; 1-23; 8-11; 11-12; 12-31
1965: 1-4; 5-21; 7-18; 12-29
1966: 1-2; 1-9; 2-22; 5-26; 5-27; 7-6
1967: 3-21
1968: 12-20
1969: 2-14; 3-22; 12-20

CYPRUS:

1960: 8-15

CZECHOSLOVAKIA:

1949: 10-4
1950: 6-14
1951: 6-21
1952: 5-6; 5-24; 7-15
1953: 3-17; 5-7; 6-24; 7-31; 8-18
1954: 1-1; 4-27; 7-17; 9-2
1955: 3-1; 4-6; 11-11; 12-3; 12-9
1956: 1-3; 1-17; 6-28; 7-4; 9-2; 9-24; 11-17; 12-8
1957: 3-6; 3-9; 9-12; 11-2
1958: 2-6; 2-18; 2-27; 3-24; 4-16; 5-7; 8-15
1959: 1-1; 3-3; 4-13; 4-30; 5-20; 12-5; 12-10; 12-11
1960: 2-2; 2-19; 5-7
1961: 2-24; 4-4; 4-10; 6-8; 10-20
1962: 3-7; 4-3; 6-22; 7-1; 7-17; 7-20; 9-30; 12-10
1963: 2-8; 4-19; 5-15; 7-15; 7-19; 8-17; 11-20
1964: 4-24; 5-27; 9-28
1965: 3-24; 4-8; 6-18; 10-26; 12-23

CZECHOSLOVAKIA— *Continued*

1966: 2-4; 5-11; 10-28
1967: 7-27
1968: 3-13; 3-26; 6-27; 8-23; 8-26; 10-19;
      10-21; 11-5
1969: 5-8; 5-31; 6-16; 8-20; 11-17

DAHOMEY:

1960: 8-1
1961: 6-19
1964: 9-13; 11-12
1966: 1-3; 1-5

DENMARK:

1950: 1-9
1956: 2-15
1957: 11-9; 12-1
1958: 4-12; 5-4
1961: 9-23
1967: 3-15
1968: 9-16
1969: 7-11

DOMINICAN REPUBLIC:

1969: 10-9

ETHIOPIA:

1961: 9-5
1964: 1-30; 4-10
1965: 6-10

FINLAND:

1952: 9-21
1953: 6-5
1954: 6-17; 6-21; 12-13
1955: 8-8
1956: 3-31; 7-31
1957: 8-7; 12-18
1958: 2-15
1959: 5-15; 12-16
1960: 2-29
1961: 4-11
1962: 3-29
1963: 5-29; 10-28
1965: 3-24; 11-23
1966: 1-26; 4-25
1968: 1-6
1969: 3-24; 4-22

FRANCE:

1950: 1-14; 11-23
1952: 4-8; 8-9
1953: 5-23; 6-5; 11-2
1956: 2-19; 11-1; 11-3
1962: 10-13

1963: 2-27; 9-28; 11-30
1964: 1-11; 1-22; 1-26; 1-27; 2-13; 9-28; 10-13
1965: 4-12; 6-7; 7-19; 10-1
1966: 6-1; 7-25; 9-19
1967: 1-29; 1-31; 2-1; 3-20
1968: 4-23; 5-7; 5-15; 5-21; 6-6
1969: 2-16; 3-14; 5-4; 5-20; 5-23; 7-14; 9-30; 12-7

GABON:

1960: 8-16

EAST GERMANY:

1949: 10-27
1950: 10-10; 11-4
1951: 10-9; 10-12
1952: 5-28
1953: 2-9; 4-30; 7-3; 7-31; 8-8; 10-30; 11-28; 12-10
1954: 1-1; 3-30; 6-10; 8-23; 8-31; 12-27
1955: 4-8; 4-24; 8-20; 9-16; 11-20; 12-8; 12-10
1956: 1-3; 1-6; 2-2; 5-20; 6-28; 9-24; 10-5; 10-24
1957: 4-5; 6-15; 9-26; 11-2; 12-16
1958: 3-24; 3-27; 4-23; 5-22; 7-31; 10-9
1959: 1-22; 2-5; 3-9; 3-17; 4-25; 12-5; 12-11
1960: 1-18; 1-19; 3-23; 3-25; 4-13
1961: 5-10; 5-15; 6-15
1962: 6-22; 7-20; 8-4; 8-14
1963: 1-16; 1-18; 2-8; 6-7; 6-22; 10-15
1964: 1-16; 7-9; 8-1; 9-2; 11-26
1965: 2-19; 5-3; 11-22
1966: 3-25; 7-4; 7-22; 8-28
1967: 4-14; 6-30
1968: 4-30; 5-4
1969: 3-8; 7-5; 10-6

WEST GERMANY:

1952: 6-25
1957: 9-8
1963: 3-14
1964: 7-27
1966: 3-18
1969: 10-5; 10-20; 10-28

GHANA:

1960: 7-3; 7-5
1961: 6-19; 8-14; 11-1; 11-2
1962: 3-28; 10-18
1963: 1-23; 3-26
1964: 1-11; 2-5; 4-10; 7-15; 7-17; 7-30; 9-22; 12-3
1965: 3-15; 5-3; 5-19; 8-5
1966: 2-24; 3-1; 3-6; 3-15; 3-31; 10-1; 10-29;
      10-30; 11-5

GUINEA:

1958: 10-7
1959: 10-4; 10-7
1960: 6-3; 9-13

GUINEA — *Continued*

1961: 6-19; 7-1; 7-4; 9-18; 9-22
1962: 7-9; 9-2
1963: 5-2
1964: 1-7; 1-21; 4-10; 5-12; 8-5; 8-31
1965: 3-15; 6-5; 9-4; 9-14; 10-2
1966: 2-9; 4-30; 6-2; 11-11
1968: 4-23; 4-30; 5-14; 5-18; 5-24; 5-31; 6-8;
      6-26; 7-23; 8-19; 9-13; 9-26; 9-28; 10-8
1969: 2-9; 2-22; 2-28; 3-1; 3-13; 4-27; 4-29; 5-1;
      6-12; 7-8; 9-29; 10-9

HUNGARY:

1949: 10-4
1951: 1-22; 2-19; 7-12
1952: 7-21; 8-20
1953: 3-30; 5-19; 7-16; 7-31; 10-3; 10-15
1954: 1-1; 4-30; 8-31; 12-28
1955: 1-10; 1-20; 4-26
1956: 1-14; 1-27; 2-29; 4-29; 6-28; 9-24; 11-6
1957: 1-16; 5-13; 6-8; 7-18; 8-3; 9-27; 11-2
1958: 3-21; 3-24; 4-3; 4-21; 5-17; 6-12; 8-8;
      8-22; 10-5
1959: 3-17; 4-3; 4-6; 5-6; 11-10; 11-17; 12-5; 12-11
1960: 2-16; 2-28; 10-20
1961: 3-8; 3-27; 7-15
1962: 2-2; 3-30; 6-22; 12-14
1963: 4-10; 5-25
1964: 1-9; 1-31; 3-24; 3-28
1965: 3-26; 5-28; 6-5
1966: 2-20; 7-20; 8-9; 11-18; 12-2
1967: 6-29
1968: 4-27; 5-4
1969: 4-21; 8-5; 11-17

INDIA:

1949: 12-30
1950: 10-30; 11-24
1951: 1-1; 5-23
1952: 4-26; 10-13
1953: 12-31
1954: 4-29; 5-5; 6-25; 7-21; 10-14; 10-19; 12-13
1955: 4-1; 5-11; 8-23; 12-16
1956: 8-28; 10-21; 11-28
1957: 1-24; 5-25; 6-7
1958: 5-15
1959: 3-30; 4-2; 4-15; 4-24; 5-25; 9-4; 9-7; 9-8;
      9-9; 9-10; 9-26; 9-29; 10-3; 10-20; 10-22;
      10-25; 11-14; 11-18; 11-20; 12-17; 12-21;
      12-26
1960: 2-15; 2-26; 4-19; 4-25; 4-29; 6-15; 11-7;
      12-9; 12-18
1961: 12-6; 12-19
1962: 2-18; 3-16; 4-13; 4-23; 4-25; 5-2; 5-8; 5-14
      5-19; 5-28; 5-30; 5-31; 6-1; 6-4; 6-7; 6-18;
      7-8; 7-10; 7-13; 7-16; 7-22; 8-11; 8-13;
      9-13; 9-19; 10-3; 10-6; 10-10; 10-13; 10-15;
      10-17; 10-21; 10-22; 10-24; 10-26; 11-5;
      11-13; 11-18; 11-19; 11-21; 11-26; 11-28;
      12-1; 12-2; 12-5; 12-6; 12-9

1963: 1-13; 1-23; 2-23; 3-1; 3-3; 3-5; 3-10; 3-14;
      3-18; 3-25; 4-2; 5-25; 8-15; 8-21
1964: 3-31; 4-10; 5-27; 6-29; 9-28; 10-9; 12-28
1965: 1-18; 5-20; 8-2; 8-23; 9-2; 9-8; 9-9; 9-12;
      9-16; 9-17; 9-19; 9-20; 9-21; 9-27;
      10-10; 11-25
1966: 1-11; 1-31; 5-4; 9-15; 9-18
1967: 3-21; 4-12; 6-13; 6-15; 6-16; 6-17; 6-18;
      7-19; 10-1
1968: 3-10; 4-8; 6-10; 8-19; 11-12
1969: 1-9; 3-13; 5-10; 6-28; 8-21; 10-15

INDONESIA:

1953: 11-30
1954: 5-5; 8-31; 12-29
1955: 4-22; 4-28; 5-26; 6-3
1956: 6-6; 8-14; 9-30; 11-3
1957: 12-27
1958: 4-17; 10-13; 11-1
1959: 10-7; 11-17; 11-19; 12-4; 12-9; 12-13
1960: 1-13; 1-23; 2-2; 3-26; 7-4; 12-9; 12-13; 12-15
1961: 3-28; 6-13; 10-11
1962: 1-20; 11-1
1963: 1-2; 1-8; 4-12; 5-10; 6-29; 10-16; 11-28; 12-1
1964: 1-28; 4-10; 5-9; 5-13; 6-6; 11-4; 11-6; 12-3
1965: 1-12; 1-21; 1-23; 3-16; 3-30; 4-3; 4-17;
      5-21; 7-24; 8-7; 8-15; 9-14; 9-30; 10-4;
      10-18; 10-23; 10-26; 11-3; 11-4; 11-26;
      12-10; 12-15; 12-18; 12-20
1966: 1-12; 1-17; 2-27; 3-9; 3-27; 3-29; 4-3; 4-5;
      4-11; 4-12; 4-15; 4-16; 4-18; 4-22; 4-25;
      4-27; 5-7; 5-13; 5-18; 5-28; 6-3; 6-9; 6-30;
      7-5; 7-23; 7-26; 8-1; 8-22; 8-31; 9-12; 10-18;
      10-21; 10-25; 11-10; 11-13
1967: 1-6; 3-1; 3-12; 3-29; 3-30; 4-11; 4-18; 4-19;
      4-21; 4-22; 4-23; 4-24; 5-27; 6-5; 6-15; 6-21;
      6-29; 7-4; 7-5; 8-5; 8-26; 9-11; 9-14; 9-15;
      9-25; 10-1; 10-5; 10-9; 10-27; 11-4
1968: 2-4; 4-9; 6-8; 7-19; 11-14
1969: 3-29

IRAQ:

1958: 7-16; 7-17
1959: 1-3; 4-4; 4-8
1960: 5-15; 5-25
1961: 10-18; 11-25
1962: 3-11
1963: 1-10; 2-12
1964: 4-10; 5-25; 9-23
1966: 6-4
1967: 11-14
1969: 11-7

ISRAEL:

1950: 1-9
1967: 6-7
1969: 3-1; 5-15

ITALY:

1957: 6-21
1962: 12-3; 12-31
1963: 12-14; 12-19
1964: 11-30
1965: 3-21; 4-9; 10-15
1966: 10-12
1967: 7-21; 8-13
1968: 8-13; 10-27
1969: 1-24; 10-5; 10-11

IRAN:

1964: 4-10

IVORY COAST:

1960: 8-6

JAMAICA:

1962: 8-5

JAPAN:

1950: 12-4
1951: 8-15; 9-4; 9-18
1952: 6-1
1953: 2-15; 3-8; 6-30; 9-28; 10-29
1954: 12-11
1955: 4-15; 5-4; 8-16; 10-16; 10-17; 11-27; 11-30
1956: 5-8; 6-21; 6-28; 10-15; 11-29
1957: 5-30; 7-16; 7-25; 9-16
1958: 2-1; 2-26; 8-5; 4-1; 5-7; 6-11
1959: 3-3; 3-5; 9-9
1960: 5-9; 6-21; 11-1
1962: 2-24; 10-28; 12-27
1963: 1-16; 1-22; 6-29; 8-20; 9-1; 9-23; 11-9
1964: 4-18; 6-27; 7-10; 10-2
1965: 4-19; 8-5; 9-18; 12-8; 12-17
1966: 1-15; 5-19; 7-5; 7-28; 8-4; 9-18; 10-1;
      11-21; 11-22
1967: 3-17; 3-23; 7-26; 9-10; 9-14; 9-28; 10-12
1968: 1-20; 2-2; 3-2; 3-6; 3-11; 3-19; 3-21; 4-4;
      4-5; 4-8; 4-10; 4-11; 4-17; 7-19; 7-21;
      8-20; 9-29; 10-8
1969: 2-14; 2-16; 3-22; 4-4; 4-9; 5-15; 6-5; 6-7;
      6-14; 7-12; 8-5; 8-12; 8-29; 9-7; 10-5;
      11-7; 11-10; 11-15; 11-21; 12-20

KENYA:

1963: 12-8
1964: 1-27; 5-20; 10-2; 12-10; 12-18
1965: 6-10
1966: 3-30
1967: 2-3; 6-29; 8-23; 11-23

NORTH :KOREA

1949: 12-25
1950: 8-18; 9-30; 10-1

1952: 2-24
1953: 7-31; 11-12
1954: 1-1; 1-25; 3-4; 3-30; 5-5; 5-20; 6-3; 6-30;
      9-4; 9-5
1955: 3-1; 3-24; 4-20; 4-21; 6-22; 7-12; 8-14; 12-21
1956: 1-12; 1-14; 5-30; 6-6; 6-28; 7-3; 8-13; 9-2;
      9-24; 10-31
1957: 1-24; 4-10; 6-7; 10-8; 11-2; 12-30; 12-31
1958: 1-21; 2-19; 4-6; 5-20; 9-27; 10-17; 10-18;
      10-26; 11-19; 11-22; 12-1; 12-16; 12-27
1959: 2-18; 2-21; 5-21; 8-25; 12-5; 12-11
1960: 2-5; 2-29; 5-23; 7-4; 8-26; 10-13; 10-18; 11-21
1961: 3-18; 3-28; 3-31; 7-11; 10-30; 11-24
1962: 1-8; 4-22; 6-15; 6-22; 9-22; 11-5
1963: 2-8; 3-29; 6-6; 6-10; 6-21; 6-29; 9-15;
      10-14; 11-25
1964: 1-24; 4-18; 4-29; 5-9; 6-10; 6-12; 9-10;
      9-12; 10-27; 12-27
1965: 2-27; 6-18; 7-30; 11-1; 11-9; 11-18; 12-2
1966: 2-25; 6-1; 7-5; 7-30; 8-12; 12-3; 12-30
1967: 12-31
1968: 1-23; 3-5; 9-9
1969: 1-24; 3-22; 6-5; 9-8; 9-30; 10-6

KUWAIT:

1965: 2-17; 6-10

LAOS:

1954: 6-1; 6-16; 6-19; 6-23
1955: 4-23
1956: 8-21
1959: 2-18; 5-18; 5-25; 9-15
1960: 11-17; 12-28
1961: 3-7; 4-20; 10-7
1962: 1-13; 6-11; 6-23; 9-7; 12-4
1963: 3-6; 3-11; 4-16; 6-29
1964: 4-4; 4-19; 5-19; 5-26; 6-13
1965: 1-20; 1-22; 11-22
1966: 2-19
1968: 2-11; 3-27; 3-29; 9-28; 9-29; 10-11
1969: 1-19; 10-11; 10-17

LEBANON:

1955: 12-31
1958: 7-16; 7-17

LIBERIA:

1964: 4-10

MALAGASY:

1960: 6-25; 7-3
1966: 8-13

MALAWI:

1964: 9-14; 12-6

MALAYSIA:

1956: 8-22; 10-3
1963: 9-29
1966: 1-12
1968: 6-20; 9-15
1969: 5-14; 8-9; 11-1

MALIAVI:

1964: 7-4; 9-29

MALI:

1960: 6-19; 7-3; 10-17
1961: 2-28; 3-4; 6-19; 7-12
1962: 7-30; 11-6
1963: 5-15; 5-17; 8-31; 12-30
1964: 1-16; 4-26; 5-12; 11-3
1965: 3-15; 3-17; 4-17; 7-14; 9-1; 9-4
1966: 5-3; 6-9
1967: 8-14
1968: 1-27; 2-10; 4-13; 5-18; 5-24; 5-31; 6-1;
       7-25; 8-19; 9-10; 9-21

MALTA:

1964: 9-20

MAURITANIA:

1965: 7-26
1967: 2-12; 10-14; 10-19
1968 11-26
1969: 4-29; 7-15; 9-27; 11-28; 11-29

MAURITIUS:

1968: 3-11

MEXICO:

1964: 1-1

MONGOLIA:

1949: 10-16
1952: 9-15; 9-29
1953: 1-16; 2-24; 7-31; 8-20
1954: 1-1; 4-7; 5-5; 12-16
1955: 3-14; 10-17; 12-21
1956: 1-4; 2-7; 2-25; 6-28; 8-29; 9-24; 10-31; 12-22
1957: 10-3; 11-2
1958: 1-17; 1-24; 1-28; 2-21; 5-20; 12-1;
       12-23; 12-29
1959: 1-5; 1-30; 12-11; 12-22
1960: 1-15; 2-23; 5-6; 5-23; 5-31; 9-20; 10-12;
       11-10; 11-21
1961: 4-7; 4-26; 8-31; 12-27
1962: 1-13; 2-25; 4-22; 5-31; 6-4; 12-26
1963: 2-8; 3-18; 3-25; 3-30; 5-25; 10-9
1964: 1-13; 1-19; 1-20; 6-3; 6-14; 6-16; 6-30;
       9-10; 12-10; 12-19

1965: 3-24; 6-9; 9-2
1966: 3-28; 5-30; 9-29
1967: 5-21; 5-26; 5-27; 8-9; 9-5
1968: 5-13
1969: 7-24

MOROCCO:

1956: 4-4
1957: 10-13
1958: 10-27; 11-1
1959: 9-30
1961: 10-27
1963: 3-30; 12-27
1964: 4-10
1965: 12-1
1966: 5-20
1969: 3-3

NEPAL:

1955: 8-1
1956: 9-20; 9-25
1957: 1-26; 3-18
1960: 3-21; 3-24; 4-26; 4-28; 6-26; 6-28; 6-30;
       8-11; 9-1; 10-26
1961: 2-15; 8-24; 9-5; 10-5; 10-31
1962: 8-14
1963: 1-13; 1-20
1964: 4-10; 4-17; 5-15; 5-19; 9-28; 10-4;
       10-11; 12-2
1965: 1-21; 3-30; 8-25; 9-3; 9-8; 10-19; 11-22
1966: 5-2; 6-25; 6-30; 10-18; 12-21
1967: 3-14; 5-21; 5-25; 5-28; 7-1; 7-4
1968: 4-28; 5-23; 5-30; 6-13; 9-19; 9-27
1969: 3-12; 4-28; 6-11; 7-12; 9-13; 9-27

NETHERLAND:

1950: 1-14; 3-27
1964: 5-6
1966: 7-19; 7-22; 12-30
1969: 1-24; 6-5

NEW ZEALAND:

1967: 3-8
1968: 3-13; 9-25; 12-25
1969: 1-18

NIGER:

1960: 8-2
1961: 6-19
1965: 2-2

NIGERIA:

1960: 9-30
1961: 6-15

NORWAY:

1950: 1-6
1958: 6-4
1961: 4-4
1963: 6-18
1966: 4-30
1969: 2-9; 8-22

PAKISTAN:

1950: 1-4
1953: 3-14
1956: 1-24; 3-19; 5-10; 10-18; 12-20
1958: 6-3; 10-4
1962: 3-2; 5-3; 12-28
1963: 1-5; 3-2; 3-4; 3-13; 6-13; 8-29; 8-30; 9-5; 9-16; 9-30
1964: 2-18; 2-19; 2-22; 2-25; 3-8; 3-15; 4-10; 7-17; 7-23; 7-31
1965: 2-13; 2-18; 3-2; 3-19; 3-25; 4-2; 6-2; 9-4; 11-1
1966: 1-12; 3-26; 4-5; 6-1; 6-23; 6-28; 7-4; 10-21; 10-22
1967: 1-17; 9-10; 9-14
1968: 2-24; 3-22; 3-23; 4-27; 4-29; 7-7; 7-19; 8-3; 9-5; 9-13; 9-28; 9-29; 11-8; 11-15; 12-14; 12-24; 12-26
1969: 1-2; 1-23; 3-22; 4-27; 5-1; 6-7; 6-20; 7-12

PHILIPPINES:

1964: 4-10

POLAND:

1949: 10-4
1950: 3-1
1951: 2-1; 6-1
1952: 2-8; 7-11
1953: 1-28; 7-31; 10-15
1954: 1-1; 2-20; 7-21; 7-26
1955: 2-11; 3-21; 6-8; 6-11; 12-21
1956: 1-28; 1-30; 2-24; 4-23; 6-21; 10-29; 12-20; 12-24
1957: 1-11; 4-1; 4-6; 10-29; 11-2; 11-4; 11-27; 12-2; 12-30
1958: 2-22; 3-24; 4-5; 4-7; 9-15
1959: 1-30; 2-14; 2-20; 3-6; 4-15; 12-5; 12-11
1960: 2-11; 2-22; 10-9; 11-30
1961: 5-15; 7-10; 7-13; 9-20
1962: 2-28; 3-27; 3-28; 5-22; 6-22; 6-25; 9-8
1963: 2-8; 4-20; 4-30; 5-4
1964: 2-5; 3-30; 5-18; 6-19; 10-16
1965: 3-16; 4-26; 5-5; 12-3
1966: 3-22; 6-20; 6-24
1967: 6-30; 10-18
1968: 4-8; 4-10
1969: 8-8; 11-17

PORTUGAL:

1952: 7-25; 8-23
1964: 10-13
1966: 12-3; 12-5; 12-10; 12-19; 12-21
1967: 1-4; 1-6; 1-14; 1-20; 1-24; 1-29
1969: 10-6

RUMANIA:

1949: 10-3
1951: 12-12
1952: 7-30
1953: 1-9; 1-19; 6-9; 7-31; 10-15
1954: 1-1; 4-19; 5-17; 5-28; 10-15
1955: 1-20; 3-10; 7-30; 10-28
1956: 1-3; 1-21; 2-13; 4-28; 6-28; 9-24; 12-12
1957: 2-21; 4-19; 9-10; 11:2
1958: 3-30; 4-12; 4-28; 7-21; 10-10; 12-31
1959: 2-13; 3-10; 3-22; 12-11
1960: 2-16; 2-29; 3-15; 6-19; 6-20
1961: 3-17; 4-28; 7-7
1962: 2-17; 5-29; 6-22; 7-17
1963: 2-8; 6-8; 7-5; 7-6; 12-27
1964: 1-24; 3-2; 9-5; 10-3; 12-9
1965: 3-23; 5-15; 12-1; 12-21
1966: 2-11; 6-16; 7-31
1967: 2-14; 3-29; 10-25; 12-18; 12-31
1968: 9-29
1969: 5-31; 6-3; 6-7; 6-17; 9-7; 9-11; 10-6; 11-17

RWANDA:

1962: 7-1

SENEGAL:

1961: 6-19

SIERRA LEONE:

1961: 4-26

SINGAPORE:

1956: 8-22; 10-3
1966: 12-17
1968: 12-16
1969: 5-6

SOMALIA:

1960: 6-15; 6-30; 7-3
1963: 1-10; 4-27; 5-15; 8-9
1964: 2-1
1965: 7-21; 8-17; 12-17
1966: 6-11; 10-23
1967: 8-16; 8-19; 11-23
1968: 4-8; 9-15
1969: 3-18; 9-21; 10-19; 12-22; 12-26

SOUTH AFRICA:
1950: 6-2
1961: 3-28

SOUTH YEMEN:

1967: 11-30
1968: 2-3; 9-18
1969: 7-17; 8-20; 12-6

SUDAN:

1956: 1-4; 4-12
1957: 12-27
1958: 11-29
1962: 5-23
1963: 3-3; 4-22; 9-1
1964: 1-27; 5-9; 5-16; 10-4
1966: 7-27; 6-20
1969: 4-1

SWEDEN:

1950: 1-14
1955: 6-24
1957: 4-8; 11-8
1964: 12-3
1967: 8-4; 8-17
1968: 7-16
1969: 2-16; 2-28; 3-1; 4-9; 5-1; 6-17; 9-27

SWITZERLAND:

1950: 1-17
1956: 12-28
1968: 5-20

SYRIA:

1955: 11-15
1956: 5-30; 7-2
1957: 7-3
1959: 2-23
1961: 10-11
1963: 2-21; 2-24; 3-15
1964: 1-6; 4-10
1965: 3-18; 9-4; 10-6
1966: 4-20
1967: 4-13; 12-11
1968: 2-1; 4-6; 8-31
1969: 5-13; 6-19; 7-19

TAIWAN:

1950: 1-5; 1-12; 4-5; 7-6; 7-31; 9-16; 9-30; 10-7;
      10-24; 11-15; 11-20
1951: 1-8; 4-20; 5-18
1954: 8-11; 8-17; 8-22; 9-3; 9-4; 9-5; 9-7; 9-9;
      9-12; 9-15; 10-10; 12-2; 12-8; 12-25
1955: 1-10; 1-18; 1-19; 1-24; 1-29; 1-31; 2-3; 2-4;
      2-5; 2-8; 2-11; 2-13; 2-23; 4-13; 4-23; 5-2;
      5-13; 7-30; 11-7; 11-10

1956: 1-18; 5-30; 6-1; 6-6; 6-28; 8-5; 8-22; 9-24
1957: 3-5; 5-7; 5-11
1958: 7-31; 8-23; 8-27; 8-29; 8-31; 9-1; 9-4; 9-6;
      9-11; 9-13; 9-15; 9-18; 9-19; 9-21; 9-22;
      9-24; 9-25; 9-30; 10-1; 10-2; 10-5; 10-6;
      10-8; 10-13; 10-14; 10-20; 10-21; 10-25;
      10-31; 11-1; 11-2
1962: 6-17
1963: 5-23; 6-20; 6-22; 11-2
1964: 2-25; 4-10; 6-12; 12-18; 12-21
1965: 1-10; 3-18; 8-6; 11-11; 11-13; 11-14; 12-4
1966: 1-9; 2-19; 3-4; 4-25; 10-17
1967: 1-13
1968: 5-31; 12-30
1969: 2-16; 3-20; 4-19; 4-30; 5-26; 6-18; 8-31;
      9-30; 12-30

TANZANIA (TANGANYIKA):

1961: 12-8
1962: 12-13
1963: 6-14
1964: 1-27; 4-10; 4-30; 6-16
1965: 1-5; 2-10; 2-16; 6-4; 6-14; 11-9
1966: 5-7; 6-8; 7-7; 10-10
1967: 6-24; 9-5
1968: 2-19; 4-6; 4-25; 4-27; 5-6; 6-18; 6-21; 8-18;
      9-22; 11-16; 12-14
1969: 2-22; 4-22; 4-25; 5-1; 5-27; 6-12; 6-24; 8-14;
      8-16; 10-18; 11-14; 12-27

THAILAND:

1955: 9-3
1956: 6-20
1968: 3-23; 8-9; 5-19; 6-7; 11-1

TOGO:

1960: 4-26; 7-3
1961: 6-19

TOBAGO:

1962: 8-30

TUNISIA:

1955: 8-28
1956: 4-4
1957: 8-2
1958: 9-25
1960: 11-30
1961: 7-14
1963: 12-27
1964: 1-9
1965: 3-1; 11-18
1967: 2-16; 9-14; 9-24

TURKEY:

1960: 5-4

UGANDA:

1962: 10-8; 10-18
1964: 1-27
1965: 4-21; 6-10; 7-11
1969: 12-24

U.S.S.R.

1949: 10-2; 10-5; 10-31; 12-16
1950: 1-20; 2-7; 2-14; 2-15; 3-27; 4-2; 4-13; 4-19;
      4-25; 7-20; 8-7; 10-25
1951: 1-2; 1-16; 3-14; 4-3; 5-22; 6-15; 7-28; 12-6
1952: 3-29; 4-12; 8-9; 8-17; 9-21; 10-2; 12-31
1953: 1-11; 2-4; 2-7; 2-14; 2-22; 2-23; 3-4; 3-6;
      3-7; 3-9; 3-21; 3-24; 3-26; 4-11; 7-31;
      8-14; 9-15; 10-8; 11-7; 12-2; 12-27
1954: 1-1; 1-23; 1-31; 5-5; 5-29; 7-31; 8-21;
      9-29; 10-2; 10-12; 12-11; 12-28; 12-30; 12-31
1955: 1-1; 1-17; 2-11; 4-15; 4-27; 4-30; 5-24;
      6-13; 8-16; 8-22; 10-5; 10-17; 11-29; 12-21
1956: 1-4; 2-4; 3-26; 4-6; 6-12; 6-14; 6-20; 6-23;
      6-28; 7-3; 7-6; 7-13; 7-25; 8-15; 8-19;
      9-18; 9-24; 10-5; 10-31; 11-6; 12-24; 12-28
1957: 1-7; 1-17; 1-18; 2-15; 2-17; 3-27; 4-10;
      4-12; 4-15; 5-26; 7-5; 7-17; 11-2; 11-21;
      12-11; 12-21; 12-22; 12-30
1958: 1-18; 3-4; 3-24; 3-28; 4-1; 4-7; 4-19; 7-4;
      7-9; 7-31; 8-8; 8-31; 9-7; 12-1; 12-21
1959: 1-17; 1-21; 1-28; 2-7; 2-26; 3-11; 3-18;
      3-19; 6-1; 6-23; 7-4; 8-5; 9-9; 9-15; 9-30;
      10-4; 10-12; 10-22; 11-15; 12-5; 12-11;
      12-12; 12-21; 12-31
1960: 1-21; 1-29; 2-20; 2-24; 3-6; 3-29; 5-7; 5-16;
      6-10; 6-20; 7-25; 8-1; 8-26; 9-10; 11-6;
      11-10; 11-21; 11-30; 12-1; 12-4; 12-8
1961: 1-31; 2-4; 2-12; 3-2; 3-20; 4-7; 4-8; 4-10;
      5-25; 5-26; 5-30; 6-19; 6-21; 7-2; 8-6; 8-26;
      8-31; 10-1; 10-6; 10-19; 12-31
1962: 1-23; 4-7; 4-17; 4-20; 4-22; 4-29; 5-7; 5-13;
      6-22; 6-23; 7-2; 7-21; 8-28; 10-13; 10-26;
      10-28; 11-6; 11-29; 12-1; 12-12; 12-15
1963: 1-1; 1-7; 1-27; 2-8; 2-10; 2-21; 2-23; 3-9;
      3-13; 4-3; 4-20; 5-9; 5-16; 6-16; 6-18; 6-19;
      6-21; 6-27; 6-29; 6-30; 7-4; 7-5; 7-7; 7-13;
      7-14; 7-18; 7-19; 7-20; 7-22; 7-31; 8-5; 8-21;
      8-30; 9-1; 9-6; 9-13; 9-16; 9-21; 9-26; 10-11;
      10-13; 10-21; 11-6; 11-18; 11-29; 12-4;
      12-6; 12-12
1964: 1-1; 1-20; 1-24; 2-3; 2-13; 2-14; 2-20; 2-25;
      2-29; 3-31; 4-1; 4-3; 4-15; 4-27; 5-4; 5-7; 5-8;
      5-13; 5-30; 6-12; 7-14; 7-20; 7-21; 7-30; 8-2;
      8-30; 9-2; 9-7; 9-8; 9-10; 9-15; 9-16; 10-14;
      10-16; 10-19; 11-1; 11-4; 11-5; 11-6; 12-12;
      12-21
1965: 1-3; 2-5; 2-10; 2-12; 2-14; 2-26; 2-27; 3-4;
      3-6; 3-12; 3-16; 3-21; 3-22; 3-29; 4-7; 4-29;
      5-5; 5-7; 5-25; 6-12; 6-13; 6-19; 6-23; 7-20;
      9-2; 11-10; 11-16; 11-18
1966: 1-4; 1-15; 2-1; 2-2; 2-6; 2-14; 3-29; 4-4;
      4-19; 4-21; 5-3; 5-12; 5-20; 6-27; 8-26; 8-31;
      9-20; 9-25; 9-29; 10-7; 10-12; 10-23; 10-26;
      11-1; 11-6; 12-12; 12-16; 12-28
1967: 1-20; 1-26; 2-2; 2-4; 2-5; 2-6; 2-9; 2-11; 3-11;
      4-30; 6-25; 6-26; 7-3; 7-27; 8-10; 8-14
1968: 1-24; 2-16; 2-23; 3-9; 3-13; 3-15; 3-21; 3-22;
      4-3; 4-4; 4-9; 4-16; 4-25; 4-29; 5-4; 5-8;

5-17; 6-1; 7-5; 7-6; 8-23; 8-26; 9-5; 9-16;
      10-1; 10-14; 10-21
1969: 1-3; 1-11; 1-31; 2-15; 3-2; 3-3; 3-4; 3-6; 3-7;
      3-10; 3-11; 3-12; 3-13; 3-15; 3-22; 3-29; 4-2;
      4-11; 5-3; 5-5; 5-6; 5-7; 5-10; 5-11; 5-23;
      5-24; 5-28; 6-3; 6-5; 6-6; 6-7; 6-11; 6-13;
      6-15; 6-18; 6-29; 7-8; 7-9; 7-10; 8-8; 8-11;
      8-13; 8-15; 8-19; 8-20; 8-28; 8-29; 9-4; 9-10;
      9-11; 9-18; 10-7; 10-8; 10-18; 10-19; 10-20;
      11-5; 11-6; 11-17; 12-14

U.A.R. (EGYPT):

1955: 5-31; 8-10; 8-22; 10-14
1956: 4-15; 5-16; 5-20; 10-22; 11-1; 11-8
1958: 2-23; 8-25; 11-28; 12-15
1960: 2-24
1961: 12-5
1962: 3-17; 10-26
1963: 1-5; 4-25; 7-14; 12-14
1964: 4-11; 5-13; 8-24; 12-21
1965: 1-13; 3-25; 4-1; 5-2; 5-4; 5-7
1967: 5-25; 6-6
1968: 7-4; 8-13
1969: 2-26; 3-5; 8-25

UNITED KINGDOM:

1950: 1-6; 4-4; 8-17; 8-24
1951: 8-15
1952: 3-7; 5-19
1953: 2-24; 7-6; 8-23
1954: 6-17; 6-28; 7-27; 8-14; 10-28
1955: 4-11
1956: 5-16; 6-1; 10-13; 10-16; 11-1; 11-3
1957: 5-31; 7-24; 10-22
1958: 4-9; 6-10; 7-18; 7-19; 8-27
1959: 1-2; 2-5
1960: 9-5; 11-15
1963: 3-21; 4-16; 4-17; 10-11; 10-24; 12-5
1964: 5-26; 10-13; 11-2
1965: 4-12
1966: 1-31; 12-17; 12-20; 12-29
1967: 3-20; 5-2; 5-12; 5-14; 5-15; 5-16; 5-17; 5-18;
      5-19; 5-21; 5-23; 5-24; 5-26; 6-1; 6-23; 6-26;
      6-29; 7-8; 7-11; 7-12; 7-16; 7-19; 7-20; 7-21;
      8-13; 8-20; 8-22; 8-30; 9-12; 9-15; 10-20;
      11-21; 11-25; 12-6
1968: 3-12; 5-27; 7-3; 7-5; 8-12; 8-26; 9-7; 10-4;
      11-15; 11-26; 12-16; 12-27
1969: 2-16; 10-4; 10-5; 10-6; 10-11; 10-16; 10-17

U.S.A.

1949: 10-4; 10-12; 10-24; 11-8; 11-22; 11-26
1950: 1-5; 1-10; 1-12; 1-14; 1-18; 6-7; 7-6; 8-31;
      9-24; 9-27; 9-30; 10-13; 11-15; 12-1; 12-16;
      12-23; 12-29
1951: 1-20; 1-23; 4-29; 5-3; 7-12; 8-15
1952: 3-8; 3-15; 4-1; 5-5
1953: 1-21; 2-2; 2-22; 8-11; 9-2; 9-5

1954: 1-12; 3-29; 6-5; 7-9; 7-21; 7-26; 8-11; 8-17; 8-22; 9-5; 9-8; 9-12; 9-13; 11-23; 12-8; 12-25

1955: 1-5; 1-19; 1-21; 1-24; 1-29; 2-28; 4-2; 4-26; 5-30; 6-1; 6-18; 7-25; 7-30; 8-1; 9-6; 9-10; 9-14; 10-9; 10-12; 10-18; 11-7; 11-10

1956: 1-6; 2-18; 3-1; 3-4; 5-30; 6-6; 6-29; 8-6; 8-22; 8-27; 8-31; 9-2; 9-10; 9-21; 9-24; 10-10; 10-16; 12-2; 12-22

1957: 2-6; 2-13; 3-7; 3-28; 4-20; 4-23; 5-6; 5-14; 5-24; 5-31; 6-5; 6-14; 6-28; 8-14; 8-22; 8-25; 8-27; 9-12; 10-5; 11-25; 12-12

1958: 1-7; 2-19; 4-12; 6-14; 6-30; 7-1; 8-3; 8-9; 8-27; 9-1; 9-4; 9-7; 9-9; 9-11; 9-14; 9-18; 9-20; 9-22; 10-4; 11-10

1959: 2-18; 2-23; 6-12; 8-5; 10-6; 10-7; 10-23

1960: 3-22; 4-10; 5-16; 6-18; 6-21; 8-1; 10-1

1961: 1-21; 1-25; 1-31; 2-1; 2-6; 2-23; 3-7; 6-27

1962: 2-14; 2-24; 3-9; 3-30; 4-21; 5-23; 6-3; 6-21; 6-23; 6-26; 6-27; 9-9; 9-13; 9-20; 10-21; 11-3

1963: 2-20; 4-16; 7-15; 8-1; 8-7; 8-12; 10-24; 11-14; 11-22; 12-13; 12-17

1964: 1-20; 1-26; 1-29; 2-1; 2-19; 2-25; 4-20; 6-13; 9-23; 9-29; 10-18; 11-15; 12-21; 12-28; 12-30

1965: 1-2; 2-15; 2-18; 3-17; 3-30; 3-31; 4-3; 4-9; 4-18; 4-30; 5-13; 6-30; 8-3; 8-16; 8-21; 9-15; 9-20; 9-23; 11-22; 12-2

1966: 1-1; 2-7; 2-20; 3-5; 3-7; 3-8; 3-9; 3-16; 3-23; 4-13; 4-14; 4-17; 4-18; 5-19; 5-20; 5-25; 6-20; 7-12; 7-16; 7-20; 8-29; 9-5; 9-16; 10-16; 11-2; 12-5; 12-16; 12-21; 12-30

1967: 1-15; 1-25; 2-21; 4-6; 4-12; 4-20; 4-24; 4-26; 4-29; 5-1; 5-2; 6-6; 6-7; 6-12; 6-25; 6-26; 8-2; 9-8; 9-19; 9-21; 9-27; 10-31; 12-24; 12-25

1968: 1-2; 1-3; 1-7; 1-8; 1-12; 1-15; 1-23; 1-24; 1-28; 1-31; 2-1; 2-13; 2-27; 3-1; 3-7; 3-12; 3-18; 3-20; 3-22; 3-24; 3-29; 4-5; 4-6; 4-15; 4-18; 4-22; 4-23; 5-9; 5-18; 5-21; 5-25; 6-2; 6-19; 6-23; 6-25; 6-28; 7-7; 7-14; 8-6; 8-7; 8-21; 8-29; 9-15; 10-23; 10-31; 11-20; 11-26; 11-29; 12-10; 12-27

1969: 1-4; 1-11; 1-18; 1-26; 1-27; 1-28; 2-4; 2-6; 2-11; 2-16; 2-19; 3-7; 3-17; 3-20; 3-27; 4-19; 5-11; 5-27; 5-28; 5-30; 6-8; 6-13; 6-23; 6-29; 7-21; 7-28; 9-7; 10-5; 10-10; 11-1; 11-3; 11-5; 11-14; 11-21; 12-7; 12-11

UPPER VOLTA:

1960: 8-4
1961: 6-19

URUGUAY:

1955: 12-17

NORTH VIETNAM:

1950: 1-19; 5-8; 8-12
1952: 4-7; 11-6
1954: 5-5; 6-1; 6-23; 7-3; 7-7; 8-2; 12-24; 12-31
1955: 2-9; 3-2; 4-23; 5-15; 5-25; 6-25; 7-7; 7-16; 8-1; 11-25; 12-30

1956: 1-24; 4-24; 6-6; 6-18; 6-28; 7-26; 9-24; 10-31; 11-18; 12-20

1957: 3-30; 4-12; 4-25; 5-15; 7-6; 7-31; 11-2; 12-11

1958: 3-12; 3-15; 3-31; 5-20; 12-1; 12-8

1959: 1-16; 1-20; 2-18; 6-20; 6-27; 8-13; 12-5; 12-11; 12-31

1960: 2-16; 3-7; 3-28; 5-14; 7-11; 8-26; 11-2; 11-21; 11-28; 12-3

1961: 1-31; 3-19; 4-18; 6-15; 7-20; 9-10

1962: 1-20; 4-22; 6-22; 7-31; 8-22; 12-5; 12-24

1963: 2-8; 5-12; 5-16; 6-29; 7-18; 8-10; 8-29; 10-24

1964: 1-24; 2-6; 3-9; 4-27; 4-29; 7-6; 7-29; 7-31; 8-12; 8-25; 9-12; 9-30

1965: 2-8; 2-13; 2-21; 3-21; 6-19; 7-11; 9-16; 11-13; 11-28; 12-3; 12-5

1966: 1-28; 1-30; 3-21; 4-22; 5-28; 6-19; 7-2; 7-22; 8-21; 8-29; 10-23

1967: 3-20; 4-9; 4-25; 5-22; 8-3; 8-5; 8-30; 9-29; 10-5

1968: 2-2; 2-3; 3-20; 6-28; 7-9; 7-20; 7-23; 8-31; 9-2; 9-21; 9-29; 9-30; 10-1; 10-5; 12-18; 12-21

1969: 2-14; 3-22; 3-23; 3-24; 6-5; 9-1; 9-2; 9-3; 9-4; 9-6; 9-26; 9-27; 10-4; 10-20; 10-25; 11-23; 12-21

VIETNAM (N.F.L.):

1964: 9-18
1965: 2-7; 3-25; 12-20
1967: 9-5; 9-29; 12-19
1968: 2-14; 3-18; 9-28; 9-29; 12-19; 12-20
1969: 2-12; 2-15; 6-10; 6-16; 7-1; 7-9; 9-29; 10-4; 10-8; 10-16; 12-19

YEMEN:

1956: 8-21
1957: 12-31
1958: 4-26
1959: 1-23
1962: 3-18; 10-6
1963: 2-15
1964: 6-1
1965: 3-23; 5-3
1966: 5-1; 5-23
1967: 1-26
1968: 3-2; 5-4; 5-13; 6-29; 7-4; 7-31
1969: 7-14; 7-19; 8-10; 11-6

YUGOSLAVIA:

1955: 1-10
1956: 2-14; 2-17; 4-27
1957: 1-4; 6-7; 11-1; 12-27
1958: 2-28; 3-29
1959: 3-18
1960: 3-25
1961: 7-15
1962: 6-28

YUGOSLAVIA — *Continued*

1963: 11-5
1964: 1-8; 6-11
1965: 5-11
1966: 6-1; 6-10
1967: 4-10
1968: 5-10
1969: 3-17; 3-22; 4-25; 6-5; 11-17

ZAMBIA:

1964: 1-17; 4-30; 10-24
1965: 6-10
1966: 8-22
1967: 4-28; 6-21; 6-23; 6-24; 6-25; 6-28; 9-5
1968: 4-8; 4-25; 9-22; 10-23
1969: 1-28; 2-23; 5-1; 6-12; 8-16; 9-26; 10-10;
       11-14; 12-2; 12-27; 12-31